Quantitative Equity Investing

The Frank J. Fabozzi Series

Quantitative Equity Investing

Techniques and Strategies

FRANK J. FABOZZI
SERGIO M. FOCARDI
PETTER N. KOLM

with the assistance of
Joseph A. Cerniglia and
Dessislava Pachamanova

John Wiley & Sons, Inc.

Library of Congress Cataloging-in-Publication Data:

Fabozzi, Frank J.
    Quantitative equity investing : techniques and strategies / Frank J. Fabozzi, Sergio M. Focardi, Petter N. Kolm ; with the assistance of Joseph A. Cerniglia and Dessislava Pachamanova.
        p. cm. — (The Frank J. Fabozzi series)
    Includes index.
    ISBN 978-0-470-26247-4 (cloth)
    1. Portfolio management. 2. Investments. I. Focardi, Sergio. II. Kolm, Petter N. III. Title.
HG4529.5.F3346 2010
332.63'2042—dc22
                                2009050962

10 9 8 7 6 5 4 3 2 1

Contents

Preface

Quantitative equity portfolio management is a fundamental building block of investment management. The basic principles of investment management have been proposed back in the 1950s in the pathbreaking work of Harry Markowitz. For his work, in 1990 Markowitz was awarded the Nobel Memorial Prize in Economic Sciences. Markowitz's ideas proved to be very fertile. Entire new research areas originated from it which, with the diffusion of low-cost powerful computers, found important practical applications in several fields of finance.

Among the developments that followed Markowitz's original approach we can mention:

- The development of CAPM and of general equilibrium asset pricing models.
- The development of multifactor models.
- The extension of the investment framework to a dynamic multiperiod environment.
- The development of statistical tools to extend his framework to fat-tailed distributions.
- The development of Bayesian techniques to integrate human judgment with results from models.
- The progressive adoption of optimization and robust optimization techniques.

Due to these and other theoretical advances it has progressively become possible to manage investments with computer programs that look for the best risk-return trade-off available in the market.

People have always tried to beat the market, in the hunt for a free lunch. This began by relying on simple observations and rules of thumb to pick the winners, and later with the advent of computers brought much more complicated systems and mathematical models within common reach. Today, so-called *buy-side quants* deploy a wide range of techniques ranging from econometrics, optimization, and computer science to data mining, machine learning, and artificial intelligence to trade the equity markets. Their strategies may range from intermediate and long-term strategies, six months to several years out, to so-called ultra-high or high-frequency strategies, at the sub-millisecond level. The modern quantitative techniques have replaced good old-fashioned experience and market insight, with the scientific rigor of mathematical and financial theories.

This book is about quantitative equity portfolio management performed with modern techniques. One of our goals for this book is to present advances in the theory and practice of quantitative equity portfolio management that represent what we might call the "state of the art of advanced equity portfolio management." We cover the most common techniques, tools, and strategies used in quantitative equity portfolio management in the industry today. For many of the advanced topics, we provide the reader with references to the most recent applicable research in the field.

This book is intended for students, academics, and financial practitioners alike who want an up-to-date treatment of quantitative techniques in equity portfolio management, and who desire to deepen their knowledge of some of the most cutting-edge techniques in this rapidly developing area. The book is written in an almost self-contained fashion, so that little background knowledge in finance is needed. Nonetheless, basic working knowledge of undergraduate linear algebra and probability theory are useful, especially for the more mathematical topics in this book.

In Chapter 1 we discuss the role and use of mathematical techniques in finance. In addition to offering theoretical arguments in support of finance as a mathematical science, we discuss the results of three surveys on the diffusion of quantitative methods in the management of equity portfolios. In Chapters 2 and 3, we provide extensive background material on one of the principal tools used in quantitative equity management, financial econometrics. Coverage in Chapter 2 includes modern regression theory, applications of Random Matrix Theory, and robust methods. In Chapter 3, we extend our coverage of financial economics to dynamic models of times series, vector autoregressive models, and cointegration analysis. Financial engineering, the many pitfalls of estimation, and methods to control model risk are the subjects of Chapter 4. In Chapter 5, we introduce the modern theory of factor models, including approximate factor models and dynamic factor models.

Trading strategies based on factors and factor models are the focus of Chapters 6 and 7. In these chapters we offer a modern view on how to construct factor models based on fundamental factors and how to design and test trading strategies based on these. We offer a wealth of practical examples on the application of factor models in these chapters.

The coverage in Chapters 8, 9, and 10 is on the use of optimization models in quantitative equity management. The basics of portfolio optimization are reviewed in Chapter 9, followed by a discussion of the Bayesian approach to investment management as implemented in the Black-Litterman framework in Chapter 9. In Chapter 10 we discuss robust optimization techniques because they have greatly enhanced the ability to implement portfolio optimization models in practice.

The last two chapters of the book cover the important topic of trading costs and trading techniques. In Chapter 11, our focus is on the issues related to trading cost and implementation of trading strategies from a practical point of view. The modern techniques of algorithmic trading are the subject of the final chapter in the book, Chapter 12.

There are three appendixes. Appendix A provides a description of the data and factor definitions used in the illustrations and examples in the book. A summary of the factors, their economic rationale, and references that have supported the use of each factor is provided in Appendix B. In Appendix C we provide a review of eigenvalues and eigenvectors.

TEACHING USING THIS BOOK

Many of the chapters in this book have been used in courses and workshops on quantitative investment management, econometrics, trading strategies and algorithmic trading. The topics of the book are appropriate for undergraduate advanced electives on investment management, and graduate students in finance, economics, or in the mathematical and physical sciences.

For a typical course it is natural to start with Chapters 1–3, 5, and 8 where the quantitative investment management industry, standard econometric techniques, and modern portfolio and asset pricing theory are reviewed. Important practical considerations such as model risk and its mitigation are presented in Chapter 4. Chapters 6 and 7 focus on the development of factor-based trading strategies and provide many practical examples. Chapters 9–12 cover the important topics of Bayesian techniques, robust optimization, and transaction cost modeling—by now standard tools used in quantitative portfolio construction in the financial industry. We recommend that a more advanced course covers these topics in some detail.

Student projects can be based on specialized topics such as the development of trading strategies (in Chapters 6 and 7), optimal execution, and algorithmic trading (in Chapters 11 and 12). The many references in these chapters, and in the rest of the book, provide a good starting point for research.

ACKNOWLEDGMENTS

We would like to acknowledge the assistance of several individuals who contributed to this book. Chapters 6 and 7 on trading strategies were co-authored with Joseph A. Cerniglia of of Aberdeen Asset Management Inc. Chapter 10 on robust portfolio optimization is coauthored with Dessislava Pachamanova of Babson College. Chapter 12 draws from a chapter by one of the authors and Lee Maclin, adjunct at the Courant Institute of Mathematical Sciences, New York University, that will appear in the *Encyclopedia of Quantitative Finance*, edited by Rama Cont and to be published by John Wiley & Sons.

We also thank Axioma, Inc. for allowing us to use several figures from its white paper series co-authored by Sebastian Ceria and Robert Stubbs.

Megan Orem typeset the book and provided editorial assistance. We appreciate her patience and understanding in working through numerous revisions.

Frank J. Fabozzi
Sergio M. Focardi
Petter N. Kolm

About the Authors

Frank J. Fabozzi is Professor in the Practice of Finance in the School of Management at Yale University and an Affiliated Professor at the University of Karlsruhe's Institute of Statistics, Econometrics and Mathematical Finance. Prior to joining the Yale faculty, he was a Visiting Professor of Finance in the Sloan School at MIT. Frank is a Fellow of the International Center for Finance at Yale University and on the Advisory Council for the Department of Operations Research and Financial Engineering at Princeton University. He is the editor of the *Journal of Portfolio Management*. He is a trustee for the BlackRock family of closed-end funds. In 2002, Frank was inducted into the Fixed Income Analysts Society's Hall of Fame and is the 2007 recipient of the C. Stewart Sheppard Award given by the CFA Institute. His recently coauthored books published by Wiley in include *Institutional Investment Management* (2009), *Finance: Capital Markets, Financial Management and Investment Management* (2009), *Bayesian Methods in Finance* (2008), *Advanced Stochastic Models, Risk Assessment, and Portfolio Optimization: The Ideal Risk, Uncertainty, and Performance Measures* (2008), *Financial Modeling of the Equity Market: From CAPM to Cointegration* (2006), *Robust Portfolio Optimization and Management* (2007), and *Financial Econometrics: From Basics to Advanced Modeling Techniques* (2007). Frank earned a doctorate in economics from the City University of New York in 1972. He earned the designation of Chartered Financial Analyst and Certified Public Accountant.

Sergio Focardi is Professor of Finance at the EDHEC Business School in Nice and the founding partner of the Paris-based consulting firm The Intertek Group. He is a member of the editorial board of the *Journal of Portfolio Management*. Sergio has authored numerous articles and books on financial modeling and risk management including the following Wiley books: *Financial Econometrics* (2007), *Financial Modeling of the Equity Market* (2006), *The Mathematics of Financial Modeling and Investment Management* (2004), *Risk Management: Framework, Methods and Practice* (1998), and *Modeling the Markets: New Theories and Techniques* (1997). He also authored two monographs published by the CFA Institute's monographs: *Challenges in Quantitative Equity Management* (2008) and *Trends in*

Quantitative Finance (2006). Sergio has been appointed as a speaker of the CFA Institute Speaker Retainer Program. His research interests include the econometrics of large equity portfolios and the modeling of regime changes. Sergio holds a degree in Electronic Engineering from the University of Genoa and a PhD in Mathematical Finance and Financial Econometrics from the University of Karlsruhe.

Petter N. Kolm is the Deputy Director of the Mathematics in Finance Masters Program and Clinical Associate Professor at the Courant Institute of Mathematical Sciences, New York University, and a Founding Partner of the New York-based financial consulting firm, the Heimdall Group, LLC. Previously, Petter worked in the Quantitative Strategies Group at Goldman Sachs Asset Management where his responsibilities included researching and developing new quantitative investment strategies for the group's hedge fund. Petter authored the books *Financial Modeling of the Equity Market: From CAPM to Cointegration* (Wiley, 2006), *Trends in Quantitative Finance* (CFA Research Institute, 2006), and *Robust Portfolio Management and Optimization* (Wiley, 2007). His interests include high-frequency finance, algorithmic trading, quantitative trading strategies, financial econometrics, risk management, and optimal portfolio strategies. Petter holds a doctorate in mathematics from Yale University, an M.Phil. in applied mathematics from the Royal Institute of Technology in Stockholm, and an M.S. in mathematics from ETH Zürich. Petter is a member of the editorial board of the *Journal of Portfolio Management*.

CHAPTER **1**

Introduction

An economy can be regarded as a *machine* that takes in input labor and natural resources and outputs products and services. Studying this machine from a physical point of view would be very difficult because we should study the characteristics and the interrelationships among all modern engineering and production processes. Economics takes a bird's-eye view of these processes and attempts to study the dynamics of the economic value associated with the structure of the economy and its inputs and outputs. Economics is by nature a quantitative science, though it is difficult to find simple rules that link economic quantities.

In most economies value is presently obtained through a market process where supply meets demand. Here is where finance and financial markets come into play. They provide the tools to optimize the allocation of resources through time and space and to manage risk. Finance is by nature quantitative like economics but it is subject to a large level of risk. It is the measurement of risk and the implementation of decision-making processes based on risk that makes finance a quantitative science and not simply accounting.

Equity investing is one of the most fundamental processes of finance. Equity investing allows allocating the savings of the households to investments in the productive activities of an economy. This investment process is a fundamental economic enabler: without equity investment it would be very difficult for an economy to properly function and grow. With the diffusion of affordable fast computers and with progress made in understanding financial processes, financial modeling has become a determinant of investment decision-making processes. Despite the growing diffusion of financial modeling, objections to its use are often raised.

In the second half of the 1990s, there was so much skepticism about quantitative equity investing that David Leinweber, a pioneer in applying advanced techniques borrowed from the world of physics to fund management, and author of *Nerds on Wall Street*,[1] wrote an article entitled: "Is

---

[1]David Leinweber, *Nerds on Wall Street: Math, Machines, and Wired Markets* (Hoboken, NJ: John Wiley & Sons, 2009).

quantitative investment dead?"[2] In the article, Leinweber defended quantitative fund management and maintained that in an era of ever faster computers and ever larger databases, quantitative investment was here to stay. The skepticism toward quantitative fund management, provoked by the failure of some high-profile quantitative funds at that time, was related to the fact that investment professionals felt that capturing market inefficiencies could best be done by exercising human judgment.

Despite mainstream academic opinion that held that markets are efficient and unpredictable, the asset managers' job is to capture market inefficiencies and translate them into enhanced returns for their clients. At the academic level, the notion of efficient markets has been progressively relaxed. Empirical evidence led to the acceptance of the notion that financial markets are somewhat predictable and that systematic market inefficiencies can be detected. There has been a growing body of evidence that there are market anomalies that can be systematically exploited to earn excess profits after considering risk and transaction costs.[3] In the face of this evidence, Andrew Lo proposed replacing the efficient market hypothesis with the *adaptive market hypothesis* as market inefficiencies appear as the market adapts to changes in a competitive environment.

In this scenario, a quantitative equity investment management process is characterized by the use of computerized rules as the primary source of decisions. In a quantitative process, human intervention is limited to a control function that intervenes only exceptionally to modify decisions made by computers. We can say that a quantitative process is a process that quantifies things. The notion of quantifying things is central to any modern science, including the dismal science of economics. Note that everything related to accounting—balance sheet/income statement data, and even accounting at the national level—is by nature quantitative. So, in a narrow sense, finance has always been quantitative. The novelty is that we are now quantifying things that are not directly observed, such as risk, or things that are not quantitative per se, such as market sentiment and that we seek simple rules to link these quantities

In this book we explain techniques for quantitative equity investing. Our purpose in this chapter is threefold. First, we discuss the relationship between mathematics and equity investing and look at the objections raised. We attempt to show that most objections are misplaced. Second, we discuss the results of three studies based on surveys and interviews of major market

[2]David Leinweber, "Is Quantitative Investing Dead?" *Pensions & Investments*, February 8, 1999.
[3]For a modern presentation of the status of market efficiency, see M. Hashem Pesaran, "Market Efficiency Today," Working Paper 05.41, 2005 (Institute of Economic Policy Research).

participants whose objective was to quantitative equity portfolio management and their implications for equity portfolio managers. The results of these three studies are helpful in understanding the current state of quantitative equity investing, trends, challenges, and implementation issues. Third, we discuss the challenges ahead for quantitative equity investing.

IN PRAISE OF MATHEMATICAL FINANCE

Is the use of mathematics to describe and predict financial and economic phenomena appropriate? The question was first raised at the end of the nineteenth century when Vilfredo Pareto and Leon Walras made an initial attempt to formalize economics. Since then, financial economic theorists have been divided into two camps: those who believe that economics is a science and can thus be described by mathematics and those who believe that economic phenomena are intrinsically different from physical phenomena which can be described by mathematics.

In a tribute to Paul Samuelson, Robert Merton wrote:

> Although most would agree that finance, micro investment theory and much of the economics of uncertainty are within the sphere of modern financial economics, the boundaries of this sphere, like those of other specialties, are both permeable and flexible. It is enough to say here that the core of the subject is the study of the individual behavior of households in the intertemporal allocation of their resources in an environment of uncertainty and of the role of economic organizations in facilitating these allocations. It is the complexity of the interaction of time and uncertainty that provides intrinsic excitement to study of the subject, and, indeed, the mathematics of financial economics contains some of the most interesting applications of probability and optimization theory. Yet, for all its seemingly obtrusive mathematical complexity, the research has had a direct and significant influence on practice[4]

The three principal objections to treating finance economic theory as a mathematical science we will discuss are that (1) financial markets are driven by unpredictable unique events and, consequently, attempts to use mathematics to describe and predict financial phenomena are futile, (2) financial phenomena are driven by forces and events that cannot be quantified, though we can use intuition and judgment to form a meaningful finan-

---

[4]Robert C. Merton, "Paul Samuelson and Financial Economics," *American Economist* 50, no. 2 (Fall 2006), pp. 262–300.

cial discourse, and (3) although we can indeed quantify financial phenomena, we cannot predict or even describe financial phenomena with realistic mathematical expressions and/or computational procedures because the laws themselves change continuously.

A key criticism to the application of mathematics to financial economics is the role of uncertainty. As there are unpredictable events with a potentially major impact on the economy, it is claimed that financial economics cannot be formalized as a mathematical methodology with predictive power. In a nutshell, the answer is that black swans exist not only in financial markets but also in the physical sciences. But no one questions the use of mathematics in the physical sciences because there are major events that we cannot predict. The same should hold true for finance. Mathematics can be used to understand financial markets and help to avoid catastrophic events.[5] However, it is not necessarily true that science and mathematics will enable unlimited profitable speculation. Science will allow one to discriminate between rational predictable systems and highly risky unpredictable systems.

There are reasons to believe that financial economic laws must include some fundamental uncertainty. The argument is, on a more general level, the same used to show that there cannot be arbitrage opportunities in financial markets. Consider that economic agents are intelligent agents who can use scientific knowledge to make forecasts.

Were financial economic laws deterministic, agents could make (and act on) deterministic forecasts. But this would imply a perfect consensus between agents to ensure that there is no contradiction between forecasts and the actions determined by the same forecasts. For example, all investment opportunities should have exactly identical payoffs. Only a perfectly and completely planned economy can be deterministic; any other economy must include an element of uncertainty.

In finance, the mathematical handling of uncertainty is based on probabilities learned from data. In finance, we have only one sample of small size and cannot run tests. Having only one sample, the only rigorous way to apply statistical models is to invoke ergodicity. An ergodic process is a stationary process where the limit of time averages is equal to time-invariant ensemble averages. Note that in financial modeling it is not necessary that economic quantities themselves form ergodic processes, only that residuals after modeling form an ergodic process. In practice, we would like the models to extract all meaningful information and leave a sequence of white noise residuals.

---

[5]This is what Nassim Taleb refers to as "black swans" in his critique of financial models in his book *The Black Swan: The Impact of the Highly Improbable* (New York: Random House, 2007).

If we could produce models that generate white noise residuals over extended periods of time, we would interpret uncertainty as probability and probability as relative frequency. However, we cannot produce such models because we do not have a firm theory known a priori. Our models are a combination of theoretical considerations, estimation, and learning; they are adaptive structures that need to be continuously updated and modified.

Uncertainty in forecasts is due not only to the probabilistic uncertainty inherent in stochastic models but also to the possibility that the models themselves are misspecified. Model uncertainty cannot be measured with the usual concept of probability because this uncertainty itself is due to unpredictable changes. Ultimately, the case for mathematical financial economics hinges on our ability to create models that maintain their descriptive and predictive power even if there are sudden unpredictable changes in financial markets. It is not the large unpredictable events that are the challenge to mathematical financial economics, but our ability to create models able to recognize these events.

This situation is not confined to financial economics. It is now recognized that there are physical systems that are totally unpredictable. These systems can be human artifacts or natural systems. With the development of nonlinear dynamics, it has been demonstrated that we can build artifacts whose behavior is unpredictable. There are examples of unpredictable artifacts of practical importance. Turbulence, for example, is a chaotic phenomenon. The behavior of an airplane can become unpredictable under turbulence. There are many natural phenomena from genetic mutations to tsunami and earthquakes whose development is highly nonlinear and cannot be individually predicted. But we do not reject mathematics in the physical sciences because there are events that cannot be predicted. On the contrary, we use mathematics to understand where we can find regions of dangerous unpredictability. We do not knowingly fly an airplane in extreme turbulence and we refrain from building dangerous structures that exhibit catastrophic behavior. Principles of safe design are part of sound engineering.

Financial markets are no exception. Financial markets are designed artifacts: we can make them more or less unpredictable. We can use mathematics to understand the conditions that make financial markets subject to nonlinear behavior with possibly catastrophic consequences. We can improve our knowledge of what variables we need to control in order to avoid entering chaotic regions.

It is therefore not reasonable to object that mathematics cannot be used in finance because there are unpredictable events with major consequences. It is true that there are unpredictable financial markets where we cannot use mathematics except to recognize that these markets are unpredictable. But we can use mathematics to make financial markets safer and more stable.[6]

Let us now turn to the objection that we cannot use mathematics in finance because the financial discourse is inherently qualitative and cannot be formalized in mathematical expressions. For example, it is objected that qualitative elements such as the quality of management or the culture of a firm are important considerations that cannot be formalized in mathematical expressions.

A partial acceptance of this point of view has led to the development of techniques to combine human judgment with models. These techniques range from simply counting analysts' opinions to sophisticated Bayesian methods that incorporate qualitative judgment into mathematical models. These hybrid methodologies link models based on data with human overlays.

Is there any irreducibly judgmental process in finance? Consider that in finance, all data important for decision-making are quantitative or can be expressed in terms of logical relationships. Prices, profits, and losses are quantitative, as are corporate balance-sheet data. Links between companies and markets can be described through logical structures. Starting from these data we can construct theoretical terms such as volatility. Are there hidden elements that cannot be quantified or described logically?

Ultimately, in finance, the belief in hidden elements that cannot be either quantified or logically described is related to the fact that economic agents are human agents with a decision-making process. The operational point of view of Samuelson has been replaced by the neoclassical economics view that, apparently, places the accent on agents' decision-making. It is curious that the agent of neoclassical economics is not a realistic human agent but a mathematical optimizer described by a utility function.

Do we need anything that cannot be quantified or expressed in logical terms? At this stage of science, we can say the answer is a qualified no, if we consider markets in the aggregate. Human behavior is predictable in the aggregate and with statistical methods. Interaction between individuals, at least at the level of economic exchange, can be described with logical tools. We have developed many mathematical tools that allow us to describe critical points of aggregation that might lead to those situations of unpredictability described by complex systems theory.

We can conclude that the objection of hidden qualitative variables should be rejected. If we work at the aggregate level and admit uncertainty,

---

[6]A complex system theorist could object that there is a fundamental uncertainty as regards the decisions that we will make: Will we take the path of building safer financial systems or we will build increasingly risky financial systems in the hope of realizing a gain?

there is no reason why we have to admit inherently qualitative judgment. In practice, we integrate qualitative judgment with models because (presently) it would be impractical or too costly to model all variables. If we consider modeling individual decision-making at the present stage of science, we have no definitive answer. Whenever financial markets depend on single decisions of single individuals we are in the presence of uncertainty that cannot be quantified. However, we have situations of this type in the physical sciences and we do not consider them an obstacle to the development of a mathematical science.

Let us now address a third objection to the use of mathematics in finance. It is sometimes argued that we cannot arrive at mathematical laws in finance because the laws themselves keep on changing. This objection is somehow true. Addressing it has led to the development of methods specific to financial economics. First observe that many physical systems are characterized by changing laws. For example, if we monitor the behavior of complex artifacts such as nuclear reactors we find that their behavior changes with aging. We can consider these changes as structural breaks. Obviously one could object that if we had more information we could establish a precise time-invariant law. Still, if the artifact is complex and especially if we cannot access all its parts, we might experience true structural breaks. For example, if we are monitoring the behavior of a nuclear reactor we might not be able to inspect it properly. Many natural systems such as volcanoes cannot be properly inspected and structurally described. We can only monitor their behavior, trying to find predictive laws. We might find that our laws change abruptly or continuously. We assume that we could identify more complex laws if we had all the requisite information, though, in practice, we do not have this information.

These remarks show that the objection of changing laws is less strong than we might intuitively believe. The real problem is not that the laws of finance change continuously. The real problem is that they are too complex. We do not have enough theoretical knowledge to determine finance laws and, if we try to estimate statistical models, we do not have enough data to estimate complex models. Stated differently, the question is not whether we can use mathematics in financial economic theory. The real question is: How much information we can obtain in studying financial markets? Laws and models in finance are highly uncertain. One partial solution is to use adaptive models. Adaptive models are formed by simple models plus rules to change the parameters of the simple models. A typical example is nonlinear state-space models. Nonlinear state-space models are formed by a simple regression plus another process that adapts continuously the model parameters. Other examples are hidden Markov models that might represent prices as formed by sequences of random walks with different parameters.

We can therefore conclude that the objection that there is no fixed law in financial economics cannot be solved a priori. Empirically we find that simple models cannot describe financial markets over long periods of time: if we turn to adaptive modeling, we are left with a residual high level of uncertainty.

Our overall conclusion is twofold. First, we can and indeed should regard mathematical finance as a discipline with methods and mathematics specific to the type of empirical data available in the discipline. Given the state of continuous change in our economies, we cannot force mathematical finance into the same paradigm of classical mathematical physics based on differential equations. Mathematical finance needs adaptive, nonlinear models that are able to adapt in a timely fashion to a changing empirical environment.

This is not to say that mathematical finance is equivalent to data-mining. On the contrary, we have to use all available knowledge and theoretical reasoning on financial economics. However, models cannot be crystallized in time-invariant models. In the future, it might be possible to achieve the goal of stable time-invariant models but, for the moment, we have to admit that mathematical finance needs adaptation and must make use of computer simulations. Even with the resources of modern adaptive computational methods, there will continue to be a large amount of uncertainty in mathematical finance, not only as probability distributions embedded in models but also as residual model uncertainty. When changes occur, there will be disruption of model performance and the need to adapt models to new situations. But this does not justify rejecting mathematical finance. Mathematical finance can indeed tell us what situations are more dangerous and might lead to disruptions. Through simulations and models of complex structure, we can achieve an understanding of those situations that are most critical.

Economies and financial markets are engineered artifacts. We can use our science to engineer economic and financial systems that are safer or we can decide, in the end, to prefer risk-taking and its highly skewed rewards. Of course we might object that uncertainty about the path our societies will take is part of the global problem of uncertainty. This objection is the objection of complex system theorists to reductionism. We can study a system with our fundamental laws once we know the initial and boundary conditions but we cannot explain how initial and boundary conditions were formed. These speculations are theoretically important but we should avoid a sense of passive fatality. In practice, it is important that we are aware that we have the tools to design safer financial systems and do not regard the path towards unpredictability as inevitable.

STUDIES OF THE USE OF QUANTITATIVE EQUITY MANAGEMENT

There are three recent studies on the use of quantitative equity management conducted by Intertek Partners. The studies are based on surveys and interviews of market participants. We will refer to these studies as the 2003 Intertek European study,[7] 2006 Intertek study,[8] and 2007 Intertek study.[9]

2003 Intertek European Study

The 2003 Intertek European study deals with the use of financial modeling at European asset management firms. It is based on studies conducted by The Intertek Group to evaluate model performance following the fall of the markets from their peak in March 2000, and explores changes that have occurred since then. In total, 61 managers at European asset management firms in the Benelux countries, France, Germany, Italy, Scandinavia, Switzerland, and the U.K. were interviewed. (The study does not cover alternative investment firms such as hedge funds.) At least half of the firms interviewed are among the major players in their respective markets, with assets under management ranging from €50 to €300 billion.

The major findings are summarized next.[10]

Greater Role for Models

In the two years following the March 2000 market highs, quantitative methods in the investment decision-making process began to play a greater role.

[7]The results of this study are reported in Frank J. Fabozzi, Sergio M. Focardi, and Caroline L. Jonas, "Trends in Quantitative Asset Management in Europe," *Journal of Portfolio Management* 31, no. 4 (2004), pp. 125–132 (Special European Section).

[8]The results of this study are reported in Frank J. Fabozzi, Sergio M. Focardi, and Caroline Jonas, "Trends in Quantitative Equity Management: Survey Results," *Quantitative Finance* 7, no. 2 (2007), pp. 115–122.

[9]The results of this study are reported in Frank J. Fabozzi, Sergio M. Focardi, and Caroline Jonas, *Challenges in Quantitative Equity Management* (CFA Institute Research Foundation, 2008) and Frank J. Fabozzi, Sergio M. Focardi, and Caroline L. Jonas, "On the Challenges in Quantitative Equity Management." *Quantitative Finance* 8, no. 7 (2008), pp. 649–655.

[10]In the quotes from sources in these studies, we omit the usual practice of identifying the reference and page number. The study where the quote is obtained will be clear.

Almost 75% of the firms interviewed reported this to be the case, while roughly 15% reported that the role of models had remained stable. The remaining 10% noted that their processes were already essentially quantitative. The role of models had also grown in another sense; a higher percentage of assets were being managed by funds run quantitatively. One firm reported that over the past two years assets in funds managed quantitatively grew by 50%.

Large European firms had been steadily catching up with their U.S. counterparts in terms of the breadth and depth of use of models. As the price of computers and computer software dropped, even small firms reported that they were beginning to adopt quantitative models. There were still differences between American and European firms, though. American firms tended to use relatively simple technology but on a large scale; Europeans tended to adopt sophisticated statistical methods but on a smaller scale.

Demand pull and management push were among the reasons cited for the growing role of models. On the demand side, asset managers were under pressure to produce returns while controlling risk; they were beginning to explore the potential of quantitative methods. On the push side, several sources remarked that, after tracking performance for several years, their management has made a positive evaluation of a model-driven approach against a judgment-driven decision-making process. In some cases, this led to a corporate switch to a quantitative decision-making process; in other instances, it led to shifting more assets into quantitatively managed funds.

Modeling was reported to have been extended over an ever greater universe of assets under management. Besides bringing greater structure and discipline to the process, participants in the study remarked that models helped contain costs. Unable to increase revenues in the period immediately following the March 2000 market decline, many firms were cutting costs. Modeling budgets, however, were reported as being largely spared. About 68% of the participants said that their investment in modeling had grown over the prior two years, while 50% expected their investments in modeling to continue to grow over the next year.

Client demand for risk control was another factor that drove the increased use of modeling. Pressure from institutional investors and consultants in particular continued to work in favor of modeling.

More generally, risk management was widely believed to be the key driving force behind the use of models.

Some firms mentioned they had recast the role of models in portfolio management. Rather than using models to screen and rank assets—which has been a typical application in Europe—they applied them after the asset manager had acted in order to measure the pertinence of fundamental analysis, characterize the portfolio style, eventually transform products through derivatives, optimize the portfolio, and track risk and performance.

Performance of Models Improves

Over one-half of the study's participants responded that models performed better in 2002 than two years before. Some 20% evaluated 2002 model performance as stable with respect to two years ago, while another 20% considered that performance had worsened. Participants often noted that it was not models in general but specific models that had performed better or more poorly.

There are several explanations for the improved performance of models. Every model is, ultimately, a statistical device trained and estimated on past data. When markets began to fall from their peak in March 2000, models had not been trained on data that would have allowed them to capture the downturn—hence, the temporary poor performance of some models. Even risk estimates, more stable than expected return estimates, were problematic. In many cases, it was difficult to distinguish between volatility and model risk. Models have since been trained on new sets of data and are reportedly performing better.

From a strictly scientific and economic theory point of view, the question of model performance overall is not easy to address. The basic question is how well a theory describes reality, with the additional complication that in economics uncertainty is part of the theory. As we observed in the previous section, we cannot object to financial modeling but we cannot pretend a priori that model performance be good. Modeling should reflect the objective amount of uncertainty present in a financial process. The statement that "models perform better" implies that the level of uncertainty has changed. To make this discussion meaningful, clearly somehow we have to restrict the universe of models under consideration. In general, the uncertainty associated with forecasting within a given class of models is equated to market volatility. And as market volatility is not an observable quantity but a hidden one, it is model-dependent.[11] In other words, the amount of uncertainty in financial markets depends on the accuracy of models. For instance, an ARCH-GARCH model will give an estimate of volatility different from that of a model based on constant volatility. On top of volatility, however, there is another source of uncertainty, which is the risk that the model is misspecified. The latter uncertainty is generally referred to as *model risk*.

---

[11]This statement is not strictly true. With the availability of high-frequency data, there is a new strain of financial econometrics that considers volatility as an observable realized volatility.

The problem experienced when markets began to fall was that models could not forecast volatility simply because they were grossly misspecified. A common belief is that markets are now highly volatile, which is another way of saying that models do not do a good job of predicting returns. Yet models are now more coherent; fluctuations of returns are synchronized with expectations regarding volatility. Model risk has been reduced substantially.

Overall, the global perception of European market participants who participated in the study was that models are now more dependable. This meant that model risk had been reduced; although their ability to predict returns had not substantially improved, models were better at predicting risk. Practitioners' evaluation of model performance can be summarized as follows: (1) models will bring more and more insight in risk management, (2) in stock selection, we will see some improvement due essentially to better data, not better models, and (3) in asset allocation, the use of models will remain difficult as markets remain difficult to predict.

Despite the improved performance of models, the perception European market participants shared was one of uncertainty as regards the macroeconomic trends of the markets. Volatility, structural change, and unforecastable events continue to challenge models. In addition to facing uncertainty related to a stream of unpleasant surprises as regards corporate accounting at large public firms, participants voiced the concern that there is considerable fundamental uncertainty on the direction of financial flows.

A widely shared evaluation was that, independent of models themselves, the understanding of models and their limits had improved. Most traders and portfolio managers had at least some training in statistics and finance theory; computer literacy was greatly increased. As a consequence, the majority of market participants understand at least elementary statistical analyses of markets.

Use of Multiple Models on the Rise

According to the 2003 study's findings, three major trends had emerged in Europe over the prior few years: (1) a greater use of multiple models, (2) the modeling of additional new factors, and (3) an increased use of value-based models.

Let's first comment on the use of multiple models from the point of view of modern financial econometrics, and in particular from the point of view of the mitigation of model risk. The present landscape of financial modeling applied to investment management is vast and well articulated.[12]

---

[12]For a discussion of the different families of financial models and modeling issues, see Sergio M. Focardi and Frank J. Fabozzi, *The Mathematics of Financial Modeling and Investment Management* (Hoboken, NJ: John Wiley & Sons, 2004).

Financial models are typically econometric models, they do not follow laws of nature but are approximate models with limited validity. Every model has an associated model risk, which can be roughly defined as the probability that the model does not forecast correctly. Note that it does not make sense to consider model risk in abstract, against every possible assumption; model risk can be meaningfully defined only by restricting the set of alternative assumptions. For instance, we might compute measures of the errors made by an option pricing model if the underlying follows a distribution different from the one on which the model is based. Clearly it must be specified what families of alternative distributions we are considering.

Essentially every model is based on some assumption about the functional form of dependencies between variables and on the distribution of noise. Given the assumptions, models are estimated, and decisions made. The idea of estimating model risk is to estimate the distribution of errors that will be made if the model assumptions are violated. For instance: Are there correlations or autocorrelations when it is assumed there are none? Are innovations fat-tailed when it is assumed that noise is white and normal? From an econometric point of view, combining different models in this way means constructing a mixture of distributions. The result of this process is one single model that weights the individual models.

Some managers interviewed for the 2003 study reported they were using judgment on top of statistical analysis. This entails that models be reviewed when they begin to produce results that are below expectations. In practice, quantitative teams constantly evaluate the performance of different families of models and adopt those that perform better. Criteria for switching from one family of models to another are called for, though. This, in turn, requires large data samples.

Despite these difficulties, application of multiple models has gained wide acceptance in finance. In asset management, the main driver is the uncertainty related to estimating returns.

Focus on Factors, Correlation, Sentiment, and Momentum

Participants in the 2003 study also reported efforts to determine new factors that might help predict expected returns. Momentum and sentiment were the two most cited phenomena modeled in equities. Market sentiment, in particular, was receiving more attention.

The use of factor models is in itself a well-established practice in financial modeling. Many different families of models are available, from the widely used classic static return factor analysis models to dynamic factor models, both of which are described later in Chapter 5. What remains a challenge is determination of the factors. Considerable resources have been devoted to studying market correlations. Advanced techniques for the robust estimation of correlations are being applied at large firms as well as at boutiques.

According to study respondents, over the three years prior to 2001, quantitative teams at many asset management firms were working on determining which factors are the best indicators of price movements. Sentiment was often cited as a major innovation in terms of modeling strategies. Asset management firms typically modeled stock-specific sentiment, while sentiment as measured by business or consumer confidence was often the responsibility of the macroeconomic teams at the mother bank, at least in continental Europe. Market sentiment is generally defined by the distribution of analyst revisions in earnings estimates. Other indicators of market confidence are flows, volume, turnover, and trading by corporate officers.

Factors that represent market momentum were also increasingly adopted according to the study. *Momentum* means that the entire market is moving in one direction with relatively little uncertainty. There are different ways to represent momentum phenomena. One might identify a specific factor that defines momentum, that is, a variable that gauges the state of the market in terms of momentum. This momentum variable then changes the form of models. There are models for trending markets and models for uncertain markets.

Momentum can also be represented as a specific feature of models. A random walk model does not have any momentum, but an autoregressive model might have an intrinsic momentum feature.

Some participants also reported using market-timing models and style rotation for the active management of funds. Producing accurate timing signals is complex, given that financial markets are difficult to predict. One source of predictability is the presence of mean reversion and cointegration phenomena.

Back to Value-Based Models

At the time of the 2003 study, there was a widespread perception that value-based models were performing better in post-2000 markets. It was believed that markets were doing a better job valuing companies as a function of the value of the firm rather than price trends, notwithstanding our remarks on the growing use of factors such as market sentiment. From a methodological point of view, methodologies based on cash analysis had increased in popularity in Europe. A robust positive operating cash flow is considered to be a better indication of the health of a firm than earnings estimates, which can be more easily massaged.

Fundamental analysis was becoming highly quantitative and automated. Several firms mentioned they were developing proprietary methodologies for the automatic analysis of balance sheets. For these firms, with the information available on the World Wide Web, fundamental analysis could be performed without actually going to visit firms. Some participants remarked that caution might be called for in attributing the good performance of value-tilted models to markets. One of the assumptions of value-based models is that there is no mechanism that conveys a large flow of funds through preferred channels, but this was the case in the telecommunications, media, and technology (TMT) bubble, when value-based models performed so poorly. In the last bull run prior to the study, the major preoccupation was to not miss out on rising markets; investors who continued to focus on value suffered poor performance. European market participants reported that they are now watching both trend and value.

Risk Management

Much of the attention paid to quantitative methods in asset management prior to the study had been focused on risk management. According to 83% of the participants, the role of risk management had evolved significantly over the prior two years to extend across portfolios and across processes.

One topic that has received a lot of attention, both in academia and at financial institutions, is the application of *extreme value theory* (EVT) to financial risk management.[13] The RiskLab in Zurich, headed by Paul Embrechts, advanced the use of EVT and copula functions in risk management. At the corporate level, universal banks such as HSBC CCF have produced theoretical and empirical work on the applicability of EVT to risk management.[14] European firms were also paying considerable attention to risk measures.

For participants in the Intertek study, risk management was the area where quantitative methods had made their biggest contribution. Since the pioneering work of Harry Markowitz in the 1950s, the objective of investment management has been defined as determining the optimal risk-return trade-off in an investor's profile. Prior to the diffusion of modeling techniques, though, evaluation of the risk-return trade-off was left to the judgment of individual asset managers. Modeling brought to the forefront the question of ex ante risk-return optimization. An asset management firm that uses quantitative methods and optimization techniques manages risk at the

---

[13]See Sergio M. Focardi and Frank J. Fabozzi, "Fat Tails, Scaling, and Stable Laws: A Critical Look at Modeling Extremal Events in Financial Phenomena," *Journal of Risk Finance* 5, no. 1 (Fall 2003), pp. 5–26.

[14]François Longin, "Stock Market Crashes: Some Quantitative Results Based on Extreme Value Theory." *Derivatives Use, Trading and Regulation* 7 (2001), pp. 197–205.

source. In this case, the only risk that needs to be monitored and managed is model risk.[15]

Purely quantitative managers with a fully automated management process were still rare according to the study. Most managers, although quantitatively oriented, used a hybrid approach calling for models to give evaluations that managers translate into decisions. In such situations, risk is not completely controlled at the origin.

Most firms interviewed for the study had created a separate risk management unit as a supervisory entity that controls the risk of different portfolios and eventually—although still only rarely—aggregated risk at the firm-wide level. In most cases, the tools of choice for controlling risk were multifactor models. Models of this type have become standard when it comes to making risk evaluations for institutional investors. For internal use, however, many firms reported that they made risk evaluations based on proprietary models, EVT, and scenario analysis.

Integrating Qualitative and Quantitative Information

More than 60% of the firms interviewed for the 2003 Intertek study reported they had formalized procedures for integrating quantitative and qualitative input, although half of these mentioned that the process had not gone very far; 30% of the participants reported no formalization at all. Some firms mentioned they had developed a theoretical framework to integrate results from quantitative models and fundamental views. Assigning weights to the various inputs was handled differently from firm to firm; some firms reported establishing a weight limit in the range of 50%–80% for quantitative input.

A few quantitative-oriented firms reported that they completely formalized the integration of qualitative and quantitative information. In these cases, everything relevant was built into the system. Firms that both quantitatively managed and traditionally managed funds typically reported that formalization was implemented in the former but not in the latter.

Virtually all firms reported at least a partial automation in the handling of qualitative information. For the most part, a first level of automation—including automatic screening and delivery, classification, and search—is provided by suppliers of sell-side research, consensus data, and news. These suppliers are automating the delivery of news, research reports, and other information.

---

[15]Asset management firms are subject to other risks, namely, the risk of not fulfilling a client mandate or operational risk. Although important, these risks were outside the scope of the survey.

About 30% of the respondents note they have added functionality over and above that provided by third-party information suppliers, typically starting with areas easy to quantify such as earnings announcements or analysts' recommendations. Some have coupled this with quantitative signals that alert recipients to changes or programs that automatically perform an initial analysis.

Only the braver will be tackling difficult tasks such as automated news summary and analysis. For the most part, news analysis was still considered the domain of judgment. A few firms interviewed for this study reported that they attempted to tackle the problem of automatic news analysis, but abandoned their efforts. The difficulty of forecasting price movements related to new information was cited as a motivation.

2006 Intertek Study

The next study that we will discuss is based on survey responses and conversations with industry representatives in 2006. Although this predates the subprime mortgage crisis and the resulting impact on the performance of quantitative asset managers, the insights provided by this study are still useful. In all, managers at 38 asset management firms managing a total of $4.3 trillion in equities participated in the study. Participants included individuals responsible for quantitative equity management and quantitative equity research at large- and medium-sized firms in North America and Europe.[16] Sixty-three percent of the participating firms were among the largest asset managers in their respective countries; they clearly represented the way a large part of the industry was going with respect to the use of quantitative methods in equity portfolio management.[17]

The findings of the 2006 study suggested that the skepticism relative to the future of quantitative management at the end of the 1990s had given way by 2006 and quantitative methods were playing a large role in equity portfolio management. Of the 38 survey participants, 11 (29%) reported that more than 75% of their equity assets were being managed quantitatively. This includes a wide spectrum of firms, with from $6.5 billion to over $650 billion in equity assets under management. Another 22 firms (58%) reported that they have some equities under quantitative management, though for 15 of these 22 firms the percentage of equities under quantitative management was less than 25%—often under 5%—of total equities under

---

[16]The home market of participating firms was a follows: 15 from North America (14 from the United States, 1 from Canada) and 23 from Europe (United Kingdom 7, Germany 5, Switzerland 4, Benelux 3, France 2, and Italy 2).

[17]Of the 38 participants in this survey, two responded only partially to the questionnaire. Therefore, for some questions, there are 36 (not 38) responses.

management. Five of the 38 participants in the survey (13%) reported no equities under quantitative management.

Relative to the period 2004–2005, the amount of equities under quantitative management was reported to have grown at most firms participating in the survey (84%). One reason given by respondents to explain the growth in equity assets under quantitative management was the flows into existing quantitative funds. A source at a large U.S. asset management firm with more than half of its equities under quantitative management said in 2006 "The firm has three distinct equity products: value, growth, and quant. Quant is the biggest and is growing the fastest."

According to survey respondents, the most important factor contributing to a wider use of quantitative methods in equity portfolio management was the positive result obtained with these methods. Half of the participants rated positive results as the single most important factor contributing to the widespread use of quantitative methods. Other factors contributing to a wider use of quantitative methods in equity portfolio management were, in order of importance attributed to them by participants, (1) the computational power now available on the desk top, (2) more and better data, and (3) the availability of third-party analytical software and visualization tools.

Survey participants identified the prevailing in-house culture as the most important factor holding back a wider use of quantitative methods (this evaluation obviously does not hold for firms that can be described as quantitative): more than one third (10/27) of the respondents at other than quant-oriented firms considered this the major blocking factor. This positive evaluation of models in equity portfolio management in 2006 was in contrast with the skepticism of some 10 years early. A number of changes have occurred. First, expectations at the time of the study had become more realistic. In the 1980s and 1990s, traders were experimenting with methodologies from advanced science in the hope of making huge excess returns. Experience of the prior 10 years has shown that models were capable of delivering but that their performance must be compatible with a well-functioning market.

More realistic expectations have brought more perseverance in model testing and design and have favored the adoption of intrinsically safer models. Funds that were using hundred fold leverage had become unpalatable following the collapse of LTCM (Long Term Capital Management). This, per se, has reduced the number of headline failures and had a beneficial impact on the perception of performance results. We can say that models worked better in 2006 because model risk had been reduced: simpler, more robust models delivered what was expected. Other technical reasons that explained improved model performance included a manifold increase in computing power and more and better data. Modelers by 2006 had available on their desk top computing power that, at the end of the 1980s, could be got only from multimillion-dollar supercomputers. Cleaner, more complete data, including intraday data and data on corporate actions/dividends, could be obtained. In addition, investment firms (and institutional clients) have learned how to use models throughout the investment management process. Models had become part of an articulated process that, especially in the case of institutional investors, involved satisfying a number of different objectives, such as superior information ratios.

Changing Role for Models in Equity Portfolio

The 2006 study revealed that quantitative models were now used in active management to find sources of excess returns (i.e., alphas), either relative to a benchmark or absolute. This was a considerable change with respect to the 2003 Intertek European study where quantitative models were reported as being used primarily to manage risk and to select parsimonious portfolios for passive management.

Another finding of the study was the growing amount of funds managed automatically by computer programs. The once futuristic vision of machines running funds automatically without the intervention of a portfolio manager was becoming a reality on a large scale: 55% (21/38) of the respondents reported that at least part of their equity assets were being managed automatically with quantitative methods; another three planned to automate at least a portion of their equity portfolios within the next 12 months. The growing automation of the equity investment process suggests that there was no missing link in the technology chain that leads to automatic quantitative management. From return forecasting to portfolio formation and optimization, all the needed elements were in place. Until recently, optimization represented the missing technology link in the automation of portfolio engineering. Considered too brittle to be safely deployed, many firms eschewed optimization, limiting the use of modeling to stock ranking or risk control functions. Advances in robust estimation methodologies (see Chapter 2) and in optimization (see Chapter 8) now allow an asset manager to construct portfolios of hundreds of stocks chosen in universes of thousands of stocks with little or no human intervention outside of supervising the models.

Modeling Methodologies and the Industry's Evaluation

At the end of the 1980s, academics and researchers at specialized quant boutiques experimented with many sophisticated modeling methodologies including chaos theory, fractals and multifractals, adaptive programming, learning theory, complexity theory, complex nonlinear stochastic models, data mining, and artificial intelligence. Most of these efforts failed to live up to expectations. Perhaps expectations were too high. Or perhaps the resources or commitment required were lacking. Emanuel Derman provides a lucid analysis of the difficulties that a quantitative analyst has to overcome. As he observed, though modern quantitative finance uses some of the techniques of physics, a wide gap remains between the two disciplines.[18]

The modeling landscape revealed by the 2006 study is simpler and more uniform. Regression analysis and momentum modeling are the most widely used techniques: respectively, 100% and 78% of the survey respondents said that these techniques were being used at their firms. With respect to regression models used today, the survey suggests that they have undergone a substantial change since the first multifactor models such as Arbitrage Pricing Theory (APT) were introduced. Classical multifactor models such as APT are static models embodied in linear regression between returns and factors at the same time. Static models are forecasting models insofar as the factors at time t are predictors of returns at time behavior $t + 1$. In these static models, individual return processes might exhibit zero autocorrelation but still be forecastable from other variables. Predictors might include financial and macroeconomic factors as well as company specific parameters such as financial ratios. Predictors might also include human judgment, for example, analyst estimates, or technical factors that capture phenomena such as momentum. A source at a quant shop using regression to forecast returns said,

> Regression on factors is the foundation of our model building. Ratios derived from financial statements serve as one of the most important components for predicting future stock returns. We use these ratios extensively in our bottom-up equity model and categorize them into five general categories: operating efficiency, financial strength, earnings quality (accruals), capital expenditures, and external financing activities.

Momentum and reversals were the second most widely diffused modeling technique among survey participants. In general, momentum and reversals were being used as a strategy, not as a model of asset returns. Momentum strategies are based on forming portfolios choosing the highest/lowest returns, where returns are estimated on specific time windows. Survey participants gave these strategies overall good marks but noted that (1) they do not always perform so well, (2) they can result in high turnover (though

---

[18]Emanuel Derman, "A Guide for the Perplexed Quant," *Quantitative Finance* 1, no. 5 (2001), pp. 476–480.

some were using constraints/penalties to deal with this problem), and (3) identifying the timing of reversals was tricky.

Momentum was first reported in 1993 by Jegadeesh and Titman in the U.S. market.[19] Nine years later, they confirmed that momentum continued to exist in the 1990s in the U.S. market.[20] Two years later, Karolyi and Kho examined different models for explaining momentum and concluded that no random walk or autoregressive model is able to explain the magnitude of momentum empirically found;[21] they suggested that models with time varying expected returns come closer to explaining empirical magnitude of momentum. Momentum and reversals are presently explained in the context of local models updated in real time. For example, momentum as described in the original Jegadeesh and Titman study is based on the fact that stock prices can be represented as independent random walks when considering periods of the length of one year. However, it is fair to say that there is no complete agreement on the econometrics of asset returns that justifies momentum and reversals and stylized facts on a global scale, and not as local models. It would be beneficial to know more about the econometrics of asset returns that sustain momentum and reversals.

Other modeling methods that were widely used by participants in the 2006 study included cash flow analysis and behavioral modeling. Seventeen of the 36 participating firms said that they modeled cash flows; behavioral modeling was reported as being used by 16 of the 36 participating firms.[22] Considered to play an important role in asset predictability, 44% of the survey respondents said that they use behavioral modeling to try to capture phenomena such as departures from rationality on the part of investors (e.g., belief persistence), patterns in analyst estimates, and corporate

---

[19]Narasimhan Jegadeesh and Sheridan Titman, "Returns to Buying Winners and Selling Losers: Implications for Stock Market Efficiency," *Journal of Finance* 48, no. 1 (1993), pp. 65–92.

[20]Narasimhan Jegadeesh and Sheridan Titman, "Cross-Sectional and Time-Series Determinants of Momentum Returns," *Review of Financial Studies* 15, no. 1 (2002), pp. 143–158.

[21]George A. Karolyi and Bong-Chan Kho, "Momentum Strategies: Some Bootstrap Tests," *Journal of Empirical Finance* 11 (2004), pp. 509–536.

[22]The term behavioral modeling is often used rather loosely. Full-fledged behavioral modeling exploits a knowledge of human psychology to identify situations where investors are prone to show behavior that leads to market inefficiencies. The tendency now is to call any model *behavioral* that exploits market inefficiency. However, implementing true behavioral modeling is a serious challenge; even firms with very large, powerful quant teams who participated in the survey reported that there is considerable work needed to translate departures from rationality into a set of rules for identifying stocks as well as entry and exit points for a quantitative stock selection process.

executive investment/disinvestment behavior. Behavioral finance is related to momentum in that the latter is often attributed to various phenomena of persistence in analyst estimates and investor perceptions. A source at a large investment firm that has incorporated behavioral modeling into its active equity strategies commented,

> The attraction of behavioral finance is now much stronger than it was just five years ago. Everyone now acknowledges that markets are not efficient, that there are behavioral anomalies. In the past, there was the theory that was saying that markets are efficient while market participants such as the proprietary trading desks ignored the theory and tried to profit from the anomalies. We are now seeing a fusion of theory and practice.

As for other methodologies used in return forecasting, sources cited nonlinear methods and cointegration. Nonlinear methods are being used to model return processes at 19% (7/36) of the responding firms. The nonlinear method most widely used among survey participants is classification and regression trees (CART). The advantage of CART is its simplicity and the ability of CART methods to be cast in an intuitive framework. A source in the survey that reported using CART as a central part of the portfolio construction process in enhanced index and longer-term value-based portfolios said,

> CART compresses a large volume of data into a form which identifies its essential characteristics, so the output is easy to understand. CART is non-parametric—which means that it can handle an infinitely wide range of statistical distributions—and nonlinear—so as a variable selection technique it is particularly good at handling higher-order interactions between variables.

Only 11% (4/36) of the respondents reported using nonlinear regime-shifting models; at most firms, judgment was being used to assess regime change. Participants identified the difficulty in detecting the precise timing of a regime switch and the very long time series required to estimate shifts as obstacles to modeling regime shifts. A survey participant at a firm where regime-shifting models have been experimented with commented,

> Everyone knows that returns are conditioned by market regimes, but the potential for overfitting when implementing regime-switching models is great. If you could go back with fifty years of data—but

we have only some ten years of data and this is not enough to build a decent model.

Cointegration was being used by 19% (7/36) of the respondents. As explained in Chapter 3, cointegration models the short-term dynamics (direction) and long-run equilibrium (fair value). A perceived plus of cointegration is the transparency that it provides: the models are based on economic and finance theory and calculated from economic data.

Optimization

Another area where much change was revealed by the 2006 study was optimization. According to sources, optimization was being performed at 92% (33/36) of the participating firms, albeit in some cases only rarely. Mean variance was the most widely used technique among survey participants: it was being used by 83% (30/36) of the respondents. It was followed by utility optimization (42% or 15/36) and, robust optimization (25% or 9/36). Only one firm mentioned that it is using stochastic optimization.

The wider use of optimization was a significant development compared to the 2003 study when many sources had reported that they eschewed optimization: the difficulty of identifying the forecasting error was behind the then widely held opinion that optimization techniques were too brittle and prone to error maximization. The greater use of optimization was attributed to advances in large-scale optimization coupled with the ability to include constraints and robust methods for both estimation and optimization. This result is significant as portfolio formation strategies rely on optimization. With optimization feasible, the door was open to a fully automated investment process. In this context, it is noteworthy that 55% of the survey respondents in the 2006 study reported that at least a portion of their equity assets is being managed by a fully automated process.

Optimization is the engineering part of portfolio construction and for this reason is discussed in Chapters 6, 7, and 8. Most portfolio construction problems can be cast in an optimization framework, where optimization is applied to obtain the desired optimal risk-return profile. Optimization is the technology behind the current offering of products with specially engineered returns, such as guaranteed returns. However, the offering of products with particular risk-return profiles requires optimization methodologies that go well beyond classical mean-variance optimization. In particular one must be able to (1) work with real-world utility functions and (2) apply constraints to the optimization process.

Challenges

The growing diffusion of models is not without challenges. The 2006 survey participants noted three: (1) increasing difficulty in differentiating products; (2) difficulty in marketing quant funds, especially to non-institutional investors; and (3) performance decay.

Quantitative equity management has now become so wide spread that a source at a long-established quantitative investment firm remarked,

> There is now a lot of competition from new firms entering the space [of quantitative investment management]. The challenge is to continue to distinguish ourselves from competition in the minds of clients.

With quantitative funds based on the same methodologies and using the same data, the risk is to construct products with the same risk-return profile. The head of active equities at a large quantitative firm with more than a decade of experience in quantitative management remarked in the survey, "Everyone is using the same data and reading the same articles: it's tough to differentiate."

While sources in the survey reported that client demand was behind the growth of (new) pure quantitative funds, some mentioned that quantitative funds might be something of a hard sell. A source at a medium-sized asset management firm servicing both institutional clients and high-net worth individuals said,

> Though clearly the trend towards quantitative funds is up, quant approaches remain difficult to sell to private clients: they remain too complex to explain, there are too few stories to tell, and they often have low alpha. Private clients do not care about high information ratios.

Markets are also affecting the performance of quantitative strategies. A report by the Bank for International Settlements (2006) noted that this is a period of historically low volatility. What is exceptional about this period, observes the report, is the simultaneous drop in volatility in all variables: stock returns, bond spreads, rates, and so on. While the role of models in reducing volatility is unclear, what is clear is that models immediately translate this situation into a rather uniform behavior. Quantitative funds try to differentiate themselves either finding new unexploited sources of return forecastability, for example, novel ways of looking at financial statements, or using optimization creatively to engineer special risk-return profiles.

A potentially more serious problem is performance decay. Survey participants remarked that model performance was not so stable. Firms are tackling these problems in two ways. First, they are protecting themselves from model breakdown with model risk mitigation techniques, namely by averaging results obtained with different models. It is unlikely that all models break down in the same way in the same moment, so that averaging with different models allows asset managers to diversify risk. Second, there is an ongoing quest for new factors, new predictors, and new aggregations of factors and predictors. In the long run, however, something more substantial might be required: this is the subject of the chapters ahead.

2007 Intertek Study

The 2007 Intertek study, sponsored by the Research Foundation of the CFA Institute, is based on conversations with asset managers, investment consultants, and fund-rating agencies as well as survey responses from 31 asset managers in the United States and Europe. In total, 12 asset managers and eight consultants and fund-rating agencies were interviewed and 31 managers with a total of $2.2 trillion in equities under management participated in the survey. Half of the participating firms were based in the United States; half of the participating firms were among the largest asset managers in their countries. Survey participants included chief investment officers of equities and heads of quantitative management and/or quantitative research.

A major question in asset management that this study focused on was if the diffusion of quantitative strategies was making markets more efficient, thereby reducing profit opportunities. The events of the summer of 2007 which saw many quantitatively managed funds realize large losses brought an immediacy to the question. The classical view of financial markets holds that market speculators make markets efficient, hence the absence of profit opportunities after compensating for risk. This view had formed the basis of academic thinking for several decades starting from the 1960s. However, practitioners had long held the more pragmatic view that a market formed by fallible human agents (as market speculators also are) offers profit opportunities due to the many small residual imperfections that ultimately result in delayed or distorted responses to news.

A summary of the findings of this study are provided next.

Are Model-Driven Investment Strategies Impacting Market Efficiency and Price Processes?

The empirical question of the changing nature of markets is now receiving much academic attention. For example, using empirical data from 1927 to

2005, Hwang and Rubesam[23] argued that momentum phenomena disappeared during the period 2000–2005, while Figelman,[24] analyzing the S&P 500 over the period 1970–2004, found new evidence of momentum and reversal phenomena previously not described. Khandani and Lo[25] show how a mean-reversion strategy that they used to analyze market behavior lost profitability in the 12-year period from 1995 to 2007.

Intuition suggests that models will have an impact on price processes but whether models will make markets more efficient or less efficient will depend on the type of models widely adopted. Consider that there are two categories of models, those based on fundamentals and those based on the analysis of time series of past prices and returns. Models based on fundamentals make forecasts based on fundamental characteristics of firms and, at least in principle, tend to make markets more efficient. Models based on time series of prices and returns are subject to self-referentiality and might actually lead to mispricings. A source at a large financial firm that has both fundamental and quant processes said,

> The impact of models on markets and price processes is asymmetrical. [Technical] model-driven strategies have a less good impact than fundamental-driven strategies as the former are often based on trend following.

Another source commented,

> Overall quants have brought greater efficiency to the market, but there are poor models out there that people get sucked into. Take momentum. I believe in earnings momentum, not in price momentum: it is a fool buying under the assumption that a bigger fool will buy in the future. Anyone who uses price momentum assumes that there will always be someone to take the asset off your hands—a fool's theory. Studies have shown how it is possible to get into a momentum-type market in which asset prices get bid up, with everyone on the collective belief wagon.

The question of how models impact the markets—making them more or less efficient—depends on the population of specific models. As long as

---

[23]Soosung Hwang and Alexandre Rubesam, "The Disappearance of Momentum" (November 7, 2008). Available at SSRN: http://ssrn.com/abstract=968176.
[24]Ilya Figelman, "Stock Return Momentum and Reversal," *Journal of Portfolio Management* 34 (2007), pp. 51–69.
[25]Amir E. Khandani and Andrew W. Lo, "What Happened to the Quants in August 2007," *Journal of Investment Management* 5 (2007), pp. 29–78.

models based on past time series of prices and returns (i.e., models that are trend followers) are being used, it will not be possible to assume that models make markets more efficient. Consider that it is not only a question of how models compete with each other but also how models react to exogenous events and how models themselves evolve. For example, a prolonged period of growth will produce a breed of models different from models used in low-growth periods.

Performance Issues

When the 2006 Intertek study was conducted on equity portfolio modeling in early 2006, quantitative managers were very heady about performance. By mid-2007, much of that headiness was gone. By July–August 2007, there was much perplexity.

Many participants in the 2007 Intertek study attributed the recent poor performance of many quant equity funds to structural changes in the market. A source at a large financial firm with both fundamental and quantitative processes said,

> The problem with the performance of quant funds [since 2006] is that there was rotation in the marketplace. Most quants have a strong value bias so they do better in a value market. The period 1998–1999 was not so good for quants as it was a growth market; in 2001–2005 we had a value market so value-tilted styles such as the quants were doing very well. In 2006 we were back to a growth market. In addition, in 2007, spreads compressed. The edge quants had has eroded.

One might conclude that if markets are cyclical, quant outperformance will also be cyclical. A leading investment consultant who participated in the survey remarked,

> What is most successful in terms of producing returns—quant or fundamental—is highly contextual: there is no best process, quant or fundamental. Quants are looking for an earnings-quality component that has dissipated in time. I hate to say it but any manager has to have the wind behind its strategies, favoring the factors.

Speaking in August 2007, the head of active quantitative research at a large international firm said,

It has been challenging since the beginning of the year. The problem is that fundamental quants are stressing some quality—be it value or growth—but at the beginning of the year there was a lot of activity of hedge funds, much junk value, much froth. In addition there was a lot of value-growth style rotation, which is typical when there is macro insecurity and interest rates go up and down. The growth factor is better when rates are down, the value factor better when rates are up. Fundamental quants could not get a consistent exposure to factors they wanted to be exposed to.

Another source said, "We tried to be balanced value-growth but the biggest danger is rotation risk. One needs a longer-term view to get through market cycles." The CIO of equities at a large asset management firm added, "Growth and value markets are cyclical and it is hard to get the timing right."

The problem of style rotation (e.g., value versus growth) is part of the global problem of adapting models to changing market conditions. Value and growth represent two sets of factors, both of which are captured, for example, in the Fama–French three-factor model.[26] But arguably there are many more factors. So factor rotation is more than just a question of value and growth markets. Other factors such as momentum are subject to the same problem; that is to say, one factor prevails in one market situation and loses importance in another and is replaced by yet another factor(s).

Other reasons were cited to explain why the performance of quantitative products as a group has been down since 2006. Among these is the fact that there were now more quantitative managers using the same data, similar models, and implementing similar strategies. A source at a firm that has both quant and fundamental processes said,

> Why is performance down? One reason is because many more people are using quant today than three, five years ago. Ten years ago the obstacles to entry were higher: data were more difficult to obtain, models were proprietary. Now we have third-party suppliers of data feeds, analytics, and back-testing capability.

A consultant concurred,

> The next 12 to 24 months will be tough for quants for several reasons. One problem is … the ease with which people can now buy and manipulate data. The problem is too many people are running

---

[26]Eugene F. Fama and Kenneth R. French, "Common Risk Factors and the Returns on Stocks and Bonds," *Journal of Financial Economics*, 47 (1993), pp. 427–465.

similar models so performance decays and it becomes hard to stay ahead. Performance is a genuine concern.

Still another source said,

> Quant performance depends on cycles and the secular trend but success breeds its own problems. By some estimates there are $4 trillion in quantitative equity management if we include passive, active, hedge funds, and proprietary desks. There is a downside to the success of quants. Because quants have been so successful, if a proprietary desk or a hedge fund needs to get out of a risk, they can't. Then you get trampled on as others have more to sell than you have to buy. The business is more erratic because of the sheer size and needs of proprietary desks and hedge funds whose clients hold 6 to 12 months against six years for asset managers.

However, not all sources agreed that the fact that quantitative managers are using the same data and/or similar models entails a loss of performance. One source said,

> Though all quants use the same data sources, I believe that there is a difference in models and in signals. There are details behind the signals and in how you put them together. Portfolio construction is one very big thing.

Another source added,

> All quants use similar data but even minor differences can lead to nontrivial changes in valuation. If you have 15 pieces of information, different sums are not trivial. Plus if you combine small differences in analytics and optimization, the end result can be large differences. There is not one metric but many metrics and all are noisy.

Investment consultants identified risk management as among the biggest pluses for a quantitative process. According to one source,

> Quantitative managers have a much greater awareness of risk. They are attuned to risk in relation to the benchmark as well as to systemic risk. Fundamental managers are often not aware of concentration in, for example, factors or exposure.

In view of the performance issues, survey participants were asked if they believed that quantitative managers were finding it increasingly difficult to generate excess returns as market inefficiencies were exploited. Just over half agreed while 32% disagreed and 16% expressed no opinion. When the question was turned around, 73% of the survey participants agreed that, though profit opportunities would not disappear, quantitative managers would find it increasingly hard to exploit them. One source remarked,

> Performance is getting harder to wring out not because everyone is using the same data and similar models, but because markets are more efficient. So we will see Sharpe ratios shrink for active returns. Managers will have to use more leverage to get returns. The problem is more acute for quant managers as all quant positions are highly correlated as they all use book to price; fundamental managers, on the other hand, differ on the evaluation of future returns'.

When asked what market conditions were posing the most serious challenge to a quantitative approach in equity portfolio management, survey respondents ranked in order of importance on a scale from one to five the rising correlation level, style rotation, and insufficient liquidity. Other market conditions rated important were a fundamental market shift, high (cross sector) volatility and low (cross) volatility. Felt less important were the impact of the dissipation of earnings and non-trending markets.

In their paper on the likely causes of the summer 2007 events, Khandani and Lo[27] note the sharp rise in correlations over the period 1998–2007. They observe that this rise in correlations reflects a much higher level of interdependence in financial markets. This interdependence is one of the factors responsible for the contagion from the subprime mortgage crisis to the equity markets in July–August 2007. When problems began to affect equity markets, the liquidity crisis started. Note that liquidity is a word that assumes different meanings in different contexts. In the study, liquidity refers to the possibility of finding buyers and thus to the possibility of deleveraging without sustaining heavy losses. One CIO commented,

> Everyone in the quant industry is using the same factors [thus creating highly correlated portfolios prone to severe contagion effects]. When you need to unwind, there is no one there to take the trade: Quants are all children of Fama and French. Lots of people are using earnings revision models.

---

[27]Khandani and Lo, "What Happened to the Quants in August 2007?"

Another source remarked, "Because quants have been so successful, if you need to get out of a risk for whatever reason, you can't get out. This leads to a liquidity sell-off."

Specific to recent market turmoil, participants identified the unwinding of long–short positions by hedge funds as by far the most important factor contributing to the losses incurred by some quant equity finds in the summer of 2007. One source said wryly, "Everyone is blaming the quants; they should be blaming the leverage."

Improving Performance

As it was becoming increasingly difficult to deliver excess returns, many quant managers had turned to using leverage in an attempt to boost performance—a strategy most sources agreed was quite risky. The events of the summer of 2007 were to prove them right. Given the performance issues, survey participants were asked what they were likely to do to try to improve performance.

The search to identify new and/or unique factors was the most frequently cited strategy and complementary to it, the intention to employ new models. A CIO of equities said,

> Through the crisis of July–August 2007, quant managers have learned which of their factors are unique and will be focusing on what is unique. There will be a drive towards using more proprietary models, doing more unique conceptual work. But it will be hard to get away from fundamental concepts: you want to hold companies that are doing well and do not want to pay too much for them.

As for the need to employ new models, the global head of quantitative strategies at a large financial group remarked,

> Regression is the art of today's tool kit. To get better performance, we will have to enlarge the tool kit and add information and dynamic and static models. People are always changing things; maybe we will be changing things just a bit quicker.

Other strategies to improve performance given by the 2007 survey participants included attempts to diversify sources of business information and data. As one investment consultant said,

All quant managers rely on the same set of data but one cannot rely on the same data and have an analytical edge; it is a tough sell. Quant managers need an informational edge, information no one else has or uses. It might be coming out of academia or might be information in the footnotes of balance sheet data or other information in the marketplace that no one else is using.

Just over 60% of the survey participants agreed that, given that everyone is using the same data and similar models, quantitative managers need a proprietary informational edge to outperform. Sources mentioned that some hedge fund managers now have people in-house on the phone, doing proprietary market research on firms.

Opinions among survey respondents diverged as to the benefits to be derived from using high-frequency (up to tick-by-tick) data. Thirty-eight percent of the participants believed that high-frequency data can give an informational edge in equity portfolio management while 27% disagreed and 35% expressed no opinion. It is true that there was still only limited experience with using high-frequency data in equity portfolio management at the time of the survey. One source remarked, "Asset managers now have more frequent updates, what was once monthly is now daily with services such as WorldScope, Compustat, Market QA, Bloomberg, or Factset. But the use of intraday data is still limited to the trading desk."

Fund Flows

Estimates of how much was under management in active quant strategies in 2007 vary from a few hundred million dollars to over $1 trillion. In a study that compared cumulative net flows in U.S. large cap quantitative and "other" products as a percentage of total assets during the 36-month period which coincided with the 2001–2005 value market, Casey, Quirk and Associates[28] found that assets grew 25% at quantitative funds and remained almost flat for other funds. A co-author of that study commented,

> What we have seen in our studies, which looked at U.S. large cap funds, is that since 2004 investors have withdrawn money from the U.S. large cap segment under fundamental managers but active quants have held on to their assets or seen them go up slightly.

---

[28]Casey, Quirk and Associates, "The Geeks Shall Inherit the Earth?" November 2005.

Addressing the question of net flows into quantitatively managed equity funds before July–August 2007, a source at a leading investment consultancy said,

> There has been secular growth for quant equity funds over the past 20 or so years, first into passive quant and, over the past 12–36 months, into active quant given their success in the past value market. Right now there is about an 80/20 market split between fundamental and active quant management. If active quants can continue their strong performance in a growth market which I think we are now in, I can see the percentage shift over the next three years to 75/25 with active quant gaining a few points every year.

Despite the high-profile problems at some long–short quantitative managed funds during the summer of 2007, 63% of the respondents indicated that they were optimistic that, overall, quantitatively managed equity funds will continue to increase their market share relative to traditionally managed funds, as more firms introduce quantitative products and exchange-traded funds (ETFs) give the retail investor access to active quant products. However, when the question was reformulated, that optimism was somewhat dampened. Thirty-nine percent of the survey participants agreed that overall quantitatively managed funds would not be able to increase their market share relative to traditionally managed funds for the year 2007 while 42% disagreed.

Many consultants who were interviewed for the study just before the July–August 2007 market turmoil were skeptical that quantitative managers could continue their strong performance. These sources cited performance problems dating back to the year 2006.

Lipper tracks flows of quantitative and non-quantitative funds in four equity universes: large cap, enhanced index funds, market neutral, and long-short funds. The Lipper data covering the performance of quantitatively and nonquantitatively driven funds in the three-year period 2005-2007 showed that quant funds underperformed in 2007 in all categories except large cap—a reversal of performance from 2005 and 2006 when quant managers were outperforming nonquantitative managers in all four categories. However, Lipper data are neither risk adjusted nor fee adjusted and the sampling of quant funds in some categories is small. For the period January 2005–June 2008, according to the Lipper data, long-only funds—both quant and nonquant—experienced a net outflow while all other categories experienced net inflows—albeit at different rates—with the exception of nonquant market neutral funds. The differences (as percentages) between quant and non-quant funds were not very large but quant funds exhibited more negative results.

In view of the preceding, the survey participants were asked if, given the poor performance of some quant funds in the year 2007, they thought that traditional asset management firms that have diversified into quantitative management would be reexamining their commitment. Nearly one third agreed while 52% disagreed (16% expressed no opinion). Those that agreed tended to come from firms at which equity assets under management represent less than 5% of all equities under management or where there is a substantial fundamental overlay to the quantitative process.

The head of quantitative equity at a large traditional manager said,

> When the firm decided back in the year 2000 to build a quant business as a diversifier, quant was not seen as a competitor to fundamental analysis. The initial role of quant managers was one of being a problem solver, for 130/30-like strategies or whereever there is complexity in portfolio construction. If quant performance is down, the firm might reconsider its quant products. Should they do so, I would expect that the firm would keep on board some quants as a support to their fundamental business.

Quantitative Processes, Oversight, and Overlay

Let's define what we mean by a quantitative process. Many traditionally managed asset management firms now use some computer-based, statistical decision-support tool and do some risk modeling. The study referred to an investment process as fundamental (or traditional) if it is performed by a human asset manager using information and judgment, and quantitative if the value-added decisions are made primarily in terms of quantitative outputs generated by computer-driven models following fixed rules. The study referred to a process as being *hybrid* if it uses a combination of the two. An example of the latter is a fundamental manager using a computer-driven stock-screening system to narrow his or her portfolio choices.

Among participants in the study, two-thirds had model-driven processes allowing only minimum (5%–10%) discretion or oversight, typically to make sure that numbers made sense and that buy orders were not issued for firms that were the subject of news or rumors not accounted for by the models. Model oversight was considered a control function. This oversight was typically exercised when large positions were involved. A head of quantitative equity said, "Decision-making is 95% model-driven, but we will look at a trader's list and do a sanity check to pull a trade if necessary."

Some firms indicated that they had automated the process of checking if there are exogenous events that might affect the investment decisions. One source said,

> Our process is model driven with about 5% oversight. We ask ourselves: "Do the numbers make sense?" and do news scanning and flagging using in-house software as well as software from a provider of business information.

This comment underlines one of the key functions of judgmental overlays: the consideration of information with a bearing on forecasts that does not appear yet in the predictors. This information might include, for example, rumors about important events that are not yet confirmed, or facts hidden in reporting or news releases that escape the attention of most investors.

Fundamental analysts and managers might have sources of information that can add to the information that is publicly available. However, there are drawbacks to a judgmental approach to information gathering. As one source said, "An analyst might fall in love with the Chief Financial Officer of a firm, and lose his objectivity."

Other sources mentioned using oversight in the case of rare events such as those of July–August 2007. The head of quantitative management at a large firm said,

> In situations of extreme market events, portfolio managers talk more to traders. We use Bayesian learning to learn from past events but, in general, dislocations in the market are hard to model."

Bayesian priors are a disciplined way to integrate historical data and a manager's judgment in the model.

Another instance of exercising oversight is in the area of risk. One source said, "The only overlay we exercise is on risk, where we allow ourselves a small degree of freedom, not on the model."

The key question is: Is there a best way to comingle judgment and models? Each of these presents pitfalls. Opinions among participants in the 2007 Intertek study differed as to the advantage of commingling models and judgment and ways that it might be done. More than two-thirds of the survey participants (68%) disagreed with the statement that the most effective equity portfolio management process combines quantitative tools and a fundamental overlay; only 26% considered that a fundamental overlay adds value. Interestingly, most investment consultants and fund-rating firms interviewed for the study shared the appraisal that adding a fundamental overlay to a quantitative investment process did not add value.

A source at a large consultancy said,

> Once you believe that a model is stable, effective over a long time, it is preferable not to use human overlay as it introduces emotion, judgment. The better alternative to human intervention is to arrive at an understanding of how to improve model performance and implement changes to the model.

Some sources believed that a fundamental overlay had value in extreme situations, but not everyone agreed. One source said,

> Overlay is additive and can be detrimental, oversight is neither. It does not alter the quantitative forecast but implements a reality check. In market situations such as of July–August 2007, overlay would have been disastrous. The market goes too fast and takes on a crisis aspect. It is a question of intervals.

Among the 26% who believed that a fundamental overlay does add value, sources cited the difficulty of putting all information in the models. A source that used models for asset managers said,

> In using quant models, there can be data issues. With a fundamental overlay, you get more information. It is difficult to convert all fundamental data, especially macro information such as the yen/dollar exchange rate, into quant models.

A source at a firm that is using a fundamental overlay systematically said,

> The question is how you interpret quantitative outputs. We do a fundamental overlay, reading the 10-Qs and the 10-Ks and the footnotes, plus looking at, for example, increases in daily sales invoices. I expect that we will continue to use a fundamental overlay: it provides a common-sense check. You cannot ignore real-world situations.

In summary, overlays and human oversight in model-driven strategies can be implemented in different ways. First, as a control function, oversight allows managers to exercise judgment in specific situations. Second, human judgment might be commingled with a model's forecasts.

Implementing a Quant Process

The 2007 survey participants were asked how they managed the model building and back-testing process. One-fourth of the participants said that their firms admitted several processes. For example, at 65% of the sources, quantitative models are built and back-tested by the asset manager him/herself; at 39% quantitative models are built and back-tested by the firm's central research center. More rarely, at 23% models might also be built by the corporate research center to the specifications of the asset manager, while at 16% models might also be built by the asset manager but are back-tested by the research center.[29]

Some sources also cited a coming together of quantitative research and portfolio management. Certainly this is already the case at some of the largest quantitative players that began in the passive quantitative arena, where, as one source put it, "the portfolio manager has Unix programming skills as a second nature."

The need to continuously update models was identified by sources as one of the major challenges to a quantitative investment process. A consultant to the industry remarked,

> The specifics of which model each manager uses is not so important as long as management has a process to ensure that the model is always current, that as a prism for looking at the universe the model is relevant, that it is not missing anything. One problem in the U.S. in the 1980s–90s was that models produced spectacular results for a short period of time and then results decayed. The math behind the models was static, simplistic, able to capture only one trend. Today, quants have learned their lesson; they are paranoid about the need to do a constant evaluation to understand what's working this year and might not work next year. The problem is one of capturing the right signals and correctly weighting them when things are constantly changing.

The need to sustain an on-going effort in research was cited by investment consultants as determinant in manager choices. One consultant said,

> When quant performance decays it is often because the manager has grown complacent and then things stop working. When we look at a quant manager, we ask: can they continue to keep doing research?

---

[29]The percentages do not add to 100 because events overlap.

One way to ensure that models adapt to the changing environment is to use adaptive modeling techniques. One quantitative manager said,

> You cannot use one situation, one data set in perpetuity. For consistently good performance, you need new strategies, new factors. We use various processes in our organization, including regime-shifting adaptive models. The adaptive model draws factors from a pool and selects variables that change over time.

The use of adaptive models and of strategies that can self-adapt to changing market conditions is an important research topic. From a mathematical point of view, there are many tools that can be used to adapt models. Among these is a class of well-known models with hidden variables, including state-space models, hidden Markov models, or regime-shifting models. These models have one or more variables that represent different market conditions. The key challenge is estimation: the ability to identify regime shifts sufficiently early calls for a rich regime structure, but estimating a rich regime shifting model calls for a very large data sample—something we rarely have in finance.

The survey participants were asked if they thought that quantitative-driven equity investment processes were moving towards full automation. By a fully automated quant investment process we intend a process where investment decisions are made by computers with little or no human intervention. An automated process includes the input of data, production of forecasts, optimization/portfolio formation, oversight, and trading. Among those expressing an opinion, as many believed that quantitative managers are moving toward full automation (38%) as not (38%). Industry observers and consultants also had difficulty identifying a trend. One source remarked, "There are all degrees of automation among quants and we see no obvious trend either towards or away from automation." It would appear that we will continue to see a diversity in management models. This diversity is due to the fact that there is no hard science behind quantitative equity investment management; business models reflect the personalities and skill sets inside an organization.

Obstacles to full automation are not due to technical shortcomings. As noted earlier, there are presently no missing links in the automation chain going from forecasting to optimization. Full automation is doable but successful implementation depends on the ability to link seamlessly a return forecasting tool with a portfolio formation strategy. Portfolio formation strategies can take the form of full optimization or might be based on some heuristics with constraints.

The progress of full automation will ultimately depend on performance and investor acceptance. Consultants that interviewed for this study were divided in their evaluation of the advisability of full automation. One source said, "All things being equal, I actually prefer a fully automated process once you believe that a model is stable, effective over a long time." However, in a divergent view, another consultant said, "I am not keen on fully automated processes. I like to see human intervention, interaction before and after optimization, and especially before trading."

Risk Management

The events of July–August 2007 highlighted once more that quantitatively managed funds can be exposed to the risk of extreme events (i.e., rare large—often adverse—events). Fundamentally managed funds are also exposed to the risk of extreme events, typically of a more familiar nature such as a market crash or a large drop in value of single firms or sectors. A head of quantitative management remarked, "There are idiosyncratic risks and systemic risks. Fundamental managers take idiosyncratic risk while the quants look at the marginal moves, sometimes adding leverage."

There seems to be a gap between state-of-the-art risk management and the practice of finance. At least, this is what appears in a number of statements made after the summer of 2007 that attributed losses to multi-sigma events in a Gaussian world. It is now well known that financial phenomena do not follow normal distributions and that the likelihood of extreme events is much larger than if they were normally distributed. Financial phenomena are governed by fat-tailed distributions. The fat-tailed nature of financial phenomena has been at the forefront of research in financial econometrics since the 1990s. Empirical research has shown that returns are not normal and most likely can be represented as fat-tailed processes.

Facts like this have an important bearing on the distribution of returns of dynamic portfolios. Consequently, the 2007 study asked survey participants if they believed that the current generation of risk models had pitfalls that do not allow one to properly anticipate risks such as those of July–August 2007. Just over two-thirds of the survey respondents evaluated agreed that, because today's risk models do not take into consideration global systemic risk factors, they cannot predict events such as those of July–August 2007. One source commented,

> Risk management models work only under benign conditions and are useless when needed. We use two risk methods, principal component analysis and rare (six-sigma) events, and risk models from

MSCI Barra and Northfield. But the risk models are mis-specified: most pairs of stocks have high correlations.

Another source added,

> There are estimation errors in everything, including in risk models. You know that they will fail, so we add heuristics to our models. Risk models do not cover downside risk but they do help control it. Studies have shown that risk models do improve the information ratio.

The growing use of derivatives in equity portfolio management is adding a new type of risk. One source commented,

> The derivatives markets are susceptible to chaos; they overheat compared to normal markets. Derivatives contracts are complex and no one knows how they will behave in various scenarios. In addition, there is credit risk/counterparty risk dealing with entities such as Sentinel—not a Wall Street firm—that can go with a puff of smoke. Their going under was blamed on the subprime crisis but it was fraud.

Sixty-three percent of the survey participants agreed that the derivative market is a market driven by its own supply and demand schedule and might present risk that is not entirely explained in terms of the underlying.

Why Implement a Quant Process?

According to survey respondents, three main objectives were behind the decision to adopt (at least partially) a quantitative-based equity investment process: tighter risk control, more stable returns, and better overall performance. The profile of a firm's founder(s) and/or the prevailing in-house culture were correlated in that they provided the requisite environment.

Other major objectives reported behind the decision to implement a quantitative equity investment process include diversification in general or in terms of new products such as 130/30-type strategies and scalability, including the ability to scale to different universes. Relative to the diversification in a global sense, a source at a large asset management firm with a small quant group said,

An important motivating factor is diversification of the overall product lineup performance. Management believes that quant and fundamental products will not move in synch.

As for the ability to offer new products such as the long–short strategies, a source at a sell-side firm modeling for the buy side remarked,

> We are seeing a lot of interest by firms known for being fundamental and that now want to introduce quant processes in the form of screens or other. These firms are trying to get into the quant space and it is the 130/30-type product that is pushing into this direction.

It was generally believed that quantitatively managed funds outperform fundamental managers in the 130/30-type arena. The ability to back-test the strategy was cited as giving quantitatively managed funds the edge. A manager at a firm that offers both fundamental and quantitative products said, "Potential clients have told us that new products such as the 130/30 strategies are more believable with extensive quant processes and testing behind them."

More generally, sources believed that quantitative processes give an edge whenever there is a complex problem to solve. An investment consultant remarked,

> Quant has an advantage when there is an element of financial engineering. The investment process is the same but quant adds value when it comes to picking components and coming up with products such as the 130/30.

Another source added,

> A quant process brings the ability to create structured products. In the U.S., institutional investors are using structured products in especially fixed income and hedge funds. Given the problem of aging, I would expect more demand in the future from private investors who want a product that will give them an income plus act as an investment vehicle, such as a combination of an insurance-type payout and the ability to decompose and build up.

As for scalability, a consultant to the industry remarked,

One benefit a quantitative process brings to the management firms is the ability to apply a model quickly to a different set of stocks. For example, a firm that had been applying quant models to U.S. large cap also tested these models on 12–15 other major markets in the backroom. Once they saw that the models had a successful in-house track record in different universes, they began to commercialize these funds.

Among survey participants, the desire to stabilize costs, revenues, and performance or to improve the cost/revenues ratio were rated relatively low as motivating factors to introduce quantitative processes. But one source at a large asset management firm said that stabilizing costs, revenues, and performance was an important factor in the firm's decision to embrace a quantitative process. According to this source, "Over the years, the firm has seen great consistency in a quant process: fees, revenues, and costs are all more stable, more consistent than with a fundamental process."

Bringing management costs down was rated by participants as the weakest factor behind the drive to implement a quantitative-driven equity investment process. A source at a large asset management firm with a small quantitative group said,

> Has management done a cost/benefit analysis of quant versus fundamental equity investment management process? Not to my knowledge. I was hired a few years ago to start up a quant process. But even if management had done a cost/benefit analysis and found quant attractive, it would not have been able to move into a quant process quickly. The average institutional investor has a seven-man team on the fund. If you were to switch to a two-man quant team, 80% of the clients would go away. Management has to be very careful; clients do not like to see change.

Barriers to Entry

The 2007 study concluded with an investigation of the barriers to entry in the business. Seventy-seven percent of the survey respondents believed that the active quantitative arena will continue to be characterized by the dominance of a few large players and a large number of small quant boutiques. Only 10% disagreed.

Participants were asked to rate a number of factors as barriers to new entrants into the quant equity investment space. The most important barrier remained the prevailing in-house culture. While one source at a fundamental-oriented firm said that very few firms are seriously opposed to trying to add discipline and improve performance by applying some quant techniques, the problem is that it is not so easy to change an organization.

A source at a large international investment consultancy commented,

> For a firm that is not quant-endowed, it is difficult to make the shift from individual judgment to a quant process. Those that have been most successful in terms of size in the active quant arena are those that began in passive quant. They chose passive because they understood it would be easier for a quantitative process to perform well in passive as opposed to active management. Most of these firms have been successful in their move to active quant management.

A source at a large firm with fundamental and quant management styles said,

> Can a firm with a fundamental culture go quant? It is doable but the odds of success are slim. Fundamental managers have a different outlook and these are difficult times for quants.

Difficulty in recruiting qualified persons was rated the second most important barrier while the cost of qualified persons was considered less of a barrier. Next was the difficulty in gaining investor confidence and the entrenched position of market leaders. An industry observer remarked,

> What matters most is the investment culture and market credibility. If an investor does not believe that the manager has quant as a core skill, the manager will not be credible in the arena of quant products. There is the risk that the effort is perceived by the investor as a backroom effort with three persons, understaffed, and undercommitted.

Among the selling points, participants (unsurprisingly) identified alpha generation as the strongest selling point for quant funds, followed by the disciplined approach and better risk management. Lower management and trading costs and a statistics-based stock selection process were rated lowest among the suggested selling points.

Survey participants were also asked to rate factors holding back investment in active quant equity products. A lack of understanding of quant processes by investors and consultants was perceived to be the most important factor holding back investments in active quant products. As one quantitative manager at an essentially fundamental firm noted, "Quant products are unglamorous. There are no 'story' stocks to tell, so it makes it a hard sell for consultants to their clients."

The need to educate consultants and investors alike, in an effort to gain their confidence, was cited by several sources as a major challenge going forward. Educating investors might require more disclosure about quant processes. At least that was what just under half of the survey participants believed, while one-fourth disagree and one-fourth have no opinion.

One CIO of equities who believes that greater disclosure will be required remarked,

> Following events of this summer [i.e., July–August 2007], quants will need to be better on explaining what they do and why it ought to work. They will need to come up with a rationale for what they are doing. They will have to provide more proof-of-concept statements.

However, among the sources that disagreed, the CIO of equities at another firm said,

> One lesson from the events of July–August 2007 is that we will be more circumspect when describing what we are doing. Disclosing what one is doing can lead to others replicating the process and thus a reduction of profit opportunities.

Lack of stellar performance was rated a moderately important factor in holding back investments in quantitative funds. Lack of stellar performance is balanced by a greater consistency in performance. A source at a fund rating service said, "Because quant funds are broadly diversified, returns are watered down. Quants do not hit the ball out of the park, but they deliver stable performance." The ability to deliver stable if not stellar performance can, of course, be turned into a major selling point.

Quantitative managers cite how Oakland Athletics' manager Billy Beane improved his team's performance using sabermetrics, the analysis of baseball through objective (i.e., statistical) evidence. Beane's analysis led him to shifting the accent from acquiring players who hit the most home runs to acquiring players with the most consistent records of getting on base.[30] Interestingly, Beane is credited with having made the Oakland Athletics the most cost-effective team in baseball though winning the American League Championship Series has proved more elusive.

---

[30]As reported in Michael Lewis, *Moneyball: The Art of Winning an Unfair Game* (New York: Norton, 2003).

LOOKING AHEAD FOR QUANTITATIVE EQUITY INVESTING

The studies we have just discussed suggested challenges that participants see in implementing quantitative strategies. We can see a number of additional challenges. Robust optimization, robust estimation, and the integration of the two are probably on the research agenda of many firms. As asset management firms strive to propose innovative products, robust and flexible optimization methods will be high on the R&D agenda. In addition, as asset management firms try to offer investment strategies to meet a stream of liabilities (i.e., measured against liability benchmarking), multistage stochastic optimization methods will become a priority for firms wanting to compete in this arena. Pan, Sornette, and Kortanek call "Intelligent Finance" the new field of theoretical finance at the confluence of different scientific disciplines.[31] According to them, the theoretical framework of intelligent finance consists of four major components: (1) financial information fusion, (2) multilevel stochastic dynamic process models, (3) active portfolio and total risk management, and (4) financial strategic analysis.

Modelers are facing the problem of performance decay that is the consequence of a wider use of models. Classical financial theory assumes that agents are perfect forecasters in the sense that they know the stochastic processes of prices and returns. Agents do not make systematic predictable mistakes: their action keeps the market efficient. This is the basic idea underlying rational expectations and the intertemporal models of Merton.[32]

Practitioners (and now also academics) have relaxed the hypothesis of the universal validity of market efficiency; indeed, practitioners have always being looking for asset mispricings that could produce alpha. As we have seen, it is widely believed that mispricings are due to behavioral phenomena, such as belief persistence. This behavior creates biases in agent evaluations—biases that models attempt to exploit in applications such as momentum strategies. However, the action of models tends to destroy the same sources of profit that they are trying to exploit. This fact receives specific attention in applications such as measuring the impact of trades. In almost all current implementations, measuring the impact of trades means measuring the speed at which models constrain markets to return to an unprofitable efficiency. To our knowledge, no market impact model attempts to measure the opposite effect, that is, the eventual momentum induced by a trade.

It is reasonable to assume that the diffusion of models will reduce the mispricings due to behavioral phenomena. However, one might reasonably

---

[31]Heping Pan, Dider Sornette, and Kenneth Kortanek, "Intelligent Finance—An Emerging Direction." *Quantitative Finance* 6, no. 4 (2006), pp. 273–277.
[32]Robert C. Merton, "An Intertemporal Capital Asset Pricing Model," *Econometrica*, 41, no. 5 (1973), pp. 867–887.

ask whether the action of models will ultimately make markets more efficient, destroying any residual profitability in excess of market returns, or if the action of models will create new opportunities that can be exploited by other models, eventually by a new generation of models based on an accurate analysis of model biases. It is far from being obvious that markets populated by agents embodied in mathematical models tend to be efficient. In fact, models might create biases of their own. For example, momentum strategies (buy winners, sell losers) are a catalyst for increased momentum, further increasing the price of winners and depressing the price of losers.

This subject has received much attention in the past as researchers studied the behavior of markets populated by boundedly rational agents. While it is basically impossible, or at least impractical, to code the behavior of human agents, models belong to a number of well-defined categories that process past data to form forecasts. Several studies, based either on theory or on simulation, have attempted to analyze the behavior of markets populated by agents that have bounded rationality, that is, filter past data to form forecasts.[33] One challenge going forward is to study what type of inefficiencies are produced by markets populated by automatic decision-makers whose decisions are based on past data. It is foreseeable that simulation and artificial markets will play a greater role as discovery devices.

---

[33]For the theoretical underpinning of bounded rationality from the statistical point of view, see Thomas J. Sargent, Bounded Rationality in Macroeconomics (New York: Oxford University Press, 1994). For the theoretical underpinning of bounded rationality from the behavioral finance perspective, see Daniel Kahneman, "Maps of Bounded Rationality: Psychology for Behavioral Economics," *American Economic Review* 93, no. 5 (2003), pp. 1449–1475. For a survey of research on computational finance with boundedly rational agents see Blake LeBaron, "Agent-Based Computational Finance," in Leigh Tesfatsion and Kenneth L. Judd (eds.) *Handbook of Computational Economics* (Amsterdam: North-Holland: 2006).

CHAPTER 2

Financial Econometrics I: Linear Regressions

Financial econometrics is a set of mathematical techniques to represent financial processes and to estimate their parameters from empirical data. Though much financial econometrics deals with the time evolution of financial processes, there are many in which the time dimension does not appear. These include financial econometrics based on analyzing cross-sectional data and panel data. Notable examples include the distribution of firm size, stock market capitalization, personal wealth, and personal income.

In this chapter we discuss the concepts and estimation techniques of covariance, correlation, linear regressions, and projections. These techniques are ubiquitous in financial econometrics. For example, the estimation of correlations and the estimation of covariances are the basis of risk management. Regressions appear in many financial applications. Static asset pricing theory, for example, is expressed through regressions. Autoregressive processes are the basis of many dynamic models including ARCH and GARCH processes.

We introduce the basic as well as the more advanced techniques currently used in quantitative equity portfolio management. These include techniques to estimate large covariance matrices, regression analysis under non-standard assumptions including quantile regression, and estimation with instrumental variables. We also discuss multivariate regressions, the basis for vector autoregressive models that will be discussed in the next chapter.

HISTORICAL NOTES

The term *econometrics*, in its modern meaning, was introduced in the economic literature by the Norwegian economist Ragnar Frisch, corecipient with Jan Timbergen of the first Nobel Memorial Prize in Economic Sciences in 1969. Frisch played a fundamental role in establishing economics as a quantitative and mathematical science and defined many of the terms we now use including the term macroeconomics. He used the term *econometrics* for the first time in his 1926 paper.[1] In this and the following chapter we will primarily describe techniques to represent the evolution of financial processes observed at discrete intervals of time. In this chapter we will first introduce the basic concepts of correlation and covariance and will outline the theory of linear regressions and projections. In the next chapter, we will introduce the theory of the linear moving average process and the autoregressive process, and we will discuss the question of the representation of time series and the concept of causality in econometrics. In Chapter 5 we will specifically deal with static and dynamic factor models.

Though the theory of stochastic processes is as old as the theory of probability, the sheer possibility of a probabilistic and statistical representation of financial and economic laws—hence of econometrics—has been the subject of debate. The main reason for skepticism was due to the fact that in most cases we only have one realization of economic processes while statistics is based on samples made by many individuals. If we analyze an economic process, we can form a sample formed by many individuals taking observations at different moments. However, classical techniques of statistical estimation assume independent samples extracted from a population with a well-defined distribution, while financial and economic time series exhibit correlations and autocorrelations and cannot be considered sequences of independent samples extracted from some distribution.

The introduction of econometrics in economics and finance theory is due to a student of Frisch, Trygve Haavelmo, who was himself a recipient of the Nobel Memorial Prize in Economic Sciences in 1989. In his 1944 paper,[2] Haavelmo introduced the idea that economic time series are "samples selected by Nature."

This notion hinges on representing the joint probability distribution of a finite sample from a time series $p(x_1, ..., x_T)$ as the product of an initial distribution and successive conditional distributions: $p(x_1,...,x_T) = p_1(x_1)p_2(x_2|x_1)\cdots p_T(x_T|x_{T-1},...,x_1)$.[3] These conditional distributions are indeed mutually independent. If, in addition, we can represent all conditional distributions with the same functional form that includes only a small number of past data, we can represent a series recursively

[1] Ragnar Frisch, "Kvantitativ formulering av den teoretiske økonomikks lover," *Statsøkonomisk Tidsskrift*, 40 (1926), pp. 299–334. ["Quantitative formulation of the laws of economic theory"].
[2] Trygve Magnus Haavelmo, "The Probability Approach in Econometrics," Supplement to *Econometrica*, 11 (1944), pp. S1–S115.
[3] For methodological issues, see David F. Hendry, *Dynamic Econometrics* (Oxford: Oxford University Press, 1995).

through a data generating process (DGP). For example, if the conditional distributions depend only on the previous time step, we can write: $p(x_1, \ldots, x_T) = p_1(x_1)p_{DGP}(x_2|x_1)\cdots p_{DGP}(x_T|x_{T-1})$. All these p_{DGP} are independent and we can form the likelihood of the sample.

Otherwise stated, econometrics is made possible by the separation of observed variables and residuals. Financial models are *probes* that extract a sequence of independent residuals from correlated observations. Residuals are formed by independent samples and therefore allow for a probabilistic treatment along the lines of classical statistics. We can apply probabilistic concepts to finance theory if we can identify simple laws that extract independent samples from observed data.

In this chapter we introduce the basic concepts and techniques used to build financial models. First we discuss the concepts of correlation and covariance and then we discuss regressions and their estimation.

COVARIANCE AND CORRELATION

Covariance and correlation are measures of linear dependence between data. Consider two sets of data indexed by the same parameter i: Y_i, X_i. Were there a deterministic linear dependence between the data, Y_i, X_i would lie on the path of some linear function $y = ax + b$. In practice, however, even if a true linear dependence exists, observed data might be corrupted by noise or might be influenced by other variables. In this case, Y_i, X_i, even if theoretically linearly dependent, would not lie on a straight line but they would be dispersed in a region of the plane as illustrated in Exhibit 2.1. The figure illustrates data generated by a model $Y_i = aX_i + b + U_i$ where the term U_i is a zero-mean, normally distributed random variable. The figures show scatterplots corresponding to different choices of the standard deviation denoted by σ. As we can see from the scatterplots in Exhibit 2.1, when the standard deviation is small, data seem to closely follow a straight line; when the standard deviation is large, data occupy a much wider region.

Assume now that we are given a set of data Y_i, X_i. We want to understand if the data have a linear functional dependence and, if so, we want to measure the strength of this linear dependence. The covariance and the correlation coefficient are measures of this dependence. Intuitively, covariance and the correlation coefficient measure how closely the two variables move together. The covariance between two random variables Y, X is defined as follows:

$$\text{cov}(Y, X) = \text{cov}(X, Y) = E\left[(Y - \bar{Y})(X - \bar{X})\right]$$
$$\bar{Y} = E(Y), \ \bar{X} = E(X)$$

EXHIBIT 2.1 Plot of the Straight Line $Y = 0.2X + 0.6$ and Scatterplot of the Same Line with Added Noise

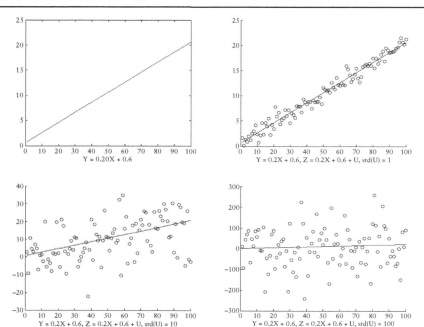

If $Y = X$, then

$$\text{cov}(X, X) = \text{var}(X) = E\left[(X - \bar{X})^2\right].$$

The covariance between two variables is normalized with respect to the mean of the variables so that it is not affected by shifts in the mean value of the variables. However, it depends on the size of the fluctuations. In particular, it depends on the scale and on the measurement unit of the variables.

We can make the covariance independent of the size of the variables by dividing by the standard deviations of the variables. The correlation coefficient is the covariance divided by the product of the standard deviations of the variables.

Given any two variables Y, X, the correlation coefficient is a real number $-1 \leq \rho_{YX} \leq 1$ defined as follows:

$$\rho_{YX} = \frac{E\left[(Y - \bar{Y})(X - \bar{X})\right]}{\sigma_Y \sigma_X}$$

$$\bar{Y} = E(Y), \ \bar{X} = E(X)$$
$$\sigma_Y = \sqrt{\mathrm{var}(Y)}, \ \sigma_X = \sqrt{\mathrm{var}(X)}$$

If the variables exhibit a linear relationship without any noise, that is, if $Y = aX + b$, then:

$$\mathrm{cov}(Y,X) = E\left[(aX + b - a\bar{X} - b)(X - \bar{X})\right] = a\sigma_X^2$$

$$\rho_{YX} = \frac{E\left[(aX + b - a\bar{X} - b)(X - \bar{X})\right]}{|a|\sigma_X^2} = \frac{aE\left[(X - \bar{X})^2\right]}{|a|\sigma_X^2} = \pm 1$$

according to the sign of a. Conversely, it can be demonstrated that if the correlation coefficient is ± 1 then the variables have a linear relationship without noise.

If the linear relationship is affected by a noise term, that is, if $Y = aX + b + \varepsilon$, then:

$$\rho_{YX} = \frac{E\left[(aX + b - a\bar{X} - b)(X - \bar{X})\right]}{|a|\sigma_X^2} = \frac{aE\left[(X - \bar{X})^2\right]}{|a|\sigma_{X+\varepsilon}\sigma_X}$$

and therefore $|\rho_{YX}| < 1$. Two random variables are said to be uncorrelated if their correlation coefficient is zero.

The linear correlation coefficient measures the strength of the eventual linear relationship between two variables but it does not measure the strength of an eventual nonlinear functional relationship between the variables. In particular, the correlation coefficient might be zero even if the variables have a deterministic nonlinear relationship. For example, if the random variable X is uniformly distributed in the interval $[-1,+1]$, the two variables X and X^2 are uncorrelated though they have a well-defined functional relationship.

Consider now the variables X and $Y = aX + b + \varepsilon$. If the noise term ε is uncorrelated with X, then the covariance between X and Y is not influenced by ε but the variance of Y depends on the variance of ε. Therefore, given a basic linear relationship between two variables X and Y, by adding a noise term uncorrelated with the variable X, correlation is lowered, covariance remains unchanged but the variance of Y increases. Note that the correlation coefficient does not depend on a and that it does not measure the steepness of the straight line $Y = aX + b$.

Estimation of the Covariance and Correlation Coefficient

Let's now discuss estimation of the covariance and correlation coefficient. Suppose a sample of N observations of the variables X and Y is given. Let's organize the sample data in two $N \times N$ vectors:

$$Y = \begin{bmatrix} Y_1 \\ \vdots \\ Y_N \end{bmatrix}, \quad X = \begin{bmatrix} X_1 \\ \vdots \\ X_N \end{bmatrix}$$

The expected value of both variables can be estimated with the empirical average:

$$\hat{Y} = \frac{\sum_{i=1}^{N} Y_i}{N}, \quad \hat{X} = \frac{\sum_{i=1}^{N} X_i}{N}$$

If we write **1** for a vector of ones, the empirical average can be also represented as:

$$\hat{Y} = \frac{\mathbf{1}^T Y}{N}, \quad \hat{X} = \frac{\mathbf{1}^T X}{N}$$

The covariance can be estimated as the empirical average of the product of X and Y:

$$
\begin{aligned}
\mathrm{cov}(Y, X) &= \frac{\sum_{i=1}^{N} (Y_i - \hat{Y})(X_i - \hat{X})}{N} \\
&= \frac{\sum_{i=1}^{N} Y_i X_i - \sum_{i=1}^{N} Y_i \hat{X} - \sum_{i=1}^{N} X_i \hat{Y} + N \hat{Y}\hat{X}}{N} \\
&= \frac{\sum_{i=1}^{N} Y_i X_i - \sum_{i=1}^{N} Y_i \hat{X} - \sum_{i=1}^{N} X_i \hat{Y} + N \hat{Y}\hat{X}}{N} \\
&= \frac{\sum_{i=1}^{N} Y_i X_i - N \hat{Y}\hat{X} - N \hat{Y}\hat{X} + N \hat{Y}\hat{X}}{N} \\
&= \frac{1}{N} \sum_{i=1}^{N} Y_i X_i - \hat{Y}\hat{X}
\end{aligned}
$$

or, in vector notation:

$$\text{cov}(Y,X) = \frac{\left(Y - \hat{Y}\right)^T \left(X - \hat{X}\right)}{N} = \frac{1}{N} Y^T X - \hat{Y}\hat{X}$$

The variance of the variables X and Y can be estimated with the empirical variance as follows:

$$\text{var}(Y) = \sigma_Y^2 = \frac{\left(Y - \hat{Y}\right)^T \left(Y - \hat{Y}\right)}{N}, \quad \text{var}(X) = \sigma_X^2 = \frac{\left(X - \hat{X}\right)^T \left(X - \hat{X}\right)}{N}$$

We can now write the estimator of the correlation coefficient as follows:

$$\text{corr}(Y,X) = \frac{\text{cov}(Y,X)}{\sigma_Y \sigma_X}$$

In the previous formulas, we obtain better small-sample properties if we divide by $N - 1$ instead of dividing by N.

Let's now consider multivariate variables. Suppose we are given a P-vector formed by P components:

$$X = (X_1, \ldots, X_P)$$

We can compute the covariance and the correlation coefficient between each pair of components and arrange them in two square $P \times P$ matrices, the covariance matrix Ω and the correlation matrix C:

$$\Omega = \{\sigma_{ij}\}, \quad \sigma_{ij} = \text{cov}(X_i, X_j)$$
$$C = \{c_{ij}\}, \quad c_{ij} = \text{corr}(X_i, X_j)$$

Both the covariance and the correlation matrices are square symmetric matrices because both the covariance and the correlation coefficient are independent of the order of the variables. The diagonal elements of the covariance matrix are the individual variances of the variables X_i while the diagonal elements of the correlation matrix are all 1.

Suppose a sample of N observations of the P variables X_i is given. Arrange the data in a $N \times P$ matrix X such that every column is formed by all observations of a variable and a row is formed by one observation of all variables. If observations take place in different moments, one row corresponds to all observations at any given moment.

$$X = \begin{bmatrix} X_{11} & \cdots & X_{N1} \\ \vdots & \ddots & \vdots \\ X_{N1} & \cdots & X_{NP} \end{bmatrix}$$

The estimation of the element σ_{ij} can be performed using the above formulas:

$$\sigma_{ij} = \frac{\sum_{s=1}^{N} X_{si} X_{sj} - N \bar{X}_i \bar{X}_j}{N}$$

In matrix notation, the covariance matrix can therefore be written as follows:

$$\Omega = \left\{ \sigma_{ij} \right\} = \frac{X^T X}{N} - \left\{ \bar{X}_i \bar{X}_j \right\}$$

Estimation Issues

There are a number of issues associated with estimating covariances and correlations. The first important issue is the time-varying nature of correlations and covariances. The previous formulas compute an average of covariances and correlations over the time window used for estimation. Clearly, the covariance and correlation at the end of the estimation period—the time of major interest in most practical financial applications—can differ significantly from the average. To mitigate this problem, a common strategy is to use a weighting scheme that assigns a heavier weight to the most recent observations. A widely used weighting scheme is the *exponentially weighted moving average* (EWMA) which assigns exponentially declining weights.

Suppose, for simplicity, that the variables X have zero mean. The EWMA consists in replacing the estimation formula

$$\sigma_{ij} = \frac{1}{N} \sum_{s=1}^{N} X_{si} X_{sj}$$

which has constant weights $1/N$ with the EWMA:

$$\sigma_{ij} = \frac{(1-\lambda)}{(1-\lambda^N)} \sum_{s=0}^{N-1} \lambda^s X_{N-s,i} X_{N-s,j}$$

where $0 < \lambda < 1$ is a parameter to be calibrated.

Another estimation strategy consists in forecasting the covariance matrix. The forecasting of volatility parameters is a major success of modern econometrics. Robert Engle introduced the notion that the volatility of economic and financial time series is time-varying and proposed the *autoregressive conditional heteroskedastic* (ARCH) family of models to model volatility.[4] Engle and Clive Granger were awarded the 2003 Nobel Memorial Prize in Economic Sciences for this discovery. The original ARCH model has since been extended in many ways. In particular, it was proposed to extend ARCH modeling to multivariate processes and therefore to the entire covariance or correlation matrix. Given the large number of parameters to be estimated, many different simplifications have been proposed.[5]

Another covariance estimation strategy was proposed by Aguilar and West.[6] They suggested forecasting the covariance matrix using dynamic factor models. In the following section of this chapter, we will discuss the general question of the attainable accuracy in estimating large covariance matrices. First we need to briefly introduce Random Matrix Theory.

Random Matrix Theory

Let us now consider the estimation of a large covariance matrix. We encounter this problem, for example, if we want to estimate the mutual covariances and correlations between the stocks in a large market, say the U.S. equity market. In such cases, the number of stocks can be in the range of several hundreds or even a few thousands. If we consider weekly returns, the number of data points, in this case, the sample of empirical returns, is at most in the range of a few hundred data points. There are two major problems in considering long time series of empirical returns. First, over a period of several years it is unlikely that correlations and covariances remain sufficiently constant; therefore empirical correlations are only an average which might be very different from true correlations at the end of the period. Second, if we consider long periods, we can select only those stocks that existed throughout the entire period. This fact, per se, creates significant biases in the estimates. We can conclude that in

---

[4]Robert F. Engle, "Autoregressive Conditional Heteroskedasticity with Estimates of Variance of United Kingdom Inflation," *Econometrica*, 50 (1982), pp. 987–1008.
[5]See for a review of these models, Robert F. Engle, Sergio Focardi, and Frank J. Fabozzi, "ARCH/GARCH Models in Applied Financial Econometrics," in Frank J. Fabozzi (ed.), *Handbook of Finance*, Vol. III (Hoboken, NJ: John Wiley & Sons, 2008).
[6]Omar Aguilar and Mike West, "Bayesian Dynamic Factor Models and Portfolio Allocation," *Journal of Business and Economic Statistics*, 18 (2000), pp. 338–357.

financial time series, the number of empirical data is often approximately of the same size as the number of variables.

When the number of observations is of the same order as the number of variables, it can be proved that estimates of covariances and correlations are subject to significant uncertainties. To gain an intuition of the uncertainties associated with estimating a large covariance matrix, consider that the number of independent entries of a covariance matrix (which is a symmetric matrix) is $N(N + 1)/2$, a number that grows with the square of the number of stocks. For example, the covariance matrix of 500 stocks includes 125,250 independent entries while the covariance matrix of 1,000 stocks includes 500,500 entries. However, the global number of data points to estimate a covariance matrix grows only linearly with the number of stocks. For example, a five-year sample of daily returns includes approximately 1,000 returns. If a portfolio includes 500 stocks, there are a total of 500,000 data points to estimate 125,250 entries, less than four data per entry. It is clear that, given these numbers, the statistical fluctuations of samples produce a large number of covariance estimates very far from the true covariances.

In order to arrive at a robust estimate of a large covariance matrix, we need to reduce the dimensionality of the matrix, that is, we need to reduce the number of independent entries. Several techniques have been proposed. One widely employed technique relies on estimating the eigenvalues of the covariance matrix and recovering a robust covariance matrix through factor analysis or principal components analysis. The problem of estimating a covariance matrix is thus shifted to the problem of estimating its eigenvalues. We can expect the eigenvalues of a large covariance matrix to exhibit a random behavior. A precise quantification of these phenomena is given by *random matrix theory* (RMT). In fact, one of the main results of RMT is the computation of the asymptotic distribution of eigenvalues.

Random matrices are matrix-variate random variables. RMT was originally developed in the 1920s to respond to specific application needs in biometrics and general multivariate statistics. In the 1950s, RMT became a key tool in quantum physics. It is now applied to many fields of science, from quantum mechanics, statistical physics, and wireless communications to number theory and financial econometrics. We will briefly sketch RMT and survey recent results with a bearing on econometrics.

A random matrix model (RMM) is a probability space (Ω, P, F) where the sample space is a set of matrices. We are particularly interested in random matrices that represent covariance matrices. Given the $m \times n$ matrix H whose columns are independent real/complex zero-mean Gaussian vectors with covariance matrix Σ, the matrix $A = HH^T$ is called a central *Wishart matrix* $W_m(n,\Sigma)$ with n degrees of freedom and covariance Σ. If the entries of H are not zero-mean, the Wishart matrix is noncentral. A Wishart matrix is an element of a probability space and we can determine its probability distribution and probability distribution function (pdf). The pdf of a central Wishart matrix with $n > m$ has the following form:

$$p_W(A) = \frac{\partial^{\frac{m(m-1)1}{2}}}{(\det \Sigma)^n \prod_{i=1}^{m}(n-i)!} \exp\left[-trace\left(\Sigma^{-1}A\right)\right] \det A^{n-m}$$

A basic insight provided by RMT is that if the number of observations is close to the number of variables, eigenvalues computed from empirical covariance matrices do not converge to the true eigenvalues when both the sample size T and the number of stocks N go to infinity keeping constant the ratio N/T. The N/T ratio is called the *aspect ratio*. The RMT distinguishes between the distribution of the *bulk* of eigenvalues and the distribution of the *edges*. Let's first discuss the bulk of the eigenvalue distribution. Results for the bulk of the distribution of eigenvalues can be summarized as follows.

Anderson (1963) proved that the empirical distribution of the eigenvalues of a square $N \times N$ matrix tends to the distribution of the eigenvalues of the true covariance matrix when the number of samples tends to infinity. However, if both the number of samples and the number of entries of the covariance matrix tend to infinity, then the empirical eigenvalues are not consistent estimators of the true eigenvalues.

A fundamental asymptotic result was proved in Marčenko and Pastur for rectangular matrices.[7] They proved that the distribution of the empirical eigenvalues of a covariance matrix tend to a well-defined distribution when the size of the matrix tends to infinity. Consider a $T \times N$ matrix H whose entries are independent and identically distribution (i.i.d.) real or complex zero mean variables with variance $1/T$ and fourth moments of order $O(1/T^2)$. Consider the matrix $A = H^T H$. As the entries of the matrix H are i.i.d. variables, the theoretical eigenvalues of the matrix A are all equal to 1. However, Marčenko and Pastur proved that the asymptotic distribution of the eigenvalues of the matrix A when $T, N \to \infty$, $N/T \to \gamma$ has the following density:

$$f_\gamma(x) = \left(1 - \frac{1}{\gamma}\right)^{+} \delta(x) + \frac{\sqrt{(x-a)(b-x)}}{2\pi\gamma x}, a = \left(1 - \sqrt{\gamma}\right)^2 \le x \le b = \left(1 + \sqrt{\gamma}\right)^2$$

$$f_\beta(x) = 0, x < a, x > b$$

---

[7]V. A. Marčenko and L. A. Pastur, "Distributions of Eigenvalues for Some Sets of Random Matrices," *Math. USSR-Sbornik*, 1 (1967), pp. 457–483.

where $(z)^+ = \max(0,z)$. Under the same assumptions, the asymptotic distribution of the eigenvalues of the matrix HH^T when $T, N \to \infty$, $N/T \to \gamma$ has the following density:

$$\tilde{f}_\gamma(x) = (1-\gamma)^+ \delta(x) + \frac{\sqrt{(x-a)(b-x)}}{2\pi x}, a = (1-\sqrt{\gamma})^2 \le x \le b = (1+\sqrt{\gamma})^2$$

$$f_\beta(x) = 0, x < a, x > b$$

If $\gamma = 1$, the distribution of singular values, which are the square roots of the corresponding eigenvalues, is the *quarter circle law*:

$$q(x) = \frac{\sqrt{4-x^2}}{\pi}, 0 \le x \le 2,$$

$$q(x) = 0, x < 0, x > 2$$

Dirac's delta at the origin reflects the fact that a fraction $(N - T)/2$ of the eigenvalues are zero if $\gamma \ge 1$.

The above result has been extended and refined in many different ways. For example, Silverstein proved an extension of Marčenko-Pastur for correlated matrices without assuming the existence of the fourth moments.[8] Suppose the entries of the $T \times N$ matrix H are i.i.d. real or complex variables with zero mean, unit variance, and finite fourth moments. Let T_N be a fixed $N \times N$ Hermitian (unitary if real) matrix. Assume the sample vector is $T_N^{\frac{1}{2}}H$. This implies that T_N is the population covariance matrix. Consider the sample covariance matrix:

$$B_N = \frac{1}{N} T_N^{\frac{1}{2}} HH' T_N^{\frac{1}{2}}$$

Silverstein proved that if the distribution of the eigenvalues of the matrices T_N tend to a nonrandom distribution, then the empirical covariance matrices B_N also tend to a nonrandom distribution. He then determined the distribution of the eigenvalues in terms of an integral equation. Burda and Jurkiewicz[9] proved the Marčenko-Pastur law using the method of the resolvent and diagrammatic techniques from quantum mechanics. Burda, Jurkie-

---

[8]Jack W. Silverstein, "Strong Convergence of the Empirical Distribution of Eigenvalues of Large Dimensional Random Matrices," *Journal of Multivariate Analysis*, 55 (1995), pp. 331–339.
[9]Zdzislaw Burda and Jerzy Jurkiewicz, "Signal and Noise in Financial Correlation Matrices," February 2004.

wicz, and Waclaw[10] extended the Marčenko-Pastur law to samples that are both correlated and autocorrelated. Burda, Goerlich, and Waclaw[11] determined explicit formulas in the case of Student-t distributions up to integrals. Similar results had already been obtained by Sengupta and Mitra.[12]

The asymptotic distribution of the eigenvalues provides a benchmark to separate meaningful eigenvalues from eigenvalues that are only noisy fluctuations around the theoretical value 1. It is therefore important to understand the behavior of the largest eigenvalues. The Marčenko-Pastur law is compatible with the existence of a few stray eigenvalues that are at the right (left) of its rightmost (leftmost) edge.

Let's first consider uncorrelated variables. Geman[13] and Silverstein[14] demonstrated that the largest eigenvalue λ_1 of the covariance matrix of a $T \times N$ i.i.d. matrix H when $T, N \to \infty$, $N/T \to \gamma$ converges almost surely to the value

$$b = \left(1 + \sqrt{\gamma}\right)^2$$

and the eigenvalue λ_k, $k = \min(T,N)$ converges to the value

$$a = \left(1 - \sqrt{\gamma}\right)^2$$

with $\lambda_{k+1} = \lambda_N = 0$ if $T < N$. That is, the largest and the smallest eigenvalues converge to the upper and lower edges of the Marčenko-Pastur law.

The latter result does not tell us anything about the asymptotic distribution of the largest eigenvalue. This distribution, called the Tracy-Widom distribution, has been determined as the solution of particular differential equations.[15] The behavior of the largest eigenvalue changes completely if the

[10]Zdzislaw Burda, Jerzy Jurkiewicz, and Bartlomiej Waclaw, "Eigenvalue Density of Empirical Covariance Matrix for Correlated Samples," August 2005.

[11]Zdzislaw Burda, Andrzej T. Görlich, and Bartlomiej Waclaw, "Spectral Properties of Empirical Covariance Matrices for Data With Power-Law Tails," April 2006.

[12]A. M. Sengupta and P. P. Mitra, "Distributions of Singular Values for Some Random Matrices, *Physical Review* E, 60 (1999).

[13]S. Geman, "A Limit Theorem for the Norm of Random Matrices," *Annals of Probability*, 8 (1980), pp. 252–261.

[14]Silverstein, "Strong Convergence of the Empirical Distribution of Eigenvalues of Large Dimensional Random Matrices."

[15]See for example, Peter J. Forrester, and Taro Nagao, "Eigenvalue Statistics of the Real Ginibre Ensemble," June 2007; Søren Johansen, "Modelling of Cointegration in the Vector Autoregressive Model," *Economic Modelling*, 17 (2000), pp. 359–373; and M. Iain Johnstone, "On the Distribution of the Largest Eigenvalue in Principal Components Analysis," *Annals of Statistics*, 29 (2001), pp. 295–327.

matrix H is heavy-tailed. Soshnikov and Fyodorov[16] and Soshnikov[17] proved that the distribution of the largest eigenvalue exhibits a weak convergence to a Poisson process. Biroli, Bouchaud, and Potters[18] showed that the largest eigenvalue of a square random matrix whose entries have distributions with power-law tails exhibits a phase transition for the Tracy-Widom law to a Frechet distribution with tail index 4.

The above results characterize the behavior of the largest eigenvalue(s) under the null hypothesis of i.i.d. entries of the matrix H. Bai and Silverstein[19] proved that similar results hold for correlated matrices in the sense there is no eigenvalue outside of the support of the asymptotic distributions of the eigenvalues of correlated matrices H. Consider the matrix

$$A = H^T H$$

under the assumption that observations are

$$H = T_N^{\frac{1}{2}} Z$$

where $T_N^{\frac{1}{2}}$ is the square root of a Hermitian matrix whose eigenvalues converge to a proper probability distribution and Z has i.i.d. standard complex entries. They proved an asymptotic exact separation theorem which states that, for any interval that separates true eigenvalues, there is a corresponding interval that separates corresponding empirical eigenvalues.

Johnstone[20] introduced the "spiked" covariance model where the population covariance matrix is diagonal with $N - r$ eigenvalues equal to 1 while the first r largest eigenvalues are larger than 1. Baik, Ben Arous, and Péché[21]

[16]Alexander Soshnikov and Yan V. Fyodorov, "On the Largest Singular Values of Random Matrices with Independent Cauchy Entries," *Journal of Mathematical Physics*, 46 (2005).

[17]Alexander Soshnikov, "Poisson Statistics for the Largest Eigenvalues in Random Matrix Ensembles," in *Mathematical Physics of Quantum Mechanics*, Vol. 690 of Lecture Notes in Physics (Berlin: Springer, 2006), pp. 351–364.

[18]Giulio Biroli, Jean-Philippe Bouchaud, and Marc Potters, "On the Top Eigenvalue of Heavy-Tailed Random Matrices," DSM/SPhT-T06/216 http://www-spht.cea.fr/articles/T06/216/.

[19]Zhidong D. Bai and Jack W. Silverstein, "Exact Separation of Eigenvalues of Large Dimensional Sample Covariance Matrices," *Annals of Probability*, 27 (1999), pp. 1536–1555.

[20]Johnstone, "On the Distribution of the Largest Eigenvalue in Principal Components Analysis."

[21]Jinho Baik, Gérard Ben Arous, and Sandrine Péché, "Phase Transition of the Largest Eigenvalue for Nonnull Complex Sample Covariance Matrices," *Annals of Probability*, 33 (2005), pp. 1643–1697.

proved a phase transition law for this "spiked" model. Consider a complex $T \times N$ matrix H whose rows are independent samples extracted from a multivariate distribution such that the eigenvalues of the covariance matrix

$$S = \frac{1}{N} H^T H$$

are

$$\left(\underbrace{l_1, \ldots, l_r}_{r}, \underbrace{1, \ldots, 1}_{N-r} \right)$$

Assume $N, T \to \infty$, $N/T \to \gamma < 1$. Then, the quantity

$$\left(1 + \sqrt{\gamma} \right)$$

is a threshold such that, if the true eigenvalues are less than

$$\left(1 + \sqrt{\gamma} \right)$$

then their empirical counterpart is buried in the bulk while, if the true eigenvalues are greater than

$$\left(1 + \sqrt{\gamma} \right)$$

then their empirical counterpart is outside of the bulk.

These results prove that given a large empirical covariance matrix obtained from T samples of N variables, we can establish a benchmark interval such that only those empirical eigenvalues that lay outside of the interval can be safely considered estimates of true eigenvalues different from 1 and therefore contribute to genuine correlations.

REGRESSIONS, LINEAR REGRESSIONS, AND PROJECTIONS

Earlier we discussed covariance and correlation as measures of the strength of the linear link between two variables. In this section we discuss the representation and the estimation of functional links between two or more random variables. We will first discuss the concept of regression as a probabilistic model and then we will discuss the estimation of regression and regression as a data model.

Consider the representation of functional relationships. A functional relationship between deterministic data is represented by a numerical function. For example, there is an approximately linear relationship, called Hooke's law, between the extension of a spring made with elastic material and the force applied to it. Though they can be approximate and/or subject to measurement errors, functional relationships of this type are considered deterministic relationships between one or more independent variable and one or more dependent variables.

In other cases, however, the dependent variable is a true random variable. For example, the distribution of market stock capitalization at different times can be modeled as a random variable function of time. In this case, time can be considered a deterministic variable while stock market capitalization can be modeled as a random variable. Still in other cases, both the dependent variables and the independent variables are true random variables with a probability distribution. For example, the relationship, if it exists, between the returns of a stock and its trading volume involves two random variables, returns and trading volumes. Of course, one might say that every empirical relationship is a relationship between random variables as there will always be measurement errors.

Let's first consider a model formed by a random variable indexed with a deterministic variable: $Y_x = Y(x)$ where the deterministic variable is generically denoted by the lower-case letter x. To each x corresponds a probability distribution and the expected value of the random variable Y_x. This model is typical of experimental situations in which the independent variables can be controlled by the observer whilst the dependent variable can randomly assume different values. Various observational settings are possible. In some instances, the experimenter can control a set of parameters but cannot control the outcome of the observation. For example, we can control the time at which we observe the return of a given stock but we cannot control the return itself, which we assume to be a random variable. In other instances, however, we randomly choose from a population. For example, in a quality control experiment, we can control the time when we perform the quality control and the parameters of the production batch from which we choose samples randomly.

With a slight abuse of notation, we define a regression function as the deterministic function $E(Y_x|x)$ obtained forming the expectation of the variable Y_x for a given x. The variable Y is called the dependent variable or the *regressand*; the variable x is called the independent variable or the *regressor*; the difference $u_x = Y_x - E(Y_x|x)$ is called the *residual of the regression*. Note that the expression $E(Y_x|x)$ is not a proper conditional expectation because the variable x is deterministic. The function $y(x) = E(Y_x|x)$ is not a random variable but a deterministic function of the variable x.

Regression is a useful tool if we can determine the functional form of the regression function. A linear regression is a linear representation of the type:

$$Y_x = ax + b + u_x$$

In the sequel of this chapter we will discuss only linear regressions. If we place no constraints on the residual terms, the above relationship is only a definition of the residual terms and is therefore always valid. Here is a set of standard constraints on the residual terms for the linear regression to become empirically identifiable:

$$E(u_x) = 0, \ \forall x$$

$$E(u_x^2) = \sigma^2, \ \forall x$$

$$E(u_x u_y), \ \forall x, y \ x \neq y$$

These constraints state that the variable Y_x can be represented as a deterministic straight line plus a residual term with zero mean, constant variance, uncorrelated for different values of the index. This definition can be immediately extended to any number of independent variables:

$$Y_x = \sum_{i=1}^{q} a_i x_i + b + u_x$$

where $x = (x_1, ..., x_q)$.

In this model, the u_x are a family of random variables indexed by the variable x, with zero mean and constant variance, uncorrelated for the different values of the index x. If we do not make any assumption as regards the higher moments, the random variables u_x are not necessarily identically distributed. For example, the residuals could have different tails in function of the regressor. If we want residuals to be identically distributed we have to make a specific assumption in that sense. If the u_x are normal variables than they are indeed identically distributed as normal variables are identified only by the mean and the variance.

Let's now consider the case in which we want to understand the functional relationships between random variables that we cannot control. For example, we might want to understand if there is any relationship between the trading volume of a given stock and the stock's returns. Both quantities are random; the correct statistical model is therefore that of a functional relationship between two random variables.

One might observe that it does not make any difference if the independent variables are deterministic or random because, in any case, we are interested in a functional relationship between different variables. It could be argued that the relationship between the different variables cannot depend on the fact that regressands are chosen by the observer or "selected by Nature," using the expression of Trygve Haavelmo. The response is that while relationships between variables cannot be influenced by how samples are selected, a statistical model where all variables are random answers questions that cannot be answered by a model where the independent variables are deterministic. For example, the correlation between the independent and the dependent variable is not a meaningful concept in a deterministic environment.

Consider now two random variables Y and X defined on the same probability space. Let's assume that a joint probability distribution $f(x, y)$ exists. Recall that the marginal distribution of X is defined as

$$f_X(x) = \int_{-\infty}^{+\infty} f(x,y)\,dy$$

while the conditional distribution of Y given X is defined as

$$f(y|x) = \frac{f(x,y)}{f_X(x)}$$

Recall also that the *conditional mean* or *conditional expectation* of Y given X is a random variable function of X defined as follows:

$$E(Y|X = x) = \int_{-\infty}^{+\infty} yf(y|x)\,dy$$

The regression function of Y on X is defined as the conditional expectation of Y given X:

$$F(X) = E(Y|X)$$

We can write $Y = F(X) + u$ where u is the residual. The conditional expectation is a random variable $F(X)$ function of X, so both $F(X)$ and u are random variables.

As in the previous case, we need to place restrictions on the residuals and make some assumptions on the functional form of the conditional expectation. Let's assume that the conditional expectation $E(Y|X)$ is a linear relationship:

$$Y = aX + b$$

and assume also that the residual is a zero-mean variable, with finite variance, uncorrelated with the variable X:

$$E(u) = 0$$
$$E(u^2) = \sigma_u^2$$
$$E(uX) = 0$$

As in the case where x is deterministic, the variable Y is called the *regressand* or the *dependent* variable while X is called the *regressor* or *independent variable*.

In summary, a linear regression function is a linear function that links the regressand and the regressor; it represents the conditional expectation of the regressand given the regressor. If the regressor is deterministic, the regression function is a deterministic relationship between deterministic variables; if the regressor is a random variable, the regression function is a linear relationship between two random variables. Exhibit 2.2 illustrates the difference between a deterministic regression function and a regression function between random variables. In the deterministic case, the values of both X and Y variables are uniformly spaced while in the case of random variables they are randomly spaced. However, the linear relationship between regressor and regressand is the same in both cases. Exhibit 2.3 illustrates the case where a normally distributed noise u is added.

EXHIBIT 2.2   Regression Function between Deterministic and Random Regressors

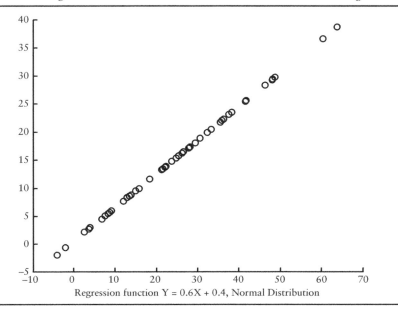

Regression function Y = 0.6X + 0.4, Normal Distribution

EXHIBIT 2.3 Regression Function between Deterministic and Random Regressors with Added Residuals

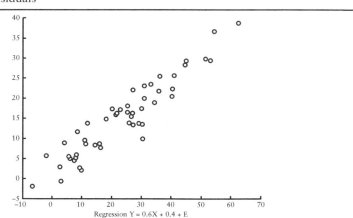

Given the above assumptions, the following relationships between the mean and the variance of Y and X holds:

$$\mu_X = E(X), \quad \mu_Y = E(Y)$$
$$\mu_Y = E(Y) = aE(X) + b = a\mu_X + b$$
$$\sigma_X^2 = E\left[(X - \mu_X)^2\right] = E\left[X^2\right] - \mu_X^2$$
$$\sigma_Y^2 = E\left[(Y - \mu_Y)^2\right] = E\left[Y^2\right] - \mu_Y^2$$

Consider now the covariance between Y and X. The following relationships hold:

$$E\left((Y - \mu_Y)(X - \mu_X)\right) = E\left[(aX + b + u - a\mu_X - b)(X - \mu_X)\right]$$
$$= aE(X^2) + E(uX) - 2a\mu_X^2 - \mu_X E(u) + a\mu_X^2$$
$$= aE(X^2) - a\mu_X^2 = a\sigma_X^2$$
$$a = \rho_{YX} \frac{\sigma_Y}{\sigma_X} = \frac{\text{cov}(Y,X)}{\sigma_Y \sigma_X} \frac{\sigma_Y}{\sigma_X} = \frac{\text{cov}(Y,X)}{\sigma_X^2}$$

Therefore the coefficient a is the correlation coefficient between Y and X multiplied by the ratio of the standard deviations of Y and X which is equivalent to the covariance between Y and X divided by the variance of X.

Consider now the linear regression of a variable Y on N variables X_i, i = 1, 2, ..., N. We write the linear regression as:

$$Y = b_1 + \sum_{i=2}^{N} b_i X_i + U$$

If we define the variable $X_1 \equiv 1$ we can write the linear regression as follows:

$$Y = \sum_{i=1}^{N} b_i X_i + U$$

The regression terminology remains unchanged: Y is the dependent variable or the regressand; the X are the independent variables or regressors; U is the residual. The regression of one regressand on multiple regressors is called a *multiple regression*, not to be confused with multivariate regression which is the regression of multiple regressands on multiple regressors. The following assumptions are the standard assumptions of regression theory:

$$E(u) = 0$$
$$E(u^2) = \sigma_u^2$$
$$E(uX_i) = 0, \quad \forall i = 1, \ldots, N$$

These standard assumptions are not the only possible assumptions and can be relaxed as we will see shortly. However, they are assumptions that define a *reasonable* model. The condition that residuals are zero-mean variables is nonrestrictive as it implies that the eventual constant value of Y is represented by the intercept b_1. The condition that the residual's variance is constant entails a significant mathematical simplification as called for by the *Ordinary Least Squares* (OLS) method. This might seem slightly unnatural as it entails that the size of the residuals is unrelated to the scale of the variable.

Lastly, the condition $E(uX) = 0$ is equivalent to the *Least Squares* (LS) principle as a population property. Here is the reasoning. Assume first that all observed variables have finite mean and finite variance:

$$-\infty < E(Y) < +\infty, \quad -\infty < E(X_i) < +\infty, \quad i = 1, \ldots, N$$
$$E(Y^2) < +\infty, \quad E(X_i^2) < +\infty, \quad i = 1, \ldots, N$$

Consequently, by the Cauchy-Schwarz inequality, all covariances exist. The least squares principle applied to the population requires that the coefficients b_i, $i = 1, \ldots, N$ minimize the expectation of the squared residual:

$$E\left(Y - \sum_{i=1}^{N} b_i X_i \right)^2$$

We can now demonstrate that the condition $E(uX) = 0$ holds if and only if the coefficients b_i, $i = 1, \ldots, N$ satisfy the least squares principle. The conditions $E(uX) = 0$ are called *orthogonality conditions* because they stipulate that residuals and regressors are uncorrelated. Uncorrelated variables are said to be orthogonal because the correlation coefficient can be interpreted as a scalar product. Hence uncorrelated variables are orthogonal because their scalar product is zero.

The expression

$$E\left(Y - \sum_{i=1}^{N} b_i X_i\right)^2$$

is minimized as a function of the b_i, $i = 1, \ldots, N$ when all of its partial derivatives with respect to the b_i are equal to zero:

$$\frac{\partial}{\partial b_i} E\left(Y - \sum_{i=1}^{N} b_i X_i\right)^2 = -2E\left(\left(Y - \sum_{i=1}^{N} b_i X_i\right) X_i\right) = 0$$

Hence equating to zero the partial derivatives of the expected squared error yields the orthogonality conditions which prove the equivalence between the orthogonality conditions and the least squares principle. Using vector notation, we can rewrite the orthogonality conditions as follows:

$$E(X^T Y) = E(X^T X)B$$

which, assuming that the matrix $E(X^T X)$ is nonsingular, yields

$$B = \left[E\left(X^T X\right)\right]^{-1} E\left(X^T Y\right)$$

In summary, the assumption of the orthogonality conditions is equivalent to imposing the choice of the regression coefficients of the linear regression; the latter minimize the expectation of the square residual. Note that this minimum expectation condition is a general property of the population, not an estimation equation: the assumption that the residuals and regressors of a linear regression are uncorrelated is equivalent to the assumption that the regression coefficient satisfies the least squares principle.[22]

When the b_j satisfy the LS orthogonality conditions, the random variable

$$\sum_{j=1}^{N} b_j X_{ij}$$

---

[22]See for example, the discussion in Thomas Sargent, *Macroeconomic Theory* (London: Academic Press, 1987).

is called the projection of Y on the X and is written as:

$$P\left(Y\middle|X_1,\ldots,X_N\right)=\sum_{j=1}^{N}b_jX_{ij}$$

A projection decomposes the variable Y into two mutually orthogonal components, the projection $P\left(Y\middle|X_1,\ldots,X_N\right)$ and the residual U. It can be demonstrated that projections obey the following recursive relationships:

$$P\left(Y\middle|X_1,\ldots,X_N,X_{N+1}\right)$$
$$=P\left(Y\middle|X_1,\ldots,X_N\right)+P\left(Y-P\left(Y\middle|X_1,\ldots,X_N\right)\middle|X_N-P\left(X\middle|X_1,\ldots,X_N\right)\right)$$

This recursive relationship shows that regressions can be constructed progressively in the sense that we can regress a variable on a partial set of variables and then add new variables progressively, without changing the previously determined coefficients.

Estimation of the Regression Coefficients

Let's now move on to the estimation of the regression parameters. Assume that we have T observations of one dependent variable Y and of N independent variables X_i, $i = 1, 2, \ldots, N$. Organize sample data in matrix forms as follows:

$$Y=\begin{bmatrix}Y_1\\Y_2\\\vdots\\Y_T\end{bmatrix},\quad X=\begin{bmatrix}X_{12}&X_{12}&\cdots&X_{1N}\\X_{22}&X_{22}&\cdots&X_{2N}\\\vdots&\vdots&\ddots&\vdots\\X_{T2}&X_{T2}&\cdots&X_{TN}\end{bmatrix},\quad U=\begin{bmatrix}U_1\\U_2\\\vdots\\U_T\end{bmatrix}$$

The matrix X is called the *design matrix*. Each row of the design matrix is an observation of the N independent variables; each column represents all T observations of an independent variable. Let's stipulate that if a constant term is needed in the regression equation, then the first column is a column of 1s. Each element of the vectors Y and U represent, respectively, an observation of the dependent variable Y and the value of the corresponding residual. Let's place all the regression coefficients in a column N-vector:

$$B = (b_1, \ldots, b_N)^T$$

To each observation corresponds a regression equation which, assuming a constant term, can be written as follows:

$$Y_1 = b_1 + b_2 X_{12} + \cdots + b_N X_{1N}$$
$$\dots\dots\dots\dots\dots\dots\dots\dots\dots\dots$$
$$Y_T = b_1 + b_2 X_{T2} + \cdots + b_N X_{TN}$$

Using matrix notation, we can compactly write all the regression equations for all observations as:

$$Y = XB + U$$

where Y and U are T-vectors, B is a N-vector, and X is a $T \times N$ matrix. All X, Y, and U are formed by random variables. Assuming that samples are independent, we can rewrite the assumptions of the regression model as follows:

$$E(U) = 0$$
$$E(UU^T) = \sigma_u^2 I_T$$

We can also assume that residuals and independent variables are independent for all variables and all lags and that the matrix X^TX is nonsingular. Under these assumptions, the Gauss-Markov theorem states that the following estimator of the regression coefficients:

$$B = (X^TX)^{-1}X^TY$$

is the *Best Linear Unbiased Estimator* (BLUE).

Let's now sketch the OLS approach to determine the estimator $B = (X^TX)^{-1}X^TY$. The OLS principle is a method of data analysis. Per se, the OLS method does not require any statistical assumption. Let's begin by illustrating the method with an example. Suppose we are given a sample of 100 pairs of data: (Y_i, X_i), $i = 1, \ldots, 100$. The Y and the design matrix for this sample are:

$Y' = [1.1877$	2.5339	–1.5088	1.6622	1.1688	–0.4077	0.5164
1.3426	4.6284	3.8694	–0.1999	4.2349	1.9754	1.2369	2.0647
1.1950	1.3259	2.9897	2.9590	3.0172	2.3215	0.4925	2.4672
3.4302	2.3389	2.9347	2.6769	1.6966	2.3439	1.3127	3.0384
1.0529	1.1811	1.4905	–0.5943	3.8384	2.7752	1.7451	3.9203
0.8885	2.5478	2.4586	3.0692	3.1129	1.9851	2.8699	2.7851
3.6277	4.1433	4.2093	2.2863	3.2774	2.0359	2.1865	3.3432
4.9326	2.6803	3.8714	3.3244	4.7174	2.5609	3.7326	4.3025
4.9006	5.3942	3.9859	2.4584	3.2577	2.9884	6.4505	3.5344
4.9481	4.0576	5.1886	3.5852	2.9977	3.0276	4.9882	4.3726

4.4039 6.0693 4.9916 4.9478 6.3877 4.0455 5.5966 5.7851
4.7563 5.2657 3.9342 4.0020 5.3049 5.9723 7.8855 4.6831
5.5873 5.3675 3.5670 5.1110 3.8053]

$$X' = \begin{bmatrix} 1 & 1 & 1 & \cdots & 1 \\ 1 & 2 & 3 & \cdots & 100 \end{bmatrix}$$

Exhibit 2.4 illustrates the scatterplot of the data.

We want to determine the straight line $y = b_1 + b_2 x$ that best approximates the linear relationship between X and Y. The least squares principle looks for the straight line that minimizes the sum of the squares of the differences between the data and the line. In this two-variable case, we want to minimize the following expression:

$$\sum_{i=1}^{100} \left(Y_i - b_1 + b_2 X_i \right)^2$$

Differentiate this expression with respect to b_1, b_2 and equate the derivatives to zero to obtain the conditions:

$$2 \sum_{i=1}^{100} \left(Y_i - b_1 - b_2 X_{i2} \right) = 0$$

$$2 \sum_{i=1}^{100} \left(Y_i - b_1 - b_2 X_{i2} \right) X_{i2} = 0$$

EXHIBIT 2.4 Scatterplot of the Sample Data

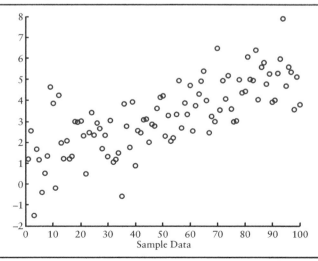

These conditions can be written in vector-matrix notation:

$$X_1^T U = 0$$
$$X_2^T U = 0$$

These conditions are called *orthogonality conditions* because they imply that the residuals are uncorrelated with the independent variables. Absence of correlation is called *orthogonality* because correlation can be interpreted algebraically as a scalar product. These conditions can be written in matrix form as:

$$X^T U = 0$$

Consider now the regression model $Y = XB + U$ and premultiply both sides by X^T thus obtaining

$$(X^T X)B = X^T Y + X^T U$$

Note that Y is a T vector and X^T is a $N \times T$ matrix. As we have just seen, the least squares condition implies $X^T U = 0$. Hence in premultiplying both sides by the inverse of $X^T X$, we obtain the estimator $B = (X^T X)^{-1} X^T Y$. If we apply this formula to our data, we obtain $B = [1.0807 \quad 0.0429]$ which is in good agreement with empirical data generated with $B = [1 \quad 0.05]$.

We can immediately generalize to any number of variables. In fact, consider a regression model $Y = XB + U$. The least squares condition seeks the coefficients that minimize:

$$\sum_{i=1}^{T} \left(Y_i - \sum_{j=1}^{N} b_j X_{ij} \right)^2$$

Differentiating and equating the derivatives to zero, we obtain the orthogonality conditions:

$$\sum_{i=1}^{T} \left[\left(Y_i - \sum_{j=1}^{N} b_j X_{ij} \right) X_{i1} \right]$$

$$\cdots\cdots\cdots\cdots\cdots\cdots\cdots\cdots\cdots$$

$$\sum_{i=1}^{T} \left[\left(Y_i - \sum_{j=1}^{N} b_j X_{ij} \right) X_{iN} \right]$$

which state that the independent variables are orthogonal to the residuals. This set of orthogonality conditions can be expressed in matrix form: $X^T U$

= 0. Using the same reasoning as above, from the orthogonality conditions we obtain

$$B = (X^T X)^{-1} X^T Y$$

Thus far we have not assumed any statistical model but we have determined a vector of coefficients B such that the sum of squared residuals

$$\sum_{i=1}^{T} \left(Y_i - \sum_{j=1}^{N} b_j X_{ij} \right)^2$$

is minimized. The OLS procedure can be applied to any set of data regardless of how they are generated. If we assume that data are generated by a statistical model $Y = XB + U$ with the sole assumptions that residuals are zero-mean variables with constant variance, mutually uncorrelated and uncorrelated with the regressors, then the B are a BLUE estimator of the true regression coefficients. Note that there are no assumptions on the distribution of residuals and regressors other than requiring zero mean and constant variance. Observe that we can look at the OLS estimator B as obtained from the orthogonality condition $E(X^T Y) = E(X^T X)B$, replacing the expectations with the empirical means.

Here is the intuition. We have seen that if we can describe a population with a regression model where regressors are uncorrelated with residuals, then the coefficients of the model satisfy the least squares condition as a population property. When we apply OLS to sample data, we estimate the population least squares property replacing expectations with empirical averages.

$$\sum_{j=1}^{N} b_j X_{ij}$$

$$P(Y | X_1, \ldots, X_N) = \sum_{j=1}^{N} b_j X_{ij}$$

$$P(Y | X_1, \ldots, X_N, X_{N+1})$$
$$= P(Y | X_1, \ldots, X_N) + P(Y - P(Y | X_1, \ldots, X_N) | X_N - P(X | X_1, \ldots, X_N))$$

The OLS method is a method of data analysis which can always be applied, regardless of the distribution of the variables, provided that second-order moments exist. The OLS estimator is not the only possible estimator. If all the variables are normally distributed, we can obtain the maximum likelikood estimator. It can be demonstrated that the maximum likelihood estimation principle yields the same estimator as the OLS method. The demonstration is straightforward. In fact, assuming normally distributed residuals with a diagonal covariance matrix, the sample likelihood L can be written as follows:

$$L(B,\sigma) = \prod_{i=1}^{T} \sigma^{-1} \exp\left(-\frac{1}{2\sigma^2}\left(Y_i - \sum_{j=1}^{N} b_j X_{ij}\right)^2\right)$$

The loglikelihood can be written as follows:

$$\log L(B,\sigma) = T\sigma^{-1} - \frac{1}{2\sigma^2}\sum_{i=1}^{T}\left(Y_i - \sum_{j=1}^{N} b_j X_{ij}\right)^2$$

The maximum likelihood is obtained maximizing the term

$$\sum_{i=1}^{T}\left(Y_i - \sum_{j=1}^{N} b_j X_{ij}\right)^2$$

This term is the sum of the squared residuals as with the OLS method.

The estimators $\hat{B}$ are random variables that depend on the sample data. The estimators $\hat{B}$ are unbiased and therefore their expectations equal the true value of the regression coefficients: $E(\hat{B}) = B$. As $\hat{B}$ is BLUE, it has the minimum variance among the linear unbiased estimators. It can be demonstrated that if residuals are uncorrelated:

$$\text{cov}(\hat{B}) = \sigma^2 (X^T X)^{-1}$$

and that an unbiased estimate s^2 of σ^2 is the following:

$$s^2 = \frac{(U^T U)}{T - N}$$

If residuals are normally distributed, the ratio $= s^2(T - N)/\sigma^2$ is distributed as a Student's t with $T-N$ degrees of freedom.

Relaxing Assumptions

We can now relax some of the assumptions we made previously on regressions.

Generalized Least Squares

Suppose that residuals might not be uncorrelated and/or that residuals do not have a constant variance. Let's therefore assume the residuals of the model $Y = XB + U$ have the following covariance matrix:

$$\text{cov}(U) = \sigma^2 \Sigma$$

where we assume that Σ is known while σ^2 is a scale parameter to be estimated. Note explicitly that this covariance matrix represents both the eventual heteroskedasticity and autocorrelation structure of the residuals. In particular, the terms on the diagonal of Σ represent the eventual time-dependence of the variance of the residuals while the off-diagonal terms represent the autocorrelations between residuals at different times.

In order to determine the regression parameters, we can use the *Generalized Least Squares* (GLS) principle. The GLS principle is the analogue of the OLS principle applied to correlated residuals. It is similar to the OLS principle insofar as it requires the minimization of the squared residuals. However, given that residuals are random variables, the sum of squared residuals depends on their covariance matrix. In fact, we can write the GLS conditions as follows:

$$\arg \min_{B} \left[\left(Y - BX \right)^T \sigma^{-2} \Sigma^{-1} \left(Y - BX \right) \right]$$

If we differentiate and equate the derivatives to zero, we obtain:

$$(X^T \Sigma^{-1} X) B = X^T \Sigma^{-1} Y$$

Assuming that the matrix $X^T \Sigma^{-1} X$ is nonsingular, the above yields the Generalized Least Squares (GLS) estimator also called Aitken's estimator:

$$\hat{B} = \left(X^T \Sigma^{-1} X \right)^{-1} X^T \Sigma^{-1} Y$$

In addition, if we premultiply the regression model by $\Sigma^{-1/2}$ we obtain another regression model $Y^* = X^* B + U^*$ where $Y^* = \Sigma^{-1/2} Y$, $X^* = \Sigma^{-1/2} X$, $U^* = \Sigma^{-1/2} U$ where $\text{cov}(U^*) = \sigma^2 I$. In other words, if the covariance matrix of the residuals is known, it is possible to transform a regression model with correlated residuals in a standard regression model with uncorrelated residuals.

The Gauss-Markov theorem extends to the GLS estimators as it can be demonstrated that the GLS estimator is the BLUE. The covariance matrix of the GLS estimator is

$$\mathrm{cov}\left(\hat{B}\right) = \sigma^2 \left(X^T \Sigma^{-1} X\right)$$

Though conceptually satisfactory, the GLS principle per se is of little use in practice as the covariance matrix of the residuals is generally not known. In practice, the GLS is replaced by the Feasible GLS (FGLS) in which the covariance matrix of residuals is replaced by an estimate of the same matrix. FGLS is applied iteratively. The first step is to estimate the multiple regression coefficients B with OLS. In general, the residuals from this initial step will show a covariance matrix $\Sigma \neq \sigma^2 I$. The second step is to use the empirical covariance matrix of the residuals obtained with OLS to produce an updated GLS-type estimate of the regression coefficients B. This procedure can be iterated until convergence is reached.

Instrumental Variables

Consider a linear model $Y = XB + U$. A variable Z_h is called an *instrumental variable* or more briefly an *instrument* if it is uncorrelated with all the residuals: $E(Z_i u) = 0$. A set of H instrumental variables $Z_1, \ldots, Z_H$ is called a *system of instrumental variables* if the variables Z_h are linearly independent, that is, no variable is a linear combination of the others, a condition which ensures that the matrix $Z^T Z$ is nonsingular.

Suppose that the linear model $Y = XB + U$ does not satisfy the orthogonality conditions but that a system of instrumental variables exist. If the number H of instrumental variables is equal to the number N of regressors, and if the matrix $Z^T X$ is nonsingular, then the instrumental variables estimator of the regression coefficients is:

$$\hat{B} = \left(Z^T X\right)^{-1} Z^T Y$$

Instrumental variables do not necessarily exist. When an instrumental variables system of the correct size do indeed exist, instrumental variables offer a way to estimate regressions where regressors and residuals are correlated.

MULTIVARIATE REGRESSION

Thus far we have discussed single equation regression where one variable is regressed on multiple regressands. However, in economics and in financial econometrics we often need to regress multiple regressands on multiple regressors. A regression of this type is called a multivariate regression.

There are different forms of multivariate regressions. The most complete specification of a regression model is given by a system of linear equations that link linearly both the Y_i and the X_j. The general form of a multiple equations model is the following:

$$Y_{t,1} = a_{21}Y_{t,2} + \cdots + a_{M1}Y_{t,M} = b_{11}X_{t1} + \cdots + b_{N1}X_{t1} + U_{t1}$$

$$\dots\dots\dots\dots\dots\dots\dots\dots\dots\dots\dots\dots\dots\dots\dots\dots\dots$$

$$Y_{t,M} = a_{1M}Y_{t,1} + \cdots + a_{M-1M}Y_{t,M} = b_{1M1}X_{t1} + \cdots + b_{NM}X_{t1} + U_{tM}$$

This system of equations can be written in matrix form as follows:

$$YA = XB + U$$

In this system, the variables Y are determined endogenously in function of the exogenous variables X. Assuming that the matrix A be nonsingular, multiplying both sides by A^{-1} the same system can be written as:

$$Y = XBA^{-1} + UA^{-1}$$
$$Y = XC + V$$

In this formulation the exogenous variables are expressed directly in function of the endogenous variables. Multivariate regressions can be estimated with the OLS method provided that residuals are zero-mean variables with constant variance and that residuals and regressors are not correlated. The estimators have the same form as for multiple regressions:

$$\hat{B} = \left(X^T X\right)^{-1} X^T Y$$

where, however, the $\hat{B}$ are now a matrix of coefficients.

Seemingly Unrelated Regressions

The *seemingly unrelated regression* (SUR) model is a multivariate regression model where all equations are independent but the residuals are mutually correlated. The SUR model was introduced by Arnold Zellner in his 1962 paper.[23] Zellner observed that if regressions use the same data, residuals can be correlated even if they refer to *seemingly unrelated* equations. The SUR model might seem to be counterintuitive as it might be difficult to see how

---

[23] Arnold Zellner, "An Efficient Method of Estimating Seemingly Unrelated Regression Equations and Tests for Aggregation Bias," *Journal of the American Statistical Association*, 57 (1962), pp. 348–368.

independent equations with different dependent and independent variables can have anything in common.

The setting of SUR is the following. Consider a number M of classical regression equations:

$$Y_{1,t} = \sum_{i=1}^{K_1} \beta_{1i} X_{i1,t} + U_{1,t}$$

$$\cdots\cdots\cdots\cdots\cdots\cdots$$

$$Y_{M,t} = \sum_{i=1}^{K_1} \beta_{Mi} X_{iM,t} + U_{M,t}$$

Assume that each equation can be estimated with OLS and that residuals are correlated with covariance matrix $\Sigma \neq \sigma^2 I$. Then the OLS estimators of each equation might not be efficient. The SUR model uses a GLS estimator applied to the global model.

QUANTILE REGRESSIONS

Thus far we analyzed classical regression models whose predictions are point estimates of the conditional mean of the dependent variable. In fact, a regression function is defined as the conditional expectation of the regressand given the regressors. It was also proved that the OLS and the GLS procedures actually estimate the conditional mean. The conditional mean is not the only possible choice of a point estimate of the distribution of the regressand. For example, another possible choise is the median.

In fact, in the eighteenth century there was a scientific debate on the relative merits of the median versus the mean as a point estimate of a distribution. The scientist and mathematician Pierre-Simon Laplace favored the median while the mathematician Karl Friedrich Gauss favored the mean and the OLS method he developed. Thereafter, the preferred point estimate became the mean and the preferred method of data analysis became the OLS regression. Reasons behind the preference for OLS include the fact that OLS is based on the minimization of the sum of squared deviations, a task that can be performed with analytical methods which yield closed-form formulas. However with the advent of fast computers and the development of more efficient optimization methods, this advantage is greatly reduced.[24]

Additional considerations might come into play. For example, the median is less sensitive to outliers than the mean, and therefore a regression

---

[24]See Stephen Portnoy and Roger Koenker, "The Gaussian Hare and the Laplacian Tortoise: Computability of Squared-Error versus Absolute-Error Estimators," *Statistical Science*, 12 (1997), pp. 279–300.

based on the conditional median as opposed to a regression based on the conditional mean is more robust. Robustness is not the only consideration. More in general, we might want to obtain more information on the distribution of the dependent variable than a point estimate of the mean or of the median. The key idea of *quantile regression* proposed by Koenker and Basset in 1978,[25] is to model the conditional quantiles, that is, to model the quantiles given the regressors.

In order to explain quantile regression, let's recall a few basic facts. First, given a set of data X_i, i = 1, ..., N, the mean and the median can be represented as a minimization problem:

$$\underset{\mu}{\arg\min}\left(\sum_{i=1}^{N}(X_i - \mu)^2\right) = \text{mean}(X_i)$$

$$\underset{\mu}{\arg\min}\left(\sum_{i=1}^{N}|X_i - \mu|\right) = \text{median}(X_i)$$

Consider now a multivariate data set which we represent as in the previous sections with a vector Y and a design matrix X whose first column is formed by 1s. The following properties hold:

$$\underset{a,b}{\arg\min}\left(\sum_{t=1}^{T}\left(Y_t - \sum_{i=1}^{N}b_i X_{ti}\right)^2\right) \text{ yields the conditional mean,}$$

$$\underset{a,b}{\arg\min}\left(\sum_{t=1}^{T}\left|Y_t - \sum_{i=1}^{N}b_i X_{ti}\right|\right) \text{ yields the conditional median.}$$

As shown in Koenker and Basset, this relationship can be generalized to any quantile. Here is how. Suppose τ, $0 < \tau < 1$ indicates the quantile. For example, τ = 0.09 indicates the upper decile. The following expression:

$$\underset{b}{\arg\min}\left(\sum_{\substack{t=1 \\ t:Y_t \geq \sum_{i=1}^{N} b_i X_{ti}}}^{T}\tau\left|Y_t - \sum_{i=1}^{N}b_i X_{ti}\right| + \sum_{\substack{t=1 \\ t:Y_t < \sum_{i=1}^{N} b_i X_{ti}}}^{T}(1-\tau)\left|Y_t - \sum_{i=1}^{N}b_i X_{ti}\right|\right)$$

yields the conditional τ quantile.

Quantile regressions have found important applications in finance. For example, quantile regressions were used by Engle and Manganelli to com-

---

[25]Roger Koenker and Gilbert Bassett, "Regression Quantiles," *Econometrica*, 46 (1978), pp. 33–50.

pute directly a risk measure known as Value at Risk (VaR) without the need to estimate the probability distribution.[26]

REGRESSION DIAGNOSTIC

Once we have estimated a regression model, we need criteria to check the quality of the regression. There are several classical ways of evaluating *in sample* the quality of a classical regression. They include the following:

- The confidence intervals of the regression coefficients.
- The *R*-square statistic.
- The *F* statistic.
- The *p* value.
- The leverage points.

In order to compute regression diagnostics we need to make an assumption about the distribution of the regression variables. The practice is to assume that residuals are normally distributed.

Under the assumption that residuals are mutually uncorrelated and uncorrelated with the regressors, if the latter are random variables, the regression coefficients are estimated by:

$$\hat{B} = \left(X^T X\right)^{-1} X^T Y$$

and the variance of the residuals is estimated by

$$\hat{\sigma}^2 = \left(\frac{1}{T-N}\right)\sum_{t=1}^{T} U_t^2$$

It can be demonstrated that the estimated variance of residuals has a Chi-square distribution with $T-N$ degrees of freedom, that the coefficients B are normally distributed, and that

$$E\left[(\hat{B}-B)(\hat{B}-B)'\right] = \hat{\sigma}^2(X^T X)$$

---

[26]Robert F. Engle and Simone Manganelli, "CAViaR: Conditional Autoregressive Value at Risk by Regression Quantiles," *Journal of Business and Economic Statistics*, 22 (2004), pp. 367–381. For a further discussion of applications in finance, see Chris Gowland, Zhijie Xiao, and Qi Zeng, "Beyond the Central Tendency: Quantile Regression as a Tool in Quantitative Investing," *Journal of Portfolio Management*, 35 (2009), pp. 106–119.

Therefore the quantities

$$\frac{\left(\hat{b}_j - b_j\right)}{\hat{\sigma}}\sqrt{a_{jj}}$$

where the a_{jj} are the diagonal elements of the matrix $(X^T X)$ have a Student's t distribution with $T - N$ degrees of freedom. This allows one to create significance intervals for the regression coefficients. A confidence interval for a given variable is an interval which includes the values of the variable within a predetermined probability. For example, a 95% confidence interval for b_1 is an interval (b_{1l}, b_{1h}) around the estimated $\hat{b}_1$ where, under the assumptions made, we will find the true value of b_1 with a 95% probability. In other words, if the model is correct, the true value of the parameter b_1 will be in the (b_{1l}, b_{1h}) interval. Of course the confidence interval is meaningful only if the model is correct.

In practice, most statistical packages will compute the N-vector

$$\begin{bmatrix} b_1 \\ \vdots \\ b_N \end{bmatrix}$$

of the estimated regression coefficients and a $N \times 2$ matrix

$$\begin{bmatrix} b_{1l} & b_{1h} \\ \vdots & \vdots \\ b_{Nl} & b_{Nh} \end{bmatrix}$$

that contains the relative confidence intervals at a specified confidence level.

The R-square statistic, also called *coefficient of determination*, evaluates the percentage of the total variation of the independent variable explained by the regression. Consider a single equation multiple regression. If we want to evaluate how well the regression fits data we can compare the total variation of the residuals with the total variation of the data. Using the notation of this chapter, we call Y the independent variable and U the residuals. The ratio

$$\frac{\sum_{t=1}^{T} U_t^2}{\sum_{t=1}^{T} Y_t^2}$$

between the total variation of the residuals and the total variation of the dependent variables measures the percentage of the data variance which is not explained by the regression. Consequently, the quantity:

$$R^2 = 1 - \frac{\sum_{t=1}^{T} U_t^2}{\sum_{t=1}^{T} Y_t^2}$$

measures the percentage of the total variation of the independent variables which is explained by the regression equation.

Defined in this way, the R^2 is misleading and might lead to serious overfitting. In fact, in sample, the percentage of total variation explained grows with the number of regressors. However, the increase of R^2 generated in this way might be a numerical artifact. For this reason it has been proposed to correct the R^2, penalizing models with many regressors. The *modified* R^2, or *adjusted* R^2, represented as R^2 used in most packages is defined as follows:

$$\tilde{R}^2 = 1 - \left(\frac{N-1}{N-K-1}\right)\frac{\sum_{t=1}^{T} U_t^2}{\sum_{t=1}^{T} Y_t^2}$$

The $\tilde{R}$ contains the factor

$$\left(\frac{N-1}{N-K-1}\right)$$

which grows with the number of the regressors and therefore penalizes the term

$$\frac{\sum_{t=1}^{T} U_t^2}{\sum_{t=1}^{T} Y_t^2}$$

which gets smaller with growing numbers of regressors.

The F statistic is a statistic computed by most statistical software packages used to test the null assumption that all regression coefficients are zero: $B = 0$. The total F statistic is defined as follows:

$$F = \frac{R^2}{1-R^2}\frac{N-K}{K-1}$$

It can be demonstrated that the F statistic is distributed as an F-distribution $F(K - 1, N - K)$ that allows one to determine the relative p values. The p

values are the probability of the distribution tail at the right of the value of a statistic. Most statistical software packages compute the F statistics and the corresponding p value from the F distribution. A small p value rejects the null of $B = 0$ because it means that the computed statistic is very unlikely given that it is far in the tail region.

ROBUST ESTIMATION OF REGRESSIONS

In this section we discuss methods for the robust estimation of regressions. Robust estimation is a topic of robust statistics. Therefore we first introduce the general concepts and methods of robust statistics and then apply them to regression analysis. In particular, we will introduce robust regression estimators and robust regression diagnostics.

Robust Statistics

Robust statistics addresses the problem of making estimates that are insensitive to small changes in the basic assumptions of the statistical models employed. The concepts and methods of robust statistics originated in the 1950s. The technical term *robust statistics* was coined by G. E. P. Box in 1953.

Statistical models are based on a set of assumptions; the most important include (1) the distribution of key variables, for example the normal distribution of errors, and (2) the model specification, for example model linearity or nonlinearity. Some of these assumptions are critical to the estimation process: if they are violated, the estimates become unreliable. Robust statistics (1) assesses the changes in estimates due to small changes in the basic assumptions and (2) creates new estimates that are insensitive to small changes in some of the assumptions. The focus of our exposition is to make estimates robust to small changes in the distribution of errors and, in particular, to the presence of outliers.

Robust statistics is also useful to separate the contribution of the tails from the contribution of the body of the data. We can say that robust statistics and classical nonrobust statistics are complementary. By conducting a robust analysis, one can better articulate important econometric findings.

As observed by Peter Huber, *robust*, *distribution-free*, and *nonparametrical* seem to be closely related properties but actually are not.[27] For example, the sample mean and the sample median are nonparametric estimates of the mean and the median but the mean is not robust to outliers.

---

[27]Huber's book is a standard reference on robust statistics: Peter J. Huber, *Robust Statistics* (New York: John Wiley & Sons, Inc., 1981).

In fact, changes of one single observation might have unbounded effects on the mean while the median is insensitive to changes of up to half the sample. Robust methods assume that there are indeed parameters in the distributions under study and attempt to minimize the effects of outliers as well as erroneous assumptions on the shape of the distribution.

A general definition of robustness is, by nature, quite technical. The reason is that we need to define robustness with respect to changes in distributions. That is, we need to make precise the concept that small changes in the distribution, which is a function, result in small changes in the estimate, which is a number. Let's first give an intuitive, nontechnical overview of the modern concept of robustness and how to measure robustness.

Qualitative and Quantitative Robustness

Here we introduce the concepts of qualitative and quantitative robustness of estimators. Estimators are functions of the sample data. Given an N-sample of data $\mathbf{X} = (x_1, \ldots, x_N)'$ from a population with a cdf $F(x)$, depending on parameter θ_∞, an estimator for θ_∞ is a function $\hat{\vartheta} = \vartheta_N(x_1, \ldots, x_N)$. Consider those estimators that can be written as functions of the cumulative empirical distribution function:

$$F_N(x) = N^{-1} \sum_{i=1}^{N} I(x_i \leq x)$$

where I is the indicator function. For these estimators we can write

$$\hat{\vartheta} = \vartheta_N(F_N)$$

Most estimators, in particular the ML estimators, can be written in this way with probability 1. In general, when $N \to \infty$ then $F_N(x) \to F(x)$ almost surely and $\hat{\vartheta}_N \to \vartheta_\infty$ in probability and almost surely. The estimator $\hat{\vartheta}_N$ is a random variable that depends on the sample. Under the distribution F, it will have a probability distribution $L_F(\vartheta_N)$. Intuitively, statistics defined as functionals of a distribution are robust if they are continuous with respect to the distribution. In 1968, Hampel introduced a technical definition of qualitative robustness based on metrics of the functional space of distributions.[28] The Hampel definition states that an estimator is robust for a given distribution F if small deviations from F in the given metric result in small deviations from $L_F(\vartheta_N)$ in the same metric or eventually in some other metric for any sequence of samples of increasing size. The definition of robustness

---

[28]F. R. Hampel, "A General Qualitative Definition of Robustness," *Annals of Mathematical Statistics*, 42 (1971), pp. 1887–1896.

can be made quantitative by assessing quantitatively how changes in the distribution F affect the distribution $L_F(\vartheta_N)$.

Resistant Estimators

An estimator is called *resistant* if it is insensitive to changes in one single observation.[29] Given an estimator $\hat{\vartheta} = \vartheta_N(F_N)$, we want to understand what happens if we add a new observation of value x to a large sample. To this end we define the *influence curve* (IC), also called *influence function*. The IC is a function of x given ϑ, and F is defined as follows:

$$IC_{\vartheta,F}(x) = \lim_{s \to 0} \frac{\vartheta((1-s)F + s\delta_x) - \vartheta(F)}{s}$$

where δ_x denotes a point mass 1 at x (i.e., a probability distribution concentrated at the single point x). As we can see from its previous definition, the IC is a function of the size of the single observation that is added. In other words, the IC measures the influence of a single observation x on a statistics ϑ for a given distribution F. In practice, the influence curve is generated by plotting the value of the computed statistic with a single point of X added to Y against that X value. For example, the IC of the mean is a straight line. Several aspects of the influence curve are of particular interest:

- Is the curve bounded as the X values become extreme? Robust statistics should be bounded. That is, a robust statistic should not be unduly influenced by a single extreme point.
- What is the general behavior as the X observation becomes extreme? For example, does it become smoothly down-weighted as the values become extreme?
- What is the influence if the X point is in the center of the Y points?

Let's now introduce concepts that are important in applied work. We then introduce the robust estimators.

The *breakdown* (BD) *bound* or *point* is the largest possible fraction of observations for which there is a bound on the change of the estimate when that fraction of the sample is altered without restrictions. For example, we can change up to 50% of the sample points without provoking unbounded changes of the median. On the contrary, changes of one single observation might have unbounded effects on the mean.

---

[29]For an application to the estimation of the estimation of beta, see R. Douglas Martin and Timothy T. Simin, "Outlier Resistant Estimates of Beta," *Financial Analysts Journal*, 59 (2003), pp. 56–58. We discuss this application later in this chapter.

The *rejection point* is defined as the point beyond which the IC becomes zero. Note that observations beyond the rejection point make no contribution to the final estimate except, possibly, through the auxiliary scale estimate. Estimators that have a finite rejection point are said to be redescending and are well protected against very large outliers. However, a finite rejection point usually results in the underestimation of scale. This is because when the samples near the tails of a distribution are ignored, an insufficient fraction of the observations may remain for the estimation process. This in turn adversely affects the efficiency of the estimator.

The *gross error sensitivity* expresses asymptotically the maximum effect that a contaminated observation can have on the estimator. It is the maximum absolute value of the IC.

The *local shift sensitivity* measures the effect of the removal of a mass at y and its reintroduction at x. For continuous and differentiable IC, the local shift sensitivity is given by the maximum absolute value of the slope of IC at any point.

Winsor's principle states that all distributions are normal in the middle.

M-estimators are those estimators that are obtained by minimizing a function of the sample data. Suppose that we are given an N-sample of data $\mathbf{X} = (x_1, \ldots, x_N)'$. The estimator $T(x_1, \ldots, x_N)$ is called an M-estimator if it is obtained by solving the following minimum problem:

$$T = \arg\min_t \left\{ J = \sum_{i=1}^{N} \rho(x_i, t) \right\}$$

where $\rho(x_{i,t})$ is an arbitrary function. Alternatively, if $\rho(x_{i,t})$ is a smooth function, we can say that T is an M-estimator if it is determined by solving the equations:

$$\sum_{i=1}^{N} \psi(x_i, t) = 0$$

where

$$\psi(x_i, t) = \frac{\partial \rho(x_i, t)}{\partial t}$$

When the M-estimator is equivariant, that is $T(x_1 + a, \ldots, x_N + a) = T(x_1, \ldots, x_N) + a$, $\forall a \in R$, we can write ψ and ρ in terms of the residuals $x - t$. Also, in general, an auxiliary scale estimate, S, is used to obtain the scaled residuals $r = (x - t)/S$. If the estimator is also equivariant to changes of scale, we can write

$$\psi(x,t) = \psi\left(\frac{x-t}{S}\right) = \psi(r)$$

$$\rho(x,t) = \rho\left(\frac{x-t}{S}\right) = \rho(r)$$

ML estimators are *M*-estimators with $\rho = -\log f$, where f is the probability density. (Actually the name *M*-estimators means maximum likelihood-type estimators.) LS estimators are also *M*-estimators.

The IC of *M*-estimators has a particularly simple form. In fact, it can be demonstrated that the IC is proportional to the function ψ:

$$IC = \text{Constant} \times \psi$$

To understand our next estimator, consider an N-sample $(x_1, \ldots, x_N)'$. Order the samples so that $x_{(1)} \le x_{(2)} \le \ldots \le x_{(N)}$. The i-th element $X = x_{(i)}$ of the ordered sample is called the *i-th order statistic*. *L-estimators* are estimators obtained as a linear combination of order statistics:

$$L = \sum_{i=1}^{N} a_i x_{(i)}$$

where the a_i are fixed constants. Constants are typically normalized so that

$$\sum_{i=1}^{N} a_i = 1$$

An important example of an *L*-estimator is the *trimmed mean*. The trimmed mean is a mean formed excluding a fraction of the highest and/or lowest samples. In this way the mean, which is not a robust estimator, becomes less sensitive to outliers.

R-estimators are obtained by minimizing the sum of residuals weighted by functions of the rank of each residual. The functional to be minimized is the following:

$$\arg\min\left\{J = \sum_{i=1}^{N} a(R_i) r_i\right\}$$

where R_i is the rank of the *i*-th residual r_i and a is a nondecreasing score function that satisfies the condition

$$\sum_{i=1}^{N} a(R_i) = 0$$

The Least Median of Squares Estimator

Instead of minimizing the sum of squared residuals, as in LS, to estimate the parameter vector, Rousseuw[30] proposed minimizing the median of squared residuals, referred to as the *least median of squares* (LMedS) *estimator*. This estimator effectively trims the $N/2$ observations having the largest residuals, and uses the maximal residual value in the remaining set as the criterion to be minimized. It is hence equivalent to *assuming* that the noise proportion is 50%.

LMedS is unwieldy from a computational point of view because of its nondifferentiable form. This means that a quasi-exhaustive search on all possible parameter values needs to be done to find the global minimum.

The Least Trimmed of Squares Estimator

The *least trimmed of squares* (LTS) *estimator* offers an efficient way to find robust estimates by minimizing the objective function given by

$$\left\{ J = \sum_{i=1}^{h} r_{(i)}^2 \right\}$$

where $r_{(i)}^2$ is the i-th smallest residual or distance when the residuals are ordered in ascending order, that is: $r_{(1)}^2 \leq r_{(2)}^2 \leq r_{(N)}^2$ and h is the number of data points whose residuals we want to include in the sum. This estimator basically finds a robust estimate by identifying the $N - h$ points having the largest residuals as outliers, and discarding (trimming) them from the data set. The resulting estimates are essentially LS estimates of the trimmed data set. Note that h should be as close as possible to the number of points in the data set that we do not consider outliers.

Reweighted Least Squares Estimator

Some algorithms explicitly cast their objective functions in terms of a set of weights that distinguish between inliers and outliers. However, these weights usually depend on a scale measure that is also difficult to estimate. For example, the *reweighted least squares* (RLS) estimator uses the following objective function:

$$\arg\min \left\{ J = \sum_{i=1}^{N} \omega_i r_i^2 \right\}$$

---

[30]P. Rousseuw, "Least Median of Squares Regression," *Journal of the American Statistical Association*, 79 (1984), pp. 871–890.

where r_i are robust residuals resulting from an approximate LMedS or LTS procedure. Here the weights ω_i trim outliers from the data used in LS minimization, and can be computed after a preliminary approximate step of LMedS or LTS.

Robust Estimators of the Center The mean estimates the center of a distribution but it is not resistant. Resistant estimators of the center are the following:[31]

- *Trimmed mean.* Suppose $x_{(1)} \le x_{(2)} \le \ldots \le x_{(N)}$ are the sample order statistics (that is, the sample sorted). The trimmed mean $T_N(\delta, 1 - \gamma)$ is defined as follows:

$$T_N(\delta, 1 - \gamma) = \frac{1}{U_N - L_N} \sum_{j=L_N+1}^{U_N} x_j$$

$$\delta, \gamma \in (0, 0.5), L_N = \text{floor}[N\delta], U_N = \text{floor}[N\gamma]$$

- *Winsorized mean.* The Winsorized mean $\bar{X}_W$ is the mean of Winsorized data:

$$y_j = \begin{cases} x_{l_N+1} & j \le L_N \\ x_j & L_N + 1 \le j \le U_N \\ x_j = x_{U_N+1} & j \ge U_N + 1 \end{cases}$$

$$\bar{X}_W = \bar{Y}$$

- *Median.* The median Med(**X**) is defined as that value that occupies a central position in a sample order statistics:

$$\text{Med}(\mathbf{X}) = \begin{cases} x_{((N+1)/2)} & \text{if } N \text{ is odd} \\ ((x_{(N/2)} + x_{(N/2+1)})/2) & \text{if } N \text{ is even} \end{cases}$$

Robust Estimators of the Spread The variance is a classical estimator of the spread but it is not robust. Robust estimators of the spread are the following:

- *Median absolute deviation.* The median absolute deviation (MAD) is defined as the median of the absolute value of the difference between a variable and its median, that is,

---

[31]This discussion and the next draw from Anna Chernobai and Svetlozar T. Rachev, "Applying Robust Methods to Operation Risk Modelling," *Journal of Operational Risk,* 1 (2006), pp. 27–41.

$$MAD = MED|X - MED(X)|$$

- *Interquartile range.* The interquartile range (IQR) is defined as the difference between the highest and lowest quartile:

$$IQR = Q(0.75) - Q(0.25)$$

where $Q(0.75)$ and $Q(0.25)$ are the 75th and 25th percentiles of the data.
- *Mean absolute deviation.* The mean absolute deviation (MAD) is defined as follows:

$$\frac{1}{N}\sum_{j=1}^{N}|x_j - MED(\mathbf{X})|$$

- *Winsorized standard deviation.* The Winsorized standard deviation is the standard deviation of Winsorized data, that is,

$$\sigma_W = \frac{\sigma_N}{(U_N - L_N)/N}$$

Robust Estimators of Regressions

Let's now apply the concepts of robust statistics to the estimation of regression coefficients, which is sensitive to outliers.

Identifying robust estimators of regressions is a rather difficult problem. In fact, different choices of estimators, robust or not, might lead to radically different estimates of slopes and intercepts. Consider the following linear regression model:

$$Y = \beta_0 + \sum_{i=1}^{N}\beta_i X_i + \varepsilon$$

The standard nonrobust LS estimation of regression parameters minimizes the sum of squared residuals,

$$\sum_{i=1}^{T}\varepsilon_t^2 = \sum_{i=1}^{T}\left(Y_i - \sum_{j=0}^{N}\beta_{ij}X_{ij}\right)^2$$

The solution of this minimization problem is

$$\hat{\boldsymbol{\beta}} = (\mathbf{X'X})^{-1}\mathbf{X'Y}$$

The fitted values (i.e, the LS estimates of the expectations) of the **Y** are

$$\hat{Y} = X(X'X)^{-1}X'Y = HY$$

The **H** matrix is called the *hat matrix* because it puts a hat on, that is, it computes the expectation $\hat{Y}$ of the **Y**. The hat matrix **H** is a symmetric $T \times T$ projection matrix; that is, the following relationship holds: $HH = H$. The matrix **H** has N eigenvalues equal to 1 and $T - N$ eigenvalues equal to 0. Its diagonal elements, $h_i \equiv h_{ii}$ satisfy:

$$0 \le h_i \le 1$$

and its trace (i.e., the sum of its diagonal elements) is equal to N:

$$\text{tr}(H) = N$$

Under the assumption that the errors are independent and identically distributed with mean zero and variance σ^2, it can be demonstrated that the $\hat{Y}$ are consistent, that is, $\hat{Y} \to E(Y)$ in probability when the sample becomes infinite if and only if $h = \max(h_i) \to 0$. Points where the h_i have large values are called *leverage points*. It can be demonstrated that the presence of leverage points signals that there are observations that might have a decisive influence on the estimation of the regression parameters. A rule of thumb, reported in Huber,[32] suggests that values $h_i \le 0.2$ are safe, values $0.2 \le h_i \le 0.5$ require careful attention, and higher values are to be avoided.

Thus far we have discussed methods to ascertain regression robustness. Let's now discuss methods to "robustify" the regression estimates, namely, methods based on *M*-estimators and *W*-estimators.

Robust Regressions Based on M-Estimators

Let's first discuss how to make *robust regressions* with Huber *M*-estimators. The LS estimators $\hat{\beta} = (X'X)^{-1}X'Y$ are *M*-estimators but are not robust. We can generalize LS seeking to minimize

$$J = \sum_{i=1}^{T} \rho \left(Y_i - \sum_{j=0}^{N} \beta_{ij} X_{ij} \right)$$

by solving the set of $N + 1$ simultaneous equations

---

[32]Huber, *Robust Statistics*.

$$\sum_{i=1}^{T} \psi \left(Y_i - \sum_{j=0}^{N} \beta_{ij} X_{ij} \right) X_{ij} = 0$$

where

$$\psi = \frac{\partial \rho}{\partial \beta}$$

Robust Regressions Based on W-Estimators

W-estimators offer an alternative form of M-estimators. They are obtained by rewriting M-estimators as follows:

$$\psi \left(Y_i - \sum_{j=0}^{N} \beta_{ij} X_{ij} \right) = w \left(Y_i - \sum_{j=0}^{N} \beta_{ij} X_{ij} \right) \left(Y_i - \sum_{j=0}^{N} \beta_{ij} X_{ij} \right)$$

Hence the $N + 1$ simultaneous equations become

$$w \left(Y_i - \sum_{j=0}^{N} \beta_{ij} X_{ij} \right) \left(Y_i - \sum_{j=0}^{N} \beta_{ij} X_{ij} \right) = 0$$

or, in matrix form

$$\mathbf{X'WX\beta = X'WY}$$

where $\mathbf{W}$ is a diagonal matrix.

The above is not a linear system because the weighting function is in general a nonlinear function of the data. A typical approach is to determine iteratively the weights through an iterative *reweighted least squares* (RLS) procedure. Clearly the iterative procedure depends numerically on the choice of the weighting functions. Two commonly used choices are the *Huber weighting function $w_H(e)$*, defined as

$$w_H(e) = \begin{cases} 1 & \text{for } |e| \le k \\ k / |e| & \text{for } |e| > k \end{cases}$$

and the *Tukey bisquare weighting function $wT(e)$*, defined as

$$w_T(e) = \begin{cases} (1 - (e / k)^2)^2 & \text{for } |e| \le k \\ 0 & \text{for } |e| > k \end{cases}$$

where k is a tuning constant often set at $1.345 \times$ (standard deviation of errors) for the Huber function and $k = 4.6853 \times$ (standard deviation of errors) for the Tukey function.

Robust Estimation of Covariance and Correlation Matrices

Variance-covariance matrices are central to modern portfolio theory. In fact, the estimation of the variance-covariance matrices is critical for portfolio management and asset allocation. Suppose returns are a multivariate random vector written as

$$\mathbf{r}_t = \boldsymbol{\mu} + \boldsymbol{\varepsilon}_t$$

The random disturbances $\boldsymbol{\varepsilon}_t$ is characterized by a covariance matrix $\boldsymbol{\Omega}$.

$$\rho_{X,Y} = \mathrm{Corr}(X, Y)$$

$$= \frac{\mathrm{Cov}(X, Y)}{\sqrt{\mathrm{Var}(X)\mathrm{Var}(Y)}} = \frac{\sigma_{X,Y}}{\sigma_X \sigma_Y}$$

The correlation coefficient fully represents the dependence structure of multivariate normal distribution. More in general, the correlation coefficient is a valid measure of dependence for elliptical distributions (i.e., distributions that are constants on ellipsoids). In other cases, different measures of dependence are needed (e.g., copula functions).[33]

The empirical covariance between two variables is defined as

$$\hat{\sigma}_{X,Y} = \frac{1}{N-1} \sum_{i=1}^{N} (X_i - \bar{X})(Y_i - \bar{Y})$$

where

$$\bar{X} = \frac{1}{N} \sum_{i=1}^{N} X_i, \quad \bar{Y} = \frac{1}{N} \sum_{i=1}^{N} Y_i$$

are the empirical means of the variables.

The empirical correlation coefficient is the empirical covariance normalized with the product of the respective empirical standard deviations:

---

[33]Paul Embrechts, Filip Lindskog, and Alexander McNeil, "Modelling Dependence with Copulas and Applications to Risk Management," in S. T. Rachev (ed.), *Handbook of Heavy Tailed Distributions in Finance* (Amsterdam: Elsevier/North-Holland, 2003).

$$\hat{\rho}_{X,Y} = \frac{\hat{\sigma}_{X,Y}}{\hat{\sigma}_X \hat{\sigma}_Y}$$

The empirical standard deviations are defined as

$$\hat{\sigma}_X = \frac{1}{N}\sqrt{\sum_{i=1}^{N}(X_i - \bar{X})^2}, \quad \hat{\sigma}_Y = \frac{1}{N}\sqrt{\sum_{i=1}^{N}(Y_i - \bar{Y})^2}$$

Empirical covariances and correlations are not robust as they are highly sensitive to tails or outliers. Robust estimators of covariances and/or correlations are insensitive to the tails. However, it does not make sense to robustify correlations if dependence is not linear.

Different strategies for robust estimation of covariances exist; among them are:

- Robust estimation of pairwise covariances.
- Robust estimation of elliptic distributions.

Here we discuss only the robust estimation of pairwise covariances. As detailed in Huber,[34] the following identity holds:

$$\text{cov}(X,Y) = \frac{1}{4ab}[\text{var}(aX + bY) - \text{var}(aX - bY)]$$

Assume S is a robust scale functional:

$$S(aX + b) = |a|S(X)$$

A robust covariance is defined as

$$C(X,Y) = \frac{1}{4ab}[S(aX + bY)^2 - S(aX - bY)^2]$$

Choose

$$a = \frac{1}{S(X)}, \quad b = \frac{1}{S(Y)}$$

A robust correlation coefficient is defined as

---

[34]Huber, *Robust Statistics*.

$$c = \frac{1}{4}[S(aX + bY)^2 - S(aX - bY)^2]$$

The robust correlation coefficient thus defined is not confined to stay in the interval [-1,+1]. For this reason the following alternative definition is often used:

$$r = \frac{S(aX + bY)^2 - S(aX - bY)^2}{S(aX + bY)^2 + S(aX - bY)^2}$$

Applications

Regression analysis has been used to estimate the market risk of a stock (beta) and to estimate the factor loadings in a factor model. Robust regressions have been used to improve estimates in these two areas.

Martin and Simin provide the first comprehensive analysis of the impact of outliers on the estimation of beta.[35] Moreover, they propose a weighted least-squares estimator with data-dependent weights for estimating beta, referring to this estimate as *resistant beta*, and report that this beta is a superior predictor of future risk and return characteristics than the beta calculated using LS. To see the potential dramatic difference between the LS beta and the resistant beta, shown below are the estimates of beta and the standard error of the estimate for four companies reported by Martin and Simin:[36]

	OLS Estimate		Resistant Estimate	
	Beta	Standard Error	Beta	Standard Error
AW Computer Systems	2.33	1.13	1.10	0.33
Chief Consolidated	1.12	0.80	0.50	0.26
Mining Co. Oil City Petroleum	3.27	0.90	0.86	0.47
Metallurgical Industries Co.	2.05	1.62	1.14	0.22

Martin and Simin provide a feeling for the magnitude of the *absolute* difference between the OLS beta and the resistant beta using weekly returns for 8,314 companies over the period January 1992 to December 1996. A summary of the distribution follows:

---

[35]Martin and Simin, "Outlier-Resistant Estimates of Beta."
[36]Reported in Table 1 of the Martin-Simin study. Various time periods were used from January 1962 to December 1996.

Absolute Difference in Beta	No. of Companies	Percent
0.0+ to 0.3	5,043	60.7
0.3+ to 0.5	2,206	26.5
0.5+ to 1.0	800	9.6
Greater than 1.0+	265	3.2

Studies by Fama and French find that market capitalization (size) and book-to-market are important factors in explaining cross-sectional returns.[37] These results are purely empirically based since there is no equilibrium asset pricing model that would suggest either factor as being related to expected return. The empirical evidence that size may be a factor that earns a risk premia (popularly referred to as the *small-firm effect* or *size effect*) was first reported by Banz.[38] Knez and Ready reexamined the empirical evidence using robust regressions, more specifically the least-trimmed squares regression discussed earlier.[39] Their results are twofold. First, they find that when 1% of the most extreme observations are trimmed each month, the risk premia found by Fama and French for the size factor disappears. Second, the inverse relation between size and the risk premia reported by Banz and Fama and French (i.e., the larger the capitalization, the smaller the risk premia) no longer holds when the sample is trimmed. For example, the average monthly risk premia estimated using LS is –12 basis points. However, when 5% of the sample is trimmed, the average monthly risk premia is estimated to be +33 basis points; when 1% of the sample is trimmed, the estimated average risk premia is +14 basis points.

CLASSIFICATION AND REGRESSION TREES

One of the limitations of utilizing regression analysis is that it treats the variable whose value we seek to predict from the perspective of averages. That is, by design, linear combinations of the explanatory variables and the regression coefficients pick up an average effect. Moreover, by only accounting for an average effect, linear combinations of the explanatory variables

---

[37]Eugene F. Fama and Kenneth R. French, "The Cross-Section of Expected Stock Returns," *Journal of Finance,* 47 (1992), pp. 427–466; and "Common Risk Factors in the Returns on Stocks and Bonds," *Journal of Financial Economics,* 33 (1993), pp. 3–56.

[38]Rolf W. Banz, "The Relationship Between Return and Market Value of Common Stocks," *Journal of Financial Economics,* 9 (1981), pp. 3–18.

[39]Peter J. Knez and Mark J. Ready, "On the Robustness of Size and Book-to-Market in Cross-Sectional Regressions," *Journal of Finance,* 52 (1997), pp. 1355–1382.

in a regression make it difficult to take into account interactions among the explanatory variables or to examine relationships on a conditional basis. A methodology popularly referred to as *classification and regression trees* (CART) can overcome these limitations of regression analysis by allowing one to (1) investigate nonlinear behavior, (2) take into consideration interactions of the explanatory variables, and (3) examine relationships on a conditional basis.[40] CART is one of the methodologies that respondents to the survey studies discussed in Chapter 1 indicated that they employ.

CART involves building decision trees that are used for regression purposes to predict dependent variables and for classification purposes to obtain categorical predictor variables. CART is a *supervised learning* method. This means that the CART methodology builds upon a known sample with known classifications or regression values. After the model is built, it is used on new cases. In a new case the CART rules are applied to predictors and the output is a classification or regression value.[41]

CART allows one to investigate relationships on a conditional basis by building a sophisticated tree-structured data analysis technique that employs a set of "if-then" decision rules. The use of if-then rules is a natural methodology for analyzing complex problems under conditions of uncertainty. The technique effectively allows a researcher to determine the most significant influences on the variable of interest (i.e., dependent variable). In applications to equity investing, for example, the variable of interest could be the behavior of the equity market. CART would allow portfolio managers to determine in the case of the equity market what might be a more important factor impacting the equity market, say, the economy or the valuation of equities. CART involves estimating the appropriate hierarchy of factors that are believed to impact the variable of interest and then assign probabilities.

---

[40]This technique was introduced in Leo Breiman, Jerome H. Friedman, Richard A. Olshen, and Charles J. Stone, *Classification and Regression Trees* (Belmont: Wadsworth, 1984).

[41]The CART methodology works by constructing binary recursive trees. Each node of the tree is split in two by a binary decision on one of the predictor variables. The optimal splitting criterion divides the sample into two subsamples which are maximally homogeneous. An often used criterion of homogeneity is based on the Gini coefficient. The splitting process can be carried on to the individual units, thereby building a complete tree. However, a complete tree would yield very poor generalization performance. Therefore, a key aspect of the learning process includes rules as to when to stop splitting the tree. Alternatively, one can build a complete tree and then "prune" it in order to reach the best performance out of sample. Once the length of the tree is decided, one has to assign a classification value to each of the last nodes. One can assign to each node the classification value that appears more frequently in the sample. After completing this step the tree is ready to be used on new cases.

To our knowledge, Sorensen, Mezrich, and Miller were the first to apply CART to quantitative investment management. [42] They applied it to relative value analysis for purposes of traditional asset allocation, one of the most common problems in quantitative investment management. The specific application was to construct optimal decision trees to model the relative performance of the S&P 500 with respect to cash. They define relative value as the earnings yield on the S&P 500 minus the long bond yield, with high relative value being indicative of higher future equity market performance. The output of their model assigned probabilities to three market states: outperform, underperform, and neutral. The question that they sought to answer is the one we mentioned earlier: What is more important in driving the equity market, the economy or the valuation of equities (as measured by price-earnings ratios)? They find, for example, that the relevance of valuation is subordinate to the economy. That is, in a strong economy, investors are not as concerned about market price-earnings ratios.

Just to provide a feel for the CART procedure, we briefly describe what was done by Sorensen, Mezrich, and Miller. They first identify the explanatory variables that they believed are the major determinants of equity returns. The explanatory variables that they used were the steepness of the yield curve, credit spread, equity risk premium, and dividend yield premium (i.e., S&P 500 dividend yield minus the long bond yield). Then CART was used to split the dependent variable, stock returns, into two distinct groups, each group being as homogeneous as possible. To accomplish this, a critical level for an explanatory variable was determined for splitting the dependent variable. The CART algorithm then continues splitting each of these two subgroups into finer subgroups each that are statistically distinguishable but homogenous within a group. The splitting continues until it can no longer improve the statistical homogeneity of each subgroup by splitting on additional explanatory variables. The resulting hierarchy of explanatory variables is such that it will have the minimum misclassification rate for the entire tree. The final product of CART is a tree-structured hierarchy of nonlinear if-then rules, where each rule is conditioning its behavior on the rules that preceded it. From this tree-structured hierarchy, a set of probabilities for reaching each state of the dependent variable can be obtained. In the application by Sorensen, Mezrich, and Miller, it is the assignment of probabilities to three market states: outperform, underperform, and neutral. They report that when the forecast probability for outperformance exceeds 70%, the model is correct almost 70% of the time.

---

[42]Eric H. Sorensen, Joseph J. Mezrich, and Keith L. Miller, "A New Technique for Tactical Asset Allocation," Chapter 12 in Frank J. Fabozzi, ed., *Active Equity Portfolio Management* (Hoboken: John Wiley & Sons, 1998).

SUMMARY

- A probabilistic description of financial time series is possible if residuals are uncorrelated white noise.
- Covariance and correlations measure the linear dependence between random variable.
- Estimating the correlations and covariances between many processes is very difficult when the sample length is of the same order of magnitude as the number of processes.
- Exponentially weighted moving averages mitigate the problem associated with estimate covariances and correlations.
- Random Matrix Theory offers a systematic analysis of the level of uncertainty associated with estimating large covariance and correlation matrices.
- Linear regressions represent linear functional links between variables.
- Standard regression models can be estimated through Ordinary Least Squares.
- Generalized Least Squares is the analog of the Ordinary Least Squares applied to correlated residuals.
- Extensions of the regression model include instrumental variables models and multivariate regressions.
- Quantile regressions can be used to obtain more information on the distribution of the dependent variable than a point estimate of the mean or of the median; the key idea is modeling the conditional quantiles (i.e., modeling the quantiles given the regressors).
- Regression diagnostics include significance tests of the coefficients and the analysis of the leverage points.
- The techniques of robust statistics address the problem of obtaining estimates that are insensitive to small changes in the basic assumptions of the statistical model employed and is also useful to separate the contribution of the tails from the contribution of the body of the data.
- Robust statistic methods can be applied to the estimation of regression coefficients, which is sensitive to outliers.
- The classification and regression trees methodology is a nonlinear regression tool that can be used to take into account interactions among the explanatory variables or to examine relationships on a conditional basis; the methodology involves building decision trees that are used to predict dependent variables and for classification purposes to obtain categorical predictor variables.

CHAPTER 3

Financial Econometrics II: Time Series

In this chapter we introduce the theory of time series and estimation methods related to time series. We begin by introducing the theory of the representation of time series in both the time and frequency domains. Next we introduce vector autoregressive processes and the concept of cointegration and discuss their estimation methods.

STOCHASTIC PROCESSES

A *stochastic process* is a time-dependent random variable. Consider a probability space (Ω, P), where Ω is the set of possible states of the world $\omega \in \Omega$ and P is a probability measure. A stochastic process is a collection of random variables X_t indexed with the time variable t. Therefore a stochastic process is a bivariate function $X(t,\omega)$ of time and states. A path of a stochastic process is a univariate function of time formed by the set of all values $X(t,\omega)$ for a given $\omega \in \Omega$. We can therefore say that a stochastic process is the collection of all of its paths. Two stochastic processes might have the same paths but different probability distributions. For example, consider a stock market. All stock price processes share the same paths but the probability distributions are different for different stocks.

A possible way to represent a stochastic process is through all the finite joint probability distributions:

$$F\left(x_1, \ldots, x_n\right) = P(X\left(t_1\right) \leq x_1, \ldots, X\left(t_n\right) \leq x_n), \ t_1 \leq \cdots \leq t_i \cdots \leq t_n$$

for any n and for any selection of n time points. The finite distributions do not determine all the properties of a stochastic process and therefore they do not uniquely identify the process.

If the finite distributions do not depend on their absolute time location but only on the differences $\tau_i = t_i - t_{i-1}$, then the process is called *stationary* or *strictly stationary*. In this case, the finite distributions can be written as $F(\tau_1, ..., \tau_{n-1})$.

In Chapter 2 we observed that the possibility of a statistical description of financial events has been the subject of debate. In fact, we have only one realization for each stock price process but the statistical model of stock price processes includes an infinite number of paths. The fact that there were doubts as to the possibility of making statistical inference from one single realization is understandable. Ultimately the solution is to assume that the statistical properties of the ensemble of paths can be inferred from the statistical properties of the set of points of one single realization. A stationary stochastic process is called *ergodic* if all the (time independent) moments are equal to the limit of the corresponding time average when time goes to infinity. For example, if a process is ergodic, the mean equals the time average. If a process is ergodic its statistical parameters can be inferred from one single realization.

The definition of a stochastic process extends naturally to multivariate processes. A *multivariate stochastic process* is a time-dependent random vector: $X_t = (X_{1,t}, ..., X_{p,t})$. Therefore, a multivariate stochastic process is a set of p bivariate functions: $X(t,\omega) = [X_1(t,\omega), ..., X_p(t,\omega)]$. The finite distributions are joint distributions of the p variables at n different instants of time. Stationarity and ergodicity are defined as in the univariate case.

TIME SERIES

If the time parameter moves in discrete increments, a stochastic process is called a *time series*. A univariate time series is a sequence of random variables:

$$X(t_1), ..., X(t_s), ...$$

Time points can be equally spaced, that is, the difference between adjacent time points is a constant: $t_s - t_{s-1} = \Delta t$. Time points can also be spaced randomly or follow a deterministic law. In the former case, the time series is more properly called a *point process*. A *multivariate time series* is a sequence of random vectors.

The number of time points of a time series is generally considered to be infinite. Time series can be infinite in both directions, from $-\infty$ to $+\infty$ or they can have a starting point t_0. Any empirical time series can be considered a sample extracted from an infinite time series. Strictly speaking, a time series can be stationary only if it is infinite in both directions.

A multivariate series is called a *covariance stationary* or *weakly stationary* or *wide-sense stationary* time series if the vector of the means is constant in time:

$$E\big(X_1(t_i),\ldots,X_N(t_i)\big)=E\big(X_1(t_j),\ldots,X_N(t_j)\big),\ \ \forall i,j$$

and if all the covariances and autocovariances, correlations, and autocorrelations depend only on the time lags:

$$\mathrm{corr}\big(X_i(t_r),X_j(t_s)\big)=\mathrm{corr}\big(X_i(t_{r+q}),X_j(t_{s+q})\big),$$
$$\forall i,j=1,\ldots,N,\ \ \forall q,r,s=\ldots-2,-1,0,1,2,\ldots$$
$$\mathrm{cov}\big(X_i(t_r),X_j(t_s)\big)=\mathrm{cov}\big(X_i(t_{r+q}),X_j(t_{s+q})\big),$$
$$\forall i,j=1,\ldots,N,\ \ \forall q,r,s=\ldots-2,-1,0,1,2,\ldots$$

If a series is covariance stationary, the covariances and correlations are constant and we can define autocorrelation and autocovariance functions as follows:

$$\rho_{ij,\tau}(\tau)=\mathrm{corr}\big(X_i(t_r),X_j(t_{r+\tau})\big)$$
$$\gamma_{ij,\tau}(\tau)=\mathrm{cov}\big(X_i(t_r),X_j(t_{r+\tau})\big)$$

Note that a strictly stationary series is not necessarily covariance stationary because the means and the covariances might not exist. If they exist, a strictly stationary series is indeed covariance stationary.

Representation of Time Series

In both theoretical and applied work, we need to characterize and represent time series. Time series might admit several different representations. A fundamental, and very general, representation of covariance stationary time series is given by the *Wold representation*, named after the statistician Herman Ole Andreas Wold. A doctoral student of Harald Cramer,[1] Wold introduced his representation in his dissertation under the supervision of Cramer. Hence, the Wold representation is often called the *Cramer-Wold representation*.

Let's first state the Wold representation for univariate series as proved by Wold in 1938.[2] Consider a zero-mean, covariance stationary series X_t.

[1] Harald Cramer, a famous Swedish mathematician, was one of the founders of actuarial science.
[2] Herman O. A. Wold, *The Analysis of Stationary Time Series* (Uppsala: Almqvist and Wicksell, 1938).

The *Wold Representation Theorem* states that X_t can be represented as the sum of two stochastic processes. The first is formed by an infinite moving average of past innovation terms; the second is a process that can be perfectly linearly predicted by the past values of X_t:

$$X_t = \sum_{j=0}^{\infty} b_j \varepsilon_{t-j} + w_t$$

$$E(\varepsilon_t) = 0, \quad E(\varepsilon_t w_s) = 0, \quad \forall t, s, \quad E(\varepsilon_t^2) = \sigma^2, \quad E(\varepsilon_t \varepsilon_s) = 0, \quad \forall t, s \ t \neq s$$

$$b_0 = 1, \quad \sum_{j=0}^{\infty} b_j^2 < \infty$$

To gain an intuition of Wold's theorem, assume that the process X_t has zero-mean and form the linear projections of X_t on $X_t, \ldots, X_{t-n}$:

$$\hat{X}_t^{(n)} = \sum_{i=1}^{n} a_i X_{t-i} = P\left[X_t \big| X_{t-1}, \ldots, X_{t-n} \right]$$

Consider now the residuals

$$w_t^{(n)} = X_t - P\left[X_t \big| X_{t-1}, \ldots, X_{t-n} \right]$$

By the orthogonality property discussed in Chapter 2, the projections and the relative residuals are orthogonal:

$$E\left(\hat{X}_t^{(n)}, P\left[X_t \big| X_{t-1}, \ldots, X_{t-n} \right] \right) = 0$$

It can be demonstrated that if we let n go to infinity then the sequence of projections

$$P\left[X_t \big| X_{t-1}, \ldots, X_{t-n} \right]$$

converges, in the mean square sense, to a well defined random variable:

$$\hat{X}_t = \sum_{i=1}^{\infty} a_i X_{t-i} = P\left[X_t \big| X_{t-1}, X_{t-2}, \ldots \right]$$

The residuals $\varepsilon_t = X_t - \hat{X}_t$ are orthogonal to all X_{t-j}. The residuals are the innovations that remain after the linear predictions

$$P\left[X_t \big| X_{t-1}, X_{t-2}, \ldots \right]$$

and hence they are linearly unpredictable. The Wold Representation Theorem states that any stationary process can be represented as the sum of two stochastic processes

$$X_t = \sum_{j=0}^{\infty} b_j \varepsilon_{t-j} + w_t$$

that are mutually orthogonal at every lag and such that the process w_t is perfectly linearly predictable from the past X_{t-j} while the process

$$\sum_{j=0}^{\infty} b_j \varepsilon_{t-j}$$

is linearly unpredictable. The process w_t is called *linearly deterministic* while the process above is called *purely nondeterministic.*

Note that, though deterministic, the process w_t is a stochastic process formed by an infinite set of different paths that are individually linearly predictable functions. The process w_t should be distinguished from deterministic trends that are not stochastic processes. An example of a linearly deterministic stationary stochastic process is given by the process $y_t = (a \sin(\omega t) + b \cos(\omega t))$ where a, b are mutually uncorrelated random variables.

The Wold decomposition carries over to the multivariate case. Consider a multivariate series $X_t = (X_{1t}, ..., X_{nt})$. In the multivariate case, the covariance function is replaced by a set of covariance matrices $\Gamma_\tau = \{\gamma_{ij,\tau}\}$ whose entries are the auto crosscovariances at lag τ: $\gamma_{ij,\tau} = E(X_{i,t} X_{j,t-\tau})$. The Wold decomposition theorem states that a multivariate process can be uniquely decomposed in two processes

$$X_t = \sum_{i=0}^{\infty} B_i U_{t-i} + W_t$$

where the terms B_i are square $n \times n$ matrices such that $B_0 = I_n$, the sum

$$\sum_{i=0}^{\infty} B_i B_t'$$

converges, the process U_t is n-variate real-valued white noise such that:

$$E(U_t) = 0, \quad E(U_t U_t^T) = \Sigma, \quad E(U_t U_{t-s}^T) = 0 \text{ for } m > 0$$

and W_t is a linearly deterministic process. Analogous to the univariate case, this latter condition means that there is an n-vector C_0 and $n \times n$ matrices C_S such that the process X_t is perfectly linearly predictable from its own past in the sense that:

$$W_t = C_0 + \sum_{s=1}^{\infty} C_s W_{t-s}$$

and

$$E\left(U_t W_{t-m}^T\right) = 0, \quad m = 0, \pm 1, \pm 2, \dots$$

As in the univariate case, the n-dimensional white noise U_t is an innovation process in the sense that U_t is the residual of the best linear forecast of X_t, that is, $U_t = X_t - P\left(X_t \big| X_{t-1}, X_{t-2}, \dots\right)$.

The Wold decomposition, as stated previously, applies to stationary processes that extend from $-\infty$ to $+\infty$. Cramer extended the Wold decomposition, proving that any process can be decomposed in a deterministic process, not necessarily linear, plus a purely nondeterministic process.[3]

The Wold decomposition is unique as a linear moving average representation but it is not the only possible representation of a stationary stochastic process. For example, a nonlinear process might have a nonlinear representation in addition to the Wold representation. It is remarkable that even nonlinear processes admit the Wold representation which is linear.

Invertibility and Autoregressive Representations

Let's first introduce the lag operator L. The operator L shifts a series back by one place: $L(X_t) = X_{t-1}$. The lag operator can be applied recursively:

$$L^0\left(X_t\right) = X_t$$
$$L^1\left(X_t\right) = X_{t-1}$$
$$L^2\left(X_t\right) = L\left(L\left(X_t\right)\right) = X_{t-2}$$
$$\dots\dots\dots\dots\dots\dots\dots\dots\dots\dots\dots$$
$$L^n\left(X_t\right) = L\left(L^{n-1}\left(X_t\right)\right) = X_{t-n}$$

Using the lag operator, the Wold representation can be written as

$$X_t = B(L)\varepsilon_t = \sum_{j=0}^{\infty} b_j L^j \varepsilon_t + w_t$$

where

[3]Harald Cramer, "On Some Classes of Non-Stationary Processes," in *Proceedings of the 4th Berkeley Symposium on Mathematical Statistics and Probability*, University of California Press, 1961, pp. 221–230.

$$B(L) = \sum_{j=0}^{\infty} b_j L^j$$

Assume that the linearly predictable part has been removed, so that X is the purely indeterministic process $X_t = B(L)\varepsilon_t$. Let's formally write the inverse of the operator $B(L)$ as follows:

$$B(L)^{-1} B(L) = I, \quad I = 1 + 0L + 0L^2 + \dots$$

We can therefore formally establish the two relationships:

$$X_t = B(L)\varepsilon_t$$
$$\varepsilon_t = B(L)^{-1} X_t$$

Not every operator $B(L)$ has an inverse. If an inverse exists, then the process is called *invertible*. In this case, a process X_t can be represented as a sum of mutually uncorrelated innovation terms and the innovation terms can be represented as an infinite sum of the past of the process.

Representation in the Frequency Domain

Let's recall a few facts related to the analysis of time series in the frequency domain.[4] The basis for spectral analysis is the Fourier series and the Fourier transforms. A periodic function $x(t)$ with period 2τ can be represented as a Fourier series formed with a denumerably-infinite number of sine and cosine functions:

$$x(t) = \frac{1}{2} a_0 + \sum_{n=1}^{\infty} \left(a_n \cos\left(\frac{\pi}{\tau} t\right) + b_n \sin\left(\frac{\pi}{\tau} t\right) \right)$$

This series can be inverted in the sense that the coefficients can be recovered as integrals through the following formulas:

$$a_n = \frac{1}{\tau} \int_{-\tau}^{+\tau} x(t) \cos\left(\frac{\pi}{\tau} t\right) dt$$

$$b_n = \frac{1}{\tau} \int_{-\tau}^{+\tau} x(t) \sin\left(\frac{\pi}{\tau} t\right) dt$$

---

[4]We follow M. B. Priestley, *Spectral Analysis and Time Series* (London: Academic Press, 1983), and D. R. Cox and H. D. Miller, *The Theory of Stochastic Processes* (Boca Raton, FL: Chapman & Hall/CRC, 1977).

If the function $x(t)$ is square integrable, it can be represented as a Fourier integral:

$$x(t) = \frac{1}{\sqrt{2\pi}} \int_{-\infty}^{+\infty} e^{i\omega t} F(\omega) d\omega$$

where the function $F(\omega)$ is called the Fourier transform of $x(t)$:

$$F(\omega) = \frac{1}{\sqrt{2\pi}} \int_{-\infty}^{+\infty} e^{-i\omega t} x(t) dt$$

In both cases, periodic and nonperiodic, *Parseval's Theorem* holds:

$$\int_{-\infty}^{+\infty} x^2(t) dt = 2\tau \sum_{n=1}^{\infty} c_n^2, c_0 = \tfrac{1}{2} a_0, c_n = \sqrt{\tfrac{1}{2}\left(a_n^2 + b_n^2\right)}$$

$$\int_{-\infty}^{+\infty} x^2(t) dt = \int_{-\infty}^{+\infty} |F(\omega)|^2 d\omega$$

The preceding Fourier analysis applies to a deterministic function $x(t)$. Suppose now that $x(t)$ is a univariate stationary stochastic process in continuous time $x(t)$. A stochastic process is a set of paths. As the process is infinite and stationary, its paths are not periodic, they do not decay to zero when time goes to infinity, and they cannot be square integrable as functions of time.

Consider the power of the signal and the power spectra. Given a stationary series (signal), its energy (i.e., the integral of its square) is infinite, but the power of the series (i.e., its energy divided by time) might tend to a finite limit.

Consider a stationary time series. Wold's theorem states that a necessary and sufficient condition for the sequence $\rho(t)$, $t = 0, \pm 1, \pm 2, \ldots$ to be the autocorrelation function of a discrete stationary process $x(t)$, $t = 0, \pm 1, \pm 2, \ldots$ is that there is a nondecreasing function $F(\omega)$ such that $F(-\pi) = 0$ and $F(+\pi) = 1$ and such that:

$$\rho(r) = \int_{-\pi}^{+\pi} e^{i\omega r} dF(\omega)$$

Assuming that the function $F(\omega)$ is differentiable and

$$\frac{dF(\omega)}{d\omega} = f(\omega)$$

we can write:

$$\rho(r) = \int_{-\pi}^{+\pi} e^{i\omega r} f(\omega) d\omega$$

This relationship can be inverted in terms of a Fourier series:

$$f(\omega) = \frac{1}{2\pi} \sum_{r=-\infty}^{r=+\infty} \rho(r) e^{-i\omega r}$$

If the series $x(t)$, $t = 0, \pm 1, \pm 2, \ldots$ is real-valued, then $\rho(r)$ is an even sequence and we can write:

$$f(\omega) = \frac{1}{2\pi} \sum_{r=-\infty}^{r=+\infty} \rho(r) \cos r\omega = \frac{1}{2\pi} + \frac{1}{\pi} \sum_{r=1}^{r=+\infty} \rho(r) \cos r\omega$$

Similar relationships can be established for covariances. In particular,

$$R(r) = \int_{-\pi}^{+\pi} e^{i\omega r} dH(\omega)$$

and if there is a density

$$\frac{dH(\omega)}{d\omega} = h(\omega)$$

the previous formula becomes:

$$R(r) = \int_{-\pi}^{+\pi} e^{i\omega r} h(\omega) d\omega$$

This expression can be inverted:

$$h(\omega) = \frac{1}{2\pi} \sum_{r=-\infty}^{r=+\infty} R(r) e^{-i\omega r}$$

If the time series is real-valued:

$$h(\omega) = \frac{1}{2\pi} \sum_{r=-\infty}^{r=+\infty} R(r) \cos r\omega = \frac{\sigma_x}{2\pi} + \frac{1}{\pi} \sum_{r=1}^{r=+\infty} R(r) \cos r\omega$$

Errors and Residuals

In statistics there is a classical distinction between errors and residuals. *Errors* are deviations from the true population mean while *residuals* are deviations from the computed sample mean. The two terms are often confused and are used almost interchangeably. However, there are fundamental differences between the two terms. For example, errors can be independent while residuals typically are not independent. To see this point, consider a sample randomly extracted from a population. As samples are supposed to be independent draws from the population, errors can be assumed to be independent. However, by construction, the residuals of the empirical sample average have zero mean which makes them surely not theoretically independent. Of course, if the sample is large, the residuals of the empirical mean are practically independent.

When discussing regressions in Chapter 2 we observed that the assumption of constant error variance implies that errors do not have the same importance in different regions of the variables. In fact, errors have a relatively smaller importance when the regression variables have large values than when they have small values. Therefore, a linear regression with constant errors is assumed to offer a better fit in the extremes of the variables than in the center.

In modeling time series, when we discuss an abstract probabilistic model we make assumptions about the model errors but when we estimate the model we observe the residuals after modeling the expected conditional mean and not the true error. We can create different probabilistic models making different assumptions about the errors. For example, we can assume that errors follow a GARCH process. Given a sample, we have to decide what model and related residuals better fit the data.

Generally speaking, we can say that any given model apportions forecasts between the model itself and its residuals. In the ideal situation, residuals are white noise that do not carry any information. In most cases, however, the main model will leave residuals with more structure. It is fundamental to restrict the structure of the residuals, otherwise the model is void of empirical content.

STABLE VECTOR AUTOREGRESSIVE PROCESSES

Consider first a univariate zero-mean stationary series. An autoregressive model of a univariate time series is a model of the form:

$$X_t = a_1 X_{t-1} + \cdots + a_q X_{t-q} + \varepsilon_t$$

where we assume that ε_t is a sequence of uncorrelated white noise terms with constant variance (homoscedastic). This series can be inverted if the roots of the equation:

$$1 - a_1 z - \cdots - a z^q = 0$$

where z is a complex variable, are all greater than one in modulus. Consider, for example, the case of $q = 1$:

$$X_t = a_1 X_{t-1} + \varepsilon_t$$
$$(1 - a_1 L) X_t = \varepsilon_t$$

$$X_t = \frac{1}{(1 - a_1 L)} = \sum_{i=1}^{\infty} a_1^i L^i \varepsilon_t$$

The series

$$\sum_{i=1}^{\infty} a_1^i L^i \varepsilon_t$$

converges if $|a_1| < 1$, a condition that implies that the real-valued solution $z = 1/a_1$ of the equation $1 - a_1 z = 0$ is greater than 1.

Consider the covariance function of a series that can be written as follows:

$$\rho(1) = E\left(X_t X_{t-1}\right) = E\left(X_{t-1}\left(a_1 X_{t-1} + \varepsilon_t\right)\right) = a_1 E\left(X_{t-1} X_{t-1}\right) = a_1 \sigma^2$$
$$\rho(2) = E\left(X_t X_{t-2}\right) = E\left(X_{t-2}\left(a_1^2 X_{t-2} + a_1 \varepsilon_{t-1} + \varepsilon_t\right)\right) = a_1^2 E\left(X_{t-2} X_{t-2}\right) = a_1^2 \sigma^2$$

$$\cdots\cdots\cdots\cdots\cdots\cdots\cdots\cdots\cdots\cdots\cdots\cdots\cdots\cdots\cdots\cdots$$

$$\rho(\tau) = E\left(X_t X_{t+\tau}\right) = a_1^q \sigma^2$$

An *autoregressive time series* $X_t = a_1 X_{t-1} + \ldots + a_q X_{t-q} + \varepsilon_t$ is a regression model of the type discussed in Chapter 2. Suppose that the roots of the equation $1 - a_1 z - \ldots - a z^q = 0$ are greater than 1 in modulus. If residuals are serially uncorrelated and have constant variance (homoscedastic) then we can estimate the autoregressive model with ordinary least squares (OLS). Let's organize sample data as we did in the case of linear regressions. An autoregressive model with q lags is a regression model with q variables plus one constant. Suppose we are given a sample time series:

$$(X_1, \ldots, X_q, X_{q+1}, \ldots, X_{T+q})'$$

We can organize the sample data and the residuals as follows:

$$X = \begin{bmatrix} X_{q+1} \\ \vdots \\ X_{q+T} \end{bmatrix}, \quad Z = \begin{bmatrix} 1 & X_q & \cdots & X_1 \\ \vdots & \vdots & \ddots & \vdots \\ 1 & X_{q+T-1} & \cdots & X_T \end{bmatrix}, \quad E = \begin{bmatrix} \varepsilon_1 \\ \vdots \\ \varepsilon_T \end{bmatrix}$$

Call $A = (a_0, a_1, \ldots, a_q)$ the vector of model coefficients. The autoregressive model can be compactly written in matrix form:

$$X = ZA + E$$

and the OLS estimator of the model is:

$$\hat{A} = \left(Z'Z \right)^{-1} Z'X$$

Let's now generalize to multivariate processes. Consider a multivariate time series:

$$X_t = (X_{1t}, \ldots, X_{Nt})'$$

and suppose that it satisfies a set of linear difference equations

$$X_{1t} = c_1 + a_{11}^{(1)} X_{1t-1} + \cdots + a_{1N}^{(1)} X_{Nt-1} + \cdots + a_{11}^{(q)} X_{1t-q} + \cdots + a_{1N}^{(q)} X_{Nt-q} + \varepsilon_{1t}$$

$$\cdots\cdots\cdots\cdots\cdots\cdots\cdots\cdots\cdots\cdots\cdots\cdots\cdots\cdots\cdots\cdots\cdots\cdots\cdots\cdots\cdots\cdots\cdots\cdots$$

$$X_{Nt} = c_N + a_{N1}^{(1)} X_{1t-1} + \cdots + a_{NN}^{(1)} X_{Nt-1} + \cdots + a_{N1}^{(q)} X_{1t-q} + \cdots + a_{NN}^{(q)} X_{Nt-q} + \varepsilon_{Nt}$$

where we assume that the residuals ε are serially uncorrelated and have constant covariance matrix Σ.

If we define the $N{\times}N$ matrices of coefficients:

$$A_1 = \begin{bmatrix} a_{11}^{(1)} & \cdots & a_{1N}^{(1)} \\ \vdots & \ddots & \vdots \\ a_{N1}^{(1)} & \cdots & a_{NN}^{(1)} \end{bmatrix}, \ldots, A_q = \begin{bmatrix} a_{11}^{(q)} & \cdots & a_{1N}^{(q)} \\ \vdots & \ddots & \vdots \\ a_{N1}^{(q)} & \cdots & a_{NN}^{(q)} \end{bmatrix}$$

and the vector of constants $C = (c_1, \ldots, c_N)'$ and the vector of residuals $E_t = (\varepsilon_{1t}, \ldots, \varepsilon_{Nt})'$, we can write the above model in matrix form:

$$X_t = C + A_1 X_{t-1} + \cdots + A_q X_{t-q} + E_t$$

A model of this type is called a *vector autoregressive model* (VAR model) of order q.

A VAR model of order q is always equivalent to a VAR model of order 1. To see this point, let's define a new time series as follows:

$$Z_t = \left(X_t', X_{t-1}', \ldots, X_{t-q+1}'\right)'$$
$$Z_{t-1} = \left(X_{t-1}', X_{t-2}', \ldots, X_{t-q}'\right)$$

The series Z satisfies the following equation:

$$Z_t = D + AZ_{t-1} + F$$

where A is the following $Nq \times Nq$ *companion matrix*:

$$A = \begin{bmatrix} A_1 & A_2 & A_3 & \cdots & \cdots & A_q \\ I & 0 & 0 & \cdots & \cdots & 0 \\ 0 & I & 0 & \cdots & \cdots & 0 \\ 0 & 0 & \ddots & \ddots & 0 & 0 \\ 0 & 0 & \ddots & I & 0 & 0 \\ 0 & 0 & \cdots & 0 & I & 0 \end{bmatrix}$$

$F = (E', 0, \ldots, 0)'$ is a $Nq \times 1$ vector whose first q elements are the residuals E, the other elements are all zero, and D is a vector of constants whose first q elements are the constants C and the other elements are all zero.

A VAR model is called *stable* if the roots of the following equation:

$$\det\left(I - A_1 z - A_q z^q\right) = 0$$

where z is a complex variable, are all outside the unit circle. Equivalently, a VAR model is stable if all the eigenvalues of the companion matrix A have modulus less than one. A stable VAR model initialized in the infinite past produces a stationary process X.

Assume that the series X_t is covariance stationary. Taking expectations of both sides of the equation $X_t = C + A_1 X_{t-1} + \ldots + A_q X_{t-q} + E_t$, we see that the unconditional mean of X_t is given by:

$$\mu = \left(I - A_1 - \cdots - A_q\right)^{-1} C$$

Subtracting the mean, we can rewrite the process in the following form:

$$X_t - \mu = A_1 \left(X_{t-1} - \mu \right) + \cdots + A_q \left(X_{t-q} - \mu \right) + E_t$$

A stable VAR model can be estimated as a multivariate regression.

Observe that the VAR model is a *seemingly unrelated regression model* (SUR model). This fact implies that the multivariate VAR, under the assumption of serially uncorrelated and homoskedastic residuals, can be estimated with OLS equation by equation.

INTEGRATED AND COINTEGRATED VARIABLES

Thus far we have considered models of stationary series, in particular covariance stationary series. A univariate series is called *integrated of order d* if it becomes stationary by differencing d times but remains nonstationary after differencing $d - 1$ times. In particular, a nonstationary series is said to be integrated of order one, or simply integrated, if it can be made stationary by differencing once. Consider a process X integrated of order one. The process X is formed by the sum of all past shocks. That is, shocks to an integrated process never decay.

The simplest example of an integrated process is the random walk defined as follows:

$$X_t = X_{t-1} + \varepsilon_t, \quad t = 0, 1, \ldots$$
$$X_t = \sum_{s=0}^{t} \varepsilon_t + X_0$$
$$\mathrm{var}\left(X_t \right) = t\,\mathrm{var}\left(\varepsilon_t \right) + \mathrm{var}\left(X_0 \right)$$

where the terms ε_t are uncorrelated white noise. The random walk is nonstationary and its variance grows linearly with time. In addition, it can be shown that the correlation coefficient between points far apart in time tends to one when the time interval between the points tends to infinity.

An integrated process is nonstationary and typically has a start in time and initial conditions, otherwise it is difficult to justify any condition on finite moments.

Therefore, a process is integrated of order d if it is nonstationary but it becomes stationary differencing at least d times. This concept is slightly ambiguous given the preceding observation that an integrated process has a starting point in time. From a strictly theoretical point of view, if we difference an integrated process which has a starting point in time we obtain another process which has a starting point in time. A process with a starting point in time cannot be stationary. We can solve the problem replacing the condition of stationarity with the condition of *asymptotic stationarity* which means that the relevant moments of the process, in particular the vector of the means and the covariance matrix tend to a finite limit when time tends to infinity. In practice, we assume that the differenced process becomes stationary after a transient period.

If we difference more than *d* times we difference a stationary series. The process of differencing a stationary series is called *overdifferencing*, and a series obtained differencing a stationary series is said to be *overdifferenced*.

If we difference a stationary series we obtain another stationary series which, however, is not invertible. In fact, the difference operator $1 - L$ cannot be inverted because we obtain

$$\left(1 - \lambda L\right)^{-1} = \sum_{i=1}^{\infty} \lambda^i L^i$$

which does not converge for $\lambda = 1$.

Let's now consider a multivariate series. The concept of an integrated multivariate series is made complex by the fact that it might occur that all the component series are individually integrated but the process is not jointly integrated in the sense that there are linear combinations of the series that are stationary. When this occurs, a multivariate series is said to be cointegrated. A VAR model, therefore, needs to consider the eventual cointegration of its component series.

Consider a multivariate time series: $X_t = (X_{1t}, ..., X_{Nt})'$. Suppose all the X_{it} are integrated of order *d*. If there are *K* independent linear combinations

$$\sum_{i=1}^{N} \alpha_i^{(k)} X_{it}, \quad i = 1, ..., K$$

that are of a lower order of integration $d' < d$, then the process X_t is said to be cointegrated of order *K*.

Nonstationary VAR Models

Consider a VAR model $X_t = A_1 X_{t-1} + ... + A_q X_{t-q} + E_t$. If one of the roots of the characteristic equation $\det(I - A_1 z - A_q z^q) = 0$ is on the unit circle, the VAR model is called *unstable*. A process defined by an unstable VAR model is nonstationary and it includes integrated variables. However, the solution of an unstable VAR model might include cointegrated variables. A key issue in the theory of unstable, nonstationary VAR models is the eventual order of the cointegration of its solutions. In order to discuss this point, we need to introduce the concept of VAR models in error correction form.

VAR Models in Error Correction Form

In order to understand how VAR analysis can be applied to integrated processes, let's first write a VAR model for a process whose components are individually integrated of order one:

$$X_t = A_1 X_{t-1} + \dots + A_q X_{t-q} + E_t$$

Let's assume that there is no constant or deterministic term. We will relax this assumption later. If we subtract X_{t-1} from both sides, we obtain the new equation:

$$X_t - X_{t-1} = (A_1 - I) X_{t-1} + \dots + A_q X_{t-q} + E_t$$
$$\Delta X_t = (1-L) X_t = (A_1 - I) X_{t-1} + A_2 X_{t-2} \dots + A_q X_{t-q} + E_t$$

Suppose now that we add and subtract $(A_1 - I)X_{t-2}$ from the right side of the equation. We obtain a new equivalent equation

$$\Delta X_t = (A_1 - I) \Delta X_{t-1} + (A_2 + A_1 - I) X_{t-2} \dots + A_q X_{t-q} + E_t$$

Suppose now that we add and subtract $(A_1 - I)X_{t-3}$ from the right side of the equation. We obtain a new equivalent equation

$$\Delta X_t = (A_1 - I) \Delta X_{t-1} + (A_2 + A_1 - I) X_{t-2} \dots + A_q X_{t-q} + E_t$$

We can continue this process up to the last term:

$$\Delta X_t = (A_1 - I) \Delta X_{t-1} + (A_2 + A_1 - I) X_{t-2} \dots + (A_{q-1} + \dots + A_1 - I) \Delta X_{t-2}$$
$$+ (A_q + \dots + A_1 - I) X_{t-q} + E_t$$

The above is the *error-correction form* of a VAR model; it shows that a VAR model can be written as a model in first differences plus an error-correction term in levels:

$$\Delta X_t = B_1 \Delta X_{t-1} + B_2 X_{t-2} \dots + B_{q-1} \Delta X_{t-2} + B_q X_{t-q} + E_t$$

The error correction term can be placed in any position. For example, an alternate, more useful formulation is the following. Start by adding and subtracting $A_q X_{t-q+1}$. We obtain:

$$X_t = A_1 X_{t-1} + \cdots + \left(A_{q-1} + A_q \right) X_{t-q+1} - A_q \Delta X_{t-q+1} + E_t$$

Next we add and subtract $(A_{q-1} + A_q) \, X_{t-q+2}$ and we obtain

$$X_t = A_1 X_{t-1} + \cdots + \left(A_{q-2} + A_{q-1} + A_q \right) X_{t-q+2} + \left(A_{q-1} + A_q \right) \Delta X_{t-q+2}$$
$$- A_q \Delta X_{t-q+1} + E_t$$

We continue until we obtain the:

$$\Delta X_t = \left(A_1 + \cdots + A_q - I \right) X_{t-1} - \left(A_2 + \cdots + A_{q-1} + A_q \right) \Delta X_{t-1} - \cdots$$
$$- \left(A_{q-1} + A_q \right) \Delta X_{t-q+2} - A_q \Delta X_{t-q+1} + E_t$$

The above is called the *vector error correction model* (VECM) representation, which is written as follows:

$$\Delta X_t = \Pi X_{t-1} + \Gamma_1 \Delta X_{t-1} + \cdots + \Gamma_{q-1} \Delta X_{t-q+1} + E_t$$
$$\Pi = \left(A_1 + \cdots + A_q - I \right), \;\; \Gamma_j = -\left(A_{j+1} + \cdots + A_q \right), \;\; j = 1, \ldots, q-1$$

Given we assume that the process X is integrated of order one, all the terms in difference are stationary of order zero and therefore the term ΠX_{t-1} must also be stationary.

The matrix $\Pi = (A_1 + \ldots + A_q - I)$ cannot have full rank because we have assumed that the process X is integrated. If the matrix $\Pi = (A_1 + \ldots + A_q - I)$ is the null matrix, there is no cointegration and the process X can be estimated in first differences.

Suppose that the matrix $\Pi = (A_1 + \ldots + A_q - I)$ has rank K with $0 < K < N$. In this case we know from matrix theory that we can represent the $N \times N$ matrix Π as the product of two $N \times K$ matrices α, β, both of rank K: $\Pi = \alpha\beta'$. The columns of β are called the cointegrating relationships. The K linear combinations $\beta'X_t$ are stationary processes. The cointegrating relationships are not unique. In fact, given any nonsingular matrix P, we obtain another decomposition $\Pi = \alpha^*\beta^{*\prime}$ choosing $\alpha^* = \alpha P$, $\beta^* = \alpha P^{-1}$.

The term ΠX_{t-1} is called the *long-term* (or the *long-run*) *part* or the *error-correction* (or *equilibrium-correction*) *term*. The entries of the matrices Γ_j are called the *short-term* (or *short-run*) *parameters*.

The order K of cointegration of the solutions of a VAR model is equal to the rank of the matrices α, β. Therefore, determining the order of cointegration of the solutions of a VAR model is obtained by determining the rank of the matrix $\Pi = \alpha\beta'$ which includes the coefficients of the terms in levels in the VECM representation.

Deterministic Terms

Thus far we have assumed that the process X has zero mean and that there is no constant term in the equation

$$X_t = A_1 X_{t-1} + \cdots + A_q X_{t-q} + E_t$$

Let's rewrite this equation as follows:

$$X_t - A_1 X_{t-1} - \cdots - A_q X_{t-q} = E_t$$
$$\left(I - A_1 L - \cdots - A_q L^q\right)X_t = E_t$$
$$A(L)X_t = E_t, \quad A(L) = \left(I - A_1 L - \cdots - A_q L^q\right)$$

To understand the interplay of a deterministic trend with a VAR model, let's consider the simplest univariate VAR model without a trend, the random walk and write:

$$x_t = x_{t-1} + \varepsilon_t, \, t = 0, \, 1, \, \ldots$$

Now add a linear trend $w_t = c_0 + c_1 t$. There is a big difference if we add a linear trend to the random walk as

$$y_t = x_t + w_t = \sum_{s=0}^{t} \varepsilon_s + c_0 + c_1 t$$

or if we write the random walk model as

$$y_t = c_0 + c_1 t + y_{t-1} + \varepsilon_t$$

The preceding yields a quadratic trend:

$$y_0 = c_0 + y_{-1} + \varepsilon_0$$
$$y_1 = c_0 + c_1 + c_0 + y_{-1} + \varepsilon_0 + \varepsilon_1$$
$$y_2 = c_0 + 2c_1 + c_0 + c_1 + c_0 + y_{-1} + \varepsilon_0 + \varepsilon_1 + \varepsilon_2$$

....

$$y_t = (t+1)c_0 + c_1 \sum_{i=0}^{t} i + \sum_{i=0}^{t} \varepsilon_i = (t+1)c_0 + c_1 \frac{t(t+1)}{2} + \sum_{i=0}^{t} \varepsilon_i$$

Exhibit 3.1 illustrates the difference between the two models by simulating two random walks obtained from the same error terms and with the same parameters of the linear trend but using one of the following models:

$$y_t = c_0 + c_1 t + y_{t-1} + \varepsilon_t$$

or

$$y_t = x_t + w_t = \sum_{s=0}^{t} \varepsilon_s + c_0 + c_1 t$$

The former model yields a quadratic trend, the latter a linear trend.

EXHIBIT 3.1 Random Walks with Linear and Quadratic Trends

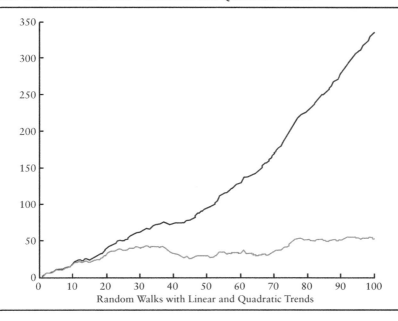

Random Walks with Linear and Quadratic Trends

Generalizing to the multivariate VAR, let's first consider the model

$$Y_t = X_t + W_t = X_t + C_0 + C_1 t$$

where X is a zero-mean stochastic process that obeys the VAR conditions Suppose now that the VAR equation includes a deterministic trend so that the model is written as follows:

$$Y_t = C_0 + C_1 t + A_1 Y_{t-1} + \cdots + A_q Y_{t-q} + E_t$$

Premultiply both sides of the equation $Y_t = X_t + C_0 + C_1 t$ by $A(L)$ and we obtain:

$$A(L)Y_t = A(L)X_t + A(L)(C_0 + C_1 t)$$
$$A(L)Y_t = E_t + A(L)(C_0 + C_1 t)$$

which gives a representation in levels of the process Y and places constraints on the deterministic terms.

Cointegration plays a fundamental role in economic and financial modeling. In Chapter 5 we will discuss the relationship of cointegration with mean reversion.

ESTIMATION OF STABLE VECTOR AUTOREGRESSIVE (VAR) MODELS

The least squares method and the maximum likelihood method apply immediately to unrestricted stable VAR models. Note that models are said to be *unrestricted* if the estimation process is allowed to determine any possible outcome, and *restricted* if the estimation process is allowed to determine parameters that satisfy given conditions, that is, restrictions on their possible range of values.

Suppose that an empirical time series is given and that the data generating process (DGP) of the series is a finite dimensional VAR(p) model. Recall that a VAR(p) model has the following form:

$$\mathbf{x}_t = \mathbf{A}_1 \mathbf{x}_{t-1} + \mathbf{A}_2 \mathbf{x}_{t-2} + \cdots + \mathbf{A}_p \mathbf{x}_{t-p} + \mathbf{v} + \boldsymbol{\varepsilon}_t$$

where

$\mathbf{x}_t$ $= (x_{1,t}, \ldots, x_{N,t})'$ is a N–dimensional stochastic time series in vector notation

$\mathbf{A}_i$ $= (a_{s,t}^i)$, $i = 1, 2, \ldots, p$, s, $t = 1, 2, \ldots, N$ are deterministic $N \times N$ matrices

$\boldsymbol{\varepsilon}_t$ $= (\varepsilon_{1,t}, \ldots, \varepsilon_{N,t})'$ is a multivariate white noise with variance-covariance matrix $\Sigma = (\sigma_1, \ldots, \sigma_N)'$

$\mathbf{v}$ $= (v_1, \ldots, v_N)'$ is a vector of deterministic terms

Though deterministic terms might be time-dependent deterministic vectors, in this section we will limit our discussion to the case of a constant intercept as this is the case commonly encountered in financial econometrics. A constant intercept in a stable VAR model yields a nonzero mean of the process.

The previous model can be written in lag notation as

$$\mathbf{x}_t = \left(\mathbf{A}_1 L + \mathbf{A}_2 L^2 + \cdots + \mathbf{A}_p L^p\right)\mathbf{x}_t + \mathbf{v} + \boldsymbol{\varepsilon}_t$$

Consider the matrix polynomial

$$\mathbf{A}(z) = \mathbf{I} - \mathbf{A}_1 z - \mathbf{A}_2 z^2 - \cdots - \mathbf{A}_p z^p, \; z \in \mathbb{C}$$

and consider the inverse characteristic equation

$$\det(\mathbf{A}(z)) = 0$$

In this section we assume that stability conditions hold

$$\det(\mathbf{A}(z)) \neq 0 \text{ for } |z| \leq 1$$

that is, the roots of the inverse characteristic equation are strictly outside of the unit circle. The result is that the VAR(p) model is stable and the corresponding process stationary. The property of stationarity applies only to processes that extend on the entire real axis, as a process that starts at a given point cannot be strictly time-invariant. In general, we will consider processes that start at $t = 1$, assuming that p initial conditions are given: $\mathbf{x}_{-p+1}, \ldots, \mathbf{x}_0$.[5] In this case, stable VAR models yield asymptotically stationary processes. When there is no risk of confusion, we will not stress this distinction.

---

[5]As in this chapter we assume that the entire time series is empirically given, the distinction between initial conditions and the remaining data is made only to simplify notation.

Recall also that the preceding N-dimensional VAR(p) model is equivalent to the following Np-dimensional VAR(1) model:

$$\mathbf{X}_t = \mathbf{A}\mathbf{X}_{t-1} + \mathbf{V} + \mathbf{U}_t$$

where

$$\mathbf{X}_t = \begin{bmatrix} \mathbf{x}_t \\ \mathbf{x}_{t-1} \\ \vdots \\ \mathbf{x}_{t-p+1} \end{bmatrix}, \mathbf{A} = \begin{bmatrix} \mathbf{A}_1 & \mathbf{A}_2 & \cdots & \mathbf{A}_{p-1} & \mathbf{A}_p \\ \mathbf{I}_N & 0 & \cdots & 0 & 0 \\ 0 & \mathbf{I}_N & \cdots & 0 & 0 \\ 0 & 0 & \ddots & \vdots & \vdots \\ 0 & 0 & \cdots & \mathbf{I}_N & 0 \end{bmatrix}, \mathbf{V} = \begin{bmatrix} \mathbf{v} \\ 0 \\ \vdots \\ 0 \end{bmatrix}, \mathbf{U}_t = \begin{bmatrix} \boldsymbol{\varepsilon}_t \\ 0 \\ \vdots \\ 0 \end{bmatrix}$$

The matrix $\mathbf{A}$ is called the *companion matrix* of the VAR(p) system.

Note that in this section we do not place any a priori computational restrictions on the model parameters, though we do assume that the model is stable. The assumption of model stability ensures that the process is stationary. This, in turn, ensures that the covariances are time-invariant. As the previous VAR(p) model is unrestricted, it can be estimated as a linear regression; it can therefore be estimated with the estimation theory of linear regression. As we consider only consistent estimators, the estimated parameters (in the limit of an infinite sample) satisfy the stability condition. However on a finite sample, the estimated parameters might not satisfy the stability condition.

We will first show how the estimation of a VAR(p) model and its VAR(1) equivalent can be performed with least squares methods or with maximum likelihood methods.

Vectoring Operators and Tensor Products

We first define the *vectoring operator*. Given an $m \times n$ matrix,

$$A = \begin{pmatrix} a_{11} & \cdots & a_{1n} \\ \vdots & \ddots & \vdots \\ a_{m1} & \cdots & a_{mn} \end{pmatrix}$$

the vectoring operator, written as vec($\mathbf{A}$),[6] stacks the matrix columns in a vector as follows:

---

[6]The vec operator should not be confused with the vech operator which is similar but not identical. The vech operator stacks the terms below and on the diagonal.

$$
\text{vec}(\mathbf{A}) = \begin{pmatrix} a_{11} \\ \vdots \\ a_{m1} \\ \vdots \\ a_{1n} \\ \vdots \\ a_{mn} \end{pmatrix}
$$

Next it is useful to define the Kronecker product. Given the $m \times n$ matrix

$$
\mathbf{A} = \begin{pmatrix} a_{11} & \cdots & a_{1n} \\ \vdots & \ddots & \vdots \\ a_{m1} & \cdots & a_{mn} \end{pmatrix}
$$

and the $p \times q$ matrix

$$
\mathbf{B} = \begin{pmatrix} b_{11} & \cdots & b_{1q} \\ \vdots & \ddots & \vdots \\ b_{p1} & \cdots & b_{pq} \end{pmatrix}
$$

we define the Kronecker product $\mathbf{C} = \mathbf{A} \otimes \mathbf{B}$ as follows:

$$
\mathbf{C} = \mathbf{A} \otimes \mathbf{B} = \begin{pmatrix} a_{11}\mathbf{B} & \cdots & a_{1n}\mathbf{B} \\ \vdots & \ddots & \vdots \\ a_{m1}\mathbf{B} & \cdots & a_{mn}\mathbf{B} \end{pmatrix}
$$

The Kronecker product, also called the *direct product* or the *tensor product*, is an $(mp) \times (nq)$ matrix. It can be demonstrated that the tensor product satisfies the associative and distributive property and that, given any four matrices $\mathbf{A}, \mathbf{B}, \mathbf{C}, \mathbf{D}$ of appropriate dimensions, the following properties hold:

$$
\text{vec}(\mathbf{A} \otimes \mathbf{B}) = (\mathbf{B}' \otimes \mathbf{I})\text{vec}(\mathbf{A})
$$

$$
(\mathbf{A} \otimes \mathbf{B})(\mathbf{C} \otimes \mathbf{D}) = (\mathbf{AC}) \otimes (\mathbf{BD})
$$

$$
(\mathbf{A} \otimes \mathbf{B})' = (\mathbf{A}') \otimes (\mathbf{B}')
$$

$$
\text{Trace}(\mathbf{A}'\mathbf{BCD}') = (\text{vec}(\mathbf{A}))'(\mathbf{D} \otimes \mathbf{B})\text{vec}(\mathbf{C})
$$

Next we discuss estimation of the model parameters using the multivariate least squares estimation method.

Multivariate Least Squares Estimation

Conceptually, the multivariate least squares (LS) estimation method is equivalent to that of a linear regression (see Chapter 2); the notation, however, is more complex. This is because we are dealing with multiple time series and because there are correlations between noise terms. Similar to what we did in estimating regressions, we now represent the autoregressive process applied to the sample and presample data as a single-matrix equation. Note that the VAR(p) process is an autoregressive process where the variables x_t are regressed over their own lagged values: The regressors are the lagged values of the dependent variable. We will introduce two different but equivalent notations.

Suppose that a sample of T observations of the N-variate variable x_t, $t = 1, \ldots, T$ and a presample of p initial conditions $x_{-p+1}, \ldots, x_0$ are given. We first stack all observations x_t, $t = 1, \ldots, T$ in a vector as was done in the case of regressions:

$$\mathbf{x} = \begin{pmatrix} x_{1,1} \\ \vdots \\ x_{N,1} \\ \vdots \\ \vdots \\ x_{1,T} \\ \vdots \\ x_{N,T} \end{pmatrix}$$

Introducing a notation that will be useful later, we can also write

$$\mathbf{x} = \text{vec}(\mathbf{X})$$

$$\mathbf{X} = \left(\mathbf{x}_1, \ldots, \mathbf{x}_T\right) = \begin{pmatrix} x_{1,1} & \cdots & x_{1,T} \\ \vdots & \ddots & \vdots \\ x_{N,1} & \cdots & x_{N,T} \end{pmatrix}$$

In other words, $\mathbf{x}$ is a ($NT \times 1$) vector where all observations are stacked, while $\mathbf{X}$ is a ($N \times T$) matrix where each column represents an N-variate observation.

Proceeding analogously with the innovation terms, we stack the innovation terms in a ($NT \times 1$) vector as follows:

$$\mathbf{u} = \begin{pmatrix} \varepsilon_{1,1} \\ \vdots \\ \varepsilon_{N,1} \\ \vdots \\ \vdots \\ \varepsilon_{1,T} \\ \vdots \\ \varepsilon_{N,T} \end{pmatrix}$$

which we can represent alternatively as follows:

$$\mathbf{u} = \text{vec}\left(\mathbf{U}\right)$$

$$\mathbf{U} = \begin{pmatrix} \varepsilon_{1,1} & \cdots & \varepsilon_{1,T} \\ \vdots & \ddots & \vdots \\ \varepsilon_{N,1} & \cdots & \varepsilon_{N,T} \end{pmatrix}$$

where $\mathbf{U}$ is a $(N \times T)$ matrix such that each column represents an N-variate innovation term.

The innovation terms have a nonsingular covariance matrix,

$$\Sigma = \left[\sigma_{i,j}\right] = E\left[\varepsilon_{i,t}\varepsilon_{j,t}\right]$$

while $E[\varepsilon_{i,t}\,\varepsilon_{j,s}] = 0$, $\forall i, j, t \neq s$. The covariance matrix of $\mathbf{u}$, $\Sigma_\mathbf{u}$ can now be written as

$$\Sigma_\mathbf{u} = \mathbf{I}_T \otimes \Sigma = \begin{pmatrix} \Sigma & \cdots & 0 \\ \vdots & \ddots & \vdots \\ 0 & \cdots & \Sigma \end{pmatrix}$$

In other words, the covariance matrix of $\mathbf{u}$ is a block-diagonal matrix where all diagonal blocks are equal to Σ. This covariance structure reflects the assumed white-noise nature of innovations that precludes autocorrelations and cross autocorrelations in the innovation terms.

In discussing the case of multivariate single-equation regressions (Chapter 2), we stacked the observations of the regressors in a matrix where each column represented all the observations of one regressor. Here we want to use the same technique but there are two differences: (1) In this case, there is no distinction between the observations of the regressors and those of the dependent variables; and (2) the multiplicity of equations requires special care in constructing the matrix of regressors. One possible solution is to construct the $(NT \times (N^2p + N))$ matrix of observations of the regressors shown in Exhibit 3.2.

This matrix can be written compactly as follows: $\mathbf{w} = (\mathbf{W}' \otimes \mathbf{I}_N)$, where

$$\mathbf{W} = \begin{pmatrix} 1 & 1 & \cdots & 1 & 1 \\ \mathbf{x}_0 & \mathbf{x}_1 & \cdots & \mathbf{x}_{T-2} & \mathbf{x}_{T-1} \\ \mathbf{x}_{-1} & \mathbf{x}_0 & \cdots & \mathbf{x}_{T-3} & \mathbf{x}_{T-2} \\ \vdots & \vdots & \ddots & \vdots & \\ \mathbf{x}_{p-1} & \mathbf{x}_{p-2} & \cdots & \mathbf{x}_{T-p-1} & \mathbf{x}_{T-p} \end{pmatrix}$$

$$= \begin{pmatrix} 1 & 1 & \cdots & 1 & 1 \\ x_{1,0} & x_{1,1} & \cdots & x_{1,T-2} & x_{1,T-1} \\ \vdots & \vdots & \ddots & \vdots & \vdots \\ x_{N,0} & x_{N,1} & \cdots & x_{N,T-2} & x_{N,T-1} \\ x_{1,-1} & x_{1,0} & \cdots & x_{1,T-3} & x_{1,T-2} \\ \vdots & \vdots & \ddots & \vdots & \vdots \\ x_{N,-1} & x_{N,0} & \cdots & x_{N,T-3} & x_{N,T-2} \\ \vdots & \vdots & \ddots & \vdots & \vdots \\ \vdots & \vdots & \ddots & \vdots & \vdots \\ x_{1,1-p} & x_{1,2-p} & \cdots & x_{1,T-p-1} & x_{1,T-p} \\ \vdots & \vdots & \ddots & \vdots & \vdots \\ x_{N,1-p} & x_{N,2-p} & \cdots & x_{N,T-p-1} & x_{N,T-p} \end{pmatrix}$$

is a $((Np + 1) \times T)$ matrix and $\mathbf{I}_N$ is the N-dimensional identity matrix.

Let us arrange all the model coefficients in a single $(N \times (Np + 1))$ matrix as

$$\mathbf{A} = \left(\mathbf{v}, \mathbf{A}_1, \ldots, \mathbf{A}_p \right)$$
$$= \begin{pmatrix} v_1 & a_{11}^1 & \cdots & a_{1N}^1 & \cdots & \cdots & \cdots & a_{11}^p & \cdots & a_{1N}^p \\ \vdots & \vdots & \ddots & \vdots & \vdots & \ddots & \vdots & \vdots & \ddots & \vdots \\ v_N & a_{N1}^1 & \cdots & a_{NN}^1 & \cdots & \cdots & \cdots & a_{N1}^p & \cdots & a_{NN}^p \end{pmatrix}$$

EXHIBIT 3.2 The Matrix of Observations of the Regressors

$$
w = \begin{pmatrix}
1 & \cdots & 0 & x_{1,0} & \cdots & 0 & x_{N,0} & \cdots & \cdots & x_{1,1-p} & \cdots & 0 & \cdots & x_{N,1-p} & \cdots & 0 \\
\vdots & \ddots & \vdots & \vdots & \ddots & \vdots & \vdots & \ddots & \vdots & \vdots & \ddots & \vdots & \vdots & \vdots & \ddots & \vdots \\
0 & \cdots & 1 & 0 & \cdots & x_{1,0} & 0 & \cdots & x_{N,0} & 0 & \cdots & x_{1,1-p} & \cdots & 0 & \cdots & x_{N,1-p} \\
1 & \cdots & 0 & x_{1,1} & \cdots & 0 & x_{N,1} & \cdots & 0 & x_{1,2-p} & \cdots & 0 & \cdots & x_{N,2-p} & \cdots & 0 \\
\vdots & \cdots & \vdots & \cdots & \ddots & \cdots & \cdots & \ddots & \cdots & \cdots & \ddots & \cdots & \cdots & \cdots & \ddots & \cdots \\
0 & \cdots & 1 & 0 & \cdots & x_{1,1} & 0 & \cdots & x_{N,1} & 0 & \cdots & x_{1,2-p} & \cdots & 0 & \cdots & x_{N,2-p} \\
\vdots & & \vdots & & \ddots & & & \ddots & & & \ddots & & & & \ddots & \\
1 & \cdots & 0 & x_{1,T-2} & \cdots & 0 & x_{N,T-2} & \cdots & 0 & x_{1,T-p-1} & \cdots & 0 & \cdots & x_{N,T-p-1} & \cdots & 0 \\
\vdots & \cdots & \vdots & \cdots & \ddots & \cdots & \cdots & \ddots & \cdots & \cdots & \ddots & \cdots & \cdots & \cdots & \ddots & \cdots \\
0 & \cdots & 1 & 0 & \cdots & x_{1,T-2} & 0 & \cdots & x_{N,T-2} & 0 & \cdots & x_{1,T-p-1} & \cdots & 0 & \cdots & x_{N,T-p-1} \\
1 & \cdots & 0 & x_{1,T-1} & \cdots & 0 & x_{N,T-1} & \cdots & 0 & x_{1,T-p} & \cdots & 0 & \cdots & x_{N,T-p} & \cdots & 0 \\
\vdots & \cdots & \vdots & \cdots & \ddots & \cdots & \cdots & \ddots & \cdots & \cdots & \ddots & \cdots & \cdots & \cdots & \ddots & \cdots \\
0 & \cdots & 1 & 0 & \cdots & x_{1,T-1} & 0 & \cdots & x_{N,T-1} & 0 & \cdots & x_{1,T-p} & \cdots & 0 & \cdots & x_{N,T-p}
\end{pmatrix}
$$

and construct the $(N(Np + 1) \times 1)$ vector as

$$\beta = \mathrm{vec}\left(\mathbf{A}\right) = \begin{pmatrix} v_1 \\ \vdots \\ v_N \\ a_{11}^1 \\ \vdots \\ a_{N1}^1 \\ \vdots \\ a_{1N}^p \\ \vdots \\ a_{NN}^p \end{pmatrix}$$

Using the preceding notation, we can now compactly write the VAR(p) model in two equivalent ways as follows:

$$\mathbf{X} = \mathbf{AW} + \mathbf{U}$$

$$\mathbf{x} = \mathbf{w}\beta + \mathbf{u}$$

The first is a matrix equation where the left and right sides are $N \times T$ matrices such that each column represents the VAR(p) equation for each observation. The second equation, which equates the two NT vectors on the left and right sides, can be derived from the first as follows, using the properties of the vec operator and the Kronecker product established previously:

$$\mathrm{vec}(\mathbf{X}) = \mathrm{vec}(\mathbf{AW}) + \mathrm{vec}(\mathbf{U})$$

$$\mathrm{vec}(\mathbf{X}) = (\mathbf{W}' \otimes \mathbf{I}_N)\mathrm{vec}(\mathbf{A}) + \mathrm{vec}(\mathbf{U})$$

$$\mathbf{x} = \mathbf{w}\beta + \mathbf{u}$$

This latter equation is the equivalent of the regression equation established in Chapter 2.

To estimate the model, we have to write the sum of the squares of residuals as we did for the sum of the residuals in a regression. However, as already mentioned, we must also consider the multivariate nature of the noise terms and the presence of correlations.

Our starting point will be the regression equation $\mathbf{x} = \mathbf{w}\beta + \mathbf{u}$ which we can rewrite as $\mathbf{u} = \mathbf{x} - \mathbf{w}\beta$. As the innovation terms exhibit a correlation structure, we have to proceed as in the case of Generalized Least Squares. We write the squared residuals as follows:

$$S = \mathbf{u}'\mathbf{\Sigma}_{\mathbf{u}}^{-1}\mathbf{u} = \sum_{t=1}^{T} \boldsymbol{\varepsilon}_t' \mathbf{\Sigma}^{-1} \boldsymbol{\varepsilon}_t$$

For a given set of observations, the quantity S is a function of the model parameters $S = S(\beta)$. The function S admits the following alternative representation:

$$S(\beta) = \text{trace}\left[(\mathbf{X} - \mathbf{AW})' \mathbf{\Sigma}_{\mathbf{u}}^{-1} (\mathbf{X} - \mathbf{AW}) \right] = \text{trace}\left[\mathbf{U}'\mathbf{\Sigma}_{\mathbf{u}}^{-1}\mathbf{U} \right]$$

In fact, we can write the following derivation:

$$S = \mathbf{u}'\mathbf{\Sigma}_{\mathbf{u}}^{-1}\mathbf{u} = (\text{vec}(\mathbf{U}))' (\mathbf{I}_T \otimes \mathbf{\Sigma})^{-1} \text{vec}(\mathbf{U})$$

$$= (\text{vec}(\mathbf{X} - \mathbf{AW}))' (\mathbf{I}_T \otimes \mathbf{\Sigma}^{-1}) \text{vec}(\mathbf{X} - \mathbf{AW})$$

$$= \text{trace}[(\mathbf{X} - \mathbf{AW})' \mathbf{\Sigma}_{\mathbf{u}}^{-1} (\mathbf{X} - \mathbf{AW})] = \text{trace}[\mathbf{U}'\mathbf{\Sigma}^{-1}\mathbf{U}]$$

These expressions are recurrent in the theory of estimation of VAR processes and multiple regressions.

We are now ready to estimate the model parameters, imposing the least squares condition: the estimated parameters $\hat{\beta}$ are those that minimize $S = S(\beta)$. The minimum of S is attained for those values of β that equate to zero the partial derivatives of S:

$$\frac{\partial S(\beta)}{\partial \beta} = 0$$

Equating these derivatives to zero yields the so-called *normal equations* of the LS method that we can derive as follows:

$$S = \mathbf{u}'\mathbf{\Sigma}_{\mathbf{u}}^{-1}\mathbf{u} = (\mathbf{x} - \mathbf{w}\beta)' \mathbf{\Sigma}_{\mathbf{u}}^{-1} (\mathbf{x} - \mathbf{w}\beta)$$

$$= \mathbf{x}'\mathbf{\Sigma}_{\mathbf{u}}^{-1}\mathbf{x} + \beta'\mathbf{w}'\mathbf{\Sigma}_{\mathbf{u}}^{-1}\mathbf{w}\beta - 2\beta'\mathbf{w}'\mathbf{\Sigma}_{\mathbf{u}}^{-1}\mathbf{x}$$

Hence the normal equations

$$\frac{\partial S(\beta)}{\partial \beta} = 2\mathbf{w}'\mathbf{\Sigma}_{\mathbf{u}}^{-1}\mathbf{w}\beta - 2\mathbf{w}'\mathbf{\Sigma}_{\mathbf{u}}^{-1}\mathbf{x} = 0$$

In addition, the Hessian is positive as

$$\frac{\partial^2 S(\beta)}{\partial\beta\partial\beta'} = 2\mathbf{w}'\Sigma_u^{-1}\mathbf{w}$$

Consequently, the LS estimator is

$$\hat{\beta} = (\mathbf{w}'\Sigma_u^{-1}\mathbf{w})^{-1}\mathbf{w}'\Sigma_u^{-1}\mathbf{x}$$

This expression—which has the same form as the Aitkin GLS estimator—is a fundamental expression in LS methods. However in this case, due to the structure of the regressors, further simplifications are possible. In fact, the LS estimator can be also written as follows:

$$\hat{\beta} = ((\mathbf{W}\mathbf{W}')^{-1}\mathbf{W} \otimes \mathbf{I}_N)\mathbf{x}$$

To demonstrate this point, consider the following derivation:

$$\begin{aligned}
\hat{\beta} &= \left(\mathbf{w}'\Sigma_u^{-1}\mathbf{w}\right)^{-1}\mathbf{w}'\Sigma_u^{-1}\mathbf{x} \\
&= \left((\mathbf{W}'\otimes\mathbf{I}_N)'(\mathbf{I}_T\otimes\Sigma)^{-1}(\mathbf{W}'\otimes\mathbf{I}_N)\right)^{-1}(\mathbf{W}\otimes\mathbf{I}_N)(\mathbf{I}_T\otimes\Sigma)^{-1}\mathbf{x} \\
&= \left((\mathbf{W}\otimes\mathbf{I}_N)(\mathbf{I}_T\otimes\Sigma^{-1})(\mathbf{W}'\otimes\mathbf{I}_N)\right)^{-1}(\mathbf{W}\otimes\mathbf{I}_N)(\mathbf{I}_T\otimes\Sigma^{-1})\mathbf{x} \\
&= \left((\mathbf{W}\mathbf{I}_T)\otimes(\mathbf{I}_N\Sigma^{-1})(\mathbf{W}'\otimes\mathbf{I}_N)\right)^{-1}(\mathbf{W}\mathbf{I}_T)\otimes(\mathbf{I}_N\Sigma^{-1})\mathbf{x} \\
&= \left((\mathbf{W}\otimes\Sigma^{-1})(\mathbf{W}'\otimes\mathbf{I}_N)\right)^{-1}(\mathbf{W}\otimes\Sigma^{-1})\mathbf{x} \\
&= \left((\mathbf{W}\mathbf{W}')^{-1}\otimes(\Sigma^{-1})\right)(\mathbf{W}\otimes\Sigma)\mathbf{x} \\
&= \left((\mathbf{W}\mathbf{W}')^{-1}\mathbf{W}\right)\otimes(\Sigma^{-1}\Sigma)\mathbf{x} \\
&= \left((\mathbf{W}\mathbf{W}')^{-1}\mathbf{W}\otimes\mathbf{I}_N\right)\mathbf{x}
\end{aligned}$$

The preceding shows that, in the case of a stable unrestricted VAR process, the multivariate LS estimator is the same as the OLS estimator obtained by minimizing the quantity $S = \mathbf{u}'\mathbf{u}$. We can therefore state that in the case of VAR processes, the LS estimators are the same as the OLS estimators computed equation by equation. Computationally, this entails a significant simplification.

We can also write another expression for the estimators. In fact, we can write the following estimator for the matrix $\mathbf{A}$:

$$\hat{A} = XW' \left(WW' \right)^{-1}$$

The preceding relationship is obtained from:

$$\hat{\beta} = \left(\left(WW' \right)^{-1} W \otimes I_N \right) x$$

$$\text{vec} \left(\hat{A} \right) = \left(\left(WW' \right)^{-1} W \otimes I_N \right) \text{vec} \left(X \right)$$

$$= \text{vec} \left(XW' \left(WW' \right)^{-1} \right)$$

To summarize, we have obtained the following results:

1. Given a VAR(p) process, the multivariate LS estimator is the same as the OLS estimator computed equation by equation.
2. The following three expressions for the estimator are equivalent:

$$\hat{\beta} = \left(w' \Sigma_u^{-1} w \right)^{-1} w' \Sigma_u^{-1} x$$

$$\hat{\beta} = \left(\left(WW' \right)^{-1} W \otimes I_N \right) x$$

$$\hat{A} = XW' \left(WW' \right)^{-1}$$

We next discuss the large-sample (asymptotic) distribution of these estimators.

The Asymptotic Distribution of LS Estimators

Estimators depend on the sample and have therefore to be considered random variables. To assess the quality of the estimators, the distribution of the estimators must be determined. The properties of these distributions are not the same in small and large samples.

It is difficult to calculate the small sample distributions of the LS estimators of the stationary VAR process determined earlier. Consider that the only restriction placed on the distribution of the white noise process is that it has a nonsingular covariance matrix. Small sample properties of a stationary VAR process can be approximately ascertained using Monte Carlo methods.

Significant simplifications hold approximately in large samples and hold asymptotically when the sample size becomes infinite. The essential result is that the distribution of the model estimators becomes normal. The asymptotic properties of the LS estimators can be established under additional assumptions on the white noise. Suppose that the white-noise process has finite and bounded fourth moments and that noise variables at different times are independent and not merely uncorrelated as we have assumed thus far. (Note that these conditions are automatically satisfied by any Gaussian white noise.) Under these assumptions, it can be demonstrated that the following properties hold:

- The $((Np + 1) \times (Np + 1))$ matrix

$$\Gamma: = \text{plim}\frac{\mathbf{WW}'}{T}$$

exists and is nonsingular.
- The $(N(Np + 1) \times 1)$ vector $\hat{\boldsymbol{\beta}}$ of estimated model parameters is jointly normally distributed:

$$\sqrt{T}\left(\hat{\boldsymbol{\beta}} - \boldsymbol{\beta}\right) \overset{d}{\to} N\left(0, \boldsymbol{\Gamma}^{-1} \otimes \boldsymbol{\Sigma}\right)$$

The $(N(Np + 1) \times N(Np + 1))$ matrix $\boldsymbol{\Gamma}^{-1} \otimes \boldsymbol{\Sigma}$ is the covariance matrix of the parameter distribution.

From the preceding, in any large but finite sample, we can identify the following estimators for the matrices Γ, $\boldsymbol{\Sigma}$:

$$\hat{\boldsymbol{\Gamma}} = \frac{\mathbf{WW}'}{T}$$

$$\hat{\boldsymbol{\Sigma}} = \frac{1}{T}\mathbf{X}\left(\mathbf{I}_T - \mathbf{W}'\left(\mathbf{WW}'\right)^{-1}\mathbf{W}\right)\mathbf{X}'$$

Note that these matrices are not needed to estimate the model parameters; they are required only to understand the distribution of the model parameters. If $N = 1$, these expressions are the same as those already established for multivariate regressions.

Estimating Demeaned Processes

In previous sections we assumed that the VAR(p) model had a constant intercept and the process variables had, in general, a nonzero mean. Note that the mean and the intercept are not the same numbers. In fact, given that the process is assumed to be stationary, we can write

$$E(\mathbf{x}_t) = \mathbf{A}_1 E(\mathbf{x}_{t-1}) + \mathbf{A}_2 E(\mathbf{x}_{t-2}) + \cdots + \mathbf{A}_p E(\mathbf{x}_{t-p}) + \mathbf{v}$$

$$\boldsymbol{\mu} - \mathbf{A}_1\boldsymbol{\mu} - \mathbf{A}_2\boldsymbol{\mu} - \cdots - \mathbf{A}_p\boldsymbol{\mu} = \mathbf{v}$$

$$\boldsymbol{\mu} = \left(\mathbf{I}_N - \mathbf{A}_1 - \mathbf{A}_2 - \cdots - \mathbf{A}_p\right)^{-1} \mathbf{v}$$

We can recast the previous reasoning in a different notation, assuming that the process variables are demeaned with a zero intercept. In this case, we can rewrite the VAR process in the following form:

$$\left(\mathbf{x}_t - \boldsymbol{\mu}\right) = \mathbf{A}_1\left(\mathbf{x}_{t-1} - \boldsymbol{\mu}\right) + \mathbf{A}_2\left(\mathbf{x}_{t-2} - \boldsymbol{\mu}\right) + \cdots + \mathbf{A}_p\left(\mathbf{x}_{t-p} - \boldsymbol{\mu}\right) + \boldsymbol{\varepsilon}_t$$

If we write $y_t = \mathbf{x}_t - \boldsymbol{\mu}$, the VAR process becomes

$$\mathbf{y}_t = \mathbf{A}_1\mathbf{y}_{t-1} + \mathbf{A}_2\mathbf{y}_{t-2} + \cdots + \mathbf{A}_p\mathbf{y}_{t-p} + \boldsymbol{\varepsilon}_t$$

This model contains N parameters less than the original model as the intercepts do not appear. If the mean is not known, it can be estimated separately as

$$\hat{\boldsymbol{\mu}} = \sum_{t=1}^{T} \mathbf{x}_t$$

The formulas previously established hold with some obvious changes. We will write down the formulas explicitly, as they will be used in the following sections:

$$\mathbf{Y} = \left(\mathbf{y}_1, \ldots, \mathbf{y}_T\right)$$
$$\mathbf{U} = \left(\boldsymbol{\varepsilon}_1, \ldots, \boldsymbol{\varepsilon}_T\right)$$
$$\mathbf{y} = \mathrm{vec}\left(\mathbf{Y}\right)$$
$$\mathbf{u} = \mathrm{vec}\left(\mathbf{U}\right)$$
$$\boldsymbol{\Sigma}_\mathbf{u} = \mathbf{I}_T \otimes \boldsymbol{\Sigma}$$
$$\mathbf{A} = \left(\mathbf{A}_1, \ldots, \mathbf{A}_p\right)$$
$$\boldsymbol{\alpha} = \mathrm{vec}\left(\mathbf{A}\right)$$
$$\mathbf{Z} = \begin{pmatrix} \mathbf{y}_0 & \cdots & \mathbf{y}_{T-1} \\ \vdots & \ddots & \vdots \\ \mathbf{y}_{1-p} & \cdots & \mathbf{y}_{T-p} \end{pmatrix}$$
$$\mathbf{z} = \left(\mathbf{Z}' \otimes \mathbf{I}_N\right)$$

The model is then written in matrix form as

$$\mathbf{y} = \mathbf{z}\alpha + \mathbf{u}$$
$$\mathbf{Y} = \mathbf{AZ} + \mathbf{U}$$

The LS estimators are then written as follows:

$$\hat{\alpha} = \left(\mathbf{z}'\Sigma_u^{-1}\mathbf{z}\right)^{-1}\mathbf{z}'\Sigma_u^{-1}\mathbf{y}$$
$$\hat{\alpha} = \left(\left(\mathbf{ZZ}'\right)^{-1}\mathbf{Z}\otimes\mathbf{I}_N\right)\mathbf{y}$$
$$\hat{\mathbf{A}} = \mathbf{YZ}'\left(\mathbf{ZZ}'\right)^{-1}$$

It can be demonstrated that the sample mean,

$$\hat{\mu} = \sum_{t=1}^{T}\mathbf{x}_t$$

is a consistent estimator of the process mean and has a normal asymptotic distribution. If the process is not demeaned and has constant estimated intercept $\hat{\mathbf{v}}$, the mean can be estimated with the following estimator:

$$\hat{\mu} = \left(\mathbf{I}_N - \mathbf{A}_1 - \mathbf{A}_2 - \cdots - \mathbf{A}_p\right)^{-1}\hat{\mathbf{v}}$$

which is consistent and has an asymptotic normal distribution.

We now turn our attention to the Maximum Likelihood estimation methods.

Maximum Likelihood Estimators

Under the assumption of Gaussian innovations, Maximum Likelihood (ML) estimation methods coincide with LS estimation methods. Recall that, given a known distribution, ML methods try to find the distribution parameters that maximize the likelihood function (i.e., the joint distribution of the sample computed on the sample itself). In the case of a multivariate mean-adjusted VAR(p) process, the given sample data are T empirical observations of the N-variate variable y_t, $t = 1, ..., T$ and a presample of p initial conditions $y_{-p+1}, ..., y_0$. If we assume that the process is stationary and that innovations are Gaussian white noise, the variables y_t, $t = 1, ..., T$ will also be jointly normally distributed.

One can derive the joint distribution of the sample y_t, $t = 1, ..., T$ in function of the sample data and apply ML methods to this distribution. However, it is easier to express the joint distribution of the noise terms in function of the data. As the white noise is assumed to be Gaussian, the noise variables at different times are independent.

The noise terms $(\varepsilon_1, ..., \varepsilon_T)$ are assumed to be independent with constant covariance matrix Σ and, therefore, $\mathbf{u} = \text{vec}(\mathbf{U})$ has covariance matrix $\Sigma_u = \mathbf{I}_T \otimes \Sigma$. Under the assumption of Gaussian noise, the density $f_u(\mathbf{u})$ of $\mathbf{u}$ is the following NT-variate normal density:

$$f_u(\mathbf{u}) = \frac{1}{(2\pi)^{\frac{NT}{2}}} |\mathbf{I}_T \otimes \Sigma|^{-\frac{1}{2}} \exp\left(-\frac{1}{2}\mathbf{u}'\left(\mathbf{I}_T \otimes \Sigma^{-1}\right)\mathbf{u}\right)$$

$$= \frac{1}{(2\pi)^{\frac{NT}{2}}} |\Sigma|^{-\frac{T}{2}} \exp\left(-\frac{1}{2}\sum_{t=1}^{T}\varepsilon_t'\Sigma^{-1}\varepsilon_t\right)$$

This density is expressed in function of the noise terms which are unobserved terms. In order to estimate, we need to express the density in terms of the observations. The density can easily be expressed in terms of observations using the VAR(p) equation:

$$\varepsilon_1 = \mathbf{y}_1 - \mathbf{A}_1\mathbf{y}_0 - \mathbf{A}_2\mathbf{y}_{-1} - \cdots - \mathbf{A}_p\mathbf{y}_{1-p}$$

$$\varepsilon_2 = \mathbf{y}_2 - \mathbf{A}_1\mathbf{y}_1 - \mathbf{A}_2\mathbf{y}_0 - \cdots - \mathbf{A}_p\mathbf{y}_{2-p}$$

$$\cdots\cdots\cdots\cdots\cdots\cdots\cdots\cdots\cdots\cdots$$

$$\varepsilon_p = \mathbf{y}_p - \mathbf{A}_1\mathbf{y}_{p-1} - \mathbf{A}_2\mathbf{y}_{p-2} - \cdots - \mathbf{A}_p\mathbf{y}_0$$

$$\varepsilon_{p+1} = \mathbf{y}_{p+1} - \mathbf{A}_1\mathbf{y}_p - \mathbf{A}_2\mathbf{y}_{p-2} - \cdots - \mathbf{A}_p\mathbf{y}_1$$

$$\cdots\cdots\cdots\cdots\cdots\cdots\cdots\cdots\cdots\cdots$$

$$\varepsilon_{T-1} = \mathbf{y}_{T-1} - \mathbf{A}_1\mathbf{y}_{T-2} - \mathbf{A}_2\mathbf{y}_{T-3} - \cdots - \mathbf{A}_p\mathbf{y}_{T-p-1}$$

$$\varepsilon_T = \mathbf{y}_T - \mathbf{A}_1\mathbf{y}_{T-1} - \mathbf{A}_2\mathbf{y}_{T-2} - \cdots - \mathbf{A}_p\mathbf{y}_{T-p}$$

The preceding can be rewritten in matrix form as follows:

$$
\begin{pmatrix} \boldsymbol{\varepsilon}_1 \\ \boldsymbol{\varepsilon}_2 \\ \vdots \\ \boldsymbol{\varepsilon}_p \\ \boldsymbol{\varepsilon}_{p+1} \\ \vdots \\ \boldsymbol{\varepsilon}_{T-1} \\ \boldsymbol{\varepsilon}_T \end{pmatrix}
=
\begin{pmatrix}
\mathbf{I}_N & 0 & \cdots & 0 & 0 & 0 & \cdots \cdots & 0 & 0 & \cdots & 0 & 0 \\
-\mathbf{A}_1 & \mathbf{I}_N & \cdots & 0 & 0 & 0 & \cdots \cdots & 0 & 0 & \cdots & 0 & 0 \\
\vdots & \vdots & \ddots & \vdots & \vdots & \vdots & \ddots \ddots & \vdots & \vdots & \ddots & \vdots & \vdots \\
-\mathbf{A}_p & -\mathbf{A}_{p-1} & \cdots & -\mathbf{A}_1 & \mathbf{I}_N & 0 & \cdots \cdots & 0 & 0 & \ddots & 0 & 0 \\
0 & -\mathbf{A}_p & \cdots & -\mathbf{A}_2 & -\mathbf{A}_1 & \mathbf{I}_N & \cdots \cdots & 0 & 0 & \ddots & 0 & 0 \\
\vdots & \vdots & \ddots & \vdots & \vdots & \vdots & \ddots \ddots & \vdots & \vdots & \ddots & \vdots & \vdots \\
0 & 0 & \cdots & 0 & 0 & 0 & \cdots & 0 & -\mathbf{A}_p & -\mathbf{A}_{p-1} & \cdots & \mathbf{I}_N & 0 \\
0 & 0 & \cdots & 0 & 0 & 0 & \cdots & 0 & 0 & -\mathbf{A}_p & \cdots & -\mathbf{A}_1 & \mathbf{I}_N
\end{pmatrix} \cdots
$$

$$
\begin{pmatrix} \mathbf{y}_1 \\ \mathbf{y}_2 \\ \vdots \\ \mathbf{y}_p \\ \mathbf{y}_{p+1} \\ \vdots \\ \mathbf{y}_{T-p} \\ \vdots \\ \mathbf{y}_{T-1} \\ \mathbf{y}_T \end{pmatrix}
+
\begin{pmatrix}
-\mathbf{A}_p & -\mathbf{A}_{p-1} & \cdots & -\mathbf{A}_1 \\
0 & -\mathbf{A}_p & \cdots & -\mathbf{A}_2 \\
\vdots & \vdots & \ddots & \vdots \\
0 & 0 & \cdots & -\mathbf{A}_p \\
\vdots & \vdots & \ddots & \vdots \\
0 & 0 & \cdots & 0
\end{pmatrix}
\begin{pmatrix} \mathbf{y}_{1-p} \\ \mathbf{y}_{2-p} \\ \\ \mathbf{y}_{-1} \\ \mathbf{y}_0 \end{pmatrix}
$$

Using these expressions and the model equation $\mathbf{y} = \mathbf{z}\boldsymbol{\alpha} + \mathbf{u}$, we can now express the density function in terms of the variables

$$
f_y(\mathbf{y}) = \left| \frac{\partial \mathbf{u}}{\partial \mathbf{y}} \right| f_u(\mathbf{u}) = \frac{1}{(2\pi)^{\frac{NT}{2}}} \left| \mathbf{I}_T \otimes \boldsymbol{\Sigma} \right|^{-\frac{1}{2}} \exp\left(-\frac{1}{2} (\mathbf{y} - \mathbf{z}\boldsymbol{\alpha})' (\mathbf{I}_T \otimes \boldsymbol{\Sigma}^{-1})(\mathbf{y} - \mathbf{z}\boldsymbol{\alpha}) \right)
$$

Using reasoning similar to what we used in the LS case, we can write the log-likelihood as follows:

$$
\begin{aligned}
\log(l) &= -\frac{NT}{2}\log(2\pi) - \frac{T}{2}\log|\boldsymbol{\Sigma}_u| - \frac{1}{2}\sum_{t=1}^{T}\boldsymbol{\varepsilon}_t'\boldsymbol{\Sigma}^{-1}\boldsymbol{\varepsilon}_t \\
&= -\frac{NT}{2}\log(2\pi) - \frac{T}{2}\log|\boldsymbol{\Sigma}_u| - \frac{1}{2}(\mathbf{y} - \mathbf{z}\boldsymbol{\alpha})'(\mathbf{I}_T \otimes \boldsymbol{\Sigma}^{-1})(\mathbf{y} - \mathbf{z}\boldsymbol{\alpha}) \\
&= -\frac{NT}{2}\log(2\pi) - \frac{T}{2}\log|\boldsymbol{\Sigma}_u| - \frac{1}{2}\operatorname{trace}(\mathbf{U}'\boldsymbol{\Sigma}_u^{-1}\mathbf{U}) \\
&= -\frac{NT}{2}\log(2\pi) - \frac{T}{2}\log|\boldsymbol{\Sigma}_u| - \frac{1}{2}\operatorname{trace}\left((\mathbf{Y} - \mathbf{A}\mathbf{Z})'\boldsymbol{\Sigma}_u^{-1}(\mathbf{Y} - \mathbf{A}\mathbf{Z}) \right)
\end{aligned}
$$

Equating the partial derivatives of this expression to zero, we obtain the very same estimators we obtained with the LS method. In the case of Gaussian noise, LS/OLS methods and ML methods yield the same result.

ESTIMATING THE NUMBER OF LAGS

In the previous sections, we assumed that the empirical process is generated by a stable VAR model. This assumption entails that the process is stationary. In both the LS and ML estimation methods, the order p of the model (i.e., the number of lags in the model) is assumed to be known. However, there is nothing in the estimation method that imposes a specific model order. Given an empirical time series, we can fit a VAR(p) model with an arbitrary number of lags.

The objective of this section is to establish criteria that allow determining a priori the correct number of lags. This idea has to be made more precise. We assume, as we did in the previous sections on the estimation of the model coefficients, that the true DGP is a VAR(p) model. In this case, we expect that the correct model order is exactly p, that is, we expect to come out with a consistent estimator of the model order. This is not the same problem as trying to determine the optimal number of lags to fit a VAR model to a process that might not be generated by a linear DGP. Here we assume that the type of model is correctly specified and discuss methods to estimate the model order under this assumption.

As observed, we can fit a model of any order to any set of empirical data. In general, increasing the model order will reduce the size of residuals but reduces the forecasting ability of the model. It is a basic tenet of learning theory that, by increasing the number of parameters, we will improve the in-sample accuracy but worsen the out-of-sample forecasting ability. In this section we consider only linear models under the assumption that the DGP is linear and autoregressive with unknown parameters.[7]

To see how increasing the number of lags can reduce the forecasting ability of the model, consider that the forecasting ability of a linear VAR model can be estimated. It can be demonstrated that the optimal forecast of a VAR model is the conditional mean. This implies that the optimal one-step forecast given the past p values of the process up to the present moment is

$$\mathbf{x}_{t+1} = \mathbf{A}_1 \mathbf{x}_t + \mathbf{A}_2 \mathbf{x}_{t-1} + \cdots + \mathbf{A}_p \mathbf{x}_{t-p+1} + \mathbf{v}$$

[7]The difference between the two approaches should not be underestimated. In its generality, learning theory deals with finding models of empirical data without any previous knowledge of the true DGP. In this section, however, we assume that a true DGP exists and is a finite VAR.

The forecasting mean square error (MSE) can be estimated. It can be demonstrated that an approximate estimate of the one-step MSE is given by the following expression:

$$\mathbf{\Sigma}_x(1) = \frac{T + Np + 1}{T} \mathbf{\Sigma}(p)$$

where $\mathbf{\Sigma}(p)$ is the covariance matrix of a model of order p. The $\mathbf{\Sigma}_x(1)$ is a covariance matrix of the forecasting errors. Based on $\mathbf{\Sigma}_x(1)$, Akaike[8] suggested a criterion to estimate the model order. First, we have to replace $\mathbf{\Sigma}(p)$ with its estimate. In the case of a zero-mean process, we can estimate $\mathbf{\Sigma}(p)$ as

$$\hat{\mathbf{\Sigma}}(p) = \frac{1}{T} \mathbf{X} \left(\mathbf{I}_T - \mathbf{W}'(\mathbf{WW}')^{-1} \mathbf{W} \right) \mathbf{X}'$$

The quantity

$$\text{FPE}(p) = \left[\frac{T + Np + 1}{T - Np + 1} \right]^N \det\left(\hat{\mathbf{\Sigma}}(p) \right)$$

is called the *final prediction error* (FPE). In 1969, Akaike[9] proposed to determine the model order by minimizing the FPE. Four years later, he proposed a different criterion based on information theory considerations. The new criterion, commonly called the *Akaike Information Criterion* (AIC), proposes to determine the model order by minimizing the following expression:

$$\text{AIC}(p) = \log\left| \hat{\mathbf{\Sigma}}(p) \right| + \frac{2pN^2}{T}$$

Neither the FPE nor the AIC estimators are consistent estimators in the sense that they determine the correct model order in the limit of an infinite sample. Different but consistent criteria have been proposed. Among them, the *Bayesian Information Criterion* (BIC) is quite popular. Proposed by Schwartz,[10] the BIC chooses the model that minimizes the following expression:

---

[8]Hirotugu Akaike, "Fitting Autoregressive Models for Prediction," *Annals of the Institute of Statistical Mathematics*, 21 (1969), pp. 243–247.
[9]Hirotugu Akaike, "Information Theory and an Extension of the Maximum Likelihood Principle," in B. N. Petrov and F. Csaki (eds.), *Second International Symposium on Information Theory* (Budapest: Akademiaio Kiado, 1973).
[10]Gideon Schwarz, "Estimating the Dimension of a Model," *Annals of Statistics*, 6 (1978), pp. 461–464.

$$\text{AIC}(p) = \log\left|\hat{\Sigma}(p)\right| + \frac{\log T}{T}2pN^2$$

There is a vast literature on model selection criteria. The justification of each criterion impinges on rather complex considerations of information theory, statistics, and learning theory.[11]

AUTOCORRELATION AND
DISTRIBUTIONAL PROPERTIES OF RESIDUALS

The validity of the LS method does not depend on the distribution of innovations provided that their covariance matrix exists. However, the LS method might not be optimal if innovations are not normally distributed. The ML method, in contrast, critically depends on the distributional properties of innovations. Nevertheless, both methods are sensitive to the eventual autocorrelation of innovation terms. Therefore, it is important to check the absence of autocorrelation of residuals and to ascertain eventual deviations from normal distributions.

The estimated VAR model distributional properties are critical in applications such as asset allocation, portfolio management, and risk management. The presence of tails might change optimality conditions and the entire optimization process.

Checking the distributional properties of an estimated VAR model can be done with one of the many available tests of autocorrelation and normality. After estimating the VAR model parameters and the model order—a process that calls for iterating the estimation process—the residuals of the process are computed. Given the linearity of the model, the normality of the model distributions can be checked by analyzing only the residuals.

The autocorrelation properties of the residuals can be checked using the Dickey-Fuller (DF) or the Augmented Dickey-Fuller (ADF) test. Both tests are widely used tests of autocorrelation implemented in most time series computer programs. The DF and ADF tests work by estimating the autoregresssion coefficient of the residuals and comparing it with a table of critical values.

---

[11]See, for example, Dean P. Foster and Robert A. Stine, "An Information Theoretic Comparison of Model Selection Criteria," Working Paper 1180, 1997, Northwestern University, Center for Mathematical Studies in Economics and Management Science.

STATIONARY AUTOREGRESSIVE DISTRIBUTED LAG MODELS

An important extension of pure VAR models is given by the family of Autoregressive Distributed Lag (ARDL) models. The ARDL model is essentially the coupling of a regression model and a VAR model. The ARDL model is written as follows:

$$y_t = v + \Phi_1 y_{t-1} + \cdots + \Phi_s y_{t-s} + P_0 x_t + \cdots + P_q x_{t-q} + \eta_t$$

$$x_t = A_1 x_{t-1} + \cdots + A_p x_{t-p} + \varepsilon_t$$

In the ARDL model, a variable y_t is regressed over its own lagged values and over the values of another variable x_t which follows a VAR(p) model. Both the η_t and the ε_t terms are assumed to be white noise with a time-invariant covariance matrix.

The previous ARDL model can be rewritten as a VAR(1) model as follows:

$$
\begin{pmatrix} y_t \\ y_{t-1} \\ \vdots \\ y_{t-s+2} \\ y_{t-s+1} \\ x_t \\ \vdots \\ \vdots \\ \vdots \\ x_{t-p} \end{pmatrix}
=
\begin{pmatrix} v \\ 0 \\ \vdots \\ 0 \\ 0 \\ 0 \\ 0 \\ \vdots \\ \vdots \\ 0 \end{pmatrix}
\begin{pmatrix}
\Phi_1 & \Phi_2 & \cdots & \Phi_{s-1} & \Phi_s & P_0 & P_1 & \cdots & P_q & \cdots & 0 & 0 \\
I & 0 & \cdots & 0 & 0 & 0 & 0 & \cdots & 0 & \cdots & 0 & 0 \\
\vdots & \vdots & \ddots & \vdots & \vdots & \vdots & \vdots & \vdots & \ddots & \vdots & \vdots & \vdots \\
0 & 0 & \cdots & I & 0 & 0 & 0 & \cdots & 0 & \cdots & 0 & 0 \\
0 & 0 & \cdots & & I & 0 & 0 & \cdots & 0 & \cdots & 0 & 0 \\
0 & 0 & \cdots & 0 & 0 & 0 & A_1 & \cdots & A_q & \cdots & A_{p-1} & A_p \\
0 & 0 & \cdots & 0 & 0 & 0 & I & \cdots & 0 & \cdots & 0 & 0 \\
\vdots & \vdots & \ddots & \vdots & \vdots & \vdots & \vdots & \vdots & \ddots & \vdots & \vdots & \vdots \\
0 & 0 & \cdots & 0 & 0 & 0 & 0 & \cdots & 0 & \cdots & 0 & 0 \\
0 & 0 & \cdots & 0 & 0 & 0 & 0 & \cdots & 0 & \cdots & I & 0
\end{pmatrix}
\begin{pmatrix} y_{t-1} \\ y_{t-2} \\ \vdots \\ y_{t-s+1} \\ y_{t-s} \\ x_t \\ x_{t-1} \\ \vdots \\ x_{t-q} \\ \vdots \\ x_{t-p} \\ x_{t-p-1} \end{pmatrix}
+
\begin{pmatrix} \eta_t \\ 0 \\ \vdots \\ 0 \\ 0 \\ \varepsilon_t \\ 0 \\ \vdots \\ 0 \end{pmatrix}
$$

The estimation of the ARDL model can therefore be done with the methods used for VAR models. Coefficients can be estimated with OLS methods and the number of lags can be determined with the AIC or BIC criteria discussed in a previous section.

The ARDL model is quite important in financial econometrics: many models of stock returns are essentially ARDL models. In particular, all models where stock returns are regressed over a number of state variables that follow a VAR model are ARDL models. We now proceed to discuss some applications of VAR processes.

ESTIMATION OF NONSTATIONARY VAR MODELS

In the previous sections we assumed that all processes were stationary and all models stable. In this section we drop this restriction and examine the estimation of nonstationary and nonstable processes. In a nonstationary process, the averages, variances, and covariances vary with time. A somewhat surprising fact is that least-squares methods can be applied to the nonstationary case although other methods are more efficient.

Consider the following VAR process:

$$\mathbf{x}_t = \mathbf{A}_1 \mathbf{x}_{t-1} + \mathbf{A}_2 \mathbf{x}_{t-2} + \cdots + \mathbf{A}_p \mathbf{x}_{t-p} + \mathbf{v} + \boldsymbol{\varepsilon}_t$$
$$\left(\mathbf{I} - \mathbf{A}_1 L - \mathbf{A}_2 L^2 - \cdots - \mathbf{A}_p L^p \right) \mathbf{x}_t = \mathbf{v} + \boldsymbol{\varepsilon}_t$$

Recall that a VAR process can be rewritten in the following error correction form:

$$\Delta \mathbf{x}_t = \mathbf{D}_1 \Delta \mathbf{x}_{t-1} + \mathbf{D}_1 \Delta \mathbf{x}_{t-2} + \cdots - \Pi \mathbf{x}_{t-p} + \mathbf{v} + \boldsymbol{\varepsilon}_t$$
$$\mathbf{D}_i = -\mathbf{I} + \sum_{q=1}^{i} \mathbf{A}_i, \ i = 1, 2, \ldots, p-1, \ \Pi = \mathbf{I} - \mathbf{A}_1 - \mathbf{A}_2 - \cdots - \mathbf{A}_p$$

In fact, we can write

$$\mathbf{x}_t - \mathbf{x}_{t-1} = \left(\mathbf{A}_1 - \mathbf{I} \right) \mathbf{x}_{t-1} + \mathbf{A}_2 \mathbf{x}_{t-2} + \cdots + \mathbf{A}_p \mathbf{x}_{t-p} + \mathbf{v} + \boldsymbol{\varepsilon}_t$$
$$\Delta \mathbf{x}_t = \left(\mathbf{A}_1 - \mathbf{I} \right) \Delta \mathbf{x}_{t-1} + \left(\mathbf{A}_2 + \mathbf{A}_1 - \mathbf{I} \right) \mathbf{x}_{t-2} + \cdots + \mathbf{A}_p \mathbf{x}_{t-p} + \mathbf{v} + \boldsymbol{\varepsilon}_t$$
$$\Delta \mathbf{x}_t = \left(\mathbf{A}_1 - \mathbf{I} \right) \Delta \mathbf{x}_{t-1} + \left(\mathbf{A}_2 + \mathbf{A}_1 - \mathbf{I} \right) \Delta \mathbf{x}_{t-2} + \cdots$$
$$- \left(\mathbf{I} - \mathbf{A}_1 - \mathbf{A}_2 - \cdots - \mathbf{A}_p \right) \mathbf{x}_{t-p} + \mathbf{v} + \boldsymbol{\varepsilon}_t$$

Alternatively, a VAR process can be rewritten in the following error correction (ECM) form:

$$\Delta \mathbf{x}_t = -\Pi \mathbf{x}_{t-1} + \mathbf{F}_1 \Delta \mathbf{x}_{t-1} + \mathbf{F}_2 \Delta \mathbf{x}_{t-2} + \cdots + \mathbf{F}_{p-1} \Delta \mathbf{x}_{t-p+1} + \mathbf{v} + \boldsymbol{\varepsilon}_t$$
$$\mathbf{F}_i = -\sum_{q=i+1}^{p} \mathbf{A}_i, \ \Pi = \mathbf{I} - \mathbf{A}_1 - \mathbf{A}_2 - \cdots - \mathbf{A}_p$$

The two formulations are equivalent for our purposes as the error correction term Π is the same. The error correction term Π could also be placed in any other intermediate position.

The integration and cointegration properties of the VAR model depend on the rank r of the matrix Π. If $r = 0$, then the VAR model does not exhibit any cointegration relationship and it can be estimated as a stable process in first differences. In this case, the process in first differences can be estimated with LS or MLE techniques for estimation of stable VAR processes as discussed in the previous sections.

If $r = N$, that is, if the matrix Π is of full rank, then the VAR model itself is stable and can be estimated as a stable process. If the rank r is intermediate $0 < r < N$, then the VAR process exhibits cointegration. In this case, we can write the matrix Π as the product $\Pi = HC'$ where both H and C are $n \times r$ matrices of rank r. The r columns of the matrix C are the cointegrating vectors of the process.

We next discuss different estimation methods for nonstationary but cointegrated VAR models, starting with the LS estimation method.

Estimation of a Cointegrated VAR with Unrestricted LS Methods

In this section on estimation of nonstationary VAR processes, we assume for simplicity $v = 0$, that is, we write a VAR process as follows:

$$\mathbf{x}_t = \mathbf{A}_1 \mathbf{x}_{t-1} + \mathbf{A}_2 \mathbf{x}_{t-2} + \cdots + \mathbf{A}_p \mathbf{x}_{t-p} + \boldsymbol{\varepsilon}_t$$

The cointegration condition places a restriction on the model. In fact, if we assume that the model has r cointegrating relationships, we have to impose the restriction rank(Π) = r, where $\Pi = I - A_1 - A_2 - L - A_p$. This restriction precludes the use of standard LS methods. However, Sims, Stock, and Watson[12] and Park and Phillips[13] demonstrated that, if we estimate the preceding model as an unconstrained VAR model, the estimators thus obtained are consistent and have the same asymptotic properties as the ML estimators that are discussed in the next section.

This last conclusion might look confusing because we say that we cannot apply LS methods due to constraints—and then apparently make a contradictory statement. To clarify the question, consider the following. We assume that the empirical data are generated by a VAR model with constraints. If we want to estimate that VAR model on a finite sample *enforcing constraints*, then we cannot apply standard LS methods. However, there is no impediment, per se, to applying unconstrained LS methods to the same data. Sims, Stock, and Watson and Park and Phillips demonstrated that, if we proceed in this way, we generate consistent estimators that respect constraints asymptotically. The model constraints will not be respected, in

---

[12]Christopher A. Sims, James H. Stock, and Mark W. Watson. 1990. "Inference in Linear Time Series Models with Some Unit Roots," *Econometrica*, 58, no. 1, pp. 161–182.

[13]Joon Y. Park and Peter C. B. Phillips, "Statistical Inference in Regressions with Integrated Processes. Part 2," *Econometric Theory*, 5 (1989), pp. 95–131.

general, on any finite sample. Intuitively, it is clear that an unconstrained estimating process, if consistent, should yield estimators that asymptotically respect the constraints. However, the demonstration is far from being obvious as one has to demonstrate that the LS procedures can be applied consistently.

To write down the estimators, we define, as in the case of stable VAR, the following notation:

$$\mathbf{X} = \left(\mathbf{x}_1, \ldots, \mathbf{x}_T \right)$$
$$\mathbf{A} = \left(\mathbf{A}_1, \ldots, \mathbf{A}_p \right)$$
$$\mathbf{Z} = \begin{pmatrix} \mathbf{x}_0 & \cdots & \mathbf{x}_{T-1} \\ \vdots & \ddots & \vdots \\ \mathbf{x}_{1-p} & \cdots & \mathbf{x}_{T-p} \end{pmatrix}$$

Using this notation, we can write the estimators of the cointegrated VAR model as the usual LS estimator of VAR models as discussed in the previous sections, that is, we can write

$$\hat{\mathbf{A}} = \mathbf{X}\mathbf{Z}' \left(\mathbf{Z}\mathbf{Z}' \right)^{-1}$$

It has also to be demonstrated that this estimator has the same asymptotic properties of the ML estimators that we are now going to discuss.

ML Estimators

The ML estimation procedure has become the state-of-the-art estimation method for systems of relatively small dimensions, where it outperforms other methods. The ML estimation methodology was developed primarily by Søren Johansen,[14] hence it is often referred to as the Johansen method. We will assume, following Johansen, that innovations are independent and identically distributed multivariate, correlated, Gaussian variables. The methodology can be extended to nonnormal distributions for innovations but computations become more complex and depend on the distribution. We will use the ECM formulation of the VAR model, that is, we will write our cointegrated VAR as follows:

$$\Delta\mathbf{x}_t = -\mathbf{\Pi}\mathbf{x}_{t-1} + \mathbf{F}_1\Delta\mathbf{x}_{t-1} + \mathbf{F}_2\Delta\mathbf{x}_{t-2} + \cdots + \mathbf{F}_{p-1}\Delta\mathbf{x}_{t-p+1} + \mathbf{\epsilon}_t$$

[14]Soren Johansen "Estimation and Hypothesis Testing of Cointegration Vectors in Gaussian Vector Autoregressive Models," *Econometrica*, 59 (1991), pp. 1551–1581.

We will first describe the ML estimation process for cointegrated processes as introduced by Banerjee and Hendry.[15] We will then make the connection with original *reduced rank regression* method of Johansen.

The method of Banerjee and Hendry is based on the idea of *concentrated likelihood*. Concentrated likelihood is a mathematical technique through which the original likelihood function (LF) is transformed into a function of a smaller number of variables, called the *concentrated likelihood function* (CLF). The CLF is better known in statistics as the *profile likelihood*. To see how CLF works, suppose that the LF is a function of two separate sets of parameters:

$$L = L\left(\vartheta_1, \vartheta_2\right)$$

In this case, the MLE principle can be established as follows:

$$\max_{\vartheta_1,\vartheta_2} L\left(\vartheta_1,\vartheta_2\right) = \max_{\vartheta_1}\left(\max_{\vartheta_2} L\left(\vartheta_1,\vartheta_2\right)\right) = \max_{\vartheta_1}\left(L^C\left(\vartheta_1\right)\right)$$

where $L^C(\vartheta_1)$ is the CLF which is a function of the parameters ϑ_1 only.

To see how this result can be achieved, recall from Chapter 2 that, assuming usual regularity conditions, the maximum of the LF is attained where the derivatives of the log-likelihood function l vanish. In particular:

$$\frac{\partial l\left(\vartheta_1,\vartheta_2\right)}{\partial \vartheta_2} = 0$$

If we can solve this system of functional equations, we obtain: $\vartheta_2 = \vartheta_2(\vartheta_1)$. The equivariance property of the ML estimators[16] now allows us to conclude that the following relationship must hold between the two sets of estimated parameters:

$$\hat{\vartheta}_2 = \vartheta_2\left(\hat{\vartheta}_1\right)$$

We see that the original likelihood function has been *concentrated* in a function of a smaller set of parameters. We now apply this idea to the ML estimation of cointegrated systems. It is convenient to introduce a notation

[15]Anindya Banerjee and David F. Hendry, "Testing Integration and Cointegration: An Overview," *Oxford Bulletin of Economics and Statistics*, 54 (1992), pp. 225–255.
[16]Recall that the equivariance property of ML estimators says that if parameter *a* is a function of parameter *b* then the ML estimator of *a* is the same function of the ML estimator of *b*.

which parallels that already introduced but is adapted to the special form of the cointegrated VAR model that we are going to use:

$$\Delta \mathbf{x}_t = -\mathbf{\Pi} \mathbf{x}_{t-1} + \mathbf{F}_1 \Delta \mathbf{x}_{t-1} + \mathbf{F}_2 \Delta \mathbf{x}_{t-2} + \cdots + \mathbf{F}_{p-1} \Delta \mathbf{x}_{t-p+1} + \mathbf{\varepsilon}_t$$

We define

$$\mathbf{X} = \left(\mathbf{x}_0, \ldots, \mathbf{x}_{T-1} \right)$$

$$\Delta \mathbf{x}_t = \begin{pmatrix} \Delta x_{1,t} \\ \vdots \\ \Delta x_{N,t} \end{pmatrix}$$

$$\Delta \mathbf{X} = \left(\Delta \mathbf{x}_1, \ldots, \Delta \mathbf{x}_T \right) = \begin{pmatrix} \Delta x_{1,1} & \cdots & \Delta x_{1,T} \\ \vdots & \ddots & \vdots \\ \Delta x_{N,1} & \cdots & \Delta x_{N,T} \end{pmatrix}$$

$$\Delta \mathbf{Z}_t = \begin{pmatrix} \Delta \mathbf{x}_t \\ \vdots \\ \Delta \mathbf{x}_{t-p+2} \end{pmatrix}$$

$$\Delta \mathbf{Z} = \begin{pmatrix} \Delta \mathbf{x}_0 & \cdots & \Delta \mathbf{x}_{T-1} \\ \vdots & \ddots & \vdots \\ \Delta \mathbf{x}_{-p+2} & \cdots & \Delta \mathbf{x}_{T-p+1} \end{pmatrix} = \begin{pmatrix} \Delta x_{1,0} & \cdots & \Delta x_{1,T-1} \\ \vdots & \ddots & \vdots \\ \Delta x_{N,0} & \cdots & \Delta x_{N,T-1} \\ \vdots & \ddots & \vdots \\ \Delta x_{1,-p+2} & \cdots & \Delta x_{1,T} \\ \vdots & \ddots & \vdots \\ \Delta x_{N,-p+2} & \cdots & \Delta x_{N,T} \end{pmatrix}$$

$$\mathbf{F} = \left(\mathbf{F}_1, \mathbf{F}_2, \ldots, \mathbf{F}_{p-1} \right)$$

Using the matrix notation, as we assume $\mathbf{\Pi} = \mathbf{HC}$, we can compactly write our model in the following form:

$$\Delta \mathbf{X} = \mathbf{F} \Delta \mathbf{Z} - \mathbf{HCX} + \mathbf{U}$$

Reasoning as we did in the case of stable VAR models, we can write the log-likelihood function as follows:

$$
\begin{aligned}
\log(l) &= -\frac{NT}{2}\log(2\pi) - \frac{T}{2}\log|\Sigma_u| - \frac{1}{2}\sum_{t=1}^{T}\varepsilon_t'\Sigma^{-1}\varepsilon_t \\
&= -\frac{NT}{2}\log(2\pi) - \frac{T}{2}\log|\Sigma_u| - \frac{1}{2}\mathrm{trace}\left(U'\Sigma_u^{-1}U\right) \\
&= -\frac{NT}{2}\log(2\pi) - \frac{T}{2}\log|\Sigma_u| - \frac{1}{2}\mathrm{trace}\left(\Sigma_u^{-1}UU'\right) \\
&= -\frac{NT}{2}\log(2\pi) - \frac{T}{2}\log|\Sigma_u| \\
&\quad - \frac{1}{2}\mathrm{trace}\left(\left(\Delta X - FZ + HCX\right)'\Sigma_u^{-1}\left(\Delta X - FZ + HCX\right)\right)
\end{aligned}
$$

We now concentrate this log-likelihood function, eliminating Σ and F. As explained previously, this entails taking partial derivatives, equating them to zero, and expressing Σ and F in terms of the other parameters. By equating to zero the derivatives with respect to Σ, it can be demonstrated that $\Sigma_C = T^{-1}UU'$. Substituting this expression in the log-likelihood, we obtain the concentrated likelihood after removing Σ:

$$
\begin{aligned}
l^{CI} &= K - \frac{T}{2}\log|UU'| \\
&= K - \frac{T}{2}\log\left|\left(\Delta X - FZ + HCX\right)\left(\Delta X - FZ + HCX\right)'\right|
\end{aligned}
$$

where K is a constant that includes all the constant terms left after concentrating.

We next eliminate the F terms. This result can be achieved taking derivatives of l with respect to F, equating them to zero and evaluating them at Σ_C. Performing all the calculations, it can be demonstrated that the evaluation at Σ_C is irrelevant and that the following formula holds:

$$
F_C = \left(\Delta X + HCX\right)\Delta Z'\left(\Delta Z\Delta Z'\right)^{-1}
$$

Substituting this expression in the formula for l^{CI}, that is, the log-likelihood after eliminating Σ_C, we obtain:

$$
l^{CII} = K - \frac{T}{2}\log\left|
\begin{array}{l}
\left(\Delta X - \left((\Delta X + HCX)\Delta Z'(\Delta Z\Delta Z')^{-1}\right)\Delta Z + HCX\right) \\
\left(\Delta X - (\Delta X + HCX)\Delta Z'(\Delta Z\Delta Z')^{-1}\Delta Z + HCX\right)'
\end{array}
\right|
$$

$$= K - \frac{T}{2} \log \frac{\left| \left(\Delta X + HCX - ((\Delta X + HCX)\Delta Z'(\Delta Z \Delta Z')^{-1})\Delta Z \right) \right|}{\left(\Delta X + HCX - (\Delta X + HCX)\Delta Z'(\Delta Z \Delta Z')^{-1} \Delta Z \right)'}$$

$$= K - \frac{T}{2} \log \frac{\left| \left((\Delta X + HCX)\left(I_T - \Delta Z'(\Delta Z \Delta Z')^{-1} \Delta Z \right) \right) \right|}{\left((\Delta X + HCX)\left(I_T - \Delta Z'(\Delta Z \Delta Z')^{-1} \Delta Z \right) \right)'}$$

$$= K - \frac{T}{2} \log \left| (\Delta X + HCX)M(\Delta X + HCX)' \right|$$

$$= K - \frac{T}{2} \log \left| \Delta X M \Delta X' + HCXM \Delta X' + \Delta X M (HCX)' + HCXM(HCX)' \right|$$

where $M = I_T - \Delta Z'(\Delta Z \Delta Z')^{-1} \Delta Z$. Matrices of the form $A = I - B'(BB')^{-1}B$ are called projection matrices. They are idempotent and symmetric, that is $A = A'$ and $AA = A^2 = A$. The latter properties were used in the last three steps of the above derivations.

We will rewrite the CLF as follows. Define $R_0 = \Delta XM$, $R_1 = XM$ and

$$S_{ij} = \frac{R_i R_j}{T}, \quad i, j = 1, 2$$

We can then rewrite the CLF as follows:

$$l^{CII}(HC) = K - \frac{T}{2} \log \left| S_{00} - S_{10}HC - S_{01}(HC)' + HCS_{11}(HC)' \right|$$

The original analysis of Johansen obtained the same result applying the method of *reduced rank regression*. Reduced rank regressions are multiple regressions where the coefficient matrix is subject to constraints. The Johansen method eliminates the terms F by regressing Δx_t and x_{t-1} on $(\Delta x_{t-1}, \Delta x_{t-2}, ..., \Delta x_{t-p+1})$ to obtain the following residuals:

$$R_{0t} = \Delta x_t - D_1 \Delta x_{t-1} + D_2 \Delta x_{t-2} + \cdots + D_{p-1} \Delta x_{t-p+1}$$
$$R_{1t} = x_{t-1} - E_1 \Delta x_{t-1} + E_2 \Delta x_{t-2} + \cdots + E_{p-1} \Delta x_{t-p+1}$$

where

$$D = (D_1, D_2, ..., D_{p-1}) = \Delta X \Delta Z'(\Delta Z \Delta Z')^{-1}$$

and

$$E = (E_1, E_2, ..., E_{p-1}) = X \Delta Z'(\Delta Z \Delta Z')^{-1}$$

The original model is therefore reduced to the following simpler model:

$$\mathbf{R}_{0t} = \mathbf{HCR}_{1t} + \mathbf{u}_t$$

The likelihood function of this model depends only on $\mathbf{R}_{0t}$, $\mathbf{R}_{1t}$. It can be written as follows:

$$l(\mathbf{HC}) = K_1 - \frac{T}{2}\log\left|(\mathbf{R}_0 + \mathbf{R}_1(\mathbf{HC}))'(\mathbf{R}_0 + \mathbf{R}_1(\mathbf{HC}))\right|$$

where we define $\mathbf{R}_0$, $\mathbf{R}_1$ as previously. If we also define S_{ij} as previously, we obtain exactly the same form for the CLF:

$$l^{\text{CII}}(\mathbf{HC}) = K - \frac{T}{2}\log\left|\mathbf{S}_{00} - \mathbf{S}_{10}\mathbf{HC} - \mathbf{S}_{01}(\mathbf{HC})' + \mathbf{HCS}_{11}(\mathbf{HC})'\right|$$

We have now to find the maximum of this CLF. Note that this problem is not well identified because, given any solution $\mathbf{H}$, $\mathbf{C}$, and any nonsingular matrix $\mathbf{G}$, the following relationships hold:

$$\mathbf{\Pi} = \mathbf{HC} = \mathbf{HGG}^{-1}\mathbf{C} = \mathbf{H}^*\mathbf{C}^*$$

so that the matrices

$$\mathbf{H}^* = \mathbf{HG}$$
$$\mathbf{C}^* = \mathbf{G}^{-1}\mathbf{C}$$

are also a solution. Additional conditions must therefore be imposed.

If the matrix $\mathbf{\Pi} = \mathbf{HC}$ were unrestricted, then maximization would yield

$$\mathbf{\Pi} = \mathbf{S}_{01}\mathbf{S}_{11}^{-1}$$

However, our problem now is to find solutions that respect the cointegration condition, that is, the rank r of $\mathbf{\Pi}$ which is the common rank of $\mathbf{H}$, $\mathbf{C}$. To achieve this goal, we can concentrate the CLF with respect to $\mathbf{H}$ and thus solve with respect to $\mathbf{C}$. By performing the rather lengthy computations, it can be demonstrated that we obtain a solution by solving the following eigenvalue problem:

$$\left|\mathbf{S}_{10}\mathbf{S}_{00}^{-1}\mathbf{S}_{01} - \lambda\mathbf{S}_{11}\right| = 0$$

This eigenvalue problem, together with normalizing conditions, will yield N eigenvalues λ_i and N eigenvectors Λ_i. In order to make this problem well determined, Johansen imposed the normalizing conditions: $\Lambda' S_{11} \Lambda = I$. Order the eigenvalues and choose the r eigenvectors Λ_i corresponding to the largest r eigenvalues. It can be demonstrated that a ML estimator of the matrix C is given by

$$\hat{C} = \left(\Lambda_1, \dots, \Lambda_r \right)$$

and an estimator of the matrix H by $\hat{H} = S_{00} \hat{C}$. The maximum of the log-likelihood is

$$l_{max} = K - \frac{T}{2} \log |S_{00}| - \frac{T}{2} \sum_{i=1}^{r} \log(1 - \lambda_i)$$

The solutions of the preceding eigenvalue problem, that is, the eigenvalues λ_i, can be interpreted as the canonical correlations between Δx_t and x_{t-1}. *Canonical correlations* can be interpreted as the maximum correlations between linear combinations of the Δx_t and x_{t-1}. We therefore see that the cointegrating relationships are those linear combinations of the levels x_{t-1} that are maximally correlated with linear combinations of the Δx_t after conditioning with the remaining terms.

Different types of normalizing conditions have been studied and are described in the literature. A general theory of long-run modeling that considers general nonlinear constraints on the matrix C was developed by Pesaran and Shin.[17] This theory goes beyond the scope of this book.

Estimating the Number of Cointegrating Relationships

The Johansen ML estimation method and its extensions critically depend on correctly estimating the number r of cointegrating relationships. Two tests, in particular, have been suggested in relationship with the Johansen method: the trace test and the maximum eigenvalue test. The *trace test* tests the hypothesis that there are at most r cointegrating vectors while the *maximum eigenvalue test* tests the hypothesis that there are $r + 1$ cointegrating vectors against the hypothesis that there are r cointegrating vectors. The mathematical details are given in the Johansen paper discussed earlier.

---

[17]M. Hashem Pesaran and Yongcheol Shin, "Long-Run Structural Modelling," Chapter 11 in S. Strom (ed.), *Econometrics and Economic Theory in the 20th Century: The Ragnar Frisch Centennial Symposium* (Cambridge, Cambridge University Press, 2001).

Lütkepohl, Saikkonen, and Trenkler[18] provide an extensive discussion of the relative merit and power of the various forms of these tests. Here we provide only a quick overview of these tests which are implemented in many standard statistical packages.

The trace test is immediately suggested by the Johansen procedure. Recall from the discussion earlier in this chapter that with the Johansen method the maximum of the log-likelihood function is

$$l_{\max} = K - \frac{T}{2}\log\left|S_{00}\right| - \frac{T}{2}\sum_{i=1}^{r}\log(1-\lambda_i)$$

The likelihood ratio test statistics for the hypothesis of at most r cointegrating vectors is

$$\lambda_{trace} = -T\sum_{i=r+1}^{r}\log(1-\lambda_i)$$

where the sum is extended to the $n - r$ smallest eigenvalues. The asymptotic distribution of this statistic is not normal. It is given by the trace of a stochastic matrix formed with functionals of a Brownian motion. Its critical values at different confidence levels have been tabulated and are used in most packages.

The likelihood ratio statistics for the maximum eigenvalue test is the following:

$$\lambda_{\max} = -T\log(1-\lambda_{r+1})$$

As for the previous test, the asymptotic distribution of this test's statistics is not normal. It is given by the maximum eigenvalue of a stochastic matrix formed with functionals of a Brownian motion. Critical values at different confidence levels have been tabulated and are used in many standard statistical packages.

MI Estimators in the Presence of Linear Trends

The previous discussion assumed a zero intercept in the model and therefore no linear trends or nonzero intercepts in the process. If we add an intercept to a VAR model, we might obtain a linear trend in the variables. With cointegrated systems there is the additional complication that a linear

---

[18]Helmut Lütkepohl, Pentti Saikkonen, and Carsten Trenkler, "Maximum Eigenvalue Versus Trace Tests for the Cointegrating Rank of a VAR Process," *Econometrics Journal*, 4 (2001), pp. 287–310.

trend might or might not be present in the cointegrated variables. In other words, the cointegrating vectors transform the I(1) variables into stationary variables or into trend-stationary variables.

The original definition of cointegration in Engle and Granger[19] excluded deterministic trends in the cointegrated variables. Now we distinguish between stochastic cointegration and deterministic cointegration. A set of I(1) variables is said to be stochastically cointegrated if there are linear combinations of these variables that are trend-stationary (i.e., stationary plus a deterministic trend). A set of I(1) variables are said to be deterministically cointegrated if there exist linear combinations which are stationary without any deterministic trend.

Therefore, when considering deterministic terms in a cointegrated VAR model, we cannot consider only constant intercepts but must include linear trends. Adding a constant term and a linear trend to the model variables as we did in the stable case, the estimation procedure described in the previous section remains valid.

ESTIMATION WITH CANONICAL CORRELATIONS

The use of canonical correlation analysis (CCA) was first proposed by Bossaerts[20] in 1988. In 1995, Bewley and Yang[21] provided a more rigorous foundation for CCA-based methodology which they called *level canonical correlation analysis* (LCCA) because the canonical correlations are computed in levels. Cointegration tests based on CCA are based on the idea that canonical correlations should discriminate those linear combinations of variables that are I(1) from those that are I(0). In fact, integrated variables should be more predictable while stationary components should be less predictable.

Bossarts proposed performing CCA and the use of the standard Dickey-Fuller (DF) test to discriminate those canonical variates that are I(1). He considers a model of the type:

$$\Delta x_t = HCx_t + \varepsilon_t$$

[19]Robert F. Engle and Clive W. J. Granger, "Cointegration and Error Correction: Representation, Estimation, and Testing," *Econometrica*, 55 (1987), pp. 251–276.
[20]Peter Bossaerts, "Common Non-Stationary Components of Asset Prices," *Journal of Economic Dynamics and Control*, 12 (1988), pp. 348–364.
[21]Ronald Bewley and Minxian Yang, "Tests for Cointegration Based on Canonical Correlation Analysis," *Journal of the American Statistical Association*, 90 (1995), pp. 990–996.

After performing the CCA between Δx_t and x_t, the canonical variates are tested for unit roots. Bossaerts conjectured, without proof, that one can use the standard critical values of the DF test.

Bewley and Yang extended the methodology, allowing for deterministic trends and other variables explaining short-run dynamics. They proposed new tests, developed the asymptotic theory, and computed the critical values to determine the number of cointegrating vectors.

Computationally, the LCCA methodology of Bewley and Yang is not very far from that of Johansen. Following Bewley and Yang, the LCCA method proceeds as follows. First, if there are additional variables, they have to be removed performing the regressions of x_t and x_{t-1} on those variables. Call R_{0t}, R_{1t} the residuals of these regressions and form the regression:

$$R_{0t} = BR_{1t} + u_t$$

We have now to determine the canonical correlations between R_{0t} and R_{1t}. This is done formally with the same equation as in the Johansen method, that is, solving the following eigenvalue problem (see Appendix B):

$$\left| S_{10}S_{00}^{-1}S_{01} - \lambda S_{11} \right| = 0$$

where

$$S_{ij} = \frac{R_i R_j}{T}, \quad i,j = 1,2$$

as in the Johansen method. However, the interpretation of these quantities is different: Here we are seeking canonical correlations between variables in levels while in the Johansen methods we correlate both levels and differences. The LCCA method picks the largest eigenvalues as does the Johansen method. Bewley and Yang developed the asymptotic theory as well as four tests for cointegration, two DF-type tests, a trace test, and a maximum eigenvalue test. For each test they determined and tabulated critical values for up to six variables. The tabulated critical values are included in their paper.

The asymptotic theory developed by Bewley and Yang showed that one can indeed use the standard unit root tests such as the Dickey-Fuller and Phillips tests, but the critical values depend on the number of variables and are not standard. Therefore, one cannot use the DF test with standard critical values, as conjectured by Bossaerts.

ESTIMATION WITH PRINCIPAL COMPONENT ANALYSIS

Thus far we have discussed methodologies based on OLS, ML, and CCA. In this section we analyze another important method based on *Principal Component Analysis* (PCA). PCA is a well known statistical methodology that, given a set of multidimensional data, finds the directions of maximum variance. PCA-based methods are used in classical factor analysis of stationary returns.

The use of PCA-based methods for integrated variables was first proposed by Stock and Watson.[22] They were the first to observe that the presence of r cointegrating vectors in n time series implies the presence of r common stochastic trends. This means that there are r independent linear combinations of the variables that are I(1) while the remaining n-r are I(0). In addition, it means that each of the n variables can be expressed as a linear combination of the common stochastic trends plus a stationary process.

Stock and Watson conjectured that those linear combinations that are I(1) must have the largest variance. Therefore, by performing a PCA on the variables in levels, one should be able to determine the cointegrating vectors by picking the largest eigenvalues. The Stock-Watson methodology proceeds as follows.

Suppose the DGP is our usual VAR(p) model:

$$\mathbf{x}_t = \mathbf{A}_1\mathbf{x}_{t-1} + \mathbf{A}_2\mathbf{x}_{t-2} + \cdots + \mathbf{A}_p\mathbf{x}_{t-p} + \boldsymbol{\varepsilon}_t$$

where we assume for the moment that the intercept term is zero. Suppose also that the number of lags p have been determined independently. Next, perform the PCA of the variables $\mathbf{x}_t$. This entails solving the following eigenvalue problem:

$$\Omega\boldsymbol{\beta} = \mu\boldsymbol{\beta}$$

where Ω is the empirical covariance matrix of the $\mathbf{x}_t$, defined as

$$\Omega = \sum_{t=1}^{T}\mathbf{x}_t\mathbf{x}_t'$$

and μ and $\boldsymbol{\beta}$ are respectively the eigenvalues and the eigenvectors to be determined.

Order the eigenvalues and choose the m largest eigenvalues μ_i, $i = 1, ...,$ m. The corresponding eigenvectors $\boldsymbol{\beta}_i$ are the candidate cointegrating vec-

---

[22]James H. Stock and Mark W. Watson, "Testing for Common Trends," *Journal of the American Statistical Association*, 83 (1988), pp. 1097–1107.

tors. Forming the linear combinations $P_{i,t} = \beta_i \mathbf{x}_t$, we obtain the vector $\mathbf{P}_t = (P_{1,t}, \ldots, P_{m,t})'$ first m principal components. We must now check the hypothesis that these principal components are $I(1)$ series and are not cointegrated among themselves.

In order to do this, the Stock and Watson method estimates the following stable VAR(p) model:

$$\Delta \mathbf{P}_t = \mathbf{A}_1 \Delta \mathbf{P}_{t-1} + \cdots + \mathbf{A}_{p-1} \Delta \mathbf{P}_{t-p+1} + \boldsymbol{\varepsilon}_t$$

and then computes

$$\hat{\mathbf{F}}_t = \mathbf{P}_t - \hat{\mathbf{A}}_1 \Delta \mathbf{P}_{t-1} - \cdots - \hat{\mathbf{A}}_{p-1} \Delta \mathbf{P}_{t-p+1}$$

Regress $\Delta \mathbf{F}_t$ on $\mathbf{F}_{t-1}$, compute the normalized eigenvalues of the regression matrix $\mathbf{B}$, and compare with the critical values tabulated in the Stock and Watson paper to test the null of m common trends against $m-q$ common trends.

If the VAR model exhibits a nonzero intercept, then there might be linear trends in the variables. This fact, in turn, raises the question of stochastic versus deterministic cointegration. The details of the computations are actually quite intricate.[23]

A major advantage of the PCA-based methodologies is that critical values depend only on the number of common trends and not on the number of time series involved. Therefore, they can be used to determine a small number of common trends in a large number of time series. This is a significant advantage in financial econometrics; we will come back to this in the section on dynamic factors later.

ESTIMATION WITH THE EIGENVALUES OF THE COMPANION MATRIX

A process is called *integrated of order one* if it can be written as: $x_t = \rho x_{t-1} + \eta_t$, where $\rho = 1$, and η_t is a stationary process. Dickey and Fuller established the asymptotic distribution of ρ and tabulated the critical values that now form the basis of the DF and ADF unit root test. Ahlgren and Nyblom[24] developed an equivalent methodology for multivariate processes. They studied a N-variate, VAR(1) process of the form:

[23]The interested reader should consult the original Stock and Watson paper.
[24]Niklas Ahlgren and Jukka Nyblom, "A General Test for the Cointegrating Rank in Vector Autoregressive Models," Working Paper No. 499, 2003, Swedish School of Economics and Business Administration.

$$\mathbf{x}_t = \mathbf{\Pi}\mathbf{x}_{t-1} + \mathbf{\varepsilon}_t$$

The major result of their work is that the number of cointegrating relationships depends on the eigenvalues of the autoregressive matrix. Ahlgren and Nyblom determined the asymptotic distribution of the eigenvalues of the autoregressive matrix estimated with OLS methods and computed critical values. The methodology can be extended to VAR models of any order by transforming the original model into a VAR(1) model and considering the companion matrix.

NONLINEAR MODELS IN FINANCE

Nonlinear models capture nonlinear relationships between returns or other financial variables. They can be applied to cross sections of data or to sequential data. The fundamental trade-off between in-sample accuracy and out-of-sample generalization capabilities is particularly important in the case of nonlinear models. In fact, in general, nonlinear models imply estimating a larger number of parameters than equivalent linear models.

This happens because in general we do not know the precise form of the nonlinear relationship and therefore we need to apply nonlinear approximation schemes. For example, suppose we want to replace a linear regression $y = ax + b + \varepsilon$ with a nonlinear regression $y = f(x) + \varepsilon$. If we knew the precise functional form $f(x)$, then the number of parameters could be the same. For example, if we could replace our original linear regression with a regression of the type $y = ax^\alpha + b + \varepsilon$, with a known α, then we would need to estimate the two parameters a, b as in the linear case. However, in general we would need to estimate a model that contains several terms. For example, in general we would need to replace the linear regression with a regression of the type $y = a_1 x + a_2 x^2 + a_3 x^3 + \dots a_n x^n + b + \varepsilon$ where many parameters a_i need to be estimated.

In addition, there are many different forms of nonlinearity with trade-offs that do not easily translate into a larger number of parameters to estimate. Given the number and the complexity of different models here, we can only list a few classes of nonlinear models that are important in finance.

Clustering Models

Clustering models create groups that are maximally homogeneous in terms of some criterion. These models can be applied to sets of multivariate data or to time series. For example, we can cluster time series of returns in terms of the level of mutual correlation. The trade-offs associated with clustering are related to the choice of the number of clusters. Among the many financial applications of clustering we can mention the clustering of balance sheet accounts or financial ratios to identify particular corporate conditions, and the clustering of time series as preprocessing of very large data sets to permit applications of statistical methods that could not work on the entire data set.

Regime Shifting Models

Regime shifting models represent a family of nonlinear models that are based on coupling a basic linear model with another model that determines the shift between different regimes, that is, that determines the choice of parameters corresponding to different regimes. The trade-offs implicit in these models are due to the need to analyze very long time series in order to capture a number of shifts sufficient to estimate the model that drives the shifting between regimes.

Models of Irregularly Spaced Data

Another family of nonlinear models that has acquired growing importance with the diffusion of high-frequency data is *models of irregularly spaced data*. High-frequency data are often irregularly spaced because they register individual transactions. Models of the distribution of the spacings are inherently nonlinear models. They are important models for understanding the behavior of returns at very short intervals.

Nonlinear DGP Models

Nonlinear DGP models are a family of models that capture those nonlinearities that are inherent to the relationships between adjacent returns. The most widely known of these models are neural networks. Neural networks can mimic any functional form of the DGP but imply the estimation of a large number of parameters with the consequent risk of overfitting and loss of forecasting ability.

CAUSALITY

The subject of causality is vast with many implications for the philosophy of science and science itself. Here we only mention the two major approaches to causality that emerged in the period after World War II: the approach of the Cowles Commission and Granger causality. The approach of the Cowles commission, which is similar to the approach to causality proposed by Herbert Simon, emphasizes the structural properties of models. In particular, the emphasis is on the the distinction between exogenous and endogenous variables. The approach of the Cowles Commission does not include any explicit element of time dependence. In this approach, whose philosophical roots go back to Bertrand Russell, causation implies a distinction between what is determined within the system of equations and what is exogenous to the system.

The approach of Granger, in contrast, is fundamentally related to time. We say that a variable X_t causes in the sense of Granger a variable Y_{t+1} if the probability $P(Y_{t+1}|$ all information dated t and earlier) is different from the probability $P(Y_{t+1}|$ all information dated t and earlier omitting information about X_t). As we do not have access to all past information, in practice Granger causality is tested by applying tests to linear regressions. Suppose, for example, that we want to test Granger causality in a bivariate model where X, Y are regressed over lagged variables of both variables. Granger causality is tested by including lagged terms of one or the other variables in either equations and testing if the explanatory power of the regression increases or decreases.

SUMMARY

- A stochastic process is a sequence of variables indexed with time; a multivariate stochastic process is a time-dependent random vector.
- If the time parameter of a stochastic process moves in discrete increments, a stochastic process is called a time series; a multivariate time series is a sequence of random vectors.
- The Wold representation theorem states that any stationary time series can be represented as the sum of two stochastic processes: a linearly predictable process and an infinite moving average process.
- A time series is invertible if it can be represented as a possibly infinite autoregressive process.
- Time series can also be represented in the frequency domain.
- Vector autoregressive (VAR) processes are models where processes are regressed over their lagged values.
- VAR can be estimated with Ordinary Least Squares methods as regressions or with Maximum Likelihood Methods if the distributions are known.
- An integrated variable is a variable that becomes stationary after differencing; over differencing produces noninvertible processes.

- Cointegrated processes are individually integrated but admit linear combinations which are stationary.
- Cointegrated processes can be represented as Error Correction Models, which are VAR models with a correction term in levels.
- Many methods for estimating cointegrated systems have been proposed including the Johansen method based on maximum likelihood and the Stock-Watson method based on principal components analysis.
- If a vector time series exhibits cointegration then we can identify a number of common trends and all series can be represented as regressions on the trends.
- There are methods based on information theory to estimate the number of lags in a VAR model.
- In applications of VAR models to asset allocation, portfolio management, and risk management, estimated model's distributional properties are critical because the presence of tails might change optimality conditions and the entire optimization process.
- There are several tests for autocorrelation and normality that can be used to test the distributional properties of an estimated VAR model such as the Dickey-Fuller or the Augmented Dickey-Fuller tests.

CHAPTER 4

Common Pitfalls in Financial Modeling

This chapter discusses the relationship between financial engineering and finance theory. There is a sharp distinction between the two. Finance theory provides the mathematical description and the foundation for forecasting quantities such as prices, returns, and interest rates. Financial engineering, on the other hand, deals with the construction and practical usability of financial products, such as derivative contracts or investment portfolios.

Financial engineering relies on finance theory, in particular on the ability to forecast financial quantities. Certainly, engineering is less formalized than theory, but needless to say, very important in getting results in the real world. This is true in the physical sciences as well as in economics. In these fields, science is able to provide the framework to perform analysis but is often ill-equipped to perform synthesis. Centuries of scientific investigations have produced an outstanding ability to model—that is—to describe our world in mathematical terms. However, our ability to synthesize purposeful artifacts, crucial for practical application, is much more limited.

We typically use human intuition to generate new designs. Designs are then analyzed with scientific tools and refined in a trial-and-error like process. Only when we are able to formalize an optimization process is our design ability at a par with our analytical ability. In this chapter we discuss how the engineering part of the portfolio formation or product design process is approached in practice.

THEORY AND ENGINEERING

An engineer synthesizes an artifact such as an airplane or a portfolio using existing knowledge. But the solution sometimes fails. One possible cause is the failure to recognize that the solution to the problem calls for a true theoretical advance. Understanding if a theoretical advance is needed to solve a given problem is critical to successfully solving an engineering problem, be it in aeronautics or in finance.

Consider the design and construction of supersonic aircraft. Airline travelers easily recognize the Boeing 747 Jumbo jet not only because of its size but also because of its characteristic hump in the front part of the fuselage. This curious looking hump, which hosts the pilot's cockpit as well as the upper passenger deck, seems at odds with a naïve view of a sleek jet-plane body. Still this hump is the result of a major breakthrough in aerodynamics—the Whitcomb area rule, or simply the area rule, also known to aeronautic engineers as *wasp-waisted* shaping. The story of the area rule is an example of how a practical problem was solved through a combination of engineering ingenuity and scientific discovery.

First discovered by Heinrich Hertel and Otto Frenzl, who were working on a transonic wind tunnel at the German airplane manufacturer Junkers between 1943 and 1945, the discovery of the area rule was lost in the general confusion at the end of World War II. It was independently rediscovered in 1952 by Richard Whitcomb, then a young aerodynamicist working for the National Advisory Committee for Aeronautics (NACA) Langley Research Center in Hampton, Virginia.

At the end of the 1940s it was believed that the ability to operate supersonic planes would represent a major military and commercial advantage. However the first trials in developing supersonic planes were disappointing: at transonic speeds (i.e., at speeds approaching the speed of sound), conventional body design experiences an increase in aerodynamic drag. The limited thrust of jet engines then available was not sufficient to overcome this drag and the aerodynamic theory of the day could not provide the solution.

It was known that the ideal shape of an airplane's body should be smoothly curved, similar to the smooth curves of a cigar. Whitcomb made the breakthrough (re)discovery that the drag was caused by the discontinuities created by the wings and that, to reduce this drag, the discontinuity between the body and the wings had to be made as smooth as possible. Whitcomb translated this discovery into a practical rule—the area rule—that could be applied to aircraft design. First used in the design of the innovative wasp-waisted plane, the Convair F-102 Delta Dagger, the Whitcomb area rule resulted in a 25% reduction of the aerodynamic drag, thus allowing the F-102 to meet the contract specifications. The Whitcomb area rule has subsequently been applied to all aircraft operating at transonic speeds.

Another example of an engineering failure due to a failure to recognize the need for a major theoretical advance comes from the field of mechanics. Metal fatigue is a phenomenon according to which a metal piece subject to repeated stresses suddenly looses its elasticity and is subject to failure. The phenomenon of metal fatigue has been known since the beginning of the nineteenth century, but until recently a theory was lacking. This lack of basic theory lead to a number of major engineering failures, such as the crash of the train from Versailles to Paris on May 8, 1842, the sinking of the oil platform Alexander Kielland on March 27, 1980, and for the series of crashes of the first commercial jet engines, the de Havilland Comet, back in 1954. In all of these cases, the design was correct given the knowledge available at the time, however, a fundamental piece of basic theory—metal fatigue—was missing.

ENGINEERING AND THEORETICAL SCIENCE

In this section we briefly discuss the concepts of science and engineering. Modern science is based on the concept of laws of nature formulated in mathematical language and (for the most part) expressed through differential equations. A differential equation is an expression that links quantities and their rates of change. For example, given a constant rate of interest r, we compute the growth of capital C through the simple differential equation:

$$\frac{dC}{dt} = Cr$$

Given initial or boundary conditions, a differential equation allows inferring the behavior of a system in the future or in other regions of space. When probabilistic laws are involved, differential equations, or their discrete counterpart, describe the evolution of probability distributions. For example, the price of an option can be expressed as a differential equation of the probability distribution of the price.

Now, differential equations are analytic and descriptive: our laws of nature allow us to analyze and describe a given physical system such as the motion of the planets or the flight of an airplane. Discovery, however, is the result of the creative efforts of humans, today typically equipped with laboratories and tools such as computers. Science is not synthetic: it does not necessarily give us a constructive methodology for making new discoveries or for engineering artifacts.

Engineering, on the other hand, is a process of synthesis in the sense that the objective of the engineering process is to construct purposeful artifacts, such as airplanes, trains or, in finance, portfolios or derivative products. In engineering, we are given a problem formulated in terms of design specifications and we attempt to synthesize a design or an artifact that meets these specifications. In finance, for example, our starting point might be the specifications of the performance of a portfolio or the requirements of a hedging instrument.

The process of engineering is based on iterating cycles of synthesis and analysis: We start by synthesizing an overall design and then we analyze the design with analytical tools based on our scientific knowledge. Science allows us to run the analysis: In the case of the design of an airplane, using sophisticated tools, engineers can test and analyze the structural stability, flight behavior, and eventual response to abnormal stresses such as storms and lightning. Typically, the analysis will suggest necessary modifications to the initial design. The design process is then iterated until the overall design can be considered satisfactory. At the end of the process, we have a complete design.

We can think of engineering as problem-solving. Since the advent of computers, much attention has been given to the question of solving problems automatically. Herbert Simon, 1978 recipient of the Nobel Prize in Economic Sciences, was among the first advocates of the notion that human problem-solving abilities can be formalized and mimicked by a computer. Following Simon's pioneering ideas, researchers in artificial intelligence (AI) devoted considerable effort to the automation of problem-solving.

The key idea of automatic problem-solving is the following. To solve a problem we proceed iteratively: we invent an approximation solution and analyze this solution with the analytical tools of science. Analysis suggests modifications to the approximate solution. Thus we produce another, hopefully better, approximate solution and proceed through another cycle. The key idea of automatic problem-solving is to define a *distance* between any approximate solution and the true or optimal solution. At every cycle we attempt to reduce the distance from the optimal solution.

Automatic problem-solving works well when solutions can be expressed as the maximization of some goal function; that is, when the problem can be cast in an optimization framework. Today, we have a vast number of theoretical tools and computer programs that allow us to solve optimization problems. However, optimizing a goal function is a far cry from the type of creative conceptual innovation that marks the development of modern science. For example, it is difficult to imagine that major scientific discoveries such as quantum mechanics can be reduced to the problem of optimizing a goal function. We do not (yet) have any realistic constructive method for making such discoveries.

Constructive methodologies are available only when we arrive at the point where we can optimize, that is, codify our design in terms of variables and express the quality of our design in terms of a goal function defined on the design variables. Once we have arrived at that level, design can be automated. Many, but not all, financial engineering problems can be cast in terms of optimization problems. (See Chapters 8, 9, and 10.)

To summarize:

- *Science is analytic*: We have the models to analyze a given system.
- *Design is a constructive process*: We need to synthesize a design starting from general high-level specifications.
- *Constructive design is performed iteratively*: We make an approximate design and analyze it. Analysis suggests modifications which lead to a change in the design and additional analysis. We iterate until the analysis tells us that our (approximate) solution and design is satisfactory.
- *Design automation*: The process of design can be automated only when we arrive at the stage of expressing the design quality in terms of a goal function. Then we can proceed with optimization—an automatic design method.

ENGINEERING AND PRODUCT DESIGN IN FINANCE

Financial engineering can be defined loosely as an engineering process whose objective is to create financial products with specified characteristics. A financial analyst who designs a derivative-based product to meet specific client needs is engaged in financial engineering. But portfolio management is also an instance of financial engineering. In fact, a portfolio manager engineers a portfolio with desired properties such as a given risk-return profile.

Indeed most financial engineering processes, including portfolio construction and derivative-based strategies, can be cast, at least theoretically, in an optimization framework.[1] This does not mean that the entire process of formulating the ideas of complex derivative instruments, risk management products, and investment products can be automated. However, once the specifications of a financial problem are defined, the engineering side can in general be theoretically formulated as an optimization problem.

Optimization depends critically on the ability to make forecasts and to evaluate the risk of those forecasts. In any optimization model, the forecasting component must be explicit. The coupling of econometric forecasting methodologies and optimization is a delicate process insofar as errors in the forecasting process can actually be maximized by the optimization process. The difficulties in this coupling have been a blocking factor in the use of optimization for many years. However, optimization can now be used more effectively, and this is for two reasons. First, we have learned how to make forecasts more robust; that is, we know how to gauge the true amount of information carried by our forecasts. Second, we have the technology neces-

---

[1]See H. Dahl, A. Meeraus, and S. Zenios, "Some Financial Optimization Models: Part I" and "Some Financial Optimization Models: Part I," in S. Zenios (ed.). *Financial Optimization* (New York: Cambridge University Press, 1993).

sary to make the optimization process more robust to measurement errors and uncertainty in the inputs. (See Chapter 10.)

In practice, in many financial applications, we do not use optimization but heuristics or human judgment. For example, a portfolio manager might use a ranking system to screen a vast universe of stocks and then form portfolios not through formal optimization but through his own judgment.

Optimization requires a careful separation between the engineering part, that is, optimization, and the basic science, that is, the econometric model which we use to perform forecasts. In some important cases, however, the separation of engineering and econometrics are somewhat blurred. Consider, for example, reversal- or momentum-based strategies. Portfolio analysts and managers form portfolios with almost mechanical rules but the detailed econometrics behind these strategies is still not fully known.

LEARNING, THEORETICAL, AND HYBRID APPROACHES TO PORTFOLIO MANAGEMENT

Let's now discuss the basic approaches to financial modeling, namely the learning approach, the theoretical approach, and the learning-theoretical approach. The learning-theoretical approach is a hybrid of the two former frameworks.

The learning approach to financial modeling is in principle a consequence of the diffusion of low-cost high-performance computers. It is based on using a family of models that (1) include an unlimited number of parameters and (2) can approximate sample data with high precision. Neural networks are a classical example. With an unrestricted number of layers and nodes, a neural network can approximate any function with arbitrary precision. We express this fact by saying that a neural network is a *universal function approximator*.

However, practice has shown that if we represent sample data with very high precision, we typically obtain poor forecasting performance. Here is why. In general, the main features of the data can be described by a simple structural model plus unpredictable noise. As the noise is unpredictable, the goal of a model is to capture the structural components. A very precise model of sample data (in-sample) will also try to match the unpredictable noise. This phenomenon called *overfitting*, leads to poor (out-of-sample) forecasting abilities. Obviously there is no guarantee that data are truly described by a simple structural model plus noise. Data might be entirely random or might be described by a truly complex model.

To avoid overfitting, the learning approach constrains the complexity of models. This is typically done by introducing what is called a penalty function. The starting point of the learning approach is a family of models. Each model has the same set of tuning parameters, but its difference from another model is in the values of the tuning parameters. Parameters are learned, that is, determined as a function of the data, by minimizing an objective function that measures the precision of the model on sample data. An example is the ordinary least squares (OLS) method that minimizes the sum of squared residuals.

However, if we use universal function approximators with a sufficient number of parameters, the objective function can become arbitrarily small. A neural network, for example, can make the sum of squared residuals arbitrarily small. A central idea in learning theory is to add a penalty term to the objective function that grows with the number of parameters but gets smaller if the number of sample points increases. If we increase the number of parameters, we make the original objective function smaller but we increase the penalty term. Therefore, the minimum of this new objective function is a trade-off between in-sample accuracy and model complexity.

At the other end of the landscape, the theoretical approach to financial modeling is based on human creativity. In this approach, models are the result of new scientific insights that have been embodied in theories. The theoretical approach is typical of the physical sciences. Laws such as the Maxwell equations of electromagnetism were discovered not through a process of learning but by a stroke of genius. Perhaps the most well-known example of a theoretical model in financial economics is the capital asset pricing model (CAPM).

The hybrid approach retains characteristics of both the theoretical and learning approaches. It uses a theoretical foundation to identify families of models but uses a learning approach to choose the correct model within the family. For example, the ARCH/GARCH family of models is suggested by theoretical considerations while, in its practical application, the right model is selected through a learning approach that identifies the model parameters.

SAMPLE BIASES

Let us now see how samples might be subject to biases that reduce our ability to correctly estimate model parameters. A well-known type of bias in financial modeling is survivorship bias, a bias exhibited by samples selected on the basis of criteria valid at the last point in the sample population. In the presence of survivorship biases in our data, return processes relative to firms that ceased to exist prior to that date are ignored. For example, while poorly performing mutual funds often close down (and therefore drop out of the sample), better performing mutual funds continue to exist (and therefore remain in the sample). In this situation, estimating past returns from the full sample would result in overestimation due to survivorship bias.

Another important bias is the selection bias intrinsic in samples from common indexes such as the Russell 1000 universe (large-cap stock).[2] The Russell 1000 includes the largest 1,000 securities (large-cap) in the Russell 3000; the Russell 3000 Index represents about 98% of the stock market capitalization in the U.S. equity market. In order to understand the selection bias, we applied a selection rule similar to that of the Russell 1000 to artificially generated random walks. Considering artificially generated random walks allows us to study the selection bias in a controlled environment, without influences from other phenomena. We formed 10,000 independent random walk price processes, each representing the price of a company's stock, over 1,000 periods using the recursive formula:

$$P_i(2) = \left(1 + R_i(2)\right) \times P_i(1) = 1 + 0.007 \times \varepsilon_i(2)$$
$$P_i(3) = \left(1 + R_i(3)\right) \times P_i(2) = \left(1 + 0.007 \times \varepsilon_i(3)\right) \times \left(1 + 0.007 \times \varepsilon_i(2)\right)$$
.
.
.
$$P_i(n) = \left(1 + 0.007 \times \varepsilon_i(n)\right) \times \cdots \times \left(1 + 0.007 \times \varepsilon_i(3)\right) \times \left(1 + 0.007 \times \varepsilon_i(2)\right)$$

where we assume $P_i(1) = 1$. The level of volatility, 0.007, is compatible with realistic market values. Let us make the simple assumption that each company has the same number of stocks outstanding. Every 50 periods, we selected the 1,000 processes with the largest market cap. Given our assumption, these are the stocks with the highest market prices. This selection rule roughly corresponds to the Russell 1000 selection rules assuming that one period represents one year. Let us call this random walk sample AR1000.

The sample paths of the random walk have the shape shown in Exhibit 4.1.

We will look at two different universes. The first is the universe were we consider only those processes selected at the latest selection date. For example, at any time between 500 and, say, 520, we include the first 1,000 processes selected at the date 500. The second universe includes all processes selected at any date in the entire period. The last universe suffers from anticipation of information as it includes, at any time except the most recent, processes whose inclusion will be known only later.

---

[2]Needless to say, many other indexes exhibit this bias: The Russell indexes were chosen as an example.

EXHIBIT 4.1   10,000 Sample Paths of a Geometric Random Walk

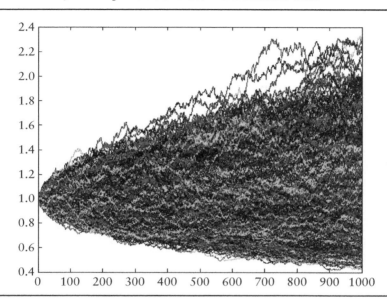

We now study the bias of averages. In other words, the latter universe includes at time t stocks whose inclusion in the universe could be known only at a time $s > t$.

THE BIAS IN AVERAGES

We will now show how data sets such as the Russell 1000 suffer from intrinsic biases when estimating averages. Note that this is not a criticism of the Russell 1000 data set: any other data set that is based on selecting the largest or the smallest firms at fixed dates exhibits similar biases. In particular we will show that computing expected returns as empirical averages or through least squares methods, two basic procedures implied by most models today, will lead to an overestimation of expected returns. In the practice of econometrics, models are estimated on moving windows. For example, the starting point for estimating a multifactor model could be estimating the expected returns and the covariance matrix over moving windows of a given length. Expected returns can be estimated as moving averages of returns. We selected a moving window of 100 periods. If one period represents one week, 100 periods correspond roughly to two years.

Continuing on our example, let's choose two moving windows that terminate at the dates 500 and 501, that is, immediately before and immediately after the selection applied at time 501. For each moving window, we plot the average of all 10,000 price processes as well as the average of the processes that were in the AR1000 at the corresponding date. Therefore, for the time window that ends at time 500, we average the 1,000 processes selected at time 451, while for the time window that ends at time 501 we average the 1,000 price processes selected at time 501. Exhibits 4.2 and 4.3 represent the three plots.

As we see in Exhibit 4.2, the average of the chosen 1,000 processes exhibits a positive inclination for the first 50 steps and then follows the same flat behavior of the grand average. However, in Exhibit 4.3 we see that the processes selected at time 501 exhibit a positive steepness for the whole period.

This behavior does not reflect any genuine growth path. In fact, by design, the paths of our artificially generated random walk do not have any intrinsic growth. The growth exhibited in Exhibits 4.1 and 4.2 is purely due to the selection process that chooses processes that grew in the previous time window. This growth, however, is a spurious bias. After the selection point, the average return is zero.

EXHIBIT 4.2 Averages of Prices in the Window before the Selection Rule is Applied

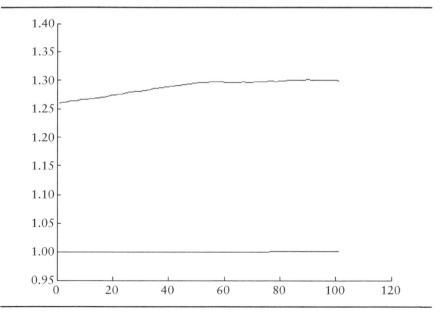

EXHIBIT 4.3   Averages of Prices in the Window after the Selection Rule is Applied

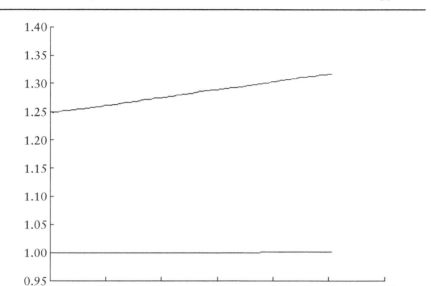

To test this result, we computed the average returns of price processes that are in the moving window selected at each moment and the average return in the period immediately after. As we are considering artificially generated independent random walks, if the sample had no bias, the empirical average of returns in any moving window should provide an estimate of the expectation of returns in the following periods. Therefore, the average of returns in the moving window and after the moving window should be the same. Instead, we obtained the following results:

Empirical average of returns in the moving window = 0.00038698%

Empirical average of returns after the moving window = 0.0030430%

Exhibit 4.4 provides an illustration of the empirical average of returns in and after the moving window.

The dotted line represents returns estimated in the moving window. Returns are higher immediately after the selection rule is applied and then get smaller, as illustrated in Exhibits 4.1 and 4.2. The continuous line represents returns after the moving window. As can be seen in Exhibit 4.4, returns

EXHIBIT 4.4   Empirical Average of Returns In and After the Moving Window

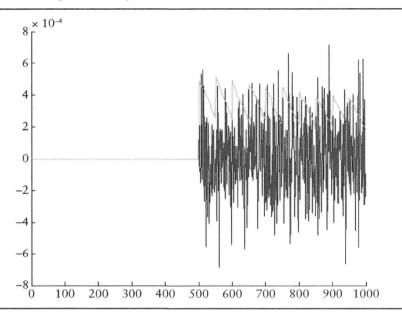

after the moving window exhibit larger fluctuations as we are considering only one period. However it is clear that, on average, returns after the moving window are smaller than average returns in the moving window.

The difference is not negligible. The empirical average of returns after the moving window is close to zero: the corresponding annualized return is 0.0002. However, the annualized returns in the moving windows exceed 2%. This means that in a data set such as the Russell 1000, estimating expected returns as empirical averages of past returns overestimates expectations by 2% just because of the sample biases.

PITFALLS IN CHOOSING FROM LARGE DATA SETS

Several investment management processes are based on selecting from a large set of price/return processes that exhibit specific characteristics. Perhaps the most obvious example is pairs trading. Pairs trading is based on selecting pairs of stocks that stay close together. It is widely believed that pairs trading was initially introduced in investment management in the 1980s by Nunzio Tartaglia, a trader working at Morgan Stanley.

Suppose we know that the price paths of two stocks will stay close together. When they are at their maximum distance, we can go long in the stock with the highest value and short in the other stock. As the paths have stayed close together in the past, we assume that they are likely to come close again and even to invert the order of their values. When their distance is reduced or changes sign a profit is realized.

Given a large universe of stocks, a pairs trading strategy will look for cointegrated pairs. A typical approach will consist in running a cointegration test on each pair. Actually a test can consist of multiple tests that each pair has to pass in order to be accepted as cointegrated.

Any statistical test, regardless of its complexity and power, will fail in a certain number of cases simply by chance. That is, a pair can appear cointegrated in a sample period purely by chance. Or a truly cointegrated pair may fail the test. In fact, any statistical test carries a significance level that tells us in what percentage of cases that test will fail purely by chance. Therefore, if we run a cointegration test on a large set of price processes and we find a number of processes that pass the cointegration test, we cannot conclude that all of these processes are really cointegrated.

To illustrate this phenomenon, let's consider a set of 1,000 artificial arithmetic random walk paths that are 1,000 steps long. Consider that in the sample set there are $(1,000 \times 1,000 - 1,000)/2 = 1,000 \times 999 \times 0.5 = 499,500$ different pairs of processes. The cointegration tests are run only on these processes. As we construct these processes as random walks, no pair selected from these random walk paths is genuinely cointegrated. However, we will find that a number of pairs of random walk paths test positive for cointegration purely by chance.

To see this point, we ran three standard cointegration tests:

1. The augmented Dickey-Fuller (ADF) test.
2. The Johansen trace test.
3. The Johansen maximum eigenvalue test.

The ADF test is based on regressing one process on the other and testing the stationarity of residuals. If residuals are stationary, then by definition the two processes are cointegrated. The Johansen trace and maximum eigenvalue tests are standard cointegration tests based on the Johansen procedure (see Chapter 3).

In practice, the application of these tests consists of comparing some test statistics with tabulated critical values. We ran the three tests on a sample set of realizations of random walk paths. The random walk is defined by the following recursive equation:

$$P_i(t) = P_i(t-1) + 0.007 \times \varepsilon_i(t)$$

where the $\varepsilon_i(t)$ are independent draws from a standard normal distribution $N(0,1)$. As before, we chose volatility to be 0.007 which is compatible with market values.

In our tests, we allow a constant term but no deterministic trend and a maximum of ten lags. Performing two sample runs, run 1 and 2, with the same parameters we obtained the following results:

- Using the ADF test at 1% significance level, in run 1, 1.1% pass the cointegration test, in run 2, 0.8%.
- Using the Johansen trace test at 99% significance level, in run 1, 2.7% pass the cointegration test, in run 2, 1.9%.
- Using the Johansen maximum eigenvalue test, in run 1, 1.7% pass the cointegration test, in run 2, 1.1%.

Using the three criteria simultaneously, in run 1, 0.5% pass the cointegration test, in run 2, 0.4%. The results are summarized in Exhibit 4.5.

These numbers refer to two samples of random walk realizations. We can see that there are large fluctuations between the two samples and large discrepancies between the three different tests. Note that the difference in the number of pairs that pass the cointegration tests is purely due to chance. We applied the same tests with the same parameterizations and used the same data generation process with the same parameters. Despite the large number of processes involved (1,000 processes), there are large differences in the number of pairs that pass the cointegration tests. We note that the critical issue is that none of the processes that pass the cointegration test is actually cointegrated. If one were to base a pairs trading strategy on these processes, one would incur losses. We can therefore reasonably conclude that given a set of price processes, the fact that some processes pass the cointegration test is not, per se, a proof that they are really cointegrated pairs.

Given a set of processes that include some truly cointegrated pairs, how can we identify the truly cointegrated pairs? We have to somehow find critical numbers for determining the number of pairs. If the number of pairs that

EXHIBIT 4.5 Number of Cointegrated Pairs in Random Walk Realizations in Two Separate Runs Using the Same Parameters

	ADF	Trace	Max Eigenvalue	All Three
Run 1	1.1%	2.7%	1.7%	0.5%
Run 2	0.8%	1.9%	1.1%	0.4%

pass the cointegration test exceeds that critical number, we can reasonably conclude that there are truly cointegrated pairs.

A simple choice of the critical number of cointegrated pairs is the level of significance multiplied by the number of pairs. That is, if our test has a significance level of 1% and if there are 499,500 different pairs, we can assume that to make safe conclusions on the existence of true cointegration, the number of pairs that pass the cointegration test must be in excess of $499,500 \times 0.01 \approx 5,000$. However, the pairs are not independent. For example, if we test pairs a,b and b,c, the pair a,c is not independent from the other two. It would be very difficult to establish mathematical criteria for small samples, hence the need for simulation.

However, as we have seen, there are large fluctuations in the number of pairs that pass the cointegration test in a random walk sample. Therefore, we may need to refine our criteria. Here, we will not further discuss the many possible approaches that might be embedded in proprietary applications: Our objective is to show by way of example that in large data sets we will always find a percentage of processes that pass specific tests. In order to draw conclusions, we must gain a better understanding, often through simulations and heuristics, of the critical numbers associated with these percentages.

TIME AGGREGATION OF MODELS AND PITFALLS IN THE SELECTION OF DATA FREQUENCY

In the physical sciences, laws of nature are typically expressed as differential equations. Differential equations establish instantaneous conditions that link functions and their derivatives. One method for solving a differential equation consists in discretizing the equation, that is, determining discrete difference equations that approximate the original differential equations.[3] In order to obtain a good approximation, the discretization steps must usually be small.

To ascertain the functional relationships between variables at distant points, we need to solve the differential equation. For example, consider the trajectory of a stone thrown in sea water. The trajectory of the stone is determined by the differential equations of dynamics and fluid dynamics plus gravitation. These equations are valid instantaneously. To ascertain the position of the stone say every second, we have to solve the equation and consider its solution at intervals of one second. In general, there will be no simple discrete equation that yields the position of the stone every second.

---

[3]This is not the only method. For example, the finite elements methods is based on totally different principles. See Thomas J. R. Hughes, *The Finite Element Method: Linear Static and Dynamic Finite Element Analysis* (Englewood Cliffs, NJ: Prentice Hall, 1987).

In financial theory, we have both discrete-time and continuous-time models. Continuous-time models are similar to the differential equations of physics. Consider, for example, the Black-Scholes option pricing equation. To ascertain the option price distribution at any given date, we have to solve the Black-Scholes equation. Under certain assumptions, the solution is known as a closed-form formula.

From this discussion, we note that in analytical models the time step is arbitrarily small (infinitesimal); we can solve for the desired quantity at any given point in time by solving the differential equation.

Let us now turn to discrete-time models. Consider, for example a vector autoregressive model of order 1, denoted by VAR(1), of the form

$$\mathbf{X}_t = \mathbf{A}\mathbf{X}_{t-1} + \mathbf{E}_t$$

Such a model is characterized by a time step. If the $\mathbf{X}$ are returns, the time steps could be days, weeks, or months. The question we want to investigate is the following: Given a process that we believe is described by a given model, can we select the time step arbitrarily? Or are different time steps characterized by different models?

If we can use the same model at different time steps, we say that our model is invariant under time aggregation. We also want to consider a companion question: Can we improve the performance of our models considering shorter time steps? This question is becoming more important with the availability of high-frequency data.

There is no general answer to these questions. Most models currently used are not invariant after time aggregation. Therefore, in the discrete world in general, we have to accept the fact that there are different models for different time steps and different horizons. We have to decide what type of dynamics we want to investigate and model. Models do not necessarily simplify at longer time horizons. Each model is an approximation that is valid for a given time step and time horizon, but might not be valid for others.

Using shorter time steps is not always advantageous; it might result in a better understanding of short-term dynamics but might not be advantageous for making longer-term forecasts: We need to understand what type of dynamics we want to capture.

MODEL RISK AND ITS MITIGATION

We conclude this chapter by realistically assuming that errors in choosing and estimating models cannot be avoided. This is because models are inevitably misspecified as they are only an approximation, more or less faithful, of the true data generating process (DGP). We discuss how to mitigate these errors. We begin by looking at the sources of error leading to model misspecification and then review remedies, in particular methods based on information theory, Bayesian methods, shrinkage, and random coefficient models. In Chapter 6, we come back to the topic of model risk in the context of factor-based trading strategies.

Sources of Model Risk

We begin our discussion by introducing the concept of model risk. In simple intuitive terms, *model risk* means that we cannot be certain that the model that we have selected to represent the data is correctly specified. If models are misspecified, forecasting errors might be significant.

To place the notion of model risk in its scientific context, note that the question of model risk is of scant interest in physics. Though at a deep philosophical level the physical sciences are hypothetical and subject to revision, a vast body of scientific knowledge is considered to be validated to a high degree. No scientist expects the laws of physics that govern the behavior of, for example, trains and planes to break down, though changes might occur at a higher conceptual level.

The notion of model risk entered science with the engineering of complex artifacts, the study of complex systems, and the widespread adoption of statistical learning methods. This is because, in tackling large artifacts and complex systems such as the economy, science begins to address problems of a different nature. When modeling complex systems such as financial markets, we might encounter one of the following characteristics:

- The phenomena under study might be very complex and thus only a simplified description is possible; this leaves open the possibility that some critical aspect is overlooked.
- The phenomena under study can be very noisy; as a consequence, the scientific endeavor consists in extracting small amounts of information from highly noisy environments.
- Being not a law of nature but the behavior of an artifact, the object under study is subject to unpredictable changes.

In financial econometrics, there are various sources of error that can lead to model misspecification (though our considerations are quite universal and apply to modeling in general, we will restrict our analysis to models of stock prices and stock returns). In particular, sources of error in financial econometrics include the following two:

1. The empirical data are nearly random but might seem to exhibit structure.
2. The empirical data have been generated by a time-varying or randomly varying DGP while the model selected is static or subject to a different time dynamics.

The first source of error—random data appearing to have structure—is due to the large amount of noise in financial time series. Thus models capture apparent regularities that are the result of mere chance. The fact that financial time series are so noisy, to the point of being almost completely random, is a weak form of market efficiency. In financial time series, any source of profit that could be easily detectable would be exploited, making it disappear. This is the principle of absence of arbitrage.

It is because of absence of arbitrage that stock price time series seem to meander randomly and stock return time series are close to random noise. The benchmark model for logprices is therefore the random walk. In addition, as return processes are strongly correlated, the benchmark model of multivariate stock logprices is that of correlated random walks. Deviations from this benchmark model allow profitable strategies. Because in the best of cases there is only very little real structure in financial time series (i.e., the data are essentially random), it is possible that we find structure where there is none. Given the sample sizes available, our statistical tests are not powerful enough to yield overwhelming evidence that data are not random.

The sheer fact that we have to filter a large amount of noise renders the filtering process uncertain. For example, estimating an unrestricted vector autoregressive (VAR) process of many stock price processes yields an estimated structure of cross autocorrelation that is almost completely spurious: the model coefficients capture noise. In Chapter 7 we discuss how to reduce the dimensionality of the model, for example with dynamic factor models, in order to capture the true information. We now come back to the same question as an issue in model risk.

The second possible source of error—that the data have some simple structure but are subject to sudden and unpredictable changes (i.e., the data have been generated by a time-varying or randomly varying DGP) not reflected in our models—is possibly the most serious source of model risk. For example, empirical data might be represented by a DGP that is stable for a given period, but then the economy is subject to change and the DGP changes as a consequence. If we had lots of data and changes were sufficiently frequent, the latter could be detected and estimated. However, as we typically have only a few years of workable homogeneous data, detecting change is problematic. A key source of model risk is the possibility that we estimate models correctly on a past sample of data but then the DGP changes and the change goes undetected.

One way of dealing with a time-varying DGP is by introducing regime-switching models (see Chapter 3). However, regime-switching models do not entirely solve the problem. In fact, any regime-switching model is a model estimated on a sample of past data. As such, it can detect only those features that are statistically relevant during the sample period. If a regime change occurs once or twice during that period, the model will not detect the change. One could investigate separately the possibility of regime changes, but doing so is complex and uncertain when applied to models that are already regime-switching.

The above considerations suggest the adoption of techniques to reduce sources of error in model selection and estimation. Possible techniques include the following:

- Information theory, to assess the complexity and the limits of the predictability of time series.
- Bayesian modeling, which assumes that models are variations of some a priori model.
- Shrinkage, a form of averaging between different models.
- Random coefficient models, a technique that averages models estimated on clusters of data.

We begin our discussion of model risk mitigation techniques with the information theory approach to model risk.

The Information Theory Approach to Model Risk

We now take a broad approach and explore how we can use information theory to mitigate model risk without making reference to any specific family of models.

We saw above that an important source of risk is due to the fact that models might mistakenly capture as stable features of the empirical data what is only random structure. To reduce this source of error, the theory of learning prescribes constraining a model's complexity using criteria based on information theory.

Intuitively, if our model shows too much structure (i.e., in the case of financial time series, if the model appears to offer ample opportunity for realizing excess returns), the model is likely to be misspecified and therefore risky. The critical questions are:

- Is it possible to estimate the maximum information extractable from a financial time series?

- Can we prescribe an information boundary such that sound robust models are not able to yield information beyond that boundary?
- Is it possible to assess the intrinsic complexity of empirical time series?

We begin our discussion on the role of information theory in mitigating model risk with a definition of the concepts of information and entropy. The concept of information is associated with the name of Claude Shannon, who laid the foundations of information theory in 1948.[4] The concept of a quantitative measure of information had been introduced in the context of communications engineering 20 years before by R. V. L. Hartley.[5]

Consider a probability distribution. Intuitively, it makes a big difference, in terms of information, if the distribution is flat or highly peaked. If one throws a fair dice, each of the six possible outcomes has the same probability and we are totally uncertain about future outcomes; the probability distribution is said to be flat. If the dice is biased, say number 6 has an 80% probability of coming up, we can be pretty confident that the next outcome will be a 6; the distribution is said to be peaked.

In a finite probability scheme,[6] with N outcomes each with probability p_i, $i = 1, 2, ..., N$ information is defined as

$$I = \sum_{i=1}^{T} p_i \log(p_i)$$

The quantity I, which is always negative, assumes a minimum

$$I = \log\left(\frac{1}{N}\right)$$

if all outcomes have the same probability; it assumes a maximum $I = 0$ if one outcome has probability 1 and all other outcomes probability 0, that is, in the case of certainty of one outcome. From the above formula it is clear that the maximum information is zero but the minimum information of an equiprobable distribution can assume any negative value.

---

[4]Claude Shannon, "The Mathematical Theory of Communication," *Bell System Technical Journal*, 27 (1948), pp. 379–423 and 623–656.
[5]Ralph V. L. Hartley, "Transmission of Information," *Bell System Technical Journal*, 7 (1928), pp. 535–564.
[6]The concept of information can be extended to continuous probability schemes, but the extension is not straightforward. For our purposes discrete probability schemes suffice.

One can add several considerations that make the quantity I a reasonable measure of information.[7] However, what really makes the concept of information so important is that we can construct a theory of information that is meaningful from the point of view of empirical science. In other words, if we associate the quantity of information to physical processes, we can establish laws that make sense empirically.

To appreciate this point, consider first that the quantity I is the opposite of a quantity H well known in physics as entropy: $I = -H$. *Entropy* is a measure of disorder.[8] A fundamental law of physics, the second law of thermodynamics states that in closed systems the global amount of entropy (i.e., disorder) can only grow or remain constant over time. Next consider that a basic result in information theory is the link between the physical characteristics of a communication channel and the rate of information that can be transmitted through that channel. It is because of physical laws such as these that the concept of information has become fundamental in physics and engineering.

We now introduce the concepts of coarse graining and symbolic dynamics. Consider an empirical financial time series. Through a process of coarse graining, we can view this series as a sequence of symbols. In fact, coarse graining means dividing the possible outcome x_t of the series into discrete segments (or partitions) and associating a symbol to each segment. For example the symbol a_i is associated to values x_t in the range $v_{i-1} < x_t < v_i$. In doing so, the original DGP of the time series entails a discrete stochastic dynamics of the corresponding sequence of symbols.

Simulation-based techniques for choosing the optimal partitioning of data have been suggested.[9] In principle, the process of coarse-graining is not restrictive as any real-world financial time series is discrete. For example, stock prices can assume only a discrete set of values. However, given the size of samples, the number of symbols that can be used in practice is much smaller than the number of possible discrete values of a series. A financial time series, for example, can be analyzed as a sequence of three symbols, while stock prices can assume any price spaced by one-tenth of a dollar.

---

[7]For a modern presentation of information theory, see, for example, Thomas M. Cover and Joy A. Thomas, *Elements of Information Theory* (New York: John Wiley & Sons, 1991).

[8]Entropy was first introduced in physics in 1864 by Rudolf Clausius in the context of thermodynamics. It was the genius of the Austrian physicist Ludwig Boltzman that made the connection between entropy as a thermodynamic concept and entropy as a measure of disorder in statistical mechanics. Isolated and poorly understood in his time, Boltzman, was to commit suicide in 1906.

[9]Ralf Steuer, Lutz Molgedey, Wierner Ebeling, and Miguel A. Jiménez-Montaño, "Entropy and Optimal Partition for Data Analysis," *European Physical Journal B*, 19 (2001), pp. 265–269.

Given the probabilistic dynamics of the symbol sequence, we can associate a probability to any sequence of n symbols $p(i_1, ..., i_n)$. Recall that the entropy H is the opposite of information as defined above, that is to say

$$H = -\sum_{i=1}^{T} p_i \log(p_i)$$

We can therefore define the entropy per block of length n (or block entropy) as follows:

$$H_n = -I_n = -\Sigma p(i_1, ..., i_n) \log p(i_1, ..., i_n)$$

From the block entropy, we can now define the conditional entropy h_n as the difference of the entropies per blocks of length $n + 1$ and n:

$$h_n = H_{n+1} - H_n = -\Sigma p(i_{n+1} | i_1, ..., i_n) \log p(i_{n+1} | i_1, ..., i_n)$$

Finally, we can define the Kolmogorov-Sinai entropy, or *entropy of the source*, as the limit for large n of the conditional entropy. The *conditional entropy* is the information on the following step conditional on the knowledge of the previous n steps. The quantity $r_n = 1 - h_n$ is called the predictability of the series.

The concepts of conditional entropy and entropy of the source are fundamental to an understanding of the complexity of a series. They supply a model-free methodology for estimating the basic predictability of a time series. Unfortunately, the concepts of entropy and information are not widely diffused in financial econometrics. Ebeling et al.[10] performed estimations of the basic predictability of financial time series with the methods of symbolic dynamics using a three-letter alphabet, that is to say, they coarse grained a times series into three symbols. They found that series such as the returns of the S&P 500 index have a limited level of predictability—in the range of 5% to 8%.

The analysis of the predictability of time series based on information theory is a basic tool for model risk assessment. It establishes a reasonable boundary to the performance of models. Models that seem to exceed by a large measure the predictability level of entropy-based estimation are also likely to exhibit a high level of model risk.

---

[10]Werner Ebeling, Lutz Molgedey, Jürgen Kurths, and Udo Schwarz, "Entropy, Complexity, Predictability and Data Analysis of Time Series and Letter Sequences," Chapter 1 in Amin Bunde, Jurgen Kropp, and Hans Joachim Schellnhuber (eds.), *Theories of Disaster: Scaling Laws Governing Weather, Body and Stock Market Dynamics* (Berlin: Springer, 2002).

While the conditional entropy and the entropy of the source of coarse-grained models give an assessment of the complexity of a series and its predictability, the recently introduced *transfer entropy*[11] gauges the information flow from one series to another. The transfer entropy is defined as: the information about future observation $I(t + 1)$ gained from past observations of I and J minus the information about future observation $I(t + 1)$ gained from past observations of I only.

This definition already shows the advantage of transfer entropy over other cross correlation statistics: It is an asymmetric measure that takes into account only statistical dependencies, and not those correlations deriving from a common external driver. Expressing the above relationship in terms of conditional entropies yields the following expression:

$$T_{I \to J}(m, l) = \Sigma p(i_1, \ldots, i_{m+1}, j_1, \ldots, j_l) \log \left[\frac{p(i_{m+1} | (i_1, \ldots, i_m, j_1, \ldots, j_l))}{p(i_{m+1} | i_1, \ldots, i_m)} \right]$$

This quantity evaluates the amount of information that flows from one series to another. Transfer entropy can be used to evaluate quantitatively cross autocorrelation in a general setting that does not depend on specific models and that might also consider nonlinear lead-lag effects.[12]

One might well ask if we can use information theory to evaluate the adequacy of specific families of models. James Hamilton introduced a series of specification tests to evaluate the adequacy of Markov switching models.[13] Hamilton's tests are based on the score of the models defined as the derivative of the conditional log-likelihood of the n-th observation with respect to the parameter vector. The approach is quite technical: the interested reader should consult the cited reference.

A very general approach to evaluating the limits of learning from finite samples comes from the Russian physicists Vapnik and Chervonenkis (VC), working in the second half of the twentieth century. They went beyond the classical information theory in the sense of Shannon, and defined a number of concepts and quantities to characterize the learning process, Vapnik entropy, empirical risk, structural risk, and the VC dimension. The VC theory establishes limits to the ability of given models to learn in a sense

---

[11]Thomas Schreiber, "Measuring Information Transfer," *Physical Review Letters*, 85 (2000), p. 461.
[12]Robert Marschinski and Lorenzo Matassini, "Financial Markets as a Complex System: A Short Time Scale Perspective," *Deutsche Bank Research Note in Economics & Statistics* (November 2001).
[13]James D. Hamilton, "Specification Testing in Markov-Switching Time-Series Models," *Journal of Econometrics*, 70 (1996), pp. 127–157.

made precise by these concepts.[14] Considered a major breakthrough, the VC theory led to the development of the *Vector Support Machine*, a learning approach based on the theory. However, the conceptual difficulty of the VC theory and the practical difficulty in applying it have thus far limited its widespread application to financial modeling.

To summarize, information theory offers a number of tools for evaluating, in a very general context and in a robust framework, limits to the forecastability of a given time series. Information theory is thus a valuable tool for evaluating model risk. Critical to the information-based approach are methods and techniques to coarse-grain time series. A number of practical information-based approaches have been proposed and are widely used in the physical sciences. Thus far, however, the use of information theory in financial econometrics has been limited to applications such as the Akaike criterion.

Bayesian Modeling

The Bayesian approach to dynamic modeling is based on Bayesian statistics. Therefore, we will begin our discussion of Bayesian modeling with a brief introduction to Bayesian statistics.

Bayesian Statistics

Bayesian statistics is perhaps the most difficult area in the science of statistics. The difficulty is not mathematical but conceptual: it resides in the Bayesian interpretation of probability. Classical statistics (which is the statistical approach used thus far in this book) adopts a *frequentist* interpretation of probability; that is to say, the probability of an event is essentially the relative frequency of its appearance in large samples. However, it is well known that pure relative frequency is not a tenable basis for probability: One cannot strictly identify probability with relative frequency. What is needed is some *bridging principle* that links probability, which is an abstract concept, to empirical relative frequency. Bridging principles have been widely discussed in the literature, especially in the philosophical strain of statistical literature but, in practice, classical statistics identifies probability with relative frequency in large samples. When large samples are not available, for example in analyzing tail events, classical statistics adopts theoretical considerations.

The frequentist interpretation is behind most of today's estimation methods. When statisticians compute empirical probability distributions, they effectively equate probability and relative frequency. The concept is

---

[14]The VC theory was exposed by Vapnik in his book *The Nature of Statistical Learning Theory* (Berlin: Springer-Verlag, 1991).

also implicit in estimation methods based on likelihood. In fact, maximum likelihood (ML) estimates of distribution parameters can be interpreted as those parameters that align the distribution as close as possible to the empirical distribution. When we compute empirical moments, we also adhere to a frequentist interpretation of probability.

In classical statistics, the probability distributions that embody a given statistical model are not subject to uncertainty. The perspective of classical statistics is that a given population has a *true* distribution: the objective of statistics is to infer the true distribution from a population sample.

Although most mathematical methods are similar to those of classical statistics, Bayesian statistics[15] is based on a different set of concepts. In particular, the following three concepts characterize Bayesian statistics:

1. Statistical models are uncertain and subject to modification when new information is acquired.
2. There is a distinction between prior probability (or prior distribution), which conveys the best estimate of probabilities given initial available information, and the posterior probability, which is the modification of the prior probability consequent to the acquisition of new information.
3. The mathematical link between prior and posterior probabilities is given by Bayes' Theorem.

The main difficulty is in grasping the meaning of these statements. On one side, the first two statements seem mere educated common sense, while the third is a rather simple mathematical statement that we illustrate in the following paragraphs. However, common sense does not make science. The usual scientific interpretation is that Bayesian statistics is essentially a rigorous method for making decisions based on the *subjectivistic* interpretation of probability.

In Bayesian statistics, probability is intended as subjective judgment guided by data. While a full exposé of Bayesian statistics is beyond the scope of this book, the crux of the problem can be summarized as follows. Bayesian statistics is rooted in data as probability judgments are updated with new data or information. However, according to Bayesian statistics there is an ineliminable subjective element; the subjective element is given by the initial prior probabilities that cannot be justified within the Bayesian theory.

---

[15]For a complete exposition of Bayesian statistics see: Donald A. Berry, *Statistics: A Bayesian Perspective* (Belmont, CA: Wadsworth Publishing, 1996) and Thomas Leonard and John Hsu, *Bayesian Methods: An Analysis for Statisticians and Interdisciplinary Researchers* (Cambridge, UK: Cambridge University Press, 1999) for a basic discussion, and Jose M. Bernardo and Adrian F. M. Smith, *Bayesian Theory* (Chichester, UK: John Wiley & Sons, 2000) for a more advanced discussion.

It would be a mistake to think that Bayesian statistics is only a rigorous way to perform subjective uncertain reasoning while classical statistics is about real data.[16] Bayesian statistics explicitly recognizes that there is some ineliminable subjectivity in probability statements and attempts to reduce such subjectivity by updating probabilities. Classical statistics implicitly recognizes the same subjectivity when setting rules that bridge from data to probabilities.

In a nutshell, the conceptual problem of both classical and Bayesian statistics is that a probability statement does not per se correspond to any empirical reality. One cannot observe probabilities, only events that are interpreted in a probabilistic sense. The real problem, both in classical and Bayesian statistics, is how to link probability statements to empirical data. If mathematically sound and interpretable probability statements are to be constructed, bridging principles are required.

Before leaving the subject of Bayesian statistics, note that in financial econometrics there is a strain of literature and related methodologies based on Empirical Bayesian Statistics. In Empirical Bayesian Statistics, priors are estimated with the usual classical methods and then updated with new information. We will come back to this subject later in this chapter.

Bayes' Theorem

We now discuss Bayes' theorem, for which there are two interpretations. One interpretation is a simple accounting of probabilities in the classical sense. Given two events A and B, the following properties, called *Bayes' theorem*, hold:

$$P(A|B) = \frac{P(B|A)P(A)}{P(B)}$$

$$P(B|A) = \frac{P(A|B)P(B)}{P(A)}$$

These properties are an elementary consequence of the definitions of conditional probabilities:

$$P(AB) = P(A|B)P(B) = P(B|A)P(A)$$

In the second interpretation of Bayes' theorem, we replace the event A with a statistical hypothesis H and the event B with the data and write

---

[16]Bayesian theories of uncertain reasoning are important in machine learning and artificial intelligence. See, for example, Judea Pearl, *Probabilistic Reasoning in Intelligent Systems: Networks of Plausible Inference* (San Francisco, CA: Morgan Kaufmann Publishers, 1988).

$$P(H|\text{data}) = \frac{P(data|H)P(H)}{P(data)}$$

This form of Bayes' theorem is the mathematical basis of Bayesian statistics. Given that P(data) is unconditional and does not depend on H, we can write the preceding as:

$$P(H|\text{data}) \propto P(\text{data}|H)P(H)$$

The probability $P(H)$ is called the *prior probability*, while the probability $P(H|\text{data})$ is called the *posterior probability*. The probability $P(\text{data}|H)$ of the data given H is called the likelihood.

Bayes' theorem can be expressed in a different form in terms of odds. The odds of H is the probability that H is false, written as $P(H^C)$. Bayes' theorem is written in terms of odds as follows:

$$\frac{P(H|\text{data})}{P(H^C|\text{data})} = \frac{P(\text{data}|H)P(H)}{P(\text{data}|H^C)P(H^C)}$$

The second interpretation of Bayes' theorem is not a logical consequence of Bayes' theorem in the first interpretation; it is an independent principle that assigns probabilities to statistical assumptions.

When applied to modeling, Bayes' theorem is expressed in terms of distributions, not probabilities. Bayes' theorem can be stated in terms of distributions as follows:

$$p(\vartheta|y) \propto L(y|\vartheta)\pi(\vartheta)$$

In this formulation, y represents the data, ϑ is the parameter set, $p(\vartheta|y)$ is the posterior distribution, $L(y|\vartheta)$ is the likelihood function, and $\pi(\vartheta)$ is the prior distribution.

A key issue in Bayesian statistics is how to determine the prior. Though considered subjective, the prior is not arbitrary; if it were, the estimation exercise would be futile. The prior represents the basic knowledge before specific measurements are taken into account. Two types of priors are often used: diffuse priors and conjugate priors. The *diffuse prior* assumes that we do not have any prior knowledge of the phenomena. A diffuse prior is a uniform distribution over an unspecified range. The *conjugate prior* is a prior such that, for a given likelihood, the prior and the posterior distribution coincide.

Bayesian Approach to Model Risk

The Bayesian handling of model risk is based on *Bayesian dynamic modeling*. Recall that the objective of model risk mitigation is to minimize the possibility of and the effects of error in model choice. The Bayesian approach to model risk assumes that though there is uncertainty as regards the model, we have a good idea of a basic form of the model. Uncertainty is expressed as a prior distribution of the model parameters where the means of the distribution determine the basic model. In other words, in the Bayesian approach to model estimation, the estimation process does not determine the model from the data but uses the data to determine deviations of the actual model from a standard idealized model. We can say that Bayesian modeling is a perturbation theory of fundamental models.

As is typical in Bayesian statistics, the quality of results depends on the priors. It might seem reasonable that those priors that express complete uncertainty lead to the same estimates obtained in the classical framework, but this is not the case. The key issue is just what priors express complete uncertainty.[17] Specifically, there is no agreement on what should be considered an uninformative prior in the case of unit root processes.

Now see how the Bayesian framework mitigates model risk. We observed that financial time series are very noisy and that we can only extract a small amount of information from all the noise. If a model appears to extract a lot of information, there is always the risk that that information is camouflaged noise.

We have already explored dimensionality reduction as one possible remedy for misspecification. Dimensionality reduction constrains model complexity, rendering effective the estimation process. In large multivariate time series, dimensionality reduction typically takes the form of factor models. The Bayesian approach to model risk assumes that we know, in the form of the prior distribution of parameters, an (idealized) robust model. For example, as we will see below, the Litterman model allows only small perturbations to the random walk. Next we see how the Bayesian approach works in practice.

Bayesian Analysis of an Univariate AR(1) Model

Let us now perform a simple Bayesian analysis of an univariate AR(1) model under the assumption of diffuse priors. Consider the following simple autoregressive model:

[17]George S. Maddala and In-Moo Kim, *Unit Roots, Cointegration, and Structural Change* (Cambridge, UK: Cambridge University Press, 1998).

$$y_t = \rho y_{t-1} + \varepsilon_t$$

Assume that the preceding model is Gaussian so that the likelihood is also Gaussian. The model being linear, Gaussian innovations entail Gaussian variables. The likelihood is a given, not a prior. We can write the likelihood, which is a function of the data parameterized by the initial conditions y_0, the autoregressive parameters ρ, and the variance σ of the innovation process as follows:

$$L(y|\rho,\sigma,y_0) = \frac{1}{\sqrt{(2\pi)^T}}\sigma^{-T}\exp\left(-\frac{\sum_{t=1}^{T}\varepsilon_t^2}{2\sigma^2}\right)$$

$$= \frac{1}{\sqrt{(2\pi)^T}}\sigma^{-T}\exp\left(-\frac{\sum_{t=1}^{T}(y_t - \rho y_{t-1})^2}{2\sigma^2}\right)$$

Assume a flat prior for (ρ, σ), that is, assume that

$$\pi(\rho,\sigma) \propto \frac{1}{\sigma}, -1 < \rho < 1, \sigma > 0$$

Then the joint posterior distribution is the following:

$$p(\rho,\sigma|y,y_0) \propto = \sigma^{-T-1}\exp\left(-\frac{\sum_{t=1}^{T}\varepsilon_t^2}{2\sigma^2}\right)$$

$$= \frac{1}{\sqrt{(2\pi)^T}}\sigma^{-T}\exp\left(-\frac{\sum_{t=1}^{T}(y_t - \rho y_{t-1})^2}{2\sigma^2}\right)$$

Let

$$\hat{\rho} = \frac{\Sigma y_t y_{t-1}}{\Sigma y_{t-1}^2}$$

be the OLS estimator of the regressive parameter and call

$$Q = \Sigma y_{t-1}^2$$

and

$$R = \Sigma(y_t - \hat{\rho}y_{t-1})^2$$

By rearranging terms and integrating, it can be demonstrated that the marginal distributions of (ρ, σ) are

$$p(\rho|y, y_0) \propto (R + (\rho - \hat{\rho})^2 Q)^{-0.5T}$$

$$p(\sigma|y, y_0) \propto \sigma^{-T} \exp\left(-\frac{R}{2\sigma^2}\right)$$

From these expressions one can see that the marginal distribution of ρ is an univariate t-distribution symmetrically distributed around the OLS estimator $\hat{\rho}$, while the marginal distribution of σ is an inverted gamma-2 distribution.

Bayesian Analysis of a VAR Model

The Bayesian VAR (BVAR) is a Bayesian specification of a VAR model. The BVAR approach is based on defining a prior distribution for the model parameters, similar to what we did above for the univariate AR(1) model. In simple and perhaps more intuitive terms, this means that the estimated VAR model is allowed only *small* deviations from a fundamental model, which is specified as a prior. The specific form of deviations from the fundamental model is prescribed by the prior distribution. For example, the fundamental model for the Litterman BVAR is a random walk. The Litterman model prescribes that the coefficients of the BVAR model be normally distributed around the coefficients of a random walk. In other words, the BVAR approach prescribes that any multivariate model of stock prices cannot differ much from a random walk.

Now see how BVAR models are estimated. Consider the following VAR(p) model:

$$\mathbf{x}_t = \mathbf{A}_1 \mathbf{x}_{t-1} + \mathbf{A}_2 \mathbf{x}_{t-2} + \ldots + \mathbf{A}_p \mathbf{x}_{t-p} + \mathbf{v} + \boldsymbol{\varepsilon}_t$$

where $x_t = (x_{1,t}, \ldots, x_{N,t})'$ is an N-dimensional stochastic time series in vector notation; $\mathbf{A}_i = (a_{s,t}^i)$, $i = 1, 2, \ldots, p$, $s,t = 1, 2, \ldots, N$ are deterministic $N \times N$ matrices; $\boldsymbol{\varepsilon}_t = (\varepsilon_{1,t}, \ldots, \varepsilon_{N,t})'$ is a multivariate white noise with variance-covariance matrix $\boldsymbol{\Sigma} = (\boldsymbol{\sigma}_1, \ldots, \boldsymbol{\sigma}_N)$; $\mathbf{v} = (v_1, \ldots, v_N)'$ is a vector of deterministic intercepts. Using the same notation used in Chapter 2, we can compactly write the VAR(p) model as follows:

$$\mathbf{X} = \mathbf{A}\mathbf{W} + \mathbf{U}$$

$$\mathbf{x} = \mathbf{w}\boldsymbol{\beta} + \mathbf{u}$$

where

$$\mathbf{X} = (\mathbf{x}_1, \ldots, \mathbf{x}_T) = \begin{pmatrix} x_{1,1} & \cdots & x_{1,T} \\ \vdots & \ddots & \vdots \\ x_{N,1} & \cdots & x_{N,T} \end{pmatrix}, \mathbf{x} = \mathrm{vec}(\mathbf{X})$$

$$\mathbf{W} = \begin{pmatrix} 1 & 1 & \cdots & 1 & 1 \\ \mathbf{x}_0 & \mathbf{x}_1 & \cdots & \mathbf{x}_{T-2} & \mathbf{x}_{T-1} \\ \mathbf{x}_{-1} & \mathbf{x}_0 & \cdots & \mathbf{x}_{T-3} & \mathbf{x}_{T-2} \\ \vdots & \vdots & \ddots & \vdots & \vdots \\ \mathbf{x}_{-p+1} & \mathbf{x}_{-p+2} & \cdots & \mathbf{x}_{T-p-1} & \mathbf{x}_{T-p} \end{pmatrix}, \mathbf{w} = (\mathbf{W}' \otimes \mathbf{I}_N)$$

$$\mathbf{U} = \begin{pmatrix} \varepsilon_{1,1} & \cdots & \varepsilon_{1,T} \\ \vdots & \ddots & \vdots \\ \varepsilon_{N,1} & \cdots & \varepsilon_{N,T} \end{pmatrix}, \mathbf{u} = \mathrm{vec}(\mathbf{U})$$

$\mathbf{\Sigma} = [\sigma_{i,j}] = E[\varepsilon_{i,t}\varepsilon_{j,t}]$ while $E[\varepsilon_{i,t}\varepsilon_{j,s}] = 0, \forall i, j, t \neq s$. The covariance matrix of $\mathbf{u}$, $\mathbf{\Sigma}_\mathbf{u}$, can therefore be written as

$$\mathbf{\Sigma}_\mathbf{u} = \mathbf{I}_T \otimes \mathbf{\Sigma} = \begin{pmatrix} \mathbf{\Sigma} & \cdots & 0 \\ \vdots & \ddots & \vdots \\ 0 & \cdots & \mathbf{\Sigma} \end{pmatrix}$$

$$\mathbf{A} = (\mathbf{v}, \mathbf{A}_1, \ldots, \mathbf{A}_p) = \begin{pmatrix} v_1 & a_{11}^1 & \cdots & a_{1N}^1 & \cdots & \cdots & \cdots & a_{11}^p & \cdots & a_{1N}^p \\ \vdots & \vdots & \ddots & \vdots & \vdots & \ddots & \vdots & \vdots & \ddots & \vdots \\ v_N & a_{N1}^1 & \cdots & a_{NN}^1 & \cdots & \cdots & \cdots & a_{N1}^p & \cdots & a_{NN}^p \end{pmatrix}$$

and

$$\boldsymbol{\beta} = \mathrm{vec}(\mathbf{A}) = \begin{pmatrix} v_1 \\ \vdots \\ v_N \\ a_{11}^1 \\ \vdots \\ a_{N1}^1 \\ \vdots \\ a_{1N}^p \\ \vdots \\ a_{NN}^p \end{pmatrix}$$

The likelihood function can be written as in the classical case:

$$l(\mathbf{x}|\boldsymbol{\beta}) = (2\pi)^{-\frac{NT}{2}} |\boldsymbol{\Sigma}|^{-\frac{T}{2}} \exp\left(-\frac{1}{2}(\mathbf{x}-\mathbf{w}\boldsymbol{\beta})'(\mathbf{I}_T \otimes \boldsymbol{\Sigma}^{-1})(\mathbf{x}-\mathbf{w}\boldsymbol{\beta})\right)$$

At this point the Bayesian estimation method departs from the classical one. In fact, in the Bayesian framework we assume that we know a priori the joint distribution of the model parameters. Suppose that the parameter vector $\boldsymbol{\beta}$ has a prior multivariate normal distribution with known mean $\boldsymbol{\beta}^*$ and covariance matrix $\mathbf{V}_\beta$; the prior density is written as

$$\pi(\boldsymbol{\beta}) = (2\pi)^{-\frac{N^2 p}{2}} |\mathbf{V}_\beta|^{-\frac{1}{2}} \exp\left(-\frac{1}{2}(\boldsymbol{\beta}-\boldsymbol{\beta}^*)'\mathbf{V}_\beta^{-1}(\boldsymbol{\beta}-\boldsymbol{\beta}^*)\right)$$

Now we form the posterior distribution $p(\boldsymbol{\beta}|\mathbf{x}) = l(\mathbf{x}|\boldsymbol{\beta})\pi(\boldsymbol{\beta})$. It can be demonstrated that the following expression holds:

$$p(\boldsymbol{\beta}|\mathbf{x}) \propto \exp\left(-\frac{1}{2}(\boldsymbol{\beta}-\bar{\boldsymbol{\beta}})'\mathbf{V}_\beta^{-1}(\boldsymbol{\beta}-\bar{\boldsymbol{\beta}})\right)$$

where the posterior mean is

$$\bar{\boldsymbol{\beta}} = [\mathbf{V}_\beta^{-1} + \mathbf{W}\mathbf{W}' \otimes \boldsymbol{\Sigma}_u^{-1}]^{-1}[\mathbf{V}_\beta^{-1}\boldsymbol{\beta}^* + (\mathbf{W}\otimes\boldsymbol{\Sigma}_u^{-1})\mathbf{x}]$$

and the posterior covariance matrix is

$$\boldsymbol{\Sigma}_\beta = [\mathbf{V}_\beta^{-1} + \mathbf{W}\mathbf{W}'\otimes\boldsymbol{\Sigma}_u^{-1}]^{-1}$$

In practice, the prior mean $\boldsymbol{\beta}^*$ and the prior covariance matrix $\mathbf{V}_\beta$ need to be specified. Set the prior mean to zero for all parameters that are considered to shrink toward zero. Litterman's choice[18] for the prior distribution, when all variables are believed to be integrated, is such that the BVAR model is a perturbation of a random walk. Litterman priors, also known as "Minnesota" priors, are normally distributed with mean set to 1 for the first lag of each equation while all other coefficients are set to zero. The prior variance of the intercept terms is infinite and that of the other coefficients is given by

$$\text{mean } v_{ij,l} = \begin{cases} (\lambda/l)^2, & i=j \\ (\lambda\vartheta\sigma_i/l\sigma_j)^2, & i\neq j \end{cases} \text{ and covariance matrix } \mathbf{V}_\beta$$

[18]Robert B. Litterman, "Forecasting with Bayesian Vector Autoregressions—Five Years of Experience," *Journal of Business and Economic Statistics*, 4 (1986), pp. 25–38.

where $v_{ij,l}$ is the prior variance of the (i,j)th element of $\mathbf{A}_l$, λ is the prior standard deviation of the diagonal elements of $\mathbf{A}_l$, θ is a constant in the interval $(0,1)$, and σ_{ij} is the i-th diagonal element of $\mathbf{\Sigma}_u$. The deterministic terms have diffused prior variance.

The Bayesian analysis of VAR models has been extended to cover the case of state-space models in general. West[19] discusses Bayesian analysis of different state-space models.

Model Averaging and the Shrinkage Approach to Model Risk

Simple model averaging to reduce model risk has been advocated by several authors. Lubos Pastor,[20] for example, recommends averaging return forecasts generated by different models. The intuition behind model averaging is simple. Here is the reasoning. Reliable estimations and forecasts from different models should be highly correlated. When they are not, this means that the estimation and forecasting processes have become dubious and averaging can substantially reduce the forecasting error. Model averaging should have only a marginal impact on forecasting performance, but should help to avoid large forecasting errors. If model averaging has a strong impact on forecasting performance, it is a sign that forecasts are uncorrelated and thus unreliable. One is advised to rethink the modeling strategy.

Averaging estimators obtained from different models can be done using a statistical estimation technique known as *shrinkage*. By averaging, estimators are shrunk closer to each other. Averaging weights can be obtained with Bayesian or Empirical Bayesian methods. Models might be based on completely different theoretical assumptions. An example comes from estimations of the covariance matrix that might be calculated using different approaches, including the empirical estimation approach, which produces highly noisy covariance matrices, or estimations based on the Capital Asset Pricing Model (CAPM), which yield covariance matrices that are highly constrained by theoretical considerations. Shrinkage *shrinks* one estimate toward the other, averaging with appropriate shrinkage coefficients. The idea can be extended to dynamic models. Different models offer different approximations to the true DGP. By averaging estimations and forecasts,

---

[19]As a detailed treatment of Bayesian modeling applied to state-space models is beyond the scope of this book, the interested reader is advised to consult Mike West and P. Jeff Harrison, *Bayesian Forecasting and Dynamic Models* (New York: Springer-Verlag, 1989).

[20]Lubos Pastor, "A Model Weighting Game in Estimating Expected Returns," in Financial Times, *Mastering Investment*, May 21, 2001, and Lubos Pastor and Robert F. Stambaugh, "Comparing Asset Pricing Models: An Investment Perspective," *Journal of Financial Economics*, 56 (2000), pp. 335–381.

one saves the common robust approximations and limits the damage when the approximations coming from any given model break down.

The method of shrinkage can be generalized to averaging between any number of models. The weighting factors can be determined by Bayesian principles if one has an idea of the relative strength of the models. Shrinkage is averaging between possibly different models. In Bayesian terms this would call for multiple priors.[21]

Random Coefficients Models

We now introduce another technique for model risk mitigation: random coefficient models. *Random coefficient models* are based on the idea of segmenting data in a number of clusters and estimating models on multiple clusters. The concept of random coefficient models was introduced in 1970 by Swamy.[22] Consider an ordinary linear regression. The regression parameters can be estimated with OLS methods using *fully pooled data*. This means that all the available data are pooled together and fed to the OLS estimator. However, this strategy might not be optimal if the regression data come from entities that have slightly different characteristics. For example, consider regressing stock returns on a predictor variable. If the returns come from companies that differ in terms of size and business sector, we might obtain different results in different sectors.

However, if our objective is to reduce model risk, we might decide to segment data into clusters that reflect different types of firms, estimate regression for each cluster, and combine the estimates. Random coefficient modeling techniques perform estimates assuming that clusters are randomly selected from a population of clusters with normal distributions.

To see how random coefficient models work, suppose that data are clustered and that each cluster has its own regression. Using the notation for regressions established in Chapter 2, we write the following regression equation for the j-th cluster:

$$\mathbf{y}_j = \mathbf{X}_j\boldsymbol{\beta}_j + \boldsymbol{\varepsilon}_j$$

where n_j is the number of elements in the j-th cluster and $\boldsymbol{\varepsilon}_j$ are mutually independent, normally distributed vectors,

[21]Raman Uppal, Lorenzo Garlappi, and Tan Wang, "Portfolio Selection with Parameter and Model Uncertainty: A Multi-Prior Approach," CEPR Discussion Paper No. 5041 (May 2005), Centre for Economic Policy Research.
[22]A. V. B. Swamy, "Efficient Inference in a Random Coefficient Regression Model," *Econometrica*, 38 (1970), pp. 311–323.

$$\varepsilon_j \sim N(0_{n_j}, \sigma^2 I_{n_j})$$

If we assume that the regression coefficients β_j are a random sample from a multivariate normal distribution,

$$\beta_j \sim N(\beta, \Sigma)$$

independent from the ε_j, we can rewrite the regression as follows:

$$y_j = X_j \beta_j + X_j \gamma_j + \varepsilon_j$$

where γ_j are the deviations of the regression coefficients from their expectations:

$$\gamma_j = \beta_j - \beta \sim N(0, \Sigma)$$

It can be demonstrated that these regressions can be estimated with MLE or LS methods.[23]

SUMMARY

- Science is analytic and we have the models to analyze a given system.
- Design is a constructive process which synthesizes a design starting from general high-level specifications.
- Constructive design is performed iteratively until the analysis indicates that the (approximate) solution and design is satisfactory.
- The process of design can be automated only when we arrive at the stage of expressing the design quality in terms of a goal function; in the latter case design reduces to optimization.
- Optimization requires a forecasting model.
- Approaches to forecast modeling include the learning approach, the theoretical approach, and the hybrid learning-theoretical approach.
- Financial samples are subject to inevitable biases.
- When we choose complex patterns from large data sets we are subject to random noise, in many cases only simulations can provide a guide; the latter problem is the opposite of the small sample problem.
- Financial models are always subject to model risk.
- Information theory, Bayesian modeling, and model averaging offer ways to mitigate the problem of model risk.

---

[23]For more on random coefficient techniques, see Nicholas T. Longford, *Random Coefficient Models* (Oxford, UK: Oxford University Press, 1993).

CHAPTER 5

Factor Models and Their Estimation

Factor models are ubiquitous in financial modeling. However, despite their apparent simplicity and widespread use, factor models entail conceptual subtleties that are not immediate to grasp. Conceptually, one must distinguish between static and dynamic factor models. Static factor models represent a large number N of *random variables* in terms of a small number K of different *random variables* called factors. Dynamic factor models represent a large number N of *time series* in terms of a small number K of different *time series* called dynamic factors. In the latter case, factor models are ultimately an instance of state-space models. In practice, dynamic models are often used in a static context—a situation that might cause some confusion. In addition, in many classical applications of factor models, we want to explain many variables that are characteristics of an individual (for example the different responses of a person to psychometric tests) while in financial applications we want to explain many variables that are idiosyncratic characteristics of many individuals (for example, a cross section of stock returns in a given moment, where each return is associated to a different firm), which is another possible source of confusion. We will first describe static models and then toward the end of the chapter turn to dynamic models. In Chapters 6 and 7 we discuss how factors and factor-based models are used in building trading strategies.

THE NOTION OF FACTORS

It is perhaps useful to start by considering the concept of factors. In everyday language, we use the term factor to indicate something that has a causal link with an event. We apply the term factor both to identifiable exogenous events and to characteristics of different events. For example, we might say that the number of inches of rain per year in a given region is a factor affecting the yield of farms in that region. In this case the number of inches of rain per year in a given region is an exogenous factor that affects the yield of each farm in that region.

However, we might also say that advertising is a factor of success, meaning that a high advertising budget contributes to the success of some products. In this latter case, the advertising budget is a characteristic of each firm and varies from firm to firm. We also have a notion of hidden factors when we make statements such as: "Her strength of will was the crucial factor for the success of her career" by which we mean that there was a mental disposition that played a crucial role though we cannot directly observe mental dispositions. Therefore, in everyday language, we already have many of the themes that are developed in the formal notion of factors.

Two important aspects of the scientific formal factors, not always present in everyday usage, should be emphasized. First, in science we call factors those variables that provide a common explanation of many other variables. In the absence of commonality, a factor model becomes a simple regression model. Second, factors as observable variables might be used to predict additional observations but often hidden nonobservable factors are the really important variables, and observations are used only to estimate them. For example, factor models were first introduced in psychometrics to find a common cause for many different psychometric observations coming from tests. Causes such as intelligence or personality traits are the important variables one wants to ascertain, while observations such as the results of psychometric tests are only used to determine hidden personality factors. In the dynamic case, factor models (i.e., state-space models) were introduced to obtain important parameters such as the position of an airplane from noisy measurements.

In the next section we will provide a more formal treatment of static linear factor models.

STATIC FACTOR MODELS

Static factor models are factor models where factors do not have any dynamics. We will consider only *linear factor models* as they represent the vast majority of models used in finance. Though we focus on factor models of returns, we will initially discuss linear factor models as general statistical models.

Linear Factor Models

A linear factor model has the form

$$x_{it} = \alpha_i + \sum_{j=1}^{K} \beta_{ij} f_{jt} + \varepsilon_{it}, \ i = 1, 2, \ldots, N, \ j = 1, 2, \ldots, K, \ t = 1, 2, \ldots, T$$

where

x_i = the *i*-th variable to explain

α_i = the average of the *i*-th variable

β_{ij} = the proportionality constant of the *i*–th variable to the *j*-th factor (the factor loading)

f_j = the *j*-th factor

ε_i = the *i*-th residual term

There are *N* variables and *K* factors in the model and we make the assumption that *N>>K*.

We can write the previous linear factor model in matrix form

$$\boldsymbol{\alpha} + \boldsymbol{\beta} \mathbf{f} + \boldsymbol{\varepsilon}$$

or explicitly

$$\begin{bmatrix} x_1 \\ \vdots \\ x_N \end{bmatrix} = \begin{bmatrix} \alpha_1 \\ \vdots \\ \alpha_N \end{bmatrix} + \begin{bmatrix} \beta_{11} & \cdots & \beta_{1K} \\ \vdots & \ddots & \vdots \\ \beta_{N1} & \cdots & \beta_{NK} \end{bmatrix} \begin{bmatrix} f_1 \\ \vdots \\ f_K \end{bmatrix} + \begin{bmatrix} \varepsilon_1 \\ \vdots \\ \varepsilon_N \end{bmatrix}$$

where

$\mathbf{x}$ = the *N*-vector of variables

$\boldsymbol{\alpha}$ = the *N*-vector of means of $\mathbf{x}$

$\boldsymbol{\beta}$ = the *N* × *K* constant matrix of factor loadings

$\mathbf{f}$ = the *K*-vector of factors

$\boldsymbol{\varepsilon}$ = the *N*-vector of residuals

We note that the vectors $\mathbf{x}$, $\mathbf{f}$, and $\boldsymbol{\varepsilon}$ are random vectors. For example, a model with three variables and two factors takes the form

$$\begin{bmatrix} x_1 \\ x_2 \\ x_3 \end{bmatrix} = \begin{bmatrix} \alpha_1 \\ \alpha_2 \\ \alpha_3 \end{bmatrix} + \begin{bmatrix} \beta_{11} & \beta_{12} \\ \beta_{21} & \beta_{22} \\ \beta_{31} & \beta_{32} \end{bmatrix} \begin{bmatrix} f_1 \\ f_2 \end{bmatrix} + \begin{bmatrix} \varepsilon_1 \\ \varepsilon_2 \\ \varepsilon_3 \end{bmatrix}$$

We see from the preceding expressions why these factor models are referred to as *static*. There are no implicit dynamics in this model. It is a lower dimensional representation (K) of a multivariate vector (N).

Given M samples, we can rewrite this model in an explicit regression form. We begin by stacking all observations, factors, and residuals in three matrices where each row corresponds to an observation:

$$x_{it} = \alpha_i + \sum_{j=1}^{K} \beta_{ij} f_{jt} + \varepsilon_{it}, \ i = 1,2,\ldots,N, \ j = 1,2,\ldots,K, \ t = 1,2,\ldots,T$$

$$\mathbf{X} = \begin{bmatrix} x_{1,1} & \cdots & x_{1,N} \\ \vdots & \ddots & \vdots \\ x_{M,1} & \cdots & x_{M,N} \end{bmatrix}, \ \mathbf{F} = \begin{bmatrix} 1 & f_{1,1} & \cdots & f_{1,K} \\ \vdots & \vdots & \ddots & \vdots \\ 1 & f_{M,1} & \cdots & f_{M,K} \end{bmatrix}, \ \mathbf{E} = \begin{bmatrix} \varepsilon_{1,1} & \cdots & \varepsilon_{1,N} \\ \vdots & \ddots & \vdots \\ \varepsilon_{M,1} & \cdots & \varepsilon_{M,N} \end{bmatrix}$$

and we create a matrix $\mathbf{B} = [\ \boldsymbol{\alpha} \ \boldsymbol{\beta} \ ]$,

$$\mathbf{B} = \begin{bmatrix} \alpha_1 & \beta_{1,1} & \cdots & \beta_{1,K} \\ \vdots & \vdots & \ddots & \vdots \\ \alpha_N & \beta_{N,1} & \cdots & \beta_{N,K} \end{bmatrix}$$

Note that in the matrix of factors $\mathbf{F}$ we add a column of 1s to represent constants. With this notation, we can write the model in regression form as

$$\mathbf{X} = \mathbf{FB}' + \mathbf{E}$$

For example, given five samples, the previous three-variable, two-factor model would be written in explicit regression form as

$$\begin{bmatrix} x_{11} & x_{12} & x_{13} \\ x_{21} & x_{22} & x_{23} \\ x_{31} & x_{32} & x_{33} \\ x_{41} & x_{42} & x_{43} \\ x_{51} & x_{52} & x_{53} \end{bmatrix} = \begin{bmatrix} 1 & f_{11} & f_{12} \\ 1 & f_{21} & f_{22} \\ 1 & f_{31} & f_{32} \\ 1 & f_{41} & f_{42} \\ 1 & f_{51} & f_{52} \end{bmatrix} \begin{bmatrix} \alpha_1 & \alpha_2 & \alpha_3 \\ \beta_{11} & \beta_{21} & \beta_{31} \\ \beta_{12} & \beta_{22} & \beta_{32} \end{bmatrix} + \begin{bmatrix} \varepsilon_{11} & \varepsilon_{12} & \varepsilon_{13} \\ \varepsilon_{21} & \varepsilon_{22} & \varepsilon_{23} \\ \varepsilon_{31} & \varepsilon_{32} & \varepsilon_{33} \\ \varepsilon_{41} & \varepsilon_{42} & \varepsilon_{43} \\ \varepsilon_{51} & \varepsilon_{52} & \varepsilon_{53} \end{bmatrix}$$

The factors $\mathbf{f}$ may or may not be observed. If factors are not observed they are called *hidden* or *latent factors,* or *latent variables.* Factor analysis and related methods such as principal components analysis are primarily concerned with determining hidden factors. If factors are given, or are observed, a factor model is a multivariate regression of $\mathbf{x}$ on $\mathbf{f}$ and factor analysis, per se, does not apply. We describe principal component analysis and factor analysis later in this chapter.

A variant of the previous linear factor model includes time dependence,

$$x_{it} = \alpha_i + \sum_{j=1}^{K} \beta_{ij} f_{jt} + \varepsilon_{it}, \; i = 1, 2, \ldots, N, \; j = 1, 2, \ldots, K, \; t = 1, 2, \ldots, T$$

or in matrix form

$$\mathbf{x}_t = \boldsymbol{\alpha} + \boldsymbol{\beta} f_t + \boldsymbol{\varepsilon}_t$$

where

$\mathbf{x}_t$ = the N-vector of variables at time t
$\boldsymbol{\alpha}$ = the N-vector of *constant* means of $\mathbf{x}_t$
$\boldsymbol{\beta}$ = the $N \times K$ matrix of constant factor loadings
$\mathbf{f}_t$ = the K-vector of factors at time t
$\boldsymbol{\varepsilon}_t$ = the N-vector of residuals both at time t

Note that in this model we have different variables at different points in time and we have to state explicitly that the means and the loadings are constants.

In this form, the linear factor model includes a time dependence. A factor model with time dependence is a model of a *stochastic process*. If all variables at different times are independent and there is no dynamics we can consider the time variable as a label of independent samples and can still apply the concepts of static linear factor models.

For the inference of a factor model of returns, we have only one realization of the process to rely on—namely, one observation from each point in time from past history. In this case, the factor model above can be expressed as

$$\mathbf{X} = \mathbf{F}\mathbf{B}' + \mathbf{E}$$

where each column of the matrices $\mathbf{X}$, $\mathbf{F}$, $\mathbf{E}$ represents a time series and each row represents an observation at a point in time ($t = 1, \ldots, N$)

$$\mathbf{X} = \begin{bmatrix} x_{1,1} & \cdots & x_{1,N} \\ \vdots & \ddots & \vdots \\ x_{T,1} & \cdots & x_{T,N} \end{bmatrix}, \; \mathbf{F} = \begin{bmatrix} 1 & f_{1,1} & \cdots & f_{1,K} \\ \vdots & \vdots & \ddots & \vdots \\ 1 & f_{T,1} & \cdots & f_{T,K} \end{bmatrix}, \; \mathbf{E} = \begin{bmatrix} \varepsilon_{1,1} & \cdots & \varepsilon_{1,N} \\ \vdots & \ddots & \vdots \\ \varepsilon_{T,1} & \cdots & \varepsilon_{T,N} \end{bmatrix}$$

There are three possible empirical settings for the above factor models. The first setting does not include any time dependence. Consider a model of personality factors. In this model, x would be a sample of test results given to a sample of individuals. Each test would include N individual questions or tests and K is the number of hidden factors to explain them. A sample might include observations of individuals in a given population without any explicit reference to time. Consider now time dependence. If we introduce a parameter t, our sample might include multiple observations for each time or it might include one single observation at each time. For example, x_t could be the observations of the tests given to all students that enter a college at the beginning of each school year. In this way we have a sample of many students for each year. Factors are common to all observations of an individual but vary from individual to individual.

Consider now a financial model where x_t represents daily returns of a universe of financial assets and f_t represents the factors at time t, N represents the number of assets in a given market and K is the number of factors to explain returns. Assuming that returns, factors, and residuals are serially independent, we can consider each x_t (and f_t if factors are observed) as an independent observation in our sample. Factors and returns are now the single realization of a multivariate time series, albeit without any time dynamics. Empirically, we have only one observation for each time point.

Consider, however, that if we perform a Monte Carlo experiment, we will simulate many possible paths for both the factors and the returns. If we compute probabilities from a Monte Carlo experiment, we are in the situation of multiple independent samples for each point in time.

Empirical Indeterminacy of the Model and Factor Rotation

Without restrictions, none of the above models is empirically determined. At first sight this might seem a complicated and counterintuitive statement but actually it is a rather obvious observation. In fact, without restrictions, a factor model is simply a definition of the residuals. We can always form linear combinations of variables: without restrictions the linear factor model states that residuals are a linear combination of observations and factors. Without restrictions on residuals, no model that includes residuals is empirically determined. In fact, if we do not place restrictions on residuals, every model is a definition of residuals.[1]

---

[1] We can make the same observation for a differential equation. For example, a first-order differential equation written in the form: $F(x,y,y') = \varphi(x)$ is effectively an equation only if we specify the term $\varphi(x)$, for example by requiring $\varphi(x) = \cos t$. Otherwise $F(x,y,y') = \varphi(x)$ is an expression that defines $\varphi(x)$ as a function of y.

From these remarks it should be clear that restrictions on the residuals of a factor model, as well as restrictions on the noise term of a regression model, are not technicalities but are an essential part of the model definition. What type of restrictions can we place on residuals? A powerful restriction consists in requiring that residuals are zero-mean variables mutually uncorrelated and uncorrelated with the factors. A linear factor model that satisfies these conditions is called a *strict factor model*. We can write the model as follows

$$\begin{aligned}
\mathbf{x} &= \boldsymbol{\alpha} + \boldsymbol{\beta}\mathbf{f} + \boldsymbol{\varepsilon} \\
E(\boldsymbol{\varepsilon}) &= 0 \\
E(\mathbf{f}) &= 0 \\
\mathrm{cov}(\mathbf{f}, \boldsymbol{\varepsilon}) &= 0 \\
\mathrm{cov}(\boldsymbol{\varepsilon}, \boldsymbol{\varepsilon}) &= \mathbf{D}, \ \ \mathbf{D} = (\sigma_1^2, \ldots, \sigma_N^2)\mathbf{I}_N \\
\mathbf{D} &= \mathrm{diag}(\sigma_1^2, \ldots, \sigma_N^2)
\end{aligned}$$

where

$$\begin{aligned}
(\sigma_1^2, \ldots, \sigma_N^2) &= \text{the vector of variances of the residuals} \\
\mathbf{I} &= \text{the unit matrix}
\end{aligned}$$

The condition that factors have zero mean is not restrictive as we can always subtract the mean from the factors. Observations are considered to be independent.

If the model is formulated with explicit time dependence, then we assume that the same strict factor model holds at each time

$$\begin{aligned}
\mathbf{x}_t &= \boldsymbol{\alpha} + \boldsymbol{\beta}\mathbf{f}_t + \boldsymbol{\varepsilon}_t \\
E(\boldsymbol{\varepsilon}_t) &= 0 \\
E(\mathbf{f}_t) &= 0 \\
\mathrm{cov}(\mathbf{f}_t, \boldsymbol{\varepsilon}_t) &= 0 \\
\mathrm{cov}(\boldsymbol{\varepsilon}_t, \boldsymbol{\varepsilon}_t) &= \mathbf{D}, \ \mathbf{D} = (\sigma_1^2, \ldots, \sigma_N^2)\,\mathbf{I}
\end{aligned}$$

and that observations and residuals in different times are independent and identically distributed (i.i.d.) variables. These conditions are the same conditions required for a multivariate regression model. Note that requiring that the residuals are mutually uncorrelated and uncorrelated with factors is different from requiring that the residuals are i.i.d. variables. The former is an assumption on the model, the latter is an assumption on how different samples are distributed.

The strict factor model conditions do not uniquely identify the factors. In fact, the factors in a factor model enter in terms of the product βf. Given any nonsingular matrix A, consider the model where the matrix of factor loadings is multiplied by A^{-1} and the vectors of factors are multiplied by A, such that $\beta^* = \beta A^{-1}$, $f^* = Af$. The new model $x = \alpha + \beta^* f^* + \varepsilon$ by virtue of

$$x = \alpha + \beta^* f^* + \varepsilon = \alpha + (\beta A^{-1})(Af) + \varepsilon x = \alpha + \beta f + \varepsilon$$

is equivalent to the original model. We conclude that factors and betas are defined only up to a linear transformation.

We can use this fact to transform factors in a set of orthonormal variables (i.e., variables whose covariance matrix is the identity matrix). In fact, if we denote Ω as the covariance matrix of factors f, the covariance matrix Ω^* of the transformed factors f^* can be written as follows:

$$\Omega^* = E[f^* f^{*\prime}] = E[(Af)(Af)'] = E[Aff'A] = A\Omega A'$$

As Ω is symmetric and positive semidefinite because it is a covariance matrix, its eigenvalues will be real non-negative numbers and the relationship $\Omega = \Omega^{-1}$ holds. Assuming the eigenvalues are all distinct and different from zero (which is generally the case for covariance matrices), if we choose the matrix A to be the matrix whose columns are the eigenvectors rescaled by the reciprocal of the square root of the corresponding eigenvalues, than the matrix Ω^* is the identity matrix: $\Omega^* = I_K$.

This transformation (i.e., the transformation that makes factors orthonormal) is not unique because it is defined up to an orthogonal rotation. In fact, suppose we rotate the orthonormal factors f with covariance matrix $\Omega^* = I_K$ by multiplying them by any orthogonal matrix (i.e., any nonsingular matrix B such that $BB' = I_K$). The rotated factors are orthonormal because the covariance matrix of the new rotated factors is $B\Omega^* B' = BIB' = I_K$.

Note that if we assume that the factor model is time dependent with i.i.d. variables, the factors become a set of independent random walks. Therefore, representing returns in terms of a strict factor model with K orthonormal factors means to represent returns as linear combinations of K independent random variables. This might seem counterintuitive because it might look as if the model does not have empirical content. Consider, however, that the empirical content of the model is represented by the means and by the factor loading matrix. Actually the assumption that returns have constant means and constant covariance matrix is a very strong empirical assumption, generally not verified.

The Covariance Matrix of Observations

Factor models are one of the tools that can be used to reduce the dimensionality of a covariance matrix of observations. In financial applications, the covariance matrix of observations is too large to be correctly estimated. Consider, for example, the covariance matrix of the returns of a universe of the size of the Russell 1000. The covariance matrix of 1,000 time series of returns has $1,000 \times 999/2 = 499,500$ different entries. Even if we estimate covariances using four years of daily return data (approximately 1,000 days), we have a total of 1 million data points to estimate for about half a million entries, that is, two data points per estimation. This sample is clearly insufficient. It can be formally demonstrated that most entries of a covariance matrix of a large universe of returns are almost all random numbers.[2]

If we can determine a strict factor model, the covariance estimation problem is dramatically simplified. In fact, in this case, we only need to determine the covariance matrix of factors plus the matrix of betas and the variances of the residuals. In the above example of 1,000 return processes, suppose we can determine a ten-factor model. The covariance matrix of factors include $100 \times 99/2 = 4,950$ entries, while the beta matrix includes $10 \times 1,000 = 10,000$ entries. Adding 1,000 residual variances we need to estimate 15,950 numbers, or 3.2% of the estimates needed for a full covariance matrix. We now have an average of 62 data points per estimate, an improvement of more than 30 times with respect to the previous case.

Consider a factor model: $x = \alpha + \beta f + \varepsilon$. We can write the covariance matrix of returns[3] as

$$\Sigma = E[(x - \alpha)(x - \alpha)'] = E[(\beta f + \varepsilon)(\beta f + \varepsilon)'] = \beta \Omega \beta' + V + 2\beta E(f\varepsilon')$$

where $V = E[\varepsilon \varepsilon']$. The last term is zero as factors and residuals are assumed to be independent. Therefore, we have

$$\Sigma = \beta \Omega \beta' + V$$

This formula simplifies further if we apply a factor rotation that transforms factors into standardized orthonormal factors whose covariance matrix is the identity matrix

---

[2]Laurent Laloux, Pierre Cizeau, Jean-Philippe Bouchaud, and Marc Potters, "Noise Dressing of Financial Correlation Matrices," *Physical Review Letters*, 83 (August 1999), pp. 1467–1470.

[3]In this and the following sections, we discuss factor models of returns. However, the methods of factor analysis described in this section can be applied to any variable and not only to returns.

$$\Sigma = \beta\,\beta' + V$$

If our factor model is a strict factor model then the matrix V becomes a diagonal matrix D and the covariance matrix takes the form

$$\Sigma = \beta\,\beta' + D$$

A strict factor model is called a *normal factor model* if all the residuals have the same variance. In this case we can write $D = \sigma^2 I_N$, and the covariance matrix becomes

$$\Sigma = \beta\,\beta' + \sigma^2 I_N$$

Using Factor Models

How do we use a factor model? Here we have to distinguish between financial and nonfinancial applications and between factor models in general and factor analysis. Factor models are primarily used in the social sciences, psychology studies, business applications such as marketing, and in some application in the physical sciences. In these domains, factor models are typically the result of factor analysis. One has a large number of observations, for example, responses to marketing questionnaires or results of psychometric tests, and wants to determine the common causes (or factors) of these observations. A marketing manager might perform factor analysis to analyze factors affecting purchases in order to design marketing strategies. A psychologist might administer psychometric tests and compute the value of factors for each individual using a model developed and tested on a large sample population. In these situations factor analysis can be useful.

In financial applications, however, the interest is in managing risk and constructing portfolios. Portfolios are constructed performing a risk-return optimization that requires computing a covariance matrix. As we observed above, computing an unrestricted covariance matrix is not feasible for large universes. Factor models reduce the calculations to computing the exposures to each factor plus the small factor covariance matrix and idiosyncratic error variances.

Factor models thus used are *risk models*. They do not have, per se, forecasting abilities. They explain returns at time t as linear combinations of factors given at time t. Risk measured by variance of returns, due to exposures to common factors is the residual undiversifiable risk. This risk cannot be diversified away regardless of how large a portfolio we choose. However, if factors can be forecasted, or if factors that explain returns at time t are known at time $t - 1$, then factor models can be used for forecasting returns.

From now onward we will only discuss factor models of returns. Factors used in factor models of returns are usually divided in three types: statistical factors, fundamental factors, and macroeconomic factors. Statistical factors are determined with factor analysis, macroeconomic factors are exogenous macroeconomic variables, and fundamental factors are determined from business fundamentals such as the balance and income statements. We discuss the resulting three methods of constructing factor models next.

FACTOR ANALYSIS AND PRINCIPAL COMPONENTS ANALYSIS

Statistical factors are determined through factor analysis. In this section we discuss factor analysis. The observed variables are the returns at a given frequency of a typically large market in a given time window. For example, we might observe daily returns of the Russell 1000 universe. Factors are not observed but must be determined together with the model. The result of the factor analysis will be:

- A (multivariate) time series of factors.
- A (multivariate) time series of residuals.
- The covariance matrix of factors.
- The factor loadings for each return process.
- The variances of each residual term.

The factor loadings represent the exposures of returns to each factor. We might use these numbers in sample (backward looking), for example to evaluate the risk associated with a fund manager's performance. However, if we need to optimize a portfolio, we have to use our estimates out of sample (forward looking). This implies that we make a forecast of risk exposures. Therefore, even risk models can be used for forecasting: they assume that factor exposures are stable and will not change in the following period. Naturally, this assumption might be unwarranted, especially in moments of market stress.

There are two basic techniques for estimating factor models: factor analysis and principal components analysis.

Let us first discuss factor analysis assuming that our returns are described by a strict factor model. Consider a strict factor model of returns with standard (orthonormal) factors. As we can always subtract the mean from returns, without loss of generality we make the additional assumption that $\alpha = 0$. If we call the returns r_t, the model can be written as

$$r_t = \beta f_t + \varepsilon_t$$

$$E(\boldsymbol{\varepsilon}_t) = 0$$
$$E(\mathbf{f}_t) = 0$$
$$E(\mathbf{r}_t) = 0$$
$$\text{cov}(\mathbf{f}_t, \boldsymbol{\varepsilon}_t) = 0$$
$$\text{cov}(\boldsymbol{\varepsilon}_t, \boldsymbol{\varepsilon}_t) = \mathbf{D}, \ \mathbf{D} = \left(\sigma_1^2, \ldots, \sigma_N^2\right)\mathbf{I}$$
$$\text{cov}(\mathbf{f}_t, \mathbf{f}_t) = \mathbf{I}$$

Under the above assumptions, the explicit regression formulation becomes

$$\mathbf{R} = \mathbf{F}\boldsymbol{\beta}' + \mathbf{E}$$

where

$$\mathbf{R} = \begin{bmatrix} \mathbf{r}_1 \\ \vdots \\ \mathbf{r}_T \end{bmatrix} = \begin{bmatrix} r_{1,1} & \cdots & r_{1,N} \\ \vdots & \ddots & \vdots \\ r_{T,1} & \cdots & r_{T,N} \end{bmatrix}, \ \mathbf{F} = \begin{bmatrix} \mathbf{f}_1 \\ \vdots \\ \mathbf{f}_T \end{bmatrix} = \begin{bmatrix} f_{1,1} & \cdots & f_{1,N} \\ \vdots & \ddots & \vdots \\ f_{T,1} & \cdots & f_{T,N} \end{bmatrix}$$

$$\mathbf{E} = \begin{bmatrix} \boldsymbol{\varepsilon}_1 \\ \vdots \\ \boldsymbol{\varepsilon}_T \end{bmatrix} = \begin{bmatrix} \varepsilon_{1,1} & \cdots & \varepsilon_{1,N} \\ \vdots & \ddots & \vdots \\ \varepsilon_{T,1} & \cdots & \varepsilon_{T,N} \end{bmatrix}, \ \boldsymbol{\beta} = \begin{bmatrix} \beta_{1,1} & \cdots & \beta_{1,K} \\ \vdots & \ddots & \vdots \\ \beta_{T,1} & \cdots & \beta_{T,K} \end{bmatrix}$$

The factor analysis procedure is a three-pass procedure: In the first pass we estimate the factor loadings of orthonormal factors, and the variances of residuals. In the second pass we estimate factors and residuals. In the third pass we might want to rotate factors to gain a better intuition of the model.

Factor Analysis via Maximum Likelihood

Various models can be used to perform factor analysis, some statistically rigorous, others only heuristics. There is a complete and rigorous procedure for linear strict factor models under the assumptions that returns, factors, and residuals are multivariate normal variables. Under this assumption, we can use the maximum likelihood estimation (MLE) principle that we will now describe.

Let us assume that our factor model is multivariate normal, that is to say that, in addition to the assumptions above, the following distributional assumptions also hold

$$\mathbf{r}_t \sim N(0, \mathbf{\Sigma})$$
$$\mathbf{f}_t \sim N(0, \mathbf{I}_K)$$
$$\mathbf{\varepsilon}_t \sim N(0, \mathbf{D})$$

Recall that, given the assumption that our model is a strict factor model with orthonormal factors, the covariance matrix of returns $\mathbf{\Sigma}$ can be represented as

$$\mathbf{\Sigma} = \mathbf{\beta\beta'} + \mathbf{D}, \ \mathbf{D} = \left(\sigma_1^2, \ldots, \sigma_N^2\right)\mathbf{I}_N$$

where $\mathbf{I}_N$ is the $N \times N$ identity matrix. Note that we can determine the empirical covariance matrix $\mathbf{\Sigma}$ using the observed data but we need to estimate the factor loadings and the residual variances.

The MLE principle estimates the parameters of a model by maximizing the *likelihood* of the model. The likelihood of a model is the product of the densities of the model's variables estimated on all samples. Under the assumption of joint normality and zero means, we can explicitly write the joint distribution of returns

$$\mathbf{r}_t \sim N(\mathbf{\alpha}, \mathbf{\Sigma}) = \left[(2\pi)^N |\mathbf{\Sigma}|\right]^{-\frac{1}{2}} \exp\left\{-\frac{1}{2}\mathbf{r}_t'\mathbf{\Sigma}^{-1}\mathbf{r}_t\right\}$$

and the likelihood is given by

$$L(\mathbf{\Sigma}) = \left[(2\pi)^N |\mathbf{\Sigma}|\right]^{-\frac{K}{2}} \prod_{t=1}^{T} \exp\left\{-\frac{1}{2}\mathbf{r}_t'\mathbf{\Sigma}^{-1}\mathbf{r}_t\right\}$$

As the logarithm is a monotone function, we can replace the likelihood function with its logarithm, forming the log-likelihood. This transformation often simplifies computations because it replaces products with sums

$$\log L(\mathbf{\Sigma}) = l(\mathbf{\Sigma}) = -\frac{NK}{2}\log(2\pi) - \frac{K}{2}\log(|\mathbf{\Sigma}|) - \frac{1}{2}\sum_{t=1}^{T}\left\{\mathbf{r}_t'\mathbf{\Sigma}^{-1}\mathbf{r}_t\right\}$$

So-called maximum likelihood expectation (MLE) method maximizes the log-likelihood $l(\mathbf{\Sigma})$ as a function of the covariance matrix $\mathbf{\Sigma}$:

$$\mathbf{\Sigma} = \arg\max_{\mathbf{\Sigma}} l(\mathbf{\Sigma})$$

using the restriction

$$\Sigma = \beta\beta' + D, \; D = \left(\sigma_1^2, \ldots, \sigma_N^2\right)I_N$$

Unless the factors are previously given, this computation cannot be performed analytically and one needs to resort to numerical methods.

The Expectation Maximization Algorithm

A numerical method for MLE is based on the *expectation maximization* (EM) algorithm that we will now describe. The EM algorithm is an iterative procedure for determining the log-likelihood when some variables are missing or when there are hidden variables. The EM was fully formulated by Dempster, Laird, and Rubin (DLR hereafter).[4] They presented EM as a coherent and complete methodology offering the mathematical and statistical justification behind it. Rubin and Thayer[5] detailed the application of the EM algorithm to factor models.

The EM algorithm assumes that besides observed data there may also be missing or so-called hidden data. The observed data are the returns r_t while the missing data are the hidden, nonobserved factors f_t. The observed returns r_t are called *incomplete data* while the set of variables that include both the observed returns r_t and the unobserved factors f_t are called *complete data*. Call z_t the vector of complete data at time t

$$z_t = \begin{bmatrix} r_t \\ f_t \end{bmatrix}$$

If factors were observed, we could apply the MLE principle in a straightforward way by maximizing the likelihood given all observed data. However, when factors are not observed, we need iterative methods to compute the model parameters.

Intuitively (albeit not precisely) speaking, the EM method is an iterative Bayesian method that alternates between two steps, the E step and the M step. The E step assumes that the model parameters are known and makes the best estimate of the hidden variables given the observed data and the model parameters estimated at the previous step. Subsequently, the M step computes new model parameters via ML estimates using the hidden data

---

[4]A. P. Dempster, N. Laird, and Donald B. Rubin, "Maximum Likelihood from Incomplete Data via the EM Algorithm," *Journal of the Royal Statistical Society*, B, 39 (1977), pp. 1–38.
[5]Donald B. Rubin and D. T. Thayer, "EM Algorithms for ML Factor Analysis," *Psychometrika*, 47 (1983), pp. 69–76.

estimated in the previous step. The new model parameters are then used to form new estimates of the hidden data and a new cycle is performed. Starting from an initial guess of the model parameters, the EM methods alternate between estimating new hidden data using old parameters and estimating new parameters using old hidden data.

This loose, simplified description highlights the Bayesian nature of the EM method in the E step where hidden factors are estimated given actual observed data. It is, however, a loose description because, as we will see in the following paragraphs, the E step does not directly estimate the hidden data but computes the expectation of the log-likelihood.

We now describe the EM algorithm formally following DLR. Call $p(\mathbf{r}_t, \mathbf{f}_t \mid \boldsymbol{\beta}, \mathbf{D})$ the joint density of the model's variables which depends on the model parameters $\boldsymbol{\beta}, \mathbf{D}$. Consider T independent samples. We write the complete data likelihood function as

$$L\left(\mathbf{r}_t, \mathbf{f}_t \mid \boldsymbol{\beta}, \mathbf{D}\right) = \prod_{t=1}^{T} p\left(\mathbf{r}_t, \mathbf{f}_t \mid \boldsymbol{\beta}, \mathbf{D}\right)$$

and the log-likelihood function as

$$\log L\left(\mathbf{r}_t, \mathbf{f}_t \mid \boldsymbol{\beta}, \mathbf{D}\right) = \log \prod_{t=1}^{T} p\left(\mathbf{r}_t, \mathbf{f}_t \mid \boldsymbol{\beta}, \mathbf{D}\right) = \sum_{i=1}^{T} \log\left(p\left(\mathbf{r}_t, \mathbf{f}_t \mid \boldsymbol{\beta}, \mathbf{D}\right)\right)$$

We can state the MLE principle in terms of the log-likelihood as follows:

$$\boldsymbol{\beta}, \mathbf{D} = \underset{\boldsymbol{\beta},\mathbf{D}}{\arg\max}\left(\log L\left(\mathbf{r}_t, \mathbf{f}_t \mid \boldsymbol{\beta}, \mathbf{D}\right)\right) = \underset{\boldsymbol{\beta},\mathbf{D}}{\arg\max}\left(\sum_{t=1}^{T} \log p\left(\mathbf{r}_t, \mathbf{f}_t \mid \boldsymbol{\beta}, \mathbf{D}\right)\right)$$

However, for each sample we have observations of the returns $\mathbf{r}_t$ but we do not have observations of the factors $\mathbf{f}_t$. Observe that we can simplify the log-likelihood function as

$$\log L = \sum_{t=1}^{T} \log p\left(\mathbf{r}_t, \mathbf{f}_t \mid \boldsymbol{\beta}, \mathbf{D}\right) = \sum_{t=1}^{T} \log\left(p\left(\mathbf{r}_t \mid \mathbf{f}_t, \boldsymbol{\beta}, \mathbf{D}\right) p\left(\mathbf{f}_t \mid \boldsymbol{\beta}, \mathbf{D}\right)\right)$$

$$= \sum_{t=1}^{T} \log p\left(\mathbf{r}_t \mid \mathbf{f}_t, \boldsymbol{\beta}, \mathbf{D}\right) + \sum_{t=1}^{T} \log p\left(\mathbf{f}_t \mid \boldsymbol{\beta}, \mathbf{D}\right)$$

As factors are assumed to be orthonormal, the density $p(\mathbf{f}_t \mid \boldsymbol{\beta}, \mathbf{D})$ does not depend on $\boldsymbol{\beta}, \mathbf{D}$, and we can therefore write

$$\log L = \sum_{t=1}^{T} \log p\left(\mathbf{r}_t \mid \mathbf{f}_t, \boldsymbol{\beta}, \mathbf{D}\right) + \sum_{t=1}^{T} \log p\left(\mathbf{f}_t\right)$$

The maximum of the log-likelihood is a function of $\boldsymbol{\beta}$ and $\mathbf{D}$, and thus the last term has no impact. Consequently, we maximize the function

$$l_C = \sum_{t=1}^{T} \log p\left(\mathbf{r}_t \left| \mathbf{f}_t, \boldsymbol{\beta}, \mathbf{D}\right.\right)$$

Observe that we have replaced the log-likelihood based on the joint distribution of the complete data with a function that depends only on conditional distribution of the observed data given the hidden factors.

The above reasoning applies to any distribution. Let's write down explicitly the log-likelihood under the assumption of joint normality. The density $p(\mathbf{r}_t|\mathbf{f}_t, \boldsymbol{\beta}, \mathbf{D})$ is the density of a normal distribution and it is therefore determined uniquely by the means and the covariances. We say that means and covariances are sufficient statistics for the log-likelihood. Given the factors, the returns are independently and normally distributed with means and covariances given by

$$E\left(\mathbf{r}_t \left| \mathbf{f}_t, \boldsymbol{\beta}, \mathbf{D}\right.\right) = E\left(\boldsymbol{\beta}\mathbf{f}_t + \boldsymbol{\varepsilon} \left| \mathbf{f}_t, \boldsymbol{\beta}, \mathbf{D}\right.\right) = \boldsymbol{\beta}\mathbf{f}_t$$

$$\mathrm{cov}\left(\mathbf{r}_t \left| \mathbf{f}_t, \boldsymbol{\beta}, \mathbf{D}\right.\right) = E\left(\mathbf{r}_t - \boldsymbol{\beta}\mathbf{f}_t \left| \mathbf{f}_t, \boldsymbol{\beta}, \mathbf{D}\right.\right) = \mathbf{D}$$

As factors are orthonormal variables, we can write:

$$\begin{aligned}
\log L &= -\frac{TK}{2}\log(2\pi) - \frac{T}{2}\log|\mathbf{D}| - \frac{1}{2}\sum_{t=1}^{T}\left(\mathbf{r}_t - \boldsymbol{\beta}\mathbf{f}_t\right)' \mathbf{D}^{-1}\left(\mathbf{r}_t - \boldsymbol{\beta}\mathbf{f}_t\right) - \frac{1}{2}\sum_{t=1}^{T}\mathbf{f}_t'\mathbf{I}_K^{-1}\mathbf{f}_t \\
&= -\frac{TK}{2}\log(2\pi) - \frac{T}{2}\log|\mathbf{D}| \\
&\quad - \frac{1}{2}\sum_{t=1}^{T}\left\{\mathbf{r}_t'\mathbf{D}^{-1}\mathbf{r}_t - \boldsymbol{\beta}\mathbf{f}_t'\mathbf{D}^{-1}\mathbf{r}_t - \mathbf{r}_t'\mathbf{D}^{-1}\boldsymbol{\beta}\mathbf{f}_t + \mathbf{f}_t''\mathbf{D}^{-1}\boldsymbol{\beta}\mathbf{f}_t\right\} - \frac{1}{2}\sum_{t=1}^{T}\mathbf{f}_t'\mathbf{f}_t \\
&= -\frac{TK}{2}\log(2\pi) - \frac{T}{2}\log|\mathbf{D}| \\
&\quad - \frac{1}{2}\sum_{t=1}^{T}\left\{\mathbf{r}_t'\mathbf{D}^{-1}\mathbf{r}_t - 2\mathbf{r}_t'\mathbf{D}^{-1}\boldsymbol{\beta}\mathbf{f}_t + \mathrm{Tr}\left[\boldsymbol{\beta}'\mathbf{D}^{-1}\boldsymbol{\beta}\mathbf{f}_t'\mathbf{f}_t\right]\right\} - \frac{1}{2}\sum_{t=1}^{T}\mathbf{f}_t'\mathbf{f}_t
\end{aligned}$$

where in the last step we used the identity $\mathbf{x}'\mathbf{Ax} = \mathrm{Tr}[\mathbf{Ax}'\mathbf{x}]$ and that for a diagonal matrix $\mathbf{A}' = \mathbf{A}$.

Following DLR, the EM algorithm can be described as follows. Suppose we are at step p of the iterative procedure and that at this step we have computed all the sufficient statistics relative to this step. In our case, suppose we have determined the matrix $\boldsymbol{\beta}_p$ and the diagonal matrix $\mathbf{D}_p$ at step p. In general, these quantities will not be the true quantities. The log-likelihood computed using these statistics is a random variable because it depends on the hidden factors that are not observed. To improve our approximation, the EM algorithm performs two steps:

1. The E-step computes the expectation of the log-likelihood (given the data) using the conditional density of the factors (given the data).
2. The M-step computes new matrices $\boldsymbol{\beta}_{p+1}$ and $\mathbf{D}_{p+1}$ maximizing the expected log-likelihood computed in the previous E step with respect to $\boldsymbol{\beta}$ and $\mathbf{D}$.

DLR observe that, in the case of factor analysis with normal distributions, the EM algorithm simplifies and can be described by the following two steps:

1. The E-step computes the expectation of the sufficient statistics of the log-likelihood given the observed data and the matrices $\boldsymbol{\beta}_p$ and $\mathbf{D}_p$ computed in the previous M step.
2. The M-step computes new matrices $\boldsymbol{\beta}_{p+1}$ and $\mathbf{D}_{p+1}$ using the sufficient statistics computed in the previous E step.

Let us see how the EM algorithm is applied to our factor model. We have to maximize the quantity

$$l_C = -\frac{T}{2}\log|\mathbf{D}| - \frac{1}{2}\sum_{t=1}^{T}\left\{ \mathbf{r}_t'\mathbf{D}^{-1}\mathbf{r}_t - 2\mathbf{r}_t'\mathbf{D}^{-1}\boldsymbol{\beta}\mathbf{f}_t + \mathrm{Tr}\left[\boldsymbol{\beta}'\mathbf{D}^{-1}\boldsymbol{\beta}\mathbf{f}_t'\mathbf{f}_t \right] \right\}$$

as the other terms of the complete likelihood do not depend on $\boldsymbol{\beta}$ and $\mathbf{D}$. First we consider the E-step.

The E-Step

The E-step computes the expectation of the log-likelihood of the complete data given the observed data. However, DLR observe that in the case of exponential distributions we need only compute the expectations of the sufficient statistics of the complete data given the observed data. The joint distribution $p(\mathbf{r}_t, \mathbf{f}_t | \boldsymbol{\beta}, \mathbf{D})$ of the complete variables is normal given the linearity of the model and yields

$$E\left(\mathbf{z}_t | \boldsymbol{\beta}, \mathbf{D}\right) = E\left(\begin{bmatrix} \mathbf{r}_t \\ \mathbf{f}_t \end{bmatrix}\right) = 0$$

$$\mathrm{cov}\left(\mathbf{z}_t\mathbf{z}_t | \boldsymbol{\beta}, \mathbf{D}\right) = \boldsymbol{\Lambda} = \begin{bmatrix} \mathrm{cov}(\mathbf{r}_t\mathbf{r}_t | \boldsymbol{\beta}, \mathbf{D}) & \mathrm{cov}(\mathbf{r}_t\mathbf{f}_t | \boldsymbol{\beta}, \mathbf{D}) \\ \mathrm{cov}(\mathbf{r}_t\mathbf{f}_t | \boldsymbol{\beta}, \mathbf{D})' & \mathrm{cov}(\mathbf{f}_t\mathbf{f}_t | \boldsymbol{\beta}, \mathbf{D}) \end{bmatrix} = \begin{bmatrix} \boldsymbol{\Lambda}_{11} & \boldsymbol{\Lambda}_{12} \\ \boldsymbol{\Lambda}_{21} & \boldsymbol{\Lambda}_{22} \end{bmatrix}$$

As $E(\mathbf{z}_t \mid \boldsymbol{\beta}, \mathbf{D}) = 0$, the complete data sufficient statistics are $\boldsymbol{\Lambda}_{11}, \boldsymbol{\Lambda}_{12}, \boldsymbol{\Lambda}_{22}$. The E-step at step p replaces the complete data sufficient statistics with their expectations given the data. We therefore need to compute the expectation of the sufficient statistics $E\left(\mathbf{z}_t \mathbf{z}_t' \mid \mathbf{r}_t, \boldsymbol{\beta}_p, \mathbf{D}_p\right)$. Following Rubin and Thayer, the sufficient statistics are

$$E\left(\boldsymbol{\Lambda}_{11} \mid \mathbf{r}_t, \boldsymbol{\beta}_p, \mathbf{D}_p\right) = E\left[\operatorname{cov}(\mathbf{r}_t \mathbf{r}_t \mid \mathbf{r}_t, \boldsymbol{\beta}_p, \mathbf{D}_p)\right] = \operatorname{cov}(\mathbf{r}_t \mathbf{r}_t) = \frac{1}{T}\sum_{t=1}^{T}\mathbf{r}_t' \mathbf{r}_t$$

$$E\left(\boldsymbol{\Lambda}_{12} \mid \mathbf{r}_t, \boldsymbol{\beta}_p, \mathbf{D}_p\right) = E\left[\operatorname{cov}(\mathbf{r}_t \mathbf{f}_t \mid \mathbf{r}_t)\right] = \boldsymbol{\beta}_p \boldsymbol{\gamma}_{p+1}$$

$$E\left(\boldsymbol{\Lambda}_{22} \mid \mathbf{r}_t, \boldsymbol{\beta}_p, \mathbf{D}_p\right) = E\left[\operatorname{cov}(\mathbf{f}_t \mathbf{f}_t \mid \mathbf{r}_t)\right] = \boldsymbol{\gamma}_{p+1}' \boldsymbol{\Lambda}_{22} \boldsymbol{\gamma}_{p+1} + \boldsymbol{\Delta}_{p+1}$$

where $\boldsymbol{\gamma}_{p+1}$ and $\boldsymbol{\Delta}_{p+1}$ are the regression coefficient matrix and the residual covariance matrix of the regression of the factors $\mathbf{f}_t$ on the returns $\mathbf{r}_t$, respectively. These quantities can be compactly described through the *sweep operator* which is explained in Appendix C:

$$SWEEP(1,2,\ldots,N)\begin{bmatrix} \boldsymbol{\beta}_p \boldsymbol{\beta}_p' + \mathbf{D}_p & \boldsymbol{\beta}_p' \\ \boldsymbol{\beta}_p & \mathbf{I}_K \end{bmatrix} = \begin{bmatrix} \left(\boldsymbol{\beta}_p \boldsymbol{\beta}_p' + \mathbf{D}_p\right)^{-1} & \boldsymbol{\gamma}_{p+1}' \\ \boldsymbol{\gamma}_{p+1} & \boldsymbol{\Delta}_{p+1} \end{bmatrix}$$

We may gain a better intuition of the E-step if we apply the E-step in its most general form, computing the expectation of l_C given the data; that is, according to the distribution $p(\mathbf{f}_t \mid \mathbf{r}_t, \boldsymbol{\beta}_p, \mathbf{D}_p)$, where parameters $\boldsymbol{\beta}_p, \mathbf{D}_p$ are those computed in the previous M-step

$$E[l_C] = E\left[-\frac{T}{2}\log|\mathbf{D}| - \frac{1}{2}\sum_{t=1}^{T}\left\{\mathbf{r}_t' \mathbf{D}^{-1}\mathbf{r}_t - 2\mathbf{r}_t' \mathbf{D}^{-1}\boldsymbol{\beta}\mathbf{f}_t + \operatorname{Tr}\left[\boldsymbol{\beta}' \mathbf{D}^{-1}\boldsymbol{\beta}\mathbf{f}_t \mathbf{f}_t'\right]\right\}\right]$$

$$= -\frac{T}{2}\log|\mathbf{D}| - \frac{1}{2}\sum_{t=1}^{T}\left\{\begin{array}{l}\mathbf{r}_t' \mathbf{D}^{-1}\mathbf{r}_t - 2\mathbf{r}_t' \mathbf{D}^{-1}\boldsymbol{\beta}E\left(\mathbf{f}_t \mid \mathbf{r}_t, \boldsymbol{\beta}_p, \mathbf{D}_p\right) \\ + \operatorname{Tr}\left[\boldsymbol{\beta}' \mathbf{D}^{-1}\boldsymbol{\beta}E\left(\mathbf{f}_t \mathbf{f}_t \mid \mathbf{r}_t, \boldsymbol{\beta}_p, \mathbf{D}_p\right)\right]\end{array}\right\}$$

Given the joint normality of the model, we need to compute only the means $E(\mathbf{f}_t \mid \mathbf{r}_t, \boldsymbol{\beta}_p, \mathbf{D}_p)$ and the covariances $E(\mathbf{f}_t' \mathbf{f}_t \mid \mathbf{r}_t, \boldsymbol{\beta}_p, \mathbf{D}_p)$. In order to compute these (sufficient) statistics, we need the distribution of factors given the data, but the model prescribes the distribution of data given the factors. Hence we employ Bayes' theorem

$$p\left(\mathbf{f}_t \mid \mathbf{r}_t, \boldsymbol{\beta}, \mathbf{D}\right) \propto p\left(\mathbf{r}_t \mid \mathbf{f}_t, \boldsymbol{\beta}, \mathbf{D}\right)p\left(\mathbf{f}_t\right)$$

The M-Step

The M-step proceeds as follows. First we replace the sufficient statistics of the log-likelihood with their expectations computed in the E-step. Then we maximize the log-likelihood equating to zero its partial derivatives with respect to β and D:

$$\frac{\partial}{\partial\beta} E[\log L] = 0, \quad \frac{\partial}{\partial D} E[\log L] = 0$$

However, given that the complete data distribution is normal, we can use a simplified process based on the regressions outlined in DLR and described in detail in Rubin and Thayer. We estimate the new model parameters directly from the covariances as follows:

$$SWEEP\left(N+1,2,\dots,N+K\right)\begin{bmatrix} \Lambda_{11} & \Lambda_{11}\gamma_{p+1} \\ \gamma'_{p+1}\Lambda_{11} & \gamma'_{p+1}\Lambda_{11}\gamma_{p+1} + \Delta_{p+1} \end{bmatrix} = \begin{bmatrix} D_{p+1} & * \\ \beta_{p+1} & * \end{bmatrix}$$

The EM algorithm has originated many other models, in particular the *expectation conditional maximization* described in Liu and Rubin.[6] These methods address the problem of the sometimes slow convergence rate of the EM algorithm. The interested reader should refer to their work.

Factor Analysis via Principal Components

Factor analysis based on the MLE principle depends critically on the assumption of normal distribution of returns. However, it is well known that returns cannot be considered normal and have tails heavier than those of the normal distribution. There are a number of estimation methods that do not depend on the assumption of normality of returns. The best known and most widely used of these methods is the *principal components analysis* (PCA) method.

Though factor analysis and PCA are similar techniques and have similar objectives, there are fundamental differences. Let us first describe in general the method of PCA, then comment on how they differ from factor analysis, and finally discuss under what conditions factor analysis and PCA are equivalent.[7]

---

[6]Chuanhai Liu and Donald B. Rubin, "Maximum Likelihood Estimation of Factor Analysis Using The ECME Algorithm With Complete and Incomplete Data," *Statistica Sinica*, 8 (1998), pp. 729–747.
[7]For a detailed analysis of PCA methodologies, see Ian T. Jolliffe, *Principal Components Analysis*, 2nd Ed. (New York: Springer 2002).

Let us first look at PCA from the point of view of the distribution of a population. Consider a random vector of N returns: $\mathbf{r} = (r_1, ..., r_N)'$. Suppose that the variables' means have been subtracted from the respective variables so that $\mathbf{r}$ is a vector of zero-mean random variables. Consider the covariance matrix Σ of $\mathbf{r}$, defined as: $\Sigma = E(\mathbf{rr}')$ or, explicitly, $\Sigma = \{\sigma_{ij}\}$, $\sigma_{ij} = E(r_i r_j)$. Being a covariance matrix, Σ is symmetric and positive semidefinite.[8]

Consider now the eigenvalues and eigenvectors of the matrix Σ. Consider the i-th eigenvalue λ_i and its corresponding eigenvector $\mathbf{h}_i$. As the matrix Σ is positive semidefinite, we have $\mathbf{h}_i'\Sigma\mathbf{h}_i = \mathbf{h}_i'\lambda_i\mathbf{h}_i \geq 0$, so all eigenvalues must be real. Let us assume that all eigenvalues are distinct and nonzero.[9] Eigenvectors are defined up to a multiplicative constant. We can therefore require that all eigenvectors have unit norm, $\mathbf{h}_i'\mathbf{h}_i = 1$.

Assembling all eigenvectors in a matrix $\mathbf{H} = [\mathbf{h}_1 \ ... \ \mathbf{h}_N]$ and all eigenvalues in a diagonal matrix $\Lambda = \text{diag}(\lambda_1 \ ... \lambda_N)$, the following relationships are valid

$$\Sigma\mathbf{H} = \mathbf{H}\Lambda$$

$$\Sigma = \mathbf{H}\Lambda\mathbf{H}^{-1}$$

$$\Lambda = \mathbf{H}\Sigma\mathbf{H}^{-1}$$

This means that the matrix of eigenvectors diagonalizes the covariance matrix. As the covariance matrix Σ is symmetric, the matrix $\mathbf{H}$ of the eigenvectors has the property $\mathbf{H}' = \mathbf{H}^{-1}$ and therefore: $\mathbf{H}'\mathbf{H} = \mathbf{I}_N$; that is, all distinct eigenvectors are mutually orthogonal and $\Sigma = \mathbf{H}\Lambda\mathbf{H}'$.

Consider now the random vector $\mathbf{r}$. The random vector $\mathbf{p} = \mathbf{Hr}$ is a vector of orthogonal random variables. In fact, the following relationships hold

$$\text{Cov}(\mathbf{p}) = E(\mathbf{pp}') = E\left((\mathbf{Hr})(\mathbf{Hr})'\right) = E(\mathbf{Hrr'H'}) = \mathbf{H}E(\mathbf{rr'})\mathbf{H}' = \mathbf{H}\Sigma\mathbf{H}' = \Lambda$$

In other words, multiplying the vector of returns $\mathbf{r}$ by the eigenvectors $\mathbf{h}_i$, we form a linear combination of the original returns that are mutually orthogonal and whose variances are equal to the corresponding eigenvalues λ_i. In addition, we can rewrite the vector $\mathbf{r}$ in terms of the orthogonal components $\mathbf{p}$ as $\mathbf{r} = \mathbf{H}'\mathbf{p}$. We say that the vectors $\mathbf{p}$ are an *orthonormal basis* for the vectors $\mathbf{r}$.

The relationship $\mathbf{r} = \mathbf{H}'\mathbf{p}$ is an exact relationship. We partition the matrix $\mathbf{H}$ in two submatrices $\mathbf{H} = [\mathbf{H}_1 \ \mathbf{H}_2]$ where $\mathbf{H}_1$ is formed by the eigenvectors corresponding to the k largest eigenvalues and partition the vector $\mathbf{p} = [\mathbf{p}_1 \ \mathbf{p}_2]$

---

[8]A matrix $\mathbf{A}$ is positive semidefinite if, for any vector $\mathbf{x}$ the relationship $\mathbf{xAx}' \geq 0$ holds.

[9]Methodologies for handling the rather unusual case of zero or equal eigenvalues are described in Jolliffe, *Principal Components Analysis*.

into two vectors $\mathbf{p}_1$, $\mathbf{p}_2$ containing the first k and the last $N\text{-}k$ components. We can therefore approximately represent the vector $\mathbf{r}$ in terms of a reduced number of eigenvectors and write the following relationship:

$$\mathbf{r} = \mathbf{H}_1'\mathbf{p}_1 + \mathbf{H}_2'\mathbf{p}_2 = \mathbf{H}_1'\mathbf{p}_1 + \mathbf{e}$$

This representation is formally similar to a factor model with k factors $\mathbf{p}_1$, loading matrix $\mathbf{H}_1$ and residuals $\mathbf{e}$. However, the residuals are generally not uncorrelated and the basic restriction of factor models is therefore not verified. Therefore, the PCA representation $\mathbf{r} = \mathbf{H}_1'\mathbf{p}_1 + \mathbf{e}$ is an approximate relationship.

Let us now move from theoretical properties of populations to samples. From the theory outlined in the above paragraphs, we infer that we can perform PCA with the following four steps:

1. Subtract the means from the sample.
2. Estimate the covariance matrix of the sample.
3. Compute the eigenvalues and eigenvectors of the covariance matrix.
4. Select the first k eigenvectors as first k PCs.

However, PCA can perhaps be better understood in terms of the *singular value decomposition of the design matrix*, which is the matrix of the sample data. Consider the same empirical setting of observations as in the previous section. A set of T observation of N returns are given. Assume that the vector of sample means has been subtracted from each observation and arrange observations in the following *design matrix*

$$\mathbf{R} = \begin{bmatrix} r_{1,1} & \cdots & r_{1,N} \\ \vdots & \ddots & \vdots \\ r_{T,1} & \cdots & r_{T,N} \end{bmatrix}$$

Suppose $T \geq N$. Consider the $N \times N$ square matrix: $\mathbf{S} = \mathbf{R}'\mathbf{R}$ and consider its eigenvectors $\mathbf{V} = [\mathbf{v}_1, ...,\mathbf{v}_N]$ and eigenvalues $[\lambda_1, ...,\lambda_N]$. The matrix $\mathbf{S}$ is proportional to the empirical covariance matrix of the sample. Let us assume, as we did in the previous section, that all eigenvalues are non-zero and distinct. The matrix $\mathbf{S}$ is symmetric since $\mathbf{S}' = (\mathbf{R}'\mathbf{R})' = \mathbf{R}'\mathbf{R} = \mathbf{S}$. We normalize eigenvectors to unitary length, so that the eigenvectors are a set of r orthonormal vectors. The $\mathbf{v}_i$ are nonzero N-vectors that are the solutions of the equation

$$\left(\mathbf{R}'\mathbf{R}\right)\mathbf{v}_i = \lambda_i\mathbf{v}_i$$

Call the positive numbers $\sigma_i = +\sqrt{\lambda_i}$ *singular values*. Consider the set of T-vectors $\mathbf{u}_i = \sigma_i^{-1} \mathbf{R} \mathbf{v}_i$. The $\mathbf{u}_i$ are a set of orthonormal vectors; in fact

$$\mathbf{u}_i' \mathbf{u}_j = \left(\sigma_i^{-1} \mathbf{R} \mathbf{v}_i\right)' \sigma_j^{-1} \mathbf{R} \mathbf{v}_j = \sigma_i^{-1} \sigma_j^{-1} \mathbf{v}_i' \mathbf{R}' \mathbf{R} \mathbf{v}_j = \sigma_i^{-1} \sigma_j^{-1} \mathbf{v}_i' \lambda_j \mathbf{v}_j$$

$$= \sigma_i^{-1} \sigma_j^{-1} \lambda_j \mathbf{v}_i' \mathbf{v}_j = \begin{cases} 0 \text{ if } i \neq j \\ \sigma_i^{-1} \sigma_i^{-1} \lambda_i = 1 \text{ if } i = j \end{cases}$$

We can construct a diagonal square $N \times N$ matrix $\boldsymbol{\Sigma}$ which has on the diagonal the values σ_i ordered by size

$$\boldsymbol{\Sigma} = \begin{bmatrix} \sigma_1 & 0 & 0 \\ 0 & \ddots & 0 \\ 0 & 0 & \sigma_N \end{bmatrix}, \; \sigma_1 \geq \sigma_2 \geq \cdots \geq \sigma_N$$

We also construct a $T \times N$ matrix $\mathbf{U}$ defined as: $\mathbf{U} = [\mathbf{u}_1, \ldots, \mathbf{u}_N]$. Using the relationships defined above, we can now state the *singular value decomposition* (SVD) relationships

$$\mathbf{RV} = \mathbf{U} \boldsymbol{\Sigma}$$

$$\mathbf{R} = \mathbf{U} \boldsymbol{\Sigma} \mathbf{V}'$$

We now see the relationship between eigenvalue decomposition and SVD: We define the matrix

$$\mathbf{R}^* = \frac{1}{\sqrt{T}} \mathbf{R}$$

and we compute the SVD of $\mathbf{R}^*$. The SVD of $\mathbf{R}^*$ determines a matrix $\mathbf{V}^*$; the columns of the matrix $\mathbf{V}^*$ are the principal components of the matrix $\mathbf{R}$. The advantage of using the PCA is that there are algorithms for performing the SVD that are more robust than the computation of eigenvalues and eigenvectors.

There is another interpretation of the PCA that is based on the Karhunen-Loéve transform. The Karhunen-Loéve transform finds the axis of maximum variance. Consider the same empirical setting as in the previous section. We want to determine the linear combination of returns with the largest possible variance, subject to the condition that the vector of coefficients has unitary length. Stated differently, we want to find a portfolio of maximum variance among all portfolios whose weights form a portfolio of unitary length.

Consider a linear combination of returns

$$\sum_{j=1}^{N} \beta_{1j} r_{tj} = \boldsymbol{\beta}_1' \mathbf{r}_t, \ \mathbf{r}_t = (r_{t1}, \ldots, r_{tN})', \ \mathbf{R} = (\mathbf{r}_1, \ldots, \mathbf{r}_T)'$$

where the weights $\boldsymbol{\beta}_1 = (\beta_{11}, \ldots, \beta_{1N})'$ satisfy the condition $\boldsymbol{\beta}_1' \boldsymbol{\beta}_1 = 1$. We want to find the weights that maximize the variance of this linear combination. Using the matrix notation developed in the previous sections, we can write:

$$\boldsymbol{\beta}_1 = \underset{\text{s.t. } \boldsymbol{\beta}_1' \boldsymbol{\beta}_1 = 1}{\mathrm{argmax}} \left(\sum_{t=1}^{T} \left(\sum_{j=1}^{N} \beta_{1j} r_{tj} \right)^2 \right) = \underset{\text{s.t. } \boldsymbol{\beta}_1' \boldsymbol{\beta}_1 = 1}{\mathrm{argmax}} \left(\sum_{t=1}^{T} \left(\boldsymbol{\beta}_1' \mathbf{r}_t \right)^2 \right)$$

As a second step, we search for those linear combinations $\boldsymbol{\beta}_2$ that have the largest variance and that are orthogonal to the first. To do this we apply the same procedure to the space of vectors: $\mathbf{r}_t^{(1)} = \mathbf{r}_t - \boldsymbol{\beta}_1 \boldsymbol{\beta}_1' \mathbf{r}$, and write the condition:

$$\boldsymbol{\beta}_2 = \underset{\text{s.t. } \boldsymbol{\beta}_2' \boldsymbol{\beta}_2 = 1, \, \boldsymbol{\beta}_1' \boldsymbol{\beta}_2 = 0}{\mathrm{argmax}} \left(\sum_{t=1}^{T} \left(\boldsymbol{\beta}_2' \mathbf{r}_t^{(1)} \right)^2 \right)$$

We proceed in this way for N steps. It can be demonstrated that the matrix $\boldsymbol{\beta}_1 = (\boldsymbol{\beta}_1, \ldots, \boldsymbol{\beta}_N)'$ coincides with the matrix of the eigenvalues of the covariance matrix.

In general, results obtained with factor analysis and with PCA do not coincide. However, it can be demonstrated that given a normal factor model with k orthonormal factors, the first K principal components coincide with the factors up to an orthogonal transformation. Recall that a normal factor model is a strict factor model where all residuals have the same variance. If this condition is not satisfied, in general the first K principal components will not coincide with the factors.

This consideration leads to the main differences between factor analysis and PCA. Both methodologies are data reduction techniques in the sense that they seek a parsimonious representation of data. Factor analysis assumes an econometric model of the data while PCA is, simply put, an eigenvalue decomposition of the covariance matrix of the data. Factor analysis yields different factors if the number of factors is changed. However, the original components of PCA do not change if additional components are added.

How to Determine the Number of Factors

The previous section discussed factor analysis and PCA as techniques to determine statistical factors. As discussed, PCA is an approximate methodology which does not require the assumption that the empirical data are generated by a specific factor model. As such, the number of principal components chosen depends on the accuracy of approximation one wants to achieve, where the approximation is measured by the percentage of variance explained by the principal components.

In the case of factor analysis, however, it is necessary to determine a priori the number of factors of the model. Determining the number of factors in a factor model has received much attention in the academic literature, and many different theoretical and heuristic solutions have been proposed.

Heuristic solutions are based on estimating the incremental gain in model quality in going from p to $p + 1$ factors. Perhaps the best known of these heuristics is the *scree test* proposed by Cattell.[10] The scree test is based on plotting the eigenvalues of the covariance matrix in order of size. Cattell observed that this plot decreases sharply up to a certain point and then slows down. The point where it starts to slow down is an approximate estimate of the number of factors.

Theoretical solutions are often based on Information Theory criteria. Information-based criteria introduce a trade-off between the size of residuals and model complexity. For example, Bai and Ng[11] propose an effective method for estimating the number of factors based on a variant of the Akaike information criterion. The advantage of the method of Bai and Ng is that it can be applied to both strict and approximate factor models.

In practice, however, the problem of estimating the number of factors is made difficult by the fact that factor models are never correctly specified. We will come back to this question after discussing approximate factor models. Note that if returns could be represented by a correctly specified strict factor model, the number of factors would be determined and factors would be empirically determined up to a linear transformation.

Note explicitly that the determination of factors through statistical analysis depends on the size of the market. If we consider only a small number of return processes, we cannot hope to reconstruct factors very accurately. On the other hand, a large market with thousands of return processes is most likely able to capture all the *causes* that determine returns. We will cover this point more fully when we discuss factor-mimicking portfolios.

---

[10]*Scree* is a geological term that indicates the debris often found at the foot of a rock. Cattell used the word scree to refer to the eigenvalues that contribute only noise. See Raymond B. Cattell, "The Scree Test for the Number of Factors," *Multivariate Behavioral Research*, 1 (1966), pp. 245–276.

[11]Jushan Bai and Serena Ng, "Determining the Number of Factors in Approximate Factor Models," *Econometrica*, 70 (2002), pp. 191–221. (See also by the same authors "Errata," 2006, Web only.)

WHY FACTOR MODELS OF RETURNS

Classical fundamental analysis as discussed, for example, in Graham and Dodd[12] consider each firm separately and assume that returns depend on characteristics of each firm. The Capital Asset Pricing Model (CAPM) as formulated by Sharpe,[13] Lintner,[14] and Mossin[15] reversed this approach. The CAPM is a factor model, albeit with only one factor and motivated by theoretical considerations. In the CAPM, the expected excess return of each stock is proportional to the global market portfolio excess return.

CAPM introduced the powerful idea that anything important for a stock's returns must be the result of the sensitivity of the same stock to one global factor, while anything idiosyncratic cannot be forecasted. This notion was extended and partially modified in the Arbitrage Pricing Theory (APT) formulated by Stephen Ross.[16] In APT, the returns of any stock are a weighted average of different factors plus, possibly, a constant. The arbitrage restrictions impose that only a small number of returns can exhibit a nonzero constant.

Both fundamental and macroeconomic factor models allow to forecast returns, as nothing in the structure of these models precludes the use of lagged factors. In these models forecasts depend only on lagged values of global factors common to the entire market. They assume that returns can be forecasted and forecasts entail sensitivity to a common cause.

The use of forecasting factor models clearly combines the ability to forecast with the ability to represent correlations. We might, however, need to consider idiosyncratic forecasts. For example, consider momentum strategies. Momentum strategies, as described for example in Figelman,[17] are nonlinear strategies where momentum is a characteristic of specific stocks in some specific moment. The result of a momentum strategy is not the same as that obtained with a factor model with a momentum factor. In the current practice of financial modeling, some firms use models that essentially trans-

---

[12]Benjamin Graham and David Dodd, *Security Analysis: Principles and Techniques* (New York: McGraw Hill, 1962).

[13]William F. Sharpe, "Capital Asset Prices: A Theory of Market Equilibrium Under Conditions of Risk," *Journal of Finance*, 19 (1964), pp. 4 25–442.

[14]John Lintner, "The Valuation of Risk Assets and the Selection of Risky Investments in Stock Portfolios and Capital Budgets," *Review of Economics and Statistics*, 47 (1965), pp. 13–37.

[15]Jan Mossin, "Equilibrium in a Capital Asset Market," *Econometrica*, 34 (1966), pp. 768–783.

[16]Stephen Ross, "The Arbitrage Theory of Capital Asset Pricing," *Journal of Economic Theory*, 13 (1976), pp. 341–360.

[17]Ilya Figelman, "Stock Return Momentum and Reversal," *Journal of Portfolio Management*, 34 (2007), pp. 51–67.

late in computer programs the reasoning of fundamental analysts. These models are idiosyncratic for each firm.

Combining the two types of models, idiosyncratic and factor requires dynamic modeling techniques that go beyond the static models analyzed thus far. We will begin by analyzing approximate factor models and then move to full-fledged dynamic factor models.

The Size of Samples and Uniqueness of Factors

Factor analysis as considered thus far assumes that the number of returns is given and eventually let the number of independent samples grow. That is, N is fixed while T can go to infinity. In statistics, we assume that the accuracy of estimates improves when the sample size grows. Letting T grow makes the sample larger and improves the accuracy of the estimates. In practice this might not be true as the model parameters might not be constant in time. However, if a strict factor model is correctly specified, from a statistical point of view increasing the sample improves accuracy.

The other dimension of factor models, the number N of returns, requires different considerations. If we let N grow, and eventually tend to infinity, we change the market and therefore the object of our study. We do not simply add samples but we change our universe and hence our model. Therefore, we cannot expect to treat the increase of the number of returns simply as an increase in the sample size.

The reason why we want to increase the number of returns in our factor analysis is twofold. The first reason is practical, as we might want to gain an insight in the behavior of a larger number of stocks. The second reason, however, is theoretical. Each return process is a probe of the market. By increasing the number of returns we expect to improve our factor analysis, to gain a more complete understanding of the factors that drive our returns.

Letting both N and T become very large, in the limit go to infinity, has a price in terms of estimation. ML estimates of factor models let only T go to infinity. Therefore, it is important to understand if it is true that a large number of returns improve factor analysis. This is indeed true. Chamberlain and Rothschild[18] demonstrate that in an infinite economy factors can be mimicked by portfolios. When we discuss approximate factor models in the following section we will take this approach: we will let both N and T become very large (go to infinity). In an economy with infinitely many assets, factors are mimicked by portfolios determined through PCA. If an

---

[18]Gary Chamberlain and Michael Rothschild, "Arbitrage, Factor Structure and Mean-Variance Analysis in Large Asset Markets," *Econometrica*, 51 (1983), pp. 1305–1324.

economy is very large, there is only one possible set of factors uniquely determined only up to an orthogonal transformation.

APPROXIMATE FACTOR MODELS OF RETURNS

The conditions of a strict factor model are too restrictive for a large cross section of returns. In practice, it is not possible to impose the condition that the residuals are mutually independent. To make factor models applicable to asset returns observed in the market, we have to relax some of the conditions of strict factor models. The first step toward a more realistic factor model is to allow for some correlation and autocorrelation of residuals. Approximate factor models allow a *moderate* level of correlation and autocorrelation among residuals. They also allow the factors themselves to be autocorrelated. The theory of approximate factor models is developed in Chamberlain and Rothschild,[19] Stock and Watson,[20] and Bai.[21]

How do we define a moderate level of correlation? Approximate factor models allow only correlations that are not marketwide. When we examine different samples at different points in time, approximate factor models admit only local autocorrelation of residuals. This condition guarantees that when the number of factors goes to infinity (i.e., when the number of assets is very large), eigenvalues of the covariance matrix remain bounded.

We will assume that autocorrelation functions of residuals decays to zero. In these models, returns are locally autocorrelated but become sequences of i.i.d. variables if the time interval between subsequent points is sufficiently long. This excludes processes with long memory or integrated processes.[22] In addition, an approximate factor model admits heteroskedastic residuals.

Therefore, we can summarize an approximate factor model as a model:

$$\mathbf{r}_t = \boldsymbol{\beta}\,\mathbf{f}_t + \boldsymbol{\varepsilon}_t$$

where all variables are *stationary* variables with zero mean (we assume that means have been subtracted). We allow factors to follow an autoregressive

---

[19]Chamberlain and Rothschild, "Arbitrage, Factor Structure and Mean-Variance Analysis in Large Asset Markets."

[20]James H. Stock and Mark W. Watson, "Forecasting Using Principal Components From a Large Number of Predictors," *Journal of the American Statistical Association*, 97 (2002), pp. 1167–1179.

[21]Jushan Bai, "Inferential Theory for Factor Models of Large Dimensions," *Econometrica*, 71 (2003), pp. 135–171.

[22]It is possible to define dynamic factor models for integrated processes but additional conditions are required.

model with a finite number of lags, and we allow residuals to mutually correlated, autocorrelated, and eventually heteroskedastic. All these conditions are quite technical and we refer the reader to the relevant literature previously referenced.

Two major conclusions of the theory of approximate factor models must be noted. The first conclusion is that PCA methods can be consistently applied to approximate factor models of large dimensions. PCA methods are easier to implement than true factor analysis and have the additional benefits that factors appear as portfolios. In fact, principal components are linear combinations of returns.

The second major conclusion is that in an economy of large dimension, PCA determines portfolios that approximately mimic all true factors. Ultimately there is only one family of factors defined up to an orthogonal transformation.

DYNAMIC FACTOR MODELS

Dynamic factor models are models that allow an asset manager to specify dynamics for factors and for the processes themselves. Dynamic factor models now have important applications outside the area of financial econometrics, for example in ecological studies.[23] The development of dynamic factor models is recent in comparison with static factor models. While modern static multifactor models were proposed by Thurstone and Hotelling in the 1930s, the first dynamic factor models were proposed in econometrics only in 1977 by Geweke[24] and by Sargent and Sims.[25] The subsequent development of dynamic factor models followed three lines: (1) dynamic factor models of stationary processes in the "finite N, large (infinite) T" case, (2) dynamic factor models of stationary processes in the "large (infinite) N, large (infinite) T" case, and (3) dynamic factor models of integrated processes. The literature on dynamic factor models of integrated processes overlaps with the large literature on cointegration.

---

[23]See, for example, A. F. Zuur, I. D. Tuck, and N. Bailey, "Dynamic Factor Analysis to Estimate Common Trends in Fisheries Time Series," *Canadian Journal of Fisheries and Aquatic Sciences,* 60 (2003), pp. 542–552.
[24]John Geweke, "The Dynamic Factor Analysis of Economic Time Series," in Dennis J. Aigner and Arthur S. Goldberger (eds.), *Latent Variables in Socio-Economic Models* (Amsterdam: North Holland, 1977).
[25]Thomas J. Sargent and Christopher Sims, "Business Cycle Modeling without Pretending to Have Too Much A Priori Economic Theory," Working Paper 55, Federal Reserve Bank of Minneapolis, 1977.

Dynamics enter factor models in three different ways: (1) specifying a dynamics for the factors, (2) specifying a dynamics for the residuals, and (3) allowing regression on lagged factors. The dynamics are typically specified as an autoregressive process.

Consider dynamic factor models with a small number of variables and a number of observations that tends to infinity. Dynamic models of this type are instances of state-space models.[26] Estimation of these models is achieved either with maximum likelihood and the Kalman filter or in the frequency domain.

Both Sargent and Sims and Geweke proposed a dynamic factor model of the type:

$$\mathbf{r}_t = \sum_{i=0}^{\infty} \boldsymbol{\beta}_i \mathbf{f}_{t-i} + \boldsymbol{\varepsilon}_t$$

where returns are an $N \times 1$ vector, the $\boldsymbol{\beta}_i$ are $N \times Q$ matrices, $\mathbf{f}_t$ is a $K \times 1$ vector for each t, and $\boldsymbol{\varepsilon}_t$ is a $N \times 1$ vector. It is assumed that N is finite, $K \ll N$ and T tends to infinity. It is also assumed that factors and residuals are uncorrelated and that residuals are mutually uncorrelated though possibly autocorrelated. This model is the dynamic equivalent of the strict factor model. Estimation is performed with maximum likelihood in the frequency domain. The number of factors is determined with a likelihood ratio test.

Quah and Sargent[27] studied larger models (N up to 60) using the Expectation Maximization algorithm.

Peña and Box[28] studied the following more general model:

$$\mathbf{r}_t = \boldsymbol{\beta}\mathbf{f}_t + \boldsymbol{\varepsilon}_t$$
$$\Phi(L)\mathbf{f}_t = \Theta(L)\boldsymbol{\eta}_t$$
$$\Phi(L) = I - \Phi_1 L - \cdots - \Phi_p L^p$$
$$\Theta(L) = I - \Theta_1 L - \cdots - \Theta_q L^q$$

where factors are stationary processes, L is the lag operator, $\boldsymbol{\varepsilon}_t$ is white noise with a full covariance matrix but is serially uncorrelated, $\boldsymbol{\eta}_t$ has a full-rank covariance matrix and is serially uncorrelated, and $\boldsymbol{\varepsilon}_t$ and $\boldsymbol{\eta}_t$ are

[26]See H. L. Lütkepohl, *Introduction to Multiple Time Series Analysis* (Berlin: Springer, 1991).
[27]Danny Quah and Thomas J. Sargent, "A Dynamic Index Model for Large Cross Sections," CEP Discussion Papers 0132, Centre for Economic Performance, London School of Economics, 1993.
[28]Danel Peña and George E. P. Box, "Identifying a Simplifying Structure in Time Series," *Journal of the American Statistical Association*, 82 (1987), pp. 836–843.

mutually uncorrelated at all lags. That is, the common dynamic structure comes only from the common factors while the idiosyncratic components can be correlated but no autocorrelation is allowed.

Peña and Box proposed the following methodology for determining the number of factors and estimating the factors. Assume that factors are normalized through the identification conditions $\beta'\beta = I$. Consider the covariance matrices

$$\Gamma_r(k) = E(r_t r_{t-k}), k = 0,1,2,\dots$$

and

$$\Gamma_f(k) = E(f_t f_{t-k}), k = 0,1,2,\dots$$

The following relationships hold:

$$\Gamma_r(0) = \beta \Gamma_f(0)\beta' + \Sigma_\varepsilon, k = 0$$
$$\Gamma_r(k) = \beta \Gamma_f(k)\beta', k \geq 1$$

Compute the eigenvalues and eigenvectors of $\Gamma_r(k) \geq 1$. The number of factors is the common rank Q of the matrices $\Gamma_r(k) \geq 1$. Use the nonzero eigenvectors of $\Gamma_r(k) \geq 1$ to estimate the loading matrix β. Use the loading matrix to recover factors.

The setting of dynamic models discussed thus far is that of classical statistics: a fixed number of time series and a number of samples that tends to infinity. In a series of papers, Stock and Watson[29] discuss the problem of forecasting a time series using a large number of predictors. This methodology is referred to as creating diffusion indexes from a large number of predictors. The motivation for suggesting this procedure is the large number of variables available to macroeconomists. Stock and Watson observed that the availability of a large number of observed time series in the range of hundreds of series makes it impossible to use the classical VAR models used by macroeconomists to model a carefully selected number of variables. They advocated a different procedure based on constructing a number of *diffusion indexes* from a large number of observed series.

Stock and Watson[30] introduced a static factor model with an infinite N and an infinite T. They observed that this model is compatible with a

---

[29]James H. Stock and Mark W. Watson, "Macroeconomic Forecasting Using Many Predictors," in Graham Elliott, Clive Granger, and Allan Timmerman (eds.), *Handbook of Economic Forecasting* (Amsterdam: North Holland, 2006).
[30]James H. Stock and Mark W. Watson, "Diffusion Indexes," NBER Working Paper 6702, August 1998.

dynamic factor model with a finite number of lags, but not with an infinite number of lags. Stock and Watson demonstrated that in the limit N, $T \to \infty$, factors can be estimated with principal components. Therefore, any dynamic factor model with a finite number of lags can be put in a static form and estimated with principal components.

Principal components do not disentangle factors from their lagged copies. Stock and Watson suggested estimating the number of factors with information criteria. The model is used to forecast one variable that is regressed on lagged factors, hence there is no need to forecast factors. They demonstrated that *feasible forecasts* (i.e., forecasts based on factors estimated with principal components) asymptotically coincide with the *unfeasible forecasts* performed using the unknown true factors.

Forni, Hallin, Lippi, and Reichlin[31] introduced the *generalized dynamic factor model*, which is a model with N, $T \to \infty$ and a finite number Q of factors, but allowing an infinite number of lags. Factors are assumed to be orthonormal white noise and factor loadings are assumed to be constant in time. The idiosyncratic components are possibly correlated and autocorrelated but uncorrelated with factors at every lag. The major difference with respect to the model described in Stock and Watson on diffusion indexes is the allowance of an infinite number of lags and the imposition of constant factor loadings.

Consider the spectral density matrix of the returns and of the idiosyncratic components. Call dynamic eigenvalues the eigenvalues of the spectral density at each frequency. Forni, Hallin, Lippi, and Reichlin assumed that the first Q dynamic eigenvalues diverge while the first dynamic eigenvalue of the idiosyncratic components is uniformly bounded. These conditions are the dynamic equivalent of the conditions on the eigenvalues of an approximate factor model. They estimated the model computing principal components in the frequency domain. Forni, Hallin, Lippi, and Reichlin[32] determined the rates of convergence in function of the convergence path $N = N(T)$, $T \to \infty$.

Thus far we have discussed two major methodologies for estimating dynamic factor models: maximum likelihood in the classical small N and T $\to \infty$ factor model and principal components in the N, $T \to \infty$ case applied in the time domain in Stock and Watson and in the frequency domain in Forni,

[31]Mario Forni, Marc Hallin, Marco Lippi, and Lucrezia Reichlin, "The Generalized Dynamic Factor Model: Identification and Estimation," *Review of Economics and Statistics*, 82 (2000), pp. 540–554.

[32]Mario Forni, Marc Hallin, Marco Lippi, and Lucrezia Reichlin, "The Generalized Dynamic Factor Model Consistency and Rates," *Journal of Econometrics*, 119 (2004), pp. 231–255.

Hallin, Lippi, and Reichlin. Doz, Giannone, and Reichlin[33] reconciled these two approaches. Their paper demonstrated that a dynamic factor model can be estimated with quasi-maximum likelihood. Their basic idea is to estimate a dynamic factor model with maximum likelihood and the Kalman filter as a misspecified exact factor model and to show that the error vanishes asymptotically.

Heaton and Solo[34] reconciled the small N and the large N approaches by introducing the signal-to-noise ratio. The setting of the paper is the same as in Stock and Watson,[35] that is, forecasting a variable using a small number of diffusion indexes. They assumed a fixed N and determined the bounds on the forecasting error in function of the signal-to-noise ratio when factors are approximated with principal components.

Dynamic Factor Models of Integrated Processes

The notion of a factor model of integrated processes is rooted in the concept of cointegration. Following Granger and Engle, who were jointly awarded the 2003 Nobel Memorial Prize in Economic Sciences for the discovery of cointegration and autoregressive conditional heteroskedasticity (ARCH) behavior, two or more integrated time series are cointegrated if there is a linear combination

$$\sum_{i=1}^{N} \alpha_i x_{it}$$

of the series that is stationary. The linear combinations

$$\sum_{i=1}^{N} \alpha_i x_{it}$$

that are stationary are referred to as *cointegrating relationships*.

---

[33]Catherine Doz, Domenico Giannone, and Lucrezia Reichlin, "A Quasy Maximum Likelihood Approach for Large Approximate Dynamic Factor Models," European Central Bank Working Paper Series No 674, September 2006.
[34]Chris Heaton and Victor Solo, "Asymptotic Principal Components Estimation of Large Factor Models," Research Papers 0303, Macquaire University, Department of Economics, 2003, and Chris Heaton, Chris and Victor Solo, "Estimation of Approximate Factor Models: Is It Important to Have a Large Number of Variables?" Presented at the North American Summer Meeting of the Econometric Society at the University of Minnesota in June 2006.
[35]Stock and Watson, "Diffusion Indexes" and James H. Stock and Mark W. Watson, "Macroeconomic Forecasting Using Diffusion Indexes," *Journal of Business and Economics Statistics*, 20 (2002), pp. 147–162.

As discussed in Chapter 3, there is a vast literature on cointegration and on determining the number of cointegrating relationships. The state-of-the-art cointegration test is the Johansen test. Johansen[36] and Hendry and Juselius[37] offer a concise presentation of cointegration.

The first link between cointegration and dynamic factor models appeared in Stock and Watson.[38] This landmark paper demonstrated that if a set of N time series is cointegrated with K cointegrating relationships, then there are $Q = N - K$ integrated common trends and the N series can be described as regressions on the common trends. The common trends are obtained performing a generalized principal components analysis, that is, the Q common trends are determined by the eigenvectors corresponding to the Q largest eigenvalues of the generalized covariance matrix

$$\Omega = \frac{1}{T}(X - \bar{X})'(X - \bar{X})$$

Escribano and Peña[39] established that common trends are equivalent to common dynamic factors in the sense that the statement that there are K cointegrating relationships is equivalent to the statement that data can be represented by $N - K$ dynamic factors.

Peña and Poncela[40] generalized the methodology put forward in Peña and Box.[41] They introduced a generalized covariance matrix for integrated processes and showed that a procedure similar to the analysis in the frequency domain holds also for integrated processes. Peña and Poncela proposed a test for the number of common factors based on analyzing the eigenvalues of the generalized covariance matrices. Factors are estimated

---

[36]Soren Johansen, "Cointegration: A Survey," in Terrence C. Mills and Kerry Patterson (eds.) *Palgrave Handbook of Econometrics: Volume 1, Econometric Theory* (New York: Palgrave MacMillan, 2006), pp. 540–577.

[37]Katarina Juselius and David Hendry, "Explaining Cointegration Analysis," University of Copenhagen, Department of Economics, Discussion Paper No. 00-20.

[38]James H. Stock and Mark W. Watson, "Testing for Common Trends," *Journal of the American Statistical Society*, 83 (1988), pp. 1097–1107.

[39]Alvaro Escribano and Daniel Peña, "Cointegration and Common Factors," *Journal Time Series Analysis*, 15 (1994), pp. 577–586.

[40]Daniel Peña, Daniel and Pilar Poncela, "Nonstationary Dynamic Factor Analysis," *Journal of Statistical Planning and Inference*, 136 (2006), pp. 1237–1257, and Peña Daniel and Pilar Poncela, "Forecasting with Nonstationary Dynamic Factor Models," *Journal of Econometrics*, 119 (2004), pp. 291–321.

[41]Peña and Box, "Identifying a Simplifying Structure in Time Series." Peña Daniel and George E. P. Box, *Identifying a Simplifying Structure in Time Series Journal of the American Statistical Association*, 82 (1987), pp. 836–843.

with maximum likelihood. They analyzed the forecasting performance of dynamic factor models with possibly integrated factors.

Illustration of Principal Components Analysis

Let's now show how PCA is performed. The data are monthly observations for the following 10 stocks: Campbell Soup, General Dynamics, Sun Microsystems, Hilton, Martin Marietta, Coca-Cola, Northrop Grumman, Mercury Interactive, Amazon.com, and United Technologies. The period considered is from December 2000 to November 2005. Exhibit 5.1 shows the graphics of the 10 return processes.

As explained earlier, performing PCA is equivalent to determining the eigenvalues and eigenvectors of the covariance matrix or of the correlation matrix. The two matrices yield different results. We perform both exercises, estimating the principal components using separately the covariance and the correlation matrices of the return processes. We estimate the covariance with the empirical covariance matrix. Recall that the empirical covariance σ_{ij} between variables (X_i, X_j) is defined as follows:

EXHIBIT 5.1   Graphics of the 10 Stock Return Processes

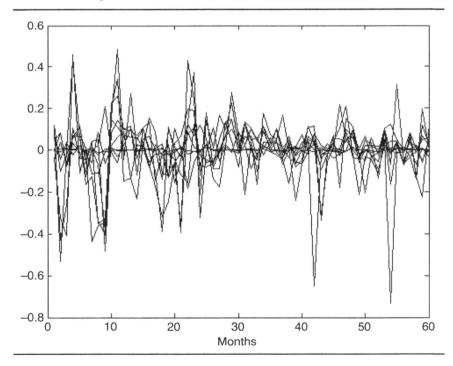

$$\hat{\sigma}_{ij} = \frac{1}{T}\sum_{t=1}^{T}(X_i(t)-\overline{X}_i)(X_j(t)-\overline{X}_j)$$

$$\overline{X}_i = \frac{1}{T}\sum_{t=1}^{T}X_i(t), \overline{X}_j = \frac{1}{T}\sum_{t=1}^{T}X_j(t)$$

Exhibit 5.2 shows the covariance matrix.

Normalizing the covariance matrix with the standard deviations, we obtain the correlation matrix. Exhibit 5.3 shows the correlation matrix. Note that the diagonal elements of the correlation matrix are all equal to one. In addition, a number of entries in the covariance matrix are close to zero. Normalization by the product of standard deviations makes the same elements larger.

Let's now proceed to perform PCA using the covariance matrix. We have to compute the eigenvalues and the eigenvectors of the covariance matrix. Exhibit 5.4 shows the eigenvectors (panel A) and the eigenvalues (panel B) of the covariance matrix.

Each column of panel A of Exhibit 5.4 represents an eigenvector. The corresponding eigenvector is shown in panel B. Eigenvalues are listed in descending order; the corresponding eigenvectors go from left to right in the matrix of eigenvectors. Thus the leftmost eigenvector corresponds to the largest eigenvalue. Eigenvectors are not uniquely determined. In fact, multiplying any eigenvector for a real constant yields another eigenvector. The eigenvectors in Exhibit 5.4 are normalized in the sense that the sum of the squares of each component is equal to 1. It can be easily checked that the sum of the squares of the elements in each column is equal to 1. This still leaves an indeterminacy, as we can change the sign of the eigenvector without affecting this normalization.

As explained earlier, if we form portfolios whose weights are the eigenvectors, we can form 10 portfolios that are orthogonal (i.e., uncorrelated). These orthogonal portfolios are called *principal components*. The variance of each principal component will be equal to the corresponding eigenvector. Thus the first principal component (i.e., the portfolio corresponding to the first eigenvalue), will have the maximum possible variance and the last principal component (i.e., the portfolio corresponding to the last eigenvalue) will have the smallest variance. Exhibit 5.5 shows the graphics of the principal components of maximum and minimum variance.

The 10 principal components thus obtained are linear combinations of the original series, $\mathbf{X} = (X_1, ..., X_N)'$ that is, they are obtained by multiplying $\mathbf{X}$ by the matrix of the eigenvectors. If the eigenvalues and the corresponding eigenvectors are all distinct, as it is the case in our illustration, we can

EXHIBIT 5.2 The Covariance Matrix of 10 Stock Returns

	SUNW	AMZN	MERQ	GD	NOC	CPB	KO	MLM	HLT	UTX
SUNW	0.02922	0.017373	0.020874	3.38E-05	-0.00256	-3.85E-05	0.000382	0.004252	0.006097	0.005467
AMZN	0.017373	0.032292	0.020262	5.03E-05	-0.00277	0.000304	0.001507	0.001502	0.010138	0.007483
MERQ	0.020874	0.020262	0.0355	-0.00027	-0.0035	-0.00011	0.003541	0.003878	0.007075	0.008557
GD	3.38E-05	5.03E-05	-0.00027	9.27E-05	0.000162	2.14E-05	-0.00015	3.03E-05	-4.03E-05	-3.32E-05
NOC	-0.00256	-0.00277	-0.0035	0.000162	0.010826	3.04E-05	-0.00097	0.000398	-0.00169	-0.00205
CPB	-3.85E-05	0.000304	-0.00011	2.14E-05	3.04E-05	7.15E-05	2.48E-05	-7.96E-06	-9.96E-06	-4.62E-05
KO	0.000382	0.001507	0.003541	-0.00015	-0.00097	2.48E-05	0.004008	-9.49E-05	0.001485	0.000574
MLM	0.004252	0.001502	0.003878	3.03E-05	0.000398	-7.96E-06	-9.49E-05	0.004871	0.00079	0.000407
HLT	0.006097	0.010138	0.007075	-4.03E-05	-0.00169	-9.96E-06	0.001485	0.00079	0.009813	0.005378
UTX	0.005467	0.007483	0.008557	-3.32E-05	-0.00205	-4.62E-05	0.000574	0.000407	0.005378	0.015017

Note: Sun Microsystems (SUNW), Amazon.com (AMZN), Mercury Interactive (MERQ), General Dynamics (GD), Northrop Grumman (NOC), Campbell Soup (CPB), Coca-Cola (KO), Martin Marietta (MLM), Hilton (HLT), United Technologies (UTX).

EXHIBIT 5.3 The Correlation Matrix of the Same 10 Return Processes

	SUNW	AMZN	MERQ	GD	NOC	CPB	KO	MLM	HLT	UTX
SUNW	1	0.56558	0.64812	0.020565	-0.14407	-0.02667	0.035276	0.35642	0.36007	0.26097
AMZN	0.56558	1	0.59845	0.029105	-0.14815	0.20041	0.1325	0.11975	0.56951	0.33983
MERQ	0.64812	0.59845	1	-0.14638	-0.17869	-0.06865	0.29688	0.29489	0.37905	0.37061
GD	0.020565	0.029105	-0.14638	1	0.16217	0.26307	-0.24395	0.045072	-0.04227	-0.02817
NOC	-0.14407	-0.14815	-0.17869	0.16217	1	0.034519	-0.14731	0.054818	-0.16358	-0.16058
CPB	-0.02667	0.20041	-0.06865	0.26307	0.034519	1	0.046329	-0.01349	-0.0119	-0.04457
KO	0.035276	0.1325	0.29688	-0.24395	-0.14731	0.046329	1	-0.02147	0.23678	0.07393
MLM	0.35642	0.11975	0.29489	0.045072	0.054818	-0.01349	-0.02147	1	0.11433	0.047624
HLT	0.36007	0.56951	0.37905	-0.04227	-0.16358	-0.0119	0.23678	0.11433	1	0.44302
UTX	0.26097	0.33983	0.37061	-0.02817	-0.16058	-0.04457	0.07393	0.047624	0.44302	1

Note: Sun Microsystems (SUNW), Amazon.com (AMZN), Mercury Interactive (MERQ), General Dynamics (GD), Northrop Grumman (NOC), Campbell Soup (CPB), Coca-Cola (KO), Martin Marietta (MLM), Hilton (HLT), United Technologies (UTX).

EXHIBIT 5.4 Eigenvectors and Eigenvalues of the Covariance Matrix

Panel A: Eigenvectors

	1	2	3	4	5	6	7	8	9	10
1	-0.50374	0.50099	0.28903	-0.59632	-0.01824	-0.01612	0.22069	-0.08226	0.002934	-0.00586
2	-0.54013	-0.53792	0.51672	0.22686	-0.06092	0.25933	-0.10967	-0.12947	0.020253	0.016624
3	-0.59441	0.32924	-0.4559	0.52998	0.051976	0.015346	0.010496	0.21483	-0.01809	-0.00551
4	0.001884	-0.00255	0.018107	-0.01185	0.013384	0.01246	-0.01398	0.01317	-0.86644	0.4981
5	0.083882	0.10993	0.28331	0.19031	0.91542	-0.06618	0.14532	-0.02762	0.011349	-0.00392
6	-0.00085	-0.01196	0.016896	0.006252	-0.00157	0.01185	-0.00607	-0.02791	-0.49795	-0.86638
7	-0.0486	-0.02839	-0.1413	0.19412	-0.08989	-0.35435	0.31808	-0.8387	-0.01425	0.027386
8	-0.07443	0.19009	0.013485	-0.06363	0.11133	-0.22666	-0.90181	-0.27739	0.010908	0.002932
9	-0.20647	-0.36078	-0.01067	-0.1424	0.038221	-0.82197	0.052533	0.35591	-0.01155	-0.01256
10	-0.20883	-0.41462	-0.5835	-0.46223	0.3649	0.27388	-0.02487	-0.14688	0.001641	-0.00174

Panel B: Eigenvalues of the Covariance Matrix

1	0.0783
2	0.0164
3	0.0136
4	0.0109
5	0.0101
6	0.0055
7	0.0039
8	0.0028
9	0.0001
10	0.0001

EXHIBIT 5.5 Graphic of the Portfolios of Maximum and Minimum Variance Based on the Covariance Matrix

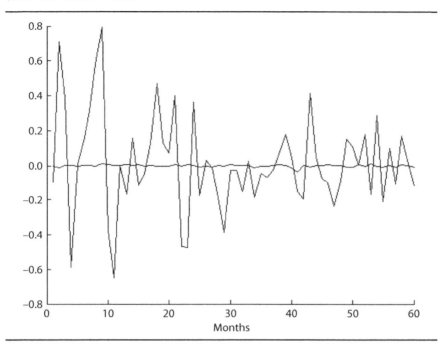

apply the inverse transformation and recover the **X** as linear combinations of the principal components.

PCA is interesting if, in using only a small number of principal components, we nevertheless obtain a good approximation. That is, we use PCA to determine principal components but we use only those principal components that have a large variance as factors of a factor model. Stated otherwise, we regress the original series **X** onto a small number of principal components. In this way, PCA implements a dimensionality reduction as it allows one to retain only a small number of components. By choosing as factors the components with the largest variance, we can explain a large portion of the total variance of **X**.

Exhibit 5.6 shows the total variance explained by a growing number of components. Thus the first component explains 55.2784% of the total variance, the first two components explain 66.8507% of the total variance, and so on. Obviously 10 components explain 100% of the total variance. The second, third, and fourth columns of Exhibit 5.7 show the residuals of the Sun Microsystem return process with 1, 5, and all 10 components,

EXHIBIT 5.6 Percentage of the Total Variance Explained by a Growing Number of Components Based on the Covariance Matrix

Principal Component	Percentage of Total Variance Explained
1	55.2784%
2	66.8508
3	76.4425
4	84.1345
5	91.2774
6	95.1818
7	97.9355
8	99.8982
9	99.9637
10	100.0000

respectively. There is a large gain from 1 to 5, while the gain from 5 to all 10 components is marginal.

We can repeat the same exercise for the correlation matrix. Exhibit 5.8 shows the eigenvectors (panel A) and the eigenvalues (panel B) of the correlation matrix. Eigenvectors are normalized as in the case of the covariance matrix.

Exhibit 5.9 shows the total variance explained by a growing number of components. Thus the first component explains 30.6522% of the total variance, the first two components explain 45.2509% of the total variance and so on. Obviously 10 components explain 100% of the total variance. The increase in explanatory power with the number of components is slower than in the case of the covariance matrix.

The proportion of the total variance explained grows more slowly in the correlation case than in the covariance case. Exhibit 5.10 shows the graphics of the portfolios of maximum and minimum variance. The ratio between the two portfolios is smaller in this case than in the case of the covariance.

The last three columns of Exhibit 5.8 show the residuals of the Sun Microsystem return process with 1, 5, and all components based on the correlation matrix. Residuals are progressively reduced, but at a lower rate than with the covariance matrix.

An Illustration of Factor Analysis

Let's now show how factor analysis is performed. To do so, we will use the same 10 stocks and return data for December 2000 to November 2005 that we used to illustrate principal components analysis.

EXHIBIT 5.7 Residuals of the Sun Microsytem Return Process with 1, 5, and All Components Based on the Covariance Matrix and the Correlation Matrix

Month/Year	Residuals Based on Covariance Matrix			Residuals Based on Correlation Matrix		
	1 Principal Component	5 Principal Components	10 Principal Components	1 Principal Component	5 Principal Components	10 Principal Components
Dec. 2000	0.069044	0.018711	1.53E-16	0.31828	0.61281	−2.00E-15
Jan. 2001	−0.04723	−0.02325	1.11E-16	−0.78027	−0.81071	1.78E-15
Feb. 2001	−0.03768	0.010533	−1.11E-16	−0.47671	0.04825	2.22E-16
March 2001	−0.16204	−0.02016	2.50E-16	−0.47015	−0.82958	−2.78E-15
April 2001	−0.00819	−0.00858	−7.63E-17	−0.32717	−0.28034	−5.00E-16
May 2001	0.048814	−0.00399	2.08E-17	0.36321	0.016427	7.22E-16
June 2001	0.21834	0.025337	−2.36E-16	1.1437	1.37	7.94E-15
July 2001	−0.03399	0.02732	1.11E-16	−0.7547	0.35591	1.11E-15
Aug. 2001	0.098758	−0.00146	2.22E-16	1.0501	0.19739	−8.88E-16
Sept. 2001	0.042674	0.006381	−5.55E-17	0.40304	0.28441	2.00E-15
Oct. 2001	0.038679	−0.00813	−5.55E-17	0.50858	0.17217	4.44E-16
Nov. 2001	−0.11967	−0.01624	1.11E-16	−0.89512	−0.8765	−7.77E-16
Dec. 2001	−0.19192	0.030744	1.67E-16	−1.001	0.047784	−1.55E-15
Jan. 2002	−0.13013	−0.00591	5.55E-17	−1.1085	−0.68171	−1.33E-15
Feb. 2002	0.003304	0.017737	0	−0.05222	0.20963	−9.99E-16
March 2002	−0.07221	0.012569	5.55E-17	−0.35765	0.13344	2.22E-16
April 2002	−0.08211	−0.00916	2.78E-17	−0.38222	−0.47647	−2.55E-15
May 2002	−0.05537	−0.02103	0	−0.45957	−0.53564	4.22E-15
June 2002	−0.15461	0.004614	1.39E-16	−1.0311	−0.54064	−3.33E-15
July 2002	0.00221	0.013057	8.33E-17	0.24301	0.37431	−1.89E-15
Aug. 2002	−0.12655	0.004691	5.55E-17	−0.8143	−0.30497	2.00E-15
Sept. 2002	−0.07898	0.039666	5.55E-17	−0.25876	0.64902	−6.66E-16
Oct. 2002	0.15839	0.003346	−1.11E-16	0.98252	0.53223	−1.78E-15
Nov. 2002	−0.11377	0.013601	1.67E-16	−0.95263	−0.33884	−2.89E-15
Dec. 2002	−0.06957	0.012352	1.32E-16	−0.10309	0.029623	−4.05E-15
Jan. 2003	0.14889	−0.00118	−8.33E-17	1.193	0.73723	5.00E-15
Feb. 2003	−0.03359	−0.02719	−4.16E-17	−0.02854	−0.38331	4.05E-15
March 2003	−0.05314	−0.00859	2.78E-17	−0.38853	−0.40615	−2.22E-16
April 2003	0.10457	−0.01442	−2.22E-16	0.73075	0.097101	−1.11E-15
May 2003	0.078567	0.022227	−5.55E-17	0.52298	0.63772	−7.77E-16
June 2003	−0.1989	−0.02905	1.39E-16	−1.4213	−1.3836	−3.55E-15
July 2003	−0.0149	−0.00955	0	0.13876	−0.1059	3.44E-15

EXHIBIT 5.7   (Continued)

	Residuals Based on Covariance Matrix			Residuals Based on Correlation Matrix		
Month/Year	1 Principal Component	5 Principal Components	10 Principal Components	1 Principal Component	5 Principal Components	10 Principal Components
Aug. 2003	−0.12529	−0.00528	8.33E-17	−0.73819	−0.51792	9.99E-16
Sept. 2003	0.10879	−0.00645	−8.33E-17	0.69572	0.25503	−2.22E-15
Oct. 2003	0.07783	0.01089	−2.78E-17	0.36715	0.45274	−1.11E-15
Nov. 2003	0.038408	−0.01181	−5.55E-17	0.11761	−0.13271	3.33E-16
Dec. 2003	0.18203	0.012593	−1.39E-16	1.2655	0.98182	3.77E-15
Jan. 2004	0.063885	−0.00042	6.94E-18	0.33717	0.038477	0
Feb. 2004	−0.12552	−0.00225	1.11E-16	−0.70345	−0.49379	0
March 2004	−0.01747	0.016836	0	−0.1949	0.35348	−1.94E-16
April 2004	0.015742	0.013764	4.16E-17	0.2673	0.46969	−5.77E-15
May 2004	−0.03556	−0.02072	−6.94E-17	−0.60652	−0.68268	0
June 2004	0.14325	0.008155	−1.94E-16	0.54463	0.59768	3.22E-15
July 2004	0.030731	−0.00285	−4.16E-17	0.13011	0.028779	7.08E-16
Aug. 2004	0.032719	−0.00179	−5.55E-17	0.26793	0.18353	2.05E-15
Sept. 2004	0.083238	0.003664	0	0.58186	0.29544	3.77E-15
Oct. 2004	0.11722	−0.00356	−1.39E-16	0.77575	0.38959	2.22E-16
Nov. 2004	−0.04794	−0.00088	0	−0.47706	−0.35464	−3.13E-15
Dec. 2004	−0.1099	−0.01903	1.11E-16	−0.69439	−0.64663	−2.22E-16
Jan. 2005	0.0479	−0.00573	2.08E-17	0.24203	−0.04065	−4.45E-16
Feb. 2005	−0.015	0.003186	1.39E-17	−0.07198	0.054412	3.28E-15
March 2005	0.005969	−0.0092	−4.16E-17	0.035251	−0.02106	3.83E-15
April 2005	−0.00742	−0.01241	−4.16E-17	−0.09335	−0.42659	−1.67E-16
May 2005	0.14998	−0.01126	6.25E-17	1.0219	0.034585	−9.05E-15
June 2005	−0.05045	−0.00363	3.47E-17	−0.25655	−0.1229	−4.66E-15
July 2005	0.065302	−0.00421	−5.20E-17	0.56136	0.16602	3.08E-15
Aug. 2005	0.006719	−0.01174	1.39E-17	0.09319	−0.22119	−2.00E-15
Sept. 2005	0.12865	−0.00259	−8.33E-17	0.95602	0.33442	3.50E-15
Oct. 2005	−0.01782	0.011827	−8.33E-17	−0.2249	0.27675	1.53E-15
Nov. 2005	0.026312	−7.72E-05	−1.39E-17	0.26642	0.19725	1.67E-15

EXHIBIT 5.8 Eigenvectors and Eigenvalues of the Correlation Matrix

Panel A: Eigenvectors

	1	2	3	4	5	6	7	8	9	10
1	-0.4341	0.19295	-0.26841	0.040065	-0.19761	0.29518	-0.11161	-0.11759	-0.72535	-0.14857
2	-0.45727	0.18203	0.20011	0.001184	0.013236	0.37606	0.05077	0.19402	0.47275	-0.55894
3	-0.47513	-0.03803	-0.16513	0.16372	-0.01282	0.19087	-0.08297	-0.38843	0.37432	0.61989
4	0.06606	0.63511	0.18027	-0.16941	-0.05974	-0.24149	-0.66306	-0.14342	0.092295	0.02113
5	0.17481	0.33897	-0.21337	0.14797	0.84329	0.23995	0.091628	-0.07926	-0.06105	0.001886
6	-0.00505	0.42039	0.57434	0.40236	-0.15072	-0.05018	0.48758	-0.07382	-0.15788	0.19532
7	-0.18172	-0.397	0.28037	0.58674	0.26063	-0.26864	-0.38592	-0.16286	-0.11336	-0.24105
8	-0.1913	0.26851	-0.55744	0.32448	-0.09047	-0.58736	0.20083	0.19847	0.15935	-0.13035
9	-0.40588	-0.0309	0.20884	-0.20157	0.29193	-0.16641	-0.08666	0.67897	-0.1739	0.37201
10	-0.32773	-0.05042	0.14067	-0.51858	0.24871	-0.41444	0.30906	-0.4883	-0.06781	-0.17077

Panel B: Eigenvalues

1	3.0652
2	1.4599
3	1.1922
4	0.9920
5	0.8611
6	0.6995
7	0.6190
8	0.5709
9	0.3143
10	0.2258

EXHIBIT 5.9   Percentage of the Total Variance Explained by a Growing Number of Components Using the Correlation Matrix

Principal Component	Percentage of Total Variance Explained
1	30.6522%
2	45.2509
3	57.1734
4	67.0935
5	75.7044
6	82.6998
7	88.8901
8	94.5987
9	97.7417
10	100.0000

EXHIBIT 5.10   Graphic of the Portfolios of Maximum and Minimum Variance Based on the Correlation Matrix

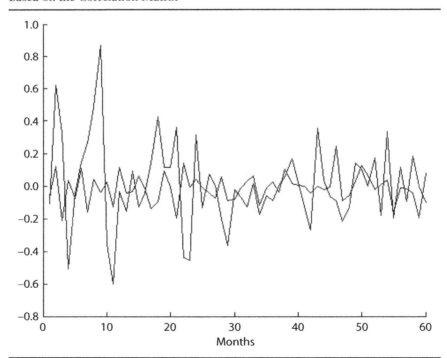

EXHIBIT 5.11   A Factor Loadings and Idiosyncratic Variances

	Factor Loadings			
	β_1	β_2	β_3	Variance
SUNW	0.656940	0.434420	0.27910	0.301780
AMZN	0.959860	−0.147050	−0.00293	0.057042
MERQ	0.697140	0.499410	−0.08949	0.256570
GD	0.002596	−0.237610	0.43511	0.754220
NOC	−0.174710	−0.119960	0.23013	0.902130
CPB	0.153360	−0.344400	0.13520	0.839590
KO	0.170520	0.180660	−0.46988	0.717500
MLM	0.184870	0.361180	0.28657	0.753250
HLT	0.593540	0.011929	−0.18782	0.612300
UTX	0.385970	0.144390	−0.15357	0.806590

To perform factor analysis, we need estimate only the factor loadings and the idiosyncratic variances of noise terms. We assume that the model has three factors. Exhibit 5.11 shows the factor loadings. Each row represents the loadings of the three factors corresponding to each stock. The last column of the exhibit shows the idiosyncratic variances.

The idiosyncratic variances are numbers between 0 and 1, where 0 means that the variance is completely explained by common factors and 1 that common factors fail to explain variance.

The p-value turns out to be 0.6808 and therefore fails to reject the null of three factors. Estimating the model with 1 and 2 factors we obtain much lower p-values while we run into numerical difficulties with 4 or more factors. We can therefore accept the null of three factors. Exhibit 5.12 shows the graphics of the three factors.

SUMMARY

- Factor models are used in all phases of asset management: portfolio construction, stock selection, and performance evaluation (return attribution analysis).
- Factor models are regression models where factors are determined either with statistical techniques or are given exogenously.
- Factor models can be classified as static models and dynamic models.

EXHIBIT 5.12   Graphics of the Three Factors

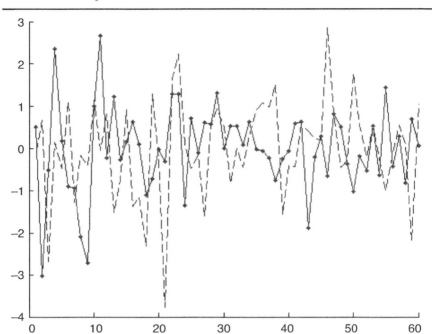

- In a static factor model, a large number of random variables is represented in terms of a small number of different random variables called factors and those factors do not have any dynamics.
- Dynamic factor models represent a large number of time series in terms of a small number of different time series called dynamic factors.
- Factor models are subject to many types of indeterminacy which can be resolved making specific assumptions.
- Statistical methods for factor analysis require the estimation of the covariance matrix.
- Covariance matrices are very noisy and only a limited number of factors can be effectively determined.
- Factors that are not observed are referred to as hidden or latent factors, or latent variables and the primary statistical tool used for determining the hidden factors is factor analysis and related methods such as principal components analysis.
- The result of factor analysis for determining the hidden factors results in a (multivariate) time series of factors, a (multivariate) time series of

residuals, the covariance matrix of factors, the factor loadings for each return process, and the variances of each residual term.

- The factor loadings represent the exposures of returns to each factor.
- The current theoretical paradigm for factor models is the approximate factor model formed by infinite time series of infinite length; this model is practically difficult to apply to return series because the empirical distribution of the eigenvalues of the covariance matrix decays very slowly.
- Dynamic factor models introduce a dynamic by regressing processes over lagged factors.
- In practice, dynamic factor models, which are ultimately an instance of state-space models, are often used in a static context—a situation that might cause some confusion.

CHAPTER 6

Factor-Based Trading Strategies I: Factor Construction and Analysis

Realizing positive excess returns in the equity markets is challenging. To achieve this objective, we need to successfully design, research, and implement an investment strategy.

Broadly we can classify investment strategies into the following categories: (1) factor-based trading strategies (also called stock selection or alpha models), (2) statistical arbitrage, (3) high-frequency strategies, and (4) event studies. The results from the Intertek surveys presented in Chapter 1 indicate that factors and factor-based models form the core of a major part of today's quantitative trading strategies. Our discussion that follows focuses on these types of models.

As background, we start our discussion of factor trading strategies briefly reviewing the evolution of thought regarding market efficiency. Neoclassical finance states that markets are efficient. Efficient market in this context means that individual investors form expectations rationally, markets aggregate information efficiently, and equilibrium prices incorporate all available information. The implication of the efficient market theory (EMT) is that there are limited, if any, opportunity to earn excess returns. Starting in the late 1970s, researchers have presented empirical results identifying anomalies and excess return opportunities. Some of the most well-known factors, their underlying basic economic rationale, and references are provided in Appendix C. Critics of neoclassical finance argue that investors are not rational and their behavior impacts the pricing of securities which in turn may lead to market inefficiencies.[1] Andrew Lo

---

[1] For a survey of behavioral finance, see Nicholas Barberis and Richard Thaler, "A Survey of Behavioral Finance," in George M. Constantinides, M. Harris, and Rene M. Stulz (eds.), *Handbook of the Economics of Finance*, (Amsterdam: Elsevier Science, 2003).

This chapter was co-authored with Joseph A. Cerniglia.

proposes a theory he calls the Adaptive Market Hypothesis that reconciles various observations about market inefficiency.[2] His theory is based on an evolutionary approach to economic interaction that incorporates cognitive neuroscience.

Most academics and practitioners agree that the efficient market hypothesis does not hold all the time and that it is possible to beat the market. The existence of the investment management and hedge fund industry provide good examples, as does the numerous published works on market predictability in academic journals. The themes and motivation for these studies differ. A number of papers show that applications of fundamental analysis[3] and financial statement analysis[4] may be able to outperform the market. Others researchers demonstrate that a range of different factors or factor-based models may have the ability to forecast the market.[5] Some models consist of a combination of multiple investing themes.[6]

We introduced the concept of factors in Chapter 5. The focus of this and the next chapter is on developing trading strategies based on factors constructed from common (cross-sectional) characteristics of stocks. For this purpose, first we give a more narrow definition of factors than that provided

[2]Andrew W. Lo, "The Adaptive Markets Hypothesis," *Journal of Portfolio Management*, 30 (2004), pp. 15–29.

[3]Jeffery S. Abarbanell and Brian J. Bushee, "Fundamental Analysis, Future Earnings, and Stock Prices," *Journal of Accounting Research*, 35 (1997), pp. 1–24; and Jeffery S. Abarbanell and Brian J. Bushee, "Abnormal Returns to a Fundamental Analysis Strategy," *Accounting Review*, 73 (1998), pp. 19–45.

[4]Jane A. Ou and Stephen H. Penman, "Financial Statement Analysis and the Prediction of Stock Returns," *Journal of Accounting and Economics*, 11 (1989), pp 295–329; Doron Nissim and Stephen H. Penman, "Ratio Analysis and Equity Valuation: From Research to Practice," *Review of Accounting Studies*, 6 (2001), pp. 109–154; and Stephen H. Penman, *Financial Statement Analysis and Security Valuation* (New York: McGraw Hill Company, 2001).

[5]Barr Rosenberg, Kenneth Reid, and Ronald Lanstein," Persuasive Evidence of Market Inefficiency," *Journal of Portfolio Management*, 11 (1985), pp 9–17; G. William Schwert, "Anomalies and Market Efficiency," in George M. Constantinides, M. Harris, Rene M. Stulz (eds.), *Handbook of the Economics of Finance, Vol. 1*, Chapter 15, 2003, pp. 939-974; Eugene F. Fama and Kenneth R. French, "The Cross-Section of Expected Stock Returns," *Journal of Finance*, 47, (1992), pp. 427–466; Robert Haugen and Nardin Baker, "Commonality in the Determinants of Expected Stock Returns," *Journal of Financial Economics*, 41(1996), pp. 401–439; Louis K. C. Chan, Jason Karceski, and Josef Lakonishok, "The Risk and Return from Factors," *Journal of Financial and Quantitative Analysis*, 33, (1998), pp 159–188; and Chu Zhang, "Factor-Mimicking Portfolios from Return-Predictive Firm-Specific Variables," Working Paper, 2003.

[6]Clifford Asness, "The Interaction of Value and Momentum Strategies," *Financial Analysts Journal*, 53 (1997), pp. 29–36.

in Chapter 5. Then, we examine the major sources of risk associated with trading strategies, and demonstrate how factors are constructed from company characteristics and market data. The quality of the data used in this process is critical. We examine several data cleaning and adjustment techniques to account for problems occurring with backfilling and restatements of data, missing data, inconsistently reported data, as well as survivorship and look-ahead biases. In the last section of this chapter we discuss the analysis of the statistical properties of factors. In the following chapter we extend this analysis to include multiple factors and cover techniques used to implement multifactor trading strategies.

In a series of examples throughout both chapters, we show the individual steps for developing a basic trading strategy. The purpose of these examples is not to provide yet another profitable trading strategy, but rather to illustrate the process an analyst may follow when performing research. In fact, the factors that we use for this purpose are well known and have for years been exploited by industry practitioners. We think that the value added of these examples is in the concrete illustration of the research and development process of a factor-based trading model.

FACTOR-BASED TRADING

Since the first version of the classic text on security analysis by Benjamin Graham and David Dodd[7]—considered to be the Bible on the fundamental approach to security analysis—was published in 1934, equity portfolio management and trading strategies have developed considerably. Graham and Dodd were early contributors to factor-based strategies because they extended traditional valuation approaches by using information throughout the financial statements[8] and by presenting concrete rules of thumb to be used to determine the attractiveness of securities.[9]

Today's quantitative managers use factors as fundamental building blocks for trading strategies. Within a trading strategy, factors determine when to buy and sell securities. In our discussion of factor-based strategies in this and the next chapter, we narrow the definition of factors given in Chapter 5. Specifically, we define a factor as a common characteristic among a group of assets. For example, a factor in the fixed income market would be the credit rating on a bond. In the equities market, it could be a

---

[7]Benjamin Graham and David Dodd, *Security Analysis* (New York: McGraw-Hill, 1962).
[8]Benjamin Graham, *The Intelligent Investor* (New York: Harper & Row, 1973).
[9]Peter L. Bernstein, *Capital Ideas: The Improbable Origins of Modern Wall Street* (New York: The Free Press, 1992).

particular financial ratio such as the price-to-earnings (P/E) or the book-to-price (B/P) ratios.

Most often this basic definition is expanded to include additional objectives. First, factors frequently are intended to capture some economic intuition. For instance, a factor may help understand the prices of assets by reference to their exposure to sources of macroeconomic risk, fundamental characteristics, or basic market behavior. Second, we should recognize that assets with similar factors (characteristics) tend to behave in similar ways. This attribute is critical to the success of a factor. Third, we would like our factor to be able to differentiate across different markets and samples. Fourth, we want our factor to be robust across different time periods.

Factors fall into three categories—macroeconomic influences, cross-sectional characteristics, and statistical factors. Macroeconomic influences are time series that measure observable economic activity. Examples include interest rate levels, gross domestic production, and industrial production. Cross-sectional characteristics are observable asset specifics or firm characteristics. Examples include, dividend yield, book value, and volatility. Statistical factors are unobservable or latent factors common across a group of assets. These factors make no explicit assumptions about the asset characteristics that drive commonality in returns. Statistical factors are not derived using exogenous data but are extracted from other variables such as returns. These factors are calculated using various statistical techniques such as principal components analysis or factor analysis as discussed in Chapter 5.

Within asset management firms, factors and forecasting models are used for a number of purposes. Those purposes could be central to managing portfolios. For example, a portfolio manager can directly send the model output to the trading desk to be executed. In other uses, models provide analytical support to analysts and portfolio management teams. For instance, models are used as a way to reduce the investable universe to a manageable number of securities so that a team of analysts can perform fundamental analysis on a smaller group of securities.

Factors are employed in other areas of financial theory such as asset pricing, risk management, and performance attribution. In asset pricing, researchers use factors as proxies for common, undiversifiable sources of risk in the economy to understand the prices or values of securities to uncertain payments. Examples include the dividend yield[10] of the market or the yield spread between a long-term bond yield and a short-term bond yield. In risk management, risk managers use factors in risk models to explain and to decompose variability of returns from securities, while portfolio managers rely on risk models for covariance construction, portfolio construction, and

---

[10]Eugene F. Fama and Kenneth R. French, "Dividend Yields and Expected Stock Returns," *Journal of Financial Economics*, 22 (1988), pp 3–25.

risk measurement. In performance attribution, portfolio managers explain past portfolio returns based on the portfolio's exposure to various factors. Within these areas, the role of factors continues to expand. Recent research presents a methodology for attributing active return, tracking error, and the information ratio to a set of custom factors.[11]

The focus in this and next chapter is on using factors to build equity forecasting models, also referred to as *alpha* or *stock selection models*. The models serve as mathematical representations of trading strategies. The mathematical representation uses future returns as dependent variables and factors as independent variables.

DEVELOPING FACTOR-BASED TRADING STRATEGIES

The development of a trading strategy has many similarities with an engineering project. We begin by designing a framework that is flexible enough so that the components can be easily modified, yet structured enough that we remain focused on our end goal of designing a profitable trading strategy.

Basic Framework and Building Blocks

The typical steps in the development of a trading strategy are:

- Defining a trading idea or investment strategy.
- Developing factors.
- Acquiring and processing data.
- Analyzing the factors.
- Building the strategy.
- Evaluating the strategy.
- Backtesting the strategy.
- Implementing the strategy.

In what follows we will take a closer look at each step.

Defining a Trading Idea or Investment Strategy

A successful trading strategy often starts as an idea based on sound economic intuition, market insight, or the discovery of an anomaly. Background research can be helpful in order to understand what others have tried or implemented in the past.

---

[11]Jose Menchero and Vijay Poduri, "Custom Factor Attribution," *Financial Analysts Journal*, 62 (2008), pp. 81–92.

We distinguish between a trading idea and trading strategy based on the underlying economic motivation. A trading idea has a more short-term horizon often associated with an event or mispricing. A trading strategy has a longer horizon and is frequently based on the exploitation of a premium associated with an anomaly or a characteristic.

Developing Factors

Factors provide building blocks of the model used to build an investment strategy. We introduced a general definition of factors earlier in this chapter. After having established the trading strategy, we move from the economic concepts to the construction of factors that may be able to capture our intuition. In this chapter we will provide a number of examples of factors based on the cross-sectional characteristics of stocks.

Acquiring and Processing Data

A trading strategy relies on accurate and clean data to build factors. There are a number of third-party solutions and databases available for this purpose such as Thomson MarketQA,[12] Factset Research Systems,[13] and Compustat Xpressfeed.[14]

Analyzing the Factors

A variety of statistical and econometric techniques must be performed on the data to evaluate the empirical properties of factors. This empirical research is used to understand the risk and return potential of a factor. The analysis is the starting point for building a model of a trading strategy.

Building the Strategy

The model represents a mathematical specification of the trading strategy. There are two important considerations in this specification: the selection of which factors and how these factors are combined. Both considerations need to be motivated by the economic intuition behind the trading strategy. We advise against model specification being strictly data driven because that approach often results in overfitting the model and consequently overestimating forecasting quality of the model.

---

[12]http://thomsonreuters.com/products_services/financial/financial_products/quantitative_analysis/quantitative_analytics.
[13]http://www.factset.com.
[14]http://www.compustat.com.

Evaluating, Back Testing, and Implementing the Strategy

The final step involves assessing the estimation, specification, and forecast quality of the model. This analysis includes examining the goodness of fit (often done in sample), forecasting ability (often done out of sample), and sensitivity and risk characteristics of the model.

We will cover the last two steps in greater detail in Chapter 7.

RISK TO TRADING STRATEGIES

In investment management, risk is a primary concern. The majority of trading strategies are not risk free but rather subject to various risks. It is important to be familiar with the most common risks in trading strategies. By understanding the risks in advance, we can structure our empirical research to identify how risks will affect our strategies. Also, we can develop techniques to avoid these risks in the model construction stage when building the strategy.

We describe the various risks that are common to factor trading strategies as well as other trading strategies such as risk arbitrage. Many of these risks have been categorized in the behavioral finance literature.[15] The risks discussed include fundamental risk, noise trader risk, horizon risk, model risk, implementation risk, and liquidity risk.

Fundamental risk is the risk of suffering adverse fundamental news. For example, say our trading strategy focuses on purchasing stocks with high earnings to price ratios. Suppose that the model shows a pharmaceutical stock maintains a high score. After purchasing the stock, the company releases a news report that states it faces class-action litigation because one of its drugs has undocumented adverse side effects. While during this period other stocks with high earnings to price ratio may perform well, this particular pharmaceutical stock will perform poorly despite its attractive characteristic. We can minimize the exposure to fundamental risk within a trading strategy by diversifying across many companies. Fundamental risk may not always be company specific, sometimes this risk can be systemic. Some examples include the exogenous market shocks of the stock market crash in 1987, the Asian financial crisis in 1997, and the tech bubble in 2000. In these cases, diversification was not that helpful. Instead, portfolio managers that were sector or market neutral in general fared better.

Noise trader risk is the risk that a mispricing may worsen in the short run. The typical example includes companies that clearly are undervalued

---

[15]See Barberis and Thaler, "A Survey of Behavioral Finance."

(and should therefore trade at a higher price). However, because noise traders may trade in the opposite direction, this mispricing can persist for a long time. Closely related to noise trader risk is *horizon risk*. The idea here is that the premium or value takes too long to be realized, resulting in a realized return lower than a target rate of return.

Model risk, also referred to as *misspecification risk*, refers to the risk associated with making wrong modeling assumptions and decisions. This includes the choice of variables, methodology, and context the model operates in. In Chapter 5 we examined different sources that may result in model misspecification. In addition, we reviewed several remedies based on information theory, Bayesian methods, shrinkage, and random coefficient models.

Implementation risk is another risk faced by investors implementing trading strategies. This risk category includes transaction costs and funding risk. Transaction costs such as commissions, bid-ask spreads and market impact can adversely affect the results from a trading strategy. If the strategy involves shorting, other implementation costs arise such as the ability to locate securities to short and the costs to borrow the securities. *Funding risk* occurs when the portfolio manager is no longer able to get the funding necessary to implement a trading strategy. For example, many statistical arbitrage funds use leverage to increase the returns of their funds. If the amount of leverage is constrained then the strategy will not earn attractive returns. Khandani and Lo confirm this example by showing that greater competition and reduced profitability of quantitative strategies today require more leverage to maintain the same level of expected return.[16]

Liquidity risk is a concern for investors. Liquidity is defined as the ability to (1) trade quickly without significant price changes, and (2) the ability to trade large volumes without significant price changes. Cerniglia and Kolm discuss the effects of liquidity risk during the "quant crisis" in August 2007.[17] They show how the rapid liquidation of quantitative funds affected the trading characteristics and price impact of trading individual securities as well as various factor-based trading strategies.

These risks can detract or contribute to the success of a trading strategy. It is obvious how these risks can detract from a strategy. What is not always clear is when any one of these unintentional risks contributes to a strategy. That is, sometimes when we build a trading strategy we take on a bias that is not obvious. If there is a premium associated with this unintended risk then a strategy will earn additional return. Later the premium to this unintended

[16]Amir E. Khandani and Andrew W. Lo, "What Happened to the Quants in August 2007?" *Journal of Investment Management*, 5 (2007), pp. 5–54.
[17]Joseph A. Cerniglia and Petter N. Kolm. "The Information Content of Order Imbalances: A Tick-by-Tick Analysis of the Equity Market in August 2007," Working Paper. Courant Institute, New York University, 2009.

risk may disappear. For example, a trading strategy that focuses on price momentum performed strongly in the calendar years of 1998 and 1999. What an investor might not notice is that during this period the portfolio became increasingly weighted toward technology stocks, particularly Internet-related stocks. During 2000, these stocks severely underperformed.

DESIRABLE PROPERTIES OF FACTORS

Factors should be founded on sound economic intuition, market insight, or an anomaly. In addition to the underlying economic reasoning, factors should have other properties that make them effective for forecasting.

It is an advantage if factors are intuitive to investors. Many investors will only invest in a particular fund if they understand and agree with the basic ideas behind the trading strategies. Factors give portfolio managers a tool in communicating to investors what *themes* they are investing in.

The search for the economic meaningful factors should avoid strictly relying on pure historical analysis. Factors used in a model should not emerge from a sequential process of evaluating successful factors while removing less favorable ones.

Most importantly, a group of factors should be parsimonious in its description of the trading strategy. This will require careful evaluation of the interaction between the different factors. For example, highly correlated factors will cause the inferences made in a multivariate approach to be less reliable. Another possible problem when using multiple factors is the possibility of overfitting in the modeling process.

Any data set contains outliers, that is, observations that deviate from the average properties of the data. Outliers are not always trivial to handle and sometimes we may want to exclude them and other times not. For example, they could be erroneously reported or legitimate abnormal values. Later in this chapter we will discuss a few standard techniques to perform data cleaning. The success or failure of factors selected should not depend on a few outliers. In most cases, it is desirable to construct factors that are reasonably robust to outliers.

SOURCES FOR FACTORS

How do we find factors? The sources are widespread with no one source clearly dominating. Employing a variety of sources seems to provide the best opportunity to uncover factors that will be valuable for developing a new model.

There are a number of ways to develop factors based on economic foundations. It may start with thoughtful observation or study of how market participants act. For example, we may ask ourselves how other market participants will evaluate the prospects of the earnings or business of a firm. We may also want to consider what stock characteristics investors will reward in the future. Another common approach is to look for inefficiencies in the way that investors process information. For instance, research may discover that consensus expectations of earnings estimates are biased.

A good source for factors is the various reports released by the management of companies. Many reports contain valuable information and may provide additional context on how management interprets the company results and financial characteristics. For example, quarterly earning reports (10-Qs) may highlight particular financial metrics relevant to the company and the competitive space they are operating within. Other company financial statements and SEC filings such as the 10-K or 8-K also provide a source of information to develop factors. It is often useful to look at the financial measures that management emphasize in their comments.

Factors can be found through discussions with market participants such as portfolio managers and traders. Factors are uncovered by understanding the heuristics experienced investors have used successfully. These heuristics can be translated into factors and models.

Wall Street analyst reports—also called sell-side reports or equity research reports—may contain valuable information. The reader is often not interested in the final conclusions, but rather in the methodology or metrics the analysts use to forecast the future performance of a company. It may also be useful to study the large quantity of books written by portfolio managers and traders that describe the process they use in stock selection.

Academic literature in finance, accounting, and economics such as those in Appendix C provides evidence of numerous factors and trading strategies that earn abnormal returns. Not all strategies will earn abnormal profits when implemented by practitioners, for example, because of institutional constraints and transaction costs. Bushee and Raedy[18] find that trading strategy returns are significantly decreased due to issues such as price pressure, restrictions against short sales, incentives to maintain an adequately diversified portfolio, and restrictions to hold no more than 5% ownership in a firm.

In uncovering factors, we should put economic intuition first and data analysis second. This avoids performing pure data mining or simply overfitting our models to past history. Research and innovation is the key to find-

---

[18]Brian J. Bushee and Jana Smith Raedy, "Factors Affecting the Implementability of Stock Market Trading Strategies," Working Paper, University of Pennsylvania and University of North Carolina, 2005.

ing new factors. Today, analyzing and testing new factors and improving upon existing ones, is itself a big industry.

BUILDING FACTORS FROM COMPANY CHARACTERISTICS

The following sections will focus on the techniques for building factors from company characteristics. Often we desire our factors to relate the financial data provided by a company to metrics that investors use when making decisions about the attractiveness of a stock such as valuation ratios, operating efficiency ratios, profitability ratios, and solvency ratios.[19] Factors should also relate to the market data such as analysts' forecasts, prices and returns, and trading volume.

WORKING WITH DATA

In this section we discuss how to work with data and data quality issues, including some well-probed techniques used to improve the quality of the data. Though the role of getting and analyzing data can be mundane and tedious, we need not forget that high-quality data are critical to the success of a trading strategy. It is important to realize model output is only as good as the data used to calibrate it. As the saying goes: "Garbage in, garbage out."[20]

Understanding the structure of financial data is important. We distinguish three different categories of financial data: time series, cross-sectional, and panel data. Time series data consist of information and variables collected over multiple time periods. Cross-sectional data consist of data collected at one point in time for many different companies (the cross-section of companies of interest). A panel data set consists of cross-sectional data collected at different points in time. We note that a panel data set may not be homogeneous. For instance, the cross-section of companies may change from one point in time to another.

Data Integrity

Quality data maintain several attributes such as providing a consistent view of history, maintaining good data availability, containing no survivorship, and

---

[19]For definition of these accounting measures, see, for example, Pamela P. Peterson and Frank J. Fabozzi, *Analysis of Financial Statements: Second Edition* (John Wiley & Sons, 2006).

[20]This phrase says to have been coined by George Fuechsel who was an IBM 305 RAMAC technician in New York. Today, it is used to describe failures in decision making due to data that is somehow incorrect, incomplete, or otherwise imprecise.

avoiding look-ahead bias. As all data sets have their limitations, it is important for the quantitative researcher to be able to recognize the limitations and adjust the data accordingly.[21]

Data used in research should provide a consistent view of history. Two common problems that distort the consistency of financial data are backfilling and restatements of data. *Backfilling of data* happens when a company is first entered into a database at the current period and its historical data are also added. This process of backfilling data creates a selection bias because we now find historical data on this recently added company when previously it was not available. Restatements of data are prevalent in distorting consistency of data. For example, if a company revises its earnings per share numbers after the initial earnings release, then many database companies will overwrite the number originally recorded in the database with the newly released figure.

A frequent and common concern with financial databases is data availability. First, data items may only be available for a short period of time. For example, there were many years when stock options were granted to employees but the expense associated with the option grant was not required to be disclosed in financial statements. It was not until 2005 that accounting standards required companies to recognize directly stock options as an expense on the income statement. Second, data items may be available for only a subset of the cross-section of firms. Some firms, depending on the business they operate in, have research and development expenses while others do not. For example, many pharmaceutical companies have research and development expenses while utilities companies do not. A third issue is that a data item may simply not be available because it was not recorded at certain points in time. Sometimes this happens for just a few observations, other times it is the case for the whole time-series for a specific data item for a company. Fourth, different data items are sometimes combined. For example, sometimes depreciation and amortization expenses are not a separate line item on an income statement. Instead it is included in cost of goods sold. Fifth, certain data items are only available at certain periodicities. For instance, some companies provide more detailed financial reports

---

[21]Many years ago one of the co-authors met Marcus C. Bogue, founder of Charter Oak Investment Systems. His firm created a Compustat Add-On Database to address the needs of the more quantitatively oriented, longer-term backtesting researchers by storing all data from current Compustat data before it gets overwritten (updated). Mr. Bogue works with most of the quantitative investment management industry. In the conversion with him the question of what distinguishes the most successful quantitative managers came up. Mr Bogue suggested that their familiarity with the data is the differentiator. Familiarity entails understanding quality, definitions, measurement, and sample characteristics of the data sets used in the investment process.

quarterly while others report more details annually. Sixth, data items may be inconsistently reported across different companies, sectors, or industries. This may happen as the financial data provider translates financial measures from company reports to the specific database items (incomplete mapping), thereby ignoring or not correctly making the right adjustments.

For these issues some databases provide specific codes to identify the causes of missing data. It is important to have procedures in place that can distinguish among the different reasons for the missing data and be able to make adjustments and corrections.

Two other common problems with databases are survivorship and look-ahead bias. *Survivorship bias* occurs when companies are removed from the database when they no longer exist. For example, companies can be removed because of a merger or bankruptcy. This bias skews the results because only successful firms are included in the entire sample. *Look-ahead bias* occurs when data are used in a study that would not have been available during the actual period analyzed. For example, the use of year-end earnings data immediately at the end of the reporting period is incorrect because the data is not released by the firm until several days or weeks after the end of the reporting period.

Data alignment is another concern when working with multiple databases. Many databases have different identifiers used to identify a firm. Some databases have vendor specific identifiers, others have common identifiers such as CUSIPs or ticker symbols. Unfortunately, CUSIPs and ticker symbols change over time and are often reused. This practice makes it difficult to link an individual security across multiple databases across time.

Example: The EBITDA/EV Factor

This example illustrates how the nuances of data handling can influence the results of a particular study. We use data from the Compustat Point-In-Time database and calculate the EBITA/EV factor.[22] This factor is defined as earnings before interest, taxes, depreciation, and amortization divided by enterprise value (EBITDA/EV). Our universe of stocks is the Russell 1000 from December 1989 to December 2008, excluding financial companies. We calculate EBITDA /EV by two equivalent but different approaches. Each approach differs by the data items used in calculating the numerator (EBITDA):

---

[22]The ability of EBITDA/EV to forecast future returns is discussed in, for example, Patricia M. Dechow, S. P. Kothari, and Ross L. Watts, "The Relation Between Earnings and Cash Flows," *Journal of Accounting and Economics*, 25 (1998), pp. 133–168.

1. EBITDA = Sales (Compustat data item 2) – Cost of Goods Sold (Compustat data item 30) – Selling and General Administrative Expenses (Compustat data item 1).
2. EBITDA = Operating Income before Depreciation (Compustat data item 21).

According to the Compustat manual, the following identity holds:

Operating Income before Depreciation
= Sales – Cost of Goods Sold – Selling and General Administrative Expenses

However, while this mathematical identity is true, this is not what we discover in the data. After we calculate the two factors, we form quintile portfolios of each factor and compare the individual holding rankings between the portfolio. Exhibit 6.1 displays the percentage differences in rankings for individual companies between the two portfolios. We observe that the results are not identical. As a matter of fact, there are large differences, particularly in the early period. In other words, the two mathematically equivalent approaches do not deliver the same empirical results.

EXHIBIT 6.1   Percentage of Companies in Russell 1000 with Different Ranking According to the EBITDA/EV Factor

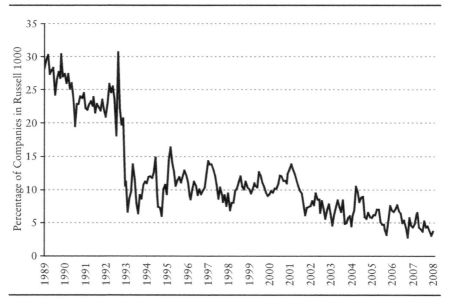

Potential Biases from Data

There are numerous potential biases that may arise from data quality issues. It is important to recognize the direct effects of these data issues are not apparent a priori. We emphasize three important effects:[23]

1. *Effect on average stock characteristics.* When calculating cross-sectional averages of various metrics such as book-to-price or market capitalization, data issues can skew statistics and lead to incorrect inference about the population characteristics used in the study.
2. *Effect on portfolio returns.* The portfolio return implications of data issues are not always clear. For example, survivor bias results in firms being removed from the sample. Typically firms are removed from the sample for one of two reasons—mergers and acquisitions or failure. In most cases firms are acquired at a premium from the prevailing stock price. Leaving these firms out of the sample would have a downward bias on returns. In cases where companies fail, the stock price falls dramatically and removing these firms from the sample will have an upward bias on returns.
3. *Effects on estimated moments of returns.* A study by Kothari, Sabino, and Zach[24] found that nonsurviving firms tend to be either extremely bad or extremely good performers. Survivor bias implies truncation of such extreme observations. The authors of the study show that even a small degree of such nonrandom truncation can have a strong impact on the sample moments of stock returns.

Dealing with Common Data Issues

Most data sets are subject to some quality issues. To work effectively, we need to be familiar with data definitions and database design. We also need to use processes to reduce the potential impact of data problems as they could cause incorrect conclusions.

The first step is to become familiar with the data standardization process vendors use to collect and process data. For example, many vendors use different templates to store data. Specifically, the Compustat US database has one template for reporting income statement data while the Worldscope Global database has four different templates depending on whether a firm

[23]Stefan Nagel, "Accounting Information Free of Selection Bias: A New UK Database 1953–1999," Working Paper, Stanford Graduate School of Business, 2001.
[24]S. P. Kothari, Jowell S. Sabino, and Tzachi Zach, "Implications of Survival and Data Trimming for Tests of Market Efficiency," *Journal of Accounting and Economics*, 39 (2005), pp. 129–161.

is classified as a bank, insurance company, industrial company, or other financial company. Other questions related to standardization a user should be familiar with include:

- What are the sources of the data—publicly available financial statements, regulatory filings, newswire services, or other sources?
- Is there a uniform reporting template?
- What is the delay between publication of information and its availability in the database?
- Is the data adjusted for stock splits?
- Is history available for extinct or inactive companies?
- How is data handled for companies with multiple share classes?
- What is the process used to aggregate the data?

Understanding of the accounting principles underlying the data is critical. Here, two principles of importance are the valuation methodology and data disclosure/presentation. For the valuation, we should understand the type of cost basis used for the various accounting items. Specifically, are assets calculated using historical cost basis, fair value accounting, or another type? For accounting principles regarding disclosure/presentation, we need to know the definition of accounting terms, the format of the accounts, and the depth of detail provided.

Researchers creating factors that use financial statements should review the history of the underlying accounting principles. For example, the cash flow statement reported by companies has changed over the years. Effective for fiscal years ending July 15, 1988, Statement of Financial Accounting Standards #85 (SFAS #85) requires companies to report the Statement of Cash Flows. Prior to the adoption of that accounting standard, companies could report one of three statements: Working Capital Statement, Cash Statement by Source and Use of Funds, or Cash Statement by Activity. Historical analysis of any factor that uses cash flow items will require adjustments to the definition of the factor to account for the different statements used by companies.

Preferably, automated processes should be used to reduce the potential impact of data problems. We start by checking the data for consistency and accuracy. We can perform time series analysis on individual factors looking at outliers and for missing data. We can use magnitude tests to compare current data items with the same items for prior periods, looking for data that are larger than a predetermined variance. When suspicious cases are identified, the cause of the error should be researched and any necessary changes made.

Methods to Adjust Factors

At first, factors consist of raw data from a database combined in an economically meaningful way. After the initial setup, a factor may be adjusted using analytical or statistical techniques to be more useful for modeling. The following three adjustments are common.

Standardization

Standardization rescales a variable while preserving its order. Typically, we choose the standardized variable to have a mean of zero and a standard deviation of one by using the transformation

$$x_i^{new} = \frac{x_i - \bar{x}}{\sigma_x}$$

where x_i is the stock's factor score, $\bar{x}$ is the universe average, and σ_x is the universe standard deviation. There are several reasons to scale a variable in this way. First, it allows one to determine a stock's position relative to the universe average. Second, it allows better comparison across stocks since means and standard deviations are the same. Third, it can be useful in combining multiple variables.

Orthogonalization

Sometimes the performance of our factor might be related to another factor. Orthogonalizing a factor for other specified factor(s) removes this relationship. We can orthogonalize by using averages or running regressions.

To orthogonalize the factor using averages according to industries or sectors, we can proceed as follows. First, for each industry we calculate the industry scores

$$s_k = \frac{\sum_{i=1}^{n} x_i \cdot ind_{i,k}}{\sum_{i=1}^{n} ind_{i,k}}$$

where x_i is a factor and $ind_{i,k}$ represent the weight of stock i in industry k. Next, we subtract the industry average of the industry scores, s_k, from each stock. We compute

$$x_i^{new} = x_i - \sum_{k \in \text{Industries}} ind_{i,k} \cdot s_k$$

where x_i^{new} is the new industry neutral factor.

We can use linear regression as described in Chapter 2 to orthogonalize a factor. We first determine the coefficients in the equation

$$x_i = a + b \cdot f_i + \varepsilon_i$$

where f_i is the factor to orthogonalize the factor x_i by, b is the contribution of f_i to x_i, and ε_i is the component of the factor x_i not related to f_i. ε_i is orthogonal to f_i (that is, ε_i is independent of f_i) and represents the neutralized factor

$$x_i^{new} = \varepsilon_i$$

In the same fashion, we can orthogonalize our variable relative to a set of factors by using the multivariate linear regression

$$x_i = a + \sum_j b_j \cdot f_j + \varepsilon_i$$

and then setting $x_i^{new} = \varepsilon_i$.

Often portfolio managers use a risk model to forecast risk and an alpha model to forecast returns. The interaction between factors in a risk model and an alpha model often concerns portfolio managers. One possible approach to address this concern is to orthogonalize the factors or final scores from the alpha model against the factors used in the risk model. Later in the chapter we will discuss this issue in more detail.

Transformation

It is common practice to apply transformations to data used in statistical and econometric models. In particular, factors are often transformed such that the resulting series is symmetric or close to being normally distributed. Frequently used transformations include natural logarithms, exponentials, and square roots. For example, a factor such as market capitalization has a large skew because a sample of large cap stocks typically includes mega-capitalization stocks. To reduce the influence of mega-capitalization companies, we may instead use the natural logarithm of market capitalization in a linear regression model.

Outlier Detection and Management

Outliers are observations that seem to be inconsistent with the other values in a data set. Financial data contain outliers for a number of reasons including data errors, measurement errors, or unusual events. Interpretation of data containing outliers may therefore be misleading. For example, our estimates could be biased or distorted, resulting in incorrect conclusions.

Outliers can be detected by several methods. Graphs such as boxplots, scatter plots, or histograms can be useful to visually identify them. Alternatively, there are a number of numerical techniques available. One common method is to compute the inter-quartile-range and then identify outliers as those values that are some multiple of the range. The inter-quartile-range is a measure of dispersion and is calculated as the difference between the third and first quartiles of a sample. This measure represents the middle 50% of the data, removing the influence of outliers.

After outliers have been identified, we need to reduce their influence in our analysis. As explained in Chapter 2, trimming and winsorization are common procedures for this purpose. Trimming discards extreme values in the data set. This transformation requires the researcher to determine the direction (symmetric or asymmetric) and the amount of trimming to occur.

Winsorization is the process of transforming extreme values in the data. First, we calculate percentiles of the data. Next we define outliers by referencing a certain percentile ranking. For example, any data observation that is greater than the 97.5 percentile or less than the 2.5 percentile could be considered an outlier. Finally, we set all values greater/less than the reference percentile ranking to particular values. In our example, we may set all values greater than the 97.5 percentile to the 97.5 percentile value and all values less than 2.5 percentile set to the 2.5 percentile value. It is important to fully investigate the practical consequences of using either one of these procedures. In the next chapter, we will apply what we learn from the following statistical summaries of the factors to build a model and implement our trading strategy.

ANALYSIS OF FACTOR DATA

After constructing factors for all securities in the investable universe, each factor is analyzed individually. Presenting the time-series and cross-sectional averages of the mean, standard deviations, and key percentiles of the distribution provide useful information for understanding the behavior of the chosen factors.

Although we often rely on techniques that assume the underlying data generating process is normally distributed, or at least approximately, most financial data is not. The underlying data generating processes that embody aggregate investor behavior and characterize the financial markets are unknown and exhibit significant uncertainty. Investor behavior is uncertain because not all investors make rational decisions or have the same goals. Analyzing the properties of data may help us better understand how uncertainty affects our choice and calibration of a model.

Below we provide some examples of the cross-sectional characteristics of various factors. For ease of exposition we use histograms to evaluate the data rather than formal statistical tests. We let particular patterns or properties of the histograms guide us in the choice of the appropriate technique to model the factor. We recommend that an intuitive exploration should be followed by a more formal statistical testing procedure. Our approach here is to analyze the entire sample, all positive values, all negative values, and zero values. Although omitted here, a thorough analysis should also include separate subsample analysis.

Example 1: EBITDA/EV

The first factor we discuss is the earnings before interest taxes and amortization to enterprise value (EBITDA/EV) factor. Enterprise value is calculated as the market value of the capital structure. This factor measures the price (enterprise value) investors pays to receive the cash flows (EBITDA) of a company. The economic intuition underlying this factor is that the valuation of a company's cash flow determines the attractiveness of companies to an investor.

Panel A of Exhibit 6.2 presents a histogram of all cross-sectional values of the EBITDA/EV factor throughout the entire history of the study. The distribution is close to normal, showing there is a fairly symmetric dispersion among the valuations companies receive. Panel B of Exhibit 6.2 shows that the distribution of all the positive values of the factor is also almost normally distributed. On the other hand, Panel C of Exhibit 6.2 shows that the distribution of the negative values is skewed to the left. However, because there are only a small number of negative values, it is likely that they will not greatly influence our model.

Example 2: Revisions

We evaluate the cross-sectional distribution of the earnings revisions factor.[25] The revisions factor we use is derived from sell-side analyst earnings forecasts from the IBES database. The factor is calculated as the number of analysts who revise their earnings forecast upward minus the number of downward forecasts, divided by the total number of forecasts. The econom-

---

[25]For a representative study see, for example, Anthony Bercel, "Consensus Expectations and International Equity Returns," *Financial Analysts Journal*, 50 (1994), pp 76-80.

EXHIBIT 6.2   Histograms of the Cross-Sectional Values for the EBITDA/EV Factor
Panel A: All Factor Values

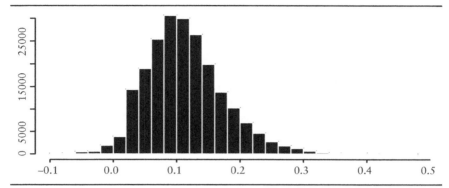

Panel B: Positive Factor Values

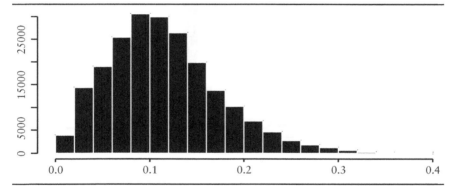

Panel C: Negative Factor Values

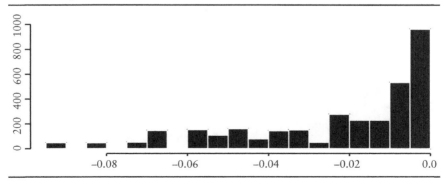

ic intuition underlying this factor is that there should be a positive relation
to changes in forecasts of earnings and subsequent returns.

In Panel A of Exhibit 6.3 we see that the distribution of revisions is
symmetric and leptokurtic around a mean of about zero. This distribution
ties with the economic intuition behind the revisions. Since business prospects of companies typically do not change from month-to-month, sell-side
analysts will not revise their earnings forecast every month. Consequently,
we expect and find the cross-sectional range to be peaked at zero. Panels B
and C of Exhibits 6.3, respectively, show there is a smaller number of both
positive and negative earnings revisions and each one of these distributions
are skewed.

EXHIBIT 6.3   Histograms of the Cross-Sectional Values for the Revisions Factor
Panel A: All Factor Values

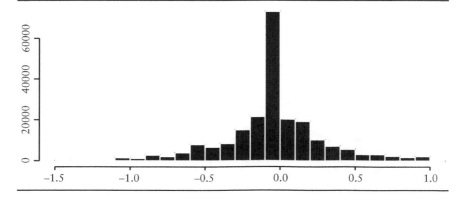

Panel B: Positive Factor Values

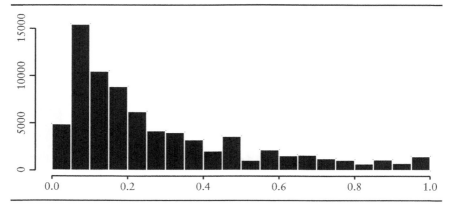

EXHIBIT 6.3　(Continued)
Panel C: Negative Factor Values

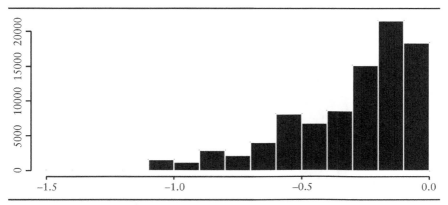

Example 3: Share Repurchase

We evaluate the cross-sectional distribution of the shares repurchases factor. This factor is calculated as the difference of the current number of common shares outstanding and the number of shares outstanding 12 months ago, divided by the number of shares outstanding 12 months ago. The economic intuition underlying this factor is that share repurchase provides information to investors about future earnings and valuation of the company's stock.[26] We expect there to be a positive relationship between a reduction in shares outstanding and subsequent returns.

We see in Panel A of Exhibit 6.4 that the distribution is leptokurtic. The positive values (see Panel B of Exhibit 6.4) are skewed to the right and the negative values (see Panel C of Exhibit 6.4) are clustered in a small band. The economic intuition underlying share repurchases is the following. Firms with increasing share count indicate they require additional sources of cash. This need could be an early sign that the firm is experiencing higher operating risks or financial distress. We would expect these firms to have lower future returns. Firms with decreasing share count have excess cash and are returning value back to shareholders. Decreasing share count could result because management believes the shares are undervalued. As expected, we find the cross-sectional range to be peaked at zero (see Panel D of Exhibit 6.4) since not all firms issue or repurchase shares on a regular basis.

---

[26]Gustavo Grullon and Roni Michaely, "The Information Content of Share Repurchase Programs," *Journal of Finance*, 59 (2004), pp 651–680.

EXHIBIT 6.4   Histograms of the Cross-Sectional Values for the Share
Repurchase Factor
Panel A: Positive Factor Values

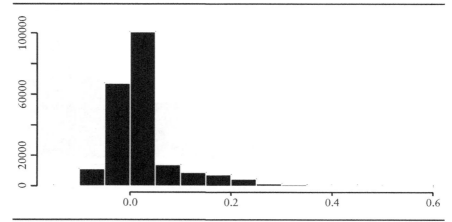

Panel B: Positive Factor Values

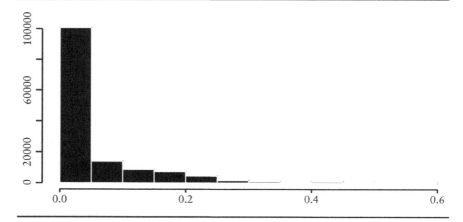

SUMMARY

- A factor is a common characteristic among a group of assets. Factors
  should be founded on sound economic intuition, market insight, or an
  anomaly.
- Factors fall into three categories—macroeconomic, cross-sectional, and
  statistical factors.

EXHIBIT 6.4 (Continued)
Panel C: Negative Factor Values

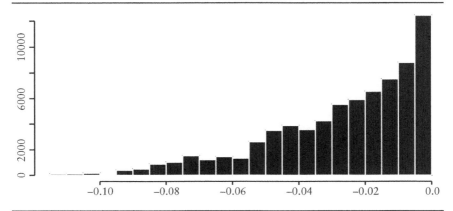

Panel D: Zero Factor Values

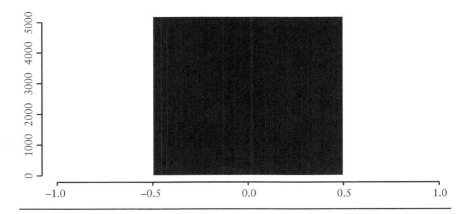

- The main steps in the development of a factor-based trading strategy are (1) defining a trading idea or investment strategy, (2) developing factors, (3) acquiring and processing data, (4) analyzing the factors, (5) building the strategy, (6) evaluating the strategy, (7) backtesting the strategy, and (8) implementing the strategy.
- Most trading strategies are exposed to risk. The main sources of risk are fundamental risk, noise trader risk, horizon risk, model risk, implementation risk, and liquidity risk.

- Factors are often derived from company characteristics and metrics, and market data. Examples of company characteristics and metrics include valuation ratios, operating efficiency ratios, profitability ratios, and solvency ratios. Example of useful market data include analysts forecasts, prices and returns, and trading volume.
- High quality data are critical to the success of a trading strategy. Model output is only as good as the data used to calibrate it.
- Some common data problems and biases are backfilling and restatements of data, missing data, inconsistently reported data, and survivorship and look-ahead biases.
- The ability to detect and adjust outliers is crucial to a quantitative investment process.
- Common methods used for adjusting data are standardization, orthogonalization, transformation, trimming, and winsorization.
- The statistical properties of factors need to be carefully analyzed. Basic statistical measures include the time-series and cross-sectional averages of the mean, standard deviations, and key percentiles.

CHAPTER 7

Factor-Based Trading Strategies II: Cross-Sectional Models and Trading Strategies

In the previous chapter we demonstrated how factors are constructed from company characteristics and market data. Subsequently, we discussed the analysis of the statistical properties of the factors. In this chapter we extend the analysis to include multiple factors with the purpose of developing a dynamic multifactor trading strategy that incorporates a number of common institutional constraints such as turnover, transaction costs, sector, and tracking error. For this purpose, we use a combination of growth, value, quality, and momentum factors. Our universe of stocks is the Russell 1000 from December 1989 to December 2008, and we construct our factors by using the Compustat Point-In-Time and IBES databases.[1]

We begin by reviewing several approaches for the evaluation of return premiums and risk characteristics to factors, including portfolio sorts, factor models, factor portfolios, and information coefficients. We then turn to techniques that are used to combine several factors into a single model—a trading strategy. In particular, we discuss the data driven, factor model, heuristic, and optimization approaches. It is critical to perform out-of-sample backtests of a trading strategy to understand its performance and risk characteristics. We cover the split-sample and recursive out-of-sample tests.

Throughout this chapter, we provide a series of examples, including backtests of a multifactor trading strategy. As noted in the previous chapter, the purpose of these examples is not to provide yet another profitable trading strategy, but rather to illustrate the process an analyst may follow when performing research. We emphasize that the factors that we use are

---

[1]Refer to Appendix A for a complete list of the factors and data sets used in this chapter.

This chapter was co-authored with Joseph A. Cerniglia.

well known and have for years been exploited by industry practitioners. We think that the value added of these examples is in the concrete illustration of the research and development process of a factor-based trading model.

CROSS-SECTIONAL METHODS FOR EVALUATION OF FACTOR PREMIUMS

There are several approaches used for the evaluation of return premiums and risk characteristics to factors. In this section, we discuss the four most commonly used approaches: portfolio sorts, factor models, factor portfolios, and information coefficients. We examine the methodology of each approach and summarize its advantages and disadvantages.

In practice, to determine the right approach for a given situation there are several issues to consider. One determinant is the structure of the financial data. A second determinant is the economic intuition underlying the factor. For example, sometimes we are looking for a monotonic relationship between returns and factors while at other times we care only about extreme values. A third determinant is whether the underlying assumptions of each approach are valid for the data generating process at hand.

Portfolio Sorts

In the asset pricing literature, the use of portfolio sorts can be traced back to the earliest tests of the capital asset pricing model (CAPM). The goal of this particular test is to determine whether a factor earns a systematic premium. The portfolios are constructed by grouping together securities with similar characteristics (factors). For example, we can group stocks by market capitalization into 10 portfolios—from smallest to largest—such that each portfolio contains stocks with similar market capitalization. The next step is to calculate and evaluate the returns of these portfolios.

The return for each portfolio is calculated by equally weighting the individual stock returns. The portfolios provide a representation of how returns vary across the different values of a factor. By studying the return behavior of the factor portfolios, we may assess the return and risk profile of the factor. In some cases, we may identify a monotonic relationship of the returns across the portfolios. In other cases, we may identify a large difference in returns between the extreme portfolios. Still in other cases, there may be no relationship between the portfolio returns. Overall, the return behavior of the portfolios will help us conclude whether there is a premium associated with a factor and describe its properties.

One application of the portfolio sort is the construction of a *factor mimicking portfolio* (FMP). A FMP is a long-short portfolio that goes long stocks with high values of a factor and short stocks with low values of a factor, in equal dollar amounts. A FMP is a zero-cost factor trading strategy.

Portfolio sorts have become so widespread among practitioners and academics alike that they elicit few econometric queries, and often no econometric justification for the technique is offered. While a detailed discussion of these topics are beyond the scope of this book, we would like to point out that asset pricing tests used on sorted portfolios may exhibit a bias that favors rejecting the asset pricing model under consideration.[2]

The construction of portfolios sorted on a factor is straightforward:

- Choose an appropriate sorting methodology.
- Sort the assets according to the factor.
- Group the sorted assets into N portfolios (usually $N = 5$, or $N = 10$).
- Compute average returns (and other statistics) of the assets in each portfolio over subsequent periods.

The standard statistical testing procedure for portfolios sorts is to use a Student's *t*-test to evaluate the significance of the mean return differential between the portfolios of stocks with the highest and lowest values of the factor.

Choosing the Sorting Methodology

The sorting methodology should be consistent with the characteristics of the distribution of the factor and the economic motivation underlying its premium. We list six ways to sort factors:

Method 1
- Sort stocks with factor values from the highest to lowest.

Method 2
- Sort stocks with factor values from the lowest to highest.

Method 3
- First allocate stocks with zero factor values into the bottom portfolio.
- Sort the remaining stocks with nonzero factor values into the remaining portfolios.

For example, the dividend yield factor would be suitable for this sorting approach. This approach aligns the factor's distributional characteristics of dividend and non-dividend-paying stocks with the economic rationale.

[2]For a good overview of the most common issues, see Jonathan B. Berk, "Sorting out Sorts," *Journal of Finance*, 55 (2000), pp. 407-427 and references therein.

Typically, non-dividend-paying stocks maintain characteristics that are different from dividend paying stocks. So we group non-dividend-paying stocks into one portfolio. The remaining stocks are then grouped into portfolios depending on the size of their nonzero dividend yields. We differentiate among stocks with dividend yield because of two reasons: (1) the size of the dividend yield is related to the maturity of the company, and (2) some investors prefer to receive their investment return as dividends.

Method 4
- Allocate stocks with zero factor values into the middle portfolio.
- Sort stocks with positive factor values into the remaining higher portfolios (greater than the middle portfolio).
- Sort stocks with negative factor values into the remaining lower portfolios (less than the middle portfolio).

Method 5
- Sort stocks into partitions.
- Rank assets within each partition.
- Combine assets with the same ranking from the different partitions into portfolios.

An example will clarify this procedure. Suppose we want to rank stocks according to earnings growth on a sector neutral basis. First, we separate stocks into groups corresponding to their sector. Within each sector, we rank the stocks according to their earnings growth. Lastly, we group all stocks with the same rankings of earning growth into the final portfolio. This process ensures that each portfolio will contain an equal number of stocks from every sector, thereby the resulting portfolios are sector neutral.

Method 6
- Separate all the stocks with negative factors values. Split the group of stocks with negative values into two portfolios using the median value as the break point.
- Allocate stocks with zero factor values into one portfolio.
- Sort the remaining stocks with nonzero factor values into portfolios based on their factor values.

For an example of method 6, recall the discussion of the share repurchase factor from Chapter 6. We are interested in the extreme positive and negative values of this factor. As we see in Panel A of Exhibit 6.4, the distribution of this factors is leptokurtic with the positive values skewed to the right and the negative values clustered in a small range. By choosing method 6 to sort this variable, we are able to distinguish between those values we view as extreme. The negative values are clustered so we want to distinguish among the magnitudes of those values. We accomplish this because our sorting method separates the negative values by the median of the negative values. The largest negative values form the extreme negative portfolio. The positive values are skewed to the right, so we want to differentiate between the larger from smaller positive values. When implementing portfolio method 6, we would also separate the zero values from the positive values.

The portfolio sort methodology has several advantages. The approach is easy to implement and can easily handle stocks that drop out or enter into the sample. The resulting portfolios diversify away idiosyncratic risk of individual assets and provide a way of assessing how average returns differ across different magnitudes of a factor.

The portfolio sort methodology has several disadvantages. The resulting portfolios may be exposed to different risks beyond the factor the portfolio was sorted on. In those instances, it is difficult to know which risk characteristics have an impact on the portfolio returns. Because portfolio sorts are nonparametric, they do not give insight as to the functional form of the relation between the average portfolio returns and the factor.

Next we provide three examples to illustrate how the economic intuition of the factor and cross sectional statistics can help determine the sorting methodology.

Example 1: Portfolio Sorts Based on the EBITDA/EV Factor

In the previous chapter, we introduced the EBITDA/EV factor. Panel A of Exhibit 7.1 contains the cross-sectional distribution of the EBITDA/EV factor. This distribution is approximately normally distributed around a mean of 0.1, with a slight right skew. We use method 1 to sort the variables into five portfolios (denoted by q1, …, q5) because this sorting method aligns the cross-sectional distribution of factor returns with our economic intuition that there is a linear relationship between the factor and subsequent return. In Panel B of Exhibit 7.1 we see that there is a large difference between the equally weighted monthly returns of portfolio 1 (q1) and portfolio 5 (q5). Therefore, a trading strategy (denoted by ls in the graph) that goes long portfolio 1 and short portfolio 5 appears to produce abnormal returns.

Example 2: Portfolios Sorts Based on the Revisions Factor

In Panel A of Exhibit 7.2 we see that the distribution of earnings revisions is leptokurtic around a mean of about zero, with the remaining values symmetrically distributed around the peak. The pattern in this cross-sectional

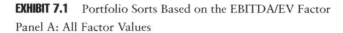

EXHIBIT 7.1 Portfolio Sorts Based on the EBITDA/EV Factor

Panel A: All Factor Values

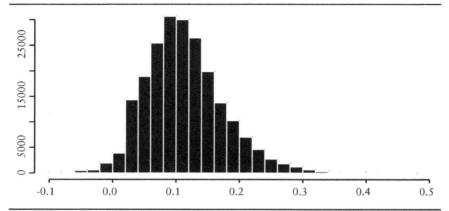

Panel B: Monthly Average Returns for the Sorted Portfolios

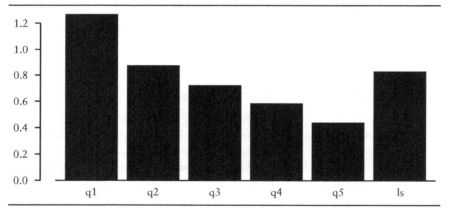

distribution provides insight on how we should sort this factor. We use method 3 to sort the variables into five portfolios. The firms with no change in revisions we allocate to the middle portfolio (portfolio 3). The stocks with positive revisions we sort into portfolios 1 and 2, according to the size of the revisions—while we sort stocks with negative revisions into portfolios 4 and 5, according to the size of the revisions. In Panel B of Exhibit 7.2 we see there is the relationship between the portfolios and subsequent monthly returns. The positive relationship between revisions and subsequent returns agrees with the factor's underlying economic intuition: we expect that firms with improving earnings should outperform. The trading strategy that goes

EXHIBIT 7.2 The Revisions Factor
Panel A: All Factor Values

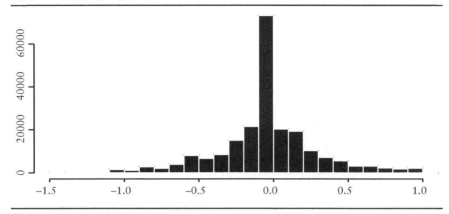

Panel B: Monthly Average Returns for the Sorted Portfolios

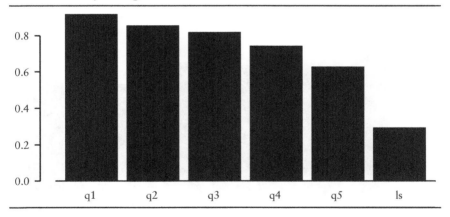

long portfolio 1 and short portfolio 5 (denoted by ls in the graph) appears to produce abnormal returns.

Example 3: Portfolio Sorts Based on the Share Repurchase Factor

In Panel A of Exhibit 7.3 we see the distribution of share repurchase is asymmetric and leptokurtic around a mean of zero. The pattern in this cross-sectional distribution provides insight on how we should sort this factor. We use method 6 to sort the variables into seven portfolios. We group stocks with positive revisions into portfolios 1 through 5 (denoted by q_1, ..., q_5 in the graph) according to the magnitude of the share repurchase factor. We

EXHIBIT 7.3 The Share Repurchase Factor
Panel A: All Factor Values

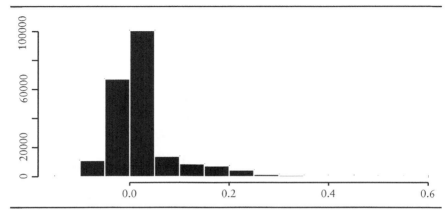

Panel B: Monthly Average Returns for the Sorted Portfolios

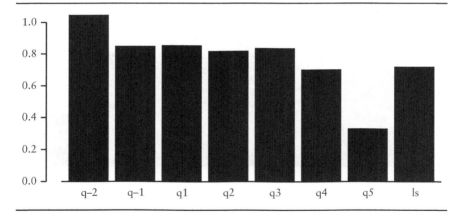

allocate stocks with negative repurchases into portfolios q–2 and q–1 where the median of the negative values determines their membership. We split the negative numbers because we are interested in large changes in the shares outstanding. In Panel B of Exhibit 7.3, unlike the other previous factors, we see that there is *not* a linear relationship between the portfolios. However, there is a large difference in return between the extreme portfolios (denoted by ls in the graph). This large difference agrees with the economic intuition of this factor. Changes in the number of shares outstanding is a potential signal for the future value and prospects of a firm. On the one hand, a large increase in shares outstanding may (1) signal to investors the need for additional cash because of financial distress, or (2) that the firm may be overvalued. On the other hand, a large decrease in the number of shares outstanding may indicate that management believes the shares are undervalued. Finally, small changes in shares outstanding, positive or negative, typically do not have an impact on stock price and therefore are not significant.

Information Ratios for Portfolio Sorts

The information ratio (IR) is a statistic for summarizing the risk-adjusted performance of an investment strategy. It is defined as the ratio of the average excess return to the standard deviation of return. For actively managed equity long portfolios, the IR measures the risk-adjusted value a portfolio manager is adding relative to a benchmark.[3] IR can also be used to capture the risk-adjusted performance of long-short portfolios from a portfolio sorts. When comparing portfolios built using different factors, the IR is an effective measure for differentiating the performance between the strategies.

New Research on Portfolio Sorts

As we mentioned earlier in this section, the standard statistical testing procedure for portfolios sorts is to use a Student's *t*-test to evaluate the mean return differential between the two portfolios containing stocks with the highest and lowest values of the sorting factor. However, evaluating the return between these two portfolios ignores important information about the overall pattern of returns among the remaining portfolios.

Recent research by Patton and Timmermann[4] provides new analytical techniques to increase the robustness of inference from portfolios sorts. The technique tests for the presence of a monotonic relationship between the portfolios and their expected returns. To find out if there is a systematic relationship between a factor and portfolio returns, they use the *monotonic*

---

[3] In Richard C. Grinold and Ronald N. Kahn, *Active Portfolio Management: A Quantitative Approach for Providing Superior Returns and Controlling Risk* (New York: McGraw-Hill, 1999), the authors discuss the differences between the *t*-statistic and the information ratio. Both measures are closely related in their calculation. The *t*-statistic is the ratio of mean return of a strategy to its standard error. Grinold and Kahn state the related calculations should not obscure the distinction between the two ratios. The *t*-statistic measures the statistical significance of returns while the IR measures the risk-reward trade-off and the value added by an investment strategy.

[4] Andrew J. Patton and Allan Timmermann, "Monotonicity in Asset Returns: New Tests with Applications to the Term Structure, the CAPM and Portfolio Sorts," Working Paper, University of California San Diego, 2009.

relation (MR) test to reveal whether the null hypothesis of no systematic relationship can be rejected in favor of a monotonic relationship predicted by economic theory. By MR it is meant that the expected returns of a factor should rise or decline monotonically in one direction as one goes from one portfolio to another. Moreover, Patton and Timmermann develop separate tests to determine the direction of deviations in support of or against the theory.

The authors emphasize several advantages in using this approach. The test is nonparametric and applicable to other cases of portfolios such as two-way and three-way sorts. This test is easy to implement via bootstrap methods. Furthermore, this test does not require specifying the functional form (e.g., linear) in relating the sorting variable to expected returns.

FACTOR MODELS

Classical financial theory states that the average return of a stock is the pay-off to investors for taking on risk. One way of expressing this risk-reward relationship is through a factor model. As we discussed in Chapter 5, a factor model can be used to decompose the returns of a security into factor-specific and asset-specific returns,

$$r_{i,t} = \alpha_i + \beta_{i,1}f_{1,t} + \ldots + \beta_{i,K}f_{K,t} + \varepsilon_{i,t}$$

where $\beta_{i,1}, \beta_{i,2}, \ldots, \beta_{i,K}$ are the factor exposures of stock i, $f_{1,t}, f_{2,t}, \ldots, f_{K,t}$ are the factor returns, α_i is the average abnormal return of stock i, and $\varepsilon_{i,t}$ is the residual.

This factor model specification is *contemporaneous*, that is, both left- and right-hand side variables (returns and factors) have the same time subscript, t. For trading strategies one generally applies a *forecasting* specification where the time subscript of the return and the factors are $t + h$ ($h \geq 1$) and t, respectively. In this case, the econometric specification becomes

$$r_{i,t+h} = \alpha_i + \beta_{i,1}f_{1,t} + \ldots + \beta_{i,K}f_{K,t} + \varepsilon_{i,t+h}$$

How do we interpret a trading strategy based on a factor model? The explanatory variables represent different factors that forecast security returns, each factor with its associated factor premium. Therefore, future security returns are proportional to the stock's exposure to the factor premium

$$E(r_{i,t+h} \mid f_{1,t}, \ldots, f_{K,t}) = \alpha_i + \beta_i'f_t$$

and the variance of future stock return is given by

$$Var(r_{i,t+h} \mid f_{1,t}, \dots, f_{K,t}) = \boldsymbol{\beta}_i' E(\mathbf{f}_t \mathbf{f}_t') \boldsymbol{\beta}_i$$

where $\boldsymbol{\beta}_i = (\beta_{i,1}, \beta_{i,2}, \dots, \beta_{i,K})'$ and $\mathbf{f}_t = (f_{1,t}, f_{2,t}, \dots, f_{K,t})'$.

We covered the estimation of linear regression and factor models in Chapters 2 and 5. In the next section we discuss some specific econometric issues regarding cross-sectional regressions and factor models.

Econometric Considerations for Cross-Sectional Factor Models

In cross-sectional regressions where the dependent variable[5] is a stock's return and the independent variables are factors, inference problems may arise that are the result of violations of classical linear regression theory as explained in Chapter 2. The three most common problems are measurement problems, common variations in residuals, and multicollinearity.

Measurement Problems

Some factors are not explicitly given, but need to be estimated. These factors are estimated with an error. The estimation errors in the factors can have an impact on the inference from a factor model. This problem is commonly referred to as the "errors in variables problem." For example, a factor that is comprised of a stock's beta is estimated with an error because beta is determined from a regression of stock excess returns on the excess returns of a market index. While beyond the scope of this book, several approaches have been suggested to deal with this problem.[6]

Common Variation in Residuals

The residuals from a regression often contain a source of common variation. Sources of common variation in the residuals are heteroskedasticity and serial correlation. We note that when the form of heteroskedasticity and serial correlation is known, we can apply generalized least squares (GLS) covered in Chapter 2. If the form is not known, it has to be estimated, for example as

---

[5]See, for example, Eugene F. Fama and Kenneth R. French, "The Capital Asset Pricing Model: Theory and Evidence," *Journal of Economic Perspectives*, 18 (2004), pp. 25-46.

[6]One approach is to use the Bayesian or model averaging techniques like the ones described in Chapter 4. For more details on the Bayesian approach, see, for example, Svetlozar T. Rachev, John S. J. Hsu, Biliana S. Bagasheva, and Frank J. Fabozzi, *Bayesian Methods in Finance* (Hoboken, NJ: John Wiley & Sons, 2008).

part of feasible generalized least squares (FGLS), also discussed in Chapter 2. We summarize some additional possibilities next.

Heteroskedasticity occurs when the variance of the residual differs across observations and affects the statistical inference in a linear regression. In particular, the estimated standard errors will be underestimated and the t-statistics will therefore be inflated. Ignoring heteroskedasticity may lead the researcher to find significant relationships where none actually exist. As we discussed in Chapter 2, several procedures have been developed to calculate standard errors that are robust to heteroskedasticity, also known as heteroskedasticity-consistent standard errors.

Serial correlation occurs when consecutive residuals terms in a linear regression are correlated, violating the assumptions of regression theory. If the serial correlation is positive then the standard errors are underestimated and the t-statistics will be inflated. Cochrane[7] suggests that the errors in cross-sectional regressions using financial data are often off by a factor of 10. Procedures are available to correct for serial correlation when calculating standard errors.

When the residuals from a regression are both heteroskedastic and serially correlated, procedures are available to correct them. One commonly used procedure, also discussed in Chapter 8, is the one proposed by Newey and West.

Petersen[8] provides guidance on choosing the appropriate method to use for correctly calculating standard errors for panel data regression when the residuals are correlated. He shows the relative accuracy of the different methods depends on the structure of the data. In the presence of firm effects, where the residuals of a given firm may be correlated across years, OLS, Newey-West (modified for panel data sets), or Fama-MacBeth,[9] corrected for first-order autocorrelation all produce biased standard errors. To correct for this, Petersen recommends using standard errors clustered by firms. If the firm effect is permanent, the fixed effects and random effects models produce unbiased standard errors. In the presence of time effects, where the residuals of a given period may be correlated across difference firms (cross-sectional dependence), Fama-MacBeth produces unbiased standard errors. Furthermore, standard errors clustered by time are unbiased when there are a sufficient number of clusters. To select the correct approach he recommends determining the form of dependence in the data and comparing the results from several methods.

[7]John H. Cochrane, *Asset Pricing* (Princeton, NJ: Princeton University Press, 2005).
[8]Mitchell A. Petersen, "Estimating Standard Errors in Finance Panel Sets: Comparing Approached," forthcoming, in *Review of Financial Studies*.
[9]We cover Fama-MacBeth regression in the next section.

Gow, Ormazabal, and Taylor[10] evaluate empirical methods used in accounting research to correct for cross-sectional and time-series dependence. They review each of the methods and discuss when each approach produces valid inferences. They analyze several methods from the accounting literature that have not previously been formally evaluated.

Multicollinearity

Multicollinearity occurs when two or more independent variables are highly correlated. We may encounter several problems when this happens. First, it is difficult to determine which factors influence the dependent variable. Second, the individual p values can be misleading—a p value can be high even if the variable is important. Third, the confidence intervals for the regression coefficients will be wide. They may even include zero. This implies that, we cannot determine whether an increase in the independent variable is associated with an increase—or a decrease—in the dependent variable. There is no formal solution based on theory to correct for multicollinearity. The best way to correct for multicollinearity is by removing one or more of the correlated independent variables. It can also be reduced by increasing the sample size.

Fama-MacBeth Regression

To address the inference problem caused by the correlation of the residuals, Fama and MacBeth[11] proposed the following methodology for estimating cross-sectional regressions of returns on factors. For notational simplicity, we describe the procedure for one factor. The multifactor generalization is straightforward.

First, for each point in time t we perform a cross-sectional regression

$$r_{i,t} = \beta_{i,t} f_t + \varepsilon_{i,t}, \quad i = 1, 2, \ldots, N$$

In the academic literature, the regressions are typically performed using monthly or quarterly data, but the procedure could be used at any frequency.

The mean and standard errors of the time series of slopes and residuals are evaluated to determine the significance of the cross-sectional regression. We estimate f and ε_i as the average of their cross-sectional estimates,

---

[10]Ian D. Gow, Gaizka Ormazabal, and Daniel J. Taylor, "Correcting for Cross-Sectional and Time-Series Dependence in Accounting Research," Working Paper, Kellogg School of Business and Stanford Graduate School, 2009.

[11]Eugene F. Fama and James D. MacBeth, "Risk, Return, and Equilibrium: Empirical Tests," *Journal of Political Economy*, 81 (1973), pp. 607–636.

$$\hat{f} = \frac{1}{T}\sum_{t=1}^{T}\hat{f}_t, \ \hat{\varepsilon}_i = \frac{1}{T}\sum_{t=1}^{T}\hat{\varepsilon}_{i,t}$$

The variations in the estimates determine the standard error and capture the effects of residual correlation without actually estimating the correlations.[12] We use the standard deviations of the cross-sectional regression estimates to calculate the sampling errors for these estimates,

$$\sigma_{\hat{f}}^2 = \frac{1}{T^2}\sum_{t=1}^{T}\left(\hat{f}_t - \hat{f}\right)^2, \ \sigma_{\hat{\varepsilon}_i}^2 = \frac{1}{T^2}\sum_{t=1}^{T}\left(\hat{\varepsilon}_{i,t} - \hat{\varepsilon}_i\right)^2$$

Cochrane[13] provides a detailed analysis of this procedure and compares it to cross-sectional OLS and pooled time-series cross-sectional OLS. He shows that when the factors do not vary over time and the residuals are cross-sectionally correlated, but not correlated over time, then these procedures are all equivalent.

Information Coefficients

To determine the forecast ability of a model, practitioners commonly use the information coefficient (IC). The IC is a linear statistic that measures the cross-sectional correlation between a factor and its subsequent realized return[14]

$$IC_{t,t+k} = corr(\mathbf{f}_t, \mathbf{r}_{t,t+k})$$

where $\mathbf{f}_t$ is a vector of cross sectional factor values at time t and $\mathbf{r}_{t,t+k}$ is a vector of returns over the time period t to $t + k$.

Just like the standard correlation coefficient, the values of the IC range from -1 to $+1$. A positive IC indicates a positive relation between the factor and return. A negative IC indicates a negative relation between the factor and return. ICs are usually calculated over an interval, for example, daily or monthly. We can evaluate how a factor has performed by examining the time series behavior of the ICs. Looking at the mean IC tells how predictive the factor has been over time.

---

[12]Fama and French, "The Capital Asset Pricing Model: Theory and Evidence."
[13]Cochrane, *Asset Pricing*.
[14]See, for example, Grinold and Kahn, *Active Portfolio Management A Quantitative Approach for Providing Superior Returns and Controlling Risk*, and Edward E. Qian, Ronald H. Hua, and Eric H. Sorensen, *Quantitative Portfolio Management: Modern Techniques and Applications* (New York: Chapman & Hall/CRC, 2007).

An alternate specification of this measure is to make f_t the rank of a cross-sectional factor. This calculation is similar to the Spearman rank coefficient. By using the rank of the factor, we focus on the ordering of the factor instead of its value. Ranking the factor value reduces the unduly influence of outliers and reduces the influence of variables with unequal variances. For the same reasons we may also choose to rank the returns instead of using their numerical value.

Sorensen, Qian, and Hua[15] present a framework for factor analysis based on ICs. Their measure of IC is the correlation between the factor ranks, where the ranks are the normalized z-score of the factor,[16] and subsequent return. Intuitively, this IC calculation measures the return associated with a one standard deviation exposure to the factor. Their IC calculation is further refined by risk adjusting the value. To risk adjust, the authors remove systematic risks from the IC and accommodate the IC for specific risk. By removing these risks, Qian and Hua[17] show that the resulting ICs provide a more accurate measure of the return forecasting ability of the factor.

The subsequent realized returns to a factor typically vary over different time horizons. For example, the return to a factor based on price reversal is realized over short horizons, while valuation metrics such as EBITDA/EV are realized over longer periods. It therefore makes sense to calculate multiple ICs for a set of factor forecasts whereby each calculation varies the horizon over which the returns are measured.

The IC methodology has many of the same advantages as regression models. The procedure is easy to implement. The functional relationship between factor and subsequent returns is known (linear).

ICs can also be used to assess the risk of factors and trading strategies. The standard deviation of the time series (with respect to t) of ICs for a particular factor $(std(IC_{t,t+k}))$ can be interpreted as the strategy risk of a factor. Examining the time series behavior of $std(IC_{t,t+k})$ over different time periods may give a better understanding of how often a particular factor may fail. Qian and Hua show that $std(IC_{t,t+k})$ can be used to more effectively understand the active risk of investment portfolios. Their research demonstrates that ex-post tracking error often exceeds the ex-ante tracking provided by risk models. The difference in tracking error occurs because tracking error is a function of both ex-ante tracking error from a risk model and the variabil-

---

[15]Eric H. Sorensen, Ronald Hua, and Edward Qian, "Contextual Fundamentals, Models, and Active Management," *Journal of Portfolio Management*, 32 (2005), pp. 23–36.
[16]A factor normalized z-score is given by the formula $z\text{-score} = (f - \bar{f}) / std(f)$ where f is the factor, $\bar{f}$ is the mean and $std(f)$ is the standard deviation of the factor.
[17]Ronald Hua and Edward Qian, "Active Risk and Information Ratio," *Journal of Investment Management*, 2 (2004), pp. 1–15.

ity of information coefficients, $std(IC_{t,t+k})$. They define the expected tracking error as

$$\sigma_{TE} = std(IC_{t.t+k})\sqrt{N}\sigma_{model}dis(\mathbf{R}_t)$$

where N is the number of stocks in the universe (breath), σ_{model} is the risk model tracking error, and $dis(\mathbf{R}_t)$ is dispersion of returns[18] defined by

$$dis(\mathbf{R}_t) = std(r_{1,t}, r_{2,t}, ..., r_{N,t})$$

Example: Information Coefficients

Exhibit 7.4 displays the time-varying behavior of ICs for each one of the factors EBITDA/EV, growth of fiscal year 1 and fiscal year 2 earnings estimates, revisions, and momentum. The graph shows the time series average of information coefficients

$$\overline{IC}_k = mean(\mathbf{IC}_{t,t+k})$$

The graph depicts the information horizons for each factor, showing how subsequent return is realized over time. The vertical axis shows the size of the average information coefficient $\overline{IC}_k$ for $k = 1, 2, ..., 15$.

EXHIBIT 7.4 Information Coefficients over Various Horizons for EBITDA/EV, Growth of Fiscal Year 1 and Fiscal Year 2 Earnings Estimates, Revisions, and Momentum Factors

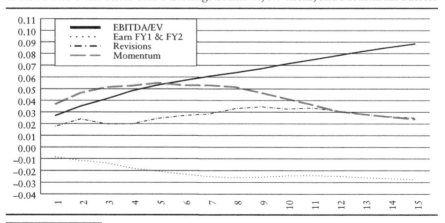

[18]We are conforming to the notation used in Qian and Hua, "Active Risk and Information Ratio." To avoid confusion Qian and Hua use $dis()$ to describe the cross-sectional standard deviation and $std()$ to describe the time series standard deviation.

Specifically, the EBITDA/EV factor starts at almost 0.03 and monotonically increases as the investment horizon lengthens from one month to 15 months. At 15 months, the EBITDA/EV factor has an IC of 0.09, the highest value among all the factors presented in the graph. This relationship suggests that the EBITDA/EV factor earns higher returns as the holding period lengthens.

The other ICs of the factors in the graph are also interesting. The growth of fiscal year 1 and fiscal year 2 earnings estimates factor is defined as the growth in current fiscal year (fy1) earnings estimates to the next fiscal year (fy2) earnings estimates provided by sell-side analysts.[19] We will call the growth of fiscal year 1 and fiscal year 2 earnings estimates factor the *earnings growth factor* throughout the remainder of the chapter. The IC is negative and decreases as the investment horizon lengthens. The momentum factor starts with a positive IC of 0.02 and increases to approximately 0.055 in the fifth month. After the fifth month, the IC decreases. The revisions factor starts with a positive IC and increases slightly until approximately the 11th month at which time the factor begins to decay.

Looking at the overall patterns in the graph, we see that the return realization pattern to different factors varies. One notable observation is that the returns to factors don't necessarily decay but sometimes grow with the holding period. Understanding the multiperiod effects of each factor is important when we want to combine several factors. This information may influence how one builds a model. For example, we can explicitly incorporate this information about information horizons into our model by using a function that describes the decay or growth of a factor as a parameter to be calibrated. Implicitly, we could incorporate this information by changing the holding period for a security traded for our trading strategy. Specifically, Sneddon[20] discusses an example that combines one signal that has short-range predictive power with another that has long-range power. Incorporating this information about the information horizon often improves the return potential of a model. Kolm[21] describes a general multiperiod model that combines information decay, market impact costs, and real world constraints.

---

[19]The earnings estimates come from the IBES database. See Appendix A for a more detailed description of the data.
[20]Leigh Sneddon, "The Tortoise and the Hare: Portfolio Dynamics for Active Managers," *Journal of Investing*, 2 (2008), pp. 106–111.
[21]Petter N. Kolm, "Multi-Period Portfolio Optimization with Transaction Costs, Alpha Decay, and Constraints", Working Paper, Courant Institute of Mathematical Sciences, New York University, 2010.

Factor Portfolios

Factor portfolios are constructed to measure the information content of a factor. The objective is to mimic the return behavior of a factor and minimize the residual risk. Similar to portfolio sorts, we evaluate the behavior of these factor portfolios to determine whether a factor earns a systematic premium.

Typically, a factor portfolio has a unit exposure to a factor and zero exposure to other factors. Construction of factor portfolios requires holding both long and short positions. We can also build a factor portfolio that has exposure to multiple attributes, such as beta, sectors, or other characteristics. For example, we could build a portfolio that has a unit exposure to book-to-price *and* small size stocks. Portfolios with exposures to multiple factors provide the opportunity to analyze the interaction of different factors.

A Factor Model Approach

By using a multifactor model, we can build factor portfolios that control for different risks.[22] We decompose return and risk at a point in time into a systematic and specific component using the regression:

$$r = Xb + u$$

where r is an N vector of excess returns of the stocks considered, X is an N by K matrix of factor loadings, b is a K vector of factor returns, and u is a N vector of firm specific returns (residual returns). Here, we assume that factor returns are uncorrelated with the firm specific return. Further assuming that firm specific returns of different companies are uncorrelated, the N by N covariance matrix of stock returns V is given by

$$V = XFX' + \Delta$$

where F is the K by K factor return covariance matrix and Δ is the N by N diagonal matrix of variances of the specific returns.

We can use the Fama-MacBeth procedure discussed earlier to estimate the factor returns over time. Each month, we perform a GLS regression to obtain

$$b = (X'\Delta^{-1}X)^{-1}X'\Delta^{-1}r$$

---

[22]This derivation of factor portfolios is presented in Grinold and Kahn, *Active Portfolio Management A Quantitative Approach for Providing Superior Returns and Controlling Risk.*

OLS would give us an unbiased estimate, but since the residuals are heteroskedastic the GLS methodology is preferred and will deliver a more efficient estimate. The resulting holdings for each factor portfolio are given by the rows of $(\mathbf{X}'\mathbf{\Delta}^{-1}\mathbf{X})^{-1}\mathbf{X}\mathbf{\Delta}^{-1}$.

An Optimization-Based Approach

A second approach to build factor portfolios uses mean-variance optimization. Using optimization techniques provide a flexible approach for implementing additional objectives and constraints.[23]

Using the notation from the previous subsection, we denote by $\mathbf{X}$ the set of factors. We would like to construct a portfolio that has maximum exposure to one target factor from $\mathbf{X}$ (the *alpha* factor), zero exposure to all other factors, and minimum portfolio risk. Let us denote the alpha factor by $\mathbf{X}_\alpha$ and all the remaining ones by $\mathbf{X}_\sigma$. Then the resulting optimization problem takes the form

$$\max_{\mathbf{w}}\left\{\mathbf{w}'\mathbf{X}_a - \frac{1}{2}\lambda\mathbf{w}'\mathbf{V}\mathbf{w}\right\}$$
$$s.t. \quad \mathbf{w}'\mathbf{X}_\sigma = 0$$

The analytical solution to this optimization problem is given by

$$b^* = \frac{1}{\lambda}\mathbf{V}^{-1}\left[\mathbf{I} - \mathbf{X}_\sigma\left(\mathbf{X}_\sigma'\mathbf{V}^{-1}\mathbf{X}_\sigma\right)^{-1}\mathbf{X}_\sigma'\mathbf{V}^{-1}\right]\mathbf{X}_\alpha$$

We may want to add additional constraints to the problem. Constraints are added to make factor portfolios easier to implement and meet additional objectives. Some common constraints include limitations on turnover, transaction costs, the number of assets, and liquidity preferences. These constraints[24] are typically implemented as linear inequality constraints, as discussed in Chapter 8, where no analytical solution is available and we have to resort to quadratic programming (QP).[25] We provide an example of this approach at the end of this chapter.

---

[23]Dimitris Melas, Raghu Suryanarayanan, and Stefano Cavaglia, "Efficient Replication of Factor Returns," *MSCI Barra Research Insight*, June 2009.

[24]An exception is the constraint on the number of assets that results in integer constraints.

[25]For a more detailed discussion on portfolio optimization problems and optimization software see, for example, Frank J. Fabozzi, Petter N. Kolm, Dessislava Pachamanova, and Sergio M. Focardi, *Robust Portfolio Optimization and Management* (Hoboken, NJ: John Wiley & Sons, 2007).

PERFORMANCE EVALUATION OF FACTORS

Analyzing the performance of different factors is an important part of the development of a factor-based trading strategy. A researcher may construct and analyze over a hundred different factors, so the means to evaluate and compare these factors is needed. Most often this process starts by trying to understand the time-series properties of each factor in isolation and then study how they interact with each other.

To give a basic idea of how this process may be performed, we use the five factors introduced earlier in this chapter: EBITDA/EV, revisions, share repurchase, momentum, and earnings growth. These are a subset of the factors that we use in the factor trading strategy model discussed later in the chapter. We choose a limited number of factors for ease of exposition. In particular, we emphasize those factors that possess more interesting empirical characteristics.

Panel A of Exhibit 7.5 presents summary statistics of monthly returns of long-short portfolios constructed from these factors. We observe that the average monthly return ranges from −0.05% for the earnings growth to 0.90% for the momentum factor. The t-statistics for the mean return are significant at the 95% level for the EBITDA/EV, share repurchase, and momentum factors. The monthly volatility ranges from 3.77% for the revisions factor to 7.13% for the momentum factor. In other words, the return and risk characteristics among factors vary significantly. We note that the greatest monthly drawdown has been large to very large for all of the factors, implying significant downside risk. Overall, the results suggest that there is a systematic premium associated with the EBITDA/EV, share repurchase, and momentum factors.

Let pctPos and pctNeg denote the fraction of positive and negative returns over time, respectively. These measures offer another way of interpreting the strength and consistency of the returns to a factor. For example, EBITDA/EV and momentum have t-statistics of 2.16 and 1.90, respectively, indicating that the former is stronger. However, pctPos (pctNeg) are 0.55 versus 0.61 (0.45 versus 0.39) showing that positive returns to momentum occur more frequently. This may provide reassurance of the usefulness of the momentum factor, despite the fact that its t-statistic is below the 95% level.

Panel B of Exhibit 7.5 presents unconditional correlation coefficients of monthly returns for long-short portfolios. The comovement of factor returns varies among the factors. The lowest correlation is −0.28 between EBITDA/EV and revisions. The highest correlation is 0.79 between momentum and revisions. In addition, we observe that the correlation between revisions and share repurchase, and between EBITDA/EV and earnings growth are close to zero. The broad range of correlations provides evidence that combining uncorrelated factors could produce a successful strategy.

EXHIBIT 7.5 Results from Portfolio Sorts

Panel A: Summary Statistics of Monthly Returns of Long-short Portfolios

	Mean	Stdev	Median	t-stat	Max	Min	pctPos	pctNeg
Revisions	0.29	3.77	0.77	1.17	10.43	−19.49	0.55	0.45
EBITDA/EV	0.83	5.80	0.72	2.16	31.61	−30.72	0.55	0.45
Share repurchase	0.72	3.89	0.43	2.78	22.01	−14.06	0.61	0.39
Momentum	0.90	7.13	0.97	1.90	25.43	−42.71	0.61	0.39
Earning growth	−0.05	4.34	0.25	−0.18	14.03	−23.10	0.53	0.47

Panel B: Correlations between Long-Short Portfolios

	Revisions	EBITDA/EV	Share Repurchase	Momentum	Earnings Growth
Revisions	1.00	−0.28	0.01	0.79	0.25
EBITDA/EV	−0.28	1.00	0.78	−0.12	0.01
Share repurchase	0.01	0.78	1.00	0.20	0.12
Momentum	0.79	−0.12	0.20	1.00	0.28
Earnings growth	0.25	0.01	0.12	0.28	1.00

289

Exhibit 7.6 presents the cumulative returns for the long-short portfolios. The returns of the long-short factor portfolios experience substantial volatility. We highlight the following patterns of cumulative returns for the different factors:

- The cumulative return of the revisions factor is positive in the early periods (12/1989 to 6/1998). While it is volatile, its cumulative return is higher in the next period (7/1998 to 7/2000). It deteriorates sharply in the following period (8/2000 to 6/2003), and levels out in the later periods (7/2003 to 12/2008).
- The performance of the EBITDA/EV factor is consistently positive in the early periods (12/1989 to 9/1998), deteriorates in the next period (10/1998 to 1/2000) and rebounds sharply (2/2000 to 7/2002), grows at slower but more historically consistent rate in the later periods (8/2002 to 4/2007), deteriorates in the next period (5/2007 to 9/2007), and returns to more historically consistent returns in last period (10/2007 to 12/2008).
- The cumulative return of the share repurchase factor grows at a slower pace in the early years (12/1989 to 5/1999), falls slightly in the middle periods (6/1999 to 1/2000), rebounds sharply (2/2000 to 7/2002), falls

EXHIBIT 7.6   Cumulative Returns of Long-Short Portfolios

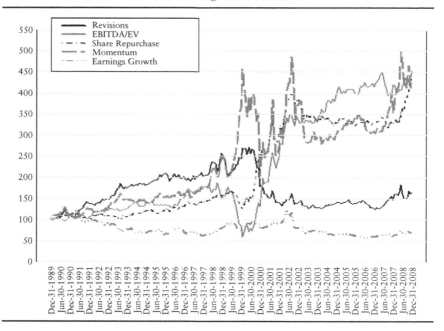

then flattens out in the next period (8/2002 to 4/2008), and increases at a large rate late in the graph (5/2008 to 12/2008).

■ The momentum factor experiences the largest volatility. This factor performs consistently well in the early period (12/1989 to 12/1998), experiences sharp volatility in the middle period (1/1999 to 5/2003), flattens out (6/2003 to 6/2007), and grows at an accelerating rate from (7/2007 to 12/2008).

The performance of the earnings growth factor is flat or negative throughout the entire period. The overall pattern of the cumulative returns among the factors clearly illustrate that factor returns and correlations are time varying.

In Panel A of Exhibit 7.7 we present summary statistics of the monthly information coefficients of the factors. The average monthly information coefficients range from 0.03 for EBITDA/EV and momentum, to 0.01 for the share repurchase factor. The t-statistics for the mean ICs are significant at the 95% level for all factors except earnings growth. With the exception of share repurchase and earnings growth, the fraction of positive returns of the factors are significantly greater than that of the negative returns.

The share repurchase factor requires some comments. The information coefficient is negative, in contrast to the positive return in the long-short portfolio sorts, because negative share repurchases are correlated with subsequent return. The information coefficient is lower than we would expect because there is not a strong linear relation between the return and the measures. As the results from the portfolio sorts indicate, the extreme values of this factor provide the highest returns.

Panel B of Exhibit 7.7 displays unconditional correlation coefficients of the monthly information coefficients. The comovement of the ICs factor returns varies among the factors. The lowest correlation is –0.66 between EBITDA/EV and share repurchases. But again this should be interpreted with caution because it is negative repurchases that we view as attractive. The highest correlation reported in the exhibit is 0.79 between momentum and revisions. Similar to the correlation of long-short factor portfolio returns, the diverse set of correlations provides evidence that combining uncorrelated factors may produce a successful strategy.

In Panel A of Exhibit 7.8 we present summary statistics of the time series average of the monthly coefficients from the Fama-MacBeth (FM) regressions of the factors. The information provided by the FM coefficients differs from the information provided by portfolio sorts. The FM coefficients show the linear relationship between the factor and subsequent returns, while the results from the portfolio sorts provide information on the extreme values of the factors and subsequent returns. The difference in

EXHIBIT 7.7 Summary of Monthly Factor Information Coefficients

Panel A: Basic Statistics for Monthly Information Coefficients

	Mean	Stdev	Median	t-stat	Max	Min	pctPos	pctNeg
Revisions	0.02	0.10	0.02	2.51	0.31	-0.29	0.58	0.42
EBITDA/EV	0.03	0.13	0.02	3.13	0.48	-0.41	0.59	0.41
Share repurchase	-0.01	0.10	-0.00	-2.13	0.20	-0.45	0.48	0.52
Momentum	0.03	0.18	0.05	2.86	0.50	-0.57	0.59	0.41
Earnings growth	-0.00	0.13	0.00	-0.56	0.26	-0.28	0.51	0.49

Panel B: Correlations for Monthly Average Information Coefficients

	Revisions	EBITDA/EV	Share Repurchase	Momentum	Earnings Growth
Revisions	1.00	-0.31	0.13	0.79	-0.14
EBITDA/EV	-0.31	1.00	-0.66	-0.26	-0.49
Share repurchase	0.13	-0.66	1.00	0.02	0.58
Momentum	0.79	-0.26	0.02	1.00	-0.05
Earnings growth	-0.14	-0.49	0.58	-0.05	1.00

EXHIBIT 7.8 Summary of Monthly Fama-MacBeth Regression Coefficients

Panel A: Basic Statistics for Fama-MacBeth Regression Coefficients

	Mean	Stdev	Median	t-stat	Max	Min	pctPos	pctNeg
Revisions	0.09	1.11	0.22	1.22	3.36	-5.26	0.59	0.41
EBITDA/EV	0.27	1.61	0.14	2.50	8.69	-7.81	0.59	0.41
Share repurchase	-0.18	0.96	-0.06	-2.90	3.21	-5.91	0.44	0.56
Momentum	0.31	2.42	0.29	1.94	9.97	-12.37	0.60	0.40
Earnings growth	-0.08	0.99	-0.04	-1.20	2.83	-4.13	0.48	0.52

Panel B: Correlations for Fama-MacBeth Regression Coefficients

	Revisions	EBITDA/EV	Share Repurchase	Momentum	Earnings Growth
Revisions	1.00	-0.27	0.05	0.77	-0.26
EBITDA/EV	-0.27	1.00	-0.75	-0.18	-0.58
Share repurchase	0.05	-0.75	1.00	-0.04	0.64
Momentum	0.77	-0.18	-0.04	1.00	-0.18
Earnings growth	-0.26	-0.58	0.64	-0.18	1.00

293

the size of the mean returns between the FM coefficients and portfolio sorts exits partially because the intercept terms from the FM regressions are not reported in the exhibit.

The average monthly FM coefficent ranges from −0.18 for share repurchase to 0.31 for the momentum factor. Again the share repurchase results should be interpreted with caution because it is negative repurchases that we view as attractive. The t-statistics for the mean ICs are significant at the 95% level for the EBITDA/EV and share repurchase factors.

Also, we compare the results of portfolio sorts in Panel A of Exhibit 7.7 with the FM coefficients in Panel A of Exhibit 7.8. The rank ordering of the magnitude of factor returns is similar between the two panels. The t-statistics are slightly higher in the FM regressions than the portfolio sorts. The correlation coefficients for the portfolio sorts in Panel B of Exhibit 7.7 are consistent with the FM coefficients in Panel B of Exhibit 7.8 for all the factors except for shares repurchases. The results for share repurchases needs to be interpreted with caution because it is negative repurchases that we view as attractive. The portfolio sorts take that into account while FM regressions do not.

To better understand the time variation of the performance of these factors, we calculate rolling 24-month mean returns and correlations of the factors. The results are presented in Exhibit 7.9. We see that the returns and correlations to all factors are time varying. A few of the time series

EXHIBIT 7.9   Rolling 24-Month Mean Returns for the Factors

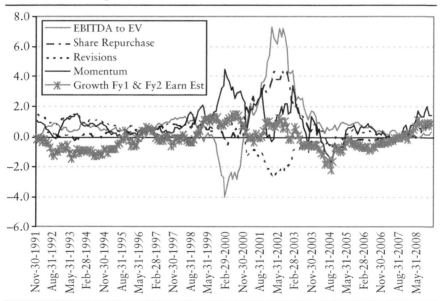

EXHIBIT 7.10 Rolling 24-Month Correlations of Monthly Returns for the Factors

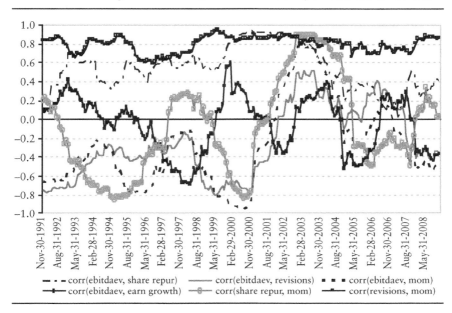

experience large volatility in the rolling 24-month returns. The EBITDA/EV factor shows the largest variation followed by the momentum and share repurchase factors. All factors experience periods where the rolling average returns are both positive and negative.

Exhibit 7.10 presents the rolling correlation between pairs of the factors. There is substantial variability in many of the pairs. In most cases the correlation moves in a wave-like pattern. This pattern highlights the time-varying property of the correlations among the factors. This property will be important to incorporate in a factor trading model. The most consistent correlation is between momentum and revisions factors and this correlation is, in general, fairly high.

MODEL CONSTRUCTION METHODOLOGIES FOR A FACTOR-BASED TRADING STRATEGY

In the previous section we analyzed the performance of each factor. The next step in building our trading strategy is to determine how to combine the factors into one model. The key aspect of building this model is to (1) determine what factors to use out of the universe of factors that we have, and (2) how to weight them.

We describe four methodologies to combine and weight factors to build a model for a trading strategy. These methodologies are used to translate the empirical work on factors into a working model. Most of the methodologies are flexible in their specification and there is some overlap between them. Though the list is not exhaustive, we highlight those processes frequently used by quantitative portfolio managers and researchers today. The four methodologies are the data driven, the factor model, the heuristic, and the optimization approaches.

It is important to be careful how each methodology is implemented. In particular, it is critical to balance the iterative process of finding a robust model with good forecasting ability versus finding a model that is a result of data mining.

The Data Driven Approach

A *data driven approach* uses statistical methods to select and weight factors in a forecasting model. This approach uses returns as the independent variables and factors as the dependent variables. There are a variety of estimation procedures, such as neural nets, classification trees, and principal components, that can be used to estimate these models. Usually a statistic is established to determine the criteria for a successful model. The algorithm of the statistical method evaluates the data and compares the results against the criteria.

Many data driven approaches have no structural assumptions on potential relationships the statistical method finds. Therefore, it is sometimes difficult to understand or even explain the relationship among the dependent variables used in the model.

Deistler and Hamann[26] provide an example of a data driven approach to model development. The model they develop is used for forecasting the returns to financial stocks. To start, they split their data sample into two parts—an in-sample part for building the model, and out-of-sample part to validate the model. They use three different types of factor models for forecasting stocks returns: quasi-static principal components, quasi-static factor models with idiosyncratic noise, and reduced rank regression. For model selection Deistler and Hamann use an iterative approach where they find the optimal mix of factors based on the Akaike's information criterion and the Bayesian information criterion (see Chapter 3). A large number of different models are compared using the out-of-sample data. They find that the reduced rank model provides the best performance. This model pro-

[26]Manfred Deistler and Eva Hamann, "Identification of Factor Models for Forecasting Returns," *Journal of Financial Econometrics*, 2 (2005), pp. 256–281.

duced the highest out-of-sample R^2s, hit rates,[27] and Diebold Mariano test statistic[28] among the different models evaluated.

The Factor Model Approach

We introduced factor models in Chapter 5. In this section we will briefly address the use of factor models for forecasting. The goal of the factor model is to develop a parsimonious model that forecast returns accurately. One approach is for the researcher to predetermine the variables to be used in the factor model based on economic intuition. The model is estimated and then the estimated coefficients are used to produce the forecasts.

A second approach is to use statistical tools for model selection. In this approach we construct several models—often by varying the factors and the number of factors used—and have them compete against each other, just like in a horse race. We then choose the best performing model.

Factor model performance can be evaluated in three ways. We can evaluate the fit, forecast ability, and economic significance of the model. The measure to evaluate the fit of a model is based on statistical measures including the model's R^2 and adjusted R^2, and F- and t-statistics of the model coefficients.

There are several methods to evaluate how well a model will forecast. West[29] discusses the theory and conventions of several measures of relative model quality. These methods use the resulting time series of predictions and prediction errors from a model. In the case where we want to compare models, West suggests ratios or differences of mean; mean-square or mean-absolute prediction errors; correlation between one model's prediction and another model's realization (also know as forecast encompassing); or comparison of utility or profit-based measures of predictive ability. In other cases where we want to assess a single model, he suggests measuring the correlation between prediction and realization, the serial correlation in one step

---

[27]The hit rate is calculated as

$$h = \frac{1}{T_2 - T_1} \sum_{t=T_1+1}^{T_2} sign(y_t^i \hat{y}_{t|t-1}^i)$$

where y_t^i is one-step ahead realized value and $\hat{y}_{t|t-1}^i$ is the one-step ahead predicted value.

[28]For calculation of this measure, see Francis X. Diebold and Roberto S. Mariano, "Comparing Predictive Accuracy," *Journal of Business and Economic Statistics*, 13 (2005), pp. 253–263.

[29]Kenneth D. West, "Forecast Evaluation," in Graham Elliot, Clive W. J. Granger, and Allan G. Timmermann (eds.), *Handbook of Economic Forecasting, Volume 1* (Amsterdam: Elsevier, 2006).

ahead prediction errors, the ability to predict direction of change, and the model prediction bias.

We can evaluate economic significance by using the model to predict values and using the predicted values to build portfolios. The profitability of the portfolios is evaluated by examining statistics such as mean returns, information ratios, dollar profits, and drawdown.

The Heuristic Approach

The heuristic approach is another technique used to build trading models. Heuristics are based on common sense, intuition, and market insight and are not formal statistical or mathematical techniques designed to meet a given set of requirements. Heuristic-based models result from the judgment of the researcher. The researcher decides the factors to use, creates rules in order to evaluate the factors, and chooses how to combine the factors and implement the model.

Piotroski[30] applies a heuristic approach in developing an investment strategy for high value stocks (high book-to-market firms). He selects nine fundamental factors[31] to measure three areas of the firm's financial condition: profitability, financial leverage and liquidity, and operating efficiency. Depending on the factor's implication for future prices and profitability, each factor is classified as either "good" or "bad." An indicator variable for the factor is equal to one (zero) if the factor's realization is good (bad). The sum of the nine binary factors the F_SCORE. This aggregate score measures the overall quality, or strength, of the firm's financial position. According to the historical results provided by Piotroski, this trading strategy is very profitable. Specifically, a trading strategy that buys expected winners and shorts expected losers would have generated a 23% annual return between 1976 and 1996.

There are different approaches to evaluate a heuristic approach. Statistical analysis can be used to estimate the probability of incorrect outcomes. Another approach is to evaluate economic significance. For example, Piotroski determines economic significance by forming portfolios based on the firm's aggregate score (F_SCORE) and then evaluates the size of the subsequent portfolio returns.

---

[30]Joseph D. Piotroski, "Value Investing: The Use of Historical Financial Statement Information to Separate Winners from Losers," *Journal of Accounting Research*, 38, Supplement (2000), pp. 1–41.

[31]The nine factors are return on assets, change in return on assets, cash flow from operations scaled by total assets, cash compared to net income scaled by total assets, change in long-term debt/assets, change in current ratio, change in shares outstanding, change in gross margin, and change in asset turnover.

There is no theory that can provide guidance when making modeling choices in the heuristic approach. Consequently, the researcher has to be careful not to fall into the data mining trap.

The Optimization Approach

In this approach, we use optimization to select and weight factors in a forecasting model. An optimization approach allows us flexibility in calibrating the model and simultaneously optimize an objective function specifying a desirable investment criteria.

There is substantial overlap between optimization use in forecast modeling and portfolio construction. We cover portfolio optimization techniques in Chapters 8 through 10. There is frequently an advantage in working with the factors directly, as opposed to all individual stocks. The factors provide a lower dimensional representation of the complete universe of the stocks considered. Besides the dimensionality reduction, which reduces computational time, the resulting optimization problem is typically more robust to changes in the inputs.

Sorensen, Hua, Qian, and Schoen[32] present a process that uses an optimization framework to combine a diverse set of factors (alpha sources) into a multifactor model. Their procedure assigns optimal weights across the factors to achieve the highest information ratio. They show that the optimal weights are a function of average ICs and IC covariances. Specifically,

$$\mathbf{w} \propto \mathrm{Cov(IC)}^{-1} \times \overline{\mathbf{IC}}$$

where $\mathbf{w}$ is the vector of factor weights, $\overline{\mathbf{IC}}$ is the vector of the average of the risk-adjusted ICs, and $\mathrm{Cov(IC)}^{-1}$ is the inverse of the covariance matrix of the ICs.

In a subsequent paper, Sorensen, Hua, and Qian[33] apply this optimization technique to capture the idiosyncratic return behavior of different security contexts. The contexts are determined as a function of stock risk characteristics (value, growth, or earnings variability). They build a multifactor model using the historical risk-adjusted IC of the factors, determining the weights of the multifactor model by maximizing the IR of the combined factors. Their research demonstrates that the weights to factors of

---

[32]Eric H. Sorensen, Ronald Hua, Edward Qian, and Robert Schoen, "Multiple Alpha Sources and Active Management," *Journal of Portfolio Management*, 40 (2004), pp. 39–45.
[33]Eric H. Sorensen, Ronald Hua, and Edward Qian, "Contextual Fundamentals, Models, and Active Management," *Journal of Portfolio Management*, 32 (2005), pp. 23–36.

an alpha model (trading strategy) differ depending on the security contexts (risk dimensions). The approach improves the ex post information ratio compared to a model that uses a one-size-fits-all approach.

Importance of Model Construction and Factor Choice

Empirical research shows that the factors and the weighting scheme of the factors are important in determining the efficacy of a trading strategy model. Using data from the stock selection models of 21 major quantitative funds, the quantitative research group at Sanford Bernstein analyzed the degree of overlap in rankings and factors.[34] They found that the models maintained similar exposures to many of the same factors. Most models showed high exposure to cash flow based valuations (e.g., EV/EBITDA) and price momentum, and less exposure to capital use, revisions, and normalized valuation factors. Although they found commonality in factor exposures, the stock rankings and performance of the models were substantially different. This surprising finding indicates that model construction differs among the various stock selection models and provides evidence that the efficacy of common signals has not been completely arbitraged away.

A second study by the same group showed commonality across models among cash flow and price momentum factors, while stock rankings and realized performance were vastly different.[35] They hypothesize that the difference between good and poor performing models may be related to a few unique factors identified by portfolio managers, better methodologies for model construction (e.g., static, dynamic, or contextual models), or good old-fashioned luck.

Example: A Factor-Based Trading Strategy

In building this model, we hope to accomplish the following objectives: identify stocks that will outperform and underperform in the future, maintain good diversification with regard to alpha sources, and be robust to

---

[34]Vadim Zlotnikov, Ann Marie Larson, Wally Cheung, Serdar Kalaycioglu, Ronna D. Lao, and Zachary A. Apoian, "Quantitative Research—January 2007: Survey of Quantitative Models—Vastly Different Rankings and Performance, Despite Similarity in Factor Exposures," Bernstein Research, January 16, 2007.
[35]Vadim Zlotnikov, Ann Marie Larson, Serdar Kalaycioglu, Ronna D. Lao, and Zachary A. Apoian, "Quantitative Research: Survey of Quantitative Models—Continued Emphasis on EV/EBIT, Momentum, Increased Focus on Capital Use; Some Evidence on Non-linear Factor Implementation; Low Return Consistency," Bernstein Research, November 21, 2007.

changing market conditions such as time varying returns, volatilities, and correlations.

We have identified 10 factors that have an ability to forecast stock returns.[36] Of the four model construction methodologies discussed previously, we use the optimization framework to build the model as it offers the greatest flexibility.

We determine the allocation to specific factors by solving the following optimization problem

$$\min_{\mathbf{w}} \mathbf{w}'\Sigma\mathbf{w}, \quad \mathbf{w} \geq 0$$

$$\sum_{v \in \text{Value}} w_v \geq 0.35$$

$$\sum_{g \in \text{Growth}} w_g \geq 0.20$$

$$3 \leq \sum_{i=1}^{10} \delta_i \leq 7$$

with the budget constraint

$$\mathbf{w}'\mathbf{e} = 1, \quad \mathbf{e} = (1, ..., 1)'$$

where Σ is the covariance matrix of factor returns, Value and Growth are the sets of value and growth factors, and δ_i is equal to one if $w_i > 0$ or zero otherwise.[37]

We constrain the minimum exposure to values factors to be greater than or equal to 35% of the weight in the model based on the belief that there is a systematic long-term premium to value.

Using the returns of our factors, we perform this optimization monthly to determine which factors to hold and in what proportions. Exhibit 7.11 displays how the factor weights change over time.

In the next step, we use the factor weights to determine the attractiveness of the stocks in our universe. We score each stock in the universe by multiplying the standardized values of the factors by the weights provided by the optimization of our factors. Stocks with high scores are deemed attractive and stocks with low scores are deemed unattractive.

To evaluate how the model performs, we sort the scores of stocks into five equally weighted portfolios and evaluate the returns of these portfolios. Panel A of Exhibit 7.12 provides summary statistics of the returns for each portfolio. Note that there is a monotonic increasing relationship among the

---

[36]We use a combination of growth, value, quality, and momentum factors. Appendix A contains definitions of all of them.

[37]See Chapter 8 for a discussion of integer constraints.

EXHIBIT 7.11 The Factor Weights of the Trading Strategy

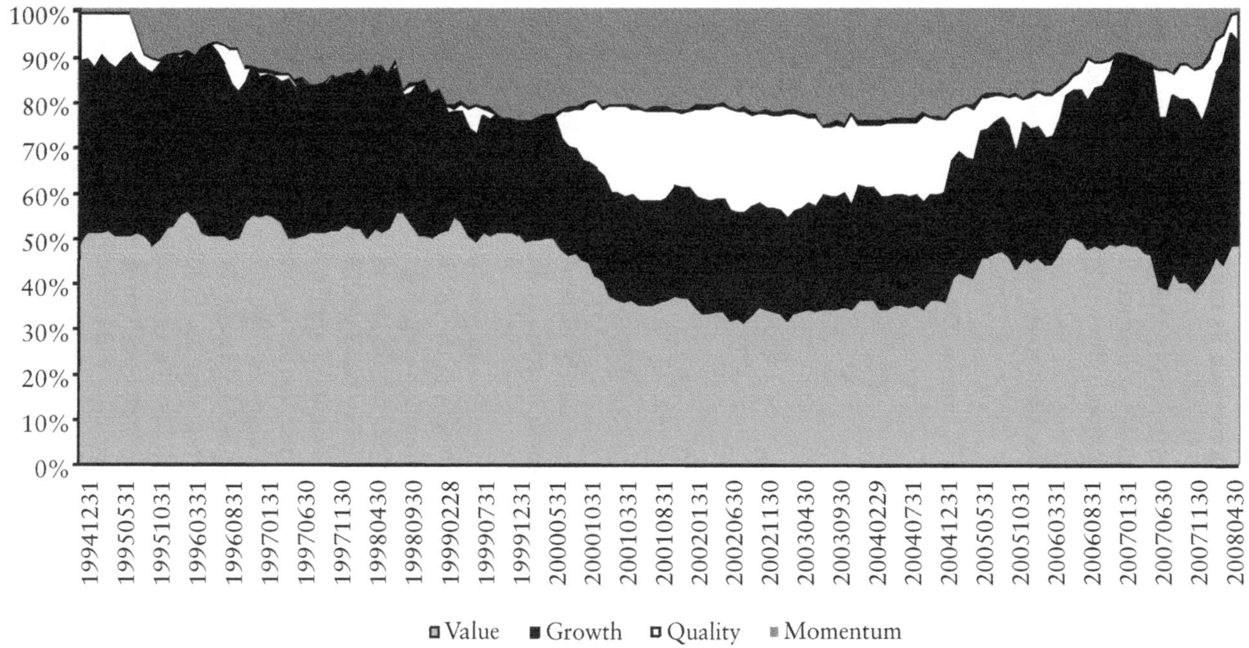

■ Value ■ Growth □ Quality ■ Momentum

EXHIBIT 7.12 Summary of Model Results
Panel A: Summary Statistics of the Model Returns

	q1	q2	q3	q4	q5	LS
Mean	1.06	0.98	0.83	0.65	0.12	0.94
Stdev	5.64	5.18	4.98	5.31	5.88	2.82
Median	1.61	1.61	1.58	1.55	1.11	0.71
Max	15.79	11.18	10.92	13.26	13.01	12.84
Min	−23.59	−23.32	−19.45	−21.25	−24.51	−6.87
Num	169	169	169	169	169	169
t-statistic	2.44	2.45	2.17	1.59	0.27	4.33
IR	0.19	0.19	0.17	0.12	0.02	0.33

Panel B: Summary Statistics of Turnover for Portfolio 1 (q1) and Portfolio 5 (q5)

	q1	q5
Mean	0.20	0.17
Stdev	0.07	0.06
Median	0.19	0.16
Max	0.53	0.39
Min	0.07	0.05
Num	169	169
t-statistic	36.74	39.17

portfolios with portfolio 1 (q1) earning the highest return and portfolio 5 (q5) earning the lowest return. Over the entire period, the long-short portfolio (LS) that is long portfolio 1 and short portfolio 5 averages about 1% per month with a monthly Sharpe ratio of 0.33. Its return is statistically significant at the 97.5% level.

Panel B of Exhibit 7.12 shows the monthly average stock turnover of portfolio 1 (q1) and portfolio 5 (q5). Understanding how turnover varies from month to month for a trading strategy is important. If turnover is too high then it might be prohibitive to implement because of execution costs. While beyond the scope of this book, we could explicitly incorporate transaction costs in this trading strategy using a market impact model such as one of the models described in Chapter 11.[38] Due to the dynamic nature

---

[38]See Joseph A. Cerniglia and Petter N. Kolm, "Factor-Based Trading Strategies and Market Impact Costs," Working Paper, Courant Institute of Mathematical Sciences, New York University, 2010.

of our trading strategy—where active factors may change from month to month—our turnover of 20% is a bit higher than what would be expected using a static approach.

We evaluate the monthly information coefficient between the model scores and subsequent return. This analysis provides information on how well the model forecasts return. The monthly mean information coefficient of the model score is 0.03 and is statistically significant at the 99% level. The monthly standard deviation is 0.08. We note that both the information coefficients and returns were stronger and more consistent in the earlier periods.

Exhibit 7.13 displays the cumulative return to portfolio 1 through portfolio 5. Throughout the entire period there is a monotonic relationship between the portfolios. To evaluate the overall performance of the model, we analyze the performance of the long-short portfolio returns. We observe that the model performs well in December 1994 to May 2007 and April 2008 to June 2008. This is due to the fact that our model correctly picked the factors that performed well in those periods. We note that the model performs poorly in July 2007–April 2008, losing an average of 1.09% a month. The model appears to suffer from the same problems many quantitative equity funds and hedge funds faced during this period.[39] The worst performance in a single month was –6.87, occurring in January 2001, and the maximum drawdown of the model was –13.7%, occurring during the period from May 2006 (peak) to June 2008 (trough).[40]

To more completely understand the return and risk characteristic of the strategy, we would have to perform a more detailed analysis, including risk and performance attribution, and model sensitivity analysis over the full period as well as over subperiods. As the turnover is on the higher side, we may also want to introduce turnover constraints or use a market impact model as described in Chapter 11.

Periods of poor performance of a strategy should be disconcerting to any analyst. The poor performance of the model during the period June 2007–March 2008 indicates that many of the factors we use were not working. We need to go back to each individual factor and analyze them in isolation over this time frame. In addition, this highlights the importance of

---

[39]Matthew S. Rothman, "Turbulent Times in Quant Land," Lehman Brothers Equity Research, August 9, 2007; and Kent Daniel, "The Liquidity Crunch in Quant Equities Analysis and Implications," Goldman Sachs Asset Management, December 13, 2007 presentation from The Second New York Fed-Princeton Liquidity Conference.

[40]We ran additional analysis on the model by extending the holding period of the model from 1 to 3 months. The results were much stronger as returns increased to 1.6% per month for a two-month holding period and 1.9% per month for a three-month holding period. The risk as measured by drawdown was higher at –17.4% for a two-month holding period and –29.5% for the three-month holding period.

EXHIBIT 7.13 Cumulative Return of the Model

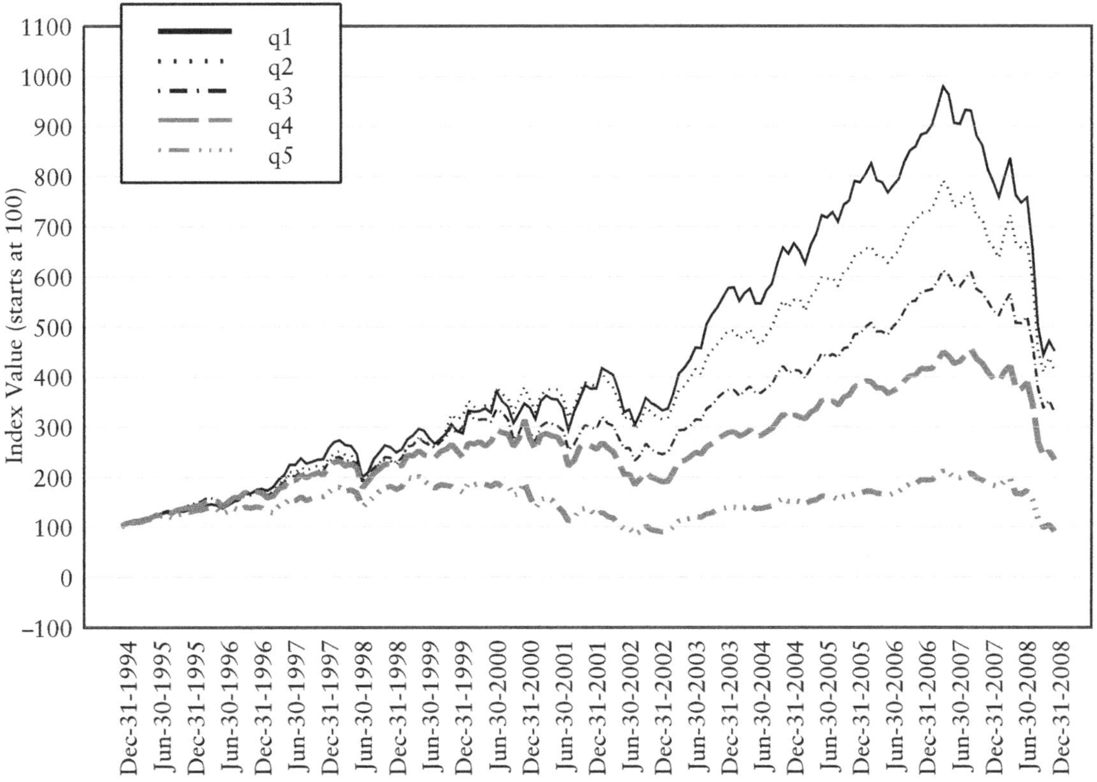

research to improve existing factors and develop new ones using novel data assets and different approaches.

BACKTESTING

In the research phase of the trading strategy, model scores are converted into portfolios and then examined to assess how these portfolios perform over time. This process is referred to as *backtesting a strategy*. The backtest should mirror as closely as possible the actual investing environment incorporating both the investment's objectives and the trading environment.

When it comes to mimicking the trading environment in backtests, special attention needs to be given to transaction costs and liquidity considerations. The inclusion of transaction costs is important because they may have a major impact on the total return. Realistic market impact and trading costs estimates affect what securities are chosen during portfolio construction. Liquidity is another attribute that needs to be evaluated. The investable universe of stocks should be limited to stocks where there is enough liquidity to be able to get in and out of positions.

Portfolio managers may use a number of constraints during portfolio construction. Frequently these constraints are derived from the portfolio policy of the firm, risk management policy, or investor objectives. Common constraints include upper and lower bounds for each stock, industry, or risk factor—as well as holding size limits, trading size limits, turnover, and the number of assets long or short.[41]

To ensure the portfolio construction process is robust we use sensitivity analysis to evaluate our results. In sensitivity analysis we vary the different input parameters and study their impact on the output parameters. If small changes in inputs give rise to large changes in outputs, our process may not be robust enough. For example, we may eliminate the five best and worst performing stocks from the model, rerun the optimization, and evaluate the performance. The results should be similar as the success of a trading strategy should not depend on a handful of stocks.

We may want to determine the effect of small changes in one or more parameters used in the optimization. The performance of the optimal portfolio should in general not differ significantly after we have made these small changes.

Another useful test is to evaluate a model by varying the investment objective. For example, we may evaluate a model by building a low tracking error portfolio, a high tracking error portfolio, and a market neutral port-

---

[41]See Chapter 8 for a discussion of the most common portfolio constraints in practice.

folio. If the returns from each of these portfolios are decent, the underlying trading strategy is more likely to be robust.

Understanding In-Sample and Out-of-Sample Methodologies

There are two basic backtesting methodologies: in-sample and out-of-sample. It is important is to understand the nuances of each.

We refer to a backtesting methodology as an in-sample methodology when the researcher uses the same data sample to specify, calibrate, and evaluate a model.

An out-of-sample methodology is a backtesting methodology where the researcher uses a subset of the sample to specify and calibrate a model, and then evaluates the forecasting ability of the model on a different subset of data. There are two approaches for implementing an out-of-sample methodology. One approach is the *split-sample method*. This method splits the data into two subsets of data where one subset is used to build the model while the remaining subset is used to evaluate the model.

A second method is the *recursive out-of-sample test*. This approach uses a sequence of recursive or rolling *windows* of past history to forecast a future value and then evaluates that value against the realized value. For example, in a rolling regression based model we will use data up to time t to calculate the coefficients in the regression model. The regression model forecasts the $t + h$ dependent values, where $h > 0$. The prediction error is the difference between the realized value at $t + h$ and the predicted value from the regression model. At $t + 1$ we recalculate the regression model and evaluate the predicted value of $t + 1 + h$ against realized value. We continue this process throughout the sample.

The conventional thinking among econometricians is that in-sample tests tend to reject the null hypotheses of no predictability more often than out-of-sample tests. This view is supported by many researchers because they reason that in-sample tests are unreliable, often finding spurious predictability. Two reasons given to support this view is the presence of unmodeled structural changes in the data and the use of techniques that result in data mining and model overfitting.

Inoune and Kilian[42] question this conventional thinking. They use asymptotic theory to evaluate the "trade-offs between in-sample tests and out-of-sample tests of predictability in terms of their size and power." They argue strong in-sample results and weak out-of-sample results are not necessarily evidence that in-sample tests are not reliable. Out-of-sample tests

---

[42]Atsushi Inoune and Lutz Kilian, "In-Sample or Out-of-Sample Tests of Predictability: Which One Should We Use?" Working Paper, North Carolina State University and University of Michigan, 2002.

using sample-splitting result in a loss of information and lower power for small samples. As a result, an out-of-sample test may fail to detect predictability while the in-sample test will correctly identify predictability. They also show that out-of-sample tests are not more robust to parameter instability that results from unmodeled structural changes.

A Comment on the Interaction between Factor-Based Strategies and Risk Models

Frequently, different factor models are used to calculate the risk inputs and the expected return forecasts in a portfolio optimization. A common concern is the interaction between factors in the models for risk and expected returns. Lee and Stefek[43] evaluate the consequences of using different factor models, and conclude that (1) using different models for risk and alpha can lead to unintended portfolio exposures that may worsen performance, (2) aligning risk factors with alpha factors may improve information ratios, and (3) modifying the risk model by including some of the alpha factors may mitigate the problem.

BACKTESTING OUR FACTOR TRADING STRATEGY

Using the model scores from the trading strategy example, we build two optimized portfolios and evaluate their performance. Unlike the five equally weighted portfolios built only from model scores, the models we now discuss were built to mirror as close as possible tradable portfolios a portfolio manager would build in real time. Our investable universe is the Russell 1000. We assign alphas for all stock in the Russell 1000 with our dynamic factor model. The portfolios are long only and benchmarked to the S&P 500. The difference between the portfolios is in their benchmark tracking error. For the low-tracking error portfolio the risk aversion in the optimizer is set to a high value, sectors are constrained to plus/minus 10% of the sector weightings in the benchmark, and portfolio beta is constrained to 1.00. For the high-tracking error portfolio, the risk aversion is set to a low value, the sectors are constrained to plus/minus 25% of the sector weightings in the benchmark, and portfolio beta is constrained to 1.00. Rebalancing is performed once a month. Monthly turnover is limited to 10% of the portfolio value for the low-tracking error portfolio and 15% of the portfolio value for the high-tracking error portfolio.

---

[43]Jyh-Huei Lee and Dan Stefek, "Do Risk Factors Eat Alphas?" *Journal of Portfolio Management*, 34 (2008), pp. 12-24.

Exhibit 7.14 presents the results of our backtest. The performance numbers are gross of fees and transaction costs. Performance over the entire period is good and consistent throughout. The portfolios outperform the benchmark over the various time periods. The resulting annualized Sharpe ratios over the full period are 0.66 for the low-tracking error portfolio, 0.72 for the high-tracking error portfolio, and 0.45 for the S&P 500.[44]

SUMMARY

- The four most commonly used approaches for the evaluation of return premiums and risk characteristics to factors are portfolio sorts, factor models, factor portfolios, and information coefficients.
- The portfolio sorts approach ranks stocks by a particular factor into a number of portfolios. The sorting methodology should be consistent with the characteristics of the distribution of the factor and the economic motivation underlying its premium.
- The information ratio (IR) is a statistic for summarizing the risk-adjusted performance of an investment strategy and is defined as the ratio of average excess return to the standard deviation of return.
- We distinguish between contemporaneous and forecasting factor models, dependent on whether both left- and right-hand side variables (returns and factors) have the same time subscript, or the time subscript of the left-hand side variable is greater.
- The three most common violations of classical regression theory that occur in cross-sectional factor models are (1) the errors in variables problem, (2) common variation in residuals such as heteroskedasticity and serial correlation, and (3) multicollinearity. There are statistical techniques that address the first two. The third issue is best dealt with by removing collinear variables from the regression, or by increasing the sample size.
- The Fama-MacBeth regression addresses the inference problem caused by the correlation of the residuals in cross-sectional regressions.
- The information coefficient (IC) is used to evaluate the return forecast ability of a factor. It measures the cross-sectional correlation between a factor and its subsequent realized return.
- Factor portfolios are used to measure the information content of a factor. The objective is to mimic the return behavior of a factor and minimize the residual risk. We can build factor portfolios using a factor

---

[44]Here we calculate the Sharpe ratio as portfolio excess return (over the risk-free rate) divided by the standard deviation of the portfolio excess return.

EXHIBIT 7.14 Total Return Report (Annualized)

From 01/1995 to 06/2008	QTD	YTD	1 Year	2 Year	3 Year	5 Year	10 Year	Since Inception
Portfolio: Low-Tracking Error	−0.86	−10.46	−11.86	4.64	7.73	11.47	6.22	13.30
Portfolio: High-Tracking Error	−1.43	−10.47	−11.78	4.15	8.29	13.24	7.16	14.35
S&P 500: Total Return	−2.73	−11.91	−13.12	2.36	4.41	7.58	2.88	9.79

model or an optimization. An optimization is more flexible as it is able to incorporate constraints.

- Analyzing the performance of different factors is an important part of the development of a factor-based trading strategy. This process begins with understanding the time-series properties of each factor in isolation and then studying how they interact with each other.

- Techniques used to combine and weight factors to build a trading strategy model include the data driven, the factor model, the heuristic, and the optimization approaches.

- An out-of-sample methodology is a backtesting methodology where the researcher uses a subset of the sample to specify a model and then evaluates the forecasting ability of the model on a different subset of data. There are two approaches for implementing an out-of-sample methodology: the split-sample approach and the recursive out-of-sample test.

- Caution should be exercised if different factor models are used to calculate the risk inputs and the expected return forecasts in a portfolio optimization.

CHAPTER 8

Portfolio Optimization: Basic Theory and Practice

Portfolio optimization today is considered an important workhorse in portfolio management. The seminal paper "Portfolio Selection" by Harry Markowitz, published in 1952 in the *Journal of Finance*, introduced the foundations of what is now popularly referred to as *mean-variance analysis*, *mean-variance optimization*, and *Modern Portfolio Theory* (MPT). Initially, mean-variance analysis generated relatively little interest outside of academia, but with time the financial community adopted the thesis. Today, financial models based on those very same principles are constantly being reinvented to incorporate new findings. In 1990, Harry Markowitz, Merton Miller, and William Sharpe were awarded the Nobel prize for their pioneering work in the theory of financial economics.[1]

In its simplest form, mean-variance analysis provides a framework to construct and select portfolios, based on the expected performance of the investments and the risk appetite of the investor. Mean-variance analysis also introduced a new terminology, which now has become the norm in the area of investment management.

Conventional wisdom has always dictated "not putting all your eggs into one basket." In more technical terms, this old adage is addressing the benefits of diversification. Markowitz quantified the concept of diversification through the statistical notion of covariance between individual securities, and the overall standard deviation of a portfolio. In essence, the old adage is saying that investing all your money in assets that may all perform poorly at the same time—that is, whose returns are highly correlated—is not a very prudent investment strategy no matter how small the chance that any one asset will perform poorly. This is because if any one single asset

---

[1]Markowitz was awarded the prize for having developed the theory of portfolio choice, Sharpe for his contributions to the theory of price formation for financial assets and the development of the Capital Asset Pricing Model, and Miller for his work in the theory of corporate finance.

performs poorly, it is likely, due to its high correlation with the other assets, that these other assets are also going to perform poorly, leading to the poor performance of the portfolio.

In this chapter, we begin with an intuitive overview of mean-variance analysis before we introduce the classical mean-variance framework. In the presence of only risky assets, the mean-variance efficient frontier has a parabolic shape. However, with the inclusion of a risk-free asset, the efficient frontier becomes linear, forming the so-called Capital Market Line. In practice when mean-variance optimization is used, portfolio managers typically add different constraints to the problem describing institutional features and investment policy decisions. We discuss the most common constraints used in practice today.

Then we discuss the estimation of the inputs required for mean-variance optimization, the expected asset returns and their covariances, using classical and practically well-probed techniques.[2]

We close the chapter with a coverage of alternative portfolio risk measures such as dispersion and downside measures, and develop a model for mean-CVaR optimization.

MEAN-VARIANCE ANALYSIS: OVERVIEW

Markowitz's starting point is that of a rational investor who, at time t, decides what portfolio of investments to hold for a time horizon of Δt. The investor makes decisions on the gains and losses he will make at time $t + \Delta t$, without considering eventual gains and losses either during or after the period Δt. At time $t + \Delta t$, the investor will reconsider the situation and decide anew. This one-period framework is often referred to as *myopic* (or *short-sighted*) behavior. In general, a myopic investor's behavior is suboptimal in comparison to an investor who makes investment decisions based upon multiple periods ahead. For example, nonmyopic investment strategies are adopted when it is necessary to make trade-offs at multiple future dates between consumption and investment or when significant trading costs related to specific subsets of investments are incurred throughout the holding period.

Markowitz reasoned that investors should decide on the basis of a trade-off between risk and expected return. Expected return of a security is defined as the expected price change plus any additional income over the time horizon considered, such as dividend payments, divided by the beginning price of the security. He suggested that risk should be measured by the variance of returns—the average squared deviation around the expected return.

---

[2]We discuss Bayesian techniques such as the Black-Litterman model in Chapter 9.

We note that it is a common misunderstanding that Markowitz's mean-variance framework relies on joint normality of security returns. Markowitz's mean-variance framework does not assume joint normality of security returns. However, the mean-variance approach is consistent with two different starting points: (1) expected utility maximization under certain assumptions; or (2) the assumption that security returns are jointly normally distributed.

Moreover, Markowitz argued that for any given level of expected return, a rational investor would choose the portfolio with minimum variance from amongst the set of all possible portfolios. The set of all possible portfolios that can be constructed is called the *feasible set*. *Minimum variance portfolios* are called *mean-variance efficient portfolios*. The set of all mean-variance efficient portfolios, for different desired levels of expected return, is called the *efficient frontier*. Exhibit 8.1 provides a graphical illustration of the efficient frontier of risky assets. In particular, notice that the feasible set is bounded by the curve I-II-III. All portfolios on the curve II-III are efficient portfolios for different levels of risk. These portfolios offer the

EXHIBIT 8.1   Feasible and Markowitz Efficient Portfolios

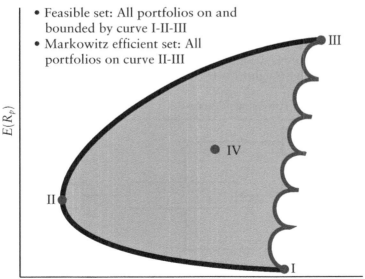

The picture is for illustrative purposes only. The actual shape of the feasible region depends on the returns and risks of the assets chosen and the correlation among them.

lowest level of standard deviation for a given level of expected return. Or equivalently, they constitute the portfolios that maximize expected return for a given level of risk. Therefore, the efficient frontier provides the best possible trade-off between expected return and risk—portfolios below it, such as portfolio IV, are inefficient and portfolios above it are unobtainable. The portfolio at point II is often referred to as the *global minimum variance portfolio* (GMV), as it is the portfolio on the efficient frontier with the smallest variance.

Exhibit 8.2 shows a schematic view of the investment process as seen from the perspective of modern portfolio theory. This process is often also referred to as *mean-variance optimization* or *theory of portfolio selection*. The inputs to the process are estimates of the expected returns, volatilities and correlations of all the assets together with various portfolio constraints. For example, constraints can be as straightforward as not allowing the short-selling of assets, or as complicated as limiting assets to be traded only in round lots. Later in this chapter, we will discuss the most commonly used portfolio constraints in practice. An optimization software package is then used to solve a series of optimization problems in order to generate the efficient frontier. Depending upon the complexity of the portfolio, the optimizations can be solved either in a spreadsheet or with more specialized optimization software. After the efficient frontier has been calculated, an optimal portfolio is chosen based on the investor's objectives such as his degree of aversion to various kinds of risk.

Though the implementation of this process can get quite involved, the theory is relatively straightforward. In the next section we present Markow-

EXHIBIT 8.2   The MPT Investment Process

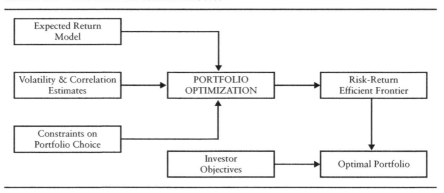

Source: Exhibit 2 in Frank J. Fabozzi, Francis Gupta, and Harry M. Markowitz, "The Legacy of Modern Portfolio Theory," *Journal of Investing*, 11 (Fall 2002), p. 8.

itz's classical framework. Our focus is on providing a practical approach to modern portfolio theory as opposed to giving a complete theoretical treatment.

CLASSICAL FRAMEWORK FOR MEAN-VARIANCE OPTIMIZATION

In this section we place the intuitive discussion thus far into a more formal mathematical context and develop the theory of mean-variance optimization. Suppose first that an investor has to choose a portfolio comprised of N risky assets.[3] The investor's choice is embodied in an N-vector $\mathbf{w} = (w_1, w_2, ..., w_N)'$ of weights, where each weight i represents the fraction of the i-th asset held in the portfolio, and

$$\sum_{i=1}^{N} w_i = 1$$

For now, we permit short selling, which means that weights can be negative.

Suppose the assets' returns $\mathbf{R} = (R_1, R_2, ..., R_N)'$ have expected returns $\mu = (\mu_1, \mu_2, ..., \mu_N)'$ and an $N \times N$ covariance matrix given by

$$\Sigma = \begin{bmatrix} \sigma_{11} & \cdots & \sigma_{1N} \\ \vdots & & \vdots \\ \sigma_{N1} & \cdots & \sigma_{NN} \end{bmatrix}$$

where σ_{ij} denotes the covariance between asset i and asset j such that $\sigma_{ii} = \sigma_i^2$, $\sigma_{ij} = \rho_{ij}\sigma_i\sigma_j$ and ρ_{ij} is the correlation between asset i and asset j. Under these assumptions, the return of a portfolio with weights $\mathbf{w} = (w_1, w_2, ..., w_N)'$ is a random variable $R_p = \mathbf{w}'\mathbf{R}$ with expected return and variance given by[4]

$$\mu_p = \mathbf{w}'\mu$$
$$\sigma_p^2 = \mathbf{w}'\Sigma\mathbf{w}$$

For now, we simply assume that expected returns, μ, and their covariance matrix, Σ, are given. Naturally, in practice these quantities have to be estimated. Later in this chapter we provide an overview of the many different techniques used for this purpose.

---

[3]Throughout this book we denote by $\mathbf{x}'$ the transpose of a vector $\mathbf{x}$.
[4]Subsequently, we will use $E(R_p)$, where R_p is the return on a portfolio, and μ_p interchangeably.

By choosing the portfolio's weights, an investor chooses among the available mean-variance pairs. To calculate the weights for one possible pair, we choose a target mean return, μ_0. Following Markowitz, the investor's problem is a constrained minimization problem in the sense that the investor must seek

$$\min_{\mathbf{w}} \frac{1}{2}\mathbf{w}'\Sigma\mathbf{w}$$

subject to the constraints[5]

$$\mu_0 = \mathbf{w}'\boldsymbol{\mu}$$
$$\mathbf{w}'\boldsymbol{\iota} = 0, \, \boldsymbol{\iota}' = [1,1,\ldots,1]$$

We will refer to this version of the classical mean-variance optimization problem as the *risk minimization formulation*.

This problem is a quadratic optimization problem with equality constraints with the solution given by[6]

---

[5]It is common in many practical applications to replace the targeted expected portfolio return constraint with $\mu_0 \leq \mathbf{w}'\boldsymbol{\mu}$, expressing the fact that the expected return should not be below a minimum value. However, with the introduction of inequality constraints (unless they are binding), the portfolio optimization problem no longer becomes analytically tractable, but has to be solved by numerical optimization techniques.

[6]This optimization problem can be solved by the method of the Lagrange multipliers. The Lagrangian becomes

$$L = \frac{1}{2}\mathbf{w}'\Sigma\mathbf{w} + \lambda(1 - \mathbf{w}'\boldsymbol{\iota}) + \gamma(\mu_0 - \mathbf{w}'\boldsymbol{\mu})$$

Differentiating with respect to $\mathbf{w}$, we obtain the first-order condition

$$\frac{\partial L}{\partial \mathbf{w}} = \Sigma\mathbf{w} - \lambda\boldsymbol{\iota} - \gamma\boldsymbol{\mu} = 0$$

Solving for $\mathbf{w}$, we get

$$\mathbf{w} = \lambda\Sigma^{-1}\boldsymbol{\iota} + \gamma\Sigma^{-1}\boldsymbol{\mu}$$

Substituting the parametrized solution for $\mathbf{w}$ into the constraints, we obtain the linear system for λ and γ

$$\boldsymbol{\iota}'\mathbf{w} = \lambda\boldsymbol{\iota}'\Sigma^{-1}\boldsymbol{\iota} + \gamma\boldsymbol{\iota}'\Sigma^{-1}\boldsymbol{\mu} \equiv 1$$
$$\boldsymbol{\mu}'\mathbf{w} = \lambda\boldsymbol{\mu}\Sigma^{-1}\boldsymbol{\iota} + \gamma\boldsymbol{\mu}'\Sigma^{-1}\boldsymbol{\mu} \equiv \mu_0$$

or in matrix form

$$\begin{pmatrix} A & B \\ B & C \end{pmatrix}\begin{pmatrix} \lambda \\ \gamma \end{pmatrix} = \begin{pmatrix} 1 \\ \mu_0 \end{pmatrix}$$

$$\mathbf{w} = \lambda\Sigma^{-1}\iota + \gamma\Sigma^{-1}\mu$$

where

$$\lambda = \frac{C - \mu_0 B}{\Delta}, \quad \gamma = \frac{\mu_0 A - B}{\Delta}$$

and

$$A = \iota'\Sigma^{-1}\iota, \quad B = \iota'\Sigma^{-1}\mu, \quad C = \mu'\Sigma^{-1}\mu$$

It is easy to see that

$$\sigma_0^2 = \mathbf{w}'\Sigma\mathbf{w}$$
$$= \frac{A\mu_0^2 - 2B\mu_0 + C}{\Delta}$$

Thus, the efficient portfolios $\mathbf{w}$ form a parabola in the (σ_0^2, μ_0)-plane, and a hyperbola in the (σ_0, μ_0)-plane referred to as the efficient frontier. Each portfolio on the efficient frontier is obtained by solving the preceding optimization problem for a different choice of μ_0.

The global minimum variance portfolio can be found by solving

$$\frac{d\sigma_0^2}{d\mu_0} = \frac{2A\mu_0 - 2B}{\Delta} = 0$$

The resulting portfolio weights are given by

$$\mathbf{w}_g = \frac{\Sigma^{-1}\iota}{A} = \frac{\Sigma^{-1}\iota}{\iota'\Sigma^{-1}\iota}$$

Mathematically, the mean-variance problem as described previously is an optimization problem referred to as a *quadratic program*. In the simple form presented, the problem can be solved analytically. In extensions involving only so-called equality constraints,[7] finding the optimum portfolio reduces to solving a set of linear equations. However, for formulations involving inequality constraints, analytical solutions are not available unless the constraints are binding. In other cases numerical optimization techniques must be used.

We note that the results of modern portfolio theory are consistent with the assumptions that either returns are jointly normally distributed, or that

---

[7]Constraints of the form $\mathbf{Aw} = \mathbf{b}$ and $\mathbf{Aw} \leq \mathbf{b}$ are referred to as equality and inequality constraints, respectively.

all investors only care about the mean and the variance of their portfolios. In practice, it is well known that asset returns are not normal and that many investors have preferences that go beyond that of the mean and the variance. The earliest studies showing nonnormality of asset returns date back to Benoit Mandelbrot[8] and Eugene Fama[9] in the early 1960s. The movement sometimes referred to as *econophysics*[10] has developed methods for the accurate empirical analysis of the distribution of asset returns that show significant deviations from the normal distribution.[11,12] In particular, there is evidence that the variances of some asset returns are not bounded, but rather that they are infinite. Moreover, one can show that in specific cases where variances are unbounded and asset returns behave like certain stable Paretian distributions, diversification may no longer be possible.[13]

The mean-variance optimization problem has several alternative but equivalent formulations that are very useful in practical applications. These formulations are equivalent in the sense that they all lead to the same efficient frontier as they trade expected portfolio return versus portfolio risk in a similar way.

First, we can choose a certain level of targeted portfolio risk, say σ_0, and then maximize the expected return of the portfolio:

$$\max_{\mathbf{w}} \mathbf{w}'\boldsymbol{\mu}$$

subject to the constraints[14]

---

[8]Benoit Mandelbrot, "The Variation in Certain Speculative Prices," *Journal of Business*, 36 (1963), pp. 394–419.

[9]Eugene F. Fama, "The Behavior of Stock Market Prices," *Journal of Business*, 38 (1965), pp. 34–105.

[10]Rosario N. Mantegna and H. Eugene Stanley, *An Introduction to Econophysics* (Cambridge: Cambridge University Press, 2000).

[11]Ulrich A. Mueller, Michel M. Dacorogna, and Olivier V. Pictet, "Heavy Tails in High-Frequency Financial Data," in Robert J. Adler, Raya E. Feldman, and Murad S. Taqqu (eds.), *A Practical Guide to Heavy Tails* (Boston, MA: Birkhaeuser, 1998), pp. 55–77.

[12]For recent empirical evidence on the distribution of asset returns and portfolio selection when distributions are nonnormal, see Svetlozar T. Rachev and Stefan Mittnik, *Stable Paretian Models in Finance* (Chichester: John Wiley & Sons, 2000); and Svetlozar T. Rachev (eds.), *Handbook of Heavy Tailed Distributions in Finance* (New York: Elsevier/North Holland, 2001).

[13]Eugene F. Fama, "Portfolio Analysis In a Stable Paretian Market," *Management Science*, 11 (1965), pp. 404–419.

[14]It is common in many practical applications that the equal sign in the risk constraint is replaced by a weak inequality, that is, $\mathbf{w}'\Sigma\mathbf{w} \leq \sigma_0^2$, expressing the fact that the risk is not allowed to be above a maximum value.

$$\mathbf{w}'\Sigma\mathbf{w} = \sigma_0^2$$
$$\mathbf{w}'\mathbf{\iota} = 1, \mathbf{\iota}' = [1,1,\ldots,1]$$

This formulation, which we will refer to as the *expected return maximization formulation* of the classical mean-variance optimization problem, is often used by portfolio managers who are required to not take more risk, as measured by the standard deviation of the portfolio return, than a certain prespecified volatility. For example, portfolios managed relative to a benchmark can be modeled in this fashion. Here the objective is to maximize the excess return of the portfolio over the benchmark and at the same time make sure that the risks in so doing do not exceed a given tracking error over the benchmark.

Alternatively, we can explicitly model the trade-off between risk and return in the objective function using a risk-aversion coefficient λ. We refer to the following formulation as the *risk aversion formulation* of the classical mean-variance optimization problem

$$\max_{\mathbf{w}} \left(\mathbf{w}'\mathbf{\mu} - \lambda \frac{1}{2} \mathbf{w}'\Sigma\mathbf{w} \right)$$

subject to

$$\mathbf{w}'\mathbf{\iota} = 1, \mathbf{\iota}' = [1,1,\ldots,1]$$

The risk aversion coefficient is also referred to as the *Arrow-Pratt risk aversion index*. When λ is small (i.e., the aversion to risk is low), the penalty from the contribution of the portfolio risk is also small, leading to more risky portfolios. Conversely, when λ is large, portfolios with more exposures to risk become more highly penalized. If we gradually increase λ from zero and for each instance solve the optimization problem, we end up calculating each portfolio along the efficient frontier. It is a common practice to calibrate λ such that a particular portfolio has the desired risk profile.

MEAN-VARIANCE OPTIMIZATION WITH A RISK-FREE ASSET

As demonstrated by William Sharpe,[15] James Tobin,[16] and John Lintner[17] the efficient set of portfolios available to investors who employ mean-variance

---

[15]William F. Sharpe, "Capital Asset Prices: A Theory of Market Equilibrium Under Conditions of Risk," *Journal of Finance*, 19 (1964), pp. 425–442.
[16]James Tobin, "Liquidity Preference as a Behavior Towards Risk," *Review of Economic Studies*, 67 (1958), pp. 65–86.
[17]John Lintner, "The Valuation of Risk Assets and the Selection of Risky Investments in Stock Portfolios and Capital Budgets," *Review of Economics and Statistics*, 47 (1965), pp. 13–37.

analysis in the absence of a risk-free asset is inferior to that available when there is a risk-free asset. We present this formulation in this section.

Assume that there is a risk-free asset, with a risk-free return denoted by R_f and that the investor is able to borrow and lend at this rate.[18] The investor has to choose a combination of the N risky assets plus the risk-free asset. The weights $\mathbf{w}'_R = (w_{R1}, w_{R2}, ..., w_{RN})$ do not have to sum to 1 as the remaining part $(1 - \mathbf{w}'_R \iota)$ is the investment in the risk-free asset. Note that this portion of the investment can be positive or negative if we allow risk-free borrowing and lending. The portfolio's expected return and variance are

$$\mu_p = \mathbf{w}'_R \mu + (1 - \mathbf{w}'_R \iota) R_f$$
$$\sigma_p^2 = \mathbf{w}'_R \Sigma \mathbf{w}_R$$

because the risk-free asset has zero variance and is uncorrelated with the risky assets.

The investor's objective is again for a targeted level of expected portfolio return, μ_0, to choose allocations by solving a quadratic optimization problem

$$\min_{\mathbf{w}_R} \mathbf{w}'_R \Sigma \mathbf{w}_R$$

subject to the constraint

$$\mu_0 = \mathbf{w}'_R \mu + (1 - \mathbf{w}'_R \iota) R_f$$

The optimal portfolio weights are given by

$$\mathbf{w}_R = C \Sigma^{-1} (\mu - R_f \iota)$$

where

$$C = \frac{\mu_0 - R_f}{(\mu - R_f \iota)' \Sigma^{-1} (\mu - R_f \iota)}$$

---

[18]We remark that, in practice, this assumption is not valid for most investors. Specifically, an investor may not be able to borrow and lend at the *same* interest rate, or may *only* be permitted to lend. If there are no short-selling restrictions on the risky assets, similar theoretical results to the ones presented in this section are obtained also for these cases. See Fischer Black, "Capital Market Equilibrium with Restricted Borrowings," *Journal of Business*, 45 (1972) pp. 444–455; and Jonathan E. Ingersoll, Jr., *Theory of Financial Decision Making* (Savage, MD: Rowan & Littlefield Publishers, Inc., 1987).

The preceding formula shows that the weights of the risky assets of any minimum variance portfolio are proportional to the vector $\boldsymbol{\Sigma}^{-1}(\boldsymbol{\mu} - R_f\boldsymbol{\iota})$, with the proportionality constant C, defined previously. Therefore, with a risk-free asset, all minimum variance portfolios are a combination of the risk-free asset and a given risky portfolio. This risky portfolio is called the *tangency portfolio*. Fama demonstrated that under certain assumptions the tangency portfolio must consist of all assets available to investors, and each asset must be held in proportion to its market value relative to the total market value of all assets.[19] Therefore, the tangency portfolio is often referred to as the *market portfolio*, or simply the *market*.[20]

We know that for a particular choice of weights, $\mathbf{w}_R^0$, such that $(\mathbf{w}_R^0)'\boldsymbol{\iota} = 0$, the portfolio only consists of the risk-free asset. On the other hand, for the choice of weights, $\mathbf{w}_R^M$, such that $(\mathbf{w}_R^M)'\boldsymbol{\iota} = 1$, the portfolio consists of only risky assets and must therefore be the market portfolio. Because

$$\mathbf{w}_R^M = C^M \boldsymbol{\Sigma}^{-1}(\boldsymbol{\mu} - R_f\boldsymbol{\iota})$$

for some C^M, we have by using $(\mathbf{w}_R^M)'\boldsymbol{\iota} = 1$ that the weights of the market portfolio are given by

$$\mathbf{w}_R^M = \frac{1}{\boldsymbol{\iota}'\boldsymbol{\Sigma}(\boldsymbol{\mu} - R_f\boldsymbol{\iota})} \cdot \boldsymbol{\Sigma}^{-1}(\boldsymbol{\mu} - R_f\boldsymbol{\iota})$$

It is also easy to verify that the market portfolio can be calculated directly from the *maximal Sharpe ratio optimization problem*

$$\max_{\mathbf{w}} \frac{\mathbf{w}'\boldsymbol{\mu} - R_f}{\sqrt{\mathbf{w}'\boldsymbol{\Sigma}\mathbf{w}}}$$

subject to $\mathbf{w}'\boldsymbol{\iota} = 1$.

In Exhibit 8.3 every combination of the risk-free asset and the market portfolio M is shown on the line drawn from the vertical axis at the risk-free rate tangent to the Markowitz efficient frontier. All the portfolios on the line are feasible for the investor to construct. The line from the risk-free rate that is tangent to the efficient frontier of risky assets is called the *Capital Market Line* (CML).

We observe that with the exception of the market portfolio, the minimum variance portfolios that are a combination of the market portfolio and

---

[19]Eugene F. Fama, "Efficient Capital Markets: A Review of Theory and Empirical Work," *Journal of Finance*, 25 (1970), pp. 383–417.

[20]Although strictly speaking it is not fully correct, we will use the terms *market portfolio* and *tangency portfolio* interchangeably throughout this book.

EXHIBIT 8.3   Capital Market Line and the Markowitz Efficient Frontier

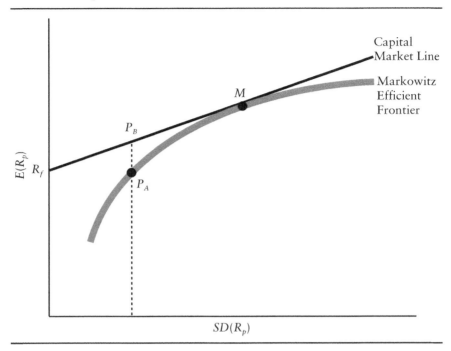

the risk-free asset are superior to the portfolio on the Markowitz efficient frontier for the same level of risk. For example, compare portfolio P_A, which is on the Markowitz efficient frontier, with portfolio P_B, which is on the CML and therefore some combination of the risk-free asset and the market portfolio M. Notice that for the same level of risk, the expected return is greater for P_B than for P_A. A risk-averse investor will prefer P_B to P_A.

With the introduction of the risk-free asset, we can now say that an investor will select a portfolio on the CML that represents a combination of borrowing or lending at the risk-free rate and the market portfolio.[21] This important property is called *separation*. Portfolios to the left of the market portfolio represent combinations of risky assets and the risk-free asset. Portfolios to the right of the market portfolio include purchases of risky assets made with funds borrowed at the risk-free rate. Such a portfolio is called a *leveraged portfolio* because it involves the use of borrowed funds.

---

[21]Today it is normal practice to use standard deviation rather than variance as the risk measure because with the inclusion of a risk-free asset, the efficient frontier in the expected return/standard deviation coordinate system is linear.

The separation property also has important implications in practice. Specifically, practical portfolio construction is normally broken down into at least the following two steps:

1. Asset allocation: Decide how to allocate the investor's wealth between the risk-free security and the set of risky securities.
2. Risky portfolio construction: Decide how to distribute the risky portion of the investment among the set of risky securities.

The first point is an integral part in devising an investment plan and policy for a particular investor. This is closely linked to an investor's strategic goals and general risk profile as well as his liquidity requirements. In this book the focus is more on the second point. In later chapters we will discuss various kinds of forecasting techniques that can be used in order to maximize different investment objectives and controlling the risk of the risky portion of the portfolio.

Deriving the Capital Market Line

We can derive a formula for the CML algebraically. Based on the assumption of homogeneous expectations regarding the inputs in the portfolio construction process, all investors can create an efficient portfolio consisting of w_f placed in the risk-free asset and w_M in the market portfolio, where w represents the corresponding percentage (weight) of the portfolio allocated to each asset. Thus, $w_f + w_M = 1$. As the expected return of the portfolio, $E(R_p)$, is equal to the weighted average of the expected returns of the two assets, we have

$$E(R_p) = w_f R_f + w_M E(R_M)$$

Since we know that $w_f = 1 - w_M$, we can rewrite $E(R_p)$ as

$$E(R_p) = (1 - w_M)R_f + w_M E(R_M)$$

which can be simplified to

$$E(R_p) = R_f + w_M[E(R_M) - R_f]$$

Since the return of the risk-free asset and the return of the market portfolio are uncorrelated and the variance of the risk-free asset is equal to zero, the variance of the portfolio consisting of the risk-free asset and the market portfolio is given by

$$\sigma_p^2 = \mathrm{var}(R_p) = w_f^2 \, \mathrm{var}(R_f) + w_M^2 \, \mathrm{var}(R_M) + 2w_f w_M \, \mathrm{cov}(R_f, R_M)$$
$$= w_M^2 \, \mathrm{var}(R_M)$$
$$= w_M^2 \sigma_M^2$$

In other words, the variance of the portfolio is represented by the weighted variance of the market portfolio.

Since the standard deviation is the square root of the variance, we can write

$$w_M = \frac{\sigma_p}{\sigma_M}$$

If we substitute the preceding result and rearrange terms, we get the explicit expression for the CML

$$E(R_p) = R_f + \left[\frac{E(R_M) - R_f}{\sigma_M} \right] \sigma_p$$

The bracketed portion of the second term in the equation for the CML

$$\left[\frac{E(R_M) - R_f}{\sigma_M} \right]$$

is often referred to as the *risk premium.*

Let us examine the economic meaning of this risk premium. The numerator of the bracketed expression is the expected return from investing in the market beyond the risk-free return. It is a measure of the reward for holding the risky market portfolio rather than the risk-free asset. The denominator is the market risk of the market portfolio. Thus, the first factor, or the slope of the CML, measures the reward per unit of market risk. Since the CML represents the return offered to compensate for a perceived level of risk, each point on the CML is a balanced market condition, or equilibrium. The slope of the CML determines the additional return needed to compensate for a unit change in risk, which is why it is also referred to as the *equilibrium market price of risk.*

In other words, the CML says that the expected return on a portfolio is equal to the risk-free rate plus a risk premium, where the risk premium is equal to the market price of risk (as measured by the reward per unit of market risk) times the quantity of risk for the portfolio (as measured by the standard deviation of the portfolio). Summarizing, we can write

$$E(R_p) = R_f + \text{Market price of risk} \times \text{Quantity of risk}$$

PORTFOLIO CONSTRAINTS COMMONLY USED IN PRACTICE

Institutional features and investment policy decisions often lead to more complicated constraints and portfolio management objectives than those present in the original formulation of the mean-variance problem. For example, many mutual funds are managed relative to a particular benchmark or asset universe (e.g., S&P 500, Russell 1000) so that their tracking error relative to the benchmark is kept small. A portfolio manager might also be restricted on how concentrated the investment portfolio can be in a particular industry or sector. These restrictions, and many more, can be modeled by adding constraints to the original formulation.

In this section, we describe constraints that are often used in combination with the mean-variance problem in practical applications. Specifically, we distinguish between linear, quadratic, nonlinear, and combinatorial/integer constraints.

Throughout this section, we denote the current portfolio weights by $\mathbf{w}_0$ and the targeted portfolio weights by $\mathbf{w}$, so that the amount to be traded is $\mathbf{x} = \mathbf{w} - \mathbf{w}_0$.

Linear and Quadratic Constraints

Some of the more commonly used linear and quadratic constraints are described next.

Long-Only Constraints

When short-selling is not allowed, we require that $\mathbf{w} \geq 0$. This is a frequently used constraint, as many funds and institutional investors are prohibited from selling stocks short.

Turnover Constraints

High portfolio turnover can result in large transaction costs that make portfolio rebalancing inefficient. One possibility is to limit the amount of turnover allowed when performing portfolio optimization. The most common turnover constraints limit turnover on each individual asset

$$|x_i| \leq U_i$$

or on the whole portfolio

$$\sum_{i \in I} |x_i| \leq U_{\text{portfolio}}$$

where I denotes the available investment universe. Turnover constraints are often imposed relative to the *average daily volume* (ADV) of a stock. For example, we might want to restrict turnover to be no more than 5% of average daily volume. Modifications of these constraints, such as limiting turnover in a specific industry or sector, are also frequently applied.

Holding Constraints

A well-diversified portfolio should not exhibit large concentrations in any specific assets, industries, sectors, or countries. Maximal holdings in an individual asset can be controlled by the constraint

$$L_i \leq w_i \leq U_i$$

where L_i and U_i are vectors representing the lower and upper bounds of the holdings of asset i. To constrain the exposure to a specific set I_i (e.g., industry or country) of the available investment universe I, we can introduce constraints of the form

$$L_i \leq \sum_{j \in I_i} w_j \leq U_i$$

where L_i and U_i denote the minimum and maximum exposures to I_i.

Risk Factor Constraints

In practice, it is very common for portfolio managers to use factor models to control for different risk exposures to risk factors such as market, size, and style.[22] Let us assume that security returns have a factor structure with K risk factors, that is

$$R_i = \alpha_i + \sum_{k=1}^{K} \beta_{ik} F_k + \varepsilon_i$$

where F_k, $k = 1, \ldots, K$ are the K factors common to all the securities, β_{ik} is the sensitivity of the i-th security to the k-th factor, and ε_i is the nonsystematic return for the i-th security.

To limit a portfolio's exposure to the k-th risk factor, we can impose the constraint

$$\sum_{i=1}^{N} \beta_{ik} w_i \leq U_k$$

---

[22]We discussed factor models in more detail in Chapter 5.

where U_k denotes maximum exposure allowed. To construct a portfolio that is neutral to the k-th risk factor (e.g., market neutral) we would use the constraint

$$\sum_{i=1}^{N} \beta_{ik} w_i = 0$$

Benchmark Exposure and Tracking Error Constraints

Many portfolio managers are faced with the objective of managing their portfolio relative to a benchmark. This is the typical situation for index fund managers and passive managers who are trying to deliver a small outperformance relative to a particular benchmark, such as the Russell 1000 or the S&P 500.

Let us denote by $\mathbf{w}_b$ the market capitalization weights (sometimes also referred to as the *benchmark weights*), and by $\mathbf{R}$ the vector of returns of the individual assets, so that $R_b = \mathbf{w}_b' \cdot \mathbf{R}$ is the return on the benchmark. A portfolio manager might choose to limit the deviations of the portfolio weights from the benchmark weights by imposing

$$\|\mathbf{w} - \mathbf{w}_b\| \leq M$$

or, similarly, for a specific industry I_i require that

$$\sum_{j \in I_i} w_j - w_{bj} \leq M_i$$

However, the most commonly used metric to measure the deviation from the benchmark is the *tracking error*. The tracking error is defined as the variance of the difference between the return of the portfolio $R_p = \mathbf{w}' \cdot \mathbf{R}$ and the return of the benchmark $R_b = \mathbf{w}_b' \cdot \mathbf{R}$, that is, $\text{TEV}_p = \text{var}(R_p - R_b)$. Expanding this definition, we get

$$\begin{aligned}
TEV_p &= \text{var}\left(R_p - R_b\right) \\
&= \text{var}\left(\mathbf{w}'\mathbf{R} - \mathbf{w}_b'\mathbf{R}\right) \\
&= (\mathbf{w} - \mathbf{w}_b)' \text{var}(\mathbf{R})(\mathbf{w} - \mathbf{w}_b) \\
&= (\mathbf{w} - \mathbf{w}_b)' \Sigma (\mathbf{w} - \mathbf{w}_b)
\end{aligned}$$

where Σ is the covariance matrix of the asset returns. In order to limit the tracking error, a constraint of the form

$$(\mathbf{w} - \mathbf{w}_b)' \Sigma (\mathbf{w} - \mathbf{w}_b) \leq \sigma_{TE}^2$$

can be added to the portfolio optimization formulation. In the next section, we provide an example that shows how the tracking error constraint formulation can be used for index tracking.

Note that a pure tracking-error constrained portfolio ignores total portfolio risk or *absolute* risk. In practice, this can result in very inefficient portfolios (in a mean-variance sense) unless additional constraints on total volatility are imposed.[23]

General Linear and Quadratic Constraints

The constraints described in this section are all linear or quadratic, that is, they can be cast either as

$$\mathbf{A}_w \mathbf{w} \le \mathbf{d}_w$$
$$\mathbf{A}_x \mathbf{x} \le \mathbf{d}_x$$
$$\mathbf{A}_b \left(\mathbf{w} - \mathbf{w}_b \right) \le \mathbf{d}_b$$

or as

$$\mathbf{w}' \mathbf{Q}_w \mathbf{w} \le q_w$$
$$\mathbf{x}' \mathbf{Q}_x \mathbf{x} \le q_x$$
$$(\mathbf{w} - \mathbf{w}_b)' \mathbf{Q}_b (\mathbf{w} - \mathbf{w}_b) \le q_b$$

These types of constraints can be dealt with directly within the quadratic programming framework, and there are very efficient algorithms available that are capable of solving practical portfolio optimization problems with thousands of assets in a matter of seconds.

Combinatorial and Integer Constraints

The following binary decision variable is useful in describing some combinatorial and integer constraints:

$$\delta_i = \begin{cases} 1, & \text{if } w_i \ne 0 \\ 0, & \text{if } w_i = 0 \end{cases}$$

where w_i denotes the portfolio weight of the i-th asset.

---

[23]Philippe Jorion, "Portfolio Optimization with Tracking-Error Constraints," *Financial Analysts Journal*, 59 (2003), pp. 70–82.

Minimum Holding and Transaction Size Constraints

The classical mean-variance optimization problem often results in a few large and many small positions. In practice, due to transaction costs and other ticket charges, small holdings are undesirable. In order to eliminate small holdings, threshold constraints of the following form are often used

$$|w_i| \geq L_{w_i} \delta_i \quad i = 1, ..., N$$

where L_{w_i} is the smallest holding size allowed for asset i.

Similarly, because of the fixed costs related to trading each individual security, it is desirable to avoid small trades. Therefore, a portfolio manager might also want to eliminate new trades, $\mathbf{x}$, smaller than a prespecified amount

$$|x_i| \geq L_{x_i} \delta_i \quad i = 1, ..., N$$

where L_{x_i} is the smallest transaction size permitted for asset i.

In practice, few portfolio managers go to the extent of including constraints of this type in their optimization framework. Instead, a standard mean-variance optimization problem is solved and then, in a *postoptimization* step, generated portfolio weights or trades that are smaller than a certain threshold are eliminated. This simplification leads to small, but often negligible, differences compared to a full optimization using the threshold constraints. Given that the mean-variance optimization problem with threshold constraints is much more complicated to solve from a numerical and computational point of view, this small discrepancy is often ignored by practitioners.

Cardinality Constraints

A portfolio manager might want to restrict the number of assets allowed in a portfolio. This could be the case when, for example, he is attempting to construct a portfolio tracking a benchmark using a limited set of assets. The cardinality constraint takes the form

$$\sum_{i=1}^{N} \delta_i = K$$

where K is a positive integer significantly less than the number of assets in the investment universe, N.

Minimum holding and cardinality constraints are related. Both of them attempt to reduce the number of small trades and the number of portfolio positions. Therefore, it is not uncommon that both constraints are used simultaneously in the same portfolio optimization. There are situations in which imposing only cardinality constraints will lead to some small trades. Conversely, with only minimum holding constraints, the resulting portfolio might still contain too many positions, or result in too many trades. Portfolio managers often have the desire not to keep the number of assets too large, and at the same time make sure that all of their holdings are larger than a certain threshold.

Round Lot Constraints

For the most part, portfolio selection models proposed in the literature are based on the assumption of a perfect *fractionability* of the investments, in such a way that the portfolio weights for each security could be represented by real numbers. In reality, securities are transacted in multiples of a minimum transaction lots, or rounds (e.g., 100 or 500 shares). In order to model transaction round lots explicitly in the optimization problem, portfolio weights can be represented as

$$w_i = z_i \cdot f_i, \quad i = 1, \ldots, N$$

where f_i is a fraction of portfolio wealth and z_i is an integer number of round lots. For example, if the total portfolio wealth is \$10 million and stock i trades at \$86 in round lots of 100, then

$$f_i = \frac{86 \cdot 100}{10^7} = 8.6 \cdot 10^{-4}$$

In applying round lot constraints, the budget constraint

$$\sum_{i=1}^{N} w_i = 1$$

may not be exactly satisfied. To accommodate this situation, the budget constraint is relaxed with undershoot and overshoot variables, $\varepsilon^- \geq 0$ and $\varepsilon^+ \geq 0$, so that

$$\sum_{i=1}^{N} f_i z_i + \varepsilon^- - \varepsilon^+ = 1$$

This formula can be written in a more compact way as

$$z' \Lambda \iota + \varepsilon^- - \varepsilon^+ = 1, \quad \iota' = [1,1,...,1]$$

where $\Lambda = \text{diag}(f_1, f_2, ..., f_N)$, that is, Λ equals the diagonal matrix of the fractions of portfolio wealth.

The undershoot and overshoot variables need to be as small as possible at the optimal point, and therefore, they are penalized in the objective function, yielding the following optimization problem:

$$\max_z \ z' \Lambda \mu - \lambda z' \Lambda \Sigma \Lambda z - \gamma (\varepsilon^- + \varepsilon^+)$$

subject to

$$z' \Lambda \iota + \varepsilon^- + \varepsilon^+ = 1, \quad \iota' = [1,1,...,1]$$
$$\varepsilon^- \geq 0, \quad \varepsilon^+ \geq 0$$

where λ and γ are parameters chosen by the portfolio manager.

Normally, the inclusion of round lot constraints to the mean-variance optimization problem only produces a small increase in risk for a prespecified expected return. Furthermore, the portfolios obtained in this manner cannot be obtained by simply rounding the portfolio weights from a standard mean-variance optimization to the nearest round lot.

In order to represent threshold and cardinality constraints we have to introduce binary (0/1) variables, and for round lots we need integer variables. In effect, the original *quadratic program* (QP) resulting from the mean-variance formulation becomes a *quadratic mixed integer program* (QMIP). Therefore, these combinatorial extensions require more sophisticated and specialized algorithms that often require significant computing time.

ESTIMATING THE INPUTS USED IN MEAN-VARIANCE OPTIMIZATION: EXPECTED RETURN AND RISK

In this section, we discuss the estimation of the inputs required for portfolio asset-allocation models. We focus on the estimation of expected asset returns and their covariances using classical and practically well-probed techniques. Modern techniques using dynamic models and hidden variable models are covered in Fabozzi, Focardi, and Kolm.[24]

An analyst might proceed in the following way. Observing weekly or monthly returns, he might use the past five years of historical data to esti-

---

[24]See Chapters 14, 15, and 16 in Frank J. Fabozzi, Sergio M. Focardi, and Petter N. Kolm, *Financial Modeling of the Equity Market: From CAPM to Cointegration* (Hoboken, NJ: John Wiley & Sons, 2006).

mate the expected return and the covariance matrix by the sample mean and sample covariance matrix. He would then use these as inputs to the mean-variance optimization, along with any ad hoc adjustments to reflect his views about expected returns on future performance. Unfortunately this historical approach most often leads to counterintuitive, unstable, or merely wrong portfolios.

Statistical estimates are noisy and do depend on the quality of the data and the particular statistical techniques used. In general, it is desirable that an estimator of expected return and risk have the following properties:

- It provides a forward-looking forecast with some predictive power, not just a backward-looking historical summary of past performance.
- The estimate can be produced at a reasonable computational cost.
- The technique used does not amplify errors already present in the inputs used in the process of estimation.
- The forecast should be intuitive, that is, the portfolio manager or the analyst should be able to explain and justify them in a comprehensible manner.

In this section we discuss the properties of the sample mean and covariance estimators as a forecast of expected returns and risk. The forecasting power of these estimators is typically poor, and for practical applications, modifications and extensions are necessary. We focus on some of the most common and widely used modifications. We postpone the treatment of Bayesian techniques such as the Black-Litterman model to Chapter 9.

The Sample Mean and Covariance Estimators

Quantitative techniques for forecasting security expected returns and risk most often rely on historical data. Therefore, it is important keep in mind that we are implicitly assuming that the past can predict the future.

It is well known that expected returns exhibit significant time variation (nonstationarity) and that realized returns are strongly influenced by changes in expected returns.[25] Consequently, extrapolated historical returns are in general poor forecasts of future returns, or as a typical disclaimer in any investment prospectus states: "Past performance is not an indication of future performance."

---

[25]See Eugene F. Fama and Kenneth R. French, "The Equity Risk Premium," *Journal of Finance,* 57 (2002), pp. 637–659; and Thomas K. Philips, "Why Do Valuation Ratios Forecast Long-Run Equity Returns?" *Journal of Portfolio Management,* 25 (1999), pp. 39–44.

One problem of basing forecasts on historical performance is that markets and economic conditions change throughout time. For example, interest rates have varied substantially, all the way from the high double digits to the low interest rate environment in the early 2000s. Other factors that change over time, and that can significantly influence the markets, include the political environment within and across countries, monetary and fiscal policy, consumer confidence, and the business cycle of different industry sectors and regions.

Of course, there are reasons why we can place more faith in statistical estimates obtained from historical data for some assets as compared to others. Different asset classes have varying lengths of histories available. For example, not only do the United States and the European markets have longer histories, but their data also tends to be more accurate. For emerging markets, the situation is quite different. Sometimes only a few years of historical data are available. As a consequence, based upon the quality of the inputs, we expect that for some asset classes we should be able to construct more precise estimates than others.

In practice, if portfolio managers believe that the inputs that rely on the historical performance of an asset class are not a good reflection of the future expected performance of that asset class, they may alter the inputs objectively or subjectively. Obviously, different portfolio managers may have different beliefs and therefore their corrections will be different.

We now turn to the estimation of the expected return and risk by the sample mean and covariance estimators. Given the historical returns of two securities i and j, $R_{i,t}$ and $R_{j,t}$, where $t = 1, \ldots, T$, the sample mean and covariance are given by

$$\overline{R}_i = \frac{1}{T}\sum_{t=1}^{T}R_{i,t}$$

$$\overline{R}_j = \frac{1}{T}\sum_{t=1}^{T}R_{j,t}$$

$$\sigma_{ij} = \frac{1}{T-1}\sum_{t=1}^{T}(R_{i,t} - \overline{R}_i)(R_{j,t} - \overline{R}_j)$$

In the case of N securities, the covariance matrix can be expressed directly in matrix form:

$$\Sigma = \frac{1}{N-1}\mathbf{X}\mathbf{X}'$$

where

$$\mathbf{X} = \begin{bmatrix} R_{11} & \cdots & R_{1T} \\ \vdots & \ddots & \vdots \\ R_{N1} & \cdots & R_{NT} \end{bmatrix} - \begin{bmatrix} \bar{R}_1 & \cdots & \bar{R}_1 \\ \vdots & \ddots & \vdots \\ \bar{R}_N & \cdots & \bar{R}_N \end{bmatrix}$$

Under the assumption that security returns are independent and identically distributed (i.i.d.), it can be demonstrated that Σ is the maximum-likelihood estimator of the population covariance matrix and that this matrix follows a Wishart distribution with $N - 1$ degrees of freedom.[26]

As mentioned before, the risk-free rate R_f does change significantly over time. Therefore, when using a longer history, it is common that historical security returns are first converted into excess returns, $R_{i,t} - R_{f,t}$, and thereafter the expected return is estimated from

$$\bar{R}_i = R_{f,t} + \frac{1}{T}\sum_{t=1}^{T}(R_{i,t} - R_{f,t})$$

Alternatively, the expected excess returns may be used directly in a mean-variance optimization framework.

Unfortunately, for financial return series, the sample mean is a poor estimator for the expected return. The sample mean is the *best linear unbiased estimator* (BLUE) of the population mean for distributions that are not heavy-tailed. In this case, the sample mean exhibits the important property that an increase in the sample size always improves its performance. However, these results are no longer valid under extreme thick-tailedness and caution has to be exercised.[27] Furthermore, financial time series are typically *not* stationary, so the mean is not a good forecast of expected return. Moreover, the resulting estimator has a large estimation error (as measured by the

---

[26]Suppose $X_1, \ldots, X_N$ are independent and identically distributed random vectors, and that for each i it holds $X_i \sim N_p(0, V)$ (that is, $E(X_i) = 0$, where 0 is a p dimensional vector, and

$$\text{Var}(\mathbf{X}_i) = E(\mathbf{X}_i\mathbf{X}_i') = \mathbf{V}$$

where V is a $p \times p$ dimensional matrix). Then, the Wishart distribution with N degrees of freedom is the probability distribution of the $p \times p$ random matrix

$$\mathbf{S} = \sum_{i=1}^{N}\mathbf{X}_i\mathbf{X}_i'$$

and we write $S \sim W_p(V, N)$. In the case when $p = 1$ and $V = 1$, then this distribution reduces to a chi-square distribution.

[27]Rustam Ibragimov, "Efficiency of Linear Estimators under Heavy-Tailedness: Convolutions of α-Symmetric Distributions," *Econometric Theory*, 23 (2007), pp. 501–517.

standard error), which significantly influences the mean-variance portfolio allocation process. As a consequence:

- Equally-weighted portfolios often outperform mean-variance optimized portfolios.[28]
- Mean-variance optimized portfolios are not necessarily well diversified.[29]
- Uncertainty of returns tends to have more influence than risk in mean-variance optimization.[30]

These problems must be addressed from different perspectives. More robust or stable (lower estimation error) estimates of expected return should be used. One approach is to impose more structure on the estimator. Most commonly, practitioners use some form of factor model to produce the expected return forecasts.[31] Another possibility is to use Bayesian (such as the Black-Litterman model) or shrinkage estimators.

Mean-variance optimization is very sensitive to its inputs. Small changes in expected return inputs often lead to large changes in portfolio weights. To some extent this is mitigated by using better estimators. However, by taking the estimation errors (whether large or small) into account in the optimization, further improvements can be made. In a nutshell, the problem is related to the fact that the mean-variance optimizer *does not know* that the inputs are statistical estimates and not known with certainty. When we are using classical mean-variance optimization, we are implicitly assuming that inputs are deterministic, and available with great accuracy. In other words, bad inputs lead to even worse outputs, or "garbage in, garbage out." Chapter 10 covers so-called robust portfolio optimization that addresses these issues.

We will now turn to the sample covariance matrix estimator. Several authors (for example, Gemmill;[32] Litterman and Winkelmann;[33] and

---

[28]J. D. Jobson and Bob M. Korkie, "Putting Markowitz Theory to Work," *Journal of Portfolio Management*, 7 (1981), pp. 70–74.

[29]Philippe Jorion, "International Portfolio Diversification with Estimation Risk," *Journal of Business*, 58 (1985), pp. 259–278.

[30]Vijay K. Chopra and William T. Ziemba, "The Effect of Errors in Means, Variances, and Covariances on Optimal Portfolio Choice," *Journal of Portfolio Management*, 19 (1993), pp. 6–11.

[31]Factor models are covered in Chapter 5.

[32]Gordon Gemmill, *Options Pricing, An International Perspective* (London: McGraw-Hill, 1993).

[33]Robert Litterman and Kurt Winkelmann, "Estimating Covariance Matrices," *Risk Management Series*, Goldman Sachs, 1998.

Pafka, Potters, and Kondor[34]) suggest improvements to this estimator using weighted data. The reason behind using weighted data is that the market changes and it makes sense to give more importance to recent, rather than to long past, information. If we give the most recent observation a weight of one and subsequent observations weights of d, d_2, d_3, ... where $d < 1$, then

$$\sigma_{ij} = \frac{\displaystyle\sum_{t=1}^{T} d^{T-t}(R_{i,t} - \bar{R}_i)(R_{j,t} - \bar{R}_j)}{\displaystyle\sum_{t=1}^{T} d^{T-1}}$$

$$= \frac{1-d}{1-d^T} \sum_{t=1}^{T} d^{T-t}(R_{i,t} - \bar{R}_i)(R_{j,t} - \bar{R}_j)$$

We observe that

$$\frac{1-d}{1-d^T} \approx 1-d$$

when T is large enough. The weighting (decay) parameter d can be estimated by maximum likelihood estimation, or by minimizing the out-of-sample forecasting error.[35]

Nevertheless, just like the estimator for expected returns, the covariance estimator suffers from estimation errors, especially when the number of historical return observations is small relative to the number of securities. The sample mean and covariance matrix are poor estimators for anything but i.i.d. time series. In the i.i.d. case, the sample mean and covariance estimator are the maximum likelihood estimators of the true mean and covariance.[36]

The sample covariance estimator often performs poorly in practice. For instance, Ledoit and Wolf[37] argue against using the sample covariance matrix for portfolio optimization purposes. They stress that the sample covariance matrix contains estimation errors that will very likely perturb and produce

---

[34]Szilard Pafka, Marc Potters, and Imre Kondor, "Exponential Weighting and Random-Matrix-Theory-Based Filtering of Financial Covariance Matrices for Portfolio Optimization," Working Paper, Science & Finance, Capital Fund Management, 2004.

[35]See Giorgio De Santis, Robert Litterman, Adrien Vesval, and Kurt Winkelmann, "Covariance Matrix Estimation," in Robert Litterman (ed.), *Modern Investment Management: An Equilibrium Approach* (Hoboken, NJ: John Wiley & Sons, 2003), pp. 224–248.

[36]See, for example, Fumio Hayashi, *Econometrics* (Princeton: Princeton University Press, 2000).

[37]Olivier Ledoit and Michael Wolf, "Honey, I Shrunk the Sample Covariance Matrix," *Journal of Portfolio Management*, 30 (2004), pp. 110–117.

poor results in a mean-variance optimization. As a substitute, they suggest applying shrinkage techniques to covariance estimation. We discuss these methods later in this chapter.

The sample covariance matrix is a nonparametric (unstructured) estimator. An alternative is to make assumptions on the structure of the covariance matrix during the estimation process. For example, one can include information on the underlying economic variables or *factors* contributing to the movement of securities. This is the basic idea behind many asset pricing and factor models that we will describe in subsequent sections. Such models are intuitive and practical, and are very widely used.

It is important to remember, however, that introducing a structure for any statistical estimator comes at a price. Structured estimators can suffer from specification error, that is, the assumptions made may be too restrictive for accurate forecasting of reality. As a solution, Jagannathan and Ma[38] proposed using portfolios of covariance matrix estimators. Their idea was to "diversify away" the estimation and specification errors to which all covariance matrix estimators are subject. Portfolios of estimators are typically constructed in a simple fashion: they are equally weighted, and easier to compute than, say, shrinkage estimators. For example, one of the portfolios of estimators suggested by Jagannathan and Ma and Bengtsson and Holst[39] consists of the average of the sample covariance matrix, a single-index matrix, and a matrix containing only the diagonal elements of the sample matrix. The latter matrix is more stable than a full asset-asset covariance matrix, as the sample covariance matrix is frequently noninvertible due to noisy data and in general may result in ill-conditioned mean-variance portfolio optimization. The single-index matrix is a covariance matrix estimator obtained by assuming that returns are generated according to Sharpe's classical single-index factor model.[40] Other portfolios of estimators add the matrix of constant correlations (a highly structured covariance matrix that assumes that each pair of assets has the same correlation). Interestingly, a recent study of several portfolio and shrinkage covariance matrix estimators using historical data on stocks traded on the New York Stock Exchange

[38]Ravi Jagannathan and Tongshu Ma, "Three Methods for Improving the Precision in Covariance Matrix Estimators," Manuscript, Kellogg School of Management, Northwestern University, 2000.
[39]Christoffer Bengtsson and Jan Holst, "On Portfolio Selection: Improved Covariance Matrix Estimation for Swedish Asset Returns," Working Paper, Lund University and Lund Institute of Technology.
[40]William Sharpe, "A Simplified Model for Portfolio Analysis," *Management Science*, 9 (1963), pp. 277–293. Sharpe suggested a single-factor model for returns, where the single factor is a market index. We will discuss factor models later in this chapter.

concluded that while portfolios of estimators and shrinkage estimators of the covariance matrix were indisputably better than the simple sample covariance matrix estimator, there were no statistically significant differences in portfolio performance over time between stock portfolios constructed using simple portfolios of covariance matrix estimators and stock portfolios constructed using shrinkage estimators of the covariance matrix, at least for this particular set of data.[41] As a general matter, it is always important to test any particular estimator of the covariance matrix for the specific asset classes and data with which a portfolio manager is dealing before adopting it for portfolio management purposes.

Further Practical Considerations

In this subsection, we consider some techniques that are important for a more successful implementation of the sample mean and covariance matrix estimators, as well as advanced estimators encountered in practice.

Heteroskedasticity and Autocorrelation Consistent Covariance Matrix Estimation

Financial return series exhibit serial correlation and heteroskedasticity.[42] *Serial correlation*, also referred to as *autocorrelation*, is the correlation of the return of a security with itself over successive time intervals. The presence of heteroskedasticity means that variances/covariances are not constant but time varying. These two effects introduce biases in the estimated covariance matrix. Fortunately, there are simple and straightforward techniques available that almost automatically correct for these biases.

Probably the most popular techniques include the approaches by Newey and West,[43] and its extension by Andrews,[44] often referred to as "Newey-West corrections" in the financial literature.[45]

---

[41]David Disatnik and Simon Bennings, "Shrinking the Covariance Matrix—Simpler is Better," *Journal of Portfolio Management*, 33 (2007), pp. 56–63.

[42]See John Y. Campbell, Andrew W. Lo, and A. Craig MacKinlay, *The Econometrics of Financial Markets* (Princeton, NJ: Princeton University Press, 1997).

[43]Whitney K. Newey and Kenneth D. West, "A Simple, Positive Semidefinite Heteroskedasticity and Autocorrelation Consistent Covariance Matrix," *Econometrica*, 56 (1987), pp. 203–208.

[44]Donald W. K. Andrews, "Heteroskedasticity and Autocorrelation Consistent Covariance Matrix Estimation," *Econometrica*, 59 (1991), pp. 817–858.

[45]However, these techniques can be traced back to work done by Jowett and Hannan in the 1950s. See G. H. Jowett, "The Comparison of Means of Sets of Observations from Sections of Independent Stochastic Series," *Journal of the Royal Statistical Society*, Series B, 17 (1955), pp. 208–227; and E. J. Hannan, "The Variance of the

Dealing with Missing and Truncated Data

In practice, we have to deal with the fact that no data series are perfect. There will be missing and errant observations, or just simply not enough data. If care is not taken, this can lead to poorly estimated models and inferior investment performance. Typically, it is tedious but very important work to clean data series for practical use. Some statistical techniques are available for dealing with missing observations; the so-called *expectation maximization* (EM) algorithm being among the most popular for financial applications.[46]

Longer daily return data series are often available from well-established companies in developed countries. However, if we turn to newer companies, or companies in emerging markets, this is often not the case. Say that we have a portfolio of 10 assets, of which five have a return history of 10 years, while the other five have only been around for three years. We could, for example, truncate the data series making all of them three years long and then calculate the sample covariance matrix. But by using the method proposed by Stambaugh,[47] we can do better than that. Simplistically speaking, starting from the truncated sample covariance matrix, this technique produces improvements to the covariance matrix that utilizes all the available data.

Data Frequency

Merton[48] shows that even if the expected returns are constant over time, a long history would still be required in order to estimate them accurately. The situation is very different for variances and covariances. Under reasonable assumptions, it can be shown that estimates of these quantities can be improved by *increasing the sampling frequency*.

However, not everyone has the luxury of having access to high-frequency or tick-by-tick data. An improved estimator of volatility can be achieved by using the daily high, low, opening, and closing prices, along with the

---

Mean of a Stationary Process," *Journal of the Royal Statistical Society*, Series B, 19 (1957), pp. 282–285.

[46]See Roderick J. A. Little and Donald B. Rubin, *Statistical Analysis with Missing Data* (New York: Wiley-Interscience, 2002); and Joe L. Schafer, *Analysis of Incomplete Multivariate Data* (Boca Raton, FL: Chapman & Hall/CRC, 1997).

[47]For a more detailed description of the technique, see Robert F. Stambaugh, "Analyzing Investments Whose Histories Differ in Length," *Journal of Financial Economics*, 45 (1997), pp. 285–331.

[48]Robert C. Merton, "On Estimating the Expected Return on the Market: An Exploratory Investigation," *Journal of Financial Economics*, 8 (1980), pp. 323–361.

transaction volume.[49] These types of estimators are typically referred to as *Garman-Klass estimators.*

Some guidance can also be gained from the option pricing literature. As suggested by Burghardt and Lane, when historical volatility is calculated for *option pricing purposes*, the time horizon for sampling should be equal to the time to maturity of the option.[50]

As Butler and Schachter point out, when historical data are used for volatility forecasting purposes, the bias found in the estimator tends to increase with the sample length.[51] However, it can be problematic to use information based on too short time periods. In this case, often the volatility estimator becomes highly sensitive to short-term regimes, such as over- and underreaction corrections.

PORTFOLIO OPTIMIZATION WITH OTHER RISK MEASURES

Generally speaking, the main objective of portfolio selection is the construction of portfolios that maximize expected returns at a certain level of risk. It is now well known that asset returns are not normal and, therefore, the mean and the variance alone do not fully describe the characteristics of the joint asset return distribution. Indeed, many risks and undesirable scenarios faced by a portfolio manager cannot be captured solely by the variance of the portfolio. Consequently, especially in cases of significant nonnormality, the classical mean-variance approach will not be a satisfactory portfolio allocation model. Since about the mid-1990s, considerable thought and innovation in the financial industry have been directed toward creating a better understanding of risk and its measurement, and toward improving the management of risk in financial portfolios. From the statistical point of view, a key innovation is the attention paid to the ratio between the bulk of the risk and the risk of the tails. The latter has become a critical statistical determinant of risk management policies. Changing situations and different portfolios may require alternative and new risk measures. The race for inventing the best risk measure for a given situation or portfolio is still ongoing. It is possible that we will never find a completely satisfactory answer

---

[49]See Mark B. Garman and Michael J. Klass, "On the Estimation of Security Price Volatilities from Historical Data," *Journal of Business,* 53 (1980), pp. 67–78; and Michael Parkinson, "The Extreme Value Method for Estimating the Variance of the Rate of Return," *Journal of Business,* 53 (1980), pp. 61–65.
[50]Galen Burghardt and Morton Lane, "How to Tell if Options Are Cheap," *Journal of Portfolio Management,* 16 (1990), pp. 72–78.
[51]John S. Butler and Barry Schachter, "Unbiased Estimation of the Black-Scholes Formula," *Journal of Financial Economics,* 15 (1986), pp. 341–357.

to the question of which risk measure to use, and the choice to some extent remains an art.

We distinguish between two different types of risk measures: (1) dispersion and (2) downside measures. We begin with an overview of the most common dispersion and downside measures.[52] We close this section with a derivation of a mean-CVaR portfolio optimization model.

Dispersion Measures

Dispersion measures are measures of uncertainty. Uncertainty, however, does not necessarily quantify risk. Dispersion measures consider *both* positive and negative deviations from the mean, and treat those deviations as equally risky. In other words, overperformance relative to the mean is penalized as much as underperformance. In this section, we review the most popular and important portfolio dispersion measures such as mean standard deviation, mean absolute deviation, and mean absolute moment.

Mean Standard Deviation and the Mean-Variance Approach

For historical reasons, portfolio standard deviation (or portfolio variance) is probably the most well-known dispersion measure because of its use in classical portfolio theory (i.e., mean-variance framework).

Mean Absolute Deviation

Konno[53] introduced the *mean absolute deviation* (MAD) approach in 1988. Rather than using squared deviations as in the mean-variance approach, here the dispersion measure is based on the absolution deviations from the mean; that is, it is defined as

$$MAD(R_p) = E\left(\left|\sum_{i=1}^{N} w_i R_i - \sum_{i=1}^{N} w_i \mu_i\right|\right)$$

where

---

[52]For a further discussion, see Sergio Ortobelli, Svetlozar T. Rachev, Stoyanov, Frank J. Fabozzi, and Almira Biglova, "The Correct Use of Risk Measures in Portfolio Theory," *International Journal of Theoretical and Applied Finance*, 8 (2005), pp. 1–27.

[53]Hiroshi Konno, "Portfolio Optimization Using L1 Risk Function," IHSS Report 88-9, Institute of Human and Social Sciences, Tokyo Institute of Technology, 1988. See also, Hiroshi Konno, "Piecewise Linear Risk Functions and Portfolio Optimization," *Journal of the Operations Research Society of Japan*, 33 (1990), pp. 139–156.

$$R_p = \sum_{i=1}^{N} w_i R_i$$

R_i and μ_i are the portfolio return, the return on asset i, and the expected return on asset i, respectively.

The computation of optimal portfolios in the case of the mean absolute deviation approach is significantly simplified, as the resulting optimization problem is linear and can be solved by standard linear programming routines.

We note that it can be shown that under the assumption that the individual asset returns are multivariate normally distributed,

$$MAD(R_p) = \sqrt{\frac{2}{\pi}}\sigma_p$$

where σ_p is the standard deviation of the portfolio.[54] That is, when asset returns are normally distributed, the mean absolute deviation and the mean-variance approaches are equivalent.

Mean Absolute Moment

The mean-absolute moment (MAMq) of order q is defined by

$$MAM_q(R_p) = \left(E\left(\left| R_p - E(R_p) \right|^q \right) \right)^{1/q}, q \ge 1$$

and is a straightforward generalization of the mean-standard deviation ($q = 2$) and the mean absolute deviation ($q = 1$) approaches.

Downside Measures

The objective in downside risk measure portfolio allocation models is the maximization of the probability that the portfolio return is above a certain minimal acceptable level, often also referred to as the *benchmark level* or *disaster level*.

Despite their theoretical appeal, downside or safety-first risk measures are often computationally more complicated to use in a portfolio context. Downside risk measures of individual securities cannot be easily aggregated into portfolio downside risk measures, as their computation requires knowledge of the entire joint distribution of security returns. Often, one has to

---

[54]Hiroshi Konno and Hiroaki Yamazaki, "Mean-Absolute Deviation Portfolio Optimization Model and its Application to Tokyo Stock Market," *Management Science*, 37 (1991), pp. 519–531.

resort to computationally intensive nonparametric estimation, simulation, and optimization techniques. Furthermore, the estimation risk of downside measures is usually greater than for standard mean-variance approaches. By the estimation of downside risk measures, we only use a portion of the original data—maybe even just the tail of the empirical distribution—and hence the estimation error increases.[55] Nevertheless, these risk measures are very useful in assessing the risk of securities with asymmetric return distributions, such as call and put options, as well as other derivative contracts.

We discuss some of the most common safety-first and downside risk measures such as Roy's safety-first, semivariance, lower partial moment, Value-at-Risk, and conditional Value-at-Risk.

Roy's Safety-First

Two very important papers on portfolio selection were published in 1952: first, Markowitz's[56] paper on portfolio selection and classical portfolio theory; second, Roy's[57] paper on *safety first*, which laid the seed for the development of downside risk measures.[58]

Let us first understand the difference between these two approaches.[59] According to classical portfolio theory, an investor constructs a portfolio that represents a trade-off between risk and return. The trade-off between risk and return and the portfolio allocation depend upon the investor's utility function. It can be hard, or even impossible, to determine an investor's actual utility function.

Roy argued that an investor, rather than thinking in terms of utility functions, first wants to make sure that a certain amount of the principal is preserved. Thereafter, he decides on some minimal acceptable return that achieves this principal preservation. In essence, the investor chooses his portfolio by solving the following optimization problem

[55]For further discussion of these issues, see Henk Grootveld and Winfried G. Hallerbach, "Variance Versus Downside Risk: Is There Really That Much Difference?" *European Journal of Operational Research*, 114 (1999), pp. 304–319.

[56]Harry M. Markowitz, "Portfolio Selection," *Journal of Finance*, 7 (1952), pp. 77–91.

[57]Andrew D. Roy, "Safety-First and the Holding of Assets," *Econometrica*, 20 (1952), pp. 431–449.

[58]See, for example, Vijay S. Bawa, "Optimal Rules for Ordering Uncertain Prospects," *Journal of Financial Economics*, 2 (1975), pp. 95–121; and Vijay S. Bawa, "Safety-First Stochastic Dominance and Portfolio Choice," *Journal of Financial and Quantitative Analysis*, 13 (1978), pp. 255–271.

[59]For a more detailed description of these historical events, we refer the reader to David Nawrocki, "A Brief History of Downside Risk Measures," *Journal of Investing* (1999), pp. 9–26.

$$\min_{w} P(R_p \leq R_0)$$

subject to

$$w'\iota = 1, \iota' = [1, 1, \ldots, 1]$$

where P is the probability function and

$$R_p = \sum_{i=1}^{N} w_i R_i$$

is the portfolio return. Most likely, the investor will not know the true probability function. However, by using Tchebycheff's inequality, we obtain[60]

$$P(R_p \leq R_0) \leq \frac{\sigma_p^2}{(\mu_p - R_0)^2}$$

where μ_p and σ_p denote the expected return and the variance of the portfolio, respectively. Therefore, not knowing the probability function, the investor will end up solving the approximation

$$\min_{w} \frac{\sigma_p}{\mu_p - R_0}$$

subject to

$$w'\iota = 1, \iota' = [1, 1, \ldots, 1]$$

We note that if R_0 is equal to the risk-free rate, then this optimization problem is equivalent to maximizing a portfolio's Sharpe ratio.

---

[60]For a random variable x with expected value μ and variance σ_x^2, Tchebycheff's inequality states that for any positive real number c, it holds that

$$P(|x - \mu| > c) \leq \frac{\sigma_x^2}{c^2}$$

Applying Tchebycheff's inequality, we get

$$P(R_p \leq R_0) = P(\mu_p - R_p \geq \mu_p - R_0) \leq \frac{\sigma_p^2}{(\mu_p - R_0)^2}$$

Semivariance

In his original book, Markowitz proposed the usage of *semivariance* to correct for the fact that variance penalizes overperformance and underperformance equally.[61] When receiving his Nobel Prize in Economic Science, Markowitz stated that "... it can further help evaluate the adequacy of mean and variance, or alternative practical measures, as criteria." Furthermore, he added "Perhaps some other measure of portfolio risk will serve in a two parameter analysis. ... Semivariance seems more plausible than variance as a measure of risk, since it is concerned only with adverse deviations."[62]

The portfolio semivariance is defined as

$$\sigma^2_{p,\min} = E\left(\min\left(\sum_{i=1}^{N} w_i R_i - \sum_{i=1}^{N} w_i \mu_i, 0 \right) \right)^2$$

where

$$R_p = \sum_{i=1}^{N} w_i R_i$$

R_i and μ_i are the portfolio return, the return on asset i, and the expected return on asset i, respectively. Jin, Markowitz, and Zhou provide some of the theoretical properties of the mean-semivariance approach both in the single-period as well as in the continuous-time setting.[63] A generalization to the semivariance is provided by the lower partial moment risk measure that we discuss in the next subsection.

Lower Partial Moment

The *lower partial moment risk measure* provides a natural generalization of semivariance that we described previously (see, for example, Bawa[64] and Fishburn[65]). The lower partial moment with *power index q* and the *target rate of return R_0* is given by

[61]Harry Markowitz, *Portfolio Selection—Efficient Diversification of Investment* (New York: Wiley, 1959).
[62]Harry Markowitz, "Foundations of Portfolio Theory," *Journal of Finance*, 46 (1991), pp. 469–477.
[63]Hanqing Jin, Harry Markowitz, and Xunyu Zhou, "A Note on Semivariance," Forthcoming in *Mathematical Finance*.
[64]Vijay S. Bawa, "Admissible Portfolio for All Individuals," *Journal of Finance*, 31 (1976), pp. 1169–1183.
[65]Peter C. Fishburn, "Mean-Risk Analysis with Risk Associated with Below-Target Returns," *American Economic Review,* 67 (1977), pp. 116–126.

$$\sigma_{R_p,q,R_0} = (E(\min(R_p - R_0, 0)^q))^{1/q}$$

where

$$R_p = \sum_{i=1}^{N} w_i R_i$$

is the portfolio return. The target rate of return R_0 is what Roy termed the *disaster level*.[66] We recognize that by setting $q = 2$ and R_0 equal to the expected return, the semivariance is obtained. Fishburn demonstrated that $q = 1$ represents a risk neutral investor, whereas $0 < q \leq 1$ and $q > 1$ correspond to a risk-seeking and a risk-averse investor, respectively.

Value-at-Risk

Probably the most well-known downside risk measure is *Value-at-Risk* (VaR), first developed by JP Morgan, and made available through the Risk-Metrics™ software in October 1994.[67] VaR is related to the percentiles of loss distributions, and measures the predicted maximum loss at a specified probability level (for example, 95%) over a certain time horizon (for example, 10 days). Today VaR is used by most financial institutions to both track and report the market risk exposure of their trading portfolios.

Formally, VaR is defined as

$$VaR_{1-\varepsilon}(R_p) = \min\{R \,|\, P(-R_p \geq R) \leq \varepsilon\}$$

where P denotes the probability function. Typical values for $(1 - \varepsilon)$ are 90%, 95%, and 99%.[68] Some of the practical and computational issues

---

[66]Roy, "Safety-First and the Holding of Assets."

[67]JP Morgan/Reuters, *RiskMetrics™—Technical Document*, 4th ed. (New York: Morgan Guaranty Trust Company of New York, 1996). See also http://www.risk metrics.com.

[68]There are several equivalent ways to define VaR mathematically. In this book, we generally use ε to denote small numbers, so the expression

$$VaR_{1-\varepsilon}(R_p) = \min \{R|P(-R_p \geq R) \leq \varepsilon\}$$

emphasizes the fact that the $(1 - \varepsilon)$-VaR is the value R such that the probability that the possible portfolio loss $(-R_p)$ exceeds R is at most some small number ε such as 1%, 5%, or 10%. For example, the 95% VaR for a portfolio is the value R such that the probability that the possible portfolio loss exceeds R is less than $\varepsilon = 5\%$.

An alternative, and equivalent way to define $(1 - \varepsilon)$-VaR is as the value R such that the probability that the maximum portfolio loss $(-R_p)$ is at most R is at least

related to using VaR are discussed in Alexander and Baptista,[69] Gaivoronski and Pflug,[70] and Mittnik, Rachev, and Schwartz.[71] Chow and Kritzman discuss the usage of VaR in formulating risk budgets, and provide an intuitive method for converting efficient portfolio allocations into value-at-risk assignments.[72] In a subsequent article, they discuss some of the problems with the simplest approach for computing the VaR of a portfolio.[73] In particular, the common assumption that the portfolio itself is lognormally distributed can be somewhat problematic, especially for portfolios that contain both long and short positions.

VaR also has several undesirable properties as a risk measure.[74] First, it is not subadditive, so the risk as measured by the VaR of a portfolio of two funds may be higher than the sum of the risks of the two individual portfolios. In other words, for VaR it *does not* hold that $\rho(R_1 + R_2) \leq \rho(R_1) + \rho(R_2)$ for all returns R_1, R_2. The subadditivity property is the mathematical description of the diversification effect. It is unreasonable to think that

some large number $(1 - \varepsilon)$ such as 99%, 95%, or 90%. Mathematically, this can be expressed as

$$VaR_{1-\varepsilon}(R_p) = \min \{R | P(-R_p \leq R) \geq 1 - \varepsilon\}$$

In some standard references, the parameter ε is used to denote the "large" probability in the VaR definition, such as 99%, 95% or 90%. VaR is referred to as α-VaR, and is defined as

$$VaR_\alpha(R_p) = \min \{R | P(-R_p \leq R) \geq \alpha\}$$

Notice that there is no mathematical difference between the VaR definitions that involve α or ε, because α is in fact $(1 - \varepsilon)$. In this book, we prefer using ε instead of α in the VaR definition so as to avoid confusion with the term *alpha* used in asset return estimation.

[69]Gordon J. Alexander and Alexandre M. Baptista, "Economic Implications of Using a Mean-VaR Model for Portfolio Selection: A Comparison with Mean-Variance Analysis," *Journal of Economic Dynamics and Control*, 26 (2002), pp. 1159–1193.
[70]Alexei A. Gaivoronski and Georg Pflug, "Value-at-Risk in Portfolio Optimization: Properties and Computational Approach," *Journal of Risk*, 7 (2005), pp. 1–31.
[71]Stefan Mittnik, Svetlotzar Rachev, and Eduardo Schwartz, "Value At-Risk and Asset Allocation with Stable Return Distributions," *Allgemeines Statistisches Archiv*, 86 (2003), pp. 53–67.
[72]George Chow and Mark Kritzman, "Risk Budgets—Converting Mean-Variance Optimization into VaR Assignments," *Journal of Portfolio Management*, 27 (2001), pp. 56–60.
[73]George Chow and Mark Kritzman, "Value at Risk for Portfolios with Short Positions," *Journal of Portfolio Management*, 28 (2002), pp. 73–81.
[74]Hans Rau-Bredow, "Value-at-Risk, Expected Shortfall and Marginal Risk Contribution," in Giorgio Szegö (ed.) *Risk Measures for the 21st Century* (Chichester: John Wiley & Sons, 2004), pp. 61–68.

a more diversified portfolio would have higher risk, so nonsubadditive risk measures are undesirable. Second, when VaR is calculated from generated scenarios, it is a nonsmooth and nonconvex function of the portfolio holdings. As a consequence, the VaR function has multiple stationary points, making it computationally both difficult and time-consuming to find the global optimal point in the optimization process for portfolio allocation.[75] Third, VaR does not take the *magnitude* of the losses beyond the VaR value into account. For example, it is very unlikely that an investor will be indifferent between two portfolios with identical expected return and VaR when the return distribution of one portfolio has a short left tail and the other has a long left tail. These undesirable features motivated the development of Conditional Value-at-Risk that we discuss next.

Conditional Value-at-Risk

The deficiencies of Value-at-Risk led Artzner et al. to propose a set of desirable properties for a risk measure.[76] They called risk measures satisfying these properties *coherent risk measures*.[77] *Conditional Value-at-Risk* (CVaR) is a coherent risk measure defined by the formula

---

[75]For some possible remedies and fixes to this problem see, Henk Grootveld and Winfried G. Hallerbach, "Upgrading Value-at-Risk from Diagnostic Metric to Decision Variable: A Wise Thing to Do?" in *Risk Measures for the 21st Century*, pp. 33–50. We will discuss computational issues with portfolio VaR optimization in more detail in Chapters 13 and 19.

[76]Philippe Artzner, Freddy Delbaen, Jean-Marc Eber, and David Heath, "Coherent Measures of Risk," *Mathematical Finance*, 9 (1999), pp. 203–228.

[77]A risk measure ρ is called a coherent measure of risk if it satisfies the following properties:

1. *Monotonicity.* If $X \geq 0$, then $\rho(X) \leq 0$
2. *Subadditivity.* $\rho(X + Y) \leq \rho(X) + \rho(Y)$
3. *Positive homogeneity.* For any positive real number c, $\rho(cX) = c\rho(X)$
4. *Translational invariance.* For any real number c, $\rho(X + c) \leq \rho(X) - c$

where X and Y are random variables. In words, these properties can be interpreted as: (1) If there are only positive returns, then the risk should be nonpositive; (2) the risk of a portfolio of two assets should be less than or equal to the sum of the risks of the individual assets; (3) if the portfolio is increased c times, the risk becomes c times larger; and (4) cash or another risk-free asset does not contribute to portfolio risk.

Interestingly, standard deviation, a very popular risk measure, is not coherent—it violates the monotonicity property. It does, however, satisfy subadditivity, which is considered one of the most important properties. The four properties required for coherence are actually quite restrictive: when taken together, they rule out a number of other popular risk measures as well. For example, semideviation-type risk measures violate the subadditivity condition.

$$CVaR_{1-\varepsilon}(R_p) = E(-R_p | -R_p \geq VaR_{1-\varepsilon}(R_p))$$

Therefore, CVaR measures the expected amount of losses in the tail of the distribution of possible portfolio losses, beyond the portfolio VaR. In the literature, this risk measure is also referred to as *expected shortfall*,[78] *expected tail loss* (ETL), and *tail VaR*. As with VaR, the most commonly considered values for $(1 - \varepsilon)$ are 90%, 95%, and 99%.

Mean-CVaR Optimization

In this subsection we develop a model for mean-CVaR optimization. Here, the objective is to maximize expected return subject to that the portfolio risk, measured by CVaR, is no larger than some value. Mathematically, we can express this as

$$\max_{\mathbf{w}} \boldsymbol{\mu}'\mathbf{w}$$

subject to

$$CVaR_{1-\varepsilon}(\mathbf{w}) \leq c_0$$

along with any other constraints on $\mathbf{w}$ (represented by $\mathbf{w} \in C_{\mathbf{w}}$), where $\boldsymbol{\mu}$ represents the vector of expected returns, and c_0 is a constant denoting the required level of risk.

Before we formulate the mean-CVaR optimization problem, we need some useful mathematical properties of the CVaR measure. To this end, let us denote by $\mathbf{w}$ the N-dimensional portfolio vector such that each component $\mathbf{w}_i$ equals the number of shares held in asset i. Furthermore, we denote by $\mathbf{y}$ a random vector describing the uncertain outcomes (also referred to as *market variables*) of the economy. We let the function $f(\mathbf{w},\mathbf{y})$ (also referred to as the *loss function*) represent the loss associated with the portfolio vector $\mathbf{w}$. Note that for each $\mathbf{w}$ the loss function $f(\mathbf{w},\mathbf{y})$ is a one-dimensional random variable. We let $p(\mathbf{y})$ be the probability associated with scenario $\mathbf{y}$.

Now, assuming that all random values are discrete, the probability that the loss function does not exceed a certain value γ is given by the cumulative probability

$$\Psi(\mathbf{w}, \gamma) = \sum_{\{\mathbf{y}|f(\mathbf{w},\mathbf{y})\leq\gamma\}} p(\mathbf{y})$$

---

[78]Strictly speaking, expected shortfall is defined in a different way, but is shown to be equivalent to CVaR (see Carlo Acerbi and Dirk Tasche, "On the Coherence of Expected Shortfall," *Journal of Banking and Finance*, 26 (2002), pp. 1487–1503).

Using this cumulative probability, we see that

$$VaR_{1-\varepsilon}(\mathbf{w}) = \min\{\gamma \,|\, \Psi(\mathbf{w},\gamma) \geq 1-\varepsilon\}$$

Since CVaR of the losses of portfolio $\mathbf{w}$ is the expected value of the losses conditioned on the losses being in excess of VaR, we have that

$$CVaR_{1-\varepsilon}(\mathbf{w}) = E(f(\mathbf{w},\mathbf{y}) | f(\mathbf{w},\mathbf{y}) > VaR_{1-\varepsilon}(\mathbf{w}))$$

$$= \frac{\sum_{\{\mathbf{y}|f(\mathbf{w},\mathbf{y})>VaR_{1-\varepsilon}(\mathbf{w})\}} p(\mathbf{y})f(\mathbf{w},\mathbf{y})}{\sum_{\{\mathbf{y}|f(\mathbf{w},\mathbf{y})>VaR_{1-\varepsilon}(\mathbf{w})\}} p(\mathbf{y})}$$

The continuous equivalents of these formulas are

$$\Psi(\mathbf{w},\mathbf{y}) = \int_{f(\mathbf{w},\mathbf{y})\leq\gamma} p(\mathbf{y})dy$$

$$VaR_{1-\varepsilon}(\mathbf{w}) = \min\{\gamma \,|\, \Psi(\mathbf{w},\gamma) \geq 1-\varepsilon\}$$

$$CVaR_{1-\varepsilon}(\mathbf{w}) = E(f(\mathbf{w},\mathbf{y}) | f(\mathbf{w},\mathbf{y}) \geq VaR_{1-\varepsilon}(\mathbf{w}))$$

$$= \varepsilon^{-1} \int_{f(\mathbf{w},\mathbf{y})\geq VaR_{1-\varepsilon}(\mathbf{w})} f(\mathbf{w},\mathbf{y})p(\mathbf{y})dy$$

We note that in the continuous case it holds that $\Psi(\mathbf{w},\gamma) = 1 - \varepsilon$ and therefore the denominator

$$\sum_{\{\mathbf{y}|f(\mathbf{w},\mathbf{y})>VaR_{1-\varepsilon}(\mathbf{w})\}} p(\mathbf{y})$$

in the discrete version of CVaR becomes ε in the continuous case.
Moreover, we see that

$$CVaR_{1-\varepsilon}(\mathbf{w}) = \varepsilon^{-1} \int_{f(\mathbf{w},\mathbf{y})\geq VaR_{1-\varepsilon}(\mathbf{w})} f(\mathbf{w},\mathbf{y})p(\mathbf{y})dy$$

$$\geq \varepsilon^{-1} \int_{f(\mathbf{w},\mathbf{y})\geq VaR_{1-\varepsilon}(\mathbf{w})} VaR_{1-\varepsilon}(\mathbf{w})p(\mathbf{y})dy$$

$$= VaR_{1-\varepsilon}(\mathbf{w})$$

because

$$\varepsilon^{-1} \int_{f(\mathbf{w},\mathbf{y})\geq VaR_{1-\varepsilon}(\mathbf{w})} p(\mathbf{y})dy = 1$$

In other words, CVaR is always at least as large as VaR, but as we mentioned above, CVaR is a coherent risk measure, whereas VaR is not. It can also be shown that CVaR is a concave function and, therefore, has a unique minimum. However, working directly with the above formulas turns out to be somewhat tricky in practice as they involve the VaR function (except for those rare cases when one has an analytical expression for VaR). Fortunately, a simpler approach was discovered by Rockefellar and Uryasev.[79]

Their idea is that the function

$$F_\varepsilon(\mathbf{w},\xi) = \xi + \varepsilon^{-1} \int_{f(\mathbf{w},\mathbf{y})\geq\gamma} (f(\mathbf{w},\mathbf{y}) - \xi)p(\mathbf{y})d\mathbf{y}$$

can be used instead of CVaR. Specifically, they proved the following three important properties:

Property 1. $F_\varepsilon(\mathbf{w},\xi)$ is a convex and continuously differentiable function in ξ.

Property 2. $VaR_{1-\varepsilon}(\mathbf{w})$ is a minimizer of $F_\varepsilon(\mathbf{w},\xi)$.

Property 3. The minimum value of $F_\varepsilon(\mathbf{w},\xi)$ is $CVaR_{1-\varepsilon}(\mathbf{w})$.

In particular, we can find the optimal value of $CVaR_{1-\varepsilon}(\mathbf{w})$ by solving the optimization problem

$$\min_{\mathbf{w},\xi} F_\varepsilon(\mathbf{w},\xi)$$

Consequently, if we denote by $(\mathbf{w}^*, \xi^*)$ the solution to this optimization problem, then $F_\varepsilon(\mathbf{w}^*, \xi^*)$ is the optimal CVaR. In addition, the optimal portfolio is given by $\mathbf{w}^*$ and the corresponding VaR is given by ξ^*. In other words, in this fashion we can compute the optimal CVaR *without* first calculating VaR.

In practice, the probability density function $p(\mathbf{y})$ is often not available, or is very difficult to estimate. Instead, we might have T different scenarios $Y = \{\mathbf{y}_1, \ldots, \mathbf{y}_T\}$ that are sampled from the probability distribution or that have been obtained from computer simulations. Evaluating the auxiliary function $F_\xi(\mathbf{w}, \xi)$ using the scenarios Y, we obtain

$$F_\varepsilon^Y(\mathbf{w},\xi) = \xi + \varepsilon^{-1}T^{-1}\sum_{i=1}^{T} \max(f(\mathbf{w},\mathbf{y}_i) - \xi, 0)$$

---

[79]See Stanislav Uryasev, "Conditional Value-at-Risk: Optimization Algorithms and Applications," *Financial Engineering News*, 14 (2000), pp. 1–5; and R. Tyrrell Rockefellar and Stanislav Uryasev, "Optimization of Conditional Value-at-Risk," *Journal of Risk*, 2 (2000), pp. 21–41.

Therefore, in this case the optimization problem

$$\min_{\mathbf{w}} CVaR_{1-\varepsilon}(\mathbf{w})$$

takes the form

$$\min_{\mathbf{w},\xi} \xi + \varepsilon^{-1}T^{-1}\sum_{i=1}^{T} \max(f(\mathbf{w},\mathbf{y}_i) - \xi, 0)$$

Replacing $\max(f(\mathbf{w}, \mathbf{y}_i) - \xi, 0)$ by the auxiliary variables z_i along with appropriate constraints, we obtain the equivalent optimization problem

$$\min \xi + \varepsilon^{-1}T^{-1}\sum_{i=1}^{T} z_i$$

subject to

$$z_i \geq 0, \, i = 1, \dots, T$$

$$z_i \geq f(\mathbf{w},\mathbf{y}_i) - \xi, \, i = 1, \dots, T$$

along with any other constraints on $\mathbf{w}$, such as no short-selling constraints or any of the constraints we discussed previously in this chapter. Under the assumption that $f(\mathbf{w},\mathbf{y})$ is linear in $\mathbf{w}$,[80] the above optimization problem is linear and can therefore be solved very efficiently by standard linear programming techniques.[81]

The formulation discussed previously can be seen as an extension of calculating the GMV and can be used as an alternative when the underlying asset return distribution is asymmetric and exhibits fat tails.

Moreover, the representation of CVaR given by the auxiliary function $F_{\varepsilon}(\mathbf{w}, \xi)$ can be used in the construction of other portfolio optimization problems. For example, the mean-CVaR optimization problem

---

[80]This is typically the case as the loss function in the discrete case is chosen to be

$$f(\mathbf{w},\mathbf{y}) = -\sum_{i=1}^{N} w_i(\mathbf{y}_i - x_i)$$

where x_i is the current price of security i.
[81]See, for example, Chapter 9 in Frank J. Fabozzi, Sergio M. Focardi, Petter N. Kolm, and Dessislava Pachamanova, *Robust Portfolio Optimization and Management* (Hoboken, NJ: John Wiley & Sons, 2007) for a discussion of numerical optimization techniques used in portfolio management.

$$\max_{\mathbf{w}} \boldsymbol{\mu}' \mathbf{w}$$

subject to

$$\mathrm{CVaR}_{1-\varepsilon}(\mathbf{w}) \leq c_0$$

along with any other constraints on $\mathbf{w}$ (represented by $\mathbf{w} \in C_{\mathbf{w}}$), where $\boldsymbol{\mu}$ represents the vector of expected returns, and c_0 is a constant denoting the required level of risk, would result in the following approximation

$$\max_{\mathbf{w}} \boldsymbol{\mu}' \mathbf{w}$$

subject to

$$\xi + \varepsilon^{-1} T^{-1} \sum_{i=1}^{T} z_i \leq c_0$$
$$z_i \geq 0, 0 = 1, \dots, T$$
$$z_i \geq f(\mathbf{w}, \mathbf{y}_i) - \xi, 0 = 1, \dots, T$$
$$\mathbf{w} \in C_{\mathbf{w}}$$

To illustrate the mean-CVaR optimization approach, we discuss an example from Palmquist, Uryasev, and Krokhmal.[82] They considered two-week returns for all the stocks in the S&P 100 Index over the period July 1, 1997 to July 8, 1999 for scenario generation. Optimal portfolios were constructed by solving the preceding mean-CVaR optimization problem for a two-week horizon for different levels of confidence. In Exhibit 8.3 we see three different mean-CVaR efficient frontiers corresponding to $(1 - \varepsilon) =$ 90%, 95%, and 99%. The two-week rate of return is calculated as the ratio of the optimized portfolio value divided by the initial value, and the risk is calculated as the percentage of the initial portfolio value that is allowed to be put at risk. In other words, when the risk is 7% and $(1 - \varepsilon)$ is 95%, this means that we allow for no more than a 7% loss of the initial value of the portfolio with a probability of 5%. We observe from the exhibit that as the CVaR constraint decreases (i.e., the probability increases) the rate of return increases.

It can be shown that for a normally distributed loss function, the mean-variance and the mean-CVaR frameworks generate the same efficient frontier. However, when distributions are nonnormal these two approaches are

---

[82]Pavlo Krokhmal, Jonas Palmquist, and Stanislav Uryasev, "Portfolio Optimization with Conditional Value-At-Risk Objective and Constraints," *Journal of Risk*, 4 (2002), pp. 11–27.

EXHIBIT 8.3   Efficient Frontiers of Different Mean-CVaR Portfolios

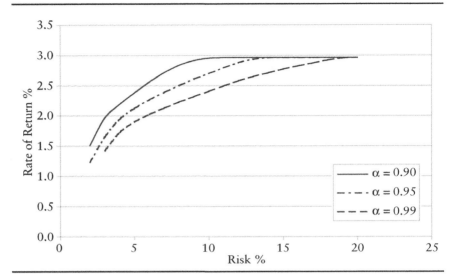

Source: Pavlo Krokhmal, Jonas Palmquist, and Stanislav Uryasev, "Portfolio Optimization with Conditional Value-At-Risk Objective and Constraints," *The Journal of Risk* 4, no. 2 (2002), p. 21. This copyrighted material is reprinted with permission from Incisive Media Plc, Haymarket House, 28-29 Haymarket, London, SW1Y 4RX, United Kingdom.

significantly different. On the one hand, in the mean-variance approach risk is defined by the variance of the loss distribution, and because the variance incorporates information from both the left as well as the right tail of the distribution, both the gains and losses are contributing equally to the risk. On the other hand, the mean-CVaR methodology only involves the part of the tail of the distribution that contributes to high losses.

In Exhibit 8.4 we can see a comparison between the two approaches for $(1 - \varepsilon) = 95\%$. The same data set is used as in the previous illustration. We note that in return/CVaR coordinates, as expected, the mean-CVaR efficient frontier lies above the mean-variance efficient frontier. In this particular example, the two efficient frontiers are close to each other and are similarly shaped. Yet with the inclusion of derivative assets such as options and credit derivatives, this will no longer be the case.[83]

---

[83]Nicklas Larsen, Helmut Mausser, and Stanislav Uryasev, "Algorithms for Optimization of Value-at-Risk," in P. Pardalos and V. K. Tsitsiringos (eds.), *Financial Engineering, e-commerce and Supply Chain* (Boston: Kluwer Academic Publishers, 2002), pp. 129–157.

EXHIBIT 8.4 Comparison Mean-CVaR95% and Mean-Variance Efficient Portfolios

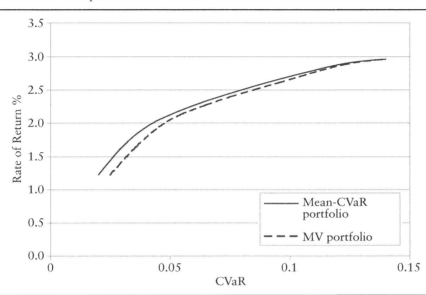

Source: Pavlo Krokhmal, Jonas Palmquist, and Stanislav Uryasev, "Portfolio Optimization with Conditional Value-At-Risk Objective and Constraints," *The Journal of Risk* 4, no. 2 (2002), p. 23. This copyrighted material is reprinted with permission from Incisive Media Plc, Haymarket House, 28-29 Haymarket, London, SW1Y 4RX, United Kingdom.

SUMMARY

■ Markowitz quantified the concept of diversification through the statistical notion of covariance between individual securities, and the overall standard deviation of a portfolio.
■ The basic assumption behind modern portfolio theory is that an investor's preferences can be represented by a function (utility function) of the expected return and the variance of a portfolio.
■ The basic principle underlying modern portfolio theory is that for a given level of expected return a rational investor would choose the portfolio with minimum variance from among the set of all possible portfolios. We presented three equivalent formulations: (1) the minimum variance formulation; (2) the expected return maximization formulation; and (3) the risk aversion formulation.
■ Minimum variance portfolios are called mean-variance efficient portfolios. The set of all mean-variance efficient portfolios is called the

efficient frontier. The efficient frontier with only risky assets has a parabolic shape in the expected return/standard deviation coordinate system.

■ The portfolio on the efficient frontier with the smallest variance is called the global minimum variance portfolio.

■ The mean-variance problem results in an optimization problem referred to as a quadratic program.

■ With the addition of a risk-free asset, the efficient frontier becomes a straight line in the expected return/standard deviation coordinate system. This line is called the *capital market line.*

■ The tangency point of the efficient frontier with only risky assets and the capital market line is called the *tangency portfolio.*

■ The *market portfolio* is the portfolio that consists of all assets available to investors in the same proportion as each security's market value divided by the total market value of all securities. Under certain assumptions it can be shown that the tangency portfolio is the same as the market portfolio.

■ The excess expected return of the market portfolio (the expected return of the market portfolio minus the risk-free rate) divided by the standard deviation of the market portfolio is referred to as the *equilibrium market price of risk.*

■ The capital market line expresses that the expected return on a portfolio is equal to the risk-free rate plus a portfolio specific risk premium. The portfolio specific risk premium is the market price of risk multiplied by the risk (standard deviation) of the portfolio.

■ Some of the most common constraints used in practice are no short-selling constraints, turnover constraints, maximum holding constraints, and tracking error constraints. These constraints can be handled in a straightforward way by the same type of optimization algorithms used for solving the mean-variance problem.

■ Integer constraints or constraints of combinatorial nature are more difficult to handle and require more specialized optimization algorithms. Some examples of these types of constraints are minimum holding constraints, transaction size constraints, cardinality constraints (number of securities permitted in the portfolio), and round lot constraints.

■ The sample means and covariances of financial return series are easy to calculate, but may exhibit significant estimation errors.

■ Serial correlation or autocorrelation is the correlation of the return of a security with itself over successive time intervals. Heteroskedasticity means that variances/covariances are not constant but changing over time.

■ In practical applications, it is important to correct the covariance estimator for serial correlation and heteroskedasticity.

■ The sample covariance estimator can be improved by increasing the sampling frequency. This is not the case for the sample expected return estimator, whose accuracy can only be improved by extending the length of the sample.

■ The mean-variance framework only takes the first two moments, the mean and the variance, into account. When investors have preferences beyond the first two moments, it is desirable to extend the mean-variance framework to include higher moments.

■ Two different types of risk measures can be distinguished: dispersion and downside measures.

■ Dispersion measures are measures of uncertainty. In contrast to downside measures, dispersion measures consider both positive and negative deviations from the mean, and treat those deviations as equally risky.

■ Some common portfolio dispersion approaches are mean standard deviation, mean-variance, mean absolute deviation, and mean absolute moment.

■ Some common portfolio downside measures are Roy's safety-first, semivariance, lower partial moment, Value-at-Risk, and Conditional Value-at-Risk.

CHAPTER 9

Portfolio Optimization: Bayesian Techniques and the Black-Litterman Model

Investment policies constructed using inferior estimates, such as sample means and sample covariance matrices, typically perform very poorly in practice. Besides introducing spurious changes in portfolio weights each time the portfolio is rebalanced, this undesirable property also results in unnecessary turnover and increased transaction costs. These phenomena are not necessarily a sign that portfolio optimization does not work, but rather that the modern portfolio theory framework is very sensitive to the accuracy of inputs.

There are different ways to address this issue. On the estimation side, one can try to produce more robust estimates of the input parameters for the optimization problems. This is most often achieved by using estimators that are less sensitive to outliers, and possibly, other sampling errors, such as Bayesian and shrinkage estimators. On the modeling side, one can constrain portfolio weights, use portfolio resampling, or apply robust or stochastic optimization techniques to specify scenarios or ranges of values for parameters estimated from data, thus incorporating uncertainty into the optimization process itself.[1]

The outline of the chapter is as follows. First, we provide a general overview of some of the common problems encountered in mean-variance optimization before we turn our attention to shrinkage estimators for expected returns and the covariance matrix. Within the context of Bayesian estimation, we focus on the Black-Litterman model. We derive the model using so-called *mixed estimation* from classical econometrics. Introducing a simple cross-sectional momentum strategy, we then show how we can combine this

---

[1]Interestingly, some new results suggest that the two approaches are not necessarily disjoint, and in some cases may lead to the same end result; see Bernd Scherer, "How Different Is Robust Optimization Really?" *Journal of Asset Management*, 7 (2007), pp. 374–387.

strategy with market equilibrium using the Black-Litterman model in the mean-variance framework to rebalance the portfolio on a monthly basis.

PRACTICAL PROBLEMS ENCOUNTERED IN MEAN-VARIANCE OPTIMIZATION

The simplicity and the intuitive appeal of portfolio construction using modern portfolio theory have attracted significant attention both in academia and in practice. Yet, despite considerable effort, it took many years until portfolio managers started using modern portfolio theory for managing real money. Unfortunately, in real world applications there are many problems with it, and portfolio optimization is still considered by many practitioners to be difficult to apply. In this section we consider some of the typical problems encountered in mean-variance optimization. In particular, we elaborate on: (1) the sensitivity to estimation error; (2) the effects of uncertainty in the inputs in the optimization process; and (3) the large data requirement necessary for accurately estimating the inputs for the portfolio optimization framework. We start by considering an example illustrating the effect of estimation error.

Example: The True, Estimated, and Actual Efficient Frontiers

Broadie introduced the terms *true frontier, estimated frontier,* and *actual frontier* to refer to the efficient frontiers computed using the true expected returns (unobservable), estimated expected returns, and true expected returns of the portfolios on the estimated frontier, respectively.[2] In this example, we refer to the frontier computed using the true, but unknown, expected returns as the true frontier. Similarly, we refer to the frontier computed using estimates of the expected returns and the true covariance matrix as the estimated frontier. Finally, we define the actual frontier as follows: We take the portfolios on the estimated frontier and then calculate their expected returns using the true expected returns. Since we are using the true covariance matrix, the variance of a portfolio on the estimated frontier is the same as the variance on the actual frontier.

From these definitions, we observe that the actual frontier will always lie below the true frontier. The estimated frontier can lie anywhere with respect to the other frontiers. However, if the errors in the expected return estimates have a mean of zero, then the estimated frontier will lie above the true

---

[2]Mark Broadie, "Computing Efficient Frontiers Using Estimated Parameters," *Annals of Operations Research: Special Issue on Financial Engineering* 45, nos. 1–4 (December 1993), pp. 21–58.

frontier with extremely high probability, particularly when the investment universe is large. We look at two cases considered by Ceria and Stubbs:[3]

1. Using the covariance matrix and expected return vector from Idzorek,[4] they randomly generate a time series of normally distributed returns and compute the average to use as estimates of expected returns. Using the expected-return estimate calculated in this fashion and the true covariance matrix, they generate an estimated efficient frontier of risk versus expected return where the portfolios were subject to no-shorting constraints and the standard budget constraint that the sum of portfolio weights is one. Similarly, Ceria and Stubbs compute the true efficient frontier using the *original* covariance matrix and expected return vector. Finally, they construct the actual frontier by computing the expected return and risk of the portfolios on the estimated frontier with the true covariance and expected return values. These three frontiers are illustrated in Exhibit 9.1.
2. Using the same estimate of expected returns, Ceria and Stubbs also generate risk versus expected return where active holdings of the assets are constrained to be ±3% of the benchmark holding of each asset. These frontiers are illustrated in Exhibit 9.2.

We observe that the estimated frontiers significantly overestimate the expected return for any risk level in both types of frontiers. More importantly, we note that the actual frontier lies far below the true frontier in both cases. This shows that the *optimal* mean-variance portfolio is not necessarily a good portfolio, that is, it is not mean-variance efficient. Since the true expected return is not observable, we do not know how far the actual expected return may be from the expected return of the mean-variance optimal portfolio, and we end up holding an inferior portfolio.

Sensitivity to Estimation Error

In a portfolio optimization context, securities with large expected returns and low standard deviations will be overweighted and conversely, securities with low expected returns and high standard deviations will be underweighted. Therefore, large estimation errors in expected returns and/or variances/

---

[3] We are grateful to Axioma Inc. for providing us with this example. Previously, it has appeared in Sebastian Ceria and Robert A. Stubbs, "Incorporating Estimation Errors into Portfolio Selection: Robust Portfolio Construction," Axioma, Inc., 2005.

[4] Thomas M. Idzorek, "A Step-By-Step Guide to the Black-Litterman Model: Incorporating User-Specified Confidence Levels," Research Paper, Ibbotson Associates, Chicago, 2005.

EXHIBIT 9.1   Markowitz Efficient Frontiers

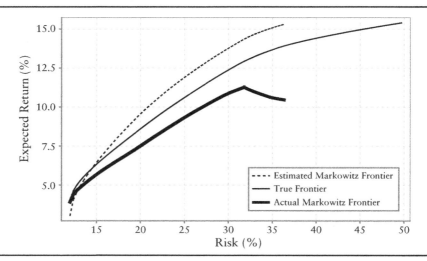

Source: Figure 2 in Sebastian Ceria and Robert A. Stubbs, "Incorporating Estimation Errors into Portfolio Selection: Robust Portfolio Construction," Axioma, Inc., 2005, p. 6. This figure is reprinted with the permission of Axioma, Inc.

EXHIBIT 9.2   Markowitz Benchmark-Relative Efficient Frontiers

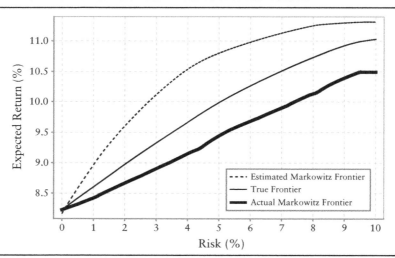

Source: Figure 3 in Sebastian Ceria and Robert A. Stubbs, "Incorporating Estimation Errors into Portfolio Selection: Robust Portfolio Construction," Axioma, Inc., 2005, p. 7. This figure is reprinted with the permission of Axioma, Inc.

covariances introduce errors in the optimized portfolio weights. For this reason, people often cynically refer to optimizers as *error maximizers.*

Uncertainty from estimation error in expected returns tends to have more influence than in the covariance matrix in a mean-variance optimization.[5] The relative importance depends on the investor's risk aversion, but as a general rule of thumb, errors in the expected returns are about 10 times more important than errors in the covariance matrix, and errors in the variances are about twice as important as errors in the covariances.[6] As the risk tolerance increases, the relative impact of estimation errors in the expected returns becomes even more important. Conversely, as the risk tolerance decreases, the impact of errors in expected returns relative to errors in the covariance matrix becomes smaller. From this simple rule, it follows that the major focus should be on providing good estimates for the expected returns, followed by the variances. In this chapter we discuss shrinkage techniques and the Black-Litterman model in order to mitigate estimation errors.

Constraining Portfolio Weights

Several studies have shown that the inclusion of constraints in the mean-variance optimization problem leads to better out-of-sample performance.[7] Practitioners often use no short-selling constraints or upper and lower bounds for each security to avoid overconcentration in a few assets. Gupta and Eichhorn suggest that constraining portfolio weights may also assist in containing volatility, increase realized efficiency, and decrease downside risk or shortfall probability.[8]

---

[5]See, Michael J. Best and Robert R. Grauer, "The Analytics of Sensitivity Analysis for Mean-Variance Portfolio Problems," *International Review of Financial Analysis,* 1 (1992), pp. 17–37; and Michael J. Best and Robert R. Grauer, "On the Sensitivity of Mean-Variance-Efficient Portfolios to Changes in Assets Means: Some Analytical and Computational Results," *Review of Financial Studies,* 4 (1991), pp. 315–342.

[6]Vijay K. Chopra and William T. Ziemba, "The Effect of Errors in Means, Variances, and Covariances on Optimal Portfolio Choice," *Journal of Portfolio Management,* 19 (1993), pp. 6–11; and Jarl G. Kallberg and William T. Ziemba, "Misspecification in Portfolio Selection Problems," in G. Bamberg and K. Spremann (eds.), *Risk and Capital: Lecture Notes in Economics and Mathematical Systems* (New York: Springer, 1984).

[7]See, for example, Peter A. Frost and James E. Savarino, "For Better Performance: Constrain Portfolio Weights," *Journal of Portfolio Management,* 15 (1988), pp. 29–34; Vijay K. Chopra, "Mean-Variance Revisited: Near-Optimal Portfolios and Sensitivity to Input Variations," Russell Research Commentary, December 1991; and Robert R. Grauer, and Frederick C. Shen, "Do Constraints Improve Portfolio Performance?" *Journal of Banking and Finance,* 24 (2000), pp. 1253–1274.

[8]Francis Gupta and David Eichhorn, "Mean-Variance Optimization for Practitioners of Asset Allocation," Chapter 4 in Frank J. Fabozzi (ed.), *Handbook of Portfolio Management* (Hoboken, NJ: John Wiley & Sons, 1998).

Jagannathan and Ma provide a theoretical justification for these observations.[9] Specifically, they show that the no short-selling constraints are equivalent to reducing the estimated asset covariances, whereas upper bounds are equivalent to increasing the corresponding covariances. For example, stocks that have high covariance with other stocks tend to receive negative portfolio weights. Therefore, when their covariance is decreased (which is equivalent to the effect of imposing no short-selling constraints), these negative weights disappear. Similarly, stocks that have low covariances with other stocks tend to get overweighted. Hence, by increasing the corresponding covariances the impact of these overweighted stocks decreases.

Furthermore, Monte Carlo experiments performed by Jagannathan and Ma indicate that when no-short-sell constraints are imposed, the sample covariance matrix has about the same performance (as measured by the global minimum variance (GMV) portfolio) as a covariance matrix estimator constructed from a factor structure.

Care needs to be taken when imposing constraints for robustness and stability purposes. For example, if the constraints used are too tight, they will completely determine the portfolio allocation—not the forecasts.

Instead of providing ad hoc upper and lower bounds on each security, as proposed by Bouchaud, Potters, and Aguilar one can use so-called *diversification indicators* that measure the concentration of the portfolio.[10] These diversification indicators can be used as constraints in the portfolio construction phase to limit the concentration to individual securities. The authors demonstrate that these indicators are related to the information content of the portfolio in the sense of information theory.[11] For example, a very concentrated portfolio corresponds to a large information content (as we would only choose a very concentrated allocation if our information about future price fluctuations is perfect), whereas an equally weighted portfolio would indicate low information content (as we would not put "all the eggs in one basket" if our information about future price fluctuations is poor).

---

[9]Ravi Jagannathan and Tongshu Ma, "Risk Reduction in Large Portfolios: Why Imposing the Wrong Constraints Helps," *Journal of Finance,* 58 (2003), pp. 1651–1683.

[10]Jean-Philippe Bouchaud, Marc Potters, and Jean-Pierre Aguilar, "Missing Information and Asset Allocation," Working Paper, Science & Finance, Capital Fund Management, 1997.

[11]The relationship to information theory is based upon the premise that the diversification indicators are generalized entropies. See, Evaldo M. F. Curado and Constantino Tsallis, "Generalized Statistical Mechanics: Connection with Thermodynamics," *Journal of Physics A: Mathematical and General,* 24 (1991), pp. L69–L72, 1991.

Importance of Sensitivity Analysis

In practice, in order to minimize dramatic changes due to estimation error, it is advisable to perform sensitivity analysis. For example, one can study the results of small changes or perturbations to the inputs from an efficient portfolio selected from a mean-variance optimization. If the portfolio calculated from the perturbed inputs drastically differ from the first one, this might indicate a problem. The perturbation can also be performed on a security by security basis in order to identify those securities that are the most sensitive. The objective of this sensitivity analysis is to identify a set of security weights that will be close to efficient under several different sets of plausible inputs.

Issues with Highly Correlated Assets

The inclusion of highly correlated securities is another major cause for instability in the mean-variance optimization framework. For example, high correlation coefficients among common asset classes are one reason why real estate is popular in optimized portfolios. Real estate is one of the few asset classes that has a low correlation with other common asset classes. But real estate in general does not have the liquidity necessary in order to implement these portfolios and may therefore fail to deliver the return promised by the real estate indexes.

The problem of high correlations typically becomes worse when the correlation matrix is estimated from historical data. Specifically, when the correlation matrix is estimated over a slightly different period, correlations may change, but the impact on the new portfolio weights may be drastic. In these situations, it may be a good idea to resort to a shrinkage estimator or a factor model to model covariances and correlations.

Incorporating Uncertainty in the Inputs into the Portfolio Allocation Process

In the classical mean-variance optimization problem, the expected returns and the covariance matrix of returns are uncertain and have to be estimated. After the estimation of these quantities, the portfolio optimization problem is solved as a deterministic problem—completely ignoring the uncertainty in the inputs. However, it makes sense for the uncertainty of expected returns and risk to enter into the optimization process, thus creating a more realistic model. Using point estimates of the expected returns and the covariance matrix of returns, and treating them as error-free in portfolio allocation, does not necessarily correspond to prudent investor behavior.

The investor would probably be more comfortable choosing a portfolio that would perform well under a number of different scenarios, thereby also attaining some protection from estimation risk and model risk. Obviously, to have some insurance in the event of less likely but more extreme cases (e.g., scenarios that are highly unlikely under the assumption that returns are normally distributed), the investor must be willing to give up some of the upside that would result under the more likely scenarios. Such an investor seeks a robust portfolio, that is, a portfolio that is assured against some worst-case model misspecification. The estimation process can be improved through robust statistical techniques such as shrinkage and Bayesian estimators discussed later in this chapter. However, jointly considering estimation risk and model risk in the financial decision-making process is becoming more important.

The estimation process frequently does not deliver a point forecast (that is, one single number), but a full distribution of expected returns. Recent approaches attempt to integrate estimation risk into the mean-variance framework by using the expected return distribution in the optimization. A simple approach is to sample from the return distribution and average the resulting portfolios (Monte Carlo approach).[12] However, as a mean-variance problem has to be solved for each draw, this is computationally intensive for larger portfolios. In addition, the averaging does not guarantee that the resulting portfolio weights will satisfy all constraints.

Introduced in the late 1990s by Ben-Tal and Nemirovski[13] and El Ghaoui and Lebret,[14] the robust optimization framework is computationally more efficient than the Monte Carlo approach. This development in optimization technology allows for efficiently solving the robust version of the mean-variance optimization problem in about the same time as the classical mean-variance optimization problem. The technique explicitly uses the distribution from the estimation process to find a robust portfolio in one single optimization. It thereby incorporates uncertainties of inputs into a deter-

---

[12]See, for example, Richard O. Michaud, *Efficient Asset Management: A Practical Guide to Stock Portfolio Optimization and Asset Allocation* (Oxford: Oxford University Press, 1998); Philippe Jorion, "Portfolio Optimization in Practice," *Financial Analysts Journal*, 48 (1992), pp. 68–74; and Bernd Scherer, "Portfolio Resampling: Review and Critique," *Financial Analysts Journal*, 58 (2002), pp. 98–109.

[13]Aharon Ben-Tal and Arkadi S. Nemirovski, "Robust Convex Optimization," *Mathematics of Operations Research*, 23 (1998), pp. 769–805; and Aharon Ben-Tal and Arkadi S. Nemirovski, "Robust Solutions to Uncertain Linear Programs," *Operations Research Letters*, 25 (1999), pp. 1–13.

[14]Laurent El Ghaoui and Herve Lebret, "Robust Solutions to Least-Squares Problems with Uncertain Data," *SIAM Journal Matrix Analysis with Applications*, 18 (1997), pp. 1035–1064.

ministic framework. The classical portfolio optimization formulations such as the mean-variance portfolio selection problem, the maximum Sharpe ratio portfolio problem, and the value-at-risk (VaR) portfolio problem all have robust counterparts that can be solved in roughly the same amount of time as the original problem.[15] In Chapter 10 we discuss robust portfolio optimization in more detail.

Large Data Requirements

In classical mean-variance optimization, we need to provide estimates of the expected returns and covariances of all the securities in the investment universe considered. Typically, however, portfolio managers have reliable return forecasts for only a small subset of these assets. This is probably one of the major reasons why the mean-variance framework has not been adopted by practitioners in general. It is simply unreasonable for the portfolio manager to produce good estimates of all the inputs required in classical portfolio theory.

We will see later in this chapter that the Black-Litterman model provides a remedy in that it blends any views (this could be a forecast on just one or a few securities, or all them) the investor might have with the market equilibrium. When no views are present, the resulting Black-Litterman expected returns are just the expected returns consistent with the market equilibrium. Conversely, when the investor has views on some of the assets, the resulting expected returns deviate from market equilibrium.

SHRINKAGE ESTIMATION

It is well known since Stein's seminal work that biased estimators often yield better parameter estimates than their generally preferred unbiased counterparts.[16] In particular, it can be shown that if we consider the problem of estimating the mean of an N-dimensional multivariate normal variable ($N > 2$), $X \in N(\mu, \Sigma)$ with known covariance matrix Σ, the sample mean $\hat{\mu}$ is not the best estimator of the population mean μ in terms of the quadratic loss function

$$L(\mu, \hat{\mu}) = (\mu - \hat{\mu})' \Sigma^{-1} (\mu - \hat{\mu})$$

[15]See, for example, Donald Goldfarb and Garud Iyengar, "Robust Portfolio Selection Problems," *Mathematics of Operations Research*, 28 (2003), pp. 1–38.
[16]Charles Stein, "Inadmissibility of the Usual Estimator for the Mean of Multivariate Normal Distribution," *Proceedings of the Third Berkeley Symposium on Mathematical Statistics and Probability*, 1 (1956), pp. 197–206.

For example, the so-called *James-Stein shrinkage estimator*

$$\hat{\mu}_{JS} = (1-w)\hat{\mu} + w\mu_0\iota$$

has a lower quadratic loss than the sample mean, where

$$w = \min\left(1, \frac{N-2}{T(\hat{\mu}-\mu_0\iota)'\Sigma^{-1}(\hat{\mu}-\mu_0\iota)}\right)$$

and $\iota = [1,1,\ldots,1]'$. Moreover, T is the number of observations, and μ_0 is an arbitrary number. The vector $\mu_0\iota$ and the weight w are referred to as the shrinkage target and the shrinkage intensity (or shrinkage factor), respectively. Although there are some choices of μ_0 that are better than others, what is surprising with this result is that it could be *any* number! This fact is referred to as the *Stein paradox*.

In effect, shrinkage is a form of averaging different estimators. The shrinkage estimator typically consists of three components: (1) an estimator with little or no structure (like the sample mean above); (2) an estimator with a lot of structure (the shrinkage target); and (3) the shrinkage intensity. The shrinkage target is chosen with the following two requirements in mind. First, it should have only a small number of free parameters (robust and with a lot of structure). Second, it should have some of the basic properties in common with the unknown quantity being estimated. The shrinkage intensity can be chosen based on theoretical properties or simply by numerical simulation.

Probably the most well-known shrinkage estimator[17] used to estimate expected returns in the financial literature is the one proposed by Jorion,[18] where the shrinkage target is given by $\mu_g\iota$ with

$$\mu_g = \frac{\iota'\Sigma^{-1}\hat{\mu}}{\iota'\Sigma^{-1}\iota}$$

and

$$w = \frac{N+2}{N+2+T(\hat{\mu}-\mu_g\iota)'\Sigma^{-1}(\hat{\mu}-\mu_g\iota)}$$

We note that μ_g is the return on the GMV portfolio discussed in Chapter 8. Several studies document that for the mean-variance framework: (1) the

---

[17]Many similar approaches have been proposed. For example, see Jobson and Korkie, "Putting Markowitz Theory to Work" and Frost and Savarino, "An Empirical Bayes Approach to Efficient Portfolio Selection."
[18]Philippe Jorion, "Bayes-Stein Estimation for Portfolio Analysis," *Journal of Financial and Quantitative Analysis*, 21 (1986), pp. 279–292.

variability in the portfolio weights from one period to the next decrease; and (2) the out-of-sample risk-adjusted performance improves significantly when using a shrinkage estimator as compared to the sample mean.[19]

We can also apply the shrinkage technique for covariance matrix estimation. This involves shrinking an unstructured covariance estimator toward a more structured covariance estimator. Typically the structured covariance estimator only has a few degrees of freedom (only a few nonzero eigenvalues) as motivated by Random Matrix Theory (see Chapter 2).

For example, as shrinkage targets, Ledoit and Wolf[20] suggest using the covariance matrix that follows from the single-factor model developed by Sharpe[21] or the constant correlation covariance matrix. In practice the single-factor model and the constant correlation model yield similar results, but the constant correlation model is much easier to implement. In the case of the constant correlation model, the shrinkage estimator for the covariance matrix takes the form

$$\hat{\Sigma}_{LW} = w\hat{\Sigma}_{CC} + (1 - w)\hat{\Sigma}$$

where $\hat{\Sigma}$ is the sample covariance matrix, and $\hat{\Sigma}_{CC}$ is the sample covariance matrix with constant correlation. The sample covariance matrix with constant correlation is computed as follows.

First, we decompose the sample covariance matrix according to

$$\hat{\Sigma} = \Lambda C \Lambda'$$

---

[19]See, for example, Michaud, "The Markowitz Optimization Enigma: Is 'Optimized' Optimal?"; Jorion, "Bayesian and CAPM Estimators of the Means: Implications for Portfolio Selection"; and Glen Larsen, Jr. and Bruce Resnick, "Parameter Estimation Techniques, Optimization Frequency, and Portfolio Return Enhancement," *Journal of Portfolio Management*, 27 (2001), pp. 27–34.

[20]Olivier Ledoit and Michael Wolf, "Improved Estimation of the Covariance Matrix of Stock Returns with an Application to Portfolio Selection," *Journal of Empirical Finance*, 10 (2003), pp. 603–621; and Olivier Ledoit and Michael Wolf, "Honey, I Shrunk the Sample Covariance Matrix," *Journal of Portfolio Management*, 30 (2004), pp. 110–119.

[21]William F. Sharpe, "A Simplified Model for Portfolio Analysis," *Management Science*, 9 (1963), pp. 277–293. Elton, Gruber, and Urich proposed the single factor model for purposes of covariance estimation in 1978. They show that this approach leads to: (1) better forecasts of the covariance matrix; (2) more stable portfolio allocations over time; and (3) more diversified portfolios. They also find that the average correlation coefficient is a good forecast of the future correlation matrix. See Edwin J. Elton, Martin J. Gruber, and Thomas J. Urich, "Are Betas Best?" *Journal of Finance*, 33 (1978), pp. 1375–1384.

where Λ is a diagonal matrix of the volatilities of returns and $\mathbf{C}$ is the sample correlation matrix, that is,

$$\mathbf{C} = \begin{bmatrix} 1 & \hat{\rho}_{12} & \cdots & \hat{\rho}_{1N} \\ \hat{\rho}_{21} & \ddots & \ddots & \vdots \\ \vdots & \ddots & \ddots & \hat{\rho}_{N-1N} \\ \hat{\rho}_{N1} & \cdots & \hat{\rho}_{NN-1} & 1 \end{bmatrix}$$

Second, we replace the sample correlation matrix with the constant correlation matrix

$$\mathbf{C}_{CC} = \begin{bmatrix} 1 & \hat{\rho} & \cdots & \hat{\rho} \\ \hat{\rho} & \ddots & \ddots & \vdots \\ \vdots & \ddots & \ddots & \hat{\rho} \\ \hat{\rho} & \cdots & \hat{\rho} & 1 \end{bmatrix}$$

where $\hat{\rho}$ is the average of all the sample correlations, in other words

$$\hat{\rho} = \frac{2}{(N-1)N} \sum_{i=1}^{N} \sum_{j=i+1}^{N} \hat{\rho}_{ij}$$

The optimal shrinkage intensity can be shown to be proportional to a constant divided by the length of the history, T.[22]

---

[22]Although straightforward to implement, the optimal shrinkage intensity, w, is a bit tedious to write down mathematically. Let us denote by $r_{i,t}$ the return on security i during period t, $1 \leq i \leq N$, $1 \leq t \leq T$,

$$\bar{r}_i = \frac{1}{T} \sum_{t=1}^{T} r_{i,t} \text{ and } \hat{\sigma}_{ij} = \frac{1}{T-1} \sum_{t=1}^{T} (r_{i,t} - \bar{r}_i)(r_{j,t} - \bar{r}_j)$$

Then the optimal shrinkage intensity is given by the formula

$$w = \max\left\{0, \min\left\{\frac{\hat{\kappa}}{T}, 1\right\}\right\}$$

where

$$\hat{\kappa} = \frac{\hat{\pi} - \hat{c}}{\hat{\gamma}}$$

and the parameters $\hat{\pi}$, $\hat{c}$, $\hat{\gamma}$ are computed as follows. First, $\hat{\pi}$ is given by

$$\hat{\pi} = \sum_{i,j=1}^{N} \hat{\pi}_{ij}$$

where

$$\hat{\pi}_{ij} = \frac{1}{T} \sum_{t=1}^{T} \left((r_{i,t} - \bar{r}_i)(r_{j,t} - \bar{r}_j) - \hat{\sigma}_{ij}\right)^2$$

In their two articles, Ledoit and Wolf compare the empirical out-of-sample performance of their shrinkage covariance matrix estimators with other covariance matrix estimators, such as the sample covariance matrix, a statistical factor model based on the first five principal components, and a factor model based on the 48 industry factors as defined by Fama and French.[23] The results indicate that when it comes to computing a GMV portfolio, their shrinkage estimators are superior compared to the others tested, with the constant correlation shrinkage estimator coming out slightly ahead. Interestingly enough, it turns out that the shrinkage intensity for the single-factor model (the shrinkage intensity for the constant coefficient model is not reported) is fairly constant throughout time with a value around 0.8. This suggests that there is about four times as much estimation error present in the sample covariance matrix as there is bias in the single-factor covariance matrix.

THE BLACK-LITTERMAN MODEL

In the Black-Litterman model an estimate of future expected returns is based on combining market equilibrium (e.g., the CAPM equilibrium) with an investor's views. As we will see, the Black-Litterman expected return is a shrinkage estimator where market equilibrium is the shrinkage target and the shrinkage intensity is determined by the portfolio manger's confidence in the model inputs. We will make this statement precise later in this section. Such views are expressed as absolute or relative deviations from equilibrium together with confidence levels of the views (as measured by the standard deviation of the views).

Second, $\hat{c}$ is given by

$$\hat{c} = \sum_{i=1}^{N} \hat{\pi}_{ii} + \sum_{\substack{i=1 \\ i \neq j}}^{N} \frac{\hat{\rho}}{2} \left(\sqrt{\hat{\rho}_{jj} / \hat{\rho}_{ii}} \, \hat{\vartheta}_{ii,ij} + \sqrt{\hat{\rho}_{ii} / \hat{\rho}_{jj}} \, \hat{\vartheta}_{jj,ii} \right)$$

where

$$\hat{\vartheta}_{ii,ij} = \frac{1}{T} \sum_{t=1}^{T} \left[\left((r_{i,t} - \overline{r}_i)^2 - \hat{\sigma}_{ii} \right) \left((r_{i,t} - \overline{r}_i)(r_{j,t} - \overline{r}_j) - \hat{\sigma}_{ij} \right) \right]$$

Finally, $\hat{\gamma}$ is given by

$$\hat{\gamma} = \left\| \mathbf{C} - \mathbf{C}_{CC} \right\|_F^2$$

where $\|\cdot\|_F$ denotes the Frobenius norm defined by

$$\|\mathbf{A}\|_F = \sqrt{\sum_{i,j=1}^{N} a_{ij}^2}$$

[23]Eugene F. Fama and Kenneth R. French, "Industry Costs of Equity," *Journal of Financial Economics*, 43 (1997), pp. 153–193.

The Black-Litterman expected return is calculated as a weighted average of the market equilibrium and the investor's views. The weights depend on (1) the volatility of each asset and its correlations with the other assets and (2) the degree of confidence in each forecast. The resulting expected return, which is the mean of the posterior distribution, is then used as input in the portfolio optimization process. Portfolio weights computed in this fashion tend to be more intuitive and less sensitive to small changes in the original inputs (i.e., forecasts of market equilibrium, investor's views, and the covariance matrix).

The Black-Litterman model can be interpreted as a Bayesian model. Named after the English mathematician Thomas Bayes, the Bayesian approach is based on the *subjective* interpretation of probability. A probability distribution is used to represent an investor's belief on the probability that a specific event will actually occur. This probability distribution, called the *prior distribution*, reflects an investor's knowledge about the probability before any data are observed. After more information is provided (e.g., data observed), the investor's opinions about the probability might change. Bayes' rule is the formula for computing the new probability distribution, called the *posterior distribution*. The posterior distribution is based on knowledge of the prior probability distribution plus the new data. A posterior distribution of expected return is derived by combining the forecast from the empirical data with a prior distribution.

The ability to incorporate exogenous insight, such as a portfolio manager's judgment, into formal models is important: such insight might be the most valuable input used by the model. The Bayesian framework allows forecasting systems to use such external information sources and subjective interventions (i.e., modification of the model due to judgment) in addition to traditional information sources such as market data and proprietary data.

Because portfolio managers might not be willing to give up control to a black box, incorporating exogenous insights into formal models through Bayesian techniques is one way of giving the portfolio manager better control in a quantitative framework. Forecasts are represented through probability distributions that can be modified or adjusted to incorporate other sources of information deemed relevant. The only restriction is that such additional information (i.e., the investor's views) be combined with the existing model through the laws of probability. In effect, incorporating Bayesian views into a model allows one to rationalize subjectivity within a formal, quantitative framework. "[T]he rational investor is a Bayesian," as Markowitz noted.[24]

---

[24]See page 57 in Harry M. Markowitz, *Mean-Variance Analysis in Portfolio Choice and Capital Markets* (Cambridge, MA: Basil Blackwell, 1987).

Derivation of the Black-Litterman Model

The basic feature of the Black-Litterman model that we discuss in this and the following sections is that it combines an investor's views with the market equilibrium. Let us understand what this statement implies. In the classical mean-variance optimization framework an investor is required to provide estimates of the expected returns and covariances of all the securities in the investment universe considered. This is of course a humongous task, given the number of securities available today. Portfolio and investment managers are very unlikely to have a detailed understanding of all the securities, companies, industries, and sectors that they have at their disposal. Typically, most of them have a specific area of expertise that they focus on in order to achieve superior returns.

This is probably one of the major reasons why the mean-variance framework has not been adopted among practitioners in general. It is simply unrealistic for the portfolio manager to produce reasonable estimates (besides the additional problems of estimation error) of the inputs required in classical portfolio theory.

Furthermore, many trading strategies used today cannot easily be turned into forecasts of expected returns and covariances. In particular, not all trading strategies produce views on *absolute* return, but rather just provide *relative* rankings of securities that are predicted to outperform/underperform other securities. For example, considering two stocks, A and B, instead of the *absolute view*, "the one-month expected return on A and B are 1.2% and 1.7% with a standard deviation of 5% and 5.5%, respectively," while a *relative view* may be of the form "B will outperform A with half a percent over the next month" or simply "B will outperform A over the next month." Clearly, it is not an easy task to translate any of these relative views into the inputs required for the modern portfolio theoretical framework. We now walk through and illustrate the usage of the Black-Litterman model in three simple steps.

Step 1: Basic Assumptions and Starting Point

One of the basic assumptions underlying the Black-Litterman model is that the expected return of a security should be consistent with market equilibrium *unless* the investor has a specific view on the security.[25] In other words, an investor who does not have any views on the market should hold the market.[26]

---

[25]Fischer Black and Robert Litterman, *Asset Allocation: Combining Investor Views with Market Equilibrium*, Goldman, Sachs & Co., Fixed Income Research, September 1990.

[26]A predecessor to the Black-Litterman model is the so-called Treynor-Black model. In this model, an investor's portfolio is shown to consist of two parts (1) a passive

Our starting point is the CAPM model:

$$E(R_i) - R_f = \beta_i(E(R_M) - R_f)$$

where $E(R_i)$, $E(R_M)$, and R_f are the expected return on security i, the expected return on the market portfolio, and the risk-free rate, respectively. Furthermore,

$$\beta_i = \frac{\text{cov}(R_i, R_M)}{\sigma_M^2}$$

where σ_M^2 is the variance of the market portfolio. Let us denote by $\mathbf{w}_b = (w_{b1}, \ldots, w_{bN})'$ the market capitalization or benchmark weights, so that with an asset universe of N securities[27] the return on the market can be written as

$$R_M = \sum_{j=1}^{N} w_{bj} R_j$$

Then by the CAPM, the expected excess return on asset i, $\Pi_i = E(R_i) - R_f$, becomes

$$\Pi_i = \beta_i(E(R_M) - R_f)$$
$$= \frac{\text{cov}(R_i, R_M)}{\sigma_M^2}(E(R_M) - R_f)$$
$$= \frac{E(R_M) - R_f}{\sigma_M^2} \sum_{j=1}^{N} \text{cov}(R_i, R_j)w_{bj}$$

We can also express this in matrix-vector form as[28]

---

portfolio/positions held purely for the purpose of mimicking the market portfolio, and (2) an active portfolio/positions based on the investor's return/risk expectations. This somewhat simpler model relies on the assumption that returns of all securities are related only through the variation of the market portfolio (Sharpe's Diagonal Model). See Jack L. Treynor and Fischer Black, "How to Use Security Analysis to Improve Portfolio Selection," *Journal of Business*, 46 (1973) pp. 66–86.

[27]For simplicity, we consider only equity securities. Extending this model to other assets classes such as bonds and currencies is fairly straightforward.

[28]Two comments about the following two relationships are of importance:

1. As it may be difficult to accurately estimate expected returns, practitioners use other techniques. One is that of *reverse optimization* also referred to as the technique of *implied expected returns*. The technique simply uses the expression $\Pi = \delta \Sigma \mathbf{w}$ to calculate the expected return vector given the market price of risk δ, the covariance matrix Σ, and the market capitalization weights $\mathbf{w}$. The technique was first introduced by Sharpe and Fisher; see William F. Sharpe, "Imput-

$$\Pi = \delta \Sigma w$$

where we define the market price of risk as

$$\delta = \frac{E(R_M) - R_f}{\sigma_M^2}$$

the expected excess return vector

$$\Pi = \begin{bmatrix} \Pi_1 \\ \vdots \\ \Pi_N \end{bmatrix}$$

and the covariance matrix of returns

$$\Sigma = \begin{bmatrix} \mathrm{cov}(R_1, R_1) & \cdots & \mathrm{cov}(R_1, R_N) \\ \vdots & \ddots & \vdots \\ \mathrm{cov}(R_N, R_1) & \cdots & \mathrm{cov}(R_N, R_N) \end{bmatrix}$$

The true expected returns μ of the securities are unknown. However, we assume that our previous equilibrium model serves as a reasonable estimate of the true expected returns in the sense that

$$\Pi = \mu + \varepsilon_\Pi, \varepsilon_\Pi \sim N(0, \tau\Sigma)$$

for some small parameter $\tau \ll 1$. We can think about $\tau\Sigma$ as our confidence in how well we can estimate the equilibrium expected returns. In other

---

ing Expected Returns from Portfolio Composition," *Journal of Financial and Quantitative Analysis*, 9 (1974), pp. 463–472; and Lawrence Fisher, "Using Modern Portfolio Theory to Maintain an Efficiently Diversified Portfolio," *Financial Analysts Journal*, 31 (1975), pp. 73–85; and is an important component of the Black-Litterman model.

2. We note that $E(R_M) - R_f$ is the market risk premium (or the equity premium) of the universe of assets considered. As pointed out by Herold and Idzorek; see Ulf Herold, "Computing Implied Returns in a Meaningful Way," *Journal of Asset Management*, 6 (2005), pp. 53–64, and Thomas M. Idzorek, "A Step-By-Step Guide to the Black-Litterman Model: Incorporating User-Specified Confidence Levels"; using a market proxy with different risk-return characteristics than the market capitalization weighted portfolio for determining the market risk premium may lead to nonintuitive expected returns. For example, using a market risk premium based on the S&P 500 for calculating the implied equilibrium return vector for the NASDAQ 100 should be avoided.

words, a small τ implies a high confidence in our equilibrium estimates and vice versa.

According to portfolio theory, because the market portfolio is on the efficient frontier, as a consequence of the CAPM an investor will be holding a portfolio consisting of the market portfolio and a risk-free instrument earning the risk-free rate. But let us now see what happens if an investor has a particular view on some of the securities.

Step 2: Expressing an Investor's Views

Formally, K views in the Black-Litterman model are expressed as a K-dimensional vector $\mathbf{q}$ with

$$\mathbf{q} = \mathbf{P}\mu + \varepsilon_q, \varepsilon_q \sim N(0,\Omega)$$

where $\mathbf{P}$ is a $K \times N$ matrix (explained in the following example) and Ω is a $K \times K$ matrix expressing the confidence in the views. In order to understand this mathematical specification better, let us take a look at an example.

Let us assume that the asset universe that we consider has five stocks ($N = 5$) and that an investor has the following two views:

1. Stock 1 will have a return of 1.5%.
2. Stock 3 will outperform Stock 2 by 4%.

We recognize that the first view is an absolute view whereas the second one is a relative view. Mathematically, we express the two views together as

$$\begin{bmatrix} 1.5\% \\ 4\% \end{bmatrix} = \begin{bmatrix} 1 & 0 & 0 & 0 & 0 \\ 0 & -1 & 1 & 0 & 0 \end{bmatrix} \begin{bmatrix} \mu_1 \\ \mu_2 \\ \mu_3 \\ \mu_4 \\ \mu_5 \end{bmatrix} + \begin{bmatrix} \varepsilon_1 \\ \varepsilon_2 \end{bmatrix}$$

The first row of the $\mathbf{P}$ matrix represents the first view, and similarly, the second row describes the second view. In this example, we chose the weights of the second view such that they add up to zero, but other weighting schemes are also possible. For instance, the weights could also be chosen as some scaling factor times one over the market capitalizations of the stock, some scaling factor times one over the stock price, or other variations thereof. We come back to these issues later in this section when we discuss how to incorporate time-series based strategies and cross-sectional ranking strategies.

We also remark at this point that the error terms ε_1, ε_2 do not explicitly enter into the Black-Litterman model—but their variances do. Quite simply, these are just the variances of the different views. Although in some instances they are directly available as a by-product of the view or the strategy, in other cases they need to be estimated separately. For example,

$$\Omega = \begin{bmatrix} 1\%^2 & 0 \\ 0 & 1\%^2 \end{bmatrix}$$

corresponds to a higher confidence in the views, and conversely,

$$\Omega = \begin{bmatrix} 5\%^2 & 0 \\ 0 & 7\%^2 \end{bmatrix}$$

represents a much lower confidence in the views. We discuss a few different approaches in choosing the confidence levels below. The off-diagonal elements of Ω are typically set to zero. The reason for this is that the error terms of the individual views are most often assumed to be independent of one another.

Step 3: Combining an Investor's Views with Market Equilibrium

Having specified the market equilibrium and an investor's views separately, we are now ready to combine the two together. There are two different, but equivalent, approaches that can be used to arrive to the Black-Litterman model. We will describe a derivation that relies upon standard econometrical techniques, in particular, the so-called *mixed estimation technique* described by Theil.[29] The approach based on Bayesian statistics has been explained in some detail by Satchell and Scowcroft.[30]

Let us first recall the specification of market equilibrium

$$\Pi = \mu + \varepsilon_\Pi, \varepsilon_\Pi \sim N(0, \tau\Sigma)$$

and the one for the investor's views

$$q = P\mu + \varepsilon_q, \varepsilon_q \sim N(0, \Omega)$$

We can stack these two equations together in the form

---

[29]Henri Theil, *Principles of Econometrics* (New York: John Wiley & Sons, 1971).
[30]Stephen Satchell and Alan Scowcroft, "A Demystification of the Black-Litterman Model: Managing Quantitative and Traditional Portfolio Construction," *Journal of Asset Management*, 1 (2000), pp. 138–150.

$$y = X\mu + \varepsilon, \varepsilon \sim N(0, V)$$

where

$$y = \begin{bmatrix} \Pi \\ q \end{bmatrix}, X = \begin{bmatrix} I \\ P \end{bmatrix}, V = \begin{bmatrix} \tau\Sigma & \\ & \Omega \end{bmatrix}$$

with I denoting the $N \times N$ identity matrix. We observe that this is just a standard linear model for the expected returns μ. Calculating the Generalized Least Squares (GLS) estimator for μ, we obtain

$$\hat{\mu}_{BL} = (X'V^{-1}X)^{-1}X'V^{-1}y$$

$$= \left(\begin{bmatrix} I & P' \end{bmatrix} \begin{bmatrix} (\tau\Sigma)^{-1} & \\ & \Omega^{-1} \end{bmatrix} \begin{bmatrix} I \\ \Pi \end{bmatrix} \right)^{-1} \begin{bmatrix} I & P' \end{bmatrix} \begin{bmatrix} (\tau\Sigma)^{-1} & \\ & \Omega^{-1} \end{bmatrix} \begin{bmatrix} \Pi \\ q \end{bmatrix}$$

$$= \left(\begin{bmatrix} I & P' \end{bmatrix} \begin{bmatrix} (\tau\Sigma)^{-1} \\ \Omega^{-1}P \end{bmatrix} \right)^{-1} \begin{bmatrix} I & P' \end{bmatrix} \begin{bmatrix} (\tau\Sigma)^{-1}\Pi \\ \Omega^{-1}q \end{bmatrix}$$

$$= \left[(\tau\Sigma)^{-1} + P'\Omega^{-1}P \right]^{-1} \left[(\tau\Sigma)^{-1}\Pi + P'\Omega^{-1}q \right]$$

The last line in the above formula is the Black-Litterman expected returns that *blend* the market equilibrium with the investor's views.

Some Remarks and Observations

Following are some comments in order to provide a better intuitive understanding of the formula. We see that if the investor has no views (that is, $q = \Omega = 0$) or the confidence in the views is zero, then the Black-Litterman expected return becomes $\hat{\mu}_{BL} = \Pi$. Consequently, the investor will end up holding the market portfolio as predicted by the CAPM. In other words, the optimal portfolio in the absence of views is the defined market.

If we were to plug return targets of zero or use the available cash rates, for example, into an optimizer to represent the absence of views, the result would be an optimal portfolio that looks very much different from the market. The equilibrium returns are those forecasts that in the absence of any other views will produce an optimal portfolio equal to the market portfolio. Intuitively speaking, the equilibrium returns in the Black-Litterman model are used to center the optimal portfolio around the market portfolio.

By using $q = P\mu + \varepsilon_q$, we have that the investor's views alone imply the estimate of expected returns $\hat{\mu} = (P'P)^{-1}P'q$. Since $P(P'P)^{-1}P' = I$ where I is the identity matrix, we can rewrite the Black-Litterman expected returns in the form

$$\hat{\mu}_{BL} = \left[(\tau\Sigma)^{-1} + P'\Omega^{-1}P \right]^{-1} \left[(\tau\Sigma)^{-1}\Pi + P'\Omega^{-1}P\hat{\mu} \right]$$

Now we see that the Black-Litterman expected return is a *confidence weighted* linear combination of market equilibrium Π and the expected return $\hat{\mu}$ implied by the investor's views. The two weighting matrices are given by

$$\mathbf{w}_\Pi = \left[(\tau\Sigma)^{-1} + P'\Omega^{-1}P \right]^{-1} (\tau\Sigma)^{-1}$$

$$\mathbf{w}_q = \left[(\tau\Sigma)^{-1} + P'\Omega^{-1}P \right]^{-1} P'\Omega^{-1}P$$

where

$$\mathbf{w}_\Pi + \mathbf{w}_q = I$$

In particular, $(\tau\Sigma)^{-1}$ and $P'\Omega^{-1}P$ represent the confidence we have in our estimates of the market equilibrium and the views, respectively. Therefore, if we have low confidence in the views, the resulting expected returns will be close to the ones implied by market equilibrium. Conversely, with higher confidence in the views, the resulting expected returns will deviate from the market equilibrium implied expected returns. We say that we tilt away from market equilibrium.

It is straightforward to show that the Black-Litterman expected returns can also be written in the form

$$\hat{\mu}_{BL} = \Pi + \tau\Sigma P'(\Omega + \tau P\Sigma P')^{-1}(q - P\Pi)$$

where we now immediately see that we tilt away from the equilibrium with a vector proportional to $\Sigma P'(\Omega + \tau P\Sigma P')^{-1}(q - P\Pi)$.

We also mention that the Black-Litterman model can be derived as a solution to the following optimization problem:

$$\hat{\mu}_{BL} = \arg\min_\mu \left\{ (\Pi - \mu)' \Sigma^{-1} (\Pi - \mu) + \tau(q - P\mu)'\Omega^{-1}(q - P\mu) \right\}$$

From this formulation we see that $\hat{\mu}_{BL}$ is chosen such that it is *simultaneously* as close to Π, and $P\mu$ is as close to q as possible. The distances are determined by Σ^{-1} and Ω^{-1}. Furthermore, the relative importance of the equilibrium versus the views is determined by τ. For example, for τ large the weight of the views is increased, whereas for τ small the weight of the equilibrium is higher. Moreover, we also see that τ is a redundant parameter as it can be absorbed into Ω.

It is straightforward to calculate the variance of the Black-Litterman combined estimator of the expected returns by the standard *sandwich formula*, that is,

$$\text{var}(\hat{\boldsymbol{\mu}}_{BL}) = (\mathbf{X'V^{-1}X})^{-1}$$
$$= \left[(\tau\boldsymbol{\Sigma})^{-1} + \mathbf{P'\Omega^{-1}P} \right]^{-1}$$

The most important feature of the Black-Litterman model is that it uses the mixed estimation procedure to adjust the *entire* market equilibrium implied expected return vector with an investor's views. Because security returns are correlated, views on just a few assets will, due to these correlations, imply changes to the expected returns on *all* assets. Mathematically speaking, this follows from the fact that although the vector $\mathbf{q}$ can have dimension $K << N$, $\mathbf{P'\Omega^{-1}}$ is an $N \times K$ matrix that propagates the K views into N components, $\mathbf{P'\Omega^{-1}q}$. This effect is stronger the more correlated the different securities are. In the absence of this adjustment of the expected return vector, the differences between the equilibrium expected return and an investor's forecasts will be interpreted as an arbitrage opportunity by a mean-variance optimizer and result in portfolios concentrated in just a few assets ("corner solutions"). Intuitively, any estimation errors are spread out over all assets, making the Black-Litterman expected return vector less sensitive to errors in individual views. This effect contributes to the mitigation of estimation risk and error maximization in the optimization process.

Practical Considerations and Extensions

In this subsection we discuss a few practical issues in using the Black-Litterman model. Specifically, we discuss how to incorporate factor models and cross-sectional rankings in this framework. Furthermore, we also provide some ideas on how the confidences in the views can be estimated in cases where these are not directly available.

It is straightforward to incorporate factor models in the Black-Litterman framework. Let us assume we have a factor representation of the returns of some of the assets, that is

$$R_i = \alpha_i + \mathbf{F}\boldsymbol{\beta}_i + \varepsilon_i, i \in I$$

where $I \subset \{1, 2, \ldots, N\}$. Typically, from a factor model it is easy to obtain an estimate of the residual variance, $\text{var}(\varepsilon_i)$. In this case, we set

$$q_i = \begin{cases} \alpha + \mathbf{F}\boldsymbol{\beta}_i, i \in I \\ 0, \text{ otherwise} \end{cases}$$

and the corresponding confidence

$$\omega_{ii}^2 = \begin{cases} \mathrm{var}(\varepsilon_i), i \in I \\ 0, \text{ otherwise} \end{cases}$$

The **P** matrix is defined by

$$p_{ii} = \begin{cases} 1, \ i \in I \\ 0, \text{ otherwise} \end{cases}$$

$$p_{ij} = 0, \ i \neq j$$

Of course in a practical implementation we would omit rows with zeros.

Many quantitative investment strategies do not a priori produce expected returns, but rather just a simple ranking of the securities. Let us consider a ranking of securities from best to worst (from an outperforming to an underperforming perspective, etc.). For example, a value manager might consider ranking securities in terms of increasing book-to-price ratio (B/P), where a low B/P would indicate an undervalued stock (potential to increase in value) and high B/P an overvalued stock (potential to decrease in value). From this ranking we form a long-short portfolio where we purchase the top half of the stocks (the group that is expected to outperform) and we sell short the second half of stocks (the group that is expected to underperform). The view **q** in this case becomes a scalar, equal to the expected return on the long-short portfolio. The confidence of the view can be decided from backtests, as we describe next. Further, here the **P** matrix is a $1 \times N$ matrix of ones and minus ones. The corresponding column component is set to one if the security belongs to the outperforming group, or minus one if it belongs to the underperforming group.

In many cases we may not have a direct estimate of the expected return and confidence (variance) of the view. There are several different ways to determine the confidence level.

One of the advantages of a quantitative strategy is that it can be backtested. In the case of the long-short portfolio strategy discussed previously, we could estimate its historical variance through simulation with historical data. Of course, we cannot completely judge the performance of a strategy going forward from our backtests. Nevertheless, the backtest methodology allows us to obtain an estimate of the Black-Litterman view and confidence for a particular view/strategy.

Another approach of deriving estimates of the confidence of the view is through simple statistical assumptions. To illustrate, let us consider the second view in the preceding example: "Stock 3 will outperform Stock 2 by 4%." If we don't know its confidence, we can come up with an estimate for it from the answers to a few simple questions. We start asking ourselves with what certainty we believe the strategy will deliver a return between 3% and 5% (4% $\pm \alpha$ where α is some constant, in this case $\alpha = 1\%$). Let us say that we believe there is a chance of two out of three that this will happen, $\frac{2}{3}$ $\approx 67\%$. If we assume normality, we can interpret this as a 67% confidence interval for the future return to be in the interval [3%, 5%]. From this confidence interval we calculate that the implied standard deviation is equal to about 0.66%. Therefore, we would set the Black-Litterman confidence equal to $(0.66\%)^2 = 0.43\%$.

Some extensions to the Black-Litterman model have been derived. For example, Satchel and Scowcroft propose a model where an investor's view on global volatility is incorporated in the prior views by assuming that τ is unknown and stochastic.[31] Idzorek introduces a new idea for determining the confidence level of a view.[32] He proposes that the investor derives his confidence level indirectly by first specifying his confidence in the tilt away from equilibrium (the difference between the market capitalization weights and the weights implied by the view alone). Qian and Gorman describe a technique based on conditional distribution theory that allows an investor to incorporate his views on *any* or *all* variances.[33]

Of course other asset classes beyond equities and bonds can be incorporated into the Black-Litterman framework.[34] Some practical experiences and implementation details have been described by Bevan and Winkelman[35] and He and Litterman.[36] A Bayesian approach, with some similarity to the Black-Litterman model, to portfolio selection using higher moments has been proposed by Harvey, et al.[37]

---

[31]Satchel and Scowcroft, "A Demystification of the Black-Litterman Model: Managing Quantitative and Traditional Portfolio Construction."

[32]Idzorek, "A Step-By-Step Guide to the Black-Litterman Model: Incorporating User-Specified Confidence Levels."

[33]Edward Qian and Stephen Gorman, "Conditional Distribution in Portfolio Theory," *Financial Analysts Journal*, 57 (2001), pp. 44–51.

[34]See, for example, Fischer Black and Robert Litterman, "Global Asset Allocation with Equities, Bonds, and Currencies," *Fixed Income Research*, Goldman Sachs, 1991; and Robert Litterman, *Modern Investment Management: An Equilibrium Approach* (Hoboken, NJ: John Wiley & Sons, 2003).

[35]Andrew Bevan and Kurt Winkelmann, "Using the Black-Litterman Global Asset Allocation Model: Three Years of Practical Experience," *Fixed Income Research*, Goldman Sachs, 1998.

[36]Guangliang He and Robert Litterman, "The Intuition Behind Black-Litterman Model Portfolios," *Investment Management Division*, Goldman Sachs, 1999.

[37]Campbell R. Harvey, John C. Liechty, Merril W. Liechty, and Peter Mueller, "Portfolio Selection with Higher Moments," Duke University, Working Paper, 2003.

The Black-Litterman Model: An Example

In this section we provide an illustration of the Black-Litterman model by combining a cross-sectional momentum strategy with market equilibrium. The resulting Black-Litterman expected returns are subsequently fed into a mean-variance optimizer. We start by describing the momentum strategy before we turn to the optimized strategy.

A Cross-Sectional Momentum Strategy

Practitioners and researchers alike have identified several ways to success-fully predict security returns based on the past history returns. Among these findings, perhaps the most popular ones are those of momentum and rever-sal strategies.

The basic idea of a momentum strategy is to buy stocks that have per-formed well and to sell the stocks that have performed poorly with the hope that the same trend will continue in the near future. This effect was first documented in academic literature by Jegadeesh and Titman[38] in 1993 for the U.S. stock market and has thereafter been shown to be present in many other international equity markets.[39] The empirical findings show that stocks that outperformed (underperformed) over a horizon of 6 to 12 months will continue to perform well (poorly) on a horizon of 3 to 12 months to follow. Typical backtests of these strategies have historically earned about 1% per month over the following 12 months.

Many practitioners rely on momentum strategies—both on shorter as well as longer horizons. Short-term strategies tend to capitalize on intraday buy and sell pressures, whereas more intermediate and long-term strategies can be attributed to over- and underreaction of prices relative to their fun-damental value as new information becomes available.[40]

Momentum portfolios tend to have high turnover so transaction and trading costs become an issue. Most studies show that the resulting profits of momentum strategies decrease if transaction costs are taken into account. For example, Korajczyk and Sadka, taking into account the different costs of buying and short-selling stocks, report that depending on the method

---

[38]Narasimhan Jegadeesh and Sheridan Titman, "Returns to Buying Winners and Selling Losers: Implications for Stock Market Efficiency," *Journal of Finance*, 48 (1993), pp. 65–91.

[39]K. Geert Rouwenhorst, "International Momentum Strategies," *Journal of Finance*, 53 (1998), pp. 267–283.

[40]Kent D. Daniel, David Hirshleifer, and Avanidhar Subrahmanyam, "Investor Psy-chology and Security Market Under- and Overreactions," *Journal of Finance*, 53 (1998), pp. 1839–1885.

of measurement and the particular strategy, profits between 17 to 35 basis points per month (after transaction costs) are achievable.[41]

While researchers seem to be in somewhat of an agreement on the robustness and pervasiveness of the momentum phenomenon, the debate is still ongoing on whether the empirical evidence indicates market inefficiency or if it can be explained by rational asset pricing theories. This discussion is beyond the scope of this book. Instead, we provide an illustration of a simple cross-sectional momentum strategy using the country indexes from the MSCI World Index.[42]

The cross-sectional momentum portfolio is constructed at a point in time t ("today") and held for one month. We sort the countries based on their "one-day lagged" past nine-month return normalized by their individual volatilities. In other words, the ranking is based on the quantity

$$z_{t,i} = \frac{P_{t-1\,\text{day},i} - P_{t-1\,\text{day}-9\,\text{months},i}}{P_{t-1\,\text{day}-9\,\text{months},i} \cdot \sigma_i}$$

where $P_{t-1\,\text{day},i}$, $P_{t-1\,\text{day}-9\,\text{months},i}$ and σ_i denote the prices of security i at one day before t, one day and nine months before t, and the volatility of security i, respectively. After the ranking, the securities in the top half are assigned a weight of

$$w_i = \frac{1}{\sigma_i \cdot \kappa}$$

where κ is a scaling factor chosen such that the resulting annual portfolio volatility is at a desirable level. In this example, we set it equal to 20%.[43] Similarly, the securities in the bottom half are assigned a weight of

$$w_i = \frac{1}{\sigma_i \cdot \kappa}$$

We make the portfolio weights a function of the individual volatilities in order not to overweight the most volatile assets. This is not a zero cost long-short portfolio as the portfolio weights do not sum up to zero. It is straightforward to modify the weighting scheme to achieve a zero cost portfolio, but for our purposes this does not matter and will not significantly change

---

[41]Robert A. Korajczyk and Ronnie Sadka, "Are Momentum Profits Robust to Trading Costs?" *Journal of Finance*, 59 (2004), pp. 1039–1082.
[42]A more detailed description of the data is provided in Appendix A.
[43]κ can be estimated from past portfolio returns at each time of rebalancing. Typically, it's value does not change significantly from period to period.

the results. The results from this simple momentum strategy are given in Exhibits 9.3 through 9.6.[44]

The momentum strategy outperforms the index on both an alpha and a Sharpe ratio basis. The Sharpe ratio of the strategy over the full period is 0.88 versus 0.62 for the index. The full period-annualized alpha is 11.7%, consistent with the standard results in the momentum literature. We also see that the beta of the strategy is very low, only 0.05 for the full sample. The realized correlation between the momentum strategy and the index is 3.5%. In other words, this momentum strategy is more or less market neutral.

It turns out that this particular implementation has an average monthly portfolio turnover of 23.7% with a cross-sectional standard deviation of 9.3%. The United Kingdom has the highest average turnover (40.6%) and New Zealand has the lowest (10.8%). For a *real-world* implementation it would therefore be important to consider the impact of transaction costs.

---

[44]The first portfolio is constructed in January 1981, as we need the previous nine-month return in order to perform the ranking.

EXHIBIT 9.3   Growth of Equity for the Momentum Strategy and the MSCI World Index

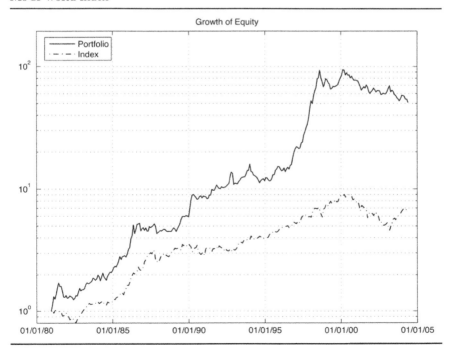

EXHIBIT 9.4   A Comparison of the Annualized Volatility of the Momentum
Strategy and the Index

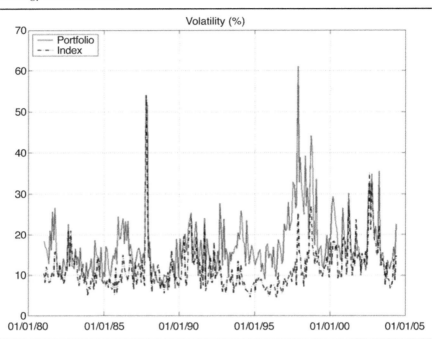

An Optimized Cross-Sectional Momentum Strategy

In the previous section we introduced a simple cross-sectional momentum strategy. In this section we demonstrate how it can be combined with
market equilibrium in a portfolio optimization framework by using the
Black-Litterman model.

In this case, we only have one view—the momentum strategy. We use the
approach described earlier where we discussed the "practical considerations
and extensions" to specify the parameters for the Black-Litterman view.

The covariance matrices needed for the portfolio optimization are calculated from daily historical data with weighting (monthly decay parameter
of $d = 0.95$) and with the correction for autocorrelation of Newey and West
(2 lags).[45] We choose $\tau = 0.1$ for the Black-Litterman model.

After computing the implied Black-Litterman expected returns, we use
the risk aversion formulation introduced in Chapter 8 of the mean-variance

---

[45]This particular covariance matrix estimator is described in Chapter 8.

EXHIBIT 9.5 Summary Statistics of the Momentum Strategy

	Start Date	End Date	Mean	Volatility	Sharpe Ratio	Skew	Kurtosis	Min	Max	Alpha	Beta
1st Qtr	Jan-81	Dec-85	23.0%	19.4%	1.18	0.12	2.82	−10.4%	17.1%	11.7%	0.25
2nd Qtr	Jan-86	Dec-91	22.1%	21.7%	1.02	0.50	4.90	−14.9%	21.8%	14.3%	0.06
3rd Qtr	Jan-92	Dec-97	26.9%	20.9%	1.29	−0.09	4.87	−18.8%	20.2%	22.3%	−0.02
4th Qtr	Jan-98	May-04	3.7%	20.8%	0.18	0.54	3.33	−13.1%	16.9%	−0.1%	−0.05
1st Half	Jan-81	Dec-91	22.5%	20.6%	1.09	0.36	4.23	−14.9%	21.8%	12.9%	0.12
2nd Half	Jan-92	May-04	14.8%	21.1%	0.70	0.23	3.82	−18.8%	20.2%	10.7%	−0.03
Full	Jan-81	May-04	18.4%	20.9%	0.88	0.29	4.01	−18.8%	21.8%	11.7%	0.05

Note: The columns Mean, Volatility, Sharpe Ratio, and Alpha are the annualized mean returns, volatilities, Sharpe ratios, and alphas of the portfolio over the different periods. Min and Max are the daily minimum and maximum portfolio returns, respectively. Skew and Kurtosis are calculated as the third and fourth normalized centered moments. Alphas and betas are calculated using one-month LIBOR.

389

EXHIBIT 9.6 Summary Statistics of the MSCI World Index

	Start Date	End Date	Mean	Volatility	Sharpe Ratio	Skew	Kurtosis	Min	Max
1st Qtr	Jan-81	Dec-85	10.2%	11.5%	0.88	−0.29	2.70	−7.6%	7.7%
2nd Qtr	Jan-86	Dec-91	13.2%	16.4%	0.81	−0.21	4.05	−14.6%	12.8%
3rd Qtr	Jan-92	Dec-97	9.6%	9.8%	0.98	0.62	3.28	−3.9%	9.5%
4th Qtr	Jan-98	May-04	2.9%	17.2%	0.17	0.17	3.49	−12.3%	16.0%
1st Half	Jan-81	Dec-91	11.8%	14.3%	0.83	−0.21	4.22	−14.6%	12.8%
2nd Half	Jan-92	May-04	6.1%	14.1%	0.43	0.15	4.32	−12.3%	16.0%
Full	Jan-81	May-04	8.8%	14.2%	0.62	−0.02	4.22	−14.6%	16.0%

Note: The columns Mean, Volatility, and Sharpe Ratio are the annualized mean returns, volatilities, and Sharpe ratios of the index over the different periods. Min and Max are the daily minimum and maximum Index returns, respectively. Skew and Kurtosis are calculated as the third and fourth normalized centered moments.

optimization problem with a risk aversion coefficient of $\lambda = 2$ (calibrated to achieve about the same volatility as the index) to calculate the optimal portfolio weights and rebalance the portfolio monthly. Before rebalancing at the end of each month, we calculate the realized portfolio return and its volatility. Results and summary statistics are presented in Exhibits 9.7 through 9.9. A comparison with the MSCI World Index is given in Exhibit 9.6.

The optimized strategy has a full sample Sharpe ratio of 0.92 versus 0.62 for the index and an alpha of 8.3%. We observe that in the last quarter the Sharpe ratio and the alpha of the strategy were negative, largely due to the general downturn in the market during that period. In contrast to the standalone momentum strategy that we discussed in the previous section, since the optimized strategy is a blend of momentum and market equilibrium, its resulting correlation with the index is significantly different from zero. For example, the full sample correlation with the index in this case is 0.36.[46]

---

[46]One possibility to decrease the correlation of the strategy with the index is to impose zero β constraints.

EXHIBIT 9.7 Growth of Equity of the Optimized Strategy and the MSCI World Index

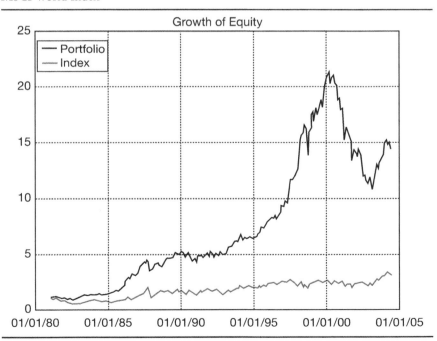

EXHIBIT 9.8 Monthly Portfolio Volatility of the Optimized Strategy Compared to Monthly Volatility of the MSCI World Index

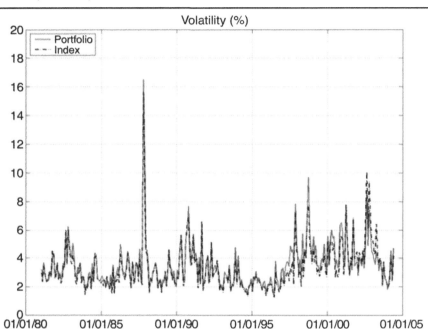

Albeit rudimentary, this illustration shows that it is possible to use portfolio theory and mean-variance optimization in the design of profitable investment strategies. The standard textbook version of the mean-variance optimization typically underperforms an equally weighted portfolio and the GMV portfolio. The main issue here is that the classical mean-variance approach is very sensitive to small changes of the expected returns of the securities. The mixed estimation procedure used in the computation of the Black-Litterman implied expected returns by blending an investor's views with market equilibrium is, in practice, an effective way to mitigate estimation errors. Simply speaking, the Black-Litterman model manages to spread out any estimation errors in individual views over all assets and thereby makes the resulting expected returns more robust to estimation risk.

EXHIBIT 9.9 Portfolio Summary Statistics of the Optimized Strategy Rebalanced Monthly

	Start Date	End Date	Mean	Volatility	Sharpe Ratio	Skew	Kurtosis	Min	Max	Alpha	Beta
1st Qtr	Jan-81	Dec-89	18.9%	15.0%	1.26	-0.33	4.39	-15.1%	13.2%	9.2%	0.28
2nd Qtr	Jan-90	Dec-94	13.8%	13.7%	1.01	0.35	3.92	-9.4%	12.8%	11.23%	0.40
3rd Qtr	Jan-95	Dec-99	23.8%	14.0%	1.70	0.19	4.12	-9.1%	14.4%	18.1%	0.39
4th Qtr	Jan-00	May-04	-2.9%	15.3%	-0.19	-0.28	2.82	-11.9%	8.5%	-5.0%	0.65
1st Half	Jan-81	Dec-94	16.5%	14.6%	1.13	-0.09	4.08	-15.1%	13.2%	11.4%	0.31
2nd Half	Jan-95	May-04	11.4%	15.2%	0.75	-0.13	3.60	-11.9%	14.4%	6.3%	0.37
Full	Jan-81	May-04	13.6%	14.9%	0.92	-0.11	3.88	-15.1%	14.4%	8.3%	0.36

Note: The columns Mean, Volatility, Sharpe Ratio, and Alpha are the annualized mean returns, volatilities, Sharpe ratios, and alphas of the portfolio over the different periods. Min and Max are the daily minimum and maximum portfolio returns, respectively. Skew and Kurtosis are calculated as the third and fourth normalized centered moments. Alphas and betas are calculated using one-month LIBOR.

SUMMARY

- Classical mean-variance optimization is sensitive to estimation error and small changes in the inputs.
- We pointed out four different approaches to make the classical mean-variance framework more robust: (1) improve the accuracy of the inputs; (2) use constraints for the portfolio weights; (3) use portfolio resampling to calculate the portfolio weights; and (4) apply the robust optimization framework to the portfolio allocation process. This chapter focused on (1) and (2).
- Typically, errors in the expected returns are about 10 times more important than errors in the covariance matrix, and errors in the variances are about twice as important as errors in the covariances.
- Estimates of expected return and covariances can be improved by using shrinkage estimation. Shrinkage is a form of averaging different estimators. The shrinkage estimator typically consists of three components: (1) an estimator with little or no structure; (2) an estimator with a lot of structure (the shrinkage target); and (3) the shrinkage intensity.
- Jorion's shrinkage estimator for the expected return shrinks toward the return of the global minimum variance portfolio.
- The sample covariance matrix should not be used as an input to the mean-variance problem. By shrinking it toward the covariance matrix with constant correlations, its quality will be improved.
- The Black-Litterman model combines an investor's views with the market equilibrium.
- The Black-Litterman expected return is a confidence weighted linear combination of market equilibrium and the investor's views. The confidence in the views and in market equilibrium determines the relative weighting.
- Factor models as well as simple ranking models can be simultaneously incorporated into the Black-Litterman model.

CHAPTER 10

Robust Portfolio Optimization

U ncertainty in the inputs to a portfolio optimization problem (for example, the expected returns and their variances and covariances) can be modeled directly in the optimization process. Robust optimization is an intuitive and efficient way to describe this form of uncertainty.

In the optimization literature, the term *robust optimization* has been used to describe several different concepts, and is therefore a little confusing. Usually, however, robust optimization refers to an area of optimization whose roots are in the robust control engineering literature. It deals with making optimization models robust with respect to constraint violations by solving so-called robust counterparts of these problems for appropriately defined uncertainty sets for the uncertain parameters. These robust counterparts are in fact worst-case formulations of the original problem in terms of deviations of the parameters from their nominal values; however, typically the worst-case scenarios are defined in clever ways that do not lead to overly conservative formulations.

We can only speculate as to why robust portfolio modeling is not more widely used by practitioners in the financial community. Probably, a major reason for this is that the technique is relatively new and is considered too technical. The implementation, however, is frequently straightforward, and has a comparable level of computational complexity to that of the original, nonrobust formulation. In this chapter, we show explicitly how the technique can be applied.

First, we discuss the robust versions of the mean-variance portfolio optimization problem when uncertainty is assumed to be present only in the expected return estimates. We show several ways of modeling the uncertainty, based on factor models and Bayesian statistics. We then extend the model to include uncertainty in the asset return covariance matrix. We conclude this section with a discussion of important considerations when using robust modeling techniques in practice, and present an example of a robust version of the mean-variance optimization problem.

This chapter is co-authored with Dessislava Pachamanova.

ROBUST MEAN-VARIANCE FORMULATIONS

We recall that the classical mean-variance problem introduced in Chapter 8 is

$$\max_{w} \boldsymbol{\mu}'\mathbf{w} - \lambda\mathbf{w}'\boldsymbol{\Sigma}\mathbf{w}$$

$$s.t. \quad \mathbf{w}'\boldsymbol{\iota} = 1$$

where $\boldsymbol{\iota} = [1,1, ..., 1]'$. In this optimization problem $\boldsymbol{\mu}, \boldsymbol{\Sigma}, \lambda$, and $\mathbf{w}$ denote the expected return, asset return covariance matrix, risk aversion coefficient, and portfolio weights, respectively.

As discussed in more detail in Chapter 9, the estimation error in the forecasts may significantly influence the resulting optimized portfolio weights. A study by Black and Litterman[1] demonstrated that small changes in the expected returns, in particular, had a substantial impact. It follows that if the estimation errors in expected returns are large—which is often the case in practice—they will significantly influence the optimal allocation. For practical applications, it is therefore crucial to incorporate the uncertainty about the accuracy of estimates in the portfolio optimization process.

Uncertainty in Expected Return Estimates

An easy way to incorporate uncertainty caused by estimation errors is to require that the investor be protected if the estimated expected return $\hat{\mu}_i$ for each asset is *around* the true expected return μ_i. The error from the estimation can be assumed to be not larger than some small number $\delta_i > 0$. A simple choice for the *uncertainty set* for $\boldsymbol{\mu}$ is the "box"

$$U_\delta(\hat{\boldsymbol{\mu}}) = \left\{ \boldsymbol{\mu} \,\middle|\, |\mu_i - \hat{\mu}_i| \le \delta_i, i = 1, ..., N \right\}$$

The δ_i's could be specified by assuming some confidence interval around the estimated expected return. For example, if expected returns are estimated using simulation (in which case the Central Limit Theorem applies)[2] or if asset returns are assumed to follow a normal distribution, then a 95% confidence interval for μ_i can be obtained by setting $\delta_i = 1.96\sigma_i / \sqrt{T}$, where T is the sample size used in the estimation.

---

[1]Fischer Black and Robert Litterman, "Global Portfolio Optimization," *Financial Analysts Journal*, 48 (1992), pp. 28–43.
[2]The Central Limit Theorem states that under mild assumptions, the mean of a sample of independent and identically distributed observations from any distribution follows an approximately normal distribution with mean equal to the actual mean of the original distribution and standard deviation equal to the standard deviation of the original distribution divided by the square root of the sample size.

The robust formulation of the mean-variance problem under the preceding assumption on $\hat{\mu}_i$ is

$$\max_{\mathbf{w}} \hat{\mu}'\mathbf{w} - \delta'|\mathbf{w}| - \lambda\mathbf{w}'\Sigma\mathbf{w}$$

$$s.t. \quad \mathbf{w}'\iota = 1$$

This formulation is in fact obvious without any involved mathematics. If the weight of asset i in the portfolio is negative, the worst-case expected return for asset i is $\mu_i + \delta_i$ (we lose the largest amount possible). If the weight of asset i in the portfolio is positive, then the worst-case expected return for asset i is $\mu_i - \delta_i$ (we gain the smallest amount possible). Note that $\mu_i w_i - \delta_i |w_i|$ equals $(\mu_i - \delta_i)w_i$ if the weight w_i is positive and $(\mu_i + \delta_i)w_i$ if the weight w_i is negative. Therefore, the mathematical expression in the objective agrees with our intuition: it tries to minimize the worst-case expected portfolio return. In this robust version of the mean-variance formulation, assets whose mean return estimates are less accurate (have a larger estimation error δ_i) are penalized in the objective function, and will tend to have smaller weights in the optimal portfolio allocation. We note that this problem has the same computational complexity as the nonrobust mean-variance formulation.[3]

To gain some additional insight, let us rewrite the robust formulation as

$$\max_{\mathbf{w}}(\hat{\mu} - \mu_{\delta,\mathbf{w}})'\mathbf{w} - \lambda\mathbf{w}'\Sigma\mathbf{w}$$

$$s.t. \quad \mathbf{w}'\iota = 1$$

where

$$\mu_{\delta,\mathbf{w}} = \begin{bmatrix} \text{sign}(w_1)\delta_1 \\ \vdots \\ \text{sign}(w_N)\delta_N \end{bmatrix}$$

---

[3]There are two well-known techniques for making this optimization problem solver-friendly by getting rid of the absolute value of the vector of weights $\mathbf{w}$, and thus converting it into a standard quadratic optimization problem. One is to introduce a new variable, ψ, to replace the absolute value. The problem can be then rewritten as

$$\max_{\mathbf{w},\psi} \hat{\mu}'\mathbf{w} - \delta'\psi - \lambda\mathbf{w}'\Sigma\mathbf{w}$$
$$s.t. \quad \mathbf{w}'\iota = 1$$
$$\psi_i \geq w_i; \psi_i \geq -w_i, i = 1,\ldots,N$$

Another way is to write $\mathbf{w}$ as a difference of two nonnegative variables $\mathbf{w}_+$ and $\mathbf{w}_-$, and replace occurrences of $|\mathbf{w}|$ by $\mathbf{w}_+ + \mathbf{w}_-$. The optimization problem becomes

$$\max_{\mathbf{w},\mathbf{w}_+,\mathbf{w}_-} \hat{\mu}'\mathbf{w} - \delta'(\mathbf{w}_+ + \mathbf{w}_-) - \lambda\mathbf{w}'\Sigma\mathbf{w}$$
$$s.t. \quad \mathbf{w}'\iota = 1$$
$$\mathbf{w} = \mathbf{w}_+ - \mathbf{w}_-, \mathbf{w}_+ \geq 0, \mathbf{w}_- \geq 0$$

Here sign(.) is the sign function (that is, $\text{sign}(x) = 1$ when $x \geq 0$ and $\text{sign}(x) = -1$ when $x < 0$). In this reformulation of the problem we see that robust optimization is related to statistical shrinkage, and the original expected return vector is shrunk to $\hat{\mu} - \mu_{\delta,w}$.

By using the equality

$$w_i \text{sign}(w_i)\delta_i = w_i \frac{w_i}{|w_i|}\delta_i = \frac{w_i}{\sqrt{|w_i|}}\delta_i \frac{w_i}{\sqrt{|w_i|}}$$

we can rewrite the problem as

$$\max_{w} \mu'w - \lambda w'\Sigma w - \hat{w}'\Delta\hat{w}$$
$$s.t. \quad w'\iota = 1$$

where

$$\hat{w} = \begin{bmatrix} \dfrac{w_1}{\sqrt{|w_1|}} \\ \vdots \\ \dfrac{w_N}{\sqrt{|w_N|}} \end{bmatrix}$$

and

$$\Delta = \begin{bmatrix} \delta_1 & & \\ & \ddots & \\ & & \delta_N \end{bmatrix}$$

Observe that this problem is yet another modification of the classical mean-variance problem. In particular, a *risk-like* term $\hat{w}'\Delta\hat{w}$ has been added to the classical formulation. This term can be interpreted as a risk adjustment performed by an investor who is averse to estimation error. The exact form of the investor's estimation error aversion is specified by the magnitude of the deltas.

One can define many other uncertainty sets for the expected returns vector μ. While more general uncertainty sets lead to more complicated optimization problems, the basic intuition and interpretation remain the same. For instance, consider the uncertainty set

$$U_\delta(\hat{\mu}) = \left\{ \mu \,\middle|\, (\mu - \hat{\mu})'\Sigma_\mu^{-1}(\mu - \hat{\mu}) \leq \delta^2 \right\}$$

It captures the idea that the investor would like to be protected in instances in which the total scaled deviation of the realized average returns from the estimated returns is within δ.[4] The derivation of the robust formulation with this uncertainty set is a bit more involved, but we show it next for illustrative purposes.

Similarly to the first example of modeling uncertainty in expected return estimates, we ask ourselves what the *worst* estimates of the expected returns would be, and how we would allocate the portfolio in this case. Mathematically, this can be expressed as

$$\max_{w} \min_{\mu \in \{\mu \mid (\mu - \hat{\mu})' \Sigma_{\mu}^{-1} (\mu - \hat{\mu}) \le \delta^2\}} \mu'w - \lambda w' \Sigma w$$

$$s.t. \quad w' \iota = 1$$

This problem is called the *robust counterpart*, or the *max-min* problem, and is not in a form that can be input into a standard optimization solver. We need to solve the *inner* problem first while holding the vector of weights w fixed, and compute the worst expected portfolio return over the set of possible values for μ:

$$\min_{\mu} \mu'w - \lambda w' \Sigma w$$

$$s.t. \quad (\mu - \hat{\mu})' \Sigma_{\mu}^{-1} (\mu - \hat{\mu}) \le \delta^2$$

The Lagrangian of this problem takes the form

$$L(\mu, \gamma) = \mu'w - \lambda w' \Sigma w - \gamma(\delta^2 - (\mu - \hat{\mu})' \Sigma_{\mu}^{-1} (\mu - \hat{\mu}))$$

Differentiating this with respect to μ, we obtain the first-order condition

$$w + 2\gamma \Sigma_{\mu}^{-1} (\mu - \hat{\mu}) = 0$$

and therefore the optimal value of μ is

$$\mu^* = \hat{\mu} - \frac{1}{2\gamma} \Sigma_{\mu} w$$

The optimal value of γ can be found by maximizing the Lagrangian after substituting the expression for the worst-case μ, that is,

---

[4]This kind of uncertainty set scales the distances between the estimated and the possible values for the expected returns by the variability (standard deviation) in the estimates. This uncertainty set ensures that the total budget of tolerance to uncertainty, δ, is distributed evenly among expected return estimates that have different variability.

$$\max_{\gamma \geq 0} L(\mathbf{\mu}, \gamma) = \mathbf{\mu}'\mathbf{w} - \lambda\mathbf{w}'\Sigma\mathbf{w} - \frac{1}{4\gamma}\mathbf{w}'\Sigma_\mu\mathbf{w} - \gamma\delta^2$$

After solving the first-order condition, we obtain

$$\gamma^* = \frac{1}{2\delta}\sqrt{\mathbf{w}'\Sigma_\mu\mathbf{w}}$$

Finally, by substituting the expression for γ^* in the Lagrangian, we obtain the robust problem

$$\max_{\mathbf{w}} \mathbf{\mu}'\mathbf{w} - \lambda\mathbf{w}'\Sigma\mathbf{w} - \delta\sqrt{\mathbf{w}'\Sigma_\mu\mathbf{w}}$$
$$s.t. \quad \mathbf{w}'\iota = 1$$

Just as in the previous problem, we interpret the term $\delta\sqrt{\mathbf{w}'\Sigma_\mu\mathbf{w}}$ as the penalty for estimation risk, where δ reflects the degree of the investor's aversion to estimation risk. We remark that the uncertainty set used here can be interpreted as an N-dimensional confidence region for the parameter vector $\hat{\mathbf{\mu}}$, defined by the estimation error covariance matrix Σ_μ.[5]

It is not immediately obvious how one can estimate Σ_μ. Note that Σ_μ is the covariance matrix of the errors in the estimation of the *expected* (average) returns. Thus, if a portfolio manager forecasts 5% active return over the next time period, but gets 1%, he cannot argue that there was a 4% error in his *expected* return—the actual error would consist of both an estimation error in the expected return and the inherent volatility in actual realized returns. In fact, critics of the approach have argued that the *realized* returns typically have large stochastic components that dwarf the *expected* returns, and hence estimating Σ_μ accurately from historical data is very hard, if not impossible.[6]

In theory, if returns in a given sample of size T are independent and identically distributed, then Σ_μ equals $(1/T) \cdot \Sigma$, where Σ is the covariance matrix of asset returns as before. However, experience seems to suggest that this may not be the best method in practice. One issue is that this approach applies only in a world in which returns are stationary. Another important issue is whether the estimate of the asset covariance matrix Σ itself is reliable if it is estimated from a sample of historical data. As we explained in

[5]In some references, the term $\sqrt{\mathbf{w}'\Sigma_\mu\mathbf{w}}$ is replaced by $\|\Sigma_\mu^{1/2}\mathbf{w}\|$, where $\|.\|$ denotes the l_2 (Euclidean, elliptic) norm of a vector. The two expressions are equivalent, but $\sqrt{\mathbf{w}'\Sigma_\mu\mathbf{w}}$ makes it evident that the new penalty term involves the standard error of the estimate, and is therefore easier to interpret.
[6]Jyh-Huei Lee, Dan Stefek, and Alexander Zhelenyak, "Robust Portfolio Optimization—A Closer Look," *MSCI Barra Research Insights* report, June 2006.

Chapter 8, computing a meaningful asset return covariance matrix requires a large number of observations—many more observations than the number of assets in the portfolio—and even then the sample covariance matrix may contain large estimation errors that may produce poor results in the mean-variance optimization. One approach when sufficient data are not available for computing the covariance matrix for all securities in the portfolio is to compute the estimation errors in expected returns at a factor (e.g., industry, country, sector) level, and use their variances and covariances in the estimation error covariance matrix for the individual asset returns.

Several approximate methods for estimating Σ_μ have been found to work well in practice.[7] For example, it has been observed that simpler estimation approaches, such as using just the diagonal matrix containing the variances of the estimates (as opposed to the complete error covariance matrix), frequently provide most of the benefit in robust portfolio optimization. In addition, standard approaches for estimating expected returns, such as Bayesian statistics and regression-based methods,[8] can produce estimates for the estimation error covariance matrix in the process of generating the estimates themselves. Practical ways to compute an effective estimation error covariance matrix include least squares regression models, the James-Stein estimator, and the Black-Litterman model.[9] We describe some of these techniques next.

Least Squares Regression Models

If expected returns are estimated based on linear regression, then one can calculate an estimate of the error covariance matrix from the regression errors. Let us assume we have the factor model for the returns

$$r = \mu + V'f + \varepsilon$$

This can be rewritten as

$$y_i = Ax_i + \varepsilon_i$$

for every asset *i* or, more generally, as

$$Y = AX + \varepsilon$$

---

[7]Robert Stubbs and Pamela Vance, "Computing Return Estimation Error Matrices for Robust Optimization," Report, Axioma, April 2005.
[8]See Chapter 2 for coverage of regression analysis.
[9]For more details, refer to Stubbs and Vance, "Computing Return Estimation Error Matrices for Robust Optimization."

where

$\mathbf{Y} = [\mathbf{y}_1,...,\mathbf{y}_N]$ is a $T \times N$ matrix of T return data observations for N assets

$\mathbf{A} = [1,\mathbf{f}_1,...,\mathbf{f}_M]$ is a $T \times (M+1)$ matrix of factor realizations

$\mathbf{X} = [\boldsymbol{\mu}, \mathbf{x}_1, ...,\mathbf{x}_M]'$ is an $(M+1) \text{ ¥ } N$ matrix of regression coefficients

If a portfolio manager decomposes the expected return forecast into factor-specific and asset-specific returns, then he is concerned about the standard error covariance matrix for the intercept term $\boldsymbol{\mu}$. This covariance matrix can be used as an estimate for $\boldsymbol{\Sigma}_{\mu}$. The matrix of estimation errors for the response corresponding to the factor realizations $(\mathbf{f}_{\tau 1},...,\mathbf{f}_{\tau M}) \in R^M$ is given by

$$\mathbf{f}_{\tau}'(\mathbf{X}\mathbf{X}')^{-1}\mathbf{f}_{\tau}\left\{\frac{1}{T}(\mathbf{Y}-\mathbf{A}\mathbf{X})'(\mathbf{Y}-\mathbf{A}\mathbf{X})\right\}$$

where $\mathbf{f}_{\tau} = (1,\mathbf{f}_{\tau 1},...,\mathbf{f}_{\tau M})'$.[10]

---

[10]To see why let us consider the linear regression model

$$y_i = \mathbf{z}_i'\boldsymbol{\beta}+\varepsilon_i, \ \varepsilon_i \sim N(0,\sigma^2)$$

where $i = 1, ..., N$. The least squares estimate of $\boldsymbol{\beta}$ is given by

$$\hat{\boldsymbol{\beta}} = (\mathbf{z}\mathbf{z}')^{-1}\mathbf{z}\mathbf{y}$$

Let us assume we want to forecast the response and determine the associated forecasting error for the factor realizations (predictor) $\mathbf{z}_0$. Let us assume that y_0, where $y_0 = \mathbf{z}_0'\boldsymbol{\beta}+\varepsilon_0$, is the true value, whereas the forecasting model gives us $\hat{y}_0 = \mathbf{z}_0'\hat{\boldsymbol{\beta}}$. Therefore, the forecasting error is given by

$$e_0 = y_0 - \hat{y}_0 = \mathbf{z}_0'(\boldsymbol{\beta}-\hat{\boldsymbol{\beta}}) + \varepsilon_0$$

and its variance is

$$\begin{aligned} Var(e_0) &= \sigma^2 + Var(\mathbf{z}_0'(\boldsymbol{\beta}-\hat{\boldsymbol{\beta}})) \\ &= \sigma^2 + \mathbf{z}_0'E((\boldsymbol{\beta}-\hat{\boldsymbol{\beta}})(\boldsymbol{\beta}-\hat{\boldsymbol{\beta}})')\mathbf{z}_0 \\ &= \sigma^2 + \mathbf{z}_0'E((\mathbf{z}\mathbf{z}')^{-1}\mathbf{z}\boldsymbol{\varepsilon}\boldsymbol{\varepsilon}'\mathbf{z}'(\mathbf{z}\mathbf{z}')^{-1})\mathbf{z}_0 \\ &= \sigma^2 + \sigma^2\mathbf{z}_0'(\mathbf{z}\mathbf{z}')^{-1}\mathbf{z}_0 \end{aligned}$$

where we used that $\hat{\boldsymbol{\beta}}=\boldsymbol{\beta}+(\mathbf{z}\mathbf{z}')^{-1}\mathbf{z}'\boldsymbol{\varepsilon}$. The forecasting variance therefore depends on two separate terms: (1) the first term is associated with the residual from the regression, and (2) the second term we define as the estimation error. To use this formula we need an estimate for σ^2. This can be obtained from observations

The James-Stein Estimator

The James-Stein estimator of expected returns is computed as a weighted average of the sample average returns (computed from a sample of size T) and a *shrinkage target* of μ_0

$$\hat{\mu}_{JS} = (1-w)\hat{\mu} + w\mu_0$$

The special form of the James-Stein shrinkage estimator proposed by Jorion[11] (named the Bayes-Stein estimator) is based on Bayesian methodology. The shrinkage target μ_0 for the Bayes-Stein estimator is computed as

$$\mu_0 = \frac{\iota'\Sigma^{-1}}{\iota'\Sigma^{-1}\iota}\hat{\mu}$$

where Σ is the *real* covariance matrix of the N returns. This matrix is unknown in practice, but one can replace Σ in the previous equation by

$$\hat{\Sigma} = \frac{T-1}{T-N-3}S$$

and S is the usual sample covariance matrix. The variance of the Bayes-Stein estimator for the expected returns is given by[12]

$$\text{var}(\hat{\mu}_{BS}) = \Sigma + \frac{1}{T+\tau}\Sigma + \frac{\tau}{T(T+\tau+1)}\frac{\mathbf{u}'}{\iota'\Sigma\iota}$$

and can be used as an estimate for the error covariance matrix Σ_μ. The parameter t is a scalar that describes the confidence in the precision of estimation of the covariance matrix Σ. Namely, the Bayes-Stein estimator assumes that the prior of the expected returns is the normal distribution with mean μ_0 and covariance matrix $(1/\tau)\Sigma$.

$$y_1 = \mathbf{z}_1'\boldsymbol{\beta}_1 + \varepsilon_1$$
$$\vdots$$
$$y_T = \mathbf{z}_T'\boldsymbol{\beta}_T + \varepsilon_T$$

(or in matrix form $\mathbf{Y} = \mathbf{ZB} + \mathbf{E}$), by the standard formula

$$\hat{\sigma}^2 = \frac{1}{T}(\mathbf{Y}-\mathbf{ZB})'(\mathbf{Y}-\mathbf{ZB})$$

[11]Philippe Jorion, "Bayes-Stein Estimation for Portfolio Analysis," *Journal of Financial and Quantitative Analysis*, 21 (1986), pp. 279–292.
[12]See Philippe Jorion, "Bayes-Stein Estimation for Portfolio Analysis."

The Black-Litterman Model

As we explained in Chapter 9, the Black-Litterman model for estimating expected returns combines the market equilibrium with an investor's views. The formula for the estimate is a weighted sum of the two estimates of expected returns

$$\hat{\mu}_{BL} = \left[(\tau\Sigma)^{-1} + \mathbf{P}'\Omega^{-1}\mathbf{P} \right]^{-1} (\tau\Sigma)^{-1}\Pi + \left[(\tau\Sigma)^{-1} + \mathbf{P}'\Omega^{-1}\mathbf{P} \right]^{-1} \left[\mathbf{P}'\Omega^{-1}\mathbf{P} \right]\mu$$

or, equivalently,

$$\hat{\mu}_{BL} = \left[(\tau\Sigma)^{-1} + \mathbf{P}'\Omega^{-1}\mathbf{P} \right]^{-1} \left[(\tau\Sigma)^{-1}\Pi + \mathbf{P}'\Omega^{-1}\mathbf{q} \right]$$

where

Σ is the $N \times N$ covariance matrix of returns
Π is $[\Pi_1, ..., \Pi_N]'$ which is the vector of expected excess returns, computed from an equilibrium model such as the CAPM
τ is a scalar that represents the confidence in the estimation of the market prior
$\mathbf{q}$ is a K-dimensional vector of K investor views
$\mathbf{P}$ is a $K \times N$ matrix of investor views
Ω is a $K \times K$ matrix expressing the confidence in the investor's views
Frequently, the matrix Ω is assumed to be diagonal, that is, investor views are assumed to be independent

As we showed in Chapter 9, the covariance of the Black-Litterman estimator of expected returns is

$$\left[(\tau\Sigma)^{-1} + \mathbf{P}'\Omega^{-1}\mathbf{P} \right]^{-1}$$

This covariance matrix can be used as an approximation for the estimation error covariance matrix Σ_μ.

Uncertainty in Return Covariance Matrix Estimates

Mean-variance portfolio optimization is less sensitive to inaccuracies in the estimate of the covariance matrix Σ than it is to estimation errors in expected returns. Nonetheless, insurance against uncertainty in these estimates can be incorporated at not too large a cost. Most generally, the robust mean-variance portfolio optimization problem can then be formulated as

$$\max_{w} \left\{ \min_{\mu \in U_{\mu}} \{ \mu'w \} - \lambda \max_{\Sigma \in U_{\Sigma}} \{ w'\Sigma w \} \right\}$$

$$s.t. \quad w'\iota = 1$$

where U_{μ} and U_{Σ} denote the uncertainty sets of expected returns and co-variances, respectively.

A few different methods for modeling uncertainty in the covariance matrix are used in practice. Some are superimposed on top of factor models for returns, while others consider confidence intervals for the individual covariance matrix entries. Benefits for portfolio performance have been observed even when the uncertainty set U_{Σ} is defined simply as a collection of several possible scenarios for the covariance matrix.[13] The latter definition of uncertainty set results in the introduction of several constraints in the optimization problem, each of which corresponds to a scenario for the covariance matrix, that is, the size of the optimization problem does not increase significantly.[14]

Factor Models

If we assume a standard factor model for returns

$$r = \mu + V'f + \varepsilon$$

then the covariance matrix of returns Σ can be expressed as

$$\Sigma = V'FV + D$$

where

V = the matrix of factor loadings
F = the covariance matrix of factor returns
D = the diagonal matrix of error term variances

It is assumed that the vector of residual returns ε is independent of the vector of factor returns f, and that the variance of μ is zero.

The statistical properties of the estimate of V naturally lead to an uncertainty set of the kind

[13]Eranda Dragoti-Cela, Peter Haumer, and Raimund Kovacevic, "Applying Robust Optimization to Account for Estimation Risk in Dynamic Portfolio Selection," Manuscript, FSC (Financial Soft Computing), Siemens AG, Vienna, Austria, 2006.
[14]See Chapter 10 in Frank J. Fabozzi, Petter N. Kolm, Dessislava Pachamanova, and Sergio M. Focardi, *Robust Portfolio Optimization and Management* (Hoboken, NJ: John Wiley & Sons, 2007).

$$S_v = \{V : V = V_0 + W, \|W_i\|_G \leq \rho_i, i = 1, \ldots, N\}$$

where W_i denotes the i-th column of W, and

$$\|w\|_G = \sqrt{w'Gw}$$

is the Euclidean (elliptic) norm of w with respect to a symmetric positive definite matrix G.[15] If we assume also that the estimates of expected returns belong to an interval uncertainty set

$$U_\delta(\hat{\mu}) = \{\mu \mid |\mu_i - \hat{\mu}_i| \leq \delta_i, i = 1, \ldots, N\}$$

we can formulate the resulting robust optimization problem as the second-order cone problem (SOCP)[16]

$$\max_{w, \psi, v, \kappa, \tau, \eta, t, s} \mu'w - \delta'\psi - \lambda(v + \kappa)$$

$$s.t. \quad \left\| \begin{matrix} 2D^{1/2}w \\ 1 - \kappa \end{matrix} \right\| \leq 1 + \kappa$$

$$w't = 1$$

$$\psi_i \geq w_i; \psi_i \geq -w_i, i = 1, \ldots, N$$

$$\tau + t't \leq v - \kappa$$

$$\eta \leq \frac{1}{l_{max}(H)}$$

where

M = the number of factors in the factor model

QLQ' = the spectral decomposition of $H = G^{-1/2}FG^{-1/2}$ (recall that G was the matrix used for defining the norm in the uncertainty set for the factor loadings matrix V)

L = a diagonal matrix with elements $l_1, \ldots, l_M$ (l_{max} is the maximum of these elements)

s = $Q'H^{1/2}G^{1/2}V_0w$

---

[15]There is a natural way to define the matrix G that is related to probabilistic guarantees on the likelihood that the actual realization of the uncertain coefficients will lie in the ellipsoidal uncertainty set S_v. Specifically, the definition of the matrix G can be based on the data used to produce the estimates of the regression coefficients of the factor model.

[16]Donald Goldfarb and Garud Iyengar, "Robust Portfolio Selection Problems," *Mathematics of Operations Research*, 28 (2003), pp. 1–38.

Constraints such as

$$\left\| \begin{bmatrix} 2\mathbf{D}^{1/2}\mathbf{w} \\ 1-\kappa \end{bmatrix} \right\| \le 1+\kappa$$

are SOCP constraints. The norm $\|\cdot\|$ simply requires taking a square root of the sum of the squared terms of the elements of the vector

$$\begin{bmatrix} 2\mathbf{D}^{1/2}\mathbf{w} \\ 1-\kappa \end{bmatrix}$$

Some specialized SOCP software may require the constraint to be input in this form, and will be more efficient if the SOCP structure is explicitly stated. However, if a general-purpose modeling language or nonlinear solver is used, this constraint can be rewritten as a general nonlinear constraint, namely,[17]

$$\sqrt{4\mathbf{w}'(\mathbf{D}^{1/2})'\mathbf{D}^{1/2}\mathbf{w} + (1-\kappa)^2} \le 1+\kappa$$

Confidence Intervals for the Entries of the Covariance Matrix

Instead of using uncertainty sets based on estimates from a factor model, one can specify intervals for the individual elements of the covariance matrix of the kind

$$\underline{\Sigma} \le \Sigma \le \overline{\Sigma}$$

If we assume that the estimates of expected returns vary in intervals

$$U_\delta(\hat{\boldsymbol{\mu}}) = \{\boldsymbol{\mu} \big| \big| \mu_i - \hat{\mu}_i \big| \le \delta_i, i = 1,\dots,N\}$$

short sales are not allowed (i.e., $\mathbf{w} \ge 0$), and the matrix $\overline{\Sigma}$ is positive semidefinite (which means that the upper bound matrix derived from data is a well-defined covariance matrix), the resulting optimization problem is very

---

[17]In some circumstances, one can raise both sides of an SOCP constraint to the second power, and obtain an equivalent quadratic constraint. This is the case here: the SOCP constraint

$$\sqrt{4\mathbf{w}'(\mathbf{D}^{1/2})'\mathbf{D}^{1/2}\mathbf{w} + (1-\kappa)^2} \le 1+\kappa$$

is equivalent to the convex quadratic constraint $\mathbf{w}'\mathbf{Dw} \le \kappa$. However, in general, quadratic and SOCP constraints are not automatically equivalent. It is therefore usually safer to input SOCP constraints directly into a nonlinear solver, without trying to convert them to quadratic constraints first.

simple to formulate. We just need to replace μ by $\mu + \delta$ and Σ by $\bar{\Sigma}$ in the mean-variance formulation, as the expression

$$\max_{w}(\hat{\mu} + \delta)'w - \lambda w'\bar{\Sigma}w$$

in fact equals

$$\max_{w}\left\{\min_{\mu \in U_{\mu}}\{\mu'w\} - \lambda \max_{\Sigma \in U_{\Sigma}}\{w'\Sigma w\}\right\}$$

under the preceding conditions.[18]

In the general case, the formulation of the robust counterpart is not as trivial, but remains a convex problem. The resulting optimization problem is in fact a semidefinite program (SDP). More precisely, assuming as before that the estimates of expected returns vary in intervals

$$U_{\delta}(\hat{\mu}) = \{\mu \,|\, |\mu_i - \hat{\mu}_i| \le \delta_i, i = 1, \ldots, N\}$$

the robust formulation of the mean-variance optimization problem is

$$\max_{w,w_+,w_-,\underline{\Lambda},\bar{\Lambda}} \hat{\mu}'w - \delta'(w_+ + w_-) - \lambda\left(\langle\bar{\Lambda},\bar{\Sigma}\rangle - \langle\underline{\Lambda},\underline{\Sigma}\rangle\right)$$

$$s.t. \quad w'\iota = 1$$

$$w = w_+ - w_-, w_+ \ge 0, w_- \ge 0$$

$$\bar{\Lambda} \ge 0, \underline{\Lambda} \ge 0$$

$$\begin{bmatrix} \bar{\Lambda} - \underline{\Lambda} & w \\ w' & 1 \end{bmatrix} \succeq 0$$

where the notation $\langle A, B \rangle$ for two symmetric matrices A, B stands for "Tr(AB)," the trace of the matrix product AB. Tr(AB) is equal to the sum of the diagonal elements of the matrix product AB.[19]

---

[18]See R. Tutuncu and M. Koenig, "Robust Asset Allocation," *Annals of Operations Research*, 132 (2004), pp. 157–187.

[19]The notation $\langle A, B \rangle$ is typically used to denote the inner product of A and B. In this case, we are dealing with an inner product on the space of symmetric matrices, defined as the trace of the product of two matrices A and B. The trace of a symmetric matrix X with N rows and N columns is mathematically defined as

$$\sum_{i=1}^{N} X_{ii}$$

that is, it is the sum of the elements of the main diagonal (left to right). It is easy to see that the trace of the product of two matrices A and B can be expressed as

$$\text{Tr}(AB) = \sum_{i=1}^{N}(AB)_{ii} = \sum_{i=1}^{N}\sum_{j=1}^{N}(A)_{ij}(B)_{ji}$$

We explained earlier the part of the robust formulation that is related to uncertainty in expected returns. In order to demystify the derivation of robust counterparts of optimization problems that are SDPs, we show how one would derive the terms related to the uncertainty in the covariance matrix.

As before, we start by asking ourselves what the worst-case value for the portfolio variance $\mathbf{w}'\Sigma\mathbf{w}$ would be if the estimates of the covariance matrix Σ vary in intervals $\underline{\Sigma} \leq \Sigma \leq \overline{\Sigma}$. For any fixed vector of portfolio weights $\mathbf{w}$, we can find it by solving the optimization problem

$$\max_{\Sigma} \mathbf{w}'\Sigma\mathbf{w}$$
$$s.t. \quad \underline{\Sigma} \leq \Sigma \leq \overline{\Sigma}$$
$$\Sigma \succeq 0$$

We use "$\geq$, $\leq$" to denote component-wise inequality, and "$\succeq$" to denote positive semidefiniteness of a matrix.[20]

The previous problem is a semidefinite program (SDP).[21] The dual problem of this semidefinite program is

$$\min_{\mathbf{w},\underline{\Lambda},\overline{\Lambda}} \langle \overline{\Lambda},\overline{\Sigma} \rangle - \langle \underline{\Lambda},\underline{\Sigma} \rangle$$
$$s.t. \quad -\mathbf{Z} + \overline{\Lambda} - \underline{\Lambda} - \mathbf{w}\mathbf{w}'$$
$$\mathbf{Z} \succeq 0, \overline{\Lambda} \geq 0, \underline{\Lambda} \geq 0$$

where $\underline{\Lambda}$ and $\overline{\Lambda}$ are the dual variables associated with the constraints $\underline{\Sigma} \leq \Sigma$ and $\Sigma \leq \overline{\Sigma}$, respectively, and $\mathbf{Z}$ is the explicit dual slack variable. This problem can be rewritten as

$$\min_{\mathbf{w},\underline{\Lambda},\overline{\Lambda}} \langle \overline{\Lambda},\overline{\Sigma} \rangle - \langle \underline{\Lambda},\underline{\Sigma} \rangle$$
$$s.t. \quad \overline{\Lambda} - \underline{\Lambda} - \mathbf{w}\mathbf{w}' \succeq 0$$
$$\overline{\Lambda} \geq 0, \underline{\Lambda} \geq 0$$

The constraint $\overline{\Lambda} - \underline{\Lambda} + \mathbf{w}\mathbf{w}' \succeq 0$ can be recast into a so-called linear matrix inequality (LMI) form which is understood by SDP solvers by using *Schur complements*[22] resulting in

---

[20] A matrix $\mathbf{X}$ is positive semidefinite, that is, $\mathbf{X} \succeq 0$, if and only if $\mathbf{z}'\mathbf{X}\mathbf{z} \geq 0$ for every real vector $\mathbf{z}$.

[21] See Chapter 9 in Fabozzi, Kolm, Pachamanova, and Focardi, *Robust Portfolio Optimization and Management* (Hoboken, NJ: John Wiley & Sons, 2007).

[22] In linear algebra, the Schur complement of a block of a square matrix $\mathbf{D}$ in a larger square matrix $\mathbf{M}$,

$$\min_{w,\underline{\Lambda},\overline{\Lambda}} \langle \overline{\Lambda}, \overline{\Sigma} \rangle - \langle \underline{\Lambda}, \underline{\Sigma} \rangle$$

$$s.t. \quad \begin{bmatrix} \overline{\Lambda} - \underline{\Lambda} & w \\ w' & 1 \end{bmatrix} \succeq 0$$

$$\overline{\Lambda} \geq 0, \underline{\Lambda} \geq 0$$

Notice that the variable Σ is not present in the preceding optimization problem. However, the optimal values of the dual problem will be at least as large as the optimal value of the primal problem. Therefore, one can use the expression

$$\min_{w,\underline{\Lambda},\overline{\Lambda}} \langle \overline{\Lambda}, \overline{\Sigma} \rangle - \langle \underline{\Lambda}, \underline{\Sigma} \rangle$$

instead of the expression

$$\max_{\Sigma} w'\Sigma w$$

in the robust mean-variance problem formulation (all of the constraints, of course, will have to be preserved in the formulation as well). This leads to the robust SDP formulation we provided previously.

SDPs are more difficult to solve than SOCPs, but are still convex problems for which interior point methods and bundle methods for large-scale (sparse) problems have been developed. Efficient SDP routines such as SeDuMi[23] (for use with MATLAB) are now available, and many modeling languages make it straightforward to solve an SDP problem.

$$M = \begin{bmatrix} A & B \\ C & D \end{bmatrix}$$

is defined as the expression $A - BD^{-1}C$. Recognizing Schur complements in nonlinear expressions is frequently a key to formulating difficult nonlinear optimization problems as computationally tractable SDPs. In particular, if we have a constraint of the kind $Q(x) - S(x)R(x)^{-1}S(x)' \succeq 0$ where x is a vector of variables, and if both $Q(x) - S(x)R(x)^{-1}S(x)' \succeq 0$ and $R(x) \succeq 0$, then we can express the constraint as the LMI

$$\begin{bmatrix} Q(x) & S(x) \\ S(x)' & R(x) \end{bmatrix} \succeq 0$$

Note that if $Q(x)$ is a scalar, then we have the nonlinear constraint $Q(x) - S(x)R(x)^{-1}S(x)' \geq 0$ in which the positive semidefiniteness sign $\succeq$ is replaced by an inequality sign $\geq$.

[23]Jos F. Sturm, "Using SeDuMi 1.02, A MATLAB Toolbox for Optimization over Symmetric Cones," *Optimization Methods and Software*, 11–12 (1999), pp. 625–653; see also SeDuMi's official site at http://sedumi.mcmaster.ca/ for tutorials and free downloads.

USING ROBUST MEAN-VARIANCE
PORTFOLIO OPTIMIZATION IN PRACTICE

As we saw in the examples earlier in this section, the computational complexity of the robust formulations of the classical portfolio optimization problems is not a real issue. Robust optimization does, however, come at the cost of additional modeling effort. The important question is whether this effort is worthwhile. In other words, what are the benefits of incorporating uncertainty in the optimization process?

Critics have argued that robust optimization does not provide more benefit than, for instance, shrinkage estimators that combine the minimum variance portfolio with a speculative investment portfolio. Indeed, under certain conditions (short sales allowed, ellipsoidal uncertainty model for expected return estimates, error covariance matrix estimated as $(1/T)\Sigma$), it can be shown that the optimal portfolio weights using robust optimization are a linear combination of the weights of the minimum variance portfolio[24] and a mean-variance efficient portfolio with speculative demand, and thus the implied expected return is equivalent to the expected return obtained using a shrinkage estimator with certain weights.[25] Robust optimization thus appears to offer a less transparent way to express investor preferences and tolerance to uncertainty than other approaches, such as shrinkage estimators and Bayesian methods, in which the shrinkage weights can be defined explicitly. In the general case, however, robust optimization is not necessarily equivalent to shrinkage estimation. They are particularly different in the presence of additional portfolio constraints. Furthermore, as we illustrated in this chapter, robust optimization can be used to account for uncertainty in parameters other than expected asset returns, making its relationship with Bayesian methods difficult to establish.

It can be argued that a difficulty with assessing the benefits of the robust optimization approach is that its performance is highly dependent on the choice (or calibration) of the model parameters, such as the aversion to the estimation error δ. However, this issue is no different from the calibration of standard parameters in the classical portfolio optimization framework, such as the length of the estimation period and the risk aversion coefficient. These and other parameters need to be determined subjectively.

We remark that other modeling devices such as Bayesian estimation (for example, James-Stein shrinkage estimators and the Black-Litterman model) have similar issues. In particular, for shrinkage estimators, the portfolio

---

[24]The minimum variance portfolio is independent of investor preferences or expected returns.

[25]See, for example, Bernd Scherer, "Can Robust Portfolio Optimisation Help to Build Better Portfolios?" *Journal of Asset Management*, 7 (2007), pp. 374–387.

manager needs to determine which shrinkage target to use and the size of the shrinkage parameter. In the Black-Litterman model, he needs to provide his confidence in equilibrium as well as his confidence in each individual view. These quantities are most often derived from subjective assumptions—or from the experience of the portfolio manager.

An advantage of the robust optimization approach is that the parameter values in the robust formulation can be matched to probabilistic guarantees. For example, if the estimates of the expected asset returns are assumed to be normally distributed, then there is an ω% chance that the true expected returns will fall in the ellipsoidal set around the manager's estimates $\hat{\boldsymbol{\mu}}$,

$$U_\delta(\hat{\boldsymbol{\mu}}) = \left\{ \boldsymbol{\mu} \big| (\boldsymbol{\mu} - \hat{\boldsymbol{\mu}})' \Sigma_\mu^{-1} (\boldsymbol{\mu} - \hat{\boldsymbol{\mu}}) \le \delta^2 \right\}$$

if δ^2 is assigned the value of the ωth percentile of a χ^2 distribution with degrees of freedom equal to the number of assets in the portfolio. More generally, if the expected returns are assumed to belong to any possible probability distribution, then assigning

$$\delta = \sqrt{\frac{1 - \omega}{\omega}}$$

guarantees that the estimates fall in the uncertainty set $U_\delta(\hat{\boldsymbol{\mu}})$ with probability at least ω%.[26,27]

Dealing with Conservatism: The Zero Net Alpha-Adjustment

Traditional uncertainty sets are frequently modified so that they can serve a particular purpose, or so that they deliver increased robustness over classical portfolio optimization without being too conservative. It has been observed in practice that the standard robust mean-variance formulation with ellipsoidal uncertainty specification for expected return estimates sometimes results in portfolio allocations that are too pessimistic. Of course, we can always make a formulation less pessimistic by considering a smaller uncertainty set. For the ellipsoidal uncertainty set, we can achieve this by decreasing the radius of the ellipsoid. However, there is a recent trend among practitioners to apply more structured restrictions. Here we

---

[26]Laurent El Ghaoui, Maksim Oks, and Francois Oustry, "Worst-Case Value-at-Risk and Robust Portfolio Optimization: A Conic Optimization Approach," *Operations Research*, 51 (2003), pp. 543–556.

[27]We note that in practice sometimes these theoretical estimates may be too conservative. Often, however, this can be detected and adjusted by explicit calibration of model parameters to historical data.

discuss a technique that has been observed to work particularly well in the practice of robust portfolio expected return modeling. The idea is to incorporate a *zero net alpha-adjustment* into the robust optimization problem.[28]

Recall that the traditional robust counterpart tries to find the optimal solution so that constraints containing uncertain coefficients are satisfied for the worst-case realization of the uncertain parameters. In particular, when trying to make a portfolio optimization problem robust with respect to errors in expected return estimates, we make the assumption that all of the actual realizations of expected returns could be worse than their expected values. Thus, the net adjustment in the expected portfolio return will always be downwards. While this leads to a more robust problem than the original one, in many instances it may be too pessimistic to assume that all estimation errors go against us. It may therefore be more reasonable, in practice, to assume that at least some of the true realizations may be above their expected values. For example, we may make the assumption that there are approximately as many realizations above the estimated values as there are realizations below the estimated values. This condition can be incorporated in the portfolio optimization problem by adding a constraint to, say, the ellipsoidal uncertainty set used for the expected returns. Namely, instead of the uncertainty set

$$U_\delta(\hat{\boldsymbol{\mu}}) = \left\{ \boldsymbol{\mu} \,\middle|\, (\boldsymbol{\mu}-\hat{\boldsymbol{\mu}})'\Sigma_\mu^{-1}(\boldsymbol{\mu}-\hat{\boldsymbol{\mu}}) \le \delta^2 \right\}$$

we can consider

$$U_\delta(\hat{\boldsymbol{\mu}}) = \left\{ \boldsymbol{\mu} \,\middle|\, \begin{matrix} (\boldsymbol{\mu}-\hat{\boldsymbol{\mu}})'\Sigma_\mu^{-1}(\boldsymbol{\mu}-\hat{\boldsymbol{\mu}}) \le \delta^2 \\ \boldsymbol{\iota}'\mathbf{D}(\boldsymbol{\mu}-\hat{\boldsymbol{\mu}}) = 0 \end{matrix} \right\}$$

for some invertible matrix **D**. When **D** = **I**, where **I** is the identity matrix, the total net adjustment to the expected returns is zero, that is, the adjustment in the expected portfolio return is zero.

It can be shown then—by using the procedure that involves optimization duality as we did earlier, but with somewhat more complicated uncertainty set restrictions—that the expected return vector in the portfolio optimization problem, $\boldsymbol{\mu}'\mathbf{w}$, should be replaced by

$$\hat{\boldsymbol{\mu}}'\mathbf{w} - \delta \left\| \left(\Sigma_\mu - \frac{1}{\boldsymbol{\iota}'\mathbf{D}\Sigma_\mu\mathbf{D}'\boldsymbol{\iota}} \Sigma_\mu \mathbf{D}'\boldsymbol{\iota}\boldsymbol{\iota}'\mathbf{D}\Sigma_\mu \right)^{1/2} \mathbf{w} \right\|$$

---

[28]Sebastian Ceria and Robert Stubbs, "Incorporating Estimation Errors into Portfolio Selection: Robust Portfolio Construction," Axioma, Inc., 2005.

instead of

$$\hat{\mu}'\mathbf{w} - \delta \left\| \mathbf{\Sigma}_\mu^{1/2} \mathbf{w} \right\|$$

as was the case with the simple ellipsoidal uncertainty set. Therefore, the zero net alpha-adjustment can be thought of as the standard robust mean-variance formulation with a modified covariance matrix of estimation errors.

There can be further variations on the zero net adjustment idea. For example, instead of restricting the adjustment of the expected return estimates, we can restrict their standard deviations. Namely, we can impose the requirement that every standard deviation of upward adjustment in the expected returns is offset by an equal downward adjustment of one standard deviation. To do this, it suffices to choose

$$\mathbf{D} = \mathbf{L}^{-1}$$

where $\mathbf{L}\mathbf{L}' = \mathbf{\Sigma}_\mu$ is the Cholesky decomposition of the covariance matrix of expected return estimates.

Similarly, if we would like to achieve a zero net adjustment in the variance of the expected return estimates, we can select

$$\mathbf{D} = \mathbf{\Sigma}_\mu^{-1}$$

It can be shown that the zero net adjustment has the desired effect on portfolio weights—that is, it does not make the portfolio unnecessarily conservative in terms of expected return. If an asset's portfolio weight is above the weight that asset would have in the portfolio that simply minimizes the estimation error in expected returns, that asset's expected return (alpha) gets adjusted downward. Conversely, if an asset's portfolio weight is below the weight that asset would have in the portfolio that simply minimizes the estimation error in expected returns, that asset's expected return (alpha) gets adjusted upward. This type of adjustment has proven to be very effective in practice.

In Exhibit 9.1 in Chapter 9, we reported results from Ceria and Stubbs[29] that showed how different the true, the estimated, and the actual Markowitz efficient frontiers can be. Exhibit 10.1 shows their results on the effect of making expected returns robust with respect to estimation error on the efficient portfolio frontiers, where the robust efficient frontier is generated by using the zero net alpha adjustment with $\mathbf{D} = \mathbf{I}$. The estimated Markowitz and the estimated robust frontier both overestimate the true frontier. How-

---

[29]Ceria and Stubbs, "Incorporating Estimation Errors into Portfolio Selection: Robust Portfolio Construction."

EXHIBIT 10.1 Robust Efficient Frontiers

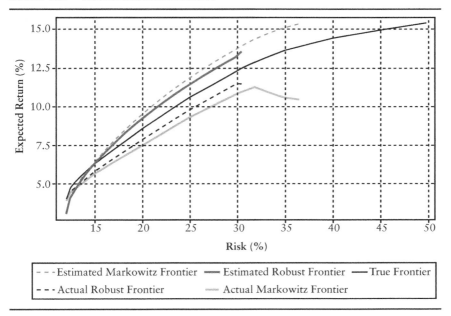

Source: Figure 4 in Sebastian Ceria and Robert Stubbs, "Incorporating Estimation Errors into Portfolio Selection: Robust Portfolio Construction," Axioma, Inc., 2005, p. 14. This copyrighted material is reprinted with permission from the authors.

ever, both the estimated and the actual realized robust efficient frontiers are closer to the true efficient frontier.

Robust optimization is, unfortunately, not a panacea. From a behavioral and decision-making point of view, few individuals have max-min preferences. Indeed, max-min preferences describe the behavior of decision makers who face great ambiguity and thus make choices consistent with the belief that the worst possible outcomes are highly likely.

By using robust portfolio optimization formulations, investors are likely to trade off the optimality of their portfolio allocation in cases in which nature behaves as they predicted for protection against the risk of inaccurate estimation. Therefore, investors using the technique should not expect to do better than classical optimization when estimation errors have little impact, or when typical scenarios occur. They should, however, expect insurance in scenarios in which their estimates deviate from the actual realized values by up to the amount they have prespecified in the modeling process. Some tests with simulated and real market data indicate that robust optimization, when inaccuracy is assumed in the expected return estimates, outperforms classical mean-variance optimization in terms of total excess return a large percentage (70% to 80%) of the time.[30] Other tests have not been as conclusive.[31] The factor that accounts for much of the difference is how the uncertainty in parameters is modeled. Therefore, finding a suitable degree of robustness and an appropriate definition of uncertainty set can have a significant impact on portfolio performance.

Independent tests by practitioners and academics using both simulated and market data appear to confirm that robust optimization generally results in more stable portfolio weights; that is, that it eliminates the extreme corner solutions resulting from traditional mean-variance optimization. This fact has implications for portfolio rebalancing in the presence of transaction costs and taxes, as transaction costs and taxes can add substantial expenses when the portfolio is rebalanced. Depending on the particular robust formulations employed, robust mean-variance optimization also appears to improve worst-case portfolio performance, and results in smoother and more consistent portfolio returns. Finally, by preventing large swings in positions, robust optimization frequently makes better use of the turnover budget and risk constraints.

SOME PRACTICAL REMARKS ON ROBUST PORTFOLIO OPTIMIZATION MODELS

The discussion in the previous sections leads to the question: So which approach is best for modeling financial portfolios? The short answer is: it depends. It depends on the size of the portfolio, the type of assets and their distributional characteristics, the portfolio strategies and trading styles involved, and existing technical and intellectual infrastructure, among others. Sometimes it makes sense to consider a combination of several techniques, such as a blend of Bayesian estimation *and* robust portfolio optimization. This is an empirical question; indeed, the only way to find out is through extensive research and testing. To offer some guidance in this regard, we provide a simple step-by-step checklist for robust quantitative portfolio management:[32]

---

[30]Ceria and Stubbs, "Incorporating Estimation Errors into Portfolio Selection: Robust Portfolio Construction."
[31]Lee, Stefek, and Zhelenyak, "Robust Portfolio Optimization—A Closer Look."
[32]By no means do we claim that this list is complete or that it has to be followed religiously. It is simply provided as a starting point and general guidance for the quantitative portfolio manager.

1. Risk forecasting: develop an accurate risk model.
2. Return forecasting: construct robust expected return estimates.
3. Classical portfolio optimization: start with a simple framework.
4. Mitigate model risk:
   a. Minimize estimation risk through the use of robust estimators.
   b. Improve the stability of the optimization framework through robust optimization.
5. Extensions.

In general, the most difficult item in this list is to calculate robust expected return estimates. Developing profitable trading strategies ("α generation") is notoriously hard, but not impossible. It is important to remember that modern portfolio optimization techniques and fancy mathematics are not going to help much if the underlying trading strategies are subpar.

Implicit in this list is that for *each step* it is important to perform thorough testing in order to understand the effect of changes and new additions to the model. It is not unusual that quantitative analysts and portfolio managers will have to revisit previous steps as part of the research and development process. For example, it is important to understand the interplay between forecast generation and the reliability of optimized portfolio weights. Introducing a robust optimizer may lead to more reliable, and often more stable, portfolio weights. However, how to make the optimization framework more robust depends on how expected return and risk forecasts are produced. Therefore, one may have to refine or modify basic forecast generation. Identifying the individual and the combined contribution of different techniques is crucial in the development of a successful quantitative framework.

Minimizing estimation risk and improving the robustness of the optimization framework can be done in either order, or sometimes at the same time. The goal of both approaches is of course to improve the overall reliability and performance of the portfolio allocation framework. Some important questions to consider here are: When/why does the framework perform well (poorly)? How sensitive is it to changes in inputs? How does it behave when constraints change? Are portfolio weights intuitive—do they make sense? How high is the turnover of the portfolio?

Many extensions are possible, starting from the simple framework of portfolio optimization. Such extensions include—the introduction of transaction costs models, complex constraints (e.g., integer constraints such as round lotting), different risk measures (e.g., downside risk measures, higher moments), dynamic and stochastic programming for incorporating intertemporal dependencies. Often these are problem specific and have to be dealt with on a case-by-case basis.

SUMMARY

- Robust portfolio optimization incorporates uncertainty directly into the optimization process. The uncertain parameters in the optimization problem are assumed to vary in prespecified uncertainty sets that are selected based on statistical techniques and probabilistic guarantees.
- Making the portfolio optimization process robust with respect to uncertainty in the parameters is not very expensive in terms of computational cost, but it may result in a worse objective value. This can be corrected by using "smart" uncertainty sets for parameters that do not make the expected portfolio return too conservative.
- There is evidence that robust optimization may reduce portfolio turnover and transaction costs, improve worst-case performance, and lead to increased and more stable returns in the long run.
- A simple step-by-step checklist for robust quantitative portfolio management:
  1. Risk forecasting: develop an accurate risk model.
  2. Return forecasting: construct robust expected return estimates.
  3. Classical portfolio optimization: start with a simple framework.
  4. Mitigate model risk:
     a. Minimize estimation risk through the use of robust estimators.
     b. Improve the stability of the optimization framework through robust optimization.
  5. Extensions.

CHAPTER 11

Transaction Costs and Trade Execution

rading is an integral component of the investment process. A poorly executed trade can eat directly into portfolio returns. This is because financial markets are not frictionless and transactions have a cost associated to them. Costs are incurred when buying or selling securities in the form of, for example, brokerage commissions, bid-ask spreads, taxes, and market impact costs.

In recent years, portfolio managers have started to more carefully consider transaction costs. Partly, this is due to the flat performance of equities, often just in the single digits, after the period in the 1990s where the stock market returned about 20% per year. In a sideway market, portfolio managers become more careful about the costs that their trades and decisions bring about. If portfolio returns can be increased by 100 to 200 basis points (bps) by reducing trading costs, that can translate into a sizable amount, especially during tougher years. Consider for example a $1 billion equity fund that has an annual turnover of 100%.[1] Transaction costs in the order of 40 basis points per trade for this fund would result in an annual turnover cost of $8 million ($1 billion × 1 × 0.004 × 2).

The literature on market microstructure, analysis and measurement of transaction costs, and market impact costs on institutional trades is rapidly expanding.[2] One way of describing transaction costs is to categorize them in terms of *explicit costs* such as brokerage and taxes, and implicit costs, which include market impact costs, price movement risk, and opportunity cost.

---

[1]By turning over a security is meant both buying and later selling the security. This amounts to two transactions.

[2]See, for example, Ian Domowitz, Jack Glen, and Ananth Madhavan, "Liquidity, Volatility, and Equity Trading Costs Across Countries and Over Time," *International Finance* 4, no. 2 (2001), pp. 221–255; and Donald B. Keim and Ananth Madhavan, "The Costs of Institutional Equity Trades," *Financial Analysts Journal* 54, no. 4 (July/August 1998) pp. 50–69.

Market impact cost is, broadly speaking, the price an investor has to pay for obtaining liquidity in the market, whereas *price movement risk* is the risk that the price of an asset increases or decreases from the time the investor decides to transact in the asset until the transaction actually takes place.

Opportunity cost is the cost suffered when a trade is not executed. Another way of seeing transaction costs is in terms of *fixed costs* versus *variable costs*. Whereas commissions and trading fees are fixed—bid-ask spreads, taxes, and all implicit transaction costs are variable.

In this chapter, we will first present a simple taxonomy of trading costs. The specification is not new and has appeared in several forms in the literature before.[3] We then discuss the linkage between transaction costs and liquidity as well as the measurement of these quantities.

Portfolio managers and traders need to be able to effectively model the impact of trading costs on their portfolios and trades. In particular, if possible, they would like to minimize the total transaction costs. To address these issues we introduce several approaches for the modeling of transaction costs.

A TAXONOMY OF TRANSACTION COSTS

Probably the easiest way to describe transaction costs is to categorize them in terms of fixed versus variable transaction costs, and explicit versus implicit transaction costs as shown below as suggested by Kissell and Glantz:[4]

	Fixed	Variable
Explicit	Commissions	Bid-Ask Spreads
	Fees	Taxes
Implicit		Delay Cost
		Price Movement Risk
		Market Impact Costs
		Timing Risk
		Opportunity Cost

[3]See Robert Kissell and Morton Glantz, *Optimal Trading Strategies* (New York: AMACOM, 2003); Bruce M. Collins and Frank J. Fabozzi, "A Methodology for Measuring Transaction Costs," *Financial Analysts Journal* 47 (1991), pp. 27–36; Ananth Madhavan, "Market Microstructure: A Survey," *Journal of Financial Markets* 3 (2000), pp. 205–258; and *The Transaction Cost Challenge* (New York: ITG, 2000).
[4]Kissell and Glantz, *Optimal Trading Strategies*.

Fixed transaction costs are independent of factors such as trade size and market conditions.[5] In contrast, variable transaction costs depend on some or all of these factors. In other words, while the fixed transaction costs are "what they are," portfolio managers and traders can seek to reduce, optimize, and efficiently manage the variable transaction costs.

Explicit transaction costs are those costs that are observable and known up front such as commissions, fees, and taxes. Implicit transaction costs, on the other hand, are nonobservable and not known in advance. Examples of transaction costs in this category are market impact and opportunity cost. In general, the implicit costs make up the dominant part of the total transaction costs.

Explicit Transaction Costs

Trading commissions and fees, taxes, and bid-ask spreads are explicit transaction costs. Explicit transaction costs are also referred to as observable transaction costs.

Commissions and Fees

Commissions are paid to brokers to execute trades.[6] Normally, commissions on securities trades are negotiable. Fees charged by an institution that holds the securities in safekeeping for an investor are referred to as *custodial fees.* When the ownership over a stock is transferred, the investor is charged a *transfer fee.*

Taxes

The most common taxes are *capital gains tax* and *tax on dividends.* The tax law distinguishes between two types of capital gains taxes: *short-term* and *long-term.* The former is according to the investor's tax bracket, whereas the latter currently stands at 15%.[7] In the United States, the tax law as of this writing requires that an asset must be held for at least one full year to qualify for the lower long-term capital gains rate. Tax planning is an important

---

[5]However, we emphasize that different exchanges and trading networks may have different fixed costs. Furthermore, the fixed costs may also be different depending upon whether a trade is an agency trade or a principal trade.

[6]For a more detailed discussion of commissions, see Alan D. Biller, "A Plan Sponsor's Guide to Commissions," Chapter 10 in Frank J. Fabozzi (ed.), *Pension Fund Investment Management: Second Edition* (Hoboken, NJ: John Wiley & Sons, 1997).

[7]There have been proposals to increase this rate in 2009.

component of many investment strategies, but this topic is outside the scope of this book.[8]

Bid-Ask Spreads

The distance between the quoted sell and buy order is called the *bid-ask spread*. The bid-ask spread is the immediate transaction cost that the market charges anyone for the privilege of trading. High immediate liquidity is synonymous with small spreads. We can think about the bid-ask spread as the price charged by dealers for supplying immediacy and short-term price stability in the presence of short-term order imbalances. Dealers act as a buffer between the investors that want to buy and sell, and thereby provide stability in the market by making sure a certain order is maintained. In *negotiated markets* such as the New York Stock Exchange (NYSE), market-makers and dealers maintain a certain minimum inventory on their books. If the dealer is unable to match a buyer with a seller (or vice versa), he has the capability to take on the exposure on his book.

However, the bid-ask spread does not necessarily represent the best prices available, and the *half spread* is, therefore, not always the minimal cost for immediate buy or sell executions. Certain price improvements are possible and occur, for example, because:

- NYSE specialists fill the incoming market orders at improved prices.[9]
- The market may have moved in favor during the time it took to route the order to the market center (a so-called *lucky saving*).
- The presence of hidden liquidity.[10]
- Buy and sell orders can be *crossed*.[11]

---

[8]Although historically tax planning has only been part of the investment strategies of institutions and wealthy individuals, this is no longer the case. In recent years, there is a trend in the mutual fund industry to provide greater availability to tax efficient mutual funds as the demand for tax efficient vehicles for individual investors has increased. See, for example, Brad M. Barber and Terrance Odean, "Are Individual Investors Tax Savvy? Evidence from Retail and Discount Brokerage Accounts," *Journal of Public Economics* 88, no. 1–2 (2004), pp. 419–442.

[9]See, for example, Lawrence E. Harris and Venkatesh Panchapagesan, "The Information Content of the Limit Order Book: Evidence from NYSE Specialist Trading Decisions," *Journal of Financial Markets* 8 (2005), pp. 25–67.

[10]For example, on *electronic communications networks* (ECNs) and on NASDAQ, although it is possible to view the limit order book, a significant portion of the book cannot be seen. This is referred to as *hidden* or *discretionary orders*.

[11]A *cross order* is an offsetting or noncompetitive matching of the buy order of one investor against the sell order of another investor. This practice is permissible only when executed in accordance with the Commodity Exchange Act, CFTC regulations,

The bid-ask spread is misleading as a true liquidity measure because it only conveys the price for small trades. For large trades, due to market impact, as we will see, the actual price will be quite different. We will elaborate more on the linkage between liquidity, trading costs, and market impact costs later in this chapter and in Chapter 12.

Implicit Transaction Costs

Investment delay, market impact cost, price movement risk, market timing, and opportunity cost are implicit transaction costs. Implicit transaction costs are also referred to as nonobservable transaction costs.

Investment Delay

Normally, there is a delay between the time when the portfolio manager makes a buy/sell decision of a security and when the actual trade is brought to the market by a trader. If the price of the security changes during this time, the price change (possibly adjusted for general market moves) represents the *investment delay cost*, or the cost of not being able to execute immediately. We note that this cost depends on the investment strategy. For example, modern quantitative trading systems that automatically submit an electronic order after generating a trading decision are exposed to smaller delay costs. More traditional approaches where investment decisions first have to be approved by, for example, an investment committee, exhibit higher delay costs. Some practitioners view the investment delay cost as part of the opportunity cost discussed later in this chapter.

Market Impact Costs

The *market impact cost* of a transaction is the deviation of the transaction price from the market (mid) price[12] that would have prevailed had the trade not occurred. The price movement is the cost, the market impact cost, for liquidity. We note that the market impact of a trade can be negative if, for example, a trader buys at a price below the no-trade price (i.e., the price that would have prevailed had the trade not taken place). In general, liquidity providers experience negative costs while liquidity demanders will face positive costs.

and the rules of the particular market. See, for example, Joel Hasbrouck, George Sofianos, and Deborah Sosebee, "New York Stock Exchange Systems and Trading Procedures," Working Paper 93-01, New York Stock Exchange, 1993, pp. 46–47.
[12]Since the buyer buys at the ask and the seller sells at the bid, this definition of market impact cost ignores the bid/ask spread which is an explicit cost.

We distinguish between two different kinds of market impact costs, temporary and permanent. Total market impact cost is computed as the sum of the two. The temporary market impact cost is of transitory nature and can be seen as the additional *liquidity concession* necessary for the liquidity provider (e.g., the market maker) to take the order, *inventory effects* (price effects due to broker/dealer inventory imbalances), or *imperfect substitution* (for example, price incentives to induce market participants to absorb the additional shares).

The permanent market impact cost, however, reflects the persistent price change that results as the market adjusts to the information content of the trade. Intuitively, a sell transaction reveals to the market that the security may be overvalued, whereas a buy transaction signals that the security may be undervalued. Security prices change when market participants adjust their views and perceptions as they observe news and the information contained in new trades during the trading day.

Traders can decrease the temporary market impact by extending the trading horizon of an order. For example, a trader executing a less urgent order can buy/sell his position in smaller portions over a period and make sure that each portion only constitutes a small percentage of the average volume. However, this comes at the price of increased opportunity costs, delay costs, and price movement risk. We will discuss this issue in more detail later in Chapter 12.

Market impact costs are often *asymmetric*; that is, they are different for buy and sell orders. For instance, Bikker and Spierdijk estimated the market impact costs from a data sample consisting of 3,728 worldwide equity trades executed during the first quarter of 2002 at the Dutch pension fund Algemeen Burgerlijk Pensioenfonds (ABP).[13] The trades, of which 1,963 were buys and 1,765 sales, had a total transaction value of €5.7 billion. They concluded that the temporary and persistent price effects of buy orders were 7.2 basis points and 12.4 basis points, respectively. For sell orders, on the other hand, these price effects were −14.5 basis points and −16.5 basis points.

This and many other empirical studies suggest that market impact costs are generally higher for buy orders. Nevertheless, while buying costs might be higher than selling costs, this empirical fact is most likely due to observations during rising/falling markets, rather than any *true* market microstructure effects. For example, a study by Hu shows that the difference in market impact costs between buys and sells is an artifact of the trade benchmark.[14]

---

[13]Jacob A. Bikker, Laura Spierdijk, and Pieter Jelle van der Sluis, "Market Impact Costs of Institutional Equity Trades," *Journal of International Money and Finance* (2007), 26(6), pp. 974–1000.

[14]Gang Hu, "Measures of Implicit Trading Costs and Buy-Sell Asymmetry," *Journal of Financial Markets* (to appear), 2008.

EXHIBIT 11.1 Distribution of Trading Volumes in the MSCI Europe in the Three-Month Period Ending December 16, 2004

	Average Daily Trading Volume < €5 million	Average Daily Trading Volume < €7.5 million	Average Daily Trading Volume < €10 million
Percentage of stocks in the MCSI Europe	17.76%	24.33%	33.75%

Data courtesy of RAS Asset Management.

(We discuss trade benchmarks later in this chapter.) When a pretrade measure is used, buys (sells) have higher implicit trading costs during rising (falling) markets. Conversely, if a posttrade measure is used, sells (buys) have higher implicit trading costs during rising (falling) markets. In fact, both pretrade and posttrade measures are highly influenced by market movement, whereas during- or average-trade measures are neutral to market movement.

Despite the enormous global size of equity markets, the impact of trading is important even for relatively small funds. In fact, a sizable fraction of the stocks that compose an index might have to be excluded or their trading severely limited. For example, RAS Asset Management, which is the asset manager arm of the large Italian insurance company RAS, has determined that single trades exceeding 10% of the daily trading volume of a stock cause an excessive market impact and have to be excluded, while trades between 5% and 10% need execution strategies distributed over several days.[15]

To appreciate the impact of these restrictions on portfolio management strategies, Exhibit 11.1 illustrates the distribution of trading volume in the MSCI Europe in the period September–December 2004 below €5 million, €7.5 million, and €10 million.

According to RAS Asset Management estimates, in practice funds managed actively with quantitative techniques and with market capitalization in excess of €100 million can operate only on the fraction of the market above the €5 million, splitting trades over several days for stocks with average daily trading volume in the range from €5 million to €10 million. They can freely operate only on two thirds of the stocks in the MSCI Europe.

Price Movement Risk

In general, the stock market exhibits a positive drift that gives rise to price movement risk. Similarly, individual stocks, at least temporarily, trend up or down. A trade that goes in the same direction as the general market or an individual security is exposed to price risk. For example, when a trader is

---

[15]Private communication RAS Asset Management.

buying in a rising market, he might pay more than he initially anticipated to fully satisfy the order. In practice, it can be difficult to separate price movement risk from the market impact cost. Typically, the price movement risk for a buy order is defined as the price increase during the time of the trade that is attributed to the general trend of a security, whereas the remaining part is market impact costs.

Market Timing Costs

The market timing costs are due to the movement in the price of a security at the time of the transaction that can be attributed to other market participants or general market volatility. Market timing cost is higher for larger trades, in particular when they are divided into smaller blocks and traded over a period of time. Practitioners often define market timing costs to be proportional to the standard deviation of the security returns times the square root of the time anticipated in order to complete the transaction.

Opportunity Costs

The cost of not transacting represents an opportunity cost. For example, when a certain trade fails to execute, the portfolio manager misses an opportunity. Commonly, this cost is defined as the difference in performance between a portfolio manager's desired investment and his actual investment after transaction costs. Opportunity costs are in general driven by price risk or market volatility. As a result, the longer the trading horizon, the greater the exposure to opportunity costs.

Identifying Transaction Costs: An Example[16]

We now consider an example to highlight the key cost components of an equity trade. Following the completion of an institutional trade, suppose that the ticker tape for XYZ stock reveals that 6,000 shares of XYZ stock were purchased at $82.00.

Although 6,000 XYZ shares were bought, Exhibit 11.2 indicates what may have happened behind the scenes—beginning with the initial security selection decision by the manager (the investment idea), to the release of

---

[16]This illustration is similar to the example provided in Wayne H. Wagner and Mark Edwards, "Implementing Investment Strategies: The Art and Science of Investing," Chapter 11 in Frank J. Fabozzi (ed.), *Active Equity Portfolio Management* (Hoboken, NJ: John Wiley & Sons, 1998). The example used here is taken from Frank J. Fabozzi and James L. Grant, *Equity Portfolio Management* (Hoboken, NJ: John Wiley & Sons, 1999), pp. 309–310.

EXHIBIT 11.2 XYZ Trade Decomposition

Equity manager wants to buy 10,000 shares of XYZ at current price of $80.
Trade desk releases 8,000 shares to broker when price is $81.
Broker purchases 6,000 shares of XYZ stock at $82 plus $0.045 (per share) commission.
XYZ stock jumps to $85, and remainder of order is canceled.
15 days later the price of XYZ stock is $88.

Source: Exhibit 1 in Chapter 11 of Frank J. Fabozzi and James L. Grant, *Equity Portfolio Management* (Hoboken, NJ: John Wiley & Sons, 1999), p. 309.

the buy order by the equity trader, to the subsequent trade execution by the broker (the essential elements of trading implementation).

We can assess the cost of trading XYZ stock as follows. The commission charge is the easiest to identify—namely, $0.045 per share, or $270 on the purchase of 6,000 shares of XYZ stock.

Since the trade desk did not release the order to buy XYZ stock until it was selling for $81, the assessed trader timing cost is $1 per share. Also, the market impact cost is $1 per XYZ share traded, as the stock was selling for $81 when the order was received by the broker—just prior to execution of the 6,000 XYZ shares at $82.

The opportunity cost—resulting from unexecuted shares—of the equity trade is more difficult to estimate. Assuming that the movement of XYZ stock price from $80 to $88 can be largely attributed to information used by the equity manager in his security selection decision, it appears that the value of the investment idea to purchase XYZ stock was 10% ($88/$80 – 1) over a 15-day trading interval. Since 40% of the initial buy order on XYZ stock was "left on the table," the opportunity cost of not purchasing 4,000 shares of XYZ stock is 4% (10% × 40%).

The basic trading cost illustration in Exhibit 11.2 suggests that without efficient management of the equity trading process, it is possible that the value of the manager's investment ideas (gross alpha) is impacted negatively by sizable trading costs in addition to commission charges, including trader timing, price or market impact cost, and opportunity cost. Moreover, trading cost management is especially important in a world where active equity managers are hard pressed to outperform a simple buy and hold approach such as that employed in a market index fund.

LIQUIDITY AND TRANSACTION COSTS

Liquidity is created by agents transacting in the financial markets when they buy and sell securities. Market makers and brokers/dealers do not create liquidity; they are intermediaries who facilitate trade execution and maintain an orderly market.

Liquidity and transaction costs are interrelated. A highly liquid market is one were large transactions can be immediately executed without incurring high transaction costs. In an indefinitely liquid market, traders would be able to perform very large transactions directly at the quoted bid-ask prices. In reality, particularly for larger orders, the market requires traders to pay more than the ask when buying, and to receive less than the bid when selling. As we discussed previously, this percentage degradation of the bid-ask prices experienced when executing trades is the market impact cost.

The market impact cost varies with transaction size: the larger the trade size the larger the impact cost. Impact costs are not constant in time, but vary throughout the day as traders change the limit orders that they have in the limit order book. A *limit order* is a conditional order; it is executed only if the limit price or a better price can be obtained. For example, a buy limit order of a security XYZ at $60 indicates that the assets may be purchased only at $60 or lower. Therefore, a limit order is very different from a *market order*, which is an unconditional order to execute at the current best price available in the market (guarantees execution, not price). With a limit order a trader can improve the execution price relative to the market order price, but the execution is neither certain nor immediate (guarantees price, not execution).

Notably, there are many different limit order types available such as pegging orders, discretionary limit orders, IOC orders, and fleeting orders. For example, fleeting orders are those limit orders that are canceled within two seconds of submission. Hasbrouck and Saar find that fleeting limit orders are much closer substitutes for market orders than for traditional limit orders.[17] This suggests that the role of limit orders has changed from the traditional view of being liquidity suppliers to being substitutes for market orders.

At any given instant, the list of orders sitting in the limit order book embodies the liquidity that exists at a particular point in time. By observing the entire limit order book, impact costs can be calculated for different transaction sizes. The limit order book reveals the prevailing supply and demand in the market.[18] Therefore, in a pure limit order market we can

---

[17]Joel Hasbrouck and Gideon Saar, "Technology and Liquidity Provision: The Blurring of Traditional Definitions," *Journal of Financial Markets* (2008).

[18]Note that even if it is possible to view the entire limit order book it does not give a *complete* picture of the liquidity in the market. This is because hidden and discretionary orders are not included. For a discussion on this topic, see Laura A. Tuttle, "Hidden Orders, Trading Costs and Information," Working Paper, Ohio State University, 2002.

EXHIBIT 11.3 The Supply and Demand Schedule of a Security

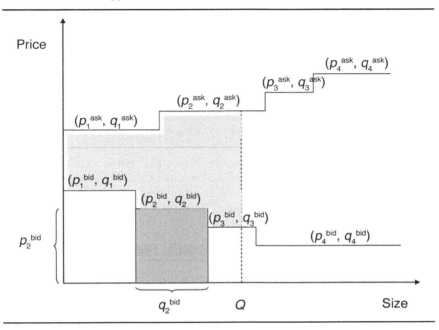

Source: Figure 1A on page 38 in Ian Domowitz and Xiaoxin Wang, "Liquidity, Liquidity Commonality and Its Impact on Portfolio Theory," Smeal College of Business Administration, Pennsylvania State University, 2002.

obtain a measure of liquidity by aggregating limit buy orders (representing the demand) and limit sell orders (representing the supply).[19]

We start by sorting the bid and ask prices, $p_1^{bid}, \ldots, p_k^{bid}$ and $p_1^{ask}, \ldots, p_l^{ask}$, (from the most to the least competitive) and the corresponding order quantities $q_1^{bid}, \ldots, q_k^{bid}$ and $q_1^{ask}, \ldots, q_l^{ask}$.[20] We then combine the sorted bid and ask prices into a supply and demand schedule according to Exhibit 11.3. For example, the block (p_2^{bid}, q_2^{bid}) represents the second best sell limit order with price p_2^{bid} and quantity q_2^{bid}.

---

[19]Ian Domowitz and Xiaoxin Wang, "Liquidity, Liquidity Commonality and Its Impact on Portfolio Theory," Smeal College of Business Administration, Pennsylvania State University, 2002; Thierry Foucault, Ohad Kadan, and Eugene Kandel, "Limit Order Book As a Market for Liquidity," *Review of Financial Studies* 18, no. 4 (2005), pp. 1171–1217.

[20]In this chapter, we diverge slightly from the notation used elsewhere in this book. Instead, we use the notation that is common in the trading and transaction cost literature and denote price by p, order quantity by q, and trade size by Q (or V).

We note that unless there is a gap between the bid (demand) and the ask (supply) sides, there will be a match between a seller and buyer, and a trade would occur. The larger the gap, the lower the liquidity and the market participants' desire to trade. For a trade of size Q, we can define its *liquidity* as the reciprocal of the area between the supply and demand curves up to Q (i.e., the "dotted" area in Exhibit 11.3).

However, few order books are publicly available and not all markets are pure limit order markets. In 2004, the NYSE started selling information on its limit order book through its new system called the *NYSE OpenBook®*. The system provides an aggregated real-time view of the exchange's limit-order book for all NYSE-traded securities.[21]

In the absence of a fully transparent limit order book, expected market impact cost is the most practical and realistic measure of market liquidity. It is closer to the true cost of transacting faced by market participants as compared to other measures such as those based upon the bid-ask spread.

MARKET IMPACT MEASUREMENTS AND EMPIRICAL FINDINGS

The problem with measuring implicit transaction costs is that the true measure, which is the difference between the price of the stock in the absence of a money manager's trade and the execution price, is not observable. Furthermore, the execution price is dependent on supply and demand conditions at the margin. Thus, the execution price may be influenced by competitive traders who demand immediate execution or by other investors with similar motives for trading. This means that the execution price realized by an investor is the consequence of the structure of the market mechanism, the demand for liquidity by the marginal investor, and the competitive forces of investors with similar motivations for trading.

There are many ways to measure transaction costs. However, in general this cost is the difference between the execution price and some appropriate benchmark, a so-called *fair market benchmark*. The fair market benchmark of a security is the price that would have prevailed had the trade not taken place, the *no-trade price*. Since the no-trade price is not observable, it has to be estimated. Practitioners have identified three different basic approaches to measure the market impact:[22]

[21]NYSE and Securities Industry Automation Corporation, *NYSE OpenBook®*, Version 1.1, 2004.
[22]Bruce M. Collins and Frank J. Fabozzi, "A Methodology for Measuring Transaction Costs," *Financial Analysts Journal* 47 (1991), pp. 27–36; Louis K. C. Chan and Joseph Lakonishok, "Institutional Trades and Intraday Stock Price Behavior," *Journal of Financial Economics* 33 (1993), pp. 173–199; and Fabozzi and Grant, *Equity Portfolio Management*.

1. *Pretrade measures* use prices occurring before or at the decision to trade as the benchmark, such as the opening price on the same-day or the closing price on the previous day.
2. *Posttrade measures* use prices occurring after the decision to trade as the benchmark, such as the closing price of the trading day or the opening price on the next day.
3. *Same-day* or *average measures* use average prices of a large number of trades during the day of the decision to trade, such as the *volume-weighted average price* (VWAP) calculated over all transactions in the security on the trade day.[23]

The volume-weighted average price is calculated as follows. Suppose that it was a trader's objective to purchase 10,000 shares of stock XYZ. After completion of the trade, the trade sheet showed that 4,000 shares were purchased at $80, another 4,000 at $81, and finally 2,000 at $82. In this case, the resulting VWAP is (4,000 × 80 + 4,000 × 81 + 2,000 × 82)/10,000 = $80.80.

We denote by χ the indicator function that takes on the value 1 or –1 if an order is a buy or sell order, respectively. Formally, we now express the three types of measures of *market impact* (MI) as follows

$$\mathrm{MI}_{\mathrm{pre}} = \left(\frac{p^{\mathrm{ex}}}{p^{\mathrm{pre}}} - 1 \right) \chi$$

$$\mathrm{MI}_{\mathrm{post}} = \left(\frac{p^{\mathrm{ex}}}{p^{\mathrm{post}}} - 1 \right) \chi$$

$$\mathrm{MI}_{\mathrm{VWAP}} = \left(\frac{\sum_{i=1}^{k} V_i \cdot p_i^{\mathrm{ex}}}{\sum_{i=1}^{k} V_i} \bigg/ p^{\mathrm{pre}} - 1 \right) \chi$$

where p^{ex}, p^{pre}, and p^{post} denote the execution price, pretrade price, and posttrade price of the stock, and k denotes the number of transactions in a particular security on the trade date. Using this definition, for a stock with market impact MI the resulting *market impact cost* for a trade of size V, *MIC*, is given by

$$\mathrm{MIC} = \mathrm{MI} \cdot V$$

---

[23]Strictly speaking, VWAP is not the benchmark here but rather the transaction type.

It is also common to adjust market impact for general market movements. For example, the pretrade market impact with market adjustment would take the form

$$\mathrm{MI}_{\mathrm{pre}} = \left(\frac{p^{\mathrm{ex}}}{p^{\mathrm{pre}}} - \frac{p_M^{\mathrm{ex}}}{p_M^{\mathrm{pre}}} \right) \chi$$

where p_M^{ex} represent the value of the index at the time of the execution, and p_M^{pre} the price of the index at the time before the trade. Market adjusted market impact for the posttrade and same-day trade benchmarks are calculated in an analogous fashion.

The above three approaches to measure market impact are based upon measuring the fair market benchmark of stock at a point in time. Clearly, different definitions of market impact lead to different results. Which one should be used is a matter of preference and is dependent on the application at hand. For example, Elkins/McSherry, a financial consulting firm that provides customized trading costs and execution analysis, calculates a same-day benchmark price for each stock by taking the mean of the day's open, close, high, and low prices. The market impact is then computed as the percentage difference between the transaction price and this benchmark. However, in most cases VWAP and the Elkins/McSherry approach lead to similar measurements.[24]

As we analyze a portfolio's return over time an important question to ask is whether we can attribute good/bad performance to investment profits/losses or to trading profits/losses. In other words, in order to better understand a portfolio's performance it can be useful to decompose investment decisions from order execution. This is the basic idea behind the *implementation shortfall approach*.[25]

In the implementation shortfall approach we assume that there is a separation between investment and trading decisions. The portfolio manager makes decisions with respect to the investment strategy (i.e., what should be bought, sold, and held). Subsequently, these decisions are implemented by the traders.

By comparing the actual portfolio profit/loss (P/L) with the performance of a hypothetical *paper* portfolio in which all trades are made at hypothetical market prices, we can get an estimate of the implementation shortfall.

---

[24]John Willoughby, "Executions Song," *Institutional Investor* 32, no. 11 (1998), pp. 51–56; and Richard McSherry, "Global Trading Cost Analysis," mimeo, Elkins/McSherry Co., Inc., 1998.
[25]Andre F. Perold, "The Implementation Shortfall: Paper Versus Reality," *Journal of Portfolio Management* 14 (1998), pp. 4–9.

For example, with a paper portfolio return of 6% and an actual portfolio return of 5%, the implementation shortfall is 1%.

There is considerable practical and academic interest in the measurement and analysis of international trading costs. Domowitz, Glen, and Madhavan[26] examine international equity trading costs across a broad sample of 42 countries using quarterly data from 1995 to 1998. They find that the mean total one-way trading cost is 69.81 basis points. However, there is an enormous variation in trading costs across countries. For example, in their study the highest was Korea with 196.85 basis points whereas the lowest was France with 29.85 basis points. Explicit costs are roughly two-thirds of total costs. However, one exception to this is the United States where the implicit costs are about 60% of the total costs.

Transaction costs in emerging markets are significantly higher than those in more developed markets. Domowitz, Glen, and Madhavan argue that this fact limits the gains of international diversification in these countries explaining in part the documented *home bias* of domestic investors.

In general, they find that transaction costs declined from the middle of 1997 to the end of 1998, with the exception of Eastern Europe. It is interesting to notice that this reduction in transaction costs happened despite the turmoil in the financial markets during this period. A few explanations that Domowitz et al. suggest are that (1) the increased institutional presence has resulted in a more competitive environment for brokers/dealers and other trading services; (2) technological innovation has led to a growth in the use of low-cost electronic crossing networks (ECNs) by institutional traders; and (3) soft dollar payments are now more common.

FORECASTING AND MODELING MARKET IMPACT

In this section we describe a general methodology for constructing forecasting models for market impact. These types of models are very useful in predicting the resulting trading costs of specific trading strategies and in devising optimal trading approaches.

As we discussed previously, the explicit transaction costs are relatively straightforward to estimate and forecast. Therefore, our focus in this section is to develop a methodology for the implicit transaction costs, and more specifically, market impact costs. The methodology is a linear factor based approach where market impact is the dependent variable. We distinguish

---

[26]Ian Domowitz, Jack Glen, and Ananth Madhavan, "International Equity Trading Costs: A Cross-Sectional and Time-Series Analysis," Technical Report, Pennsylvania State University, International Finance Corp., University of Southern California, 1999.

between *trade-based* and *asset-based* independent variables or forecasting factors.

Trade-Based Factors

Some examples of trade-based factors include:

- Trade size
- Relative trade size
- Price of market liquidity
- Type of trade (information or noninformation trade)
- Efficiency and trading style of the investor
- Specific characteristics of the market or the exchange
- Time of trade submission and trade timing
- Order type

Probably the most important market impact forecasting variables are based on absolute or relative trade size. Absolute trade size is often measured in terms of the number of shares traded, or the dollar value of the trade. Relative trade size, on the other hand, can be calculated as number of shares traded divided by average daily volume, or number of shares traded divided by the total number of shares outstanding. Note that the former can be seen as an explanatory variable for the temporary market impact and the latter for the permanent market impact. In particular, we expect the temporary market impact to increase as the trade size to the average daily volume increases because a larger trade demands more liquidity.

Each type of investment style requires a different need for immediacy.[27] Technical trades often have to be traded at a faster pace in order to capitalize on some short-term signal and therefore exhibits higher market impact costs. In contrast, more traditional long-term value strategies can be traded more slowly. These types of strategies can in many cases even be liquidity providing, which might result in negative market impact costs.

Several studies show that there is a wide variation in equity transaction costs across different countries.[28] Markets and exchanges in each country are different, and so are the resulting market microstructures. Forecast-

---

[27]Donald B. Keim and Ananth Madhavan, "Transaction Costs and Investment Style: An Inter-Exchange Analysis of Institutional Equity Trades," *Journal of Financial Economics* 46 (1997), pp. 265–292.
[28]See Domowitz, Glen, and Madhavan, "Liquidity, Volatility, and Equity Trading Costs Across Countries and Over Time," and Chiraphol N. Chiyachantana, Pankaj K. Jain, Christine Jian, and Robert A. Wood, "International Evidence on Institutional Trading Behavior and Price Impact," *Journal of Finance* 59 (2004), pp. 869–895.

ing variables can be used to capture specific market characteristics such as liquidity, efficiency, and institutional features.

The particular timing of a trade can affect the market impact costs. For example, it appears that market impact costs are generally higher at the beginning of the month as compared to the end of it.[29] One of the reasons for this phenomenon is that many institutional investors tend to rebalance their portfolios at the beginning of the month. Because it is likely that many of these trades will be executed in the same stocks, this rebalancing pattern will induce an increase in market impact costs. The particular time of the day a trade takes place does also have an effect. Many informed institutional traders tend to trade at the market open as they want to capitalize on new information that appeared after the market close the day before.

As we discussed earlier in this chapter, market impact costs are asymmetric. In other words, buy and sell orders have significantly different market impact costs. Separate models for buy and sell orders can therefore be estimated. However, it is now more common to construct a model that includes dummy variables for different types of orders such as buy/sell orders, market orders, limit orders, and the like.

Asset-Based Factors

Some examples of asset-based factors are:

- Price momentum
- Price volatility
- Market capitalization
- Growth versus value
- Specific industry or sector characteristics

For a stock that is exhibiting positive price momentum, a buy order is liquidity demanding and it is, therefore, likely that it will have higher market impact cost than a sell order.

Generally, trades in high volatility stocks result in higher permanent price effects. It has been suggested by Chan and Lakonishok[30] and Smith et al.[31] that this is because trades have a tendency to contain more information

---

[29]F. Douglas Foster and S. Viswanathan, "A Theory of the Interday Variations in Volume, Variance, and Trading Costs in Securities Markets," *Review of Financial Studies* 3 (1990), pp. 593–624.

[30]Louis K. C. Chan and Joseph Lakonishok, "Institutional Equity Trading Costs: NYSE versus Nasdaq," *Journal of Finance* 52 (1997), pp. 713–735.

[31]Brian F. Smith, D. Alasdair, S. Turnbull, and Robert W. White, "Upstairs Market for Principal and Agency Trades: Analysis of Adverse Information and Price Effects," *Journal of Finance* 56 (2001), pp. 1723–1746.

when volatility is high. Another possibility is that higher volatility increases the probability of hitting and being able to execute at the liquidity providers' price. Consequently, liquidity suppliers display fewer shares at the best prices to mitigate adverse selection costs.

Large-cap stocks are more actively traded and therefore more liquid in comparison to small-cap stocks. As a result, market impact cost is normally lower for large-caps.[32] However, if we measure market impact costs with respect to relative trade size (normalized by average daily volume, for instance) they are generally higher. Similarly, growth and value stocks have different market impact cost. One reason for that is related to the trading style. Growth stocks commonly exhibit momentum and high volatility. This attracts technical traders that are interested in capitalizing on short-term price swings. Value stocks are traded at a slower pace and holding periods tend to be slightly longer.

Different market sectors show different trading behaviors. For instance, Bikker and Spierdijk show that equity trades in the energy sector exhibit higher market impact costs than other comparable equities in nonenergy sectors.[33]

A Factor-Based Market Impact Model

One of the most common approaches in practice and in the literature in modeling market impact is through a linear factor model of the form

$$MI_t = \alpha + \sum_{i=1}^{I} \beta_i x_i + \varepsilon_t$$

where α, β_i are the factor loadings and x_i are the factors. Frequently, the error term ε_t is assumed to be independently and identically distributed. Recall that the resulting market impact cost of a trade of (dollar) size V is then given by $MIC_t = MI_t \cdot V$. However, extensions of this model including conditional volatility specifications are also possible. By analyzing both the mean and the volatility of the market impact, we can better understand and manage the trade-off between the two. For example, Bikker and Spierdijk use a specification where the error terms are jointly and serially uncorrelated with mean zero, satisfying

---

[32]Keim and Madhavan, "Transaction Costs and Investment Style," and Laura Spierdijk, Theo Nijman, and Arthur van Soest, "Temporary and Persistent Price Effects of Trades in Infrequently Traded Stocks," Working Paper, Tilburg University and Center, 2003.
[33]Bikker, Spierdijk, and van der Sluis, "Market Impact Costs of Institutional Equity Trades."

$$\mathrm{Var}(\varepsilon_t) = \exp\left(\gamma + \sum_{j=1}^{J} \delta_j z_j\right)$$

where γ, δ_j, and z_j are the volatility, factor loadings, and factors, respectively.

Although the market impact function is linear, this of course does not mean that the dependent variables have to be. In particular, the factors in the previous specification can be nonlinear transformations of the descriptive variables.

Consider, for example, factors related to trade size (e.g., trade size and trade size to daily volume). It is well known that market impact is nonlinear in these trade size measures. One of the earliest studies in this regard was performed by Loeb,[34] who showed that for a large set of stocks the market impact is proportional to the square root of the trade size, resulting in a market impact cost proportional to $V^{3/2}$. Typically, a market impact function linear in trade size will underestimate the price impact of small- to medium-sized trades whereas larger trades will be overestimated.

Chen, Stanzl, and Watanabe suggest to model the nonlinear effects of trade size (dollar trade size V) in a market impact model by using the Box-Cox transformation;[35] that is,

$$\mathrm{MI}(V_t) = \alpha_b + \beta_b \frac{V_t^{\lambda_b} - 1}{\lambda_b} + \varepsilon_t$$

where t and τ represent the time of transaction for the buys and the sells, respectively. In their specification, they assumed that ε_t and ε_τ are independent and identically distributed with mean zero and variance σ^2. The parameters α_b, β_b, λ_b, α_s, β_s, and λ_s were then estimated from market data by nonlinear least squares for each individual stock. We remark that λ_b, $\lambda_s \in [0,1]$ in order for the market impact for buys to be concave and for sells to be convex.

In their data sample (NYSE and Nasdaq trades between January 1993 and June 1993), Chen et al. report that for small companies the curvature parameters λ_b, λ_s are close to zero, whereas for larger companies they are not far away from 0.5. Observe that for $\lambda_b = \lambda_s = 1$ market impact is linear in the dollar trade size. Moreover, when $\lambda_b = \lambda_s = 0$ the impact function is logarithmic by the virtue of

---

[34]Thomas F. Loeb, "Trading Costs: The Critical Link between Investment Information and Results," *Financial Analysts Journal* 39, no. 3 (1983), pp. 39–44.
[35]Zhiwu Chen, Werner Stanzl, and Masahiro Watanabe, "Price Impact Costs and the Limit of Arbitrage," Yale School of Management, International Center for Finance, 2002.

$$\lim_{\lambda \to 0} \frac{V^\lambda - 1}{\lambda} = \ln(\lambda)$$

As just mentioned, market impact is also a function of the characteristics of the particular exchange where the securities are traded as well as of the trading style of the investor. These characteristics can also be included in the general specification outlined previously. For example, Keim and Madhavan proposed the following two different market impact specifications[36]

1. $MI = \alpha + \beta_1 \chi_{OTC} + \beta_2 \frac{1}{p} + \beta_3 |q| + \beta_4 |q|^2 + \beta_5 |q|^3 + \beta_6 \chi_{Up} + \varepsilon$

    where
    χ_{OTC} is a dummy variable equal to one if the stock is an OTC traded stock or zero otherwise
    p is the trade price
    q is the number of shares traded over the number of shares outstanding
    χ_{Up} is a dummy variable equal to one if the trade is done in the upstairs[37] market or zero otherwise

2. $MI = \alpha + \beta_1 \chi_{Nasdaq} + \beta_2 q + \beta_3 \ln(MCap) + \beta_4 \frac{1}{p} + \beta_5 \chi_{Tech} + \beta_6 \chi_{Index} + \varepsilon$

    where
    χ_{NASDAQ} is a dummy variable equal to one if the stock is traded on NASDAQ or zero otherwise
    q is the number of shares traded over the number of shares outstanding,
    MCap is the market capitalization of the stock
    p is the trade price
    χ_{Tech} is a dummy variable equal to one if the trade is a short-term technical trade or zero otherwise

---

[36]Donald B. Keim and Ananth Madhavan, "Transactions Costs and Investment Style: An Inter-Exchange Analysis of Institutional Equity Trades," *Journal of Financial Economics* 46 (1997), pp. 265–292; and Donald B. Keim and Ananth Madhavan, "The Upstairs Market for Large-Block Transactions: Analysis and Measurement of Price Effects," *Review of Financial Studies* 9 (1996), pp. 1–36.
[37]A securities transaction not executed on the exchange but completed directly by a broker in-house is referred to as an upstairs market transaction. Typically, the upstairs market consists of a network of trading desks of the major brokerages and institutional investors. The major purpose of the upstairs market is to facilitate large block and program trades.

χ_{Index} is a dummy variable equal to one if the trade is done for a portfolio that attempts to closely mimic the behavior of the underlying index or zero otherwise

These two models provide good examples for how nonlinear transformations of the underlying dependent variables can be used along with dummy variables that describe specific market or trade characteristics.

Several vendors and broker/dealers such as MSCI Barra[38] and ITG[39] have developed commercially available market impact models. These are sophisticated multimarket models that rely upon specialized estimation techniques using intraday data or tick-by-tick transaction-based data. However, the general characteristics of these models are similar to the ones described in this section.

We emphasize that in the modeling of transaction costs it is important to factor in the objective of the trader or investor. For example, one market participant might trade just to take advantage of price movement and hence will only trade during favorable periods. His trading cost is different from an investor who has to rebalance a portfolio within a fixed time period and can therefore only partially use an opportunistic or liquidity searching strategy. In particular, this investor has to take into account the *risk of not completing* the transaction within a specified time period. Consequently, even if the market is not favorable, he may decide to transact a portion of the trade. The market impact models described previously assume that orders will be fully completed and ignore this point.

INCORPORATING TRANSACTION COSTS IN ASSET-ALLOCATION MODELS

Standard asset-allocation models generally ignore transaction costs and other costs related to portfolio and allocation revisions. However, the effect of transaction costs is far from insignificant. On the contrary, if transaction costs are not taken into consideration, they can eat into a significant part of the returns. Whether transaction costs are handled efficiently or not by the portfolio or fund manager can therefore make all the difference in attempting to outperform the peer group or a particular benchmark.

The typical asset-allocation model consists of one or several forecasting models for expected returns and risk. Small changes in these forecasts can result in reallocations which would not occur if transaction costs had

---

[38]Nicolo G. Torre and Mark J. Ferrari, "The Market Impact Model," Barra Research Insights.
[39]"ITG ACE—Agency Cost Estimator: A Model Description," 2003, www.itginc.com.

been taken into account. Therefore, it is to be expected that the inclusion of transaction costs in asset-allocation models will result in a reduced amount of trading and rebalancing.

In this section we demonstrate how transaction costs models can be incorporated into standard asset-allocation models. For simplicity, we will use the mean-variance model to describe the basic approach. However, it is straightforward to extend this approach into other frameworks.

In 1970, Pogue gave one of the first descriptions of an extension of the mean-variance framework that included transaction costs.[40] Several other authors including, for example, Schreiner,[41] Adcock and Meade,[42] Lobo, Fazel, and Boyd,[43] Mitchell and Braun,[44] have provided further extensions and modifications to this basic approach. These formulations can be summarized by the mean-variance risk aversion formulation with transaction costs, given by

$$\max_{\mathbf{w}} \mathbf{w}'\boldsymbol{\mu} - \lambda \mathbf{w}'\boldsymbol{\Sigma}\mathbf{w} - \lambda_{\mathrm{TC}} \cdot \mathrm{TC}$$

subject to $\iota'\mathbf{w} = 1$, $\iota = [1,1,\ldots,1]'$ where TC denotes a transaction cost penalty function and λ_{TC} a transaction cost aversion parameter. In other words, the objective is to maximize expected return less the cost of risk and transaction costs. The transaction costs term in the utility function introduces resistance or friction in the rebalancing process that makes it costly to reach the mean-variance portfolio, which would have been the result had transaction costs not been taken into account. We can imagine that as we increase the transaction costs, at some point it will be optimal to keep the current portfolio.

Transaction costs models can involve complicated nonlinear functions. Although there exists software for general nonlinear optimization problems, the computational time required for solving such problems is often too long

[40]Gerry A. Pogue, "An Extension of the Markowitz Portfolio Selection Model to Include Variable Transactions' Costs, Short Sales, Leverage Policies and Taxes," *Journal of Finance* 25, no. 5 (1970), pp. 1005–1027.

[41]John Schreiner, "Portfolio Revision: A Turnover-Constrained Approach," *Financial Management* 9, no. 1 (Spring 1980), pp. 67–75.

[42]Christopher J. Adcock and Nigel Meade, "A Simple Algorithm to Incorporate Transaction Costs in Quadratic Optimization," *European Journal of Operational Research* 79, no. 1 (1994), pp. 85–94.

[43]Miguel Sousa Lobo, Maryam Fazel, and Stephen Boyd, "Portfolio Optimization with Linear and Fixed Transaction Costs and Bounds on Risk," *Annals of Operations Research* 152, no. 1 (2007), pp. 376–394.

[44]John E. Mitchell and Stephen Braun, "Rebalancing an Investment Portfolio in the Presence of Transaction Costs," Technical Report, Department of Mathematical Sciences, Rensselaer Polytechnic Institute, 2002.

for realistic investment management applications, and the quality of the solution is frequently not guaranteed. Very efficient and reliable software is available, however, for linear and quadratic optimization problems. It is therefore common in practice to approximate a complicated nonlinear optimization problem by simpler problems that can be solved quickly. In particular, portfolio managers frequently employ approximations of the transaction cost penalty function in the mean-variance framework.[45]

One of the most common simplifications to the transaction cost penalty function is to assume that it is a separable function dependent only on the portfolio weights $\mathbf{w}$, or more specifically on the portion to be traded $\mathbf{x} = \mathbf{w} - \mathbf{w}_0$, where $\mathbf{w}_0$ is the original portfolio and $\mathbf{w}$ is the new portfolio after rebalancing. Mathematically, we can express this as

$$TC(\mathbf{x}) = \sum_{i=1}^{N} TC_i(x_i)$$

where TC_i is the transaction cost function for security i and x_i is the portion of security i to be traded. The transaction cost function TC_i is often parameterized as a quadratic function of the form

$$TC_i(x_i) = \alpha_i \cdot \chi_{\{x_i \neq 0\}} + \beta_i |x_i| + \gamma_i |x_i|^2$$

where the coefficients α_i, β_i, and γ_i may be different for each asset, and $\chi_{\{x_i \neq 0\}}$ is the indicator function that is equal to one when $x_i \neq 0$ and zero otherwise.

When all $\alpha_i = 0$, the resulting optimization problem is a quadratic optimization problem of the form

$$\max_{\mathbf{w}} \mathbf{w}'\boldsymbol{\mu} - \lambda \mathbf{w}'\Sigma\mathbf{w} - \lambda_{TC}(\beta'|\mathbf{x}| + |\mathbf{x}|' \, \Gamma |\mathbf{x}|)$$

subject to the usual constraints, where $\beta' = (\beta_1, \ldots, \beta_N)$ and

$$\Gamma = \begin{bmatrix} \gamma_1 & 0 & \cdots & \cdots & 0 \\ 0 & \gamma_2 & \ddots & & \vdots \\ \vdots & \ddots & \ddots & \ddots & \vdots \\ \vdots & & \ddots & \ddots & 0 \\ 0 & \cdots & \cdots & 0 & \gamma_N \end{bmatrix}$$

---

[45]See, for example, Andre F. Perold, "Large-Scale Portfolio Optimization," *Management Science* 30, no. 10 (1984), pp. 1143–1160; and Hiroshi Konno and Annista Wijayanayake, "Portfolio Optimization Problem under Concave Transaction Costs and Minimal Transaction Unit Constraints," *Mathematical Programming and Finance* 89, no. 2 (2001), pp. 233–250.

In particular, as this is a quadratic optimization problem, it can be solved with exactly the same software that is capable of solving the classical mean-variance optimization problem.

Alternatively, piecewise-linear approximations to transaction cost function models can be used. An example of a piecewise-linear function of transaction costs for a trade of size t of a particular security is illustrated in Exhibit 11.4. The transaction cost function illustrated in the graph assumes that the rate of increase of transaction costs (reflected in the slope of the function) changes at certain threshold points. For example, it is smaller in the range 0% to 15% of some reference volume (Vol) than in the range 15% to 40%. Mathematically, the transaction cost function in Exhibit 11.4 can be expressed as

$$TC(x)$$
$$= \begin{cases} s_1 x, & 0 \leq x \leq 0.15 \cdot \text{Vol} \\ s_1(0.15 \cdot \text{Vol}) + s_2(x - 0.15 \cdot \text{Vol}), & 0.15 \cdot \text{Vol} \leq x \leq 0.40 \cdot \text{Vol} \\ s_1(0.15 \cdot \text{Vol}) + s_2(0.25 \cdot \text{Vol}) + s_3(x - 0.40 \cdot \text{Vol}), & 0.40 \cdot \text{Vol} \leq x \leq 0.55 \cdot \text{Vol} \end{cases}$$

where s_1, s_2, s_3 are the slopes of the three linear segments on the graph.

Including piecewise-linear functions for transaction costs in the objective function of the mean-variance (or any general mean-risk) portfolio

EXHIBIT 11.4 An Example of Modeling Transaction Costs (TC) as a Piecewise-Linear Function of Trade Size t

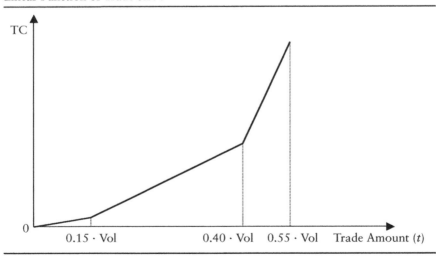

optimization problem is straightforward.[46] We can introduce new decision variables that correspond to the number of pieces in the piecewise-linear approximation of the transaction cost function (in this case, there are three linear segments, so we introduce variables y_1, y_2, y_3), and write the penalty term in the objective function for an individual asset as

$$\lambda_{TC}(s_1 \cdot y_1 + s_2 \cdot y_2 + s_3 \cdot y_3)$$

If there are N assets in the portfolio, the total transaction cost will be the sum of the transaction costs for each individual asset. That is, the penalty term becomes

$$\lambda_{TC}\sum_{i=1}^{N}(s_{1,i} \cdot y_{1,i} + s_{2,i} \cdot y_{2,i} + s_{3,i} \cdot y_{3,i})$$

In addition, one needs to specify the following constraints on the new decision variables:

$$0 \le y_{1,i} \le 0.15 \cdot \text{Vol}_i$$
$$0 \le y_{2,i} \le 0.25 \cdot \text{Vol}_i$$
$$0 \le y_{3,i} \le 0.15 \cdot \text{Vol}_i$$

Note that because of the increasing slopes of the linear segments and the goal of minimizing that term in the objective function, the optimizer will never set the decision variable corresponding to the second segment, $y_{2,i}$, to a number greater than 0 unless the decision variable corresponding to the first segment, $y_{1,i}$, is at its upper bound. Similarly, the optimizer would never set $y_{3,i}$ to a number greater than 0 unless both $y_{1,i}$ and $y_{2,i}$ are at their upper bounds. This set of constraints allows us to compute the total traded amount of asset i as $y_{1,i} + y_{2,i} + y_{3,i}$.

Of course, one also needs to link the traded amount of asset i to the optimal portfolio allocation. This is done by adding another set of constraints. We introduce variables z_i, one for each asset in the portfolio, that would represent the amount traded (but not the direction of the trade), and would be nonnegative. Then, we would require that

$$z_i = y_{1,i} + y_{2,i} + y_{3,i} \quad \text{for each asset } i$$

---

[46]See, for example, Dimitris Bertsimas, Christopher Darnell, and Robert Soucy, "Portfolio Construction through Mixed-Integer Programming at Grantham, Mayo, Van Otterloo and Company," *Interfaces* 29, no. 1 (1999), pp. 49–66.

and also that z_i equals the change in the portfolio holdings of asset i. The latter condition is imposed by writing the constraint

$$z_i = \left| w_i - w_{0,i} \right|$$

where $w_{0,i}$ and w_i are the initial and the final amount of asset i in the portfolio, respectively.[47]

Despite their apparent complexity, piecewise-linear approximations for transaction costs are very solver-friendly, and save time (relative to nonlinear models) in the actual portfolio optimization. Although modeling transaction costs this way requires introducing new decision variables and constraints, the increase in the dimension of the portfolio optimization problem does not affect significantly the running time or the performance of the optimization software, because the problem formulation is *easy*.

INTEGRATED PORTFOLIO MANAGEMENT: BEYOND EXPECTED RETURN AND PORTFOLIO RISK

Equity trading should not be viewed separately from equity portfolio management. On the contrary, the management of equity trading costs is an integral part of any successful investment management strategy. In this context, MSCI Barra points out that superior investment performance is based on careful consideration of four key elements:[48]

1. Forming realistic return expectations.
2. Controlling portfolio risk.
3. Efficient control of trading costs.
4. Monitoring total investment performance.

Unfortunately, most discussions of equity portfolio management focus solely on the relationship between expected return and portfolio risk—with little if any emphasis on whether the selected securities in the optimal or target portfolio can be acquired in a cost efficient manner.

---

[47]This constraint can be written in an equivalent, more optimization solver-friendly form, namely,

$$z_i \geq w_i - w_{0,i}$$
$$z_i \geq -(w_i - w_{0,i})$$

[48]The trading cost factor model described in this section is based on MSCI Barra's Market Impact Model™. A basic description of the model is covered in a three-part newsletter series. See Nicolo Torre, "The Market Impact Model™," Equity Trading: Research, Barra Newsletters 165–167 (Barra, 1998).

To illustrate the seriousness of the problem that can arise with suboptimal portfolio decisions, Exhibit 11.5 highlights the typical versus ideal approach to (equity) portfolio management. In the typical approach (top portion of Exhibit 11.5), portfolio managers engage in fundamental and/ or quantitative research to identify investment opportunities—albeit with a measure of investment prudence (risk control) in mind. Upon completion, the portfolio manager reveals the list of securities that form the basis of the target portfolio to the senior trader. At this point, the senior trader informs the portfolio manager of certain nontradable positions—which causes the portfolio manager to adjust the list of securities either by hand or some other ad hoc procedure. This, in turn, causes the investor's portfolio to be suboptimal.

Exhibit 11.5 also shows that as the trader begins to fill the portfolio with the now suboptimal set of securities, an additional portfolio imbalance may occur as market impact costs cause the prices of some securities to "run away" during trade implementation. It should be clear that any ad hoc adjustments by the trader at this point will in turn build a systematic imbalance in the investor's portfolio—such that the portfolio manager's actual portfolio will depart permanently from that which would be efficient from a return-risk and trading cost perspective.

A better approach to equity portfolio management (lower portion of Exhibit 11.5) requires a systematic integration of portfolio management

EXHIBIT 11.5 Typical versus Ideal Portfolio Management

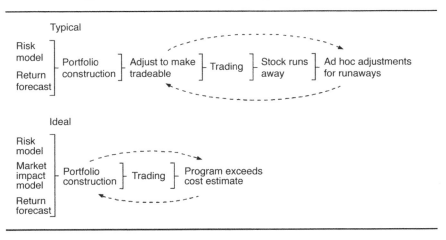

Source: Figure 4 in Nicolo Torre, "The Market Impact Model™—First in a Series: The Market Impact Problem," *Equity Trading: Research,* Barra Newsletters 165 (Barra, 1998), pp. 7–8.

and trading processes. In this context, the returns forecast, risk estimates, and trading cost program are jointly combined in determining the optimal investment portfolio. In this way, the portfolio manager knows up front if (complete) portfolio implementation is either not feasible or is too expensive when accounting for trading costs.

Accordingly, the portfolio manager can incorporate the appropriate trading cost information into the portfolio construction and risk control process—before the trading program begins. The portfolio manager can then build a portfolio of securities whereby actual security positions are consistent with those deemed to be optimal from an integrated portfolio context.

SUMMARY

- Trading and execution are integral components of the investment process. A poorly executed trade can eat directly into portfolio returns because of transaction costs.
- Transaction costs are typically categorized in two dimensions: *fixed costs* versus *variable costs*, and *explicit costs* versus *implicit costs*.
- In the first dimension, fixed costs include commissions and fees. Bid-ask spreads, taxes, delay cost, price movement risk, market impact costs, timing risk, and opportunity cost are variable trading costs.
- In the second dimension, explicit costs include commissions, fees, bid-ask spreads, and taxes. Delay cost, price movement risk, market impact cost, timing risk, and opportunity cost are implicit transaction costs.
- Implicit costs make up the larger part of the total transaction costs. These costs are not observable and have to be estimated.
- Liquidity is created by agents transacting in the financial markets by buying and selling securities.
- Liquidity and transaction costs are interrelated: In a highly liquid market, large transactions can be executed immediately without incurring high transaction costs.
- A limit order is an order to execute a trade only if the limit price or a better price can be obtained.
- A market order is an order to execute a trade at the current best price available in the market.
- In general, trading costs are measured as the difference between the execution price and some appropriate fair market benchmark. The fair market benchmark of a security is the price that would have prevailed had the trade not taken place.

- Typical forecasting models for market impact costs are based on a statistical factor approach. Some common trade-based factors are: trade size, relative trade size, price of market liquidity, type of trade, efficiency and trading style of the investor, specific characteristics of the market or the exchange, time of trade submission, trade timing, and order type. Some common asset-based factors are: price momentum, price volatility, market capitalization, growth versus value, and specific industry/sector characteristics.
- Transaction costs models can be incorporated into standard asset-allocation models such as the mean-variance framework.
- Efficient equity portfolio management requires a systematic integration of trading costs management, trading execution, and portfolio management.

CHAPTER 12

Investment Management and Algorithmic Trading

Technology continues to have an increasingly significant impact on how securities are traded in today's markets. Many trading floors have been replaced by electronic trading platforms and more than a third of the trading volume in the United States can be attributed to *algorithmic trading*. Every large broker-dealer provides algorithmic trading services to their institutional clients in order to assist their trading. The algorithms used by institutional investors, hedge funds, and many other market participants are used to make trading decisions about the timing, price, and size of trades, with the objective of reducing risk-adjusted costs.

In a broad sense, the term algorithmic trading is used to describe trading in an automated fashion according to a set of rules. It is often used interchangeably with statistical trading or statistical arbitrage, which may or may not be automated, but is based on signals derived from statistical analyses or models. *Smart order routing*, *program trading*, and *rules-based trading* are some of the other terms associated with algorithmic trading. More recently, the range of functions and activities associated with algorithmic trading has grown to include market impact modeling, execution risk analytics, cost aware portfolio construction, and the use of market microstructure effects.

In this chapter, we first explain the basic ideas of market impact and optimal execution from both the sell- and buy-side perspectives. We then provide an overview of the most popular algorithmic trading strategies. We close the chapter with a discussion on the "high-frequency arms race" and the impact of algorithmic trading on the markets.

This chapter draws from Petter N. Kolm and Lee Maclin, "Algorithmic Trading," to appear in Rama Cont (ed.), *Encyclopedia of Quantitative Finance*, John Wiley & Sons, 2010.

MARKET IMPACT AND THE ORDER BOOK

The limit order book contains resting limit orders. These orders rest in the book and provide liquidity as they wait to be matched with nonresting orders, which represent a demand for liquidity. The three most common types of nonresting orders are marketable limit orders, market orders, and fill-or-kill orders.

The bid side of the limit book contains resting bids to buy a certain number of shares of stock at a certain price. The offer side contains resting offers to sell a certain number of shares of stock at a certain price.

A *market order* is a demand for an immediate execution of a certain number of shares at the best possible price. To get the best possible price, a market order sweeps through one side of the limit order book—starting with the best price—matching against resting orders until the full quantity of the market order is filled or the book is completely depleted.

Unlike a market order, a marketable limit order can be executed only at a specified price or better. For example, a marketable limit order to buy 100 shares at $90.01 can match with a resting limit order to sell 200 shares at $90.00. The trade print—the price at which the trade would take place—would be $90.00.

The following examples illustrate how market orders to sell interact with resting limit orders to buy.

Exhibit 12.1 shows the idealized market impact of a two hundred share market order to sell. The horizontal and vertical axes display the time and price, respectively.

EXHIBIT 12.1   Idealized Market Impact Model Showing Sell of 200 Shares

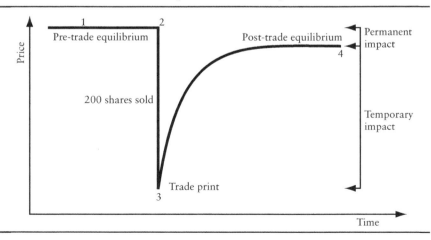

The bid side of the limit order book contains bids to buy a certain number of shares of stock at a certain price. Resting limit orders—orders that sit in the order book—are said to *provide liquidity* by mitigating the market impact of orders that must be filled immediately. The state of the book establishes a pre-trade equilibrium (1), which is disturbed by a market order to sell 200 shares (2). Market orders must be filled immediately, and therefore represent a demand for liquidity.

As the sell order depletes the bid book by matching with limit orders to buy, it obtains an increasingly less favorable (lower) trade price, resulting in the trade print (3). Assuming no other trading activity, over time liquidity providers replenish the bid book to (4), which is the post-trade equilibrium.

The difference between (4) and (1) is an information-based effect called *permanent market impact*. It is the market's response to information that a market participant has decided not to own 200 shares of this stock. This effect is typically modeled as immediate and linear in total number of shares executed. Huberman and Stanzl[1] show that, if the effect were not linear and immediate, buying and selling at two different rates could produce an arbitrage profit.

The difference between (4) and (3) is called *temporary market impact*. The trader who initiated the trade is willing to obtain a less favorable fill price (3) to get his trade done immediately. This *cost of immediacy* is typically modeled as a linear or square root function. Under the assumption of square root impact, with all other factors held constant, a trade of 200 shares executed over the same period of time as a trade of 100 shares would have square root of two times more temporary impact per share.

Exhibit 12.2 shows what would happen if the same trader were willing to wait sometime between trades. The trade print from Exhibit 12.1 is shown as a shaded line (1). As in Exhibit 12.1, a pre-trade equilibrium (2) is disturbed by a 100 share market order to sell (3). As the market order depletes the bid book by matching with limit orders to buy, it obtains a fill price (4). Over time (5), liquidity providers refill the bid book with limit orders to buy. But the new post-trade equilibrium (6) is lower than the pre-trade equilibrium because it incorporates the information of the executed market order.

Our trader then places another market sell order for 100 shares (6) and obtains a trade print (7). Over time the temporary impact—(8) minus (7)—decays and results in a new post-trade equilibrium (8). As the permanent impact is assumed to be linear and immediate, the post-trade equilibrium is shown to be the same for one order of 200 shares as it is for two orders of 100 shares each.

---

[1] Gur Huberman and Werner Stanzl, "Price Manipulation and Quasi-Arbitrage," *Econometrica* 72, no. 4 (2004), pp. 1247–1275.

EXHIBIT 12.2   Idealized Market Impact Model Showing Two Sells of 100 Shares Each

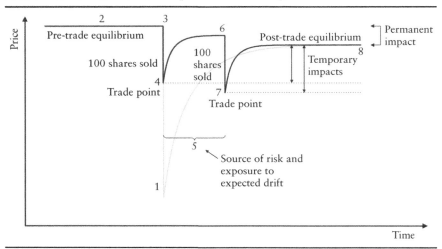

OPTIMAL EXECUTION

While our trader waits between trades (5), he incurs price risk—the risk that his execution will be less favorable due to the random movement of prices. In this context, a *shortfall* is the difference between the effective execution price and the arrival price—the prevailing price at the start of the execution period. If we use the variance of *shortfall* as a proxy for risk, a trader's aversion to risk establishes a risk/cost trade-off. In the first scenario, he pays a higher cost—the difference between (8) and (1)—to eliminate risk. In the second scenario, he pays a lower cost—the average of the differences between (8) and (4), and (8) and (7)—but takes on a greater dispersion of shortfalls associated with the waiting time between trades (5). This is the trade-off considered in the seminal paper of Almgren and Chriss.[2]

Risk aversion increases a trader's sense of urgency and makes it attractive to pay some premium to reduce risk. The premium the trader pays is in the form of higher temporary market impact. All other factors held constant, a higher expected temporary market impact encourages slower trading, while a higher expected risk or risk aversion encourages faster trading.

Risk aversion embodies the notion that people dislike risk. For a risk-averse agent, the utility of a fair game, $u(G)$, is less than the utility of having the expected value of the game, $E(u(G))$, with certainty. The degree of risk

[2]Robert Almgren and Neil Chriss, "Optimal Execution of Portfolio Transactions," *Journal of Risk* 3, no. 2 (2000), pp. 5–39.

aversion may be captured by the risk aversion parameter λ, which is used to translate risk into a *certain dollar cost equivalent*—the smallest certain dollar amount that would be accepted instead of the uncertain payoff from the fair game. For an agent with quadratic utility the certain dollar cost equivalent is given by $E(G) - \lambda Var(G)$. Hence, his degree of risk aversion is characterized by the family of risk/return pairs with the same constant trade-off between expected return and risk. An annualized target return and standard deviation imply a risk aversion, and may be translated to a risk aversion parameter of the type used in some optimal execution algorithms.

Another factor that influences the decision to trade more quickly or more slowly is the expectation of price change. For the purpose of execution, a *positive alpha* is an expectation of profits per share per unit time for unexecuted shares. A faster execution captures more of the profits associated with this expectation of price change. A *negative alpha* is the expectation of losses per share per unit time for unexecuted shares. A slower execution incurs less of the losses associated with this expectation of price change.

For example, a trader has positive alpha if he expects prices to move lower while he is executing his sell orders. He may choose to front-weight his trade schedule—execute more rapidly at the beginning of the execution period—to obtain better execution prices. Similarly, a seller who believes that prices are moving higher may back-weight his trade schedule or delay the execution.

The general form of the optimal execution problem is finding the best trade-off between the effects of risk, market impact, and alpha by minimizing risk-adjusted costs relative to a prespecified benchmark. Common benchmarks are volume weighted average price (VWAP) and arrival price (the price prevailing at the beginning of the execution period).

The first formulations of this problem go back to the seminal papers of Bertsimas and Lo,[3] and Almgren and Chriss.[4] Assuming a quadratic utility function, a general formulation of this problem takes the form

$$\min_{x_t} E(C(x_t)) + \lambda Var(C(x_t))$$

where $C(x_t)$ is the cost of deviating from the benchmark. The solution is given by the trade schedule x_t that represents the number of shares that remains to buy/sell at time t. The trader's optimal trade schedule is a function of his level of risk aversion—$\lambda \geq 0$—which determines his urgency to trade, and dictates the preferred trade-off between execution cost and risk.

In the following two subsections we describe the sell- and buy-side perspectives of the typical arrival price optimal execution models.

[3]Dimitris Bertsimas and Andrew W. Lo, "Optimal Control of Execution Costs," *Journal of Financial Markets* 1, no. 1 (1998), pp. 1–50.
[4]Almgren and Neil, "Optimal Execution of Portfolio Transactions."

The Sell-Side Perspective

The typical optimal execution model uses arrival price as a benchmark and balances the trade-off between market impact, price risk, and opportunity cost. Alpha is assumed to be greater than or equal to zero, which means that delaying execution may carry an associated opportunity cost, but does not carry an expectation of profit. The optimal strategy lies somewhere between two extremes: (1) trade everything immediately at a known cost, or (2) reduce market impact by spreading the order into smaller trades over a longer horizon at the expense of increased price risk and opportunity cost.

Bertsimas and Lo[5] proposed an algorithm for the optimal execution problem that finds the minimum expected cost of trading over a fixed period of time for a risk neutral trader, $\lambda = 0$, facing an environment where price movements are assumed to be serially uncorrelated.

Almgren and Chriss[6] extended this concept using quadratic utility to embody the trade-off between expected cost and price risk. The more aggressive (passive) trade schedules incur higher (lower) market impact costs and lower (higher) price risk. Similar to classical portfolio theory, as λ varies the resulting set of points (Var (λ), $E(\lambda)$) traces out the *efficient frontier of optimal trading strategies*. The two extreme cases $\lambda = 0$ and $\lambda \to \infty$ correspond to the minimum impact strategy—trading at a constant rate throughout the execution period—and the minimum variance strategy—a single execution of the entire target quantity at the start of the execution period.

Let us consider selling X shares, that is, we want $x_0 = X$ and $x_T = 0$. Under the assumptions that asset prices follow an arithmetic Brownian motion, permanent impact is immediate and linear in total shares executed, and temporary impact is linear in the rate of trading, the solution of the Almgren and Chriss model is

$$x_t = X \frac{\sinh(\kappa(T-t))}{\sinh(\kappa T)}$$

where

$$\kappa = \sqrt{\frac{\lambda \sigma^2}{\eta}}$$

Here σ and η represent stock volatility and linear temporary market impact cost.

Note that the solution is effectively a decaying exponential $X \exp(-\kappa t)$ adjusted such that $x_T = 0$. It does not depend on the permanent market impact, consistent with the discussion in the previous section. The urgency

[5]Bertsimas and Lo, "Optimal Control of Execution Costs."
[6]Almgren and Chriss, "Optimal Execution of Portfolio Transactions."

of trading is embodied in κ. This parameter determines the speed of liquidation independent of the order size X. For a higher risk aversion parameter or volatility—for example, representing increased perceived risk—the speed of trading increases as well. We also see that for a higher expected temporary market impact cost, the speed of trading decreases.

IMPACT MODELS

An impact model is used to predict changes in price due to trading activity. This expectation of price change may be used to inform execution and portfolio construction decisions. Several well-known models have been proposed. The models by Hasbrouck,[7] Lillo et al.,[8] and Almgren et al. are examples.[9]

Almgren et al. use a proprietary data set obtained from Citigroup's equity trading desk in which a trade's direction (buyer or seller initiated) is known. Note that for most public data sets, trade direction is not available and has to be estimated by a classification algorithm. Classification errors in algorithms such as Lee and Ready,[10] and Ellis, Michaely, and O'Hara[11] introduce a bias that produces an overestimate of the true trading cost.

In Almgren et al., trades serve as a proxy for trading imbalance. The authors assume that, sometime after the complete execution of a parent order, only permanent impact remains. This allows them to separate impact into its temporary and permanent components.

The model parameters can then be calculated from a regression, giving the following results. First, permanent impact cost is linear in trade size and volatility. Second, temporary impact cost is linear in volatility and roughly proportional to the square root—Almgren et al. find a power ⅗—of the fraction of volume represented by one's own trading during the period of execution. Hence, for a given rate of trading, a less volatile stock with large average daily volume has the lowest temporary impact costs.

---

[7]Joel Hasbrouck, "Measuring the Information Content of Stock Trades," *Journal of Finance* 46, no. 1 (1991), pp. 179–207.

[8]Lillo Fabrizio, J. Doyne Farmer, and Rosario N. Mantegna, "Master Curve for Price-Impact Function," *Nature* 421, no. 6919 (2003), p. 129.

[9]Robert Almgren, Chee Thum, Emmanuel Hauptmann, and Hong Li, "Equity Market Impact," *Risk* 18, no. 7 (2005), pp. 57–62.

[10]Charles M. C. Lee and Mark J. Ready, "Inferring Trade Direction from Intraday Data," *Journal of Finance* 46, no. 2 (1991), pp. 733–746.

[11]Katrina Ellis, Roni Michaely, and Maureen O'Hara, "The Accuracy of Trade Classification Rules: Evidence from Nasdaq," *Journal of Financial and Quantitative Analysis* 35, no. 4 (2000), pp. 529–551.

The Buy-Side Perspective

Optimal execution algorithms have less value to a typical portfolio manager if analyzed separately from the corresponding returns earned by his trading strategy. In fact, high transaction costs are not bad per se—they could simply prove to be necessary for generating superior returns. At present, the typical sell side perspective of algorithmic trading does not take expectation of profits or the client's portfolio objectives into account. Needless to say, this is an important component of execution.

The decisions of the trader and the portfolio manager are based on different objectives. The trader decides on the timing of the execution, breaking large parent orders into a series of child orders that, when executed over time, represent the correct trade-off between opportunity cost, market impact, and risk. The trader sees only the trading assets, whereas the portfolio manager sees the entire portfolio, which includes both the trading assets and the static—nontrading—positions.

The portfolio manager's task is to construct a portfolio by optimizing the trade-off between opportunity cost, market impact, and risk for the full set of trading and nontrading assets. In general, the optimal execution framework described by Almgren and Chriss is not appropriate for the portfolio manager.

Engle and Ferstenberg[12] proposed a framework that unites these objectives by combining optimal execution and classical mean-variance optimization models. In their model, trading takes place at discrete time intervals as the portfolio manager rebalances his portfolio holdings $\mathbf{w}_t$ at times $t = 0, 1, \ldots, T$ subject to changing expected returns, $\boldsymbol{\mu}_t$, and risk (as measured by the covariance matrix of returns), $\boldsymbol{\Omega}_t$, until he reaches the portfolio that reflects his final view

$$\mathbf{w}_T = \frac{1}{2\lambda}\boldsymbol{\Omega}_T^{-1}\boldsymbol{\mu}_T$$

The joint dynamic optimization problem has the form

$$\max_{\{\mathbf{w}_t\}} \sum_{t=1}^{T}\left(\mathbf{w}_T'\boldsymbol{\mu}_T - \lambda\mathbf{w}_T'\boldsymbol{\Omega}_T\mathbf{w}_T\right)$$

$$-\sum_{t=1}^{T}\left\{\Delta\mathbf{w}_T'\boldsymbol{\tau}_t + (\mathbf{w}_T - \mathbf{w}_{t-1})'\boldsymbol{\mu}_t + \lambda(\mathbf{w}_T - \mathbf{w}_{t-1})'\boldsymbol{\Omega}_t(\mathbf{w}_T - \mathbf{w}_{t-1})\right\}$$

$$+2\lambda\sum_{t=1}^{T}(\mathbf{w}_T - \mathbf{w}_{t-1})'\boldsymbol{\Omega}_t\mathbf{w}_T$$

---

[12]Robert F. Engle and Robert Ferstenberg, "Execution Risk," *Journal of Portfolio Management* 33, no. 2 (2007), pp. 34–44.

where $\tau_t = \tau_t(\Delta\mathbf{w}_t)$ is the temporary market impact function (for simplicity of exposition we ignore permanent impacts). This is a dynamic programming problem that has to be solved by numerical techniques.

Each one of the three terms in the objective function above has an intuitive interpretation. The first term represents the standard mean-variance optimization problem. The second term corresponds to the optimal execution problem. The third term is the covariance between the remaining shares to be traded and the final position. In the single asset case, the third term is positive (negative) for buying (selling) orders, which implies that risk is reduced (increased). If this term is ignored, which occurs when portfolio allocation and optimal execution are performed separately, then the measurement of total risk is biased.

POPULAR ALGORITHMIC TRADING STRATEGIES

A small number of execution strategies have become de facto standards and are offered by most technology providers, banks, and institutional broker/ dealers. However, even among these standards, the large number of input parameters makes it difficult to compare execution strategies directly.

Typically, a strategy is motivated by a *theme*, or *style* of trading. The objective is to minimize either absolute or risk-adjusted costs relative to a *benchmark*. For strategies with mathematically defined objectives, an *optimization* is performed to determine how to best use the strategy to maximize a trader's or portfolio manager's utility. A *trade schedule*—or *trajectory*—is planned for strategies with a target quantity of shares to execute. The *order placement* engine—sometimes called the *microtrader*—translates from a strategy's broad objectives to individual orders. User defined *input parameters* control the trade schedule and order placement strategy.

In this section we review some of the most common algorithmic trading strategies.

Volume-Weighted Average Price

Six or seven years ago, the volume weighted average price (VWAP) execution strategy represented the bulk of algorithmic trading activity. Currently, it is second in popularity only to arrival price. The appeal of benchmarking to VWAP is that the benchmark is easy to compute and intuitively accessible.

The typical parameters of a VWAP execution are the start time, the end time, and the number of shares to execute. Additionally, optimized forms of this strategy require a choice of risk aversion.

The most basic form of VWAP trading uses a model of the fractional daily volume pattern over the execution period. A trade schedule is calculated to match this volume pattern. For example, if the execution period is one day, and 20% of a day's volume is expected to be transacted in the first hour, a trader using this basic strategy would trade 20% of his target accumulation or liquidation in the first hour of the day. Since the daily volume pattern has a U shape—with more trading in the morning and afternoon and less in the middle of the day—the volume distribution of shares executed in a VWAP pattern would also have this U shape.

VWAP is an ideal strategy for a trader who meets all of the following criteria:

- His trading has little or no alpha during the execution period.
- He is benchmarked against the volume weighted average price.
- He believes that market impact is minimized when his own rate of trading represents the smallest possible fraction of all trading activity.
- He has a set number of shares to buy or sell.

Deviation from these criteria may make VWAP strategies less attractive. For example, market participants who trade over the course of a day and have strong positive alpha may prefer a front-weighted trajectory, such as those that are produced by an arrival price strategy.

The period of a VWAP execution is most typically a day or a large fraction of a day. Basic VWAP models predict the daily volume pattern using a simple historical average of fractional volume. Several weeks to several months of data are commonly used. However, this forecast is noisy. On any given day, the actual volume pattern deviates substantially from its historical average, complicating the strategy's objective of minimizing its risk-adjusted cost relative to the VWAP benchmark. Some models of fractional volume attempt to increase the accuracy of volume pattern prediction by making dynamic adjustments to the prediction based on observed trading results throughout the day.

Several variations of the basic VWAP strategy are common. The ideal VWAP user (as defined previously) can lower his expected costs by increasing his exposure to risk relative to the VWAP benchmark. For example, assuming an alpha of zero, placing limit orders throughout the execution period and catching up to a target quantity with a market order at the end of the execution period will lower expected cost while increasing risk. This is the highest risk strategy. Continuously placing small market orders in the fractional volume pattern is the lowest risk strategy, but has a higher expected cost. For a particular choice of risk aversion, somewhere between the highest and lowest risk strategies, is a compromise optimal strategy that perfectly balances risk and costs.

For example, a risk-averse VWAP strategy might place one market order of 100 shares every 20 seconds while a less risk-averse strategy might place a limit order of 200 shares, and, 40 seconds later, place a market order for the difference between the desired fill of 200 and the actual fill (which may have been smaller). The choice of the average time between market orders in a VWAP execution implies a particular risk aversion.

For market participants with a positive alpha, a frequently used rule-of-thumb optimization is compressing trading into a shorter execution period. For example, a market participant may try to capture more profits by doing all of his VWAP trading in the first half of the day instead of taking the entire day to execute.

In another variant of VWAP—*guaranteed VWAP*—a broker commits capital to guarantee his client the VWAP price in return for a predetermined fee. The broker takes on a risk that the difference between his execution and VWAP will be greater than the fee he collects. If institutional trading volume and individual stock returns were uncorrelated, the risk of guaranteed VWAP trading could be diversified away across many clients and many stocks. In practice, managing a guaranteed VWAP book requires some complex risk calculations that include modeling the correlations of institutional trading volume.

Time-Weighted Average Price

The time-weighted average price execution strategy (TWAP) attempts to minimize market impact costs by maintaining an approximately constant rate of trading over the execution period. With only a few parameters—start time, end time, and target quantity—TWAP has the advantage of being the simplest execution strategy to implement. As with VWAP, optimized forms of TWAP may require a choice of risk aversion. Typically, the VWAP or arrival price benchmarks are used to gauge the quality of a TWAP execution. TWAP is hardly ever used as its own benchmark.

The most basic form of TWAP breaks a parent order into small child orders and executes these child orders at a constant rate. For example, a parent order of 300 shares with an execution period of 10 minutes could be divided into three child orders of 100 shares each. The child orders would be executed at the 3:20, 6:40, and 10:00 minute marks. Between market orders, the strategy may place limit orders in an attempt to improve execution quality.

An ideal TWAP user has almost the same characteristics as an ideal VWAP user, except that he believes that the lowest *trading rate*—not the lowest *participation rate*—incurs the lowest market impact costs.

TWAP users can benefit from the same type of optimization as VWAP users by placing market orders less frequently, and using resting limit orders to attempt to improve execution quality.

Participation

The *participation strategy* attempts to maintain a constant fractional trading rate. That is, its own trading rate as a fraction of the market's total trading rate should be constant throughout the execution period. If the fractional trading rate is maintained exactly, participation strategies cannot guarantee a target fill quantity.

The parameters of a participation strategy are the start time, end time, fraction of market volume the strategy should represent, and max number of shares to execute. If the max number of shares is specified, the strategy may complete execution before the end time. Along with VWAP and TWAP, participation is a popular form of nonoptimized strategies, though some improvements are possible with optimization.

VWAP and arrival price benchmarks are often used to gauge the quality of a participation strategy execution. The VWAP benchmark is particularly appropriate because the volume pattern of a perfectly executed participation strategy is the market's volume pattern during the period of execution. An ideal user of participation strategies has all of the same characteristics as an ideal user of VWAP strategies, except that he is willing to forego certain execution to maintain the lowest possible fractional participation rate.

Participation strategies do not use a trade schedule. The strategy's objective is to participate in volume as it arises. Without a trade schedule, a participation strategy can't guarantee a target fill quantity. The most basic form of participation strategies waits for trading volume to show up on the tape, and follows this volume with market orders. For example, if the target fractional participation rate is 10%, and an execution of 10,000 shares is shown to have been transacted by other market participants, a participation strategy would execute 1,000 shares in response.

Unlike a VWAP trading strategy, which for a given execution may experience large deviations from an execution period's actual volume pattern, participation strategies can closely track the actual—as opposed to the predicted—volume pattern. However, close tracking has a price. In the preceding example, placing a market order of 1,000 shares has a larger expected market impact than slowly following the market's trading volume with smaller orders. An optimized form of the participation strategy amortizes the trading shortfall over some period of time. Specifically, if an execution of 10,000 shares is shown to have been transacted by other market participants, instead of placing 1,000 shares all at once, a 10% participation strategy might place 100 share orders over some period of time to amortize the shortfall of 1,000 shares. The result is a lower expected shortfall, but a higher dispersion of shortfalls.

Market-on-Close

The market-on-close strategy is popular with market participants who either want to minimize risk-adjusted costs relative to the closing price of the day, or want to manipulate—*game*—the close to create the perception of a good execution. The ideal market-on-close user is benchmarked to the close of the day and has low or negative alpha. The parameters of a market-on-close execution are the start time, the end time, and the number of shares to execute. Optimized forms of this strategy require a risk-aversion parameter.

When market-on-close is used as an optimized strategy, it is similar in its formulation to an arrival price strategy. However, with market-on-close, a back-weighted trade schedule incurs less risk than a front-weighted one. With arrival price, an infinitely risk averse trader would execute everything in the opening seconds of the execution period. With market-on-close, an infinitely risk averse trader would execute everything at the closing seconds of the day. For typical levels of risk aversion, some trading would take place throughout the execution period. As with arrival price optimization, positive alpha increases urgency to trade and negative alpha encourages delayed execution.

In the past, market-on-close strategies were used to manipulate—or *game*—the close, but this has become less popular as the use of VWAP and arrival price benchmarks have increased. Gaming the close is achieved by executing rapidly near the close of the day. The trade print becomes the closing price or very close to it, and hence shows little or no shortfall from the closing price benchmark. The true cost of the execution is hidden until the next day when temporary impact dissipates and prices return to a new equilibrium.

Arrival Price

The arrival price strategy—also called the *implementation shortfall strategy*—attempts to minimize risk-adjusted costs using the arrival price benchmark. Arrival price optimization is the most sophisticated and popular of the commonly used algorithmic trading strategies.

The ideal user of arrival price strategies has the following characteristics.

- He is benchmarked to the arrival price.
- He is risk averse and knows his risk-aversion parameter.
- He has high positive or high negative alpha.
- He believes that market impact is minimized by maintaining a constant rate of trading over the maximum execution period while keeping trade size small.

Most implementations are based on some form of the risk-adjusted cost minimization introduced by Almgren and Chriss[13] that we discussed earlier. In the most general terms, an arrival price strategy evaluates a series of trade schedules to determine which one minimizes risk-adjusted costs relative to the arrival price benchmark. As discussed in the section on optimal execution, under certain assumptions, this problem has a closed form solution.

The parameters in an arrival price optimization are alpha, number of shares to execute, start time, end time, and a risk aversion parameter. For buyers (sellers) positive (negative) alpha encourages faster trading. For both buyers and sellers, risk encourages faster trading, while market impact costs encourage slower trading.

For traders with positive alpha, the feasible region of trade schedules lies between the immediate execution of total target quantity and a constant rate of trading throughout the execution period.

A more general form of arrival price optimization allows for both buyers and sellers to have either positive or negative alpha. For example, under the assumption of negative alpha, shares held long and scheduled for liquidation are—without considering one's own trading—expected to go up in price over the execution period. This would encourage a trader to delay execution or stretch out trading. Hence, the feasible region of solutions that account for both positive and negative alpha includes back-weighted as well as front-weighted trade schedules.

Other factors that necessitate back-weighted trade schedules in an arrival price optimization are expected changes in liquidity and expected crossing opportunities. For example, an expectation of a cross later in the execution period may provide enough cost savings to warrant taking on some price risk and the possibility of a compressed execution if the cross fails to materialize. Similarly, if market impact costs are expected to be lower later in the execution period, a rational trader may take on some risk to obtain this cost savings.

A variant of the basic arrival price strategy is *adaptive arrival price*. A favorable execution may result in a windfall in which an accumulation of a large number of shares takes place at a price significantly below the arrival

---

[13]Almgren and Chriss, "Optimal Execution of Portfolio Transactions."

price. This can happen by random chance alone. Almgren and Lorenz[14] demonstrated that a risk-averse trader should use some of this windfall to reduce the risk of the remaining shares. He does this by trading faster and thus incurring a higher market impact. Hence, the strategy is adaptive in that it changes its behavior based on how well it is performing.

Crossing

Though crossing networks have been around for some time, their use in algorithmic trading strategies is a relatively recent development. The idea behind crossing networks is that large limit orders—the kind of orders that may be placed by large institutional traders—are not adequately protected in a public exchange. Simply displaying large limit orders in the open book of an electronic exchange may leak too much information about institutional traders' intentions. This information is used by prospective counter-parties to trade more passively in the expectation that time constraints will force traders to replace some or all of large limit orders with market orders. In other words, information leakage encourages *gaming* of large limit orders. Crossing networks are designed to limit information leakage by making their limit books opaque to both their clients and the general public.

A popular form of cross is the *mid-quote cross*, in which two counter-parties obtain a mid-quote fill price. The mid-quote is obtained from a reference exchange, such as the NYSE or other public exchange. Regulations require that the trade is then printed to a public exchange to alert other market participants that it has taken place. The cross has no market impact but both counterparties pay a fee to the crossing network. These fees are typically higher than the fees for other types of algorithmic trading because the market impact savings are significant while the fee is contingent on a successful cross.

More recently, crossing networks have offered their clients the ability to place limit orders in the crossing networks' dark books. Placing a limit order in a crossing network allows a cross to occur only at a certain price. This makes crossing networks much more like traditional exchanges, with the important difference that their books are opaque to market participants.

To protect their clients from price manipulation, crossing networks implement antigaming logic. As previously explained, opaqueness is itself a form of antigaming, but there are other strategies. For example, some crossing networks require orders above a minimum size, or orders that will

[14]Robert Almgren and Julian Lorenz, "Adaptive Arrival Price," in Brian R. Bruce (ed.), *Algorithmic Trading III: Precision, Control, Execution* (London: Euromoney Institutional Investor, 2007), pp. 59–66.

remain in the network longer than a minimum time commitment. Other networks will cross only orders of similar size. This prevents traders from pinging—sending small orders to the network to determine which side of the network's book has an order imbalance.

Another approach to antigaming prevents crosses from taking place during periods of unusual market activity. The assumption is that some of this unusual activity is caused by traders trying to manipulate the spread in the open markets to get a better fill in a crossing network.

Some networks also attempt to limit participation by active traders, monitoring their clients' activities to see if their behavior is more consistent with normal trading than with gaming.

There are several different kinds of crossing networks. A *continuous crossing network* constantly sweeps through its book in an attempt to match buy orders with sell orders. A *discrete crossing network* specifies points in time when a cross will take place, say every half hour. This allows market participants to queue up in the crossing network just prior to a cross instead of committing resting orders to the network for extended periods of time. Some crossing networks allow scraping—a one-time sweep to see if a single order can find a counterparty in the crossing network's book—while others allow only resting orders.

In *automated* crossing networks, resting orders are matched according to a set of rules, without direct interaction between the counterparties. In *negotiated* crossing networks, the counterparties first exchange indications of interest, then negotiate price and size via tools provided by the system.

Some traditional exchanges now allow the use of *invisible orders*, resting orders that sit in their order books but are not visible to market participants. These orders are also referred to as *dark liquidity*. The difference between these orders and those placed in a crossing network is that traditional exchanges offer no special antigaming protection.

Private dark pools are collections of orders that are not directly available to the public. For example, a bank or pension manager might have enough order flow to maintain an internal order book that, under special circumstances is exposed to external scraping by a crossing network or *crossing aggregator*.

A *crossing aggregator* charges a fee for managing a single large order across multiple crossing networks. Order placement and antigaming rules differ across networks, making this task fairly complex. A crossing aggregator may also use information about historical and real-time fills to direct orders. For example, failure to fill a small resting buy order in a crossing network may betray information of a much larger imbalance in the network's book. This makes the network a more attractive destination for future sell orders. In general, the management of information across crossing networks should give crossing aggregators higher fill rates than exposure to any individual network.

Crossing lends itself to several optimization strategies. Longer exposure to a crossing network increases the chances of an impact-free fill, but also increases the risk of a large and compressed execution if an order fails to obtain a fill. Finding an optimal exposure time is one type of crossing optimization. A more sophisticated version of this approach is solving for a *trade-out*, a schedule for trading shares out of the crossing network into the open markets. As time passes and a cross is not obtained, the strategy mitigates the risk of a large, compressed execution by slowly trading parts of the order into the open markets.

Other Algorithms

Two other algorithms are typically included in the mix of standard algorithmic trading offerings. The first is *liquidity seeking* where the objective is to soak up available liquidity. As the order book is depleted, trading slows. As the order book is replenished, trading speeds up.

The second algorithm is *financed trading*. The idea behind this strategy is to use a sale to finance the purchase of a buy with the objective of obtaining some form of hedge. This problem has all of the components of a full optimization. For example, if, after a sell, a buy is executed too quickly, it will obtain a less favorable fill price. On the other hand, executing a buy *leg* too slowly increases the tracking error between the two components of the hedge and increases the dispersion of costs required to complete the hedge.

WHAT IS NEXT?

The average trade size for IBM, as reported in the Trade and Quote (TAQ) database, declined from 650 shares in 2004 to 240 shares in 2007. Falling trade sizes are evidence of the impact of algorithmic trading. Large, infrequent portfolio rebalancing and trading are being replaced by *small delta continuous trading*.

The antithesis of the small delta continuous trading approach is embodied in the idea of *lazy portfolios*, in which portfolios are rebalanced infrequently to reduce market impact costs. The first argument against lazy portfolios is that as time passes, the weights drift further and further away from optimal target holdings, in both alpha and risk dimensions. Second, use of an optimizer after long holding periods tends to produce large deviations from current holdings. When executed—often relatively quickly—these deviations result in significant market impact costs.

Engle and Ferstenberg[15] show that to correctly measure risk we must take both existing positions and unexecuted shares into account. This idea unites execution risk with portfolio risk. Portfolio construction and optimal execution are similarly united by incorporating market impact costs directly into the portfolio construction process.

Ideally, the portfolio manager would like to solve a problem similar in nature to the multiperiod consumption-investment problem,[16] that in addition takes market impact costs and changing probability distributions for a large universe of securities into account. This *dynamic portfolio* or *small delta continuous trading* problem represents the next step in the evolution of institutional money management. However, it presents some mathematical and computational challenges. As has been pointed out by Sneddon,[17] dynamic portfolio problem differs in several important ways from the classical multiperiod consumption-investment problem. First, the return probability distributions change throughout time. Second, the objective functions for active portfolio management do not depend on predicted alpha/risk, but rather on realized return/risk. Finally, the dynamics of the model may be far more complex. Grinold[18] provides an elegant and analytically tractable but greatly simplified model. Kolm and Maclin[19] describe a full-scale simulation-based framework that incorporates realistic constraints and a transaction cost model.

Other efforts of ongoing research in algorithmic trading are extending market microstructure and optimal execution models to futures, options, and fixed-income products. These initiatives follow the dominant theme of algorithmic trading, the creation of a unified view, an all encompassing framework for the entire trading process, including modeling, portfolio construction, risk analytics, and execution across all tradable asset classes.

---

[15]Engle and Ferstenberg, "Execution Risk."

[16]Robert C. Merton, "Lifetime Portfolio Selection under Uncertainty: The Continuous-Time Case," *Review of Economics and Statistics* 51, no. 3 (1969), pp. 247–257.

[17]Leigh Sneddon, "The Dynamics of Active Portfolios," Westpeak Global Advisors, 2005.

[18]Richard Grinold , "Dynamic Portfolio Analysis," *Journal of Portfolio Management* 34, no. 1 (2007), p. 12–26.

[19]Petter N. Kolm and Lee Maclin, "A Practical Method for Dynamic Portfolio Optimization," Working Paper, New York, Courant Institute, New York University, 2009.

SOME COMMENTS ABOUT THE HIGH-FREQUENCY ARMS RACE[20]

An often-quoted—but unattributed—fact is that a one millisecond reduction in latency is worth about $100 million per year for some exchanges and high-frequency trading firms. Needless to say, this is a substantial amount of money. Why are companies willing to pay these large sums of money?

The main argument is that by being faster they can react to changes in the market before everyone else, thereby gaining an advantage. Their competitive advantage arises from being able to process and disseminate information sooner and faster than other market participants. This so-called *millisecond game* involves using anything from faster computers located as close to the exchanges as possible,[21] to the usage of highly specialized computer codes where, for example, the message packet sizes have been optimized.

These sophisticated high-frequency trading firms, representing about 2% of the approximately 20,000 trading firms in the United States, are believed to be responsible for almost three-quarters of all U.S. equity trading volume. These businesses include hundreds of the most secretive prop shops, proprietary trading desks at the major investment banks, and maybe about 100 or so of the most sophisticated hedge funds.[22] The TABB Group estimates that total annual profits of these high-frequency trading firms were about $21 billion in 2009.[23]

Algorithmic traders are liquidity providers that profit from the spread (about a cent) and the rebate (also referred to as the *maker taker* fee). Liquidity providers that post orders to buy or sell at fixed prices are offered a rebate from the exchange if their quotes result in trades. Today, most markets offer rebates as a form of volume discount to attract high-frequency traders. For example, in July 2009 Direct Edge paid a rebate of 0.25 cents per share to subscribing firms that provide liquidity and charged liquidity takers a fee of 0.28 cents.

---

[20]The area of algorithmic and high-frequency trading has been rapidly developing over the last few years, and is continuing to do so. The facts and comments reported in this section are based on the information available as of the time of the writing of this book. As this landscape is continuing to change and evolve, so may the facts and results presented in this section.

[21]This practice is referred to as *colocation*. As of August 2009, at NASDAQ about 100+ firms colocated their servers at a rate of about $7,000 per rack and month.

[22]Rob Iati, "The Real Story of Trading Software Espionage," *Advanced Trading*, July 10, 2009.

[23]Larry Tabb and Robert Iati, "Equity Trading in Transition: New Business Models for a Brave New World," Tabb Group, 2009.

Every time the exchange receives an updated quote the fastest firms are able to receive that information and update their quotes accordingly before anyone else. Therefore, they have a greater chance of having their liquidity providing order executed. The successful execution provides them with a small gain that includes the spread (if any) and the rebate.

Latency

Certainly, one part of being faster means reducing *latency*. While latency is a very important component of high-frequency trading, there is no common and agreed-upon definition. A definition is to consider the so-called end-to-end latency, also referred to as total latency, which consists of two components: (1) exchange latency, and (2) member latency. The former is the latency associated with the price discovery and dissemination from the exchange, while the latter refers to the time it takes to get the information to and processing it at the firm. These two components can in turn be further broken down into the following steps:

1. Price dissemination and distribution at the exchange.
2. Transmission of price information from the exchange to the firm.
3. Preparation of the order at the firm.
4. Distribution of the order to the exchange.
5. Place the order in order book.
6. Order acknowledgment from the exchange.
7. Final report on the order execution from the exchange.

A survey conducted by Greene and Robin,[24] concluded that the timings for each one of the previous steps varies quite a bit from exchange to exchange, and from firm to firm. The results from the survey are as follows: (1) 500 microseconds–5 milliseconds,[25] (2) 4–5 milliseconds, (3)+(4) around

[24]James Greene and Peter Robin, "The Competitive Landscape for Global Exchanges: What Exchanges Must Do to Meet User Expectations," Cisco Internet Business Solutions Group, 2008. The authors interviewed 40 senior executives representing a broad cross-section from buy and sell-side firms and exchanges/alternative trading systems such as AllianceBernstein, Cantor Fitzgerald/eSpeed, Credit Suisse, D.E. Shaw, Deutsche Börse, E*TRADE, Goldman Sachs, Highbridge Capital, HSBC Securities, ISE, ITG, Lehman Brothers, London Stock Exchange (LSE), Madoff Investment Securities, Morgan Stanley, and the New York Stock Exchange (NYSE). The exchanges that the participants were asked to rank and comment upon were CME, Deutsche Börse, Euronext, ISE, LSE, NASDAQ, NYSE, and TSE.
[25]NASDAQ (1 millisecond), BATS Trading (400–500 microseconds), LSE (2 milliseconds), NYSE (2–5 milliseconds), Deutsche Börse (2 milliseconds).

100 milliseconds,[26] (5) 5–25 milliseconds,[27] and (6) 500 microseconds–2 milliseconds.[28] The study did not address (7).

An important part of latency is the remote location data transfers. These transfers are typically between the firm and the exchange, but may involve other parties as well (or multiple exchanges). With the current technology available these transfers can be done in about 7 milliseconds between New York and Chicago, and in about 35 milliseconds between the West and East coasts.[29]

High-Frequency Trading and Liquidity

The most critical component of an exchange is to be able to provide market participants with liquidity. For the purposes of this discussion, we can loosely define liquidity as: (1) the ability to *trade quickly* without significant price changes, and (2) the ability to *trade large volumes* without significant price changes.

At the time of the writing of this chapter, there is an ongoing debate both in the technical as well as popular press whether algorithmic and high-frequency traders enhance market efficiency and provide increased liquidity.

Decreasing latency changes the competitive factors in the demand and supply of liquidity and how quotes are updated to reflect public information. As a consequence of business profit incentives, algorithmic traders consume liquidity when it is cheap and supply liquidity when it is expensive, thereby smoothing out liquidity over time. This in turn facilitates moving price toward its efficient price as the algorithmic traders compete by trying to provide the best quotes.

Henderschott, Jones, and Menkveld[30] show that increased algorithmic trading leads to narrower quoted and effective spreads for large-cap stocks.

---

[26]According to the study, some firms reported that they can handle prices within 2–3 milliseconds.

[27]Average/median execution times: LSE (8–14 milliseconds), NYSE (10–25 milliseconds), NASDAQ (15 milliseconds), BATS Trading (5 milliseconds). However, the study reports that outliers can be up to 250–500 milliseconds for execution.

[28]This is a confirmation that the order has been *received* at the exchange, and not necessarily that it has been placed on the book: BATS Trading (500 microseconds), LSE (1 millisecond), NASDAQ (1 millisecond), NYSE (2 milliseconds).

[29]These are one-way transfers as reported by John Barr, "Low Latency: What's It All About?" *451 Market Insight Service*, 2008. At the speed of light it would take about 11 milliseconds at the shortest distance from the East Coast to the West Coast (this is 2,092 miles or 3347 kilometers, and is from (approximately) Jacksonville, FL to San Diego, CA. The speed of light is 299.792458 kilometers/millisecond.

[30]Terrence J. Hendershott, Charles M. Jones, and Albert J. Menkveld, "Does Algorithmic Trading Improve Liquidity?" (April 26, 2008). WFA 2008 paper; received the WFA NYSE-Euronext award for best paper in equity trading.

The narrower spreads result from a decrease in the amount of price discovery associated with trades (i.e., a decrease in adverse selection).

Interestingly, the authors suggest that the revenues of liquidity suppliers also increase with algorithmic trading. This is consistent with that algorithmic liquidity suppliers have a form of market power as they introduce their new algorithms and are able to capture some of the surplus for themselves.

High-frequency and algorithmic traders are often accused for the recent increase in market volatility. A recent study by Riordan and Henderschott[31] in the 30 DAX stocks on the Deutsche Börse seems to indicate the opposite. In particular, the authors find no evidence that algorithmic traders demanding liquidity during times of low liquidity increased volatility. In addition, they also show that when algorithmic traders do not supply liquidity, there is no impact on volatility.

Obviously, there are physical limitations as to how much latency can be decreased. Standard arguments of economic theory suggest that over time through competition the profit margins of high-frequency trading will decrease. Most players will at some point have about the same technological infrastructure, but not necessarily the same algorithms. As in many other areas, it will come down to who has the best (the "smartest") algorithms. It is believed by some that the true edge in high-frequency trading already is coming from the usage of superior algorithms—that are not always the fastest—but that are able to make the better decisions.

SUMMARY

- *Algorithmic trading* is used to describe trading in an automated fashion according to a set of rules. Smart order routing, program trading, and rules-based trading are other terms associated with algorithmic trading.
- We distinguish two forms of market impact: an information-based effect called *permanent market impact*, and an order book-based effect referred to as *temporary market impact*. The temporary market impact is due to the depletion of limit orders in the order book. Its size depends on how long it takes to replenish the order book.
- The *shortfall* is the difference between the effective execution price and the arrival price (the price at the start of the execution).
- *Optimal execution* algorithms determine the optimal trade trajectory by optimizing a trade-off between execution cost and risk. The Almgren and Chriss model minimizes expected shortfall minus a risk aversion coefficient times the variance of shortfall.

---

[31]Ryan Riordan and Terrence Hendershott, "Algorithmic Trading and Information," Working Paper, 2009.

- An *impact model* is used to predict changes in price due to trading activity.
- The decisions of the trader and the portfolio manager are based on different objectives. The trader decides on the timing of the execution, breaking large parent orders into child orders that represent the optimal trade-off between opportunity cost, market impact, and risk.
- The portfolio manager's task is to construct a portfolio by optimizing the trade-off between opportunity cost, market impact, and risk for the full set of trading and nontrading assets.
- The trader sees only the trading assets, whereas the portfolio manager sees the entire portfolio, which includes both the trading assets and the static—nontrading—positions. Therefore, the standard optimal execution framework is in general not appropriate for the portfolio manager.
- Some well-established sell-side algorithmic trading strategies include: *volume weighted average price* (VWAP), *time-weighted average price* (TWAP), *participation, Market-on-Close, arrival price* (also called *implementation shortfall*), and *crossing*.
- The *dynamic portfolio* and *small delta continuous trading problems* refer to multiperiod models that optimize the trade-off between opportunity cost, market impact, alpha decay, and risk (or a subset thereof) for the full set of trading and nontrading assets.
- The *high-frequency arms race* and the *millisecond game* refer to the increased competition in the high-frequency and algorithmic trading space to reduce latency in order to be faster than other market participants, thereby obtaining a trading and informational advantage.
- Latency can be broken down into the following seven components: (1) price dissemination and distribution at the exchange, (2) transmission of price information from the exchange to the firm, (3) preparation of the order at the firm, (4) distribution of the order to the exchange, (5) place the order in order book, (6) order acknowledgment from the exchange, and (7) final report on the order execution from the exchange.

Data Descriptions and Factor Definitions

Some of the examples throughout this book use different data sets, including the MSCI World Index and its individual constituents, one-month LIBOR, and the Compustat Point-In-Time and IBES Consensus databases. In this appendix we provide an overview and summary statistics of these data sets. In addition, in Chapters 6 and 7 we use several value, quality, growth, and momentum factors. In this appendix we provide detailed definitions of these factors.

THE MSCI WORLD INDEX

We obtained daily levels and returns of the MSCI World Index and all its constituents along with market capitalization weights over the period 1/1/1980 through 5/31/2004 directly from Morgan Stanley Capital International, Inc.[1] The levels and returns are given from the perspective of an investor in the United States.

The MSCI World Index is a free float-adjusted market capitalization index that is designed to measure global developed market equity performance. As of December 2004, the MSCI World Index consisted of the following 23 constituents (developed market country indexes): Australia, Austria, Belgium, Canada, Denmark, Finland, France, Germany, Greece, Hong Kong, Ireland, Italy, Japan, the Netherlands, New Zealand, Norway, Portugal, Singapore, Spain, Sweden, Switzerland, the United Kingdom, and the United States. Other constituents that were part of the index at some point throughout the time period January 1980 through May 2004 were Malaysia, Mexico, and South African Gold Mines.

---

[1]We would like to thank Morgan Stanley Capital International, Inc., http://www.msci.com, for providing us with the data set. In particular, we thank Nicholas G. Keyes for preparing and for answering all our questions in regards to the data set.

The different constituents of the index as of January in the years 1985, 1995, and 2004 along with their market capitalization in billions of U.S. dollars and percentage weight, and their ranking (in terms of market capitalization) are displayed in Exhibit A.1. We observe that the relative rankings among the different countries have been relatively stable throughout time. Nevertheless, the total market capitalization of the MSCI World Index has grown from about $1.8 trillion as of January 1985 to $17.4 trillion as of May 2004. Details about how the country indexes are constructed are available in the *MSCI Standard Methodology Book*.[2]

In Exhibits A.2, A.3, and A.4, we display some basic statistical properties of the data set. For simplicity, as all of the constituents that were part of the index as of May 2004 also were part of the index in January 1988, we only display statistics calculated over this period. The statistics are calculated over the full period as well as over each half; the first half is January 1988 through December 1994, and the second half is January 1995 through May 2004.

We report the mean returns, return volatilities, and Sharpe ratios in annual terms. The minimum return (Min) and the maximum return (Max) are all in daily terms. The skew and kurtosis are calculated as the third and fourth normalized centered moments. The definition of the Sharpe ratio used in this book is the annualized mean return divided by the annualized volatility for the period under consideration.

We observe that the performance of the MSCI World Index as well as for most of its constituents was very good over the period considered. The average annual mean return for the index over the full period was 6.4% with an annual volatility of 12.9%. The average mean return in the first and the second halves were virtually the same (6.4% versus 6.3%), but the volatility increased from 11.1% to 14.0%. The individual country returns over the full sample range from 1.1% (Japan) to 13.7% (Finland), whereas volatilities range from 16.0% (Canada) to 33.2% (Finland).

If we rank the performance of individual countries in terms of their Sharpe ratio, Denmark and Switzerland (both with 0.65) come out ahead followed by the United States (0.62). Interestingly enough, comparing the rankings between the two periods based on the Sharpe ratio, we see that there is virtually no persistence at all. Indeed, the Spearman rank correlation coefficient (the correlation between the rankings of the two periods) is –0.07.

There is significant time variation in volatilities. Exhibit A.5 demonstrates this fact for some of the countries in the sample, showing the one-year rolling standard deviation for the MSCI World Index, Singapore, Spain, Sweden, Switzerland, the United Kingdom, and the United States.

---

[2]*MSCI Standard Methodology Book*, Morgan Stanley Capital International Inc., May 11 version, 2004.

EXHIBIT A.1 Market Capitalization Weights of the MSCI World Index and Its Constituents as of the First Business Day in January in the Years 1985, 1995, and 2004

	1985			1995			2004		
	$US (billion)	Percent	Rank	$US (billion)	Percent	Rank	$US (billion)	Percent	Rank
World	1,765.1	100.00		7,650.8	100.00		17,416.4	100.00	
Australia	27.8	1.57	6	125.1	1.63	10	373.6	2.15	9
Austria	0.8	0.05	20	18.0	0.23	20	16.0	0.09	22
Belgium	7.6	0.43	15	49.3	0.64	16	77.5	0.45	15
Canada	71.7	4.06	4	171.1	2.24	7	463.9	2.66	7
Denmark	3.6	0.20	17	35.3	0.46	17	55.5	0.32	17
Finland	26.7	0.35	18	122.8	0.71	13			
France	23.1	1.31	9	265.6	3.47	5	727.6	4.18	4
Germany	49.1	2.78	5	300.1	3.92	4	530.8	3.05	6
Greece							33.3	0.19	20
Hong Kong	14.7	0.83	12	136.5	1.78	9	118.5	0.68	14
Ireland	12.5	0.16	23	54.1	0.31	18			
Italy	15.1	0.85	10	102.9	1.34	12	285.3	1.64	10
Japan	367.5	20.82	2	2,145.7	28.04	2	1,576.7	9.05	3
Malaysia	1.7	0.10	19	105.6	1.38	11			
Mexico									
Netherlands	25.7	1.46	8	167.9	2.19	8	380.8	2.19	8

EXHIBIT A.1 (Continued)

	1985			1995			2004		
	$US (billion)	Percent	Rank	$US (billion)	Percent	Rank	$US (billion)	Percent	Rank
New Zealand				17.3	0.23	21	15.8	0.09	23
Norway	2.7	0.15	18	19.9	0.26	19	35.7	0.20	19
Portugal							26.5	0.15	21
Singapore	14.7	0.84	11	56.8	0.74	15	60.4	0.35	16
South African Gold Mines	12.4	0.70	13	13.6	0.18	22			
Spain	7.0	0.40	16	74.3	0.97	14	271.3	1.56	11
Sweden	11.8	0.67	14	76.1	1.00	13	167.7	0.96	12
Switzerland	26.4	1.49	7	215.0	2.81	6	545.0	3.13	5
United Kingdom	131.2	7.43	3	731.1	9.56	3	1,906.4	10.95	2
United States	950.4	53.85	1	2,784.6	36.40	1	9,571.3	54.96	1

EXHIBIT A.2 Statistics of Daily Returns over the Period January 1988 through May 2004

	Mean (%)	Volatility (%)	Sharpe Ratio	Rank	Skew	Kurtosis	Min (%)	Max (%)
World	6.4	12.9	0.49	6	−0.06	6.19	−5.1	4.9
Australia	7.3	17.6	0.42	15	−0.20	6.02	−8.5	7.7
Austria	7.7	19.1	0.41	17	−0.17	9.68	−12.6	9.7
Belgium	8.3	18.1	0.46	8	0.31	9.19	−8.6	9.1
Canada	7.2	16.0	0.45	9	−0.54	9.73	−9.3	5.4
Denmark	11.9	18.1	0.65	1	−0.25	6.16	−9.0	7.0
Finland	13.7	33.2	0.41	16	−0.14	9.76	−18.2	17.3
France	10.5	19.9	0.53	5	−0.13	5.89	−9.7	7.6
Germany	9.4	22.5	0.42	14	−0.29	7.87	−12.9	7.3
Greece	12.7	29.9	0.43	13	0.30	8.54	−11.1	17.3
Hong Kong	11.5	26.3	0.44	11	−0.47	20.42	−23.0	17.4
Ireland	8.7	19.3	0.45	10	−0.14	6.94	−7.5	7.2
Italy	6.4	22.3	0.29	21	−0.12	5.88	−10.5	6.9
Japan	1.1	23.2	0.05	24	0.41	7.41	−8.1	13.1
Netherlands	9.2	18.7	0.49	7	−0.14	7.20	−8.1	6.8
New Zealand	2.8	22.1	0.13	23	−0.14	10.16	−14.6	11.7
Norway	9.2	21.3	0.43	12	−0.26	8.23	−11.6	10.3
Portugal	2.8	18.6	0.15	22	−0.03	8.63	−9.6	9.2
Singapore	7.6	21.0	0.36	20	0.21	11.76	−10.2	12.6
Spain	8.4	21.1	0.40	19	−0.05	7.02	−10.6	9.6
Sweden	13.5	25.0	0.54	4	0.07	7.00	−9.3	12.1
Switzerland	11.6	17.9	0.65	2	−0.14	7.08	−9.0	7.0
United Kingdom	6.8	16.9	0.40	18	−0.04	5.52	−5.2	7.5
United States	10.1	16.1	0.62	3	−0.14	7.24	−6.7	5.8

Note: The columns Mean, Volatility, and Sharpe Ratio are the annualized mean returns, volatilities, and Sharpe ratios of each country index. Rank is the numerical rank based on each country's Sharpe ratio. Min and Max are the daily minimum and maximum returns, respectively. Skew and Kurtosis are calculated as the third and fourth normalized centered moments.

EXHIBIT A.3 Statistics of Daily Returns over the Period January 1988 through December 1994

	Mean (%)	Volatility (%)	Sharpe Ratio	Rank	Skew	Kurtosis	Min (%)	Max (%)
World	6.4	11.1	0.57	12	0.04	7.70	−5.1	4.9
Australia	9.0	17.4	0.51	14	−0.43	5.98	−8.5	4.5
Austria	11.2	21.2	0.53	13	−0.08	11.80	−12.6	9.7
Belgium	10.2	15.8	0.64	7	0.32	12.84	−8.6	8.5
Canada	2.7	10.6	0.25	19	−0.35	5.08	−3.8	3.2
Denmark	13.2	17.4	0.76	5	−0.28	7.97	−9.0	7.0
Finland	5.7	21.7	0.26	18	0.08	5.86	−7.9	7.3
France	11.4	17.8	0.64	8	−0.30	7.93	−9.7	7.6
Germany	12.1	20.1	0.61	10	−0.77	14.54	−12.9	7.3
Greece	15.7	31.9	0.49	16	0.51	10.29	−11.1	17.3
Hong Kong	20.3	24.1	0.84	3	−2.28	37.08	−23.0	8.6
Ireland	10.1	19.8	0.51	15	0.01	7.49	−7.5	7.2
Italy	3.0	22.2	0.14	21	−0.29	7.12	−10.5	6.9
Japan	4.3	22.6	0.19	20	0.47	8.53	−8.1	11.4
Netherlands	11.7	13.6	0.87	2	−0.46	6.11	−6.4	3.4
New Zealand	2.2	22.7	0.10	22	0.02	7.83	−10.0	8.4
Norway	13.1	22.4	0.59	11	−0.15	9.09	−11.6	10.3
Portugal	−3.1	19.3	−0.16	24	0.06	12.10	−9.6	9.2
Singapore	18.8	16.2	1.16	1	−0.52	11.49	−9.1	5.5
Spain	1.2	19.1	0.06	23	−0.20	11.16	−10.6	9.6
Sweden	13.2	21.0	0.63	9	0.05	7.59	−9.3	8.3
Switzerland	13.4	17.0	0.79	4	−0.41	8.47	−9.0	6.5
United Kingdom	6.8	16.1	0.42	17	0.09	6.13	−5.2	7.5
United States	9.0	12.6	0.71	6	−0.55	9.30	−6.5	3.8

Note: The columns Mean, Volatility, and Sharpe Ratio are the annualized mean returns, volatilities, and Sharpe ratios of each country index. Rank is the numerical rank based on each country's Sharpe ratio. Min and Max are the daily minimum and maximum returns, respectively. Skew and Kurtosis are calculated as the third and fourth normalized centered moments.

EXHIBIT A.4 Statistics of Daily Returns over the Period January 1995 through May 2004

	Mean (%)	Volatility (%)	Sharpe Ratio	Rank	Skew	Kurtosis	Min (%)	Max (%)
World	6.3	14.0	0.45	9	−0.09	5.39	−4.4	4.7
Australia	6.1	17.7	0.35	16	−0.03	6.05	−6.8	7.7
Austria	5.2	17.3	0.30	20	−0.29	5.11	−6.1	4.0
Belgium	6.9	19.7	0.35	15	0.30	7.57	−6.2	9.1
Canada	10.6	19.0	0.56	4	−0.54	8.11	−9.3	5.4
Denmark	10.9	18.7	0.58	3	−0.22	5.10	−6.1	5.7
Finland	19.7	39.7	0.50	7	−0.17	7.99	−18.2	17.3
France	9.8	21.3	0.46	8	−0.06	4.93	−6.1	6.1
Germany	7.4	24.1	0.31	18	−0.08	5.18	−7.5	7.1
Greece	10.5	28.2	0.37	14	0.07	6.11	−9.4	8.8
Hong Kong	4.9	27.8	0.18	21	0.42	13.03	−12.9	17.4
Ireland	7.6	19.0	0.40	11	−0.28	6.44	−7.5	6.1
Italy	8.9	22.3	0.40	10	0.01	4.97	−6.9	6.9
Japan	−1.3	23.7	−0.06	24	0.38	6.70	−6.9	13.1
Netherlands	7.2	21.7	0.33	17	−0.06	6.18	−8.1	6.8
New Zealand	3.2	21.7	0.15	22	−0.28	12.18	−14.6	11.7
Norway	6.3	20.5	0.31	19	−0.37	7.20	−9.0	7.5
Portugal	7.1	18.1	0.39	12	−0.10	5.23	−6.3	5.2
Singapore	−0.7	24.0	−0.03	23	0.41	10.40	−10.2	12.6
Spain	13.7	22.5	0.61	1	0.01	5.18	−6.2	7.3
Sweden	13.7	27.6	0.50	6	0.07	6.32	−9.2	12.1
Switzerland	10.2	18.5	0.55	5	0.02	6.29	−6.9	7.0
United Kingdom	6.8	17.5	0.39	13	−0.11	5.15	−5.1	5.4
United States	10.8	18.3	0.59	2	−0.03	6.05	−6.7	5.8

Note: The columns Mean, Volatility, and Sharpe Ratio are the annualized mean returns, volatilities, and Sharpe ratios of each country index. Rank is the numerical rank based on each country's Sharpe ratio. Min and Max are the daily minimum and maximum returns, respectively. Skew and Kurtosis are calculated as the third and fourth normalized centered moments.

EXHIBIT A.5 One-Year Rolling Volatility (Standard Deviation) of the MSCI World Index, Singapore, Spain, Sweden, Switzerland, United Kingdom, and the United States

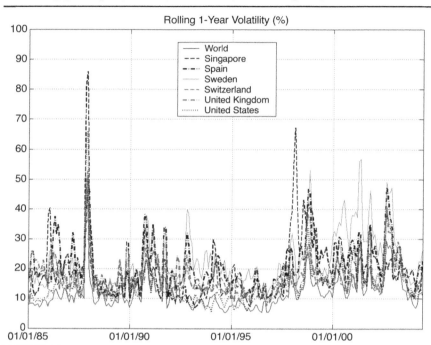

The correlation matrix for the full period is given in Exhibit A.6. Correlations between the different countries range from 0.01 (United States and Italy) to 0.76 (Canada and the Netherlands). We would therefore expect there to be some benefits of diversification.

Also, the correlations exhibit time variation. For example, in Exhibit A.7 the two-year rolling correlations of United States with Germany, Hong Kong, Italy, Japan, and the Netherlands are depicted. Note that while some correlations have increased (United States versus Germany) others have decreased (United States versus Hong Kong). In fact, a further analysis of this data set shows that the correlations between the different countries have actually *decreased* over time whereas the volatilities have *increased*. This result is consistent with several academic studies.[3] If we perform a decompo-

---

[3]See, for example, Richard O. Michaud, Gary L. Bergstrom, Ronald D. Frashure, and Brian K. Wolahan, "Twenty Years of International Equity Investing," *Journal of Portfolio Management* 23, no. 1 (Fall 1996), pp. 9–22; and William N. Goetzmann, Lingfeng Li, and K. Geert Rouwenhorst, "Long-Term Global Market Correlations," *Journal of Business* 78, no. 1, pp. 1–38, 2005.

EXHIBIT A.6 Correlation Matrix of the MSCI World Index and the Individual Constituents over the Period 1/5/1988 through 5/31/2004

		1	2	3	4	5	6	7	8	9	10	11	12	13	14	15	16	17	18	19	20	21	22	23	24
World	1	1.00																							
Australia	2	0.29	1.00																						
Austria	3	0.34	0.24	1.00																					
Belgium	4	0.53	0.24	0.48	1.00																				
Canada	5	0.61	0.20	0.14	0.25	1.00																			
Denmark	6	0.41	0.24	0.45	0.53	0.21	1.00																		
Finland	7	0.46	0.22	0.26	0.37	0.33	0.38	1.00																	
France	8	0.65	0.23	0.41	0.62	0.38	0.50	0.51	1.00																
Germany	9	0.65	0.26	0.49	0.63	0.38	0.53	0.48	0.71	1.00															
Greece	10	0.24	0.16	0.28	0.30	0.12	0.29	0.20	0.27	0.29	1.00														
Hong Kong	11	0.31	0.37	0.21	0.18	0.18	0.21	0.24	0.23	0.26	0.15	1.00													
Ireland	12	0.42	0.30	0.42	0.48	0.20	0.46	0.33	0.48	0.49	0.31	0.23	1.00												
Italy	13	0.50	0.22	0.37	0.50	0.28	0.44	0.40	0.60	0.56	0.22	0.19	0.39	1.00											
Japan	14	0.53	0.31	0.26	0.25	0.15	0.23	0.19	0.23	0.23	0.19	0.29	0.26	0.19	1.00										
Netherlands	15	0.64	0.26	0.40	0.65	0.37	0.50	0.50	0.76	0.71	0.26	0.25	0.49	0.56	0.23	1.00									
New Zealand	16	0.19	0.51	0.22	0.18	0.10	0.17	0.16	0.16	0.20	0.14	0.25	0.23	0.16	0.22	0.19	1.00								
Norway	17	0.42	0.31	0.40	0.42	0.25	0.47	0.37	0.48	0.48	0.26	0.25	0.43	0.38	0.24	0.51	0.22	1.00							
Portugal	18	0.37	0.21	0.41	0.47	0.20	0.45	0.34	0.45	0.47	0.30	0.17	0.40	0.39	0.22	0.43	0.18	0.36	1.00						
Singapore	19	0.34	0.36	0.24	0.23	0.18	0.23	0.24	0.25	0.27	0.20	0.54	0.26	0.21	0.35	0.26	0.28	0.29	0.20	1.00					
Spain	20	0.59	0.25	0.43	0.57	0.34	0.49	0.45	0.71	0.64	0.28	0.28	0.44	0.60	0.24	0.65	0.18	0.45	0.48	0.26	1.00				
Sweden	21	0.57	0.29	0.35	0.47	0.36	0.47	0.61	0.63	0.59	0.25	0.27	0.42	0.51	0.26	0.59	0.20	0.49	0.40	0.30	0.58	1.00			
Switzerland	22	0.58	0.24	0.46	0.63	0.29	0.52	0.41	0.68	0.68	0.30	0.21	0.49	0.53	0.25	0.70	0.17	0.48	0.46	0.24	0.62	0.55	1.00		
United Kingdom	23	0.64	0.24	0.34	0.51	0.36	0.43	0.44	0.68	0.58	0.21	0.24	0.50	0.50	0.24	0.70	0.16	0.43	0.36	0.25	0.57	0.54	0.60	1.00	
United States	24	0.78	0.06	0.08	0.24	0.62	0.14	0.24	0.34	0.35	0.07	0.11	0.14	0.24	0.08	0.33	0.01	0.17	0.12	0.13	0.30	0.29	0.26	0.34	1.00

481

EXHIBIT A.7 Two-Year Rolling Correlations of United States with Germany, Hong Kong, Italy, Japan, and the Netherlands

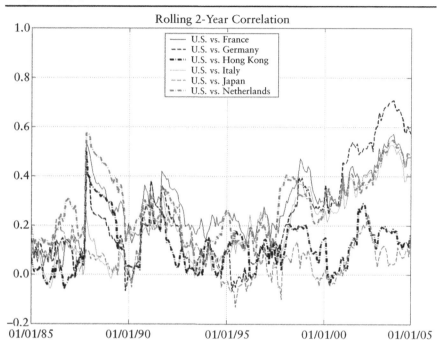

sition of the correlation throughout the sample, we find that about half the benefits of diversification available today to the international investor are due to the increasing number of available markets, and the other half is due to the lower average correlation among the different markets.

ONE-MONTH LIBOR

In some examples in this book we use one-month LIBOR.[4] LIBOR, which stands for the London Interbank Offered Rate, is one of the most widely used benchmarks for short-term interest rates. It is the variable interest rate at which banks can borrow funds from each other in the London interbank market. The one-month LIBOR is depicted in Exhibit A.8.

---

[4]British Bankers' Association, http://www.bbalibor.com.

EXHIBIT A.8   One-Month LIBOR

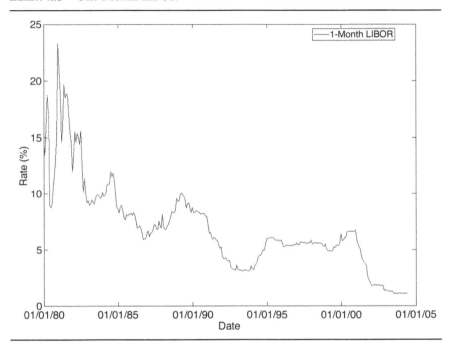

THE COMPUSTAT POINT-IN-TIME, IBES CONSENSUS DATABASES AND FACTOR DEFINITIONS

The factors used in Chapters 6 and 7 were constructed on a monthly basis with data from the Compustat Point-In-Time and IBES Consensus databases. Our sample includes all stocks contained in the Russell 1000 index over the period December 31, 1989 to December 31, 2008.

The Compustat Point-In-Time database[5] contains quarterly financial data from the income, balance sheet, and cash flow statements for active and inactive companies. This database provides a consistent view of historical financial data, both reported data and subsequent restatements, the way it appeared at the end of any month. Using this data allows the researcher to avoid common data issues such as survivorship and look-ahead bias. The data is available from March 1987.

---

[5]http://www.compustat.com.

The Institutional Brokers Estimate System (IBES) database[6] provides actual earnings from companies and estimates of various financial measures from sell-side analysts. The estimated financial measures include estimates of earnings, revenue/sales, operating profit, analyst recommendations, and other measures. The data is offered on a summary (consensus) level or detailed (analyst-by-analyst) basis. The U.S. data covers reported earnings estimates and results since January 1976.

The factors used in Chapters 6 and 7 are defined as follows.[7]

Value Factors

Operating Income Before Depreciation to Enterprise Value = EBITDA/EV

where

$$EBITDA = \text{Sales LTM (Compustat Item 2)} \\ - \text{Cost of goods Sales LTM (Compustat Item 30)} \\ - \text{SG\&A Exp (Compustat Item 1)}$$

and

$$EV = [\text{Long-Term Debt (Compustat Item 51)} \\ + \text{Common Shares Outstanding (Computstat Item 61)} \\ \times \text{Price (PRCCM)} - \text{Cash (Compustat Item 36)}]$$

$$\text{Book to price} = \text{Stockholders' Equity Total (Computstat Item 60)} \\ \div [\text{Common Shares Outstanding (Computstat Item 59)} \\ \times \text{Price (PRCCM)}]$$

$$\text{Sales to price} = \text{Sales LTM (Computstat Item 2)} \\ \div [\text{Common Shares Outstanding (Computstat Item 61)} \\ \times \text{Price (PRCCM)}]$$

Quality Factors

$$\text{Share repurchase} = [\text{Common Shares Outstanding (Computstat Item 61)} \\ - \text{Common Shares Outstanding (Computstat Item 61) from 12 months ago}] \\ \div \text{Common Shares Outstanding (Computstat Item 61) from 12 months ago}$$

---

[6]http://www.thomsonreuters.com.
[7]LTM refers to the last four reported quarters.

Asset Turnover = Sales LTM (Computstat Item 2)/[(Assets (Computstat Item 44)
  − Assets (Computstat Item 44) from 12 months ago)/ 2]

Return on Invested Capital = Income/Invested Capital

where

  Income = Income Before Extra Items LTM (Computstat Item 8)
    + Interest Expense LTM (Computstat Item 22)
    + Minority Interest Expense LTM (Computstat Item 3)

and

  Invested Capital = Common Equity (Computstat Item 59)
    + Long-Term Debt (Computstat Item 51)
    + Minority Interest (Computstat Item 53)
    + Preferred Stock (Computstat Item 55)

Debt to Equity = Total Debt/Stockholder's Equity

where

  Total Debt = [Debt in Current Liabilities (Computstat Item 45)
    + Long-Term Debt − Total (Computstat Item 51)]

and

  Stockholder's Equity = Stockholder's Equity (Computstat Item 60)

Chg Debt to Equity = (Total Debt − Total Debt from 12 months ago)
    ÷ [(Stockholder's Equity
    + Stockholder's Equity from 12 months ago)/2]

Growth

  Revisions = [Number of UP Revisions (IBES item NUMUP)
    − Number of Down Revisions (IBES item NUMDOWN)]
    ÷ Number of Estimates Revisions (IBES item NUMEST)

  Growth of Fiscal Year 1 and Fiscal Year 2 Earnings Estimates
  = Consensus Mean of FY2 (IBES item MEAN FY2)
    ÷ Consensus Mean of FY1 (IBES item MEAN FY1) − 1

Momentum

Momentum = Total return of last 11 months excluding the most returns from the most recent month.

Summary Statistics

Exhibit A.9 contains monthly summary statistics of the factors defined previously. Factor values greater than the 97.5 percentile or less than the 2.5 percentile are considered outliers. We set factor values greater than the 97.5 percentile value to the 97.5 percentile value, and factor values less than the 2.5 percentile value to the 2.5 percentile value, respectively.

EXHIBIT A.9   Summary Statistics

	Mean	Standard Deviation	Median	25 Percentile	75 Percentile
EBITDA/EV	0.11	0.06	0.11	0.07	0.15
Book to price	0.46	0.30	0.40	0.24	0.62
Sales to price	0.98	0.91	0.69	0.36	1.25
Share repurchase	0.03	0.09	0.00	−0.01	0.03
Asset Turnover	1.83	1.89	1.46	0.64	2.56
Return on Invested Capital	0.13	0.11	0.11	0.07	0.17
Debt to Equity	0.97	1.08	0.62	0.22	1.26
Change in Debt to Equity	0.10	0.31	0.01	−0.04	0.17
Revisions	−0.02	0.33	0.00	−0.17	0.11
Growth of Fiscal Year 1 and Fiscal Year 2 Earnings Estimates	0.37	3.46	0.15	0.09	0.24
Momentum	13.86	36.03	11.00	−7.96	31.25

Summary of Well-Known Factors and Their Underlying Economic Rationale

Dividend Yield

Economic rationale: Investors prefer to immediately receive receipt of their investment returns.

References:
Ray Ball, "Anomalies in Relationships Between Securities' Yields and Yield-Surrogates," *Journal of Financial Economics*, 6 (1978), pp. 103–126.

Value

Economic rationale: Investors prefer stocks with low valuations.

References:
Kent Daniel and Sheridan Titman, "Evidence on the Characteristics of Cross-Sectional Variation in Stock Returns," *Journal of Finance*, 52 (1997), pp. 1–33.
Jennifer Conrad, Michael Cooper, and Gautam Kaul, "Value versus Glamour," *Journal of Finance*, 58 (2003), pp. 1969–1996.
Eugene F. Fama and Kenneth R. French, "The Cross-Section of Expected Stock Returns," *Journal of Finance*, 47 (1992), pp. 427–466.
Eugene F. Fama and Kenneth R. French, "Common Risk Factors in the Returns on Stocks and Bonds," *Journal of Financial Economics*, 33 (1993), pp. 3–56.
Eugene F. Fama and Kenneth R. French, "Multifactor Explanations of Asset Pricing Anomalies," *Journal of Finance*, 51 (1996), pp. 55–84.

Size (Market Capitalization)

Economic rationale: Smaller companies tend to outperform larger companies.

References:
Rolf W. Banz, "The Relationship Between Return and Market Value of Common Stocks," *Journal of Financial Economics*, 9 (1981), pp. 3–18.
Josef Lakonishok, Andrei Shleifer, and Robert W. Vishny, "Contrarian Investment, Extrapolation, and Risk," *Journal of Finance*, 49 (1994), pp. 1541–1578.

Asset Turnover

Economic rationale: This measure evaluates the productivity of assets employed by a firm. Investors believe higher turnover correlates with higher future return.

References:
Patricia M. Fairfield and Teri Lombardi Yohn, "Using Asset Turnover and Profit Margin to Forecast Changes in Profitability," *Review of Accounting Studies*, 6 (2001), pp. 371–385.

Earnings Revisions

Economic rationale: Positive analysts' revisions indicate stronger business prospects and earnings for a firm.

References:
Kent L. Womack, "Do Brokerage Analysts' Recommendations Have Investment Value?" *Journal of Finance*, 51 (1996), pp. 137–167.
Harrison Hong, Terence Lim, and Jeremy C. Stein, "Bad News Travels Slowly: Size, Analyst Coverage and the Profitability of Momentum Strategies," *Journal of Finance*, Vol. 55, Issue 1, Feb. 2000, pp. 265–295.
Narasimhan Jegadeesh, Joonghyuk Kim, Susan D. Krische, and Charles M. C. Lee, "Analyzing the Analysts: When Do Recommendations Add Value? "*Journal of Finance*, 59 (2004), pp. 1083–1124.

Growth of Fiscal Year 1 and Fiscal Year 2 Earnings Estimates

Economic rationale: Investors are attracted to companies with growing earnings.

References:
Robert D. Arnott, "The Use and Misuse of Consensus Earnings," *Journal of Portfolio Management*, 11 (1985), pp. 18–27.
Gary A. Benesh and Pamela P. Peterson, "On the Relation Between Earnings Changes, Analysts' Forecasts and Stock Price Fluctuation," *Financial Analysts Journal*, (1986), pp 29–39.

Momentum

Economic rationale: Investors prefer stocks that have had good past performance.

References:
Narasimhan Jegadeesh, "Evidence of Predictable Behavior of Security Returns," *Journal of Finance*, 45 (1990), pp. 881–898.
Narasimhan Jegadeesh and Sheridan Titman, "Returns to Buying Winners and Selling Losers: Implications for Stock Market Efficiency," *Journal of Finance*, 48 (1993), pp. 65–91.

Return Reversal

Economic rationale: Stocks overreact to information, that is, stocks with the highest returns in the current month tend to earn lower returns the following month.

References:
Narasimhan Jegadeesh, "Evidence of Predictable Behavior of Security Returns," *Journal of Finance,* 45 (1990), pp. 881–89.

Idiosyncratic Risk

Economic rationale: Stocks with high idiosyncratic risk in the current month tend to have lower returns the following month

References:
Andrew Ang, Robert J. Hodrick, Yuhang Xing, and Xiaoyan Zhang, "The Cross-Section of Volatility and Expected Returns," *Journal of Finance* 61 (2006), pp. 259–299.

Earnings Surprises

Economic rationale: Investors like positive earnings surprises and dislike negative earnings surprises

References:
Ray Ball and Philip Brown, "An Empirical Evaluation of Accounting Income Numbers," *Journal of Accounting Research*, 6 (1968), pp. 159–177.
Dan Givoly and Josef Lakonishok, "The Information Content of Financial Analysts' Earnings Forecasts," *Journal of Accounting and Economics*, 1 (1979), pp. 165–185.
Victor Bernard and Jacob Thomas, "Post-Earnings-Announcement Drift: Delayed Price Response or Risk Premium?" *Journal of Accounting Research*, 27 (1989), pp. 1–48.
Victor Bernard and Jacob Thomas, "Evidence that Stock Prices Do Not Fully Reflect the Implications of Current Earnings for Future Earnings," *Journal of Accounting and Economics*, Vol. 13, 1990, pp. 305–340.
Narasimhan Jegadeesh and Joshua Livnat, "Revenue Surprises and Stock Returns," *Journal of Accounting and Economics*, 41 (2006), pp. 147–171.

Accounting Accruals

Economic rationale: Companies with earnings that have a large cash component tend to have higher future returns.

References:
Richard G. Sloan, "Do Stock Prices Fully Reflect Information in Accruals and Cash Flows about Future Earnings?" *The Accounting Review*, 71 (12996), pp. 289–315.

Corporate Governance

Economic rationale: Firms with better corporate governance tend to have higher firm value, higher profits, higher sales growth, lower capital expenditures, and fewer corporate acquisitions.

References:
Michael C. Jensen and William H. Meckling, "Theory of the Firm: Managerial Behavior Agency Costs, and Ownership Structure," *Journal of Financial Economics*, 3 (1976), pp 305–360.

Executive Compensation Factors

Economic rationale: Firms that align compensation with shareholders interest tend to outperform.

References:
Paul A. Gompers, Joy L. Ishii, and Andrew Metrick, "Corporate Governance and Equity Prices," *Quarterly Journal of Economics*, 118 (2003), pp. 107–155
Holthausen, R., D. Larcker, and R. Sloan, "Annual Bonus Schemes and the Manipulation of Earnings," *Journal of Accounting and Economics*, 19 (1995), pp. 29–74.
David Yermack, "Good Timing: CEO Stock Option Awards and Company News Announcements," *Journal of Finance*, 52 (1997), pp. 449–476.
John E. Core, Robert W. Holthausen, and David F. Larcker, "Corporate Governance, Chief Executive Officer Compensation, and Firm Performance," *Journal of Financial Economics*, 51 (1999), pp. 371–406.

Accounting Risk Factors

Economic rationale: Companies with lower accounting risk tend to have higher future returns.

References:
David Burgstahler and Ilia Dichev, "Earnings Management to Avoid Earnings Decreases and Losses," *Journal of Accounting and Economics*, 24 (1997), pp. 99–126.
Siew Hong Teoh, Ivo Welch, and T. J. Wong, "Earnings Management and the Underperformance of Seasoned Equity Offerings," *Journal of Financial Economics*, 50 (1998), pp. 63–99.
Douglas J. Skinner and Richard G. Sloan, "Earnings Surprises, Growth Expectations and Stock Returns, or, Don't Let a Torpedo Stock Sink Your Portfolio," *Review of Accounting Studies*, 7 (2002), pp. 289–312.

APPENDIX **C**

Review of Eigenvalues
and Eigenvectors

In this appendix, we will provide a review of eigenvalues and eigenvectors, as well as the SWEEP operator.

The eigenvalues and the eigenvectors of a generic $N \times N$ square matrix **A** are those numbers and those non-zero vectors that satisfy the equation

$$\mathbf{A}\mathbf{x} = \lambda \mathbf{x}$$

The eigenvalues are the roots of the characteristic equation $\det(A - \lambda \mathbf{I}_N) = 0$. There are at most N distinct eigenvalues and eigenvectors. In general, eigenvalues can be real or complex numbers. If an eigenvalue is a complex number, then its complex conjugate is also an eigenvalue. Two or more eigenvalues and eigenvectors might coincide. If the matrix **A** is positive semidefinite, that is, if the condition $\mathbf{x}'\mathbf{A}\mathbf{x} \geq 0$, $\forall \mathbf{x}$ holds, then its eigenvalues are all real non-negative numbers. In fact, $\mathbf{x}'\mathbf{A}\mathbf{x} = \mathbf{x}'\lambda\mathbf{x} \geq 0$. Covariance matrices are positive semidefinite and therefore their eigenvalues are real but can be zero, and two or more can coincide.

Suppose the eigenvalues λ_i are all real, distinct, and non-zero. Let us arrange the eigenvalues in a diagonal matrix

$$\Lambda = \begin{bmatrix} \lambda_1 & 0 & 0 \\ 0 & \ddots & 0 \\ 0 & 0 & \lambda_N \end{bmatrix}$$

and the corresponding eigenvectors $\mathbf{h}_i$ in a matrix

$$\mathbf{H} = \begin{bmatrix} \mathbf{h}_1 & \mathbf{h}_N \end{bmatrix}$$

As $\mathbf{A}\mathbf{h}_i = \lambda_i \mathbf{h}_i$, the matrix relationships $\mathbf{A}\mathbf{H} = \mathbf{\Lambda}\mathbf{H}$ and $\mathbf{H}^{-1}\mathbf{A}\mathbf{H} = \mathbf{\Lambda}$ hold. We say that we have diagonalized the matrix $\mathbf{A}$. If we premultiply $\mathbf{H}$ by the matrix

$$
\mathbf{\Lambda}^{-\frac{1}{2}} = \begin{bmatrix} \dfrac{1}{\sqrt{\lambda_1}} & 0 & 0 \\ 0 & \ddots & 0 \\ 0 & 0 & \dfrac{1}{\sqrt{\lambda_N}} \end{bmatrix}
$$

then $\mathbf{\Lambda}^{-\frac{1}{2}}(\mathbf{\Lambda}^{-\frac{1}{2}}) = \mathbf{\Lambda}^{-1}$ and $(\mathbf{\Lambda}^{-\frac{1}{2}}\mathbf{H})^{-1}\mathbf{A}(\mathbf{\Lambda}^{-\frac{1}{2}}\mathbf{H}) = \mathbf{I}_N$.

THE SWEEP OPERATOR

The Sweep operator greatly simplifies the notation of linear regression. Consider an $N \times N$ matrix $\mathbf{A}$. We define the operation of sweeping $\mathbf{A}$ on its kth diagonal element, $\text{SWEEP}(k)\mathbf{A} = \mathbf{B}$ as the mapping $\mathbf{A} \mapsto \mathbf{B}$ defined by

$$
B_{kk} = \frac{1}{A_{kk}}
$$

$$
B_{ik} = -\frac{A_{ik}}{A_{kk}}, \; i \neq k \; \left(k^{th} \text{ column} \right)
$$

$$
B_{kj} = \frac{A_{kj}}{A_{kk}}, \; j \neq k \; \left(j^{th} \text{ row} \right)
$$

$$
B_{ij} = A_{ij} - \frac{A_{ik}A_{kj}}{A_{kk}}, \; i \neq k, \; j \neq k
$$

If $\mathbf{B}_1 = \text{SWEEP}(k_1)\mathbf{A}$, $\mathbf{B}_2 = \text{SWEEP}(k_2)\mathbf{B}_1$, ..., $\mathbf{B} = \text{SWEEP}(k_r)\mathbf{B}_{r-1}$, we write $\mathbf{B} = \text{SWEEP}(k_1, ..., k_r)\mathbf{A}$. The following property holds:

If $\mathbf{A} = \begin{bmatrix} \mathbf{B} & \mathbf{C} \\ \mathbf{D} & \mathbf{E} \end{bmatrix}$ where $\mathbf{B}, \mathbf{C}, \mathbf{D}, \mathbf{E}$ are matrices of dimension

$(r \times r), (r \times s), (s \times r), (s \times s), s + r = N$

respectively, then

$$\text{SWEEP}(1,2,\ldots,r)\,\mathbf{A} = \begin{bmatrix} \mathbf{B}^{-1} & \mathbf{B}^{-1}\mathbf{C} \\ -\mathbf{D}\mathbf{B}^{-1} & \mathbf{E}-\mathbf{D}\mathbf{B}^{-1}\mathbf{C} \end{bmatrix}$$

$$\text{SWEEP}(r+1,r+2,\ldots,r+s)\,\mathbf{A} = \begin{bmatrix} \mathbf{B}-\mathbf{C}\mathbf{E}^{-1}\mathbf{D} & -\mathbf{C}\mathbf{E}^{-1} \\ \mathbf{E}^{-1}\mathbf{D} & \mathbf{E}^{-1} \end{bmatrix}$$

The SWEEP operator allows us to express the quantities in a linear regression in a compact way,

$$\text{SWEEP}(1,2,\ldots,N)\begin{bmatrix} \mathbf{R'R} & \mathbf{R'f} \\ \mathbf{Rf'} & \mathbf{f'f} \end{bmatrix} = \begin{bmatrix} \left(\mathbf{R'R}\right)^{-1} & \boldsymbol{\beta} \\ \boldsymbol{\beta'} & \mathbf{D} \end{bmatrix}$$

The SWEEP operator is a highly versatile statistical operators that is used in

■ Least squares (ordinary, generalized, multiple regression, and the general linear model)
■ Multivariate analysis of variance
■ All possible regressions

The SWEEP operator provides an intuition for most inversion operations because each element of the matrix being operated on is readily identifiable and has statistical meaning.

Index